ADMINISTERING vSPHERE® 5: PLANNING, IMPLEMENTING, AND TROUBLESHOOTING

JOHN HALES, BRIAN EILER, AND STEVE JONES

Course Technology PTR
A part of Cengage Learning

COURSE TECHNOLOGY
CENGAGE Learning™

Australia • Brazil • Japan • Korea • Mexico • Singapore • Spain • United Kingdom • United States

COURSE TECHNOLOGY
CENGAGE Learning·

Administering vSphere® 5: Planning, Implementing, and Troubleshooting
John Hales
Brian Eiler
Steve Jones

Publisher and General Manager, Course Technology PTR: Stacy L. Hiquet

Associate Director of Marketing: Sarah Panella

Manager of Editorial Services: Heather Talbot

Senior Marketing Manager: Mark Hughes

Acquisitions Editor: Heather Hurley

Project Editor: Jenny Davidson

Technical Reviewer: Rob Markovic

Interior Layout Tech: MPS Limited, a Macmillan Company

Cover Designer: Mike Tanamachi

Indexer: Valerie Haynes Perry

Proofreader: Michael Beady

For product information and technology assistance, contact us at
Cengage Learning Customer & Sales Support, 1-800-354-9706
For permission to use material from this text or product,
submit all requests online at
www.cengage.com/permissions
Further permissions questions can be emailed to
permissionrequest@cengage.com

Library of Congress Control Number: 2012930789

ISBN-13: 978-1-4354-5654-9

ISBN-10: 1-4354-5654-8

Course Technology, a part of Cengage Learning
20 Channel Center Street
Boston, MA 02210
USA

Cengage Learning is a leading provider of customized learning solutions with office locations around the globe, including Singapore, the United Kingdom, Australia, Mexico, Brazil, and Japan. Locate your local office at: **international.cengage.com/region**

Cengage Learning products are represented in Canada by Nelson Education, Ltd.

For your lifelong learning solutions, visit **courseptr.com**

Visit our corporate website at **cengage.com**

Printed in the United States of America
1 2 3 4 5 6 7 14 13 12

John Hales
I would like to dedicate this book to my parents, Bob and Betty Hales, whose encouragement to explore computer technology started in the earliest days of personal computers and has never wavered since.

Brian Eiler
I would like to dedicate this book to my wife, Eve. Without you and all your incredible support, this and so many of my other projects would never have seen the light of day. I love you!

Steve Jones
I would like to dedicate this book to my parents and my grandfather, Ernest Alford, who taught me that I could achieve any goal if I was willing to work hard enough.

ACKNOWLEDGMENTS

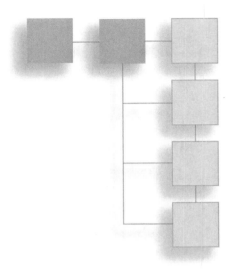

FROM THE GROUP

We would like to begin by thanking the team at Cengage Learning for bringing this work to life, especially Heather Hurley who first contacted us about writing this book, and Jenny Davidson, our incredibly patient, and very meticulous editor. We'd also like to thank our technical editor, Rob Markovic, for his help in checking our facts. Their help has been appreciated and they put us in the best light possible.

A big thanks goes out to Trevor Foster at Visio Café for allowing us to use their wonderfully crafted stencils in our diagrams. Their handiwork really brings diagrams to life!

JOHN HALES

I would like to thank my family for their undying support that they have offered throughout this project and the many previous writing projects I've undertaken. Without that support, this book would not have been possible. A special shout out to my wife is warranted for all of her help and support. I love you!!

I would like to thank my sister, Lori Aldrich, who has reviewed the manuscript and polished it before turning it over to Cengage Learning for their expert review, and for her expert help in creating many graphics that helped make complex concepts easier to understand.

Finally, my co-authors, Steve Jones and Brian Eiler have taught me a lot about the product with their own areas of expertise and backgrounds. The calls, meetings, and coordination were worth it!

BRIAN EILER

First, I'd like to thank my family and my partners at VUmbrella for allowing me the time to work on this project; books always look simpler to write than they really are. Special thanks go out to Jeantet Fields at VUmbrella for handling my duties while I was abroad and working on this book. Your communication skills are truly amazing!

I would like to thank my co-authors, John Hales and Steve Jones: Thank you for your terrific contributions during all our late night conference calls. While it took almost a year, we finally got this massive tome on the shelf!

Finally, I would like to give special thanks to all the men and women serving in the Armed Forces as well as to all the civilian contractors supporting them. I wrote a good percentage of this book while teaching at the Kandahar Airfield in Afghanistan. After spending a few months in "Rocket City" and experiencing just some of what you guys go through, I have a newfound appreciation for all the work you do for the rest of us. Thank you!

STEVE JONES

I would like to take this time to thank my family, whose understanding and support were a critical factor in undertaking and completing this project. I especially would like to thank my wife who has gone the second and third mile to allow me the time to not only learn about vSphere 5, but to put those new concepts and ideas on paper. Her support has been unending.

I would also like to thank John Hales and Brian Eiler for their contributions to my content and the "second set of eyes" that provided valuable insight. Also, thanks for the con calls and the advice and perspective that helped make this the best book that it could be.

ABOUT THE AUTHORS

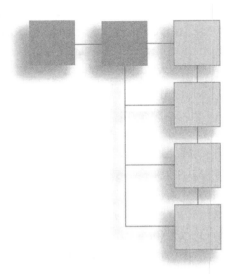

JOHN HALES

John Hales has been working in the IT industry for more than 16 years, and with VMware products for 12+ years. He has earned many vendor certifications over the years, including EMC, VMware, Microsoft, Novell, and CompTIA. His certifications include: VCP 3, 4, and 5; VCAP; VCI; MCSE (NT 4, Windows 2000, and 2003); MCDBA; MCT; CAN; CNE 3, 4, 5, and 6; EMCSA; Network+; A+; and CTT+. He has taught and developed courses (and consulted on many of these technologies) for both public clients and Fortune 500 companies. He has taught in North America, Europe, Asia, the Middle East, and Australia.

His experience with virtualization began with VMware Workstation and progressed through various desktop and server products and releases, becoming a strong proponent of virtualization, especially using VMware products.

Today, he teaches a variety of classes for various vendors, specializing in VMware's vSphere 4 and 5, SRM, and View, Dell, and EMC storage, and how applications (such as SQL and Exchange) can best exploit these technologies. He is the president of Hales Technologies, a company specializing in courseware development, training, and solution-oriented consulting. John lives in Sunrise, Florida, with his wife and four children and can be contacted at johnh@halestechnologies.com.

BRIAN EILER

Brian Eiler has been working in the IT trenches since 1995. Over the years he has worn many hats, including consultant, trainer, systems administrator, and manager. He holds vendor certifications from VMware, Microsoft, Citrix, and CompTIA, including VMware's VCI, VCP (3, 4, and 5), VCAP4-DCA, and VCAP4-DCD certifications. Brian has also worked for Microsoft's Training and Certification group in the development of the Exchange Server and Active Directory exams.

Brian began using VMware products with an early version of Workstation in 1999, later expanding into server virtualization in 2004 with ESX version 2.0. He has used every version of ESX/vSphere since, and has deployed hundreds of ESX servers throughout the world, both as a consultant and as a full-time systems administrator. Brian currently consults and teaches classes for VMware around the world, most recently for the military in Afghanistan.

In addition to consulting and teaching around the world, Brian works as the Director of Professional Services for VUmbrella, a provider of training and consulting services specifically focused on virtualization. Brian resides in Indiana with his wife and two wonderful children, and can be reached at beiler@vumbrella.com.

STEVE JONES

Steve Jones began in the IT industry in 1985, working with DOS 2.1 and performing warranty work on IBM PC 5150, XT 5160, and the IBM AT 5170 personal computers. He has performed component-level repair on system boards, disk controllers, printers, monitors, modems, and mainframe terminals. He has worked as an assistant service manager for 8 years, and supported both in-house technicians and end-users on technical issues.

Steve has earned industry certifications through CompTIA (A+, Security+, Network+, Server+, and CTT), Novell (CNA 3, CNE 4.11, 5, and 6), HP (AIS on Proliant Servers), Dell (DCSNP), Microsoft (MCSE NT4, Windows Server 2000, 2003, MCSA on Windows Server 2000 and 2003, MCTS on Windows Server 2008, and MCT since 2003), and VMware (VCP 3, 4, and 5, and VCI). Steve has been training since 2000 and performing courseware development since 2002.

Steve worked on the team that designed and installed the VMware training facility at the Dell Training Center in Round Rock, Texas, and co-wrote a course for Dell and EqualLogic emphasizing the deployment of Hyper-V virtualization environments using EqualLogic storage solutions.

Today, Steve develops courseware and teaches classes for companies of varying sizes, including classes covering Microsoft technologies, virtualization using VMware's Virtual Infrastructure 3, vSphere 4 and 5, and Microsoft's Hyper-V technologies, EMC storage, and classes that cover performance optimization of those technologies.

Steve is the Owner/Managing Member of MicroTrain, LLC, and a founding member of The Courseware Group. He can be reached at stevej@thecoursewaregroup.com or mctxtd@yahoo.com.

Contents

Introduction

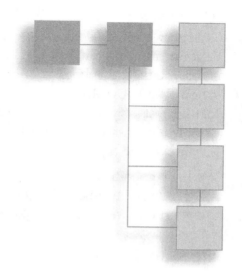

A Word About This Book

Welcome to *Administering vSphere 5: Planning, Implementing, and Troubleshooting*! Whether this is your first vSphere installation or your 50th, this book will save you effort and time (and maybe even money) while planning, configuring, and maintaining your vSphere 5 environment. We have worked very hard to prepare material covering all these areas because each area is important to a successful vSphere implementation project. In some cases we have written complete examples on how to install or configure a particular feature. Other areas are focused more on the best practices we've learned for planning or for maintenance. In the end, we hope you find the book to be well balanced and a helpful resource throughout your project.

In addition to all the normal guidance, we've compiled tips, tricks, and examples we use when teaching people how to work with vSphere. Your friendly neighborhood authors are also experienced consultants and trainers. Our "day jobs" happen to be educating and explaining vSphere, so we thought: "why not write a book?" There never seems to be quite enough time during class or even during our consulting engagements to cover all the nuts and bolts of vSphere. This seemed like the perfect opportunity to fill in many of those gaps.

We realized early that we didn't want or need to re-invent what VMware has already provided in their product documentation. Instead we wanted to create a more comprehensive guide; a book that fills in the gaps these other documents leave. For instance, VMware's product documentation is an exceptionally well-written resource material; however, those documents weren't designed to train you in any particular area. We wrote this book with your education specifically in mind. We want you to LEARN how to do this, not just read about it.

Though we feel this book is very complete, a 900-page book is no substitute for the depth of information you would receive if you attended an official VMware training course. Rather, this book should be considered complementary to instructor-led education. We know that many people in our classes take notes. This book was written for the rest of you. The ones who had to take that call in the middle of class and completely missed the discussion on vNetwork Distributed Switches (or any of a hundred other topics).

We have gone to great lengths to make this as error free as humanly possible and at the same time to make it engaging and easy to read. We hope you'll agree and let us know on our webpage at http://www.AdministeringvSphere.com.

Bonus DVD

A bonus vSphere 5 training DVD created by TrainSignal is included at the back of the book. It includes more than three hours of video training on the following topics:

Lesson 1: Getting Started with VMware vSphere 5 Training Course

Find out who should watch this course and what vSphere 5 topics are covered in this video training course.

Lesson 2: Lab Setup

Learn why you should build your own lab, the options for creating your lab, and the various vSphere lab environments used in the creation of this course.

Lesson 3: Course Scenario

In this lesson you will learn the details of the course scenario.

Lesson 4: Overview of VMware vSphere 5

In this lesson, we'll cover the components that make up vSphere, how it's priced, and how the VMware cloud infrastructure relates.

Lesson 5: Installing VMware ESXi 5

Learn the system requirements and how to install ESXi 5, step by step.

Lesson 6: Installing vCenter 5

There's more to installing vCenter than the traditional Windows App. Properly installing vCenter means analyzing the hardware/software and database requirements. Additionally, learn how to download the vSphere 60-day evaluation, which contains the latest vCenter.

Lesson 7: Installing vCenter 5 as a Linux Appliance (vCSA)

NEW in vSphere 5, the vCenter Server appliance allows you to deploy vCenter 5 without a Windows license or installation. Additionally, there is no vCenter install to perform so you can have vCenter up and running, faster than ever before!

Lesson 8: Using the vSphere 5 Web Client

NEW in vSphere 5, the vSphere web-based client has been introduced. Learn what this new client can and can't do as well as what makes it unique (and very cool). Also, you'll learn how to install the required web-client server that makes it all work.

Lesson 9: What's New in vSphere 5

In this lesson, you'll learn all the new features of vSphere 5, what they do, and how they can help you. Watch this one to catch up on all that is new in VMware's most exciting release yet.

DVD-ROM Downloads

If you purchased an ebook version of this book, and the book had a companion DVD-ROM, you may download the contents from www.courseptr.com/downloads. Please note that you will be redirected to the Cengage Learning site.

If your book has a DVD-ROM, please check our website for any updates or errata files. You may download files from www.courseptr.com/downloads. Please note that you will be redirected to the Cengage Learning site.

PART I

WHERE DO I START?

Installing vSphere 5 may not seem like rocket science, but to the uninitiated, making it work the way you intended can be a daunting task. In this first part of the book, we want to help you understand what the vSphere product can do, and how you can take advantage of the different features of the product.

In Chapter 1 we introduce both the features and limitations of vSphere and what you should consider when designing a vSphere infrastructure (or upgrading one). Chapter 2 includes a lesson on how to properly plan a virtualization project (or any project for that matter, but we focus on virtualization). Chapter 3 discusses the various upgrade considerations, including how to upgrade ESX, ESXi, and vCenter to version 5. Finally, Chapter 4 wraps up this part of the book with an introduction to automation and scripting so that you can make your vSphere environment easier to manage.

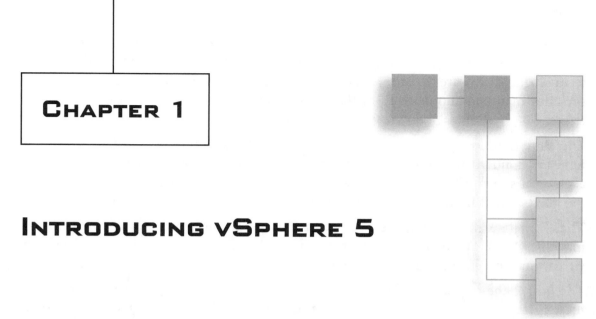

CHAPTER 1

INTRODUCING vSPHERE 5

For those of you with prior vSphere experience you might recall vSphere 4 being more of a network/management-centric release (Distributed Switches, 64-bit computing, VDR, etc.). vSphere 5 will likely be known as the storage-centric release because of all the improvements like policy-based VM storage, Storage DRS, a completely new Storage vMotion technique, and a rewritten HA solution that uses shared storage to communicate host availability. Much has changed, yet the product will still feel familiar.

And now for those of you just joining us, you may be asking, "What is vSphere anyway?" Well, would you believe that it's really just a marketing term? vSphere encompasses a lot of products and technologies, but what do you think of when you hear the word vSphere? If you said virtualization, cloud computing, ESXi server, or vCenter, you'd be right on track. And, at the risk of sounding like we've been bribed to drive the company line (unfortunately for us, we weren't), vSphere 5 is all of these things and more.

Note

The name vSphere originated with the release of VMware's ESX and ESXi server version 4.0 suite of products. It subsequently has referred to version 4.1 and now 5.0. The vSphere name can be thought of as a logical wrapper around many different virtualization features that VMware has provided in their products. Some of these features are less obvious than others because they make up the foundation of the virtual infrastructure. In this chapter we will explore the various components of vSphere and its related product suite.

VMware vSphere 5 is VMware's next-generation virtualization product suite, which includes their industry-leading hypervisor (VMware ESXi) and management technologies (VMware vCenter server, and additional vCenter Suite products). It also provides many additional features that we'll soon discuss. But first, let's define some terms.

The first term is *hypervisor*. No, that's not a Microsoft product. Hypervisor is an industry-standard name for the software that manages and controls virtualization on a physical server. The hypervisor is a resource traffic cop of sorts. Its job is to control the guest virtual machines' access to the physical host's hardware resources.

There are two more terms we need to define: guest and host. A *guest* is a virtual machine (VM). Hopefully if you're reading this book you have some idea of what a virtual machine is, but if not don't worry. We discuss VMs thoroughly in Chapter 9.

The *host* is the physical server that "hosts" the various guest VMs through the use of the hypervisor software. You'll see later in Chapter 5, when we discuss ESXi, that we can manage each host individually using vSphere client, but to take advantage of all the cool features of vSphere you need to use something called vCenter server. vCenter is the management server for vSphere products, and we discuss it in more detail in Chapter 6.

If you're just joining the vSphere bandwagon, but you have experience using ESX version 3.x, you might be wondering what happened to VMware Virtual Infrastructure. The answer is basically "nothing." Virtual Infrastructure, or VI, which contained ESX 3.5 and Virtual Center 2.5, has just been upgraded. Both of these components remain part of VMware's vSphere suite of products. VMware vSphere is just an evolution of the VI product line, with many more features and enhancements to tackle the complexities of building and managing virtualized datacenters, and especially cloud-centric solutions.

VMware vSphere Editions

Before we dive into all the great features of vSphere, it might be a good time to talk about how you can get your hands on vSphere. As with version 4, the VMware vSphere 5 suite is sold in different license levels, or bundles. This helps us because not every company or project will call for every feature VMware offers. In order to keep the prices competitive, they offer product bundles that offer fewer features at a reduced cost (as compared to the Enterprise Plus license level). The more features you need, the more you pay. That being said, Table 1.1 describes the VMware vSphere 5 editions and their respective features.

Table 1.1   vSphere 5 Edition Comparison

Included Features	60-day Evaluation*	Free Version	Essentials	Essentials Plus	Standard	Enterprise	Enterprise Plus
vRAM per CPU License	96GB	32GB	32GB	32GB	32GB	64GB	96GB
vCPUs per VM	32-way	8-way	8-way	8-way	8-way	8-way	32-way
ESXi Hypervisor	X	X	X	X	X	X	X
Manageable via vCenter	X		X	X	X	X	X
Update Manager	X		X	X	X	X	X
vStorage APIs for Data Protection	X		X	X	X	X	X
Thin Provisioning	X		X	X	X	X	X
High Availability **	X			X	X	X	X
Data Recovery	X			X	X	X	X
vMotion	X			X	X	X	X
Virtual Serial Port Concentrator	X					X	X
Hot Add Virtual Hardware	X				X	X	X

(Continues)

Table 1.1 vSphere 5 Edition Comparison (*Continued*)

Included Features	60-day Evaluation*	Free Version	Essentials	Essentials Plus	Standard	Enterprise	Enterprise Plus
vShield Zones	X					X	X
Fault Tolerance	X					X	X
vStorage APIs for Array Integration	X					X	X
Storage vMotion **	X					X	X
DRS & DPM	X					X	X
Distributed Switches	X						X
Storage & Network I/O Control	X						X
Host Profiles	X						X
Auto Deploy ***	X						X
Policy-Driven Storage ***	X						X
Storage DRS ***	X						X

* The 60-day evaluation period expires exactly 60 days from the date you install the ESXi software, and it cannot be restarted unless you reinstall the ESXi software on the server.
** Rewritten in vSphere 5
*** New Feature in vSphere 5

Caution

This information pertains to licensing; any or all of it may change at any time without notice. Contact your local VMware reseller or visit http://www.vmware.com for the most up-to-date information.

Tip

vSphere 5, like its predecessors, is available with a 60-day unlimited evaluation period. The term "unlimited" here refers to the fact that the evaluation version includes all the functioning components of the Enterprise Plus version, which licenses all the possible features. After the 60-day time period expires, you must obtain a valid license from VMware to continue using the server properly. Note that even the free edition requires a license key (they just want your e-mail address).

As you can see, there's a lot of variety in the menu, and like anything, the prices are subject to change. You will want to contact your nearest VMware reseller, or VMware's website for the most current pricing. The one main thing you might notice if you have a background in vSphere 4 is that VMware eliminated the Advanced bundle, splitting up the features between the Standard and Enterprise editions.

Let's go through the various editions, explaining their features in a bit more detail. As you can see from the chart of features, each edition builds on the previous edition. The license editions are Standard, Enterprise, and Enterprise Plus, with two special-edition bundles called Essentials and Essentials Plus. These last two are packaged slightly differently as you'll see further on. As we discuss each of these editions, we'll also highlight the features that make them unique, so that you'll have a better understanding of which edition is right for you, and your needs.

Standard Edition

VMware vSphere Standard Edition is your entry-level choice into server virtualization and management. Standard Edition provides everything you need in order to start virtualizing and consolidating your environment. Standard Edition also provides some basic availability functionality. Here's a breakdown of the features included with Standard Edition:

- VMware ESXi
- 8-way Virtual Symmetric Multi-Processing (vSMP)
- Data Recovery
- vMotion
- High Availability

As you see, Standard Edition includes quite a few features, but, what do they all do? Let's have a look:

VMware ESXi

VMware ESXi is the foundation of the vSphere virtualization stack, providing the platform upon which the remainder of the vSphere suite is built. ESXi is the hypervisor platform provided with VMware vSphere, as well as the central virtual layer on which everything resides.

There are two types of hypervisors. ESXi and the previous version of ESX are considered a type 1, or bare metal, hypervisor. A bare metal hypervisor doesn't require another operating system to be installed first because it *is* the operating system. The other type of hypervisor, type 2, is referred to as "hosted" because it resides as an application or service on another operating system such as Microsoft Windows or Linux.

We will cover more aspects about host design, including bare metal versus hosted hypervisors later in Chapter 5, "ESXi—Your Host."

ESX: Bare metal or Hosted?

But wait, wasn't ESX based on RedHat? Shouldn't it be considered "hosted"? The answer to this is "No." Let us explain: VMware ESX server (unlike ESXi) was found only in prior versions of vSphere. It consisted of two key components: the VMkernel (the hypervisor) and the Linux-based Service Console (the management interface).

VMware called their hypervisor "VMkernel." It is the core of their virtualization process. The VMkernel is a purpose-built virtualization layer that provides your virtual machines access to the physical hardware. The VMkernel is also responsible for providing the following services: CPU scheduling, disk access, virtual network switching, and memory management.

This leaves us with the Service Console. In vSphere 5, the ESX Service Console no longer exists. It was a management layer for the previous ESX platforms, which was confined to a single ESX host. This means it was the part of the server you interacted directly with, but it couldn't be used to manage any other ESXi hosts. It provided an interface for you to interact with both the VMkernel and that host's virtual machines (from a management perspective only). The Service Console was Linux based, specifically a distribution of RHEL (Red Hat Enterprise Linux), which is where the above-mentioned question comes from. It should be noted, however, that while it resembled RHEL, and in fact has many of the same services, the similarities were only surface deep in that the Service Console was stripped down to the bare minimums required to support virtualization management.

In vSphere 5, the ESX service console was replaced with remote functionality such as the vCLI, VMA, and PowerCLI. These tools are discussed in greater detail in Chapter 4 when we discuss automation tools.

8-way Virtual Symmetric Multi-Processing (vSMP)

Symmetric Multi-Processing, or SMP, is what allows us to effectively use more than one CPU in a server. SMP has been around for decades on the physical servers, and it is what allows us to take advantage of all these additional CPU cores we have today. From a slightly more technical perspective, SMP allows an operating system to schedule and execute CPU instructions on different logical CPUs (cores or hyper-threads) in an attempt to improve CPU execution concurrency for the programs.

The reason for virtual SMP is similar to the reason for physical SMP; it gives us the ability to concurrently execute multiple processes in the VM. Unfortunately, not all applications take advantage of SMP, so be selective in which VMs you grant multiple vCPUs; not using SMP properly can cause performance issues. In the Standard and Enterprise editions of vSphere, the hypervisor is able to support virtual machines with up to 8 virtual CPUs (vCPUs). As with vSphere 4, we have the ability to assign vCPUs in multiples of 1, instead of the traditional 1, 2, or 4 vCPU increments. So if you want a VM with 3 vCPUs, you can do it as long as your guest operating system supports it.

Note

While you are limited to 8 vCPUs in the Standard and Enterprise editions, in Enterprise Plus edition you can give a VM up to 32 vCPUs! Remember though, less is more. Don't allocate more vCPUs that absolutely necessary. Refer to Chapters 9 and 10 for more information.

Data Recovery

VMware Data Recovery, or VDR, leverages the VMware vStorage APIs to allow you to create backups of your virtual machines and store them in a deduplicated format either on network storage or a VMFS volume. By leveraging technology such as data deduplication, you can store a highly reduced footprint of your required storage space by simply eliminating duplicate data. In addition to creating whole-VM back-ups, the product also includes the ability to create multiple restore points, and an application that can restore single files from a VDR backup. We talk about VDR a bit more in Chapter 9 when we discuss VMs and their backup options.

vMotion

Have you ever wanted to perform invasive hardware maintenance during the day but couldn't due to production time constraints? Maybe you needed to swap power feeds or upgrade some firmware. In the past you would need to power off your server to perform this task. vMotion solves this dilemma—for virtual machines anyway. We can migrate a running virtual machine from one ESXi host to another without down-time. Really.

You will never forget watching your first VMware vMotion. Watching a virtual machine with an active workload, like streaming video or a very active database, move from one physical server to another is eye-opening. This live migration feat is what VMware calls VMware vMotion. Using vMotion, you are able to take a planned maintenance on a physical host, which would normally cause an outage, and turn it into a zero downtime event.

vMotion is also extremely useful in normal day-to-day operations, as we can also leverage vMotion to load balance the virtual machines across ESXi hosts in your environment. Some of this load balancing can even be automated, as you'll see later when we discuss the vMotion in depth in Chapter 9 and the Distributed Resource Scheduler (DRS) in Chapter 11.

High Availability

What does VMware mean by High Availability (HA)? VMware's HA has the ability to seamlessly and automatically restart virtual machines on different hosts in a clustered vSphere environment. This might happen, for example, if one ESXi host experiences a power failure or other major hardware failure. In vSphere 5, HA was completely rewritten from the ground up to eliminate many of the weaknesses of the previous AAM-based model.

VMware HA has a few basic requirements such as shared storage and appropriately licensed ESXi hosts, but it can bring a degree of high availability to virtual machines and their applications that may otherwise never have support for high availability. Of course there are some planning aspects to consider, but VMware HA can be enabled with nothing more difficult on the part of the administrator than a few clicks!

We cover VMware HA in depth in Chapter 12, where we've dedicated an entire chapter to it and all of its associated features.

Enterprise Edition

This is the VMware vSphere edition that VMware has put together for enterprises and large business deployments. What a bundle it is too, including all of the features we have discussed to this point, and adding to it critical virtual machine resource management tools. These additional features are as follows:

- Virtual Serial Port Concentrator
- Hot Add
- vShield Zones
- Fault Tolerance
- vStorage APIs for Array Integration (VAAI)

- Storage vMotion
- Distributed Resource Scheduling (DRS)
- Distributed Power Management (DPM)

Virtual Serial Port Concentrator

The virtual serial port concentrator is part of an API that allows a VM to maintain virtual serial port connections through a special proxy server. The advantage of using the serial port concentrator is that these connections remain active even when the VM is migrated to another host via vMotion. The proxy server maintains the telnet or serial connection to the target device, and the VM and proxy server communicate via the network.

VMware Hot Add

Planning is good, but as we all know, you can't plan for everything. For instance, you created your virtual machine with what was at the time an appropriate amount of RAM, CPU, and hard disk. Now you have a new application that requires more of everything and you can't reboot the server because it is in production. VMware Hot Add is a feature that helps us overcome some of these issues.

As the name suggests, Hot Add allows the virtual machine administrator to make hardware changes, in the form of CPU, RAM, disks, and even network cards to a running virtual machine with no downtime. Of course, this requires an operating system that supports this ability; otherwise, the OS may crash or at best, not recognize the change. We discuss this ability, along with other virtual machine functions in Chapter 9.

VMware vShield Zones

VMware vShield Zones was released in vSphere 4. It allows administrators to dynamically provision new sub-networks while maintaining compliance with your security policies and other regulatory requirements. It does this by building on vSphere's already robust virtual networking to add virtual firewalls and fenced networks. What makes this unique is that the vShield appliance is able to maintain the virtual machine's security policy for its entire lifecycle, including vMotion migrations and management traffic. This in turn reduces your requirement for multiple physical firewalls. We don't go into a great amount of detail in this book on vShield Zones, as it is more of a cornerstone component for vShield Director than a traditional vSphere implementation.

VMware Fault Tolerance

VMware Fault Tolerance was initially released in the vSphere 4 suite. Fault Tolerance (FT) allows us to simultaneously execute one VM on multiple ESXi hosts to provide hardware-level high availability. Now, this isn't some sort of grid computing project; this is for redundancy. The second VM is running, but you can think of it more like a shadow of the first VM. The hypervisors don't allow both VMs to communicate on the network unless one of them fails. What makes FT special is that the shadow VM picks up right where the primary left off, making a near-seamless transition, potentially avoiding any downtime for the protected VM.

FT takes advantage of high-speed network connections between the ESXi hosts and the vLockstep technology to seamlessly maintain a virtual machine's state on two separate ESXi hosts. You can think of it as an active-passive cluster where every CPU instruction for a single VM is mirrored on the second ESXi host. What this means is that should you lose either of these two ESXi hosts due to an unplanned hardware outage, your FT-protected virtual machines would stay running on the other node, as if nothing happened. No reboot required.

Furthermore, if you have another surviving host in the cluster or the first node recovers, FT will automatically create a new secondary, or shadow, virtual machine, ensuring that the protected virtual machines stay that way.

For many applications that are not cluster state aware, this is the highest form of high availability that can be achieved. Like the VMware HA feature, this too requires no additional configuration at the virtual machine level, but it does have limitations. Read more about FT in Chapter 12 where we discuss the various high availability options in vSphere 5.

vStorage APIs for Array Integration (VAAI)

These APIs can dramatically improve the performance and efficiency of your storage arrays. Some of the functions can reduce the number of SCSI reservations made on the arrays, while others are designed to offload intense copy processes to the backend arrays. These APIs were present in vSphere 4; however, in vSphere 5 these APIs also affect NAS devices and NFS datastores.

VMware Storage vMotion

If you're anything like the rest of us, you've accidentally deployed a VM to the wrong datastore, or you've somehow managed to fill up a datastore. Either way, you need to move a VM somewhere with more space, and of course you can't take any downtime to do it. VMware Storage vMotion comes to the rescue by bringing the concepts of vMotion to the storage world. It allows virtual machine administrators the flexibility to migrate a virtual machine disk between datastores even if the datastores are on different SAN arrays. Oh, and it does it all without downtime for the virtual machine.

This allows an administrator to move virtual machines to a new SAN, or between high-cost and low-cost storage, without the need for downtime or extended mainte-nance. This is a great tool in any administrator's belt to lower their amount of down-time in the datacenter. We cover this feature in greater detail in Chapter 9.

VMware Distributed Resource Scheduler (DRS)

VMware Distributed Resource Scheduler (DRS) is a clustering feature that can lever-age vMotion to load balance your VMs across multiple ESXi hosts. DRS uses a rule base and performance-based algorithms to decide how best to distribute the server load over the VMware cluster during different workload periods.

There are additional features, which allow you to either group or separate virtual machines over multiple hosts to create a pattern that best suits your business and availability requirements. DRS is covered in Chapter 11.

VMware Distributed Power Management (DPM)

VMware Distributed Power Management (DPM) is an extension to DRS that auto-matically evacuates and powers down unused ESXi hosts during periods of low usage. When the cluster's resource demand increases, DPM uses server remote management functions to power on the ESXi hosts to provide the additional horsepower.

With servers these days taking more and more power, and with power costs going up, this becomes a great way to lower infrastructure costs and create a better Return on Investment (ROI) for your virtualization initiative. DPM is covered in detail with DRS in Chapter 11.

Enterprise Plus Edition

- 32-way Virtual Symmetric Multi-Processing (vSMP)
- Distributed Switches
- Host Profiles
- Storage/Network I/O Controls
- Auto Deploy

- Policy-Driven Storage
- Storage DRS

32-way Virtual Symmetric Multi-Processing (vSMP)

As with 8-way vSMP, you have the ability to assign multiple virtual CPUs to a single virtual machine to increase the processing cores available to your applications. In the case of Enterprise Plus we now have the ability to allocate up to 32 of these virtual CPUs per VM. Though adding 32 vCPUs to a VM may seem like a good thing, as we'll discuss later in Chapter 10, more vCPUs may not be the answer if you have performance woes.

Distributed Switches

VMware vNetwork Distributed Switches (vDS) add scalability to VMware's traditional virtual networking model. Their predecessor, the vNetwork Standard Switches, are basic "layer 2" devices that operate and are managed on each ESXi host. Configuration changes on a standard switch must be made on each affected ESXi host, and all traffic through these switches stays on each ESXi host.

In comparison, the vDS operates slightly different. Though all the data traffic still remains on each ESXi host, with vDS, VMware moved the control plane (management functions) off of the ESXi host and into the vCenter server.

So what is the benefit to this? Moving the management of these switches into vCenter server reduces the amount of manual reconfiguration necessary, and it enables you to maintain a consistent vSwitch setup over a group of hosts. There are many other features of the vDS, and we go into each of these in Chapter 7 when we talk about networking.

VMware Host Profiles

VMware Host Profiles are designed to help VMware administrators with the task of maintaining a consistent configuration or set of configurations on their ESXi hosts. Why? Picture yourself 12 months from now, vSphere has caught on like wild fire in your organization, and suddenly you have 200 ESXi hosts and 3000 VMs. These ESXi hosts, despite your best efforts, have grown organically with networking changes here, local user accounts there, and you have to somehow manage all of this.

Enter host profiles. You can create a baseline profile for what a good configuration looks like, and then deploy that configuration to all or some of your ESXi hosts. Well, it's almost as simple as that, but we'll cover the details when we get to Chapter 13 where we discuss Configuration and Patch Management.

Storage/Network I/O Controls

Storage I/O Control gives us the ability to apply rules and constraints to the VMs to keep the disk performance at an optimal level. This involves constraining the number of IOPS and using a proportional share-based system on a per-VM basis.

Network I/O Control permits a form of Quality of Service (QoS) and a proportional share-based system to keep network traffic at optimal levels. Using these tools, we can keep less important, yet very active VMs from monopolizing the resources on an ESXi host.

Auto Deploy

Auto Deploy is a feature that enables state less ESXi hosts. These hosts have no hard drives or permanent storage installed. They boot from the network using PXE and download a customized executable image of ESXi via TFTP server. Once online, the hosts download their configuration "personality" from vCenter and begin hosting VMs.

This not only accelerates the deployment of new hosts, but it alleviates the trouble of backing up the hosts and replacing failed hosts. Coupled with host profiles, configuration deployment and drift become a thing of the past.

Policy-Driven Storage

Not all storage is created equal. Some storage devices are intended for heavy production databases, whereas others are optimized for archival storage. We also have different tiers of VMs, ranging from high-end database servers to low-key file servers. The goal of policy-driven storage is to match these VMs to the appropriate storage in a dynamic environment. We can assign different profiles and policies to the datastores and VMs to allow vCenter to adjust the layout as needed to maintain the most optimal performance settings possible.

Storage DRS

Following policy-driven storage is a new feature that leverages the power of Storage vMotion to dynamically move VMs between datastores without downtime. Storage DRS constantly monitors the storage structure and health just like regular DRS monitors the CPU and RAM of the ESXi hosts. With Storage DRS, we can be certain that the VMs are on the best-suited storage devices available.

Essentials and Acceleration Kits

Now that we've covered the basic editions and all of the features they come bundled with, let's take a moment to discuss the Acceleration Kits and Essentials editions.

Table 1.2   Acceleration Kit Entitlement

Kit Name	vCenter Edition	CPU Licenses	Maximum Pooled vRAM
Essentials Kit	vCenter for Essentials	6 CPUs*	192GB
Essentials Plus Kit	vCenter for Essentials	6 CPUs*	192GB
Standard Acceleration Kit	vCenter Standard	8 CPUs	256GB
Enterprise Acceleration Kit	vCenter Standard	6 CPUs	384GB
Enterprise Plus Acceleration Kit	vCenter Standard	6 CPUs	576GB

* The Essentials and Essentials Plus Kits only allow up to 3 physical ESXi hosts with a maximum of two CPU sockets in each host.

Simply put, these editions include your basic virtualization features. They've been created to help jumpstart a small/medium business (SMB) that wants to deploy a virtualization infrastructure, but reduce its initial capital investment.

Each kit comes bundled with a certain number of CPUs, an edition of vCenter server, and a limit on the amount of pooled vRAM. See Table 1.2.

Caution

This information pertains to licensing; any or all of it may change at any time without notice. Contact your local VMware reseller or visit http://www.vmware.com for the most up-to-date information.

There are also versions of the vSphere Essentials and Essentials Plus for Retail and Branch Office environments available from VMware. While these editions mirror the functionality of the Essentials and Essentials Plus versions described previously, these editions are designed to be licensed and managed either from a branch office or from the corporate datacenter. These packages require the additional purchase of a support and update subscription for 1 calendar year, and also require a starter kit purchase that includes a total of 10 sites, at a maximum of 3 physical hosts per site. In this package, additional sites can be added as business needs change.

THE NEW LICENSING MODEL

The vSphere licensing model has been modified to better meld with the licensing model for vCloud Director and other Infrastructure as a Service (IaaS) offerings. Here are some of the changes.

Sockets versus Cores

Licenses for vSphere 5 are exclusively tied to CPU sockets, not cores. The licenses are no longer based on the number of cores per socket. This model worked well when CPU manufacturers were releasing processors with 2, 4, or even 6 cores, but when the market expanded to 12+ cores per socket, this model became a problem. The core-based license model was eliminated in vSphere 5.

Physical RAM Limits

Like the CPU socket licensing mentioned above, vSphere is no longer licensed based on the amount of physical RAM in the ESXi host. In vSphere 4 Standard, Advanced, and Enterprise editions hosts were limited to 256GB of physical RAM; whereas Enterprise Plus was unlimited. Under vSphere 5, all editions are unlimited in regards to physical RAM in the ESXi host. The physical RAM-based license model was replaced with vRAM Entitlement licensing, which is discussed next.

vRAM Entitlement

vRAM Entitlement is a term that had the virtualization industry in an uproar within days of its announcement. The blogosphere was saturated by complaints, commentary, and disgust. Customers were upset, saying the new licensing model was unfair and called it a money-grab by VMware. Soon after the announcement, VMware revised the licensing model, increasing the vRAM limits substantially. But what did it all mean, and how does this new version of vRAM Entitlement affect you?

First, a little definition and explanation: vRAM Entitlement is a system to control the amount of virtual RAM (vRAM) that can be assigned to VMs on a particular host or in a vCenter environment. Each vSphere CPU license provides an incremental increase in the pooled vRAM. As you can see in the vSphere editions chart at the beginning of this chapter, the vRAM entitlement per CPU increases by the edition of your vSphere license. A Standard Edition license gives us 32GB per CPU socket; whereas a single socket Enterprise Plus license provides 96GB to the vRAM pool.

When the ESXi hosts are managed under a vCenter server, the vRAM pool is used by VMs across the entire infrastructure, so a relatively inactive ESXi host will contribute the unused portion of its vRAM entitlement to a more active ESXi server. From a technical perspective, all of this is maintained in vCenter and operates in the background. The only time this comes into play is when you attempt to power on a VM with more vRAM allocated to it than what is remaining in the vRAM pool in vCenter. Remember, vRAM is accumulated throughout your environment and pooled at the vCenter level instead of allocating a specific amount of vRAM per host. Also, vCenter does not impose a hard stop limit; instead, it logs the license violation in the event list. Only vCenter for Essentials (a special, limited-functionality release of vCenter server) imposes any sort of hard limit on vRAM provisioning.

So why was this such a big deal? In previous versions of vSphere, VMware had no such model or limits on a per VM basis. This new model seemed to unfairly tax customers who assigned large quantities of vRAM to their VMs, and it went right in the face of the announcement that a VM could now utilize as much as 1TB of vRAM.

VMware responded with a change that essentially doubled the vRAM Entitlement per license and declared that a single VM would never be charged for more than 96GB of vRAM, even if it had 1TB of vRAM actually assigned to it.

In the end, the vRAM licensing model is helpful for administrators because it tangibly limits VM sprawl. For years managers and users alike have expected near immediate on-demand deployment of VMs, yet in many cases they assumed there was almost no cost associated with the new VM (it's virtual right?). Now, we as administrators have the ability to associate a real cost with each of these VMs, which in turn makes it easier to justify careful planning and resource conservation.

VMware vSphere Management Interfaces

Now that we've covered all the wonderful things that vSphere can do, we need to briefly touch on the interfaces and services you will use to manage your vSphere environment. Please bear in mind that we are only introducing these components at this point, and we will go into much greater detail in the chapters to follow.

Your management tools will primarily be:

- VMware vSphere web client
- VMware vSphere client for Windows
- VMware vCenter server
- vSphere Command Line Interface (vCLI)
- vSphere PowerCLI (PowerShell)
- vSphere Management Assistant (vMA)
- vSphere vCenter Orchestrator

VMware vSphere Web Client

For years the web client for vCenter and ESX was so feature-deprived that it could hardly be called a client at all. With the release of vSphere 5, VMware has revamped the web client. While it still heavily favors VM management tasks instead of host or cluster tasks, we can use this in lieu of the installable Windows client in many cases to maintain a vSphere environment. We cover the web client in more depth, along with the vCenter editions, in Chapter 6.

VMware vSphere Client for Windows

Even though we have a much more robust web client, some things must still be configured using the vSphere client for Windows. This is the upgrade to the traditional client VMware has offered since vCenter was first released. It is a Windows-based application designed to connect either directly to an ESXi host or to a VMware vCenter server. Unfortunately there is no installable client for the Mac or Linux platforms.

VMware vCenter Server

Unless you are only using the free version of ESXi, you will likely want to purchase a license for VMware vCenter server, commonly referred to as vCenter. vCenter is the management server for your vSphere environment. Your ESXi hosts are controlled and configured via the vCenter management interfaces.

Historically, vCenter has always been a Windows-based application server. Now in version 5, VMware has released a new virtual appliance that becomes your vCenter server in a pre-build Linux virtual machine. You just import it on an ESXi server and in minutes you are up and running. The Windows version of vCenter is still available and we discuss the installation and configuration of both editions later in Chapter 6.

In both editions, the basic management tasks include creating virtual machine clones, templates, guest operating system customization, vSphere security, and the deployment of new virtual machines. It also includes the ability to manage ESXi hosts, datastores, virtual networking, and other advanced host configuration.

vSphere Command Line Interface (vCLI)

The vSphere Command Line Interface, or vCLI is a remote command set for managing ESXi and vCenter server systems. It is very common to use the vCLI to create and execute scripts that automate administrative processes such as storage reconfiguration or the creation of virtual network switches. This toolset is built on top of the vSphere SDK for Perl. This has the added benefit of making this management tool quite flexible, in that it will run on any platform that supports Perl. We cover the vCLI in Chapter 4 along with the automation tools.

vSphere PowerCLI (PowerShell)

VMware vSphere PowerCLI, or PowerCLI for short, is what the VMware Toolkit for Windows (PowerShell) turned into. The PowerCLI is a Windows PowerShell snap-in provided by VMware for the management of vSphere ESXi hosts as well as vCenter server. By utilizing many specialized commands, known as cmdlets, it allows a Windows admin to perform most any task that can be performed from the vSphere Client. By using PowerShell for this tool, VMware reduces the learning curve for automating the virtual infrastructure for the Windows administrator significantly. We will cover PowerCLI in Chapter 4.

vSphere Management Assistant (vMA)

The vSphere Management Assistant is a prebuilt Linux virtual appliance that comes installed with the vCLI and VMware Software Development Kit (SDK) and APIs. vMA is a free download from VMware's website. This allows administrators and developers to manage their vSphere environment from a command line. For ESXi it provides a platform for vendor-provided agents, as well as centralized logging, and authenticated non-interactive logins (scripts). This is the logical replacement for much of the functionality provided in the former ESX Service Console. We explain how to install and configure vMA in Chapter 4.

VMware vCenter Orchestrator

vCenter Orchestrator, as the name suggests, is a component of vCenter server. Orchestrator provides an automation framework for your virtual infrastructure that is workflow based, which can simplify the management and automation of your environment. To help kick-start the workflow automation process, VMware ships Orchestrator with several out-of-the-box workflows. We discuss Orchestrator in a bit more detail in Chapter 4.

VMWARE VSPHERE BOLT-ON PRODUCTS

As complete as vCenter is, there are additional modules that VMware sells to extend the functionality of your vSphere environment. Some of these products are for management, while others assist with troubleshooting or disaster recovery. Here are some of these bolt-on products:

- VMware vSphere Cloud Director
- VMware vCenter Site Recovery Manager
- VMware vCenter Chargeback

- VMware vCenter server heartbeat
- VMware vCenter CapacityIQ
- VMware vCenter AppSpeed

Many of these products are simply too vast to cover at an appropriate amount of detail in this book, but we at least wanted to make you aware of them. In Chapter 15 we touch on each of these products briefly.

SUMMARY

Let's take a step back and review what we've covered thus far. We talked about how best to use this book, the various vSphere editions and their respective features, and how you will manage your new vSphere infrastructure. Now that we have a good foundation for understanding the vSphere suite, we'll move into planning your vSphere installation!

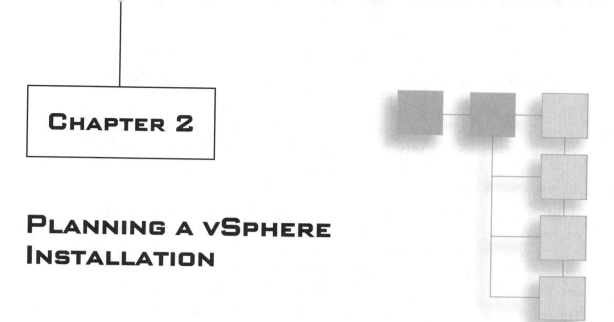

CHAPTER 2

PLANNING A VSPHERE INSTALLATION

Nearly every vSphere book has a chapter dedicated to planning. After all, the product will form the foundation of your virtual datacenter. Without proper planning you may achieve your immediate goals, but in the process you'll likely create some interesting "troubleshooting opportunities."

In this book, instead of giving you a chapter dedicated to all the various permutations of settings and hardware choices, we decided to incorporate planning into the beginning of every chapter. This way, you get the relevant information at the same time we explain how to use it. So, instead of just listing all the various choices you *could* make during your planning process, we give you the tools to decide for yourself what a good plan should include.

This planning chapter will focus on all the aspects that go into creating a successful plan—meaning, we leave the details of the plan up to you, but we guide you though the process of creating that plan. If it helps, you can think of this chapter as a blueprint of a successful vSphere project PLAN rather than of a successful vSphere implementation (though we also want your implementation to be successful).

These pages represent some tried-and-true project management methodologies that we have used with great success. The first task will be to familiarize you with the methodology, and then we will task you with gathering information and assembling your team. The methodology we will use is structured as follows:

- **Architecture vision.** Define the project and any limiting factors.
- **Architecture analysis.** Determine what you have and what you will need.

- **Technology architecture.** Develop your plans and diagram the solution.
- **Migration planning.** Bridge the gap between what "is" and what "will be."

Throughout this chapter we will beat this idea like a dead horse: "Document Everything." Record your rationale for decision making even if the rationale seems obvious. Your decision may become invalid if a limitation is changed or removed. Documenting your rationale for each decision will make it easy to identify cascading changes resulting from a single upstream change.

In addition to solid documentation, a good plan should be highly repeatable. So now you're wondering why in the world you would ever want to repeat this crazy endeavor. Well, a repeatable design doesn't mean you *must* repeat it, it simply means that you *could* repeat it. In other words, the design isn't so overly complex that the only place and time where this design could ever be implemented is here and now.

This doesn't necessarily mean you can change a few names and the plan can be repurposed. It means that you have followed a very detailed process and you can easily identify the logic behind your choices, including the potential alternative options. In this way, you can alter your constraints, requirements, or even risks, and quickly identify suitable options. A plan that is highly repeatable is one that can be quickly adapted should your environment change.

DEFINE YOUR PROJECT—ARCHITECTURE VISION

The architectural vision phase is really just the initial information gathering process, and getting all the involved parties to agree on a fixed set of terms for the project. The goal of this phase is to achieve approval and authorization to proceed with your project. By identifying the various limiting factors you can design a solution that addresses these concerns before they derail your project.

You will learn about all those limiting factors from people known as Subject Matter Experts (SMEs). A SME is someone who is considered by your organization to be the expert in a particular area. That doesn't mean they know everything about that area; it means they are authoritative. For example, for financial matters your SME may be the CFO or Corporate Controller of your organization. For security concerns the SME may be a hired consultant your organization trusts for guidance.

You will interview these SMEs to learn what the business must do to make this project a success. The most important thing to remember is to transcribe your interviews with the SMEs and keep in touch with them throughout the project. You will later refer back to these interview notes when making design decisions. It is important to include these notes in your design document to justify your design decisions.

During your interviews, your SMEs will give you a lot of information. You should organize this information into the following categories, and remember: Document Everything.

- **Business goals.** What does the business hope to gain from this project?
- **Stakeholders/objectives.** Who are the players, and what do they want?
- **Project scope.** What are the boundaries of the project?
- **Requirements.** What must we accomplish to be successful?
- **Constraints.** Have we been restricted in accomplishing the objectives?
- **Assumptions.** What aspects must we assume to be true without proof?
- **Risks.** What other factors pose a threat to the success of the project?

Business Goals

The ultimate driver of your project should be the goals of your business or organization. This may sound obvious, but it is rather startling the number of projects we have seen initiated just "because we can" instead of "because we should." If you are uncertain, ask yourself the following questions:

- Do we have executive/business leader support?
- Have we performed a Return on Investment (ROI) study for the project?
- Are we solving a problem for the customers or clients?
- If we cancelled this project, would the revenue/profits be negatively affected?

If you were able to answer "yes" to at least one of these questions, you likely have a business case for completing your project. If you were unable to answer "yes" to any of these questions, you may be chasing new technology or you're in desperate need of a hobby.

A business goal should be measurable, but it doesn't need to be exact. For example, you might have a goal to reduce the electricity costs in your datacenter. The goal "Reduce datacenter electricity costs" is a bit too vague even though it is measurable. You might rephrase the goal to "Reduce datacenter electricity costs by 25%." Now we've added a measurable aspect to your goal, which makes it possible to determine if/when we have achieved that goal.

A goal should also provide direction for the product selections in your project. In the above example we know that energy costs are important, and therefore we should include options that allow us to reduce these costs. In this case, one option could be to use VMware Converter to consolidate physical servers to reduce costs. Another might be to leverage specific technologies such as Distributed Power Management to reduce operational costs during non-peak hours.

In any case, a business goal should involve real business problems and solutions, whether they be cost-related or customer-related. The thing to remember is that these are goals, not requirements. We may not achieve these goals, but this design will make a best effort to do so.

Stakeholders/Objectives

A stakeholder is anyone who has something to gain or lose as a result of this project. Every project has stakeholders, and every stakeholder has an objective (hidden or otherwise). In a virtualization project you may have a large number of stakeholders because your project will involve most of your organization's IT infrastructure. Here are some examples:

- Executive leadership
- Enterprise application support
- Server administrators
- Database administrators
- Network administrators
- End user support (help desk)
- Backup/Disaster recovery personnel

These same stakeholders are likely also to be your Subject Matter Experts (SMEs). You will need to consult with each of them to determine their objectives and to learn if their support will help you sell your project to upper management or other departments.

Your stakeholders' objectives may later become requirements, but in the initial stages of your project you should consider each stakeholder's objectives independently. In some cases you may receive conflicting objectives such a helpdesk administrator's desire for full access while on call, whereas the security administrator wants complete lockdown of every system at all times. It might seem like a good idea to get in the middle of this debate, but instead just record these objectives and let management figure out who wins.

Project Scope

"Scope creep" is the bane of consultants everywhere. Defining and adhering to the scope of a project is one of the most important components of project management. A project scope defines what is to be included (and excluded) from the project. The project owners will typically set an initial project scope when the project is proposed. Over the course of the design meetings this scope will likely change based on feedback from each of the stakeholders in the project. When the design meetings have concluded, it should be relatively easy to determine what will comprise the project boundaries.

For example, as the project owner you may propose a vSphere upgrade project. In your initial scope of work you might define that all branch offices within your company will be included in the project. Later, as you determine financial backing, you agree to limit your initial scope to include only your main office due to insufficient project funding. As your project design meetings progress it may become necessary to broaden or further restrict the scope to achieve all the stakeholders' objectives or requirements.

Requirements

Requirements may be imposed on your project by internal or external sources. In the case of publicly traded companies, governmental bodies may impose requirements in the form of laws or regulations. In the United States, two such regulations are HIPPA and Sarbanes/Oxley. Each requires a specific level of security, auditing, or documentation that may affect the project design.

Though both business goals and requirements carry consequences for not meeting them, a requirement will typically have a very negative effect on the organization. For example, not meeting the security requirements of the HIPPA laws can carry significant financial penalties and/or civil court charges.

Internal requirements may have less dramatic consequences, but they tend to be just as important. For example, your CIO may require you to reuse your existing server hardware during your project. This isn't a requirement that will be easy to break—you simply can't buy any new hardware. The repercussions of this requirement however may impose wide-reaching limits on other design elements and potentially even other requirements.

During your design, careful consideration should be taken to ensure that each requirement remains met as other design decisions are made. It is entirely possible that while working to achieve one requirement you make a design decision that violates another requirement.

Constraints

A constraint defines how something must be accomplished. It doesn't typically dictate a specific outcome of the project, but it will certainly restrict how you go about achieving your desired outcomes. Constraints take on many forms. Some constraints are political in nature, while others are based on financial means, technical concerns, or even time.

For example, when meeting with your CIO you learn that he significantly favors one provider of professional services over another. While you could likely make a compelling case for using the other vendor, you feel it is unlikely that he would change his mind. In this case, we consider the vendor choice a constraint and not a requirement because the project isn't focused on *who* performs the work; it is focused on what work is to be performed. The CIO is constraining your options for implementation services providers, not dictating requirements.

Another example of a constraint would be a limitation on the budget available for the project. This constraint is present in nearly all projects, though it isn't often called out explicitly unless the budget is reduced mid-plan, or if during the planning meetings a stakeholder indicates a need that will exceed the original budget. In some cases the budget constraint could even be elastic in the sense that depending on the objective, additional funding might become available.

Lastly, time can also be a constraint. We're not referring to a due date or milestone date in this case. Time, as a constraint, is a limitation on when you can work, or how much work can be performed in a given time period. For example, you may only have access to the site from 8am until 5pm Monday through Friday. If you know there is 120 hours of work to be performed, you must either choose to be onsite for three weeks, or employ three people to work simultaneously. That constraint may be linked to other constraints such as tasks that must be completed in sequence versus in parallel.

Assumptions

Making assumptions is a good thing. Well, let's rephrase that.... Identifying assumptions is a good thing. Whenever we design something we also typically assume some things as well. Those things may seem insignificant or even obvious, but if we base some of the design decisions on assumptions, we could be in for a big surprise. Assumptions may later prove inaccurate or the thing being assumed may change without notice.

This is why it's vital for us to carefully document the logic behind the design decisions. For example, if we are considering the use of iSCSI for storage, there may be several factors to consider. This decision is based on the assumption that the networking team will deliver a dedicated 10Gbps LAN for the iSCSI use. It is reasonable to assume that a dedicated 10Gbps LAN should have sufficient capacity to support an iSCSI network, but we still need to document this as an assumption. The reason is because we aren't directly responsible for the delivery of the 10Gbps LAN (the networking team is), but that delivery has been assumed when we were making the design decisions to use iSCSI. For example, if we *assume* they will deliver the dedicated 10Gbps network, but instead it is delivered as a shared resource, the bandwidth available to iSCSI may change, and we may have insufficient bandwidth for the storage network.

Noting these assumptions will help throughout the design because we can later verify that the assumptions haven't changed, and therefore the design decisions are still valid. In the above example, we should confer with the networking team to ensure they know their responsibilities before we finalize the project. Think of this as expectation management. It's always better to go over the expectations again, rather than assume everyone knows his/her responsibilities.

Risks

Every project has a risk or two. Some risks are more obvious than others, and in many cases risks and assumptions are very closely related. The chief difference between a risk and an assumption is that an assumption is something that we believe to be true without proof because we have no reason to believe otherwise. A risk on the other hand is something we hope is true, but we know there is a potential that it may prove inaccurate or the circumstances surrounding the assumption may change easily.

For the purposes of your project, you should identify risks that pose a real threat to the success of your project. While it would be great to identify every conceivable risk, some risks may mitigate or don't pose a significant threat to the overall project. Focus on areas that would be impacted the most if the risk manifests itself into a credible threat. For example, you might label executive sponsorship/approval as a risk if the project is being run from the lower ranks and presented to upper management. If the executive team decides not to fund the project, the project dies.

Another risk may be timing. There could be a window of opportunity where you will have the ability to leverage a specific and critical resource for your project. Missing that window of opportunity should be listed as a risk because if you miss the window, you may not be able to successfully complete your project on time (or at all).

ASSESSING WHAT WE HAVE—ARCHITECTURE ANALYSIS

Before you draw up a grand plan of buying new servers, storage, and other things you can't afford, it might be a good idea to determine what equipment and resources you already have in your environment. It's not necessarily about saving money; it's about interoperability. Though some elements of your network or storage architecture will likely be replaced during your project, it isn't likely that you'll start over from scratch. Even consultants designing new vSphere implementations rarely find true "green field" environments where they can build everything from the ground up. In many cases, you will need to reuse or even repurpose existing equipment for your project. In all but the most rare circumstances you will be required to interoperate with the existing network or storage infrastructure. Determining what you have before you start planning will help you design an appropriate and compatible solution.

Collecting Information

To begin collecting information about your environment, you need to know what to look for. That may sound absurd because after all it is *your* environment; you know everything there is to know about it. We're going to cover it anyway because in this sense we're going to look in great detail at some areas, while other areas will be glossed over at a much higher level. Not all the information in your environment will be relevant to a vSphere design, and you will likely find that you are missing some key information as you flip through these pages.

Tip

Did you know that there are tools available both from VMware and third parties to help you collect some of this information? VMware provides a tool called Capacity Planner that can help identify virtualization candidates based on their resource usage. You will still need to collect empirical data about your environment, but these tools can be of great help, especially if you have large number of servers.

To simplify the process, we'll break your environment down into some bite-sized chunks.

- Servers/hosts
- Networking
- Storage
- Data protection
- Staff
- Facilities

Servers/Hosts

Depending on their age, your servers, or "hosts" as we call them in a virtual infrastructure, may be reusable in your vSphere 5 environment. Age alone is not a solid guarantee of compatibility. We need to know the hardware make up of each host; that is, the manufacturer, model, and any specific hardware components within the servers.

The most important information is the number of logical processors, the CPU type and model, the amount of RAM, the type of network adapters, and the storage devices/adapters in the host. Other details such as redundant fans and power supplies, serial numbers, video cards, and other hardware accessories can be left out for now. That information may be useful to you at some point, but it won't likely impact our decision of whether to install ESX on the host.

The next step will feel like a time-sink, but it is worth it in the long run. You need to collect the CPU and RAM utilization statistics from all the servers you intend to virtualize. It may take you a considerable amount of time depending on the number of servers you have, but once you have collected it the information will prove invaluable. That information will be your chief indicator as to which servers are good virtualization candidates. It will also help you determine the size and number of ESX hosts you will need for the project. Without these statistics, you'll make blind decisions based on assumptions, and we know how well that works (or doesn't).

Gather this information for each of your hosts and place it in a spreadsheet. We will add to this spreadsheet over the next few sections, and then finally put it to use when we enter the next phase of the planning process: The Current State Analysis.

Networking

The networking components could be broken down even further, but for the sake of brevity we will discuss three key areas: endpoints, transport, and the separation of your networks.

The endpoints are your servers; more accurately we're referring to the NICs in your servers. What speed are they? How many are active/disabled? What IP addresses are assigned to each? How heavily utilized are the NICs (Mbps and packets/second)? These questions should represent additional columns in your spreadsheet for each server you intend to virtualize.

When we refer to transport, we are talking about the various upstream switches that will connect your servers to the rest of your network. Depending on the size and scale of your network, these switches may be your "core switches," a "distribution" layer, or even just an "access" layer. Whatever you call it, we need to know what type of switches you possess, their link speeds, their capabilities, and the number of available ports.

The capabilities of your switches may include things such as VLAN trunking, port aggregation, and spanning tree. These functions may be necessary to implement proper network separation in your vSphere design. As before, gather this information in a spreadsheet so we can analyze it later, but it would be best to create a new page or tab because this information isn't directly related to the servers.

The final category we mentioned was the separation of your networks. This can be accomplished in a number of ways and they reflect the age-old OSI model: Physical, Ethernet, and TCP/IP.

Physical separation is just that, it is a physically separate network. There are no uplinks that tie that network to another. Common examples here include dedicated iSCSI networks, DMZs or extranets, and isolated lab environments. You need to know how many of these isolated physical networks you must support in your virtual environment. For instance, if you intend to host VMs that are in your DMZ along side VMs that are in your production network, you must have separate network adapters in the host to keep these networks separate.

The next type of separation is based on Ethernet or layer 2. We use VLANs to logically break up a single physical network into multiple broadcast domains. Each broadcast domain is mutually exclusive and broadcast (or unicast traffic) does not cross between each other. You need to understand how many VLANs you have and what each is used for. In addition, you should determine if you can create additional VLANs dedicated for virtualization use (vMotion, Fault Tolerant Logging, and/or Management).

Finally we have layer 3 segmentation, IP subnets. You may have multiple subnets in a given VLAN or sharing a single physical network. It is important to determine how your network is organized, including the number of routers and firewalls that separate the traffic. Don't forget to record the link speeds of those routers and firewalls. If you must pass traffic between two IP subnets you may find that you have a bottleneck at the router or firewall. Just because you have a 10Gbps LAN doesn't necessarily mean that your routers and firewalls have 10Gbps interfaces. The traffic crossing those devices will slow down to the speed of their interfaces, resulting in a bottleneck where your network speed is reduced to 1Gbps or even 100Mbps.

Knowing how your network is segmented or physically separated will define the number and type of your virtual switches. Document this information in the form of a network map, but also list the VLANs, IP subnets, and any physical networks in your spreadsheet (possibly a new sheet/tab).

Storage

Storage is easily one of the more overlooked and underemphasized aspects of pre-planning, yet it arguably has the most profound impact on a virtualization design.

Unlike in a physical environment where storage is dedicated to each server, in a virtual environment we share storage among the virtual machines. Part of the reason storage is often overlooked is because virtualization projects are typically initiated and organized by people who have always dealt with storage in local, non-shared capacities. The storage they're most familiar with is dedicated and locally attached to their servers. Each server has its own storage, and disk contention either doesn't exist or has never been diagnosed as a problem.

Not factoring in the effects of shared storage can result in a virtualization design that suffers from disk contention right out of the gate. A common mistake in virtualization projects is to assume that you can cram every server you have into a single storage array. While you might be able to pull it off, a better plan would be to find out your storage requirements *before* you try it.

Storage Requirements   When it comes to storage, it's not just the size that matters; it's how you use it. Pub humor aside, that statement is absolutely true. Disk capacity has an impact in your design, but it isn't the most important aspect. We need to know how you are using your storage. We can measure the utilization in I/O Operations Per Second (IOPS) and in bandwidth. The IOPS will tell us how many transactions are going to and from your disks to meet the demands of your workload (such as a mail server or database server). The bandwidth is a measure of how much data we're sending in a given second. You can equate these two figures to a network; packets per second versus Mbps. Just because you are not utilizing 4Gbps of data throughput doesn't mean you don't have a lot of packets of data. In storage, the more packets you send, the more the backend storage processor must process. The more it has to process, the slower its response. This leads us to the final requirement: latency. Latency is the amount of time we must wait for the storage system to process the requests. The higher the latency, the slower the workload behaves.

You will need to collect information about your physical servers' IOPS, bandwidth, average latency, and yes, disk sizes before we will know how many workloads can coexist on the same storage array. This information can be obtained within the operating system of your servers using tools such as perfmon for Windows, and iostat for Linux/Unix systems. There are also automated third-party tools available that can help you automate the collection of this information from your servers.

Again, enter this information into your spreadsheet. You can just add a few extra columns in your server spreadsheet because we will use this information along with the CPU, RAM, and network statistics when defining virtualization candidates. The storage information will also be used to define the type and number of disk storage systems required for your project.

Data Protection

Wouldn't it be nice if virtualization eliminated the need for backups? Unfortunately for you, it doesn't. In fact, it adds a new dimension of backups that can be either a blessing or a curse depending on your job. We'll discuss the various ways we can backup virtual machines and the data they hold later in this book. This section focuses on identifying your existing backup strategy so that when you are done with your project your data protection level is either at the same level or better than when you started.

You can add a couple more columns to your spreadsheet of servers. These columns should define the frequency and type of backup performed on each server. You might have daily full backups, or hourly incrementals. Whatever the case, enter it here. We won't use this to size the environment, but it will be helpful when you are choosing your backup strategy later.

You might also want to note your data retention policies and any disaster recovery information relevant to your servers. This will be helpful when determining how long you must keep your disk-based or tape-based backups later. Some servers may have different retention periods, so record this information on your server spreadsheet even if it is the same for all servers.

Staff

This one may not seem like it fits in a project plan, but believe us, it does. The people behind the project matter as much as the equipment you select. It's important to assess your team to determine their capabilities. This will tell you if training is required, whether consultants will be needed, and who will maintain and manage the environment once the project has been completed.

Assessing the technical ability of your team can be a sensitive topic, especially if any member of the team is a bit insecure. Despite the challenges it must be done, even if informally. When possible, make it known what you are doing and involve the team members. Your impression of a person's technical abilities may not be representative of their actual abilities. Ask them, involve them, and explain why you need to know; it will ultimately benefit them.

Depending on your project budget, this is where training may play a part. If you determine that the key component you lack is technical know-how, allocate funding to train your team. The training will likely pay for itself quickly if you can avoid or minimize the use of contractors. In addition, the training will help you maintain and manage the environment in the long run.

Tip

Did you know that VMware has a wide array of training offerings? While some vender training is aimed exclusively toward certification, VMware's educational materials are designed to help you in the field. They offer classes ranging from Installation/Configuration of vSphere to advanced troubleshooting and design workshops. Refer to VMware's Education website for more details. http://www.vmware.com/education.

Consultants and contractors may be an option if you don't have the technical expertise and can't reasonably expect your team to bear the burden of a large project. Labor can quickly drive up the cost of a project, so be wary of how much you intend to use consultants and limit their scope appropriately to avoid nasty surprises. This is another case of expectation management. Things work best if you make your expectations crystal clear (in writing) and the consultants understand what is expected of them (and agree to it in writing).

Finally, you need to understand who will maintain the virtual environment in your organization. Identify who is expected to maintain the systems and determine if they have the available resources and technical ability to do so. Keep in mind that there will be a transitional period where both physical and virtual systems are in production. Leveraging your existing system administrators may be possible, but you may need to augment their headcount during that transition while they determine the most efficient means to support the new environment. After all, there's no point in building a grand design if no one will be able to keep it running after it has been built.

Facilities

Another easily overlooked area is the capacity and functionality of your datacenter. Do you have sufficient power to run both the new servers and the old servers simultaneously while you migrate to the virtual environment? You need to verify that the UPS can handle the additional load, and then determine if the HVAC in the datacenter will handle the increased heat output of the new equipment. If a generator is available, does it have sufficient capacity to start the equipment if the UPS were to fail?

This might seem like a lot to consider, but there is an alternative. If upgrading your datacenter is no trivial matter, you might consider migrating to a public cloud provider. Private clouds are expandable environments that you own entirely, and likely maintain yourself. On the other hand, a public cloud is owned and maintained by someone else. The facilities are someone else's problem. You lease a part of their infrastructure and migrate your servers into their virtual environment.

There are costs with either option, and there is no guaranteed answer that we can give you on whether or not to use a public cloud provider. We can only guide you to analyze the costs associated with each option and pick the option that has the longest reaching benefits. Don't choose either option based on a 1–2 year plan.

Current State Analysis

Collecting the information is a time-consuming process, so it might take awhile before you're ready to begin analyzing the data. Don't rush things. The data you collect now will be your only true gauge of how things were running before you virtualized them. In addition to helping you refute claims of performance degradation due to virtualization, the data will help you size your virtual infrastructure and help determine which components of your infrastructure must be replaced or upgraded.

The analysis of your current environment or current state isn't a one-time meeting where you pour over all the data and make executive decisions about the future. It is a process that involves reviewing your findings and comparing them to your architectural vision parameters such as business goals, requirements, constraints, and overall project scope. You will use this information to further refine your plan and potentially adjust your requirements and scope if what you have found is different from what you had initially expected to find.

For example, you may have initially assumed that your Microsoft SQL Server system was not a virtualization candidate because it seemed to be over utilized. During your information gathering process you determined that its daily CPU average was 5%–10%, with periodic bursts of 70%–80% throughout the day. After analyzing the disk utilization, you determined that the I/O requirements could still be met if virtualized, but your DBA recommended that you assign a dedicated set of hard disks for the transaction logs.

Throughout this book we will discuss various areas of planning and the questions you should ask while creating your plan. You will use the data collected in your current state analysis to answer these questions and help form a solid design that fits your environment. The result of the current state analysis is the technology architecture, which we cover next.

DESIGN CONSIDERATIONS—TECHNOLOGY ARCHITECTURE

At this point you've determined the boundaries and goals of your project and you've learned as much about your existing environment as you ever wanted to know (or perhaps even more than you wanted to know). The next step is to develop a design that meets the needs of the business while being ever mindful of what you uncovered during your current state analysis.

The technology architecture involves creating both documentation and diagrams that identify and support your design decisions for the new environment. I know we've said it a couple times already, but it bears repeating. Documenting your decisions is critical, even if you believe the decision is obvious. This will become more apparent if you start to change aspects of the design and later ask "why did we choose five hosts versus six?" or "why didn't we include host profiles?"

Designs and Diagrams

This is the part where we create a bunch of pretty pictures and write a book to explain how to build everything. Okay, well maybe not a book, but you might come close to it if you have a complex design with a lot of decisions to justify. As you can guess, there is a lot more to designing than opening Visio and drawing a couple of diagrams. We have to explain what to do with those diagrams.

Note

In our experience, pictures do say a thousand words, but they aren't always the words you intended to say. A well-crafted diagram may give an installer all the information he/she needs to build the system, but it won't provide any supporting information. A design document will fill in those voids and help the installer understand your line of thinking (and therefore keep on track) even if you overlooked something.

In the next few sections we'll discuss the design document as well as a couple different types of design diagrams. That's right, there are different types of diagrams, and each has a specific purpose and time when it is most useful. You may not even need or create all these diagrams, but you won't know until you read about them.

Make your diagraming life easier by using Visio stencils whenever possible. In this book we used the artwork and stencils from VisioCafe.com. We've used their stencils for years because they are both gorgeous and easily recognized by most IT people. Just remember to ask the author for permission before republishing any stencil/shape you intend to use for commercial purposes.

Tip

Check out VisioCafe.com for some rather spectacular stencils, ranging from logical concepts to actual physical hardware. Always use detail where appropriate: logical diagrams should use logical concepts; whereas physical connectivity diagrams should actually depict the physical devices whenever possible.

- **The design document.** The comprehensive justification for all your decisions.
- **Conceptual diagrams.** Whiteboard sketches and other things written on napkins.

- **Logical diagrams.** The high-level connectivity and assembly diagrams.
- **Physical diagrams.** A very, very detailed diagram used at install time.

The Design Document

So now you might be thinking: "Hey, I'm the one who will be installing all this stuff; I don't need a document to justify my decisions!" Well, even if you are the designer, implementer, and maintainer all rolled up into one nice package, you still need to write out a plan to explain to anyone else that has to support this mess…er…project, after you get promoted. You do intend to move on at some point, right? Documentation doesn't endanger your job; it allows you to move up and on to bigger and better projects. Trust us. We know.

Of course an organized document would probably be helpful to anyone reading it, but the design document doesn't have to follow a fancy format. It can be a Word document with references to hardware and software quotes, Visio diagrams, and pages in VMware's documentation. Yes, you can reference someone else's documentation; why reinvent the wheel? Just be sure to cite your source. It isn't about plagiarism; in this case, the risk is that VMware may change their documentation without sending you an email first (I know, the nerve, right?). If you have noted your source, you can always check your sources later.

Note

> Remember, this document is your design document. It isn't a run-book to install the product. Keep it concise and refer to other documents for clarification and installation steps.

In the course of justifying your design decisions, you will likely also make references back to your initial design meetings. You should include all those notes and interviews in this document. Record the required timetables, budget, and even your current state analysis. Again, all of that is part of your justification for each decision in your design. You should reference this material so that it is evident where your decision originated. Don't reinvent the wheel and re-explain something that was written well during an interview with one of your SMEs.

Design Decision Example

> This can be a lot to take in, so here's an example of something you might include in your design document:
>
> During your project planning meetings, the network security manager mentions that your extranet currently exposes your public-facing servers to a lot of unnecessary risk because all the servers are part of the same VLAN and IP subnet. If one server becomes compromised the others would be completely exposed.

Instead of creating a bunch of little VLANs and wasting IP subnets for each, he asks you to consider using private VLANs to isolate the traffic between your hosts. You know that the vNetwork Distributed Switches can support this.

In your design document you will need to specify that vNetwork Distributed Switches are to be used for the extranet. Your rationale can be very concise: these switches support private VLANs, which were recommended by the network security manager.

> **Decision.** A vNetwork Distributed Switch will be configured for systems in the extranet.

> **Rationale.** These switches support private VLANs, which were recommended by the network security manager; see SME-NSM Interview #1 paragraph 6.

Again, you don't have to re-write the context of that meeting, just reference it as shown in the example. You're really just trying to record the reasons (aka the features) that drove you to include a vNetwork Distributed Switch in your design so that if someone later asks you to downgrade your vSphere version, you can explain what you will give up as a result.

The final result of your design document should be a comprehensive story describing your process and logic throughout your project. There should be very little, if anything, in your project left to guesswork or speculation. Of course, getting this detailed doesn't guarantee the project will go exactly as you intended. What it does mean, however, is that if something changes during the course of your project, you will have a reasonable chance to determine which other areas of the project may have just been put at risk.

Conceptual Diagrams

Have you ever had a brainstorm at lunch or dinner and just started scribbling stuff on the nearest writable surface? Hopefully you at least found a bar napkin because you wouldn't want to lose those precious diagrams. You might not think much of them, but these conceptual diagrams are the foundation for future diagrams and discussions. We refer to these diagrams as "conceptual" because they don't necessarily represent a system or even a collection of systems. They represent thought processes.

So now you're wondering why you should bother including scribbles in a professional project plan, right? Well the answer is that they lead us to create the more detailed diagrams later, and they help you remember past discussions. Those discussions may invoke new thoughts as your project progresses, so retaining these diagrams is a way to ensure that nothing is left out, even the colorful, less-than-sober ideas.

Figure 2.1 is an example of a conceptual diagram. We decided not to show you a crumpled up paper napkin diagram because it didn't look very nice, but the effect is the same. Conceptual diagrams don't have a lot of detail. They represent ideas rather than actual components and addresses.

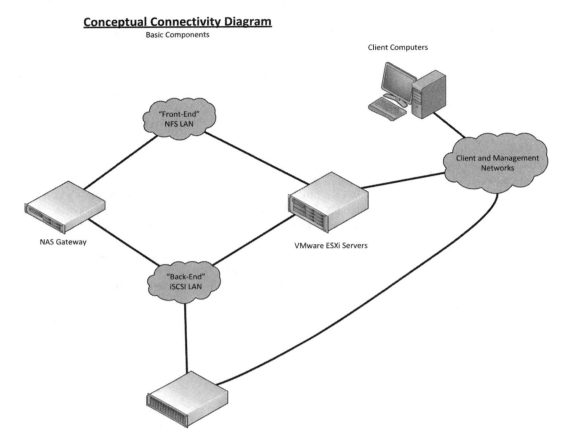

Figure 2.1
Basic conceptual diagram.

Logical Diagrams

As you see, a conceptual diagram isn't going to help us much at install time; we need something with a bit more detail, but not so much detail that we get lost in a sea of physical connectors and interfaces. A logical diagram targets that middle ground by illustrating abstractions and, you guessed it, logical connectivity. These diagrams may be focused on network connectivity, security topologies, server deployment work-flows, storage diagrams, and more.

Logical diagrams are really the catchall diagram type between the more conceptual "artwork" diagrams and the highly detailed and specific physical diagrams. As a result, this is the most common type of diagram used in planning and in post-install documentation. Another reason is that they provide a lot of detail, but lack the aspects that are likely to change at install time. Also, remember that you can

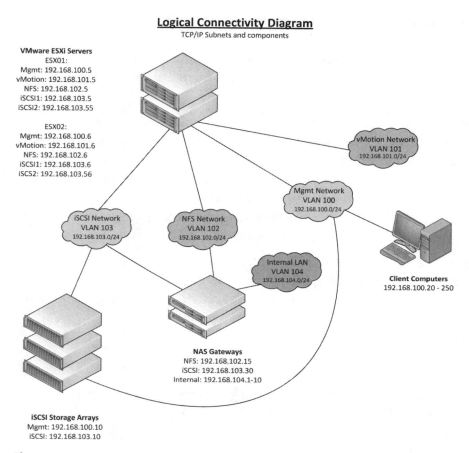

Figure 2.2
Logical diagram.

obtain Visio stencils of logical concepts too. Using standardized shapes can greatly help your readers understand your diagrams without needing a key to explain everything.

In Figure 2.2, we've expanded upon the conceptual diagram to include the TCP/IP interfaces of the networking components. This logical diagram is used when configuring the various servers and storage devices, and it serves as documentation after the project has been completed.

Physical Diagrams

So, the logical diagram added more information, but it didn't really tell us where to connect all those cables. That need brings us to the high-detail physical diagrams. These diagrams are helpful at install time, but they can also be helpful during troubleshooting should something change with your storage or network cabling. Physical diagrams depict how everything is actually cabled. We show the exact interfaces for the cables and how they connect to each other. If someone changed the configuration of a port on a switch, or if they moved a network cable, you can refer to these diagrams to set things right. They also remove ambiguity for the installers when building the system.

In some cases, physical diagrams can be photos scanned in and annotated. Other times they rely on specialized Visio stencils with pre-drawn images of server, networking, and storage objects. A physical diagram doesn't have to look exactly like the physical devices, but it certainly helps. Physical diagrams just need to show the relationship between the physical connectors. That means you can use boxes inside of boxes if you have to. Just be sure to label your diagram because physical diagrams aren't typically bundled with many extra documents and notes.

In Figure 2.3, you can see a mess of cables and connectors. Trust us, it looks better in color, and it actually becomes readable when printed on large-scale paper. That is typical with physical diagrams. You are trying to represent a physical environment,

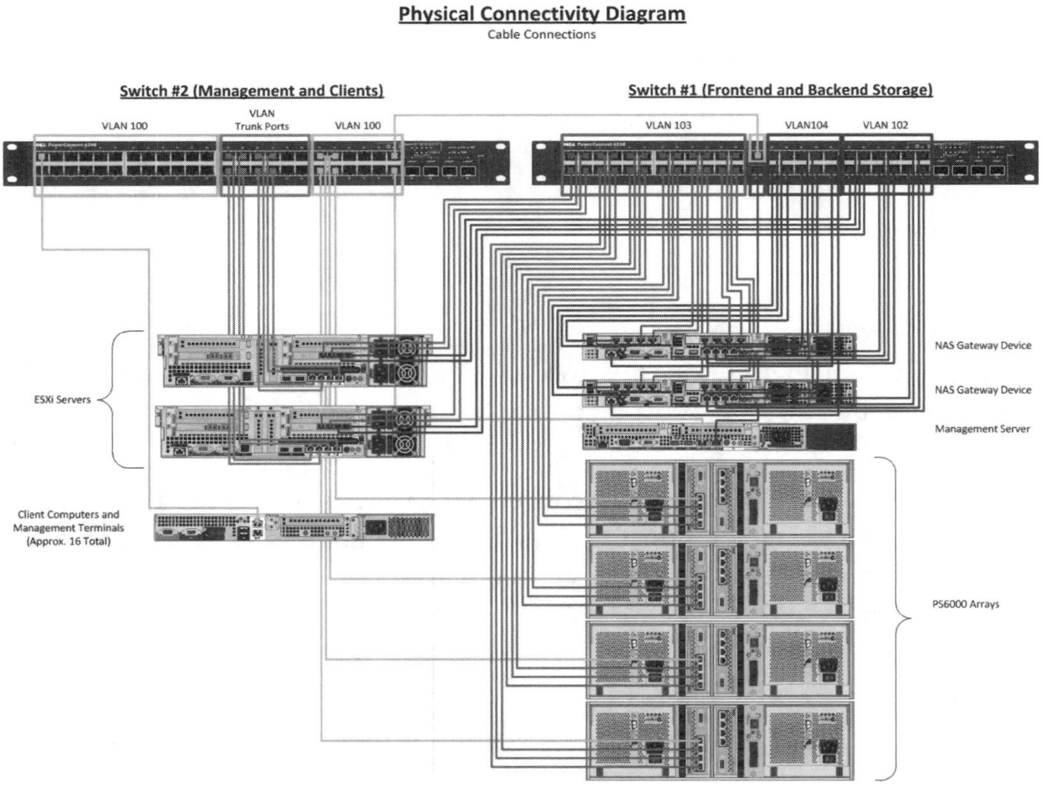

Figure 2.3
Physical diagram.

so occasionally these diagrams become life-size. In this case, the diagram was used to explain which ports were to be cabled to each switch port. You can also see how it maps to the previous example of the logical diagram.

High-Level Overview

At the beginning of this chapter we said that the intricate details of planning would be contained in each chapter throughout this book. We're going to stick with that plan, but in this section we wanted to outline just a few of the topics we discuss in later chapters of this book.

Hosts

- How many hosts should we have?
- How do you know how to size the hosts?
- Should we use Active Directory authentication on the hosts?
- Do we need to configure/alter the ESXi firewall?

vCenter

- Will vCenter be a VM or a physical server?
- Will vCenter be installed on Windows or as a vApp?
- What type of database can we use?
- How do we configure permissions and security in vCenter

Networking

- How many vSwitches do we need?
- Should we use Standard or Distributed Switches?
- Do we need VLANs?
- Should we consider using network I/O control?

Storage

- What's the difference between Fibre Channel, iSCSI, and NAS storage?
- Should we use Storage vMotion and Storage DRS?
- Do we have a need to use storage I/O control?
- How should I configure my new VMFS LUNs?

Virtual Machines

- How many vCPUs should I allocate to a VM?

- Do I want to be stingy with RAM, or pass it out freely to the VMs?

- Where will each VM store its disks?

- Should we convert the physical servers or start from scratch?

Cluster

- How many hosts should we have in each cluster?

- How should we assign resources to the VMs?

- How should you configure High Availability (HA) for the cluster?

- Should we utilize DRS in fully automated mode?

Management

- How can we use host profiles?

- How will we patch the ESXi hosts?

- How will we manage the configuration of the environment?

- What should we consider when converting physical machines to VMs?

PUTTING THE PLAN INTO MOTION—MIGRATION PLANNING

Up to now, we've gathered information, determined what we have, built a plan for what we want, and drawn an assortment of pictures to help us bring it all together, but there is something missing. We need an implementation plan that can take us from where we are to where we want to be.

This design document isn't an implementation plan; it's a story of how the plan was created. The Migration Plan is your implementation plan and guide. But before we can make such a plan, we must first perform a brief gap analysis to see how far we are from our goal.

The "Gap Analysis"

A gap analysis is a study that compares two configuration states to determine the "gap" or the differences between them. In this case, the two configuration states are the current state and the final plan represented in the design document. The gap analysis needs to show which components are to be replaced, and the order of the implementation events. Like the design document, we don't want to include all the verbose detail of how to perform these tasks in the gap analysis. Instead we use the gap analysis to create another document that breaks down what must be done to implement the design. We'll call that document the implementation guide.

Before we get into the implementation guide, we should talk about how to organize and complete the gap analysis. This document should be task-based, but it is not a run-book. Also, some tasks will have dependencies; therefore a Gantt chart may be the easiest way to represent the Migration Plan.

To begin the gap analysis, you must compare your current analysis with your design documents. Look for things such as new hardware or software. Determine how long it will take to receive those items, and then how long you estimate the installation process will take. If you organize the tasks and task dependencies in your Gantt chart you will have built a gap analysis that can be easily converted into an Implementation Plan.

The Implementation Plan

Once you have created the Gantt chart you know what tasks must be performed and can begin the final phase of the plan: the Implementation Plan or run-book. This document will list the steps and process required to install the environment. There could be more than one document, broken into functional areas, and then distributed to the implementation team. For instance, the server team may be charged with the responsibility of installing the hardware and software for ESXi hosts, whereas the storage team may be responsible for configuring the SAN and the associated connectivity.

This guide might give step-by-step instructions, or it might make references to the vender documentation. Either option is fine as long as the steps are made available to the installation team.

SUMMARY

So how do you know when you're finished with the plan? When you have reviewed the plan with your team and no one has any questions. Okay, that sounds a bit ambiguous, but that's because we can't tell you when you will be done.

The thought we will leave you with is this: You won't ever answer 100% of the questions, nor can you plan for 100% of the situations. Strive for 80% and then trust your team to make up the difference with their own good judgment. If you have documented your decision rationale properly, they may know what you had in mind without even having to ask.

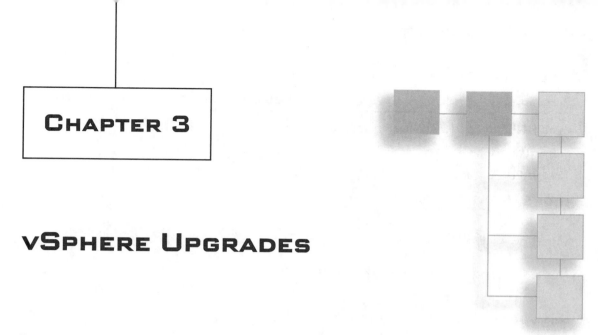

CHAPTER 3

vSphere Upgrades

In many environments, System Administrators are faced with a dilemma when a new version of an existing operating system is released. Many wonder if there is something in this new release that they need. The benefits offered by the new version must be evaluated against the possible risk of a change in the environment; current applications and drivers must be evaluated for compatibility with the proposed new software, backups must be taken, and the possibility of a maintenance period exists for the duration of the upgrade process.

If possible, a good practice is to deploy a test environment with representative operating systems and applications to verify that the new revisions of vSphere 5 and vCenter will meet production environment needs, and will provide a seamless transition to the new deployment. This provides a means to verify that all drivers and updates will be compatible, and configuration changes can be tested in a non-production environment.

Once the installation has been documented and tested, it is also possible to deploy new servers with the updated vSphere 5 operating system and all necessary drivers and updates. If the storage is configured to be shared between the old and new servers, the virtual machines can be migrated and upgraded in one process, minimizing the impact to the production installation.

Fresh Install versus Upgrading from a Previous Version

In this chapter, we will examine the process of upgrading an existing vCenter instance to a vCenter 5 installation. As we will see, most of the existing components

Table 3.1   Fresh Install versus Upgrading an Existing Version

Procedure	Installing vCenter	Upgrading vCenter
Install .NET 3.5 and Windows Installer 4.5	Yes	Yes
Select Language	Yes	Yes
Accept EULA	Yes	Yes
Provide Customer Information	Yes	Yes (Edit Existing Information)
Install New Database	Yes	No (Upgrade Existing Database)
Upgrade vCenter Agents on each ESXi Host	No	Yes
Provide Login Credentials	Yes	Yes
Select Destination Folder	Yes	Yes
Select Folder for Inventory Service	Yes	Yes
Choose Linked Mode Options	Yes	No
Choose Ports for vCenter	Yes	Yes
Choose Ports for Inventory Service	Yes	Yes
Choose JVM Configuration	Yes	Yes

will seamlessly upgrade to the new version, but how does this upgrade process compare to a fresh install of vCenter? In Table 3.1, we compare the two methods of obtaining a vCenter 5 installation.

Note that many of the steps are common between the two approaches; however, there are differences:

- In the new installation, a new database is created, while an upgrade provides the option to upgrade the existing table structure or to create a new database to store the vCenter content.

- In the installation process, the vCenter agents are installed on each ESXi host when that host is added to the vCenter inventory; the upgrade will locate those legacy vCenter agents and offer to upgrade them.

- The upgrade process does not provide the option to modify the Linked Mode configuration, while Linked Mode can be initiated as part of the installation.

Once the decision has been made to perform the upgrade, you must determine if an upgrade path is available that will allow you to smoothly transition to a new version, or will you simply install the new version and migrate over existing processes? Fortunately, VMware has made the decision a bit easier by providing an upgrade path from legacy versions of the ESX/ESXi virtualization platform, including versions of ESX and ESXi 3.5 and later, and also allows the migration from Virtual Center 2.5 Update 6 and later. Please note that if an environment contains versions of ESX and Virtual Center earlier than those specified, those hosts will need to be upgraded to those minimum levels before upgrading to vSphere 5.

It is important to mention the relevance of the VMware communities resource. This is a great place to obtain pre-installation information based on the experiences of others who may be using the same hardware and adapters as you. Also, there are several blogs that are written by VMware engineers and consultants that can provide insight into VMware technologies and implementation advice. These blogs are accessible from the blogs.vmware.com web page.

UPGRADE PATHS

In the upgrade process, there are several components that will need to be upgraded. These include:

- VirtualCenter/vCenter
- The ESX/ESXi host(s)
- vSphere modules
- VMFS
- Orchestrator
- vNetwork Standard/Distributed Switch
- VMware Tools/Virtual Machine Hardware
- Update Manager
- vSphere Client
- VMware View

We will begin by examining the process to upgrade an existing vCenter instance. vCenter is the "command and control" center of the VMware environment, and many of the components that are considered to be Enterprise level are contained solely within the vCenter realm. Once we have upgraded vCenter itself, we have additional options to upgrade the ESX/ESXi hosts. To begin the process, consider the following:

- Verify that any existing vCenter plug-ins are compatible with the new vSphere 5 platform. The VMware Product Interoperability Matrix can be accessed at https://www.vmware.com/resources/compatibility/sim/interop_matrix.php.

- Verify that all hardware is compatible with the new virtualization environment in the VMware Compatibility Guide at http://www.vmware.com/resources/compatibility/search.php.

- It is important to mention here that vCenter 5 is backward-compatible with versions of VMware back to VI 3.5 Update 6, and can fully manage and communicate with these legacy installations. However, Virtual Center 2.5 cannot communicate with any version of vSphere, so any implementation that will include multiple revisions of VMware will need to be managed through vSphere 5.

First, as always, a complete backup of the existing host(s) should be created. This allows the administrator to return to the previous version should the need present itself. Once the backup has been verified, the upgrade process can begin in earnest.

vCenter Server

Upgrading previous versions of vCenter can take two forms: those that begin with versions of Virtual Center, and those that are based on vCenter. Versions of Virtual Center prior to Update 6 are not supported with vCenter 5 and must be updated to version 6 before a data migration is possible.

Versions of vCenter 4.0 and later can be upgraded in-place as long as the operating system is a 64-bit version. Any 32-bit installations must use the Data Migration tool to complete the upgrade. Table 3.2 summarizes the possibilities for upgrading to vCenter 5.

At the same time, the vSphere Client must also be upgraded to accommodate the new vCenter 5 platform. Table 3.3 summarizes the requirements for upgrading the vSphere Client.

Prerequisites for Upgrading the vCenter Database

As you are considering the process of upgrading the various components of your VMware environment, it is helpful to remember that each component will have some considerations associated with it. Spending a little time to verify that these issues are remedied at this stage will result in a smoother and easier transition. In this section, we will look at the "little gotchas" that are related to the vCenter database.

Table 3.2 vCenter Upgrade Support

Version of vCenter	Upgrade Supported?	Comments
Prior to Virtual Center Update 6	No	
Virtual Center 2.5 Update 6	Yes	This version can be upgraded by migrating to the vCenter 5 on a separate physical or virtual machine using the Data Migration tool. If the database is located on a separate device, the database can simply be upgraded. This upgrade will extend the schema of the data to ensure compatibility with vCenter 5.
vCenter 4.0	Yes	If the vCenter platform is installed on a 64-bit operating system, an in-place upgrade can be performed. If vCenter is installed on a 32-bit operating system, the Data Migration tool must be used to complete the migration.
vCenter 4.1	Yes	In-place upgrade.

Table 3.3 vSphere Client Upgrade Support

Version of the Client	Upgrade?	Comments
vSphere Client 4.0	No	No upgrade supported
vSphere 4.1	Yes	In-place upgrade

Note

The information below is accurate as of the Generally Available (GA) release of vSphere 5. Please check your release notes for the version of vSphere 5 that you are installing for any relevant updates to these prerequisites.

IBM DB2 9.5

- The correct version of the IBM DB2 Native Client for the database must be installed. A minimum of Fix pack 5 is required, and Fix pack 7 is recommended.
- The IBM Data Server Runtime Client will need to be installed if the database is located on a separate physical or virtual machine.
- Verify that the ODBC data source name entry reflects the correct database server and credentials for the environment.

- Verify that the directory for the DB2 binaries is in the system path statement. This sub-directory is often found in the C:\Program Files\IBM\SQLLIB\BIN folder.

- Remember that the Windows server that hosts the vCenter platform may require a reboot in order to locate and recognize the database correctly.

IBM DB2 9.7

- The same prerequisites apply as those listed for DB2 version 9.5.

- A minimum of Fix pack 2 is required, and Fix pack 3a is recommended.

Microsoft SQL Server 2005

- SP3 is required for 32-bit and 64-bit versions of SQL Server 2005 for compatibility with vCenter 5.

- Verify that the ODBC data source name entry reflects the correct database server and credentials for the environment.

- If you are planning to implement the new vCenter Server Appliance, SQL Server is not compatible with vCenter and cannot be used as the database.

Microsoft SQL Server 2008 Express

- In previous versions of Virtual Center or vCenter SQL Server, Express was included in the distribution media and was an option for smaller deployments that did not exceed 5 hosts and 50 virtual machines.

- This included database is not an option for an upgrade to vCenter 5. If you wish to use this version of the database, it must be installed prior to the upgrade, or a new, fresh installation of vCenter must be performed.

- If you are planning to implement the new vCenter Server Appliance, SQL Server is not compatible with vCenter and cannot be used as the database.

Microsoft SQL Server 2008 and SQL Server 2008 R2

- Verify that the ODBC data source name entry reflects the correct database server and credentials for the environment.

- If you are planning to implement the new vCenter Server Appliance, SQL Server is not compatible with vCenter and cannot be used as the database.

Oracle 10g R2

- In order to prepare for the upgrade to vCenter, patch 10.2.0.4 must be installed on both the existing vSphere Client and vCenter server, and then patch 5699495 can be applied to the client.

- Verify that the ODBC data source name entry reflects the correct database server and credentials for the environment.

- When the Oracle 10g client is installed, it contains the ojdbc14.jar driver set. By default, it installs to Oracle client install location\oracle\product\10.2.0\instance_name\jdbc\lib. The vCenter server will then copy the file from the default location to the directory for the vCenter Tomcat server (vCenter installation folder\Infrastructure\tomcat\lib). If the file is not located during the installation, you will need to download the file from the Oracle website and install it manually.

Oracle 11g

- Verify that the ODBC data source name entry reflects the correct database server and credentials for the environment.

- When the Oracle 10g client is installed, it contains the ojdbc14.jar driver set. By default, it installs to Oracle client install location\oracle\product\10.2.0\instance_name\jdbc\lib. The vCenter server will then copy the file from the default location to the directory for the vCenter Tomcat server (vCenter installation folder\Infrastructure\tomcat\lib). If the file is not located during the installation, you will need to download the file from the Oracle website and install it manually.

- Both Oracle 11g R1 11.1.0.7 and Oracle 11g R2 11.2.0.1 with patch 5 (9966926) are fully supported for compatibility with vCenter 5.

Upgrading a Previous Version of vCenter

As stated earlier, this process of upgrading vCenter, should, in an ideal situation, be performed first in a test lab. This allows you to resolve any issues that may arise from the upgrade process before transitioning into the production side. Following are some basic considerations that may make the job of upgrading your environment a simpler process.

Back Up the Existing Environment   It is a best practice to perform a complete backup of the existing environment prior to initiating the upgrade process. This provides a means to return to a previous installation if the upgrade results are not as planned. This will minimize downtime until the issues can be resolved. The two most important components that require a backup are the vCenter database and any SSL certificates that are in use.

Note

If for some reason the database and certificates are not backed up prior to the upgrade, there is no path back to the original environment.

To back up the current certificates, copy the SSL certificate folder found under %ALLUSERSPROFILE%\Application Data\VMware\VMware VirtualCenter and place it in a safe place.

As a rule, you may also wish to document the existing vCenter environment, such as IP address, FQDN, NTP and DNS configuration, vCenter DSN information, and any ports in use that deviate from the defaults.

Run the vCenter Host Agent Pre-Upgrade Checker The first step is to determine if any issues exist that may cause a failure or an incompatibility in the upgrade process. This can be accomplished by running the vCenter Host Agent Pre-Upgrade Checker tool. This tool is found on the distribution media for vCenter, and it is designed to evaluate any upgrades from vCenter 4.x to vCenter 5 for potential problems.

In order to reduce any possible issues, when the Host Agent Pre-Upgrade Checker is initialized, it accesses www.vmware.com and will download any required updates that apply to the Checker itself.

During the analysis, the Pre-Upgrade Checker will determine:

- If the ESX/ESXi server can be accessed through the network
- Whether there is enough disk space for the upgrade to proceed
- If the network configuration is correct
- Whether there are existing file system issues
- The existing patching level of the host

While the testing is designed to uncover possible inconsistencies, the Pre-Upgrade Checker cannot resolve issues on its own. Nor can it detect all possible issues, as it is designed to locate and detect issues that are known by the development team at VMware. As new issues present themselves, the Checker update is made available on the VMware website.

In order to use the Agent Pre-Upgrade Checker, verify that the vCenter server has both Microsoft .NET 3.5 SP1 and Microsoft VJ #2.0 SE installed. Note that both packages are included in the vCenter distribution media. Once the two Microsoft packages are installed, you will need to install the Agent Pre-Upgrade Checker application. This can be done by using the autorun feature of the vCenter distribution media, or by browsing the media for the AgentUpgradeChecker.exe file located in the \vpx\agentupgradecheck folder.

Once the install has completed, you will have the option to scan all ESXi hosts using the Standard Mode option, or to specify individual hosts by using the Custom Mode option. When the scan has completed, you can use the View Report link to review the findings, and the report will also contain links to VMware Knowledge Base (KB) articles that will help to resolve any issues that may have been detected.

The ESX System Analyzer   A new utility to aid in the detection and remediation of pre-upgrade issues is the ESX System Analyzer, which is available as a free download from VMware at the following URL:

http://labs.vmware.com/flings/esx-system-analyzer

This utility is designed to smooth the transition from an ESX installation to an ESXi installation. Since ESXi does not have a local Linux installation, there are potential incompatibilities that exist when migrating to a new ESXi server. This utility will scan the prospective ESXi server and discover information such as:

1. Is the server hardware at the correct level to support the new vSphere 5 ESXi installation?

2. Are there any virtual machines that are located on internal datastores that will need to be migrated to a shared SAN volume?

3. Have any RPM packages been added to the local service console that must be addressed?

4. Are there CRON jobs that must be transitioned, if possible, to a vCLI or PowerCLI script?

For documentation purposes, the ESX System Analyzer will enumerate the virtual machines that are in the ESX server's inventory and detail the version of VMware Tools and virtual machine hardware that is presented to each VM.

The requirements for the ESX System Analyzer appliance are listed in Table 3.4.

Table 3.4 ESX System Analyzer Requirements

Component	Requirements
CPU1	vCPU
RAM	512MB
Disk	20GB
Virtual Center Support	2.5, 4.x, 5
ESX Host Support	3.5, 4.x
Browser Support	IE 7 and 8, Firefox 6.0.2, Chrome 13.0.782

As you can see, this is not a high-resource appliance. After the appliance has been downloaded, you configure it by opening a web browser to the FQDN of the appliance and using the following credentials to log in:

Username: admin

Password: admin.

To scan the ESX servers in the environment once you have logged in, you will need to associate a vCenter instance with the appliance.

Software Prerequisites to the Upgrade

If you are attempting to upgrade from VirtualCenter 2.x or later, the host operating system must be a version of Microsoft Windows that is compatible with vCenter server. The supported versions are as follows:

- Windows Server 2003 Standard, Enterprise, Datacenter, 64-bit SP2
- Windows Server 2003 R2 Standard, Enterprise, Datacenter, 64-bit SP1
- Windows Server 2008 Standard, Enterprise, Datacenter, 64-bit SP2
- Windows Server 2008 R2, Standard, Enterprise, Datacenter, 64-bit

As part of the upgrade, vCenter requires the installation of the Microsoft .NET 3.5 SP1 framework. The installer will assess the system and determine if the framework is installed. By default, the installer will install the package if necessary, and may require Internet access to download additional files to complete the installation. If the .NET framework is installed by the installer, the vCenter server will require a reboot to continue.

Once you have verified that you are installing to a supported version of Microsoft Windows, it is a good time to create a current backup of the vCenter database. This will allow you to "roll back" to the previous version of vCenter if necessary. At this point, you can go to downloads.vmware.com and download the installation package for vCenter 5.

As in previous versions of vCenter, there is a 60-day evaluation period for vCenter 5, but you may wish to have your license key handy in order to properly license your new installation. You will need to close all instances of the Client package for Virtual Center (the VI Client) or vCenter (the vSphere Client), and you need to log in to the Virtual Center or vCenter server with credentials that have administrative permissions in order to perform the upgrade.

Note at this point that if you have an instance of Guided Consolidation installed, you must uninstall it before proceeding.

Also, if the existing installation of vCenter contains add-in components that may be incompatible with the new version of vCenter, such as Update Manager or Converter, these add-ons will be de-registered during the upgrade process. These components can be manually installed at a later time. Update Manager is installed from the vCenter Upgrade wizard; Converter is installed by browsing the vCenter distribution media to the Converter folder.

If you are currently employing what is termed a "hybrid" environment, one in which you are supporting both ESX 3.5 and vSphere 4 hosts in the same HA cluster, you will need to verify that each ESX host has been upgraded to patch level 24. This update is required for ESX 3.5 hosts because once vCenter has been upgraded, hosts that have an earlier patch level will not be added to the HA Cluster, nor can they exit Maintenance Mode. The patch can be accessed at http://www.vmware.com/patch/download.

One main concern when upgrading vCenter is the status of the contents of the vCenter database. As a best practice, a current backup of the database content should be created. As we are discussing an upgrade, there are options:

If the current database is installed on a device separate from the vCenter server, and the envisioned configuration will be to use a separate device in the new environment, you can maintain the database location as it is.

If, however, the current database is installed on the same device as the vCenter application, and the new environment calls for a local installation in the new environment, the following options exist:

Note

The information below is accurate as of the Generally Available (GA) release of vSphere 5. Please check your release notes for the version of vSphere 5 that you are installing for any relevant updates to these prerequisites.

- **Microsoft SQL Server Express.** If the vCenter database was deployed as part of the vCenter installation process, you can create a current backup and leverage the Data Migration tool to move the current content to the new location. If, however, the database was installed in a separate process, a simple backup and restore process is available.

- **Microsoft SQL Server.** If the current vCenter database is installed using a full SQL Server database, you can simply back up the existing content, detach the database from the SQL Server instance, and attach it to the new vCenter installation.

- **Oracle and IBM DB2.** If you are currently using either IBM DB2 or Oracle as your vCenter database, you can perform a backup prior to the upgrade and restore the database content after the upgrade has completed successfully.

Since the release of the vSphere 4.1 platform, VMware supports 64-bit installation exclusively. This means that when you are prepared to connect your vCenter to its new database, you will need to create a 64-bit DSN.

If you used the Data Migration tool to migrate the previous database contents, the Migration tool will create the new 64-bit DSN as part of the migration process.

Using the Migration Tool to Upgrade vCenter

The process of upgrading an existing installation of vCenter begins with the process of preserving the existing contents of the vCenter database. The database is critically important to maintain as it contains information for all of the objects in the vCenter inventory and their associated parameters. The Data Migration tool provides a seamless mechanism to back up the contents of an embedded SQL Server database prior to the actual vCenter upgrade process. This should be a primary consideration as you move forward with the upgrade.

Backing Up the Old vCenter Database Data

The vCenter Upgrade includes the Data Migration tool as a means to create a copy of the existing vCenter configuration such as SSL certificates, TCP/IP port configurations, and VMware licenses that may be installed. Once the upgrade has been completed, this configuration data can be restored to the new database. This process is designed to be performed on a database created using SQL Server Express.

Something to consider here is that if the database has been in production for some time, there may be empty table space within the database. To minimize the amount of time and space required to perform the backup, you may want to consider shrinking the database prior to performing the data migration. This can easily be accomplished using the SQL Server Management Studio or by simply taking your DBA to lunch.

To back up the existing vCenter database, extract the contents of the datamigration ZIP file that is located on the vCenter distribution media, and copy them to a local folder. Use the backup.bat file to back up the current contents of the vCenter database.

In the scenario in which Orchestrator is also installed on the same virtual or physical machine as vCenter, the Data Migration tool will make a copy of the Orchestrator configuration, but will not copy or back up the actual Orchestrator database.

Similarly, if Update Manager is installed on the same machine as vCenter, the Data Migration tool will make a copy of the Update Manager configuration, but unlike Orchestrator, the Update Manager database can be backed up if it is installed on a local SQL Server Express database. Note that the patch binaries are not backed up as part of the process.

Using the Data Migration Tool to Upgrade vCenter

If the original vCenter installation used a SQL Server Express database, and the data migration was utilized to create a backup of the original vCenter database content, the Data Migration tool can be leveraged to assist in the upgrade to the new version of vCenter.

As a prerequisite, verify that the Microsoft Installer 4.5 and the Microsoft .NET 3.5 framework are installed on the new server that will function as vCenter. Also, delete any existing VIM_SQLEXP or SQLEXP_VIM databases that may exist on the destination server. These may be the result of a previous installation of vCenter 5, and will cause the process to fail.

To start the upgrade, you will need to copy the datamigration folder from the original vCenter installation and paste it to the new server. Verify that the vCenter distribution media is in the appropriate drive, and open a command prompt. Change directories to the location of the data migration files. Use the Install batch file to initiate the upgrade.

Verify the correct host name, and enter the location of the installation files. The Install batch file will browse to the specified directory, and invoke the vCenter installer.

You will need to specify environment parameters such as user name and organization, and you will have the option to provide a license key. If a key is not provided, the vCenter will install in evaluation mode, and a key can be added later.

Choose the SQL Server Express option for the vCenter database and complete the installation wizard by defining the amount of RAM that will be allocated for the Tomcat web server, and provide the number of ephemeral ports for the new environment. At this point, clicking on Install will start the installation. The content from the legacy version of the vCenter database will be restored and the upgrade will complete. You may want to review the logs as a precautionary process, or copy the restore.log from the \logs folder to document the process.

You can reinstall any vCenter modules that were in use in the old infrastructure.

The Upgrade Process for vCenter

As you would expect, the upgrade process involves time. In fact, you can expect that the vCenter upgrade process will complete in approximately 40 to 50 minutes. A major factor in this upgrade time is the size of the existing database; a small database will involve a shorter amount of time than a large database. Something to consider here is whether to shrink the size of the existing vCenter database to minimize this upgrade timeframe.

Rollup scripts are used by VMware to reduce the size of the vCenter database, which, in a large environment, can grow very large, very quickly. These rollup scripts are normally executed by the SQL Server Agent as a background process. However, if you are using a full SQL Server instance to host your vCenter database, you can manually execute these scripts before performing the backup of the vCenter database by using the SQL Query Analyzer. Keep in mind that these scripts work only for the full version of SQL Server, as this process is handled by vCenter itself for SQL Server Express. These scripts will take the average value from the previous period and use that value to represent a much longer time (taking the average of a series of 20-second intervals and representing that for a single 5-minute interval).

You can also delete any legacy data from the vCenter database by using one of two scripts that are available from VMware: for SQL Server the script is named VCDB_Purge_MSSQL.zip and the script for Oracle is VCDB_Purge_Oracle.zip. Please note that these scripts are intended to be used by experienced DBAs and can cause unintended data loss if misused. An important note here is that the scripts can take quite a long time to process all the old data, so this is a factor to add to the upgrade process.

Added to this time will be the amount of time required to add each ESXi host into the inventory. Also, the DRS algorithm will not be running during the upgrade, therefore cluster load-balancing will not occur. The VMs themselves will remain accessible, and any HA clusters will continue to function normally.

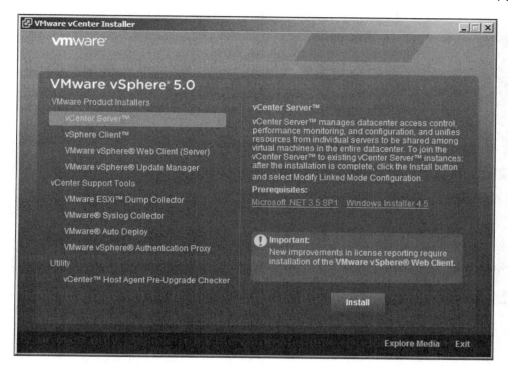

Figure 3.1
The vCenter Installation wizard.

At the initial vCenter screen, you will have the option to install the required Microsoft .NET SP1 and Windows Installer 4.5 as they are installed on the vCenter server. Highlight the vCenter server link and click Install. You will need to select the desired installation language.

In Figure 3.1, the vCenter Installation wizard main page is displayed. Note there are two hyperlinks available to access the Microsoft .NET 3.5 SP1 and the Windows Installer 4.5 components. Also, the Install button will initiate the installer for the vCenter upgrade process.

In Figure 3.2, the installer has discovered a previous revision of vCenter and it will be upgraded. The installer checks for the presence of an existing license, provides a reminder that any previous licenses may be invalid, and will require an upgraded version as well.

In Figure 3.3, the installer scans the previous installation and discovers any existing license keys for vCenter. The installer then provides a reminder that all hosts and the vCenter instance will require updated licenses to ensure continued functionality.

At this point, keep in mind that the ODBC driver located by the installer should be the SQL Native Client, not the SQL Server driver. Remember that Microsoft SQL Server 2000 is no longer considered a supported database for the vCenter installation.

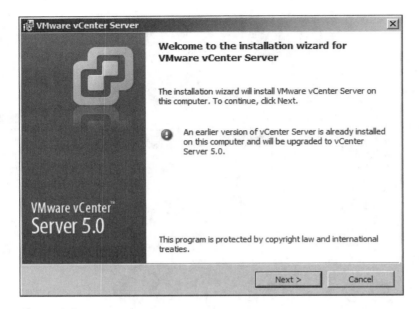

Figure 3.2
Previous versions.

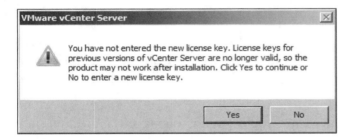

Figure 3.3
Upgrades and licenses.

As a part of the installation process, the installer will evaluate the system to determine if any of the vCenter add-on modules are installed. In the case of VMware Orchestrator, it will be upgraded as part of the upgrade of vCenter. Converter, on the other hand, is no longer supported as an add-on for vCenter; you will need to use the Standalone version instead. For further information on the Standalone version, refer to Chapter 14.

In Figure 3.4, if an existing Update Manager installation is located, a warning is displayed alerting that the legacy version of Update Manager will not be compatible with the new version of vCenter, and it must be upgraded separately.

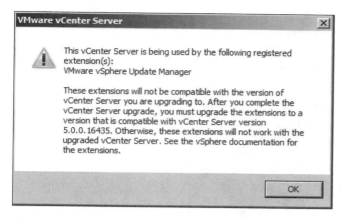

Figure 3.4
Upgrades and vCenter add-ons.

In Figure 3.5, the installer scans the current vCenter instance and attempts to locate an existing vCenter database.

If a current vCenter database is found, the installer will recognize that the current database is incompatible with the new software. The installer will upgrade the existing database format after verification is provided that backup copies of the database and any SSL certificates have been made.

In Figure 3.6, the installer provides the option to upgrade the existing vCenter agent on each host in the vCenter inventory.

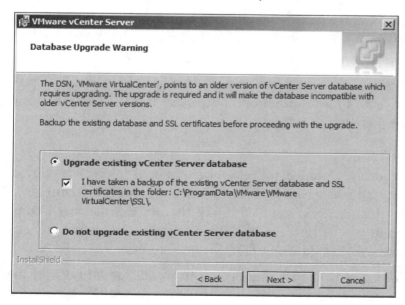

Figure 3.5
Upgrading the vCenter database.

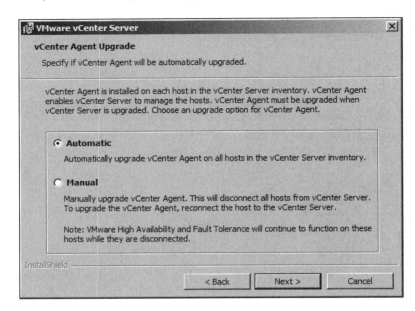

Figure 3.6
Upgrading the vCenter agents.

As part of the upgrade process, the vCenter agent on each ESXi server in the inventory will need to be upgraded as well. You have the option of allowing the installer to perform the upgrade to each vCenter agent, or you can upgrade each agent manually.

The installer will proceed to upgrade the vCenter agents (if selected), query for the account to be used for the vCenter server service, and will ask for the installation folders. As in previous versions, you have the option to modify the ports that will be used by the vCenter installation, including the Inventory Service.

The vCenter Inventory Service will be installed as a component of the upgrade process and is responsible for providing information concerning the current configuration and licensing status of the environment.

Using the Data Migration Tool

The vCenter Upgrade includes the Data Migration tool as a means to create a copy of the existing vCenter configuration such as SSL certificates, TCP/IP port configurations, and VMware licenses that may be installed. Once the upgrade has been completed, this configuration data can be restored to the new database. This process can also be performed on a database created using SQL Server Express.

When installing Update Manager, you have the option to install the add-on on the same server as vCenter, or it can be installed on a separate device. If the current Update Manager installation is on the same server as the vCenter instance, the vCenter 5 distribution media includes a utility to back up the Update Manager database in preparation for the upgrade.

When the backup of the original databases is complete, insert the vCenter distribution media and open the Autorun application from the root folder.

Using Windows Explorer, open the vCenter distribution media and browse to the datamigration folder. Extract the contents of the datamigration compressed folder, and use the backup.bat batch file to back up the existing contents of the Update Manager database in preparation for the upgrade. The backup.bat invokes the backup.py script that actually performs the backup operation. Please note at this point that the backup script does not back up any patch binary files.

Prior to performing the backup, verify that the existing version of vCenter is compatible with the upgrade process. The vCenter instance should be a minimum of Virtual Center Update 6 or a current version of vCenter. You will also need to stop the Virtual Center or vCenter server service before continuing with the backup process.

If you used the included SQL Server Express database for the vCenter database, verify that named pipes are enabled, and that the name of the named pipes is \\.\pipe\sql\ query.

Finally, verify that the DSN for the existing database is "VMware VirtualCenter" or the backup process will be unable to locate the database, and the backup will fail.

In the scenario in which Orchestrator is also installed on the same virtual or physical machine as vCenter, the Data Migration tool will make a copy of the Orchestrator configuration, but will not copy or back up the actual Orchestrator database.

Similarly, if Update Manager is installed on the same machine as vCenter, the Data Migration tool will make a copy of the Update Manager configuration, but unlike Orchestrator, the Update Manager database can be backed up if it is installed on a local SQL Server Express database. Note that the patch binaries are not backed up as part of the process.

If the administrator used the Data Migration tool to back up the SQL Server Express database content for vCenter, he or she can use the Data Migration tool to install the new vCenter instance and restore the SQL Express data to the new database. Note that the name for the new vCenter server should be the same as the old vCenter installation.

To start, verify that Microsoft Windows Installer version 4.5 and .NET 3.5 are pre-installed on the new server. Note that the installation of vCenter requires that any existing SQL Express databases that were used with a previous instance of vCenter will need to be deleted before proceeding.

On the new server, extract the contents of the datamigration folder to the new server, and use the install.bat batch file to install the new vCenter application. You will need to browse to the vCenter 5 installation executable file. The install.bat file will verify the backup data is accessible, and will proceed through the installation wizard. Once the installation completes, the backup database content is automatically restored.

If the Update Manager database was backed up as well, the Update Manager installation wizard will initiate and proceed through the installation process. Once complete, the database content will restore automatically to the new destination.

Post-Upgrade Tasks

After the vCenter installation has completed successfully, you can restore the contents of the previous vCenter database to the new database, and verify that the vCenter instance is correctly configured. Verify the locations of the e-mail server and SNMP destination for alerting if necessary.

Also, you will need to install the new version of Converter and verify functionality. Converter is found on the vCenter distribution in the Converter folder.

Again, if desired, you can execute the rollup scripts to reduce the amount of data stored in the vCenter database before placing the instance into production.

ESX/ESXi Hosts

Now that vCenter has been upgraded, turn your attention to the physical hosts. Before beginning the process of upgrading the hosts, verify that the following prerequisites have been met.

- Verify that all hardware is compatible with the new virtualization environment in the VMware Compatibility Guide at http://www.vmware.com/resources/compatibility/search.php.

- Verify that there is enough free disk space available on the ESX/ESXi host. The upgrade from the vSphere 4 environment to the new vSphere 5 installation will require a minimum of 50MB on a VMFS datastore.

- Unless you plan to use the new ESXi host in a Boot from SAN implementation, verify that all SAN cabling is removed from the host's HBA. This will eliminate the possibility of placing the vSphere installation on an unintended datastore.

First, as always, a complete backup of the existing host(s) should be created. This allows the administrator to return to the previous version should the need present itself. Once the backup has been verified, the upgrade process can begin in earnest.

Previous versions of the ESX/ESXi platform can be easily upgraded to the new version in several ways. Table 3.5 details the acceptable methods to perform the upgrade.

Changes to Resource Pools

Once the upgrade has been completed, existing resource pools may be affected by the larger amount of system RAM used by the operating system. As a result of this higher system resource utilization, there may be resource pools that are configured to use a large amount of their provided resources in which VMs may not have enough RAM to meet power-on requirements. Should this occur, the system will generate an alert viewable through the Alt + F11 key sequence. Affected resource pools may require reconfiguration to remedy this change.

Changes to Networking

The major change to the networking in vSphere 5 is that the Service Console port no longer exists. As part of the upgrade, any Service Console ports are replaced by VMkernel ports.

This conversion also means that if a Service Console port configuration supplies the default route for the ESX server, that particular port is removed and is replaced by a VMkernel port. If this Service Console port utilized a DHCP-provided IP configuration, the Peer DNS configuration is converted to a DhcpDNS setting. Peer DNS is a configuration in which the networking settings are provided through DHCP, and name resolution is provided through a peer server. In the new environment, PeerDNS is changed to DhcpDNS to obtain the DNS settings from the DHCP server along with the IP address, subnet mask, and default gateway.

Additional Service Console ports, such as those providing redundancy for management or HA heartbeats are converted into VMkernel ports attached to new port groups. It would be a good idea to verify networking configuration as a post-upgrade task.

Changes to the Firewall

After the host has completed the upgrade process, the host is rebooted, and the esx.conf is consulted to configure the firewall for the first boot. A new ESXi 5.0 rulesets list is created and takes the place of the ESX 4.x version as a part of the upgrade process. If any rulesets are present that do not have matching values in the esx.conf file, those rulesets are loaded in the enabled or open status.

Table 3.5 Upgrade Support in vSphere 5

Version of ESX/ESXi Software	Direct Upgrade?	Migration?	Fresh Install?	Comments
ESX and ESXi 3.x hosts	No	No	Yes	Both ESX and ESXi 3.x hosts will require an upgrade to vSphere 4.x first; then the upgrade to vSphere 5 can proceed.
ESX and ESXi hosts with vSphere 4 that may have a partition compatibility issue with vSphere 5.	No	No	No	These type of installations typically were an upgrade from ESX 3.x and the partitioning is compatible only if there is at least one VMFS partition that begins after sector 1843200. A fresh install is required if this criteria is not met. To maintain any VMs, they must be migrated to another host during the upgrade.
Upgrade from ESX and ESXi vSphere 4 hosts using Update Manager	Yes	Yes	Yes	This type of upgrade is fully supported.
ESX and ESXi hosts using a direct manual upgrade.	Yes	Yes	Yes	Partitions can be individually upgraded, or all partitions can be upgraded at the same time.
Scripted upgrades from vSphere 4 ESX and ESXi hosts	Yes	Yes	Yes	This type of upgrade is supported if the disk partitioning is compatible with vSphere 5. There must be at least one VMFS partition that begins after sector 1843200.
Upgrades from a ESX or ESXi vSphere 4.x host using boot from SAN or SSD devices	Yes	Yes	Yes	A fresh installation of vSphere is required to optimize or change the partitioning scheme.
An upgrade for an ESX host that has a corrupted Service Console.	No	No	Yes	If the installer detects any corruption during the upgrade process, it will recommend a fresh installation.
ESX or ESXi hosts with custom driver implementations	Yes	Yes	Yes	It is recommended that VMware Image Builder be used to create a custom installation package.

The esx.conf is read and any existing enabled/disabled configurations are migrated along with the allowed IP configured through the use of the esxcfg-firewall command line tool.

After the first boot, traffic is passed for any rulesets that have a value of 0 in both the blockIncoming and blockOutgoing fields of the default policy. Any other traffic is denied by default. Any ports that were opened through the use of the esxcfg-firewall syntax are closed after the upgrade.

As is the case with any major upgrade, there are some considerations that we must be aware of:

- Verify that the correct licensing has been arranged for your new deployment.

- Verify that all backups are current and valid.

- Note that this is considered a major upgrade and does not provide a "rollback" option.

Migration Effects on the ESXi Configuration and Files

The following files will be directly migrated to the new installation as part of the upgrade process:

- /etc/sfcb/sfcb.cfg
- /etc/ntp.conf
- /etc/ntp.drift
- /etc/ntp.keys
- /etc/sysconfig/keyboard
- /etc/vmware/vmkiscsid/*
- /etc/vmware/esx.conf
- /etc/vmware/hostd/*
- /etc/hosts
- /etc/resolv.conf
- /etc/nsswitch.conf
- /etc/ssh
- /etc/security/access.conf

- /etc/motd
- /etc/security/login.map

The following files are migrated with caveats:

- /etc/syslog.conf—Migrated for ESX hosts only.
- /etc/sysconfig/network—VMKernel ports will be created from any Service Console ports.
- /etc/pam.d—The upgrade will reset any modifications to the default values in system-auth.
- /etc/snmp/snmp.conf—Contents converted into /etc/vmware/snmp.xml.
- /etc/fstab—All NFS entries are migrated; any other entries are not.
- /etc/passwd—Root user password is converted; any others are not.

These files are migrated as part of the upgrade process to provide compatibility for the likewise environment:

- /etc/krb.conf
- /etc/krb5.log
- /etc/krb.realms
- /etc/likewise/*
- /etc/krb5.conf
- /etc/krb5.mkey
- /etc/krb5.acl
- /etc/krb5.keytab

The following files are not migrated due to a lack of backwards-compatibility with previous versions of ESX/ESXi:

- /etc/logrotate.conf
- /etc/vmware/hostd/config.xml
- /etc/rc.d/rc*.d/*
- /etc/vmware/hostd/proxy.xml
- /etc/vmware/Init
- /etc/sysconfig/syslog

The following files are not migrated because their function is not supported in the vSphere 5 version of ESXi.

- /etc/localtime
- /etc/openldap
- /etc/sysconfig/i18n
- /etc/sudoers
- /etc/sysconfig/clock
- /etc/sysconfig/xinetd
- /etc/yp.conf
- /etc/xinetd.conf
- /etc/ldap.conf
- /etc/login.defs

Supported Upgrade Methods

The actual upgrade of the ESX/ESXi host can be accomplished in several ways: directly, using the vSphere 5 distribution media, and by using Update Manager. In this section we will take a look at each of the methods of upgrading our ESX/ESXi hosts.

Direct Upgrade   The first method of upgrading an ESXi host can be termed a direct upgrade in that you are using the ESXi distribution media to perform a local process.

As shown in Figure 3.7, when the ESX/ESXi host boots from the distribution media, it automatically determines that there is a pre-existing installation and provides the option to boot from the local disk, execute the installation routine, or you can also specify a disk to boot from by using the Tab key.

Figure 3.7
The initial upgrade screen.

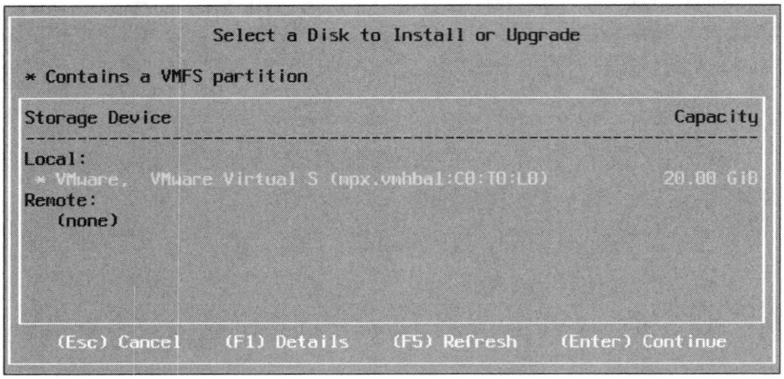

Figure 3.8
Choosing the destination disk.

As shown in Figure 3.8, the installer will scan the ESX/ESXi host to locate any local or SAN-based disks that are available for the install. In this example, the installer has found a 20GB local, but no remote or SAN-based devices. Note here, that the term "mpx.vmhba1" is used. The term "vmhba" or virtual machine host bus adapter is probably familiar, but the prefix "mpx" may not be so familiar. "mpx" represents the term VMware Multiplex Device. This generally refers to an internal device, such as a disk connected to an internal RAID controller or an internal CD or DVD device.

At this point, we can choose the destination disk by highlighting it and clicking Continue.

As depicted in Figure 3.9, if the installer discovers an existing installation on the selected disk, you will be prompted to determine what to do with the existing content. You have the option to migrate the installation and preserve the datastore, you

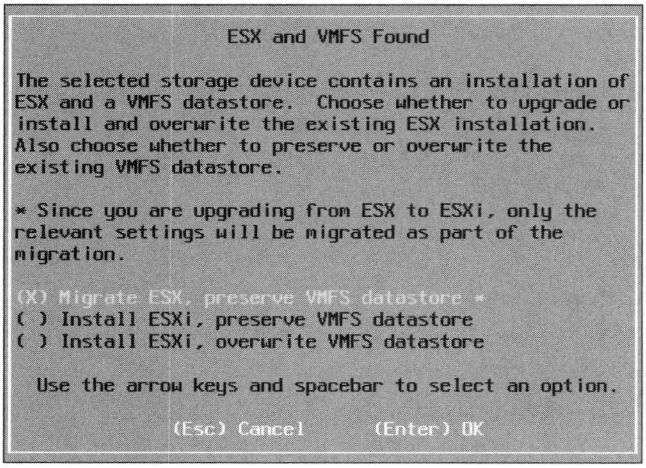

Figure 3.9
Discovering existing installations.

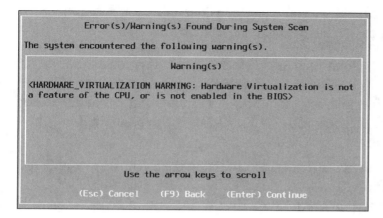

Figure 3.10
Hardware virtualization warning.

can install the new version over the old installation and preserve existing datastores, or you can install the new revision and overwrite any existing datastores.

Note that during the actual upgrade process, the installer queries the hardware to determine the compatibility of the hardware configuration with the new version of ESXi. If any potential issues are located during this query, the installer will display a warning to alert you of any changes or modification that you may need to address after the installation has completed. These warnings may not be "show stoppers," but they do warrant consideration. As depicted in Figure 3.10, this particular installation began with hardware virtualization disabled in the BIOS. Since VMware heavily leverages hardware virtualization, this is something that is easily overlooked, and should be enabled in the BIOS once the installation has finished.

As shown in Figure 3.11, after all of the bits and pieces have been installed, the process will display a completion message that reminds you that you have a 60-day free

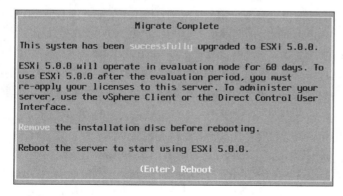

Figure 3.11
Upgrade completion.

trial to evaluate the product. After that, you must consider licensing to continue to use the full product. Licensing topics will be covered later in this chapter.

vSphere Update Manager   The first step in performing an upgrade with Update Manager is to create a baseline. A baseline is a specific set of patches or updates that you wish to make available to hosts or VMs. A baseline will be defined that includes the upgrade from ESX/ESXi 4.x to ESXi 5.0 and then the baseline is attached to a host folder, cluster, or a single physical host.

When Update Manager performs an upgrade, the individual ESX hosts are updated first, then virtual appliances and virtual machines. Once these initial upgrades complete successfully, upgrades for virtual machine hardware and VMware Tools can also be scheduled. These upgrades are best performed through leveraging DRS (Distributed Resource Scheduler) clustering. Depending on how the DRS cluster is configured, the first host in the cluster can be upgraded by using VMotion to move any virtual machines to another host in the cluster, placing the host in Maintenance Mode, performing the upgrade, restoring the host from Maintenance Mode, and then allowing DRS to re-balance the cluster. Then we can simply move through each of the hosts in the cluster in the same manner. Using this scheme allows the update to occur without affecting the availability of the virtual machines themselves, and should be transparent to end users.

Keep in mind that the same process used to upgrade a cluster is also used to upgrade a stand-alone host. Any VMs that are currently running on the ESX/ESXi host will need to be either powered off or moved to another host using VMotion. Then the host can be placed into Maintenance Mode, updated, and then resumed from Maintenance Mode. VMs can then be powered on, or moved back to the host, again using VMotion.

After all of the physical hosts have been upgraded, a baseline can be created that defines the upgrades for the virtual hardware presented to the VMs, and any upgrades to the VMware Tools. Virtual machine upgrades can be scheduled based on the power state of the VMs. Powered-on VMs can be scheduled first, followed by suspended VMs, and finally, powered-off VMs. Tiering the upgrades in this manner can reduce the workload presented to the underlying datastores.

If the candidate ESX/ESXi host was originally an ESX 3.x host that was upgraded to vSphere 4.x, these hosts typically will not have enough disk space in the /boot partition to allow Update Manager to update these hosts. There must be a minimum of 350MB free space available in the /boot partition for Update Manager to complete the upgrade successfully. If the host does not have enough free space, you can use an interactive upgrade, or a script can also be used to upgrade this host.

Using Update Manager with HA, DPM, and FT   As stated earlier, Update Manager can leverage the DRS cluster functionality by updating physical hosts without impacting the availability of the VMs. However, there are other vCenter components that must be taken into consideration. HA (High Availability), DPM (Distributed Power Management), and FT (Fault Tolerance) can also impact the ability of Update Manager to complete the upgrade.

These topics will be covered more in-depth in succeeding chapters, but it may be advantageous to temporarily disable DPM, HA admission control, and FT for the cluster while the upgrade is in progress.

Please note that unlike virtual machines, which can be powered on and updated, physical hosts cannot be powered on and updated if they are in a powered-off state.

As part of its normal process, Update Manager will scan all of the necessary devices, and then disable DPM and HA admission control before applying the patch or upgrade. Once the upgrade has been completed, Update Manager will then restore the normal configuration of the cluster.

For example, if DPM encounters a physical ESX/ESXi host that has no virtual machines currently powered on, the DPM process may attempt to place that host into standby mode depending on the HA configuration of the cluster. While this is the normal use of DPM, if an Update Manager upgrade is currently in progress, this could interfere with the completion of the upgrade for that particular host. Normally, if DPM has placed a host into standby mode, Update Manager can resume the host, perform the upgrade, and then allow DPM to place the host in standby mode again. If however, the physical host is in standby, and DPM has been disabled, Update Manager will not update the host.

Similarly, Update Manager will attempt to update any physical hosts in an HA cluster if FT is enabled for a VM in that cluster. As a best practice, all hosts in a cluster should be maintained at the same patch and update level.

Also new in vSphere 5, the updating of ESX/ESXi hosts in a cluster can proceed either sequentially or in parallel. This means that a cluster remediation will take less time than in previous versions of ESX.

Update Manager and PXE-Boot Hosts   There are environments in which the ESXi hosts boot from a PXE-Boot environment, rather than booting from internal or SAN-based storage. These environments can be easily upgraded as well.

If you open the Update Manager component of vCenter and open the Configuration tab, you can leverage solutions such as the new ESX Agent Manager to deploy the

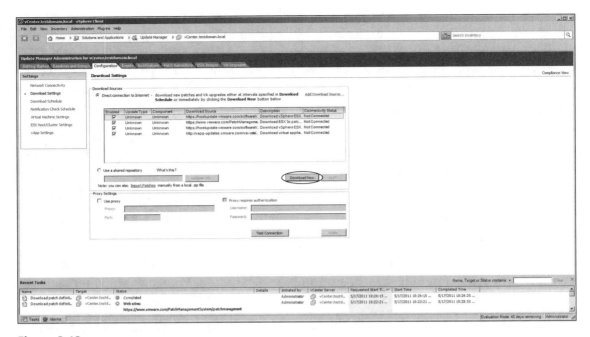

Figure 3.12
Download ESXi upgrades packages.

upgrade package. The Update Manager Remediate wizard also allows PXE-Boot hosts to be updated by selecting the Enable Patch Management of Powered-on ESXi Hosts option.

Either of these options will update a PXE-Boot host, but the updates may be discarded after the host is rebooted. You will need to update the PXE-Boot image itself to make the upgrade permanent.

In Figure 3.12, using the Admin View, we must first verify that the update has been downloaded from the https://hostupdate.vmware.com website.

Click on the Configuration tab, select Download Settings, then Download Now. This will ensure that we have the most current updates.

After the updates have been downloaded successfully, the baseline must be created to contain our updates. Select the Baselines and Groups tab; note that there are two baselines already defined: Critical Host Patches and Non-Critical Host Patches. Select the Create link, and select Host Upgrade Baseline from the New Baseline Group wizard. Choose Create a New Host Upgrade Baseline. Specify a name for the baseline and verify that Host Upgrade is selected. Select the upgrade package that you wish to use and click Next, then Finish.

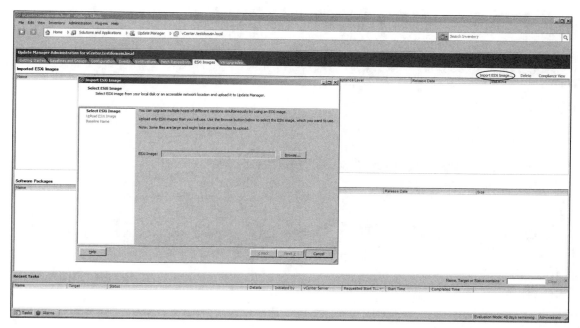

Figure 3.13
Importing the ESXi image.

Once the import is completed, the new baseline will appear in the Baselines and Groups pane. Click on Compliance View and attach the update to the appropriate cluster or physical hosts.

As an alternative, an ISO version of the new operating system can by imported from a local disk or a network and made available to Update Manager. This is done by using the ESXi Images tab.

In Figure 3.13, from the ESXi Images tab, select Import ESXi Image, and browse to the correct image using the Browse button. This image can now become the basis for our upgrade.

Select the Baselines and Groups tab and create a new baseline using the ISO image that we imported. Once the baseline has been defined, we can attach it to the appropriate cluster, folder, or stand-alone hosts.

In Figure 3.14, now that the baseline was successfully created, we can now right-click on the folder, cluster, or host that we wish to upgrade and select Scan for Updates.

Update Manager will then evaluate the designated object or objects against the baseline that we created. The resultant view in Update Manager will show which hosts are compliant, and those that are not. We can then select the hosts and Remediate them, which will place the host(s) in Maintenance Mode, and apply the upgrade.

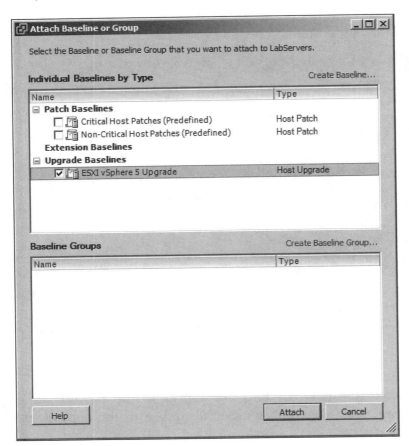

Figure 3.14
Attaching the baseline.

Remediation can be performed in several ways:

- Right-click on the Cluster or stand-alone and select Remediate to immediately update the host, or the remediation can be staged for a later timeframe.

- Highlight the host in the results pane, and either select Stage or Remediate.

Upgrading Manually Using the ISO File   The same options exist when upgrading a physical ESX/ESXi host as are available when performing a new installation: the install process can be started by booting from the ESXi distribution media or from a USB drive.

It is considered a best practice to perform a backup of the host before initiating the upgrade.

This provides a "safety net" in case the installation fails for any reason, and you need to go back to the original configuration with a minimum of downtime while a problem is resolved.

Perform an Interactive Installation from a DVD   Upgrading an existing ESX/ESXi host is almost identical to the process used to perform a new installation. Download the ISO from the web and burn the image to a CD or DVD ROM. You will need to verify that the server boot order is configured to boot from the CD/DVD drive. If the boot order is correct, place the ISO image in the CD/DVD drive and reboot the host.

You will need to verify the correct destination disk for the upgrade. At this point, you may wish to disconnect any SAN-based devices to reduce the possibility of installing on the wrong disk.

If you selected the correct disk, the installer should be able to locate an existing installation. You will be given three options:

- **Upgrade ESXi, preserve VMFS datastore.** This selection will perform the upgrade and also allows any existing VMs and templates to be preserved.

- **Install ESXi, preserve VMFS datastore.** This selection will perform a new installation, preserving any existing VMs or templates, but there will be no migration of current configurations.

- **Install ESXi, overwrite VMFS datastore.** This selection will upgrade the host, but will not maintain the existing datastore contents.

Once the installer has completed the upgrade, reboot the host.

Perform an Upgrade Using a USB Key as the Source   To create a USB key that contains the ESXi ISO image, you will need to connect the USB key to a Linux device. Since the ESXi platform is based on RHEL, the disk formatting will be the same. Create an active FAT32 primary partition on the USB key using the following procedure:

Use the `fdisk/dev/sdb1` command located in the sbin folder to invoke the fdisk process and reference the device specified by the sdb1 identifier. Begin by typing "d" to remove any pre-existing partitions, type "n" to add a new primary partition, type "t" to set the file system type, and type "a" to mark the new partition as "Active." Type "w" to write the new partition information to the USB key, and format the partition using the `./sbin/mkfs.vfat -F 32 /dev/sdb1` command. At this point, the USB key should be ready to receive the ISO image. Use the `mount /dev/sdb1 /boot-disk` command to mount the USB key to the "bootdisk" device name. Mount the CD/DVD containing the ISO to a device named "mydisk" using the `mount -o loop`

`VMware-VMvisor-Installer-5.0.0-XXXXXX.x86_64.iso /mydisk` command. We can now copy the ISO image from the CD/DVD to the USB key using the `cp -r mydisk/* /bootdisk` command.

When the files have been copied, use the `mv /bootdisk/isolinux.cfg /bootdisk/syslinux.cfg` command to rename the isolinux.cfg file to syslinux.cfg. Now we can unmount the USB key using `umount /bootdisk`. The USB key can now be used to upgrade the ESX/ESXI hosts. Be sure to configure the server boot order accordingly.

Using a Script to Upgrade an ESX/ESXi Host   An existing ESX/ESXi host can be upgraded to vSphere 5 by booting an existing host from the ISO file. We discussed the process of utilizing a script, sometimes called a "kickstart" script to perform an unattended install. The same process is applicable here. You will need to create a script that defines all of the parameters for the upgrade process and make it available either locally in the form of a USB key or CD/DVD, or in the form of a network-accessible location that can use HTTP, HTTPS, or NFS.

vSphere Modules

vCenter has optional modules available that can extend the functionality provided in the environment. These add-ons can be accessed through the vCenter distribution media, in the case of Update Manager, or by adding optional appliances such as the VDR (VMware Data Recovery) or vMA (vSphere Management Assistant). Please note that the appliances must be added and configured manually.

vSphere Update Manager (VUM)

As part of an upgrade process to vCenter 5, the additional components should be upgraded as well to maintain compatibility.

In Figure 3.15, after inserting the vCenter 5 distribution media, highlight the VMware vSphere Update Manager link and click Install, as you did to upgrade the vCenter environment.

If the Autorun process does not begin automatically, browse the contents of the CD/DVD drive and manually locate the Autorun executable.

In Figure 3.16, the installer will attempt to locate a current installation of Update Manager.

Once you select the installation language, you will receive a dialog box that states that a previous installation of Update Manager has been discovered by the installer. Clicking on the OK button will initiate the upgrade process.

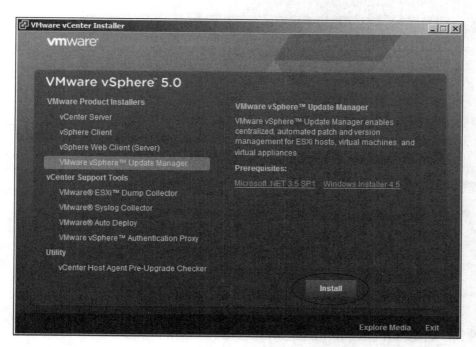

Figure 3.15
Installing Update Manager.

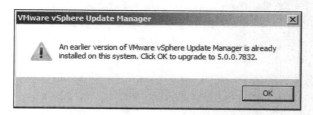

Figure 3.16
Locating current installations.

The installation will proceed through computing resource requirements for the upgrade and the new version of Update Manager, then a dialog is displayed that presents options for proceeding.

In Figure 3.17, note the line that states "Update Manager 5.0 does not support the patching of VM applications and operating systems."

This is a big change from vSphere 4.x and previous versions of Update Manager. In previous versions, Update Manager had the capacity to download operating system and application updates and include those in baselines for deployment to virtual machines as well. Also note that Update Manager can only upgrade ESX/ESXi hosts

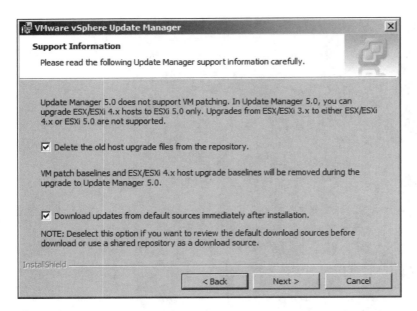

Figure 3.17
Resolving legacy upgrade content.

4.x and later; previous versions of ESX/ESXi will need to first be upgraded to version 4.x through some other mechanism (scripted upgrade, manual process) before Update Manager can be used in the upgrade process.

In the default configuration, Update Manager will delete any legacy baselines that were defined for ESX/ESXi hosts during the upgrade process. Update Manager will also automatically connect to the Internet and any other pre-defined resources in an attempt to download any new updates for the environment.

As we discussed with the installation of vCenter, Update Manager will then confirm the DSN for the new environment, and display the default driver that will be used to access the database.

At this point, the upgrade for Update Manager is very similar to what we discussed for upgrading vCenter:

1. You will verify the driver selected to access the Update Manager database.

2. Select either to upgrade the existing database, in which case you will need to select the "I have taken a backup of the existing Update Manger database" option, or you can opt not to upgrade the database.

3. At this point, the installer will verify the IP address, port usage, and credentials as in previous versions, and then complete the install. A reboot will finalize the upgrade.

As in previous versions of Update Manager, after the reboot you will need to log in to the vCenter server using the vSphere Client and download the Update Manager plug. This enables interaction with the Update Manager component. Please remember that this is a physical file install; it is not a profile that follows a user. It will need to be installed on all workstations that will be used to manage Update Manager.

vCenter Converter

This feature is no longer supported or functional in vSphere 5. You must uninstall these modules before upgrading vCenter to version 5. As mentioned earlier, you can still use the Standalone version of Converter. This is discussed more in Chapter 14.

Guided Consolidation

This feature is no longer supported or functional in vSphere 5. You must uninstall these modules before upgrading vCenter to version 5.

VMFS

The features available in VMFS 5 and the process of performing this upgrade are detailed in Chapter 8.

vNetwork Standard to/from vNetwork Distributed Switch

The new features available in vSphere 5 and the process of upgrading existing virtual switches are detailed in Chapter 7.

VM Hardware and VMware Tools

During an upgrade, it is important to also upgrade VMware Tools as you upgrade the remainder of the environment. VMware Tools provides critical driver functionality that greatly enhances the capabilities and performance of the VM. You can upgrade VMware tools manually, or you can configure virtual machines to check for and install newer versions of VMware Tools.

Within each VM, the current version of VMware Tools is evaluated as the VM is powered on. Because of this evaluation, if the VM has a Microsoft operating system, the user can be notified when a newer version is available. This notification takes the form of a yellow caution indicator located in the taskbar, near the time display.

For Windows-based VMs, VMware Tools can also be configured to automatically upgrade during the next power cycle, or when the VM is rebooted. Since the installation of VMware Tools incorporates the installation of newer drives, the VM may need to be rebooted to fully utilize the new driver set. As an alternative, the driver modules may be unloaded and reloaded to allow Linux-based VMs to utilize the new drivers.

As a best practice, the version of VMware Tools should always match the virtual machine hardware revision that is present in the environment.

There are two main methods to upgrade VMware Tools: the first is to use vCenter to manually specify which virtual machines are to be upgraded, or Update Manager can be used to stage the upgrade to comply with environmental requirements.

The term virtual machine hardware revision refers to the hardware set that is presented to the VM when it is powered on. This defines the simulated hardware devices that the VM will have as resources.

When a VM is defined on a vSphere 5 host, it will, by default, use virtual machine version 8. Keep in mind that this revision of the VM hardware is incompatible with previous releases of the VMware environment. Even though virtual machines with a legacy hardware set will function on a vSphere 5 host, it will not have access to the latest capabilities until the virtual hardware is updated.

If this will be a hybrid environment, one in which there will be a mixture of vSphere 5 and legacy versions, consideration must be given to selecting virtual machine hardware version 7 to provide backward compatibility.

Update Manager is used to upgrade the virtual machine hardware through defining a baseline, identically to the process for upgrading VMware Tools.

Upgrading Licensing

After you have evaluated the options and upgraded all of the components in your environment, the process is not complete until you have considered upgrading your licensing. In many cases, you will want to maintain the components that you were using in the previous version. To assist you in this decision, VMware is offering the vSphere Licensing tool. This tool can be downloaded from the following link: http://downloads.vmware.com/d/details/licenseadv10/ZHcqYnQldHdiZCpwcA==. Note that

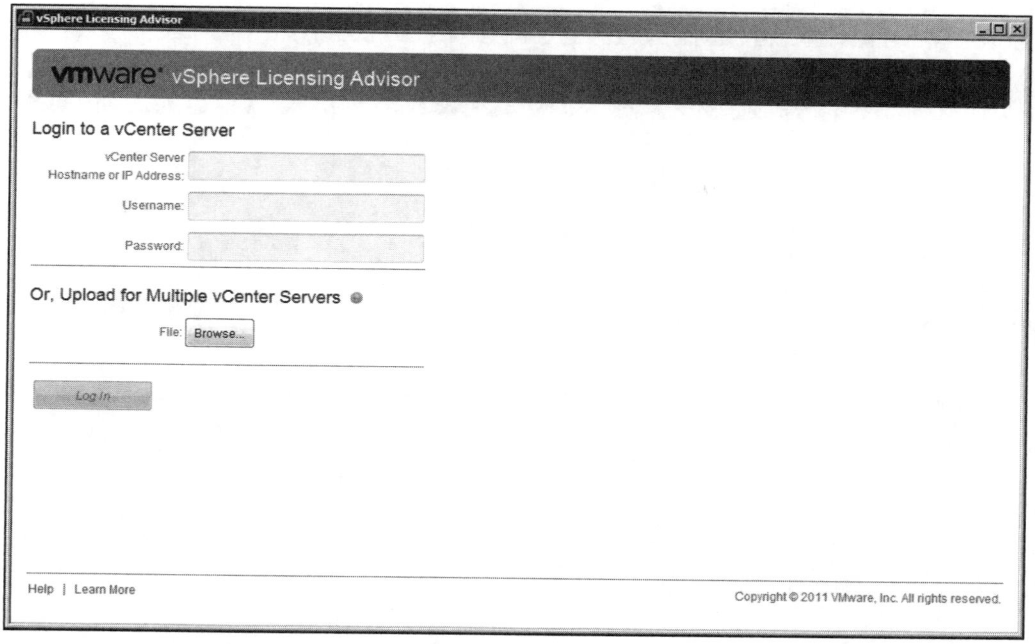

Figure 3.18
Log in to the vSphere Licensing Advisor.

this utility requires a recent version of Java. If you do not have Java on your vCenter server, you will need to download and install a copy before proceeding.

As shown in Figure 3.18, you will need to install the tool and provide connectivity information (FQDN or IP address) and Administrator credentials, and then the licensing tool will poll the vCenter database. If you have vCenter servers that are connected via linked mode, you will need to log in to each of the vCenter server instances individually.

The utility allows the administrator to log in to a single vCenter instance by providing the correct credentials, or multiple vCenter servers can be evaluated by providing a text file containing the FQDN and IP address of each vCenter server.

As shown in Figure 3.19, the Licensing Advisor will analyze the current environment and display the current virtual machines in the inventory, their RAM usage, the uptime of the VM, the power state of the VM, the current host of the VM, and the current edition of vSphere installed in the environment. The RAM values will assist administrators in determining the correct levels of VMware licensing that applies to their current and planned deployments.

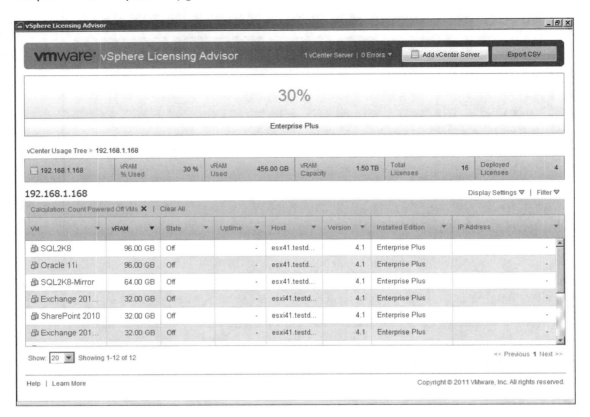

Figure 3.19
Licensing Advisor results.

Summary

In this chapter, we looked at the different methods that are available to upgrade existing vCenter instances and ESX/ESXi servers. All of these options will not apply to every environment, but VMware has covered a lot of bases in providing utilities and tools to make the upgrading process more efficient.

In Chapter 4, we will take a look at how we can use scripting and the command line to automate processes and tasks within vSphere 5.

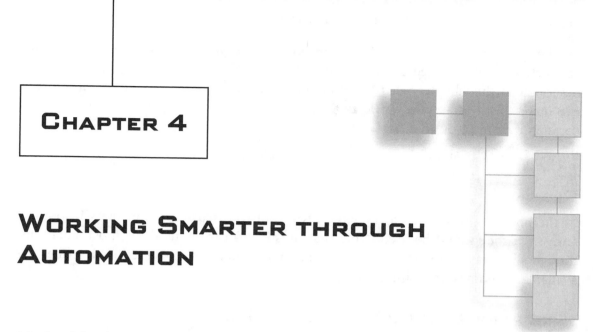

CHAPTER 4

WORKING SMARTER THROUGH AUTOMATION

Much of this book is designed around the premise of using the vSphere Client GUI to manage your virtual infrastructure, and in many, if not most, cases, this is the tool you will probably use. However, for repetitive tasks, nothing beats a script. On the other hand, sometimes the GUI isn't working and the only way to fix things is from the command line. For some people, a GUI is not their favorite user interface (UI), and they prefer working from a command line. Today, both the GUI and CLI make calls to the same set of APIs on the ESXi host or the vCenter server, so it becomes more of a preference in most cases. This chapter deals with the various scripting and other available automation resources.

You might be wondering why we're dealing with this at the beginning of the book. Why not teach everything using the GUI and then just include a chapter covering this stuff at the end? Good question. The reason is that we want to show you how to do things in the GUI and then provide some examples of how to do them in one or more command line (aka TUI—Textual User Interface) ways. For that to make any sense, we need to explain what the tools are early on in the book and describe the installation and configuration necessary to use them first.

If you don't like TUIs, simply ignore this chapter and skip the examples throughout the book (at least until you run into a troubleshooting problem that requires their use— then come back and review this chapter).

One final note on the scripts throughout this book: They are not full scripts, but rather just the code needed to illustrate the solution to the problem described; in programmer language, they are "code snippets" that could be modified and used in scripts you create. For example, none of the vCLI examples will include references to the server or the credentials needed and all PowerCLI examples assume you have already connected to either vCenter or the desired server. This is required as the CLI tools described in this chapter need to know on which server(s) you'd like the commands executed; this was implied with ESX as the commands were run locally from the command prompt on that host.

Ready? Let's get started!

PLANNING

In the planning section of this chapter, we want to discuss some of the CLI options and when they might be used. Note that most tools can be used for most situations, though some tasks are better suited to one tool or another. This section describes the available Windows and Linux tools.

What Automation Options Are Available?

Let's begin with a quick review of which tools are at our disposal, the platform(s) they can be used on, and a few notes on each.

vCLI

The first tool is the vCLI (the vSphere Command Line Interface). It was introduced in vSphere 4.0 as the replacement for the rCLI (remote Command Line Interface) that was pioneered in 3.5. This tool didn't exist before ESX 3.5 because it was designed to be the primary CLI for ESXi, which was introduced with version 3.5 and does not have a full-service console like ESX had. ESX servers used the service console locally on each host to perform any desired Linux-based CLI operations.

The vCLI was renamed not only to use an initial "v" like most products in the vSphere family, but also because it really was version 2 in terms of features and functionality of the CLI.

One of the great advances made in the vCLI in version 4 is the ability to authenticate commands against the native Linux-style users (usually *root*) as well as vCenter users (usually Active Directory users). This means that administrators can run these commands without having to know the root password, and it also provides a measure of accountability by logging who runs what command.

The vCLI is an executable that can be installed on either Linux or Windows platforms and is designed to be run from administrators' desktops and laptops. It is based on Perl (a common programming/scripting language in Linux and UNIX) scripts and those scripts access the vSphere APIs to perform their assigned tasks.

Most people do not use this tool, however, favoring the vMA (vSphere Management Assistant) instead.

vMA

The vMA is a VA (Virtual Appliance) that is configured as follows:

- 1 vCPU
- 600MB RAM
- 3GB Virtual Disk
- 64-bit Novell SUSE Linux Enterprise (SLES) 11

It includes the following software preinstalled and configured:

- VMware Tools
- vCLI for Linux
- vSphere SDK for Perl
- Java JRE version 1.6

The vMA has some functionality that the vCLI does not, including the following:

- The ability to configure a list of servers with stored credentials, meaning that every vCLI command entered does not need to include the credentials explicitly. This is configured and administered via vifp, which will be discussed in the security section later in this chapter. This feature is known as fastpass.

- When mcli.pl is used, a command can be run against a group of servers instead of a single server per command without scripting; this will be discussed in more detail in the installation section for the vMA later in this chapter.

- It can be used as a central storage repository of scripts, much like service console scripts were formerly on each ESX server, but with the advantage that they don't need to be copied between those servers.

- It implements CIM (Common Information Model) and thus can be used by programmers and OEMs to implement agents that were formerly run in the service console of ESX servers to work now in the vMA with ESXi.

PowerCLI

PowerCLI is VMware's tool to manage the vSphere environment from a Windows-based command line. It is based on Microsoft's PowerShell, which in turn depends on the .NET infrastructure. .NET is standard in Windows 2008, Vista, and later, and can be installed in Windows 2003 and XP as well. VMware has found PowerCLI to be very popular and has added a lot of functionality to it over the years since its first introduction with VI 3.5. VMware has also added PowerCLI functionality to manage other applications as well, such as the new PowerCLI for VUM (vSphere Update Manager) and for View, and is the only mechanism for managing Auto Deploy (discussed in Chapter 5).

PowerCLI is an object-based set of tools, and thus is used differently than many Linux commands or batch files. To take advantage of what it can do, you should be familiar with PowerShell, which is far beyond the scope of this book. For a good primer on PowerShell, refer to the following resources:

- **www.powershell.com.** This site has a lot of information on PowerShell, including tips and tricks; a tip of the day; forums to ask questions; webcasts; and our favorite feature, a free e-book, *Mastering PowerShell*, available at: powershell.com/cs/blogs/ebook/.

- **blogs.msdn.com/b/powershell/.** The official blog from Microsoft on the subject, with news and events, a link to the latest downloadable help, and other resources.

- **www.powershellpro.com/.** This site has lots of downloadable scripts to solve many common problems, a lot of great tutorials (from the simple to the advanced), and a link to most (if not all) of the PowerShell books currently on the market.

While on the subject, here are a few great resources for PowerCLI:

- **www.vmware.com/support/developer/PowerCLI/index.html.** The official site of the actual product documentation from VMware is the best place to get started with PowerCLI. It includes the installation guide, the administrators and developers guides, and a link to all of the PowerCLI cmdlets.

- **blogs.vmware.com/vipowershell/.** The official PowerCLI blog from VMware, featuring many tips and tricks and links to cool resources.

- **twitter.com/powercli.** A Twitter feed focused strictly on PowerCLI.

Finally, though not a specific website, if you search the Internet for "PowerCLI poster," you will find a poster that divides all of the commands into various tasks, provides common switches and links to other resources, etc. It is a one-page poster that you can save or print and use as a great reference.

Many of the examples of automation throughout this book will be based on PowerCLI.

Onyx Fling

VMware creates a lot of cool tools that may or may not be integrated into future products. Many can be found at http://labs.vmware.com/flings. Flings are usually simple tools that may prove very useful. Some examples (at the time of writing—subject to change at any time) include:

- **Inventory Snapshot.** Inventories many of the objects in vCenter (including permissions, roles, custom settings, and clusters), and creates a PowerCLI script that can be used to recreate those objects in a different vCenter (for example, to take a development environment and recreate a new production environment based on it).

- **ThinApped vSphere Client.** VMware has packaged the standard vSphere Client using ThinApp (which is a VMware tool that allows applications to be executed without installing them natively on the computer on which the applications are run—a concept called Application Virtualization that separates the application from the operating system in much the same way the virtualization described in this book separates the operating system from the underlying hardware) to make it easy to run in any environment (XP, Vista, or Windows 7) without installing anything.

- **esxplot.** Allows the large volume of data that can be captured by saving resxtop information to a file and allows you to graph it—there are no known limits to either the number of rows or columns, unlike many other tools.

- **IOBlazer.** A storage benchmarking tool that runs on many platforms and allows a lot of customization in creating any kind of IO load you want to simulate (even more than IOMeter, which has been used for years in storage benchmarking). It runs on Linux, Windows, and Mac OSX.

- **VGC.** VMware Guest Console provides access to the guest VMs themselves (for example, to copy a file to each and then run it, view processes, etc.) as well as to manage VMware snapshots en masse for large groups of VMs.

- **vCMA.** vCenter Mobile Access is a VA that allows you to manage your vCenter infrastructure from a smart phone or tablet with a UI that is formatted for smaller, lower resolution devices. It can't do everything, but for many common tasks, it is very useful.

For our purposes here, we'll focus on Onyx. You can watch an overview of the tool at http://www.youtube.com/watch?v=6ab_tMI2a8Y (and there are links there to other related videos as well). This video was current for the release of the Alpha version (a very early stage in development) of the project, so it is a little dated, but it does showcase it very well. This tool is similar in purpose to Exchange Administrator in Exchange 2007 and later, namely to help convert GUI tasks into PowerShell (or in our case PowerCLI) code. The basic idea is that you complete tasks in the vSphere Client and the corresponding method of accomplishing the task with PowerCLI based on the options you selected will automatically be generated for you.

Orchestrator

Orchestrator is a workflow automation tool designed to help automate a group of tasks, such as the following:

1. A programmer makes a request for an Active Directory domain controller, SQL server, two web servers, and one each of an XP, Vista, and Windows 7 client using an online form for that purpose.

2. His manager receives an e-mail with the request and approves it.

3. The approved request is parsed and the requested Virtual Machines created automatically from templates.

4. The programmer is notified that the process is complete and his VMs are ready.

This tool is relatively complex to set up and is aimed at programmers more than administrators trying to automate tasks with the other mechanisms described here. This tool is thus beyond the scope of this book.

More information on Orchestrator can be found at the following sites:

■ **www.vmware.com/files/pdf/VMware-vCenter-Orchestrator-DS-EN.pdf.** A quick sales sheet type of document that describes in simple terms what Orchestrator is and what it does.

■ **www.vmware.com/support/pubs/orchestrator_pubs.html.** The official product documentation, including installation and administrators guides, as well as a developers guide and an API plug-in reference to Orchestrator.

■ **blogs.vmware.com/orchestrator/.** The official VMware blog on Orchestrator, with cool new tools and features, tips, and tricks, etc.

■ **www.vcoteam.info/.** The Orchestrator team's own website with links to other places to get information.

Common Areas in Which Automation Works Well

Automation is most useful in larger installations where tasks are repetitive. Small environments often complete these tasks only once or a few times, so the overhead of creating the scripts is probably more than the benefits received. Even in these environments, however, some of the techniques described in this chapter and illustrated throughout this book are very useful for troubleshooting and resolving problems that may not be fixable without them (short of a reinstall).

Common examples of when automation works well, or in some cases tasks that are easier or even only possible from the command line, include those listed in this section.

Scripted Installations

While there are not many question asked during an ESXi install, there are still configuration tasks that need to be undertaken once the install finishes. These can be completed manually, but to do so error free when installing tens or hundreds of servers is both a challenge as well as boring. Host Profiles (described in Chapter 5) could be used, but that requires the Enterprise Plus edition. vSphere Auto Deploy could be used (as described in Chapter 5) as well. Scripted installations make it easy to quickly and repeatedly install servers. Those familiar with using Linux Kick Start for installation will be able to quickly create the necessary files.

Large or Repeating Maintenance Tasks

Many times reconfiguring the environment requires a lot of effort and time; for example, if an unused network adapter (e.g., vmnic3) needs to be added to a new virtual switch (e.g., vSwitch5) and a VMkernel port (e.g., VMotion) created on that switch that is configured for VMotion (with an IP address in the 192.168.10.x range), it's just a few clicks in the GUI. But if there are 100 ESX servers that need those same changes made on each of them, that is a time-consuming process. As previously described with scripted installations, you could use Host Profiles, but again, that requires the Enterprise Plus edition and even then, you'd be prompted for 100 IP addresses (and you'd also have to make sure you didn't have any typos or duplicates). It would be much simpler to just write a simple script to do the job like this (Note the line starting with $VirtualSwitch is one long line of code. It had to be broken up to stay within the margins of this book.):

```
$VMotionIp = 10
ForEach ($EsxHost in (get-vmhost))
{
$VirtualSwitch = New-VirtualSwitch -VMHost $EsxHost -Name vSwitch5 -nic vmnic3 $VMotion
= New-VirtualPortGroup -VirtualSwitch $VirtualSwitch -Name VMotion New-VmHost-
NetworkAdapter -VMHost $EsxHost -PortGroup VMotion -VirtualSwitch $VirtualSwitch -IP
192.168.10.$VMotionIp -SubnetMask 255.255.255.0 -VMotionEnabled: $true
$VMotionIp++
}
```

This simple script will automatically create a new virtual switch on all of the ESXi servers in vCenter named `vSwitch5` using `vmnic3`, create a new port group called `VMotion`, and then convert the port group into a VMkernel port that is VMotion enabled. The IP address on the first server will be `192.168.10.10` and each subsequent server will increment the last number of the IP address by one.

Reporting

Many times you'll need to report to management on the status of the environment. There are a lot of great third-party tools that will do this, but this may cost money and may not give you exactly what you want. For example, maybe you're running low on disk space and need a weekly report on VMs that have snapshots larger than 1GB in size. A simple, though not pretty, way to do this is with this one-line script:

```
Get-Vm | Get-Snapshot | Where-Object {$_.SizeMB -gt 1024} | Select VM, Name, SizeMB
```

One quick note on this code: The `Where-Object` cmdlet uses curly braces {}, not parentheses ().

The output could be formatted in HTML if desired and even be configured to automatically e-mail the output with a few simple PowerCLI commands. Just schedule the script to run weekly with Windows Scheduler (or any other scheduler you want) and your problem is solved.

In other situations, it is not necessary to run the script on a repeating basis. For example, maybe you are preparing for an upgrade and want to determine the version of all of your ESXi servers. You could look at them one by one in the GUI, but why do that when a simple script will do the trick? All you need is this one-liner:

```
Get-VmHost | % {$EsxHost = $_ | Get-View; $EsxHost.Config.Product | Select {$EsxHost.Name}, Version, Build, FullName}
```

Configuring Settings That Can't Be Set in the GUI

Some things just don't have a GUI way to do them—for example, enabling CDP (Cisco Discovery Protocol) on a standard vSwitch. These tasks must be performed at the command line. To set the CDP mode to both (meaning that an ESXi server will listen to the physical switches for their configuration and broadcast its own configuration to the switches) on `vSwitch0` via the vCLI (or the vMA) use:

```
vicfg-vswitch -B both vSwitch0
```

These and many more tasks can be done at the command line. These examples use the vCLI, but PowerCLI could also have been used; sometimes we'll illustrate one method and sometimes the other. Some things are easier to do in one or the other, but a discussion on when to use a certain approach is beyond the scope of this book.

Troubleshooting

Sometimes you need to troubleshoot an issue, and the command line may be the simplest way to do so. For many issues, you can use the vCLI, vMA, or PowerCLI, but for some issues (especially those dealing with networking), you may need to log in to the console on the server. This is covered in the troubleshooting section of Chapter 5. From there, you could check network connectivity to a SAN array (with an IP address of 192.168.10.20)—for example, by using vmkping (which sends a ping out a VMkernel port) like this:

```
vmkping 192.168.10.20
```

IMPLEMENTATION AND MANAGEMENT

Now that we know why we might want or need to use various CLI tools, we need to cover their installation and some basic configurations. We'll also look at keeping the tools up-to-date, matching the version of the tool with the version(s) of ESX or ESXi in use, and converting old scripts that may have been designed to be used at the service console in ESX to scripts that will run in the vCLI and vMA with ESXi.

How to Install and Use the vCLI

The vCLI is typically installed on administrators' computers to allow them to remotely run commands and scripts against their ESXi servers and to help troubleshoot them. As mentioned previously, many people use the vMA instead and just use SSH (for example, via putty) to access the vMA VM, in which case you can skip this section and jump to the section on the vMA.

Requirements

The installation process and requirements are vastly different for Linux and Windows. We will briefly touch on the Linux installation and refer you to the Linux documentation for more details, as each variant of Linux has its own requirements and prerequisite software. Also, VMware recommends that you use the vMA unless you are "an experienced Linux administrator" as you may have to manually install or uninstall various prerequisite applications and/or manually update various components to get it to work.

The Windows installation is very straightforward and will automatically install all required components; it can also be uninstalled like any other application.

Linux VMware recommends use of the Linux version of vCLI only if you are an experienced Linux administrator; for all others, it recommends the prepackaged vMA instead because all of the prerequisite software is preinstalled.

The following distributions of Linux are supported (though the vCLI may run on many others, it is not supported on those platforms):

- Red Hat Enterprise Linux 5.5 Server (32 bit and 64 bit)
- SLES (SUSE Linux Enterprise Server, by Novell) 10 SP1 and 11 (32 bit and 64 bit)
- Ubuntu 10.04 (32 bit and 64 bit)

In addition, the following Linux packages must already be installed before installation begins (the installation will check for them and fail if any or all are not present):

- **OpenSSL.** Used to encrypt the communications between the system running vCLI and the system(s) you are running the commands against.
- **LibXML2.** Used to parse XML, which is also used (internally) by many of the commands.
- **e2fsprogs.** Utilities to manage the file system, which are required by some components of Perl. This component is called uuid-dev on SLES distributions.

The installation will check on the presence and version of many Perl modules and then proceed in one of three ways:

- If they are not present, they will automatically be installed using CPAN (assuming you have an Internet connection). If you don't have an Internet connection, installation will stop and you will see an error message.
- If they are present and the version is lower than the recommended version, installation will proceed, but each of the modules listed in a message at the end of the installation process will need to be updated manually using the native OS tools.
- If they are present and higher than the recommend version, installation will complete with no messages.

Windows The vCLI is only supported on the following versions of Windows:

- Vista Enterprise SP1 (32 and 64 bit)
- 7 (32 and 64 bit)
- 2008 (64 bit)

It is much simpler to install—in fact, all required prerequisites are installed with the application (that primarily means ActivePerl by ActiveState Software to provide the needed Perl support) and removed if the application is uninstalled. The only exception to this is that if you want to run esxcli commands, you must manually install Visual C++ 2008 32-bit edition (the filename is vcredist_x86.exe) before they will work.

Installation

The actual installation of vCLI (assuming you've met all of the prerequisites for Linux or Windows) is fairly straightforward. You will need to download the software from the VMware website where you downloaded all of the other VMware components.

Linux   To install the vCLI, follow these steps (logged in as root or someone with superuser permissions or the equivalent):

1. Untar (extract) the installation files from the version you downloaded by running this command:

   ```
   tar -zxvf VMware-vSphere-CLI-5.X.X-XXXXX.i386.tar.gz
   ```

2. It will automatically create a vmware-vsphere-vcli-distrib directory below the current directory. Change to that directory.

3. Run the following command (you may need to use sudo depending on who you logged in as and the privileges associated with that user):

   ```
   ./vmware-install.pl
   ```

4. Agree to the license terms.

5. If prerequisite Perl modules are missing, it will connect to CPAN and download and install them; this may be a lengthy process.

6. Enter the directory to install in or accept the default (/usr/bin).

7. Review the installation result and manually update any Perl modules noted (if any).

Windows   The installation on Windows is fairly simple:

1. Run the downloaded installer

2. If prompted, remove any old files so that everything can be upgraded to the new version.

3. Accept the default installation location (C:\Program Files\VMware\VMware vSphere CLI) or select your own.

4. Reboot when finished (to make sure the path information is properly updated; otherwise, the application may not function correctly).

Connecting and Entering Commands

Once the vCLI is installed, to use it, simply open a command prompt (Windows) or a terminal session (Linux) and change to the directory where it was installed.

Tip

In Windows, you can go to Start > All Programs > VMware > VMware vSphere CLI > Command Prompt to open a command prompt that defaults to the installation directory.

Note that in Windows, most commands (except for esxcli) have a .pl extension, and that extension must be entered as part of every command; that is not required in Linux. This book will not show the .pl extension in any commands.

The commands (most starting with `vicfg-`) are run from the prompt. Typically, the command is entered followed by command line options that include the server to authenticate against (`--server`); the username (`--username`); the password for the specified user (`--password`); and if the server specified is a vCenter server, the ESXi (or ESX for pre-version-5 versions) server to run the command against (`--vihost`), finally followed by any options relevant to the command entered. If the `--password` option is not entered, the user will be prompted for the password.

For example, to list the NICs on an ESXi server, use the following command from a command prompt where the vCLI is installed:

```
vicfg-nics --server vc01.testdomain.local --username administrator --password mypass
--vihost esxi01.testdomain.local -l
```

In this command, `vicfg-nics` is the command to be executed, and the only option (besides the authentication options) necessary for this command is `-l` to list the NICs on the host.

How to Install and Use vMA

Although you can install and use vCLI any place you want, many administrators prefer to have a central server that they connect to and run commands against. One of the most-liked features is the ability to run commands without constantly entering credentials for those commands (which will be described below in the security section). It is simple and easy to set up and use.

Just a quick note before we begin: This section will review the installation and use of vMA; vifp is an optional (but very useful) feature that can be used with vMA, but as it is primarily security focused, it will be discussed in the security section of this chapter. Nevertheless, there are several references to it in this section, because many of the topics logically belong here and not specifically under security.

Requirements

The requirements for this are minimal, namely it must be run on an ESXi 4.0 U2 (Update 2), 4.1, or 5 host that is capable of running 64-bit VMs (meaning either Intel VT must be present and enabled in the BIOS [for Intel-based servers] or for AMD-based servers, an Opteron rev E. or later must be used), but it can manage ESX and ESXi 3.5 U5, 4.0 U2, 4.1, and 5 hosts (optionally via vCenter 4.0 or later). As mentioned above, the requirements for the VM are very modest (1 vCPU and 600MB of RAM).

Installation

Before you can install it, you must download vMA from the VMware website where you downloaded the other vSphere components. Once downloaded, unzip it and note the location for use in the Deploy OVF Template wizard.

Installation is very straightforward. To install it, do the following (note that some references to concepts described later in the book, such as thick and thin provisioning and datastores will not be described here—this procedure assumes you've already got a vSphere environment running, and indeed this must be the case before you can install the vMA):

1. Open the vSphere Client and connect to your vCenter (or ESXi if vCenter is not used) server.

2. Select the server (or cluster) you want to install it on.

3. Select File > Deploy OVF Template.

4. Select Deploy from File or URL then browse to the location you downloaded it from and click Next.

5. Review the template details and click Next.

6. Review the License agreement, click Accept, and click Next.

7. Give the vMA a name or accept the default vSphere Management Assistant (vMA), select the inventory location if you are connected to vCenter (datacenter and/or folder), and click Next.

8. Select the desired datastore, thick or thin provisioning option, and click Next.

9. Select the port group for the VM that also has access to vCenter and the ESXi servers and click Next.

10. Select the IP policy that you will use to give the VM an IP (Fixed—assigned within the VM, Transient—a kind of DHCP that is managed by vCenter for Virtual Appliances and vApps, or DHCP—standard DHCP) and click Next.

11. If Fixed was selected in the previous step, enter the static IP and click Next.

12. Click Finish and the VM will be deployed.

Connecting and Entering Commands

The first time you power up the vMA VM, it will prompt for a password for the vi-admin account. This account is a root equivalent (the root account is disabled in VMA—if you get error messages about running any commands that require root, use *sudo* and the command—only the vi-admin account is configured to be able to use `sudo`). This password should be a strong password, especially if you use the vifp feature because it will have admin access to all of your servers with stored credentials. In fact, if you try to use a simple (or even a moderately complex) password, you'll get a "Bad Password" message and will need to enter a new one. The password must be at least eight characters and contain one uppercase, one lowercase, and one special symbol (by default). These parameters can be modified if desired; to do so, refer to http://www.novell.com/support/viewContent.do?externalId=7008156&sliceId=1 for the method and http://content.hccfl.edu/pollock/AUnix2/PAM-Help.htm in the Some Notes Regarding pam_cracklib section for an explanation of the parameters. This is beyond the scope of the book and thus won't be discussed further.

You will also be prompted for the networking configuration you want to use. (DHCP or static IP address; if a static configuration, the IP, DNS, default gateway, etc.) Make sure that this information is valid on the *management* network, not the standard VM network (if they are different, and they really should be different). This VA will be used to manage the rest of the environment from the command line.

The initial setup process is illustrated in Figure 4.1 and is as follows:

1. If additional IPv6 addresses are required (beyond the default ones), type *y* to configure additional IPv6 addresses (for most scenarios, this is not necessary).

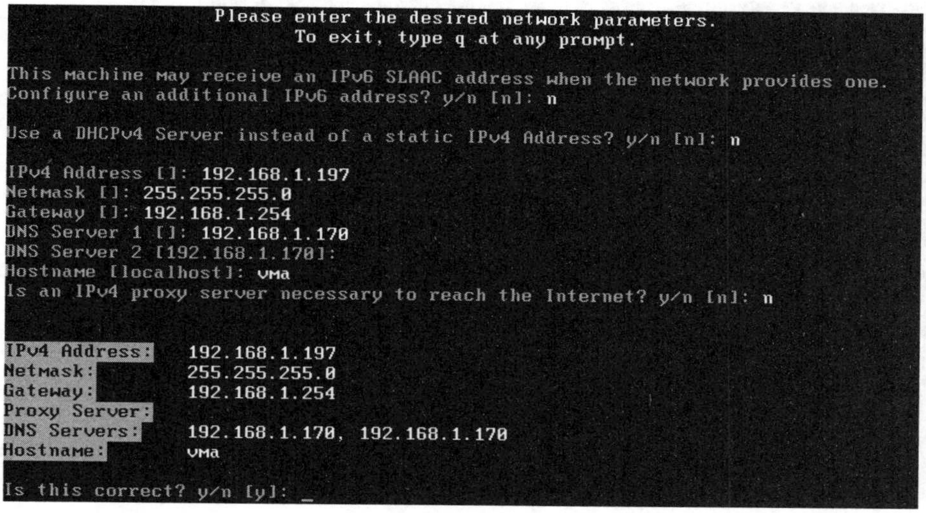

```
                    Please enter the desired network parameters.
                       To exit, type q at any prompt.

This machine may receive an IPv6 SLAAC address when the network provides one.
Configure an additional IPv6 address? y/n [n]: n

Use a DHCPv4 Server instead of a static IPv4 Address? y/n [n]: n

IPv4 Address []: 192.168.1.197
Netmask []: 255.255.255.0
Gateway []: 192.168.1.254
DNS Server 1 []: 192.168.1.170
DNS Server 2 [192.168.1.170]:
Hostname [localhost]: vMa
Is an IPv4 proxy server necessary to reach the Internet? y/n [n]: n


IPv4 Address:     192.168.1.197
Netmask:          255.255.255.0
Gateway:          192.168.1.254
Proxy Server:
DNS Servers:      192.168.1.170, 192.168.1.170
Hostname:         vMa

Is this correct? y/n [y]: _
```

Figure 4.1
vMA network configuration prompts.

2. If you are using DHCP to configure the IPv4 address, type *y* and skip to Step 4 below; otherwise, select *n* and continue on to the next step.

3. Type the IP address, subnet mask, default gateway, DNS server addresses (two are allowed) as prompted, pressing Enter after each.

4. When prompted, enter the host name for the vMA—to use this name on the network, you'll also need to make sure an A (host) record is created in DNS. In the screenshot, we chose a local name, not planning on referencing it by name in the future. You can open a console and access it directly or allow IP access.

5. If a proxy server is required for Internet access (to update the vMA later), type *y* and enter the proxy details; if a proxy isn't used or Internet access is not allowed, type *n*.

6. Review the settings and confirm they are correct, then type *y* to continue. You can change them later by using standard Linux commands, the Configure Network option when you open a console to the vMA, or via a web browser. You could also simply delete and redeploy the vMA, but that is a rather drastic step and will destroy any configuration and data you had in the vMA VA. Next, the vi-admin password needs to be set, as shown in Figure 4.2

7. After displaying the IP configuration, the system will inform you that the root user has been disabled and that all access to vMA is done via the vi-admin user instead. Type the old password (it is blank—just hit Enter), then type a new

```
The root account is disabled in this vMA virtual machine, which means no one can
 log in as root. The administrator account for vMA is called "vi-admin". In orde
r to log in to vMA, you need to log in as this user. This user has been pre-crea
ted in the vMA, and its password needs to be set now. Please enter a secure pass
word for the account now.

Please provide a password for the vi-admin user. If you are prompted for an old
password for this user, press <enter>.
Old Password:
New UNIX password:
BAD PASSWORD: it is too short
passwd: Authentication token manipulation error

Please provide a password for the vi-admin user. If you are prompted for an old
password for this user, press <enter>.
Old Password:
New UNIX password:
BAD PASSWORD: it is based on a dictionary word
passwd: Authentication token manipulation error

Please provide a password for the vi-admin user. If you are prompted for an old
password for this user, press <enter>.
Old Password:
New UNIX password:
Retype new UNIX password: _
```

Figure 4.2
Setting the vMA vi-admin password.

password. If the password does not meet the complexity requirements described above, you'll get various error messages as shown in Figure 4.2. Repeat this step until an acceptable password is entered.

8. Confirm the password and the system will finalize the initial configuration. Be sure to write down this password, because if it is lost or forgotten, there is no way to get it back (without redeploying the vMA).

Once the initial setup has been completed, you can access vMA either by opening a console window to it (but others could also open and people could watch others and/ or interfere by having multiple people type at once on the same console window) or by using an SSH client (such as PuTTY) to connect to the server, with each person getting his/her own session (the usual route for all but the smallest IT shops).

When you open a console, the screen shown in Figure 4.3 will be displayed.

Note that setting the time zone and/or reconfiguring the network can be done from this screen, as well as by opening a browser to the IP address displayed on the screen. We'll discuss the browser approach later in this chapter when we discuss updating vMA.

Tip

When using the browser, don't forget the https:// at the beginning of the address, nor the :5480 at the end or the URL won't work.

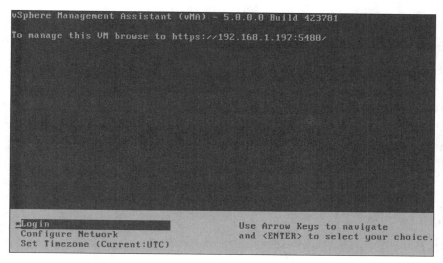

```
vSphere Management Assistant (vMA) - 5.0.0.0 Build 423781

To manage this VM browse to https://192.168.1.197:5480/
```

```
*Login                          Use Arrow Keys to navigate
 Configure Network              and <ENTER> to select your choice.
 Set Timezone (Current:UTC)
```

Figure 4.3
vMA main screen.

On the other hand, if you use an SSH client (such as PuTTY), you'll just be prompted for the name and password. You will not see the screen and other options shown above.

Once connected to vMA, simply log in and then enter commands as you would with vCLI.

Caution

If you want to delete vMA for any reason (for example, to upgrade it to a new version) and you don't want to or can't use the update feature in the browser, you should remove all vifp targets first or you will end up with multiple vi-user and vi-admin accounts (with a unique numerical ID each time you do) on each server. Removing the target first will also remove the user accounts created when they were added.

If you want, you can enable the vi-user account, which will allow read-only access to the servers in the environment (for example, for reporting purposes or to allow junior admins limited access). This account can't be used with AD-based targets (either ESXi servers that have been joined to the domain or vCenter servers); for that you'll need to either join vMA to the domain and use an AD account to log in to VMA or use the vi-admin account. This limits the functionality of this account, but may nevertheless be useful in some scenarios. To enable the account, follow these steps:

1. Log in to vMA as the vi-admin user.

2. Run the following command:

```
sudo passwd vi-user
```

3. Enter (and confirm) the password for the account. If the password does not meet the same complexity requirements previously described for the vi-admin user, you'll need to repeat Steps 2 and 3 again until they are met.

Integrating vMA into a Windows Domain

If you are operating in an AD environment and want to join vMA to a domain so you can log in with your AD account instead of the vi-admin or other local Linux account, you'll need to follow these steps:

1. Log in to vMA as vi-admin.

2. Run the following command:

```
sudo domainjoin-cli join <domain name> <domain admin user name>
```

3. Type the password for the vi-admin user (required by sudo) as well as the domain admin user account specified (required by AD).

4. Reboot vMA. Note that you need to reboot vMA or you will see strange errors, have trouble adding new fastpass targets using AD authentication, etc. You can do this by running the command:

```
sudo reboot
```

You can always verify the domain that the vMA belongs to by running this command:

```
sudo domainjoin-cli query
```

If you want to leave the domain, run the following command:

```
sudo domainjoin-cli leave
```

Here, let us also present a couple of tips that make the integration with AD even easier: setting a default domain so you don't need to enter the domain along with the user each time you log in and adding an AD group to the /etc/sodoers file, allowing them to use the sudo command as needed.

Setting a Default AD Domain for Login   Normally when you join vMA to a domain and then want to log in to vMA using your domain credentials, you need to enter them in the format *Domain\User*. If you do that a lot or if the domain name is particularly long or complex, it might be much simpler to set the default domain to the one that vMA belongs to. To do so, follow these steps:

1. Log in to vMA as an admin user (with permissions to run sudo—unless you've already done the procedure in the next section, you'll need to log in as the local vi-admin).

2. Run the following command to use `vi` to edit the configuration file used to configure the parameters used with AD:

```
sudo vi /etc/likewise/lsassd.conf
```

3. Locate the following line and delete the comment character (the # sign) at the beginning so the default domain will be used:

```
# assume-default-domain = yes
```

4. Save the file and exit `vi` by typing the following:

```
:wq!
```

5. Reload the configuration file to make the change take effect by running this command (otherwise the change will not take effect until the vMA is rebooted):

```
sudo /opt/likewise/bin/lw-refresh-configuration
```

The references to `likewise` in the steps above (and in the next section) are because VMware leverages Likewise's Open product for AD integration. You can learn more about the underlying technology by going to: http://www.likewise.com/products/likewise_open/.

Adding an AD Group to the Sudoers File   The `/etc/sudoers` file is used in Linux to configure who can use the `sudo` command, which allows non-root users to run commands that normally only the root user can run. This is relatively common and easy for Linux users, but what if you've configured AD authentication and want to allow AD users or groups to use these commands as well? No problem, you just need to configure the file appropriately (after you've joined the vMA to the domain).

1. Log in to vMA as the local vi-admin user (which can run `sudo` by default).

2. The `sudoers` file is the configuration file used to configure the list of users authorized to run `sudo`. It is read-only by default, so you must use a special tool (basically `vi`, which also allows write access to the file) to update the file:

```
sudo visudo
```

3. At the bottom of the file, add the following line (you can repeat this step as many times as you need to add multiple users and/or groups):

```
%<Domain Name>\\<User or Group name> ALL=(ALL) ALL
```

Note that the domain name must be preceded by the % sign, the \ between the domain and user must be typed twice (the backslash is a special character, so it tells

Linux the next character is a special character), and any embedded spaces in a user or group name must have a \ before the space (for the same reason). For example, the group ESX Admins in the testdomain domain would be entered as follows:

```
%testdomain\\ESX\ Admins ALL=(ALL) ALL
```

4. Save the file and exit sudo by typing the following:

```
:wq!
```

To verify that the user (or group) now has access to sudo, log in as the desired user (or a member of the desired group) and run the following command:

```
id
```

It should return all of the AD groups the user belongs to; this will let you verify that the user has the correct access. Verify it by running:

```
sudo -l
```

This should report the commands you can run, and it should say "(ALL) ALL."

Working with Groups of Servers

Sometimes you may want to run the same command against a group of servers; we've provided several reasons you might want to do so already earlier in this chapter. Also, as previously mentioned, one of the advantages of using the vMA over the vCLI is this capability. To do so, you can take advantage of one of the sample scripts that comes with the vMA called mcli.pl.

The mcli.pl script is located in /opt/vmware/vma/samples/perl and also has an accompanying README file that further documents its use and purpose.

To use this tool, follow these steps:

1. Use the vifp tool to add all of the targets you want to run the command against (if they haven't already been added). The procedures to do so are covered in the Security section of this chapter under "vMA—Using Fastpass."

2. Optionally, verify that all of the desired targets are all on the list by running this command:

```
vifp listservers -l
```

3. Create a file that contains all of the servers you want to run the command against. If you want, you could create multiple files with different servers in them for different purposes.

4. Set the vifp target to the first server in that list with this command:

```
vifptarget -s <hostname>
```

5. Run the command using `mcli.pl` this way (substituting `filename` for the file you created in step 3 and `command` for any vCLI command you want, along with any optional parameters it requires, but without any authentication or server parameters):

```
/opt/vmware/vma/samples/perl/mcli.pl filename command
```

This is a great way to do much of what PowerCLI can do using standard Linux syntax for those not interested in learning and using PowerCLI and doing things the Windows way.

How to Install and Use PowerCLI

PowerCLI is fairly straightforward to set up and use. It only runs on Windows and installs like any other Windows application.

Requirements

PowerCLI is supported on Windows XP or 2003 SP2, Vista, 7, and 2008 (both 32-bit and 64-bit versions). It works with vCenter 2.5 Update 6, 4.0 Update 1 and 2, 4.1, and 5.0, as well as ESX servers back to 3.03 Update 1 and all versions of ESXi.

In addition to the base OS, PowerCLI requires either PowerShell 1.0 or 2.0 to be installed (this may be a component that can be installed as part of the OS or may need to be downloaded separately from Microsoft, depending on the OS you're installing on). PowerShell requires the .NET framework 2.0 SP1 to function, so this must be installed before PowerShell if it is not already installed.

That's it for the prerequisites—pretty simple really, now let's move on to the installation.

Installation

Before you can install it, you must download PowerCLI from the VMware website where you downloaded the other vSphere components; it is also available at www .vmware.com/go/powercli.

Note

There are several PowerCLI applications available—the base PowerCLI, as well as versions for managing VUM (vSphere Update Manager), View, and other VMware products. This book will only discuss using the base PowerCLI components.

Once downloaded, run the application and follow the installation wizard as follows:

1. At the beginning, before the formal wizard even starts, you may be notified that VMware VIX is required and will automatically be installed; click OK to acknowledge that this will occur. The installation wizard will then automatically install it before starting the PowerCLI installation.

2. If you have not used PowerShell before, the security level will be set to a high level to ensure that rogue scripts don't damage your computer, steal information, etc. If that is the case, the dialog box shown in Figure 4.4 will appear; click Continue for now and make a note that you may need to adjust that when PowerShell is run.

3. At the introduction screen, click Next.

4. Review the license agreement, agree to it, and click Next.

5. Accept the default installation location (C:\Program Files (x86)\VMware\Infrastructure\vSphere PowerCLI\) or click Change, select a new one, and click Next. Note that the (x86) after Program Files will not be there on a 32-bit OS.

6. Click Install.

7. Click Finish when the installation completes.

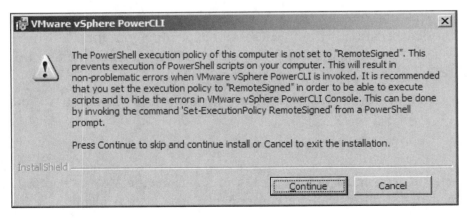

Figure 4.4
Execution policy warning.

You should notice a new icon on your desktop called VMware vSphere PowerCLI, and if you installed it on a 64-bit OS, a second icon called VMware vSphere Power-CLI (32-Bit). In addition, you should find under All Programs > VMware > VMware vSphere PowerCLI the above two programs (actually they just launch PowerShell and configure the environment, loading the required files for PowerCLI), as well as documentation including the Admin guide and a help file on the PowerCLI cmdlets.

Connecting and Entering Commands

To begin using PowerCLI, just run the application; note that it will take a few minutes to start as the .NET framework must be initialized, PowerShell loaded, and PowerCLI cmdlets loaded, so be patient. If you got the error message about your execution policy being too restrictive, you will also see the error message shown in Figure 4.5 when you launch PowerCLI. In that case, PowerCLI will not be properly configured until you lower the execution policy setting.

Let's briefly review the execution policy settings (from most restrictive to least restrictive):

- **Restricted.** No scripts can run (interactive commands only). The default setting is the most secure, but prevents the script that configures PowerCLI from running. It is recommended that you select a lower setting.

- **AllSigned.** Only digitally signed scripts from trusted providers can be executed, whether written by you or downloaded from the Internet. You can use this, but you'll need to refer to the PowerShell documentation on signing scripts if you want to do any scripting.

- **RemoteSigned.** Any scripts downloaded from the Internet must be signed by a trusted provider and any local script can run. This is VMware's recommended option so that local scripts you write can be executed, but anything you download must first be signed to prevent malicious use of PowerShell.

Figure 4.5
PowerCLI initialization error.

■ **Unrestricted.** Any scripts can run; this is the least secure option, but the simplest to use. Many people use this setting, but be aware that by doing so you have circumvented the native controls put in place by Microsoft to protect your security.

To view the current policy, run this command:

```
Get-ExecutionPolicy
```

Note

> To change the execution policy on Windows Vista, 2008, or later, you must run PowerShell as an administrator by right-clicking the application and selecting *Run as administrator*. If you are not currently logged in as a local administrator, you will need to specify the credentials of a local administrator to change this setting.

To set the execution policy, open PowerShell or PowerCLI (as an administrator, if necessary, depending on the OS you're running), and run the following command (where `Level` is any of the options described above):

```
Set-ExecutionPolicy <Level>
```

Before you begin using PowerCLI, you should check that everything is properly installed and that the computer it was installed on has access to the vCenter and ESXi servers. The simplest way to do this is to connect to one of them by running this command:

```
Connect-VIServer -Server <Server name or IP> -User <UserName> -Password <Password>
```

In the above command, replace the parameters in <> with the appropriate values. Note that the server can be either an ESXi server or a vCenter server and that you will need to specify credentials appropriate to the server specified.

If that command doesn't work, you probably don't have network access to the server you specified.

Keeping Your Tools Up to Date

One of the important tasks you'll face as an administrator is keeping the tools you use up to date; this is especially true when you upgrade versions of vSphere or vCenter, but also true in normal use to gain access to the latest features available to patch the software, fix bugs, and plug vulnerabilities. The method for doing this depends on the tool in question. The documentation for each tool is at the URL listed in each section; at each one there is also a Download link at the top of the page that can be used to download the tool itself.

vCLI

You can always find the latest version of vCLI at www.vmware.com/support/developer/vcli/. Usually a new version of the tool is released about the same time as a new version of vSphere is released; sometimes they also release a new version when an update is released, but this is not as common unless new functionality is exposed that they want to provide command line access to. You may want to check the above site whenever you download a new version of vSphere. Installation and upgrade of the tool were previously described.

vMA

You can always download vMA to update it like you would the vCLI by going to www.vmware.com/go/vma/. This works, but this tool in particular has another option to keep not only the vCLI and related components, but also the OS itself up to date, and that is through the use of the browser interface previously mentioned. To use this tool, do the following:

- Open a web browser to the vMA IP (the IP address and port can be seen when you open a console to vMA).

Tip

Remember to use https:// and the port (5480) for this to work. Also, if you have joined vMA to the domain and want to log in using domain credentials, you must specify the domain and the username in the Domain\User format. If a default domain has been specified, it is ignored when logging in via the browser.

- Optionally, select the Network tab and then click the Proxy button on the second row of tabs. Verify the proxy settings to make sure you can access the Internet; you can modify it if required by selecting the "Use a proxy server" check box, setting the Proxy Server to the name or IP address, and Proxy Port to the desired port. Optionally, you can also specify a username and password to authenticate against the proxy server.

- Select the Update tab and click the Check Updates button to see if a new version is available. The system will return the results of the last check, and if an update is available, simply click Install Updates to update vMA.

That's all there is to it. As simple as it was in vSphere 4, it is that much easier (and graphical) in 5. This does require Internet access to work. If Internet access is not possible, you can manually download and install the patches, but that is more complicated and beyond the scope of this book. You can also simply download the latest version of vMA and deploy the VA again, but all of your settings will be lost; you'll need to reconfigure the environment as previously described.

PowerCLI

Each new version of PowerCLI exposes more and more functionality, so it is important to make sure that the PowerCLI version you are using has the features required by the script you are running or the command you are using. To determine the PowerCLI version, simply run this command inside PowerCLI:

```
Get-PowerCLIVersion
```

Note that several snap-ins may be loaded, and each will be listed, along with the version of each.

Similarly to the vCLI, you can always find the latest version of PowerCLI at www.vmware.com/go/PowerCLI. Usually a new version of the tool is released about the same time an update or a new version of vSphere is released. You may want to check that site whenever you download a new version of vSphere.

Matching Your Host/vCenter Version to Your Automation Tools

As mentioned in the previous section, you should always make sure that any automation tools you choose to use are at the same or higher level than what you want to manage; for example, PowerCLI 4.0 supports vSphere 4.0 and ESX 3 servers, but not vSphere 4.1 servers. Make it a habit that whenever you plan on performing any version or even update patches to your vSphere environment (ESXi and/or vCenter) to check with VMware and make sure you also get the latest tools to manage those servers. Generally, we like to complete the tools upgrade at the same time we perform the vCenter upgrade. You can also upgrade the tools prior to a vCenter upgrade if you want.

Upgrading the vCLI was covered in the sections above for both Windows and Linux; updating PowerCLI will upgrade the environment to the new version. The vMA can be run side-by-side with older versions as they run in separate VMs, so this makes it simple to keep the old one available until the new one is thoroughly tested and any configuration from the old one migrated to the new one. Even then, the old version of the vMA can be kept for a period of time after switching to the new version in case any issues arise.

Converting ESX Scripts to vCLI/vMA Scripts

Many scripts that have been written for execution on the ESX service console can be modified to run remotely via the vCLI or vMA. Figure 4.6 reviews the issues that

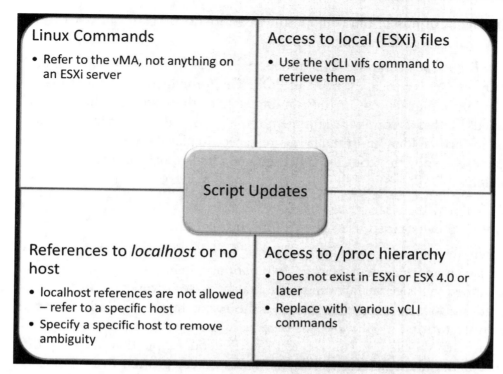

Linux Commands
- Refer to the vMA, not anything on an ESXi server

Access to local (ESXi) files
- Use the vCLI vifs command to retrieve them

Script Updates

References to *localhost* or no host
- localhost references are not allowed – refer to a specific host
- Specify a specific host to remove ambiguity

Access to /proc hierarchy
- Does not exist in ESXi or ESX 4.0 or later
- Replace with various vCLI commands

Figure 4.6
Script conversion issues and suggested solutions.

must be addressed to convert those scripts to run in the vMA environment. The issues fall into four broad categories (references to vMA apply equally to the host where vCLI is running):

- **Linux commands.** Any commands in the script will run on and refer to vMA where the script is running, not to anything on an ESXi server. Depending on what commands are run, that may or may not be an issue.

- **Access to local (ESXi) files.** Any local files referenced in the script will also be local to vMA, not an ESXi server; if you need access to files on the ESXi server itself, you can use the vCLI command vifs to retrieve them. This command will allow you to create and delete directories and files, copy files to/from the ESXi server, etc. Note that wild card characters and relative paths are not supported, so some minor script modifications may be required in this area as well.

- **References to either localhost or no host.** localhost references are not allowed as they would refer to vMA, not an ESXi host. Remedy this by specifying the particular host in question or by using various programming techniques to loop through a series of hosts. You could also use the `mcli.pl` script in vMA to run the script against a group of hosts.

■ **Access to the /proc hierarchy.** This functionality was available in ESX 3.5 and lower only, and never in any version of ESXi. The /proc hierarchy is a virtual file system in Linux that represents the running state of the system, including modules loaded, hardware configuration, memory, etc. ESXi is not based on Linux and has no /proc folder, and thus it was replaced. Replace any references in this directory structure with various vCLI commands that return equivalent information.

SECURITY

Security is often an afterthought in many phases of vSphere design and deployment, and nowhere is this more evident than in automation. We just want things to work so we throw something together or we assume that because it works for us, the master vSphere administrator, that when we give the script to a help desk person or another administrator that it will work for them as well, and when they subsequently have trouble, we are shocked. If you aspire to write good scripts that are truly time and effort savers, think about security early on and in every project. Even if you just use the tool interactively without writing any scripts, you still must authenticate before any commands can run.

In this section, we'll begin by taking a brief look at interactive authentication (which is often used in troubleshooting from the command line) and then we'll look at ways to authenticate within scripts. Note that for the second section, the tool or tools that can be used with that method will be listed in the section header; if none are listed, it can be used with any of the tools. A summary table with this information is included at the start of the section as well to help keep the options straight.

Interactive Authentication

One of the most common ways to authenticate is interactively, by entering credentials on commands as they are entered. Any of the methods described below for scripting can also be used interactively as commands are entered as well.

If the server specified is a vCenter server or an ESXi host that has been joined to the domain, and the vMA has also been joined to the same domain, then instead of entering the username and password options, the `--passthroughauth` option can be specified to use the current user's Windows credentials instead.

Script Authentication

While interactive authentication is okay for troubleshooting, it doesn't work very well when you scale that out to creating a script. You don't want usernames and passwords on every line, especially those with administrative access. Nor do you want to stop at every command and be prompted for the password. Not to worry: each automation tool has its own abilities in this area to in some manner or another securely get the credentials and use them as required. Table 4.1 lists the available options.

Hard Coding Credentials in Individual Commands

This is the simplest technique to implement, but is the least secure and will require the most maintenance to keep up with username and password changes. All that must be done to use this technique is add the usual credentials (`--server`, `--password`, etc.) previously described on each command that requires authentication. The problem is that scripts are stored in plain text and anyone with access to the script will then be able to read all of the usernames and passwords. In addition, many maintenance tasks require administrative access (at least to varying degrees), so that makes the environment even less secure. We wouldn't ever recommend using this approach in any script.

vMA—Using Fastpass

Before we begin discussing how to use fastpass, we should take a minute and discuss what happens to each ESXi server when it is added to fastpass from a security perspective. When you use vMA for scripting, you have two options as previously described—use AD accounts or use native Linux accounts. There are also two modes of authentication: `--fpauth`, which is the native fastpass mechanism and uses Linux users; and `--adauth`, which was introduced in vMA 4.1 and uses AD accounts. The `--adauth` mechanism is considered much more secure as credentials are not stored on any server (except the domain controllers of course), whereas `--fpauth` uses a relatively simple XOR cipher to encrypt the password and is relatively simple to break.

Table 4.1   Tools and Authentication Options Summary Matrix

Tool	Hard Code	Fastpass	Session File	Get-Credential
vCLI	X		X	
vMA	X	X	X	
PowerCLI	X			X

If you choose to use the native Linux accounts (and thus `--fpauth`), then the vi-admin user will be added as a user on each server with administrative access and the vi-user account will be added as a user on each server with read-only permissions (even if the account has not been enabled—this is in case you choose to enable it later). When you remove a server from the list of available servers in fastpass, the two user accounts will be removed as well.

On the other hand, if you choose to use AD, then each user who adds a server to the fastpass list will need to have administrator permissions on the server (either as a user or due to a group that he/she belongs to that has administrative privileges on that host). When using AD, the two Linux users previously mentioned will not be added either, as AD is being used.

Caution

The two mechanisms should not be mixed in the same vMA, with some ESXi servers added using the Linux users (with `--fpauth`) and some ESXi servers using AD users (with `--adauth`), as you will always be prompted for each command for a username and password for the servers not using the type of user you logged into vMA as (Linux or AD).

We've said this before, but we want to repeat our note one more time: it is better to join vMA to the domain as described in the implementation portion of this chapter and use AD credentials to log in and access vMA than to use the vi-admin account, as using the vi-admin account will store each server you add as a target in its own credentials store instead of all the credentials residing in AD. Using AD credentials may also harden the environment, with minimum and maximum password lengths, ages, etc.

You begin using fastpass by adding targets—things you want to run commands against someday. Targets are either ESXi servers or vCenter servers, and you may want to add both to give you options as you create scripts and run commands. For example, sometimes you may want to choose things in vCenter (including both vCenter configuration options and ESXi server options), while other times you may want to target a specific server directly. Note that in a few cases, commands must be run directly against the server itself instead of the server through vCenter.

To add a target using `--fpauth` (the vi-admin account), type the following command:

```
sudo vifp addserver <ESXi or vCenter FQDN> --username root
```

It is possible to use a different account other than `root` if desired (for example, the administrator account for Windows when specifying a vCenter server), as long as it has administrator permissions to the server specified. No matter what user was specified, you'll be prompted for the password after you press Enter; type it and the target is added. Note that when you add a vCenter server, you'll also get a note that the credentials will be stored and this is a security risk (as we've previously explained); type **yes** to confirm that you want the server added.

To add a server while using an AD account, a similar process is followed, except the command is a little different, namely:

```
sudo vifp addserver <ESXi or vCenter FQDN> --authpolicy adauth --username <Domain>\\
<User>
```

Note the double backslash (\\) in the example above—that is required because \ is an "escape" character to Linux meaning "do something special with the next character." You would use this same syntax if a user or group had a space in it, such as ESX Admins, which you would specify as follows:

```
<domain>\\ESX\ Admins
```

You can also omit the username switch, in which case you'll be prompted for the AD account to be used to add the target (which like with --fpauth requires that the account be an administrator for the server). You'll need to specify the domain name and username in the typical <Domain>\<User> format (without the extra backslash as this is in a prompt, not a command line option).

Tip

An advantage of using the AD method is that when adding multiple targets together, after you enter the AD account's password once, it does not keep prompting for the password, whereas the Linux approach prompts for a password every time.

To confirm that the servers have been added, run the following command (the switch is the letter l for list, not the number 1):

```
vifp listservers -l
```

The server name, type, and authentication type will be displayed, as shown in Figures 4.7 and 4.8. Note that you can have some targets added with --adauth and some with --fpauth, but that makes the situation trickier—as previously mentioned, we'd suggest you stick to one or the other. The vMA documentation discusses how to set up Kerberos tickets and keep them refreshed when you log in as the vi-admin and then run commands against a target that was added with --adauth. It is somewhat difficult and a fairly rare situation—hence our earlier recommendation to stick to one or the other when adding targets and later using them.

```
vi-admin@localhost:~> vifp listservers -l
esx01.testdomain.local  ESXi    fpauth
esx02.testdomain.local  ESXi    fpauth
esx03.testdomain.local  ESXi    fpauth
```

Figure 4.7
Servers added with `--fpauth`.

```
vma:~> vifp listservers -l
esx01.testdomain.local  ESXi    adauth
esx02.testdomain.local  ESXi    adauth
esx03.testdomain.local  ESXi    adauth
```

Figure 4.8
Servers added with `--adauth`.

Before a target can be used, it must be initialized, which sets the focus of all commands to that server (until you log out or change the focus by running the command again and pointing to a different server). To do so, run this command:

```
vifptarget --s <FQDN of a previously added target>
```

Note that this will also change your command prompt in the vMA so that you can see both who you are logged as (which is always displayed as shown in Figure 4.7) as well as the target server just specified.

Once that is done, commands can be entered without specifying any credentials or even the server itself—very similar to how commands were formerly run on ESX servers. The only exception to this rule is that if a vCenter server is the target, then your commands must specify the `--vihost` option to denote which ESXi server managed by vCenter you want to run the command against (it does not need to be a target in fastpass to use it).

If you want to set the context back to nothing (no target server), use this command:

```
vifptarget -c
```

vCLI and/or vMA—Using Session Files

The vCLI (and thus the vMA as it runs vCLI commands) can use session files to store credentials securely for a short period of time. To use them, a file is created (in this example `/tmp/mycred`) using the following syntax:

```
/usr/share/doc/vmware-vcli/samples/session/save_session.pl --savesessionfile /tmp/
mycred --server <server name or IP> --username <user> --password <password>
```

Note

Any credentials will be accepted, whether valid or not—all this command does is encode the supplied credentials.

The username and password specified are encrypted and then saved in the specified file (along with the specified server). One advantage of this method is that you can create any number of files, each with its own credentials for any number of servers (one set of credentials per server per file). Specifying the password on a command line is not considered a good practice as the password will be in plain text and reviewing the command history could reveal the password. This is less of an issue if you use PuTTY instead of the console itself.

To use the session file, simply specify a vCLI command and use the `--sessionfile` parameter and omit the `--username`, `--password`, and `--server` parameters that are typically specified. For example, to view the physical NICs on a server, using the file from the previous step, type this command:

```
vicfg-nics --sessionfile /tmp/mycred -l
```

One very important note about session files: they only are valid for thirty minutes after they are last used, so you don't need to worry about the credentials in the file being a security risk (at least for very long).

PowerCLI—Using Get-Credential

Get-Credential is a PowerShell cmdlet, and thus not unique to PowerCLI, but it can be used with PowerCLI. When this is used in a script, you can prompt for a username and password or the script can supply the username and only prompt for the password and the result stored in a variable. The variable is protected so that you can't view the contents and see the username and password, but you can use the variable any time that credentials are needed by simply passing the variable that contains the username and password. For example, to connect to an ESXi server named esx01.testdomain.local, you could use the following code:

```
$Cred=Get-Credential
Connect-ViServer esx01.testdomain.local -Credential $Cred
```

This way, you don't need to know the credentials in advance nor do you need to hardcode them anywhere. At the same time, the credentials can be reused as needed and are stored securely.

TROUBLESHOOTING

While it would be great if we never ran into any issues, that is not practical—we run into them all of the time. Not counting simple problems like misspellings, there are some common areas that are prone to errors in the field of automation; we'll look at things that go wrong in scripts as well as some common issues with the tools themselves.

Common Script Problems

Let's begin with some of the common issues that arise when creating, using, and maintaining scripts.

Authentication

The first area is relatively simple to diagnose—you run the script and you see errors about not being connected to either the vCenter server or ESXi host or you see errors that specifically state bad username or password. This happens when passwords are changed and the credentials are not updated or authentication methods change (such as authenticating through AD instead of to local usernames and passwords) and the script developer is unaware of the changes. Make it a habit before changing the environment to test the impact on scripts in a development environment and never hard code credentials in scripts, environmental variables, files, etc. Not only is this a terrible security practice, but when those credentials change, and they *will* change, the script will break and it may take a lot of investigation to figure out where the credential was stored.

Name Resolution

Never hard code names or IP addresses in scripts, as servers get upgraded (and renamed), new servers added, etc. It is far simpler to prompt for them or explicitly refer to them in a file with a comment at the beginning stating how to update it. Alternatively, place the server names or IPs in variables at the beginning of the script and then use the variables throughout the script. Also, as previously mentioned, never use localhost as it is virtually never what you think it is referring to, especially as scripts get moved to other servers, modified by others, etc. Planning for this at the earliest stages of the script development process will save you a lot of time and effort later. We know that many scripts start out as a quick solution to a problem and were never intended to even become scripts, much less to be used all over the place by many administrators, but a few minutes spent documenting the script will save hours of troubleshooting later—trust us, we know! We often hear, "But I don't have time to document," and we understand, believe us, but if that is the case, you'll have even less time to troubleshoot later when there is a problem.

Version Mismatch

Make sure you place a comment at the beginning of the script stating what version of the tool the script was written for, so if it stops working later, you can refer to the release notes between that version and the one you are trying to use to see what changed. There are even functions for PowerCLI on the Internet (such as this one: http://wannemacher.us/?p=274) that you can add to all of your scripts that will do this check and alert you if the version has changed. To make the function even more useful, simply create a variable that contains the version of PowerCLI used in writing the script, and pass that parameter to the version checker previously mentioned. If script updates are needed, simply update the script and the variable to the new version of PowerCLI and you are back in business.

Hard-coded Variables Are Incorrect

Many scripts are not developed with the thought of them ever becoming scripts; in other words, commands typed interactively are simply copied and pasted into a file that becomes a script with no thought of how the new script will be maintained. A simple way to make sure that you get into trouble is to think this way.

A better way is to think of the variables needed by the commands in the script and then create a variable for each parameter at the top of the script with some documentation (in the format of a comment for each) as to what they are for and what they do. This simple process will take some time and effort at first, but you will soon see that scripts you write often need many of the same variables, so you can copy them from one script to the next. This makes creating a new script much simpler and faster.

Another option is to refer to files that have these variables in them and read the parameters from them. This takes more time and effort, but has the advantage that the same file can be used by multiple scripts if desired, instead of making the same change to multiple scripts.

Common Tool Issues

Many of the common tool issues were addressed previously, but it bears repeating that problems may arise with the use of any automation tool, so a brief troubleshooting section may prove useful.

Incorrect Version of a Tool Compared to ESXi or vCenter

Often, a problem arises when the vSphere environment is upgraded with new versions of ESXi and/or vCenter but the tools have not been upgraded. People often forget the dependencies on these tools when planning for upgrades. As mentioned previously, we suggest that you upgrade the tools at the beginning of any upgrade process, either before or at the same time as vCenter, which should always be the first thing upgraded.

Tool Functionality and/or Parameters Changed

Oftentimes, between versions of a given tool, functionality will be removed or a parameter will be changed (redefined, syntax modified, etc.). These will be noted in the release notes that accompany each version of the tool. Typically VMware will announce that support will be removed for a feature or parameter in a future version and then a version or two later it will actually be removed, giving you time to modify scripts. This is a great reason to review the release notes each time a tool is updated (besides noting new functionality, bugs fixed, etc.).

Tool Connectivity

If everything appears to be okay with your tool configuration, but you can't connect and manage the servers as you expect, check the IP and DNS configuration; often one (or both) are incorrect and need to be updated for proper connectivity. You may also find that your management is done on a different vLAN than your management station is connected to—this is especially true for the vMA, which must be connected to the correct port group (the one containing the management ports of your ESXi servers as well as vCenter) to function correctly.

Another thing you can try to verify connectivity is to use the Managed Object Browser (MOB). The MOB is a web-based interface on all ESXi and vCenter servers that provides access to the objects available for management, including the properties and methods available for each. This is a useful tool, especially for programmers, to understand the object model that VMware uses, and is also a useful tool to prove connectivity to the server—if you can't connect via a web browser as described below, the tools will not be able to either and you will need to diagnose the root cause (often it is network or firewall related or a bad username and password combination).

To use this tool, follow these steps:

1. Open a web browser to the FQDN or IP address of either the vCenter or ESXi server you want to test, followed by /mob. The URL will be in this format: https://<name *or IP*>/mob.

2. Enter a valid username and password for the specified server.

It is possible to disable SSL access to the server, so if the above procedure fails, try to connect with http instead.

vMA Has Authentication Issues When Using an AD Account

There have been some reports and community questions about issues with AD authentication. While we've not experienced them, most of the time people have reported a simple solution: remove vMA from the domain, reboot, delete the computer account in AD, and then rejoin the domain. The directions on how to leave and return to the domain were given in the implementation section for vMA. If this doesn't resolve the issue, you may need to repeat the process removing both the ESXi hosts and vMA and then adding them both back again as just described. It is also possible that with fastpass you added servers before they joined the domain and now credentials are jumbled. To remedy the situation, simply remove the fastpass targets and add them back again.

SUMMARY

We hope that you've caught the vision of the kinds of things that can be done via the command line and some great reasons to do so. We hate doing the same things over and over again, especially things that are simple but very repetitive. We love using scripts for these kinds of tasks.

PowerCLI will be the primary CLI tool for administrators that primarily use Windows, while the vMA will probably be the main tool for those using Linux. For those getting started with PowerCLI, remember to leverage Onyx to help you get started.

Now let's turn our attention to installing ESXi servers and building the infrastructure needed to get started with vSphere. This chapter concludes the introductory section and we'll now turn to the bulk of the infrastructure design and configuration in Part II.

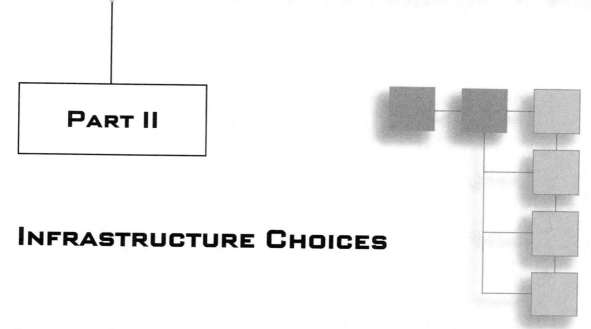

PART II

INFRASTRUCTURE CHOICES

In previous chapters, we discussed the process of planning a new deployment, upgrading from an earlier version of ESX/ESXi and vCenter, and we found that automation was a valid option in the virtualized environment.

In this part, we will detail the differences between vSphere 4.x and vSphere 5, and discuss the details of installing a new ESXi 5 server, the basic configuration of the new ESXi server, basic management tools, permissions, using ESXi logs, and gathering performance metrics using resxtop.

CHAPTER 5

ESXi—YOUR HOST

In this chapter, we will discuss the installation of ESXi, vCenter, vCenter add-on modules, and plan for those installations. In the past several years, virtualization has evolved from a "testing-only environment" into a re-evaluation of current datacenter design, application requirements, and considerations relative to meshing a virtualized deployment with physical networking and storage. If we do not assess the physical environment in a detailed manner, the end result may not perform as desired, or, in a worst-case scenario, may result in unplanned downtime.

PLANNING

One of the key primary considerations is how well you know your environment. For example, do you know at this very moment how much RAM is in use in one of the physical servers in your environment? How much CPU is currently in use? If you do not know the amount of physical resources that each of the applications requires to remain functional, how can you virtualize them? Remember, when you define a VM, you have to define the amount of resources that the VM will have access to. This directly affects the performance that the VM will deliver.

In a best-case scenario, you should perform a pre-virtualization assessment before the virtualization project begins in earnest. There are several tools available that can show you the real resources that the servers and applications will require. You also must remember to perform this assessment during a representative timeframe that will give you a true indication of your server's utilization. For example, an accounting firm typically is at its highest system utilization during the December to May timeframe; it doesn't make sense to assess the physical servers during June or July.

VMware offers the Capacity Planner application as an option to evaluate the physical servers. Capacity Planner is available as a service from an authorized VMware partner, and can be used to accurately evaluate the hardware requirements of physical servers and desktops that may be virtualized as a part of the deployment.

For those deployments that contain only Windows devices, the Microsoft Assessment and Planning Toolkit (MAP) can be used to gain insight into the resource utilization. The MAP toolkit can be downloaded from Microsoft's Technet at http://technet.microsoft.com/en-us/library/bb977556.aspx and installed locally in the network. To maintain the assessment data, MAP requires a SQL database to store the accumulated metrics. The database can be a full instance of SQL Server 2005, 2008, or 2008 R2. If desired, you can also use a SQL Server Express 2008 instance that will be installed by default along with the toolkit.

In either case, this assessment will allow us to plan our physical server hardware much more effectively than if we simply "guessed." In many cases, hardware is either sadly under-deployed, or money is spent on hardware that may never be fully utilized. These requirements can be termed "the 5 food groups" of virtualization. The first four of these food groups are CPU, RAM, disk, and network. The fifth food group, office politics, is no less important than the hardware requirements.

Office politics can improve the deployment of a virtualized environment, or it can lead to seemingly endless bottlenecks centered around who owns an environment, who will manage the environment, and who pays for it. It is vitally important to involve key players in the decision-making and planning processes, and to keep them constantly updated as to the progress of the deployment.

VMware Auto Deploy

Auto Deploy is a new provisioning option available in vSphere 5. Auto Deploy is used in conjunction with vCenter to allow an administrator to simultaneously deploy large numbers of ESXi hosts with a minimum of effort. The Auto Deploy installation files are found on the vCenter distribution media.

As a physical server is powered on, vCenter consults Auto Deploy to determine if the host has been "designated" for deployment. If so, Auto Deploy leverages PXE boot to provide the imaging for the server; then a Host Profile can be used to configure more specific parameters automatically. This means that a generic installation profile can be created, and then location or host-specific configurations can be applied later.

The installable software that will be deployed on the server is defined using the Image Builder PowerCLI utility and is stored in the Image Profile. The actual configuration, such as firewall settings or network port definitions, is stored in an associated Host Profile.

Even though the Auto Deploy installation maintains much of the configuration state in secure locations, the actual dynamic state content is still stored in local DRAM and is subject to loss in the event of a power event.

If any current virtual machines are stored on a physical host that is designated for deployment with Auto Deploy, any information relative to those virtual machines must be maintained. If the host is member of an HA cluster, Auto Deploy will store this information. If the host is not in an HA cluster, vCenter is required to "fill in the blanks."

Finally, if any information is required that would normally be provided by a user, this information is saved in the form of an answer file.

Initially, the Auto Deploy package must be installed on the vCenter server. This vCenter server instance will manage the Auto Deploy feature for all hosts in its own inventory. Auto Deploy can also be installed on a separate Microsoft Windows–based server or virtual machine, and Auto Deploy will need to be registered with a vCenter instance to deploy successfully.

Please note that the new vCenter appliance can also be used as a valid platform for Auto Deploy. In this scenario, the appliance is added to an existing ESXi 5 host, and it contains the Auto Deploy components, a DHCP server, and a built-in TFTP server to provide access to the image files.

Licensing Considerations

As the hosts are deployed through Auto Deploy, you have the option to assign license keys to each host as it is deployed. This means that the host is completely configured between the installation files, the Host Profile, and the licensing as it completes the deployment. This licensing process is performed using PowerCLI. You always have the option to manually configure the licensing as the host is added to vCenter.

How ESXi 5 Differs from Previous Versions

Okay, we have taken a look at the process of planning for a new vSphere 5 host, but are there any changes to the environment that I have been used to? Yes, there are. To start, there is no ESX platform in the new release of vSphere 5; all vSphere 5 servers are going to be ESXi. This means a fundamental change to standard processes if you have been using the local Service Console for management tasks or to run scripts.

But, what else is different?

ESX Server and the Service Console

With the release of vSphere 5, there are significant changes to the ESX environment. To start with, there is no upgraded version of ESX. The management tasks that were performed locally in the Service Console are now modified and will be executed solely through the vMA (vSphere Management Assistant) or the vCLI (vSphere Command Line Interface). ESXi will continue to utilize the Management network, a VMkernel port for access through the vSphere Client, and vCenter, just as in previous releases.

Changes to the Installation Process

There are several modifications to the ESXi install process. There is now a unified installer that supports both new installations and upgrades from previous versions. The new vSphere Auto Deploy utility allows an image to be stored locally in RAM on the Auto Deploy server, and the same image can now be deployed across multiple servers.

The capability to perform upgrades and migration using the command line has been deprecated as well; support has not been maintained for vihostupdate and esxupdate tools in vSphere 5. However, once the vSphere 5 installation or upgrade has been completed successfully, patching can still be performed using the vCLI (vSphere Command Line Interface).

Virtualization of Apple Servers

Also available is the capability to virtualize Apple Mac OS X servers. This allows Apple virtual machines to co-exist on the same physical host as virtual machines based on other operating systems.

When a virtual machine is created, either EFI (Extensible Firmware Interface) or BIOS firmware is available, and this choice is based on the operating system selected. Both EFI and BIOS firmware provide basic I/O functions required by the VM before the OS is installed. Once the OS is loaded, control is passed to the drivers within the OS.

vSphere 5 now fully supports the virtualization of Apple's Mac OS X operating system. The key point here is that Mac OS X only supports EFI and is not compatible with a BIOS.

If you decide to deploy a virtual machine with an Apple Mac OS X, please remember that if, after the VM is deployed, the EFI firmware configuration is modified to the BIOS setting, the VM will not boot until the original configuration is restored.

To deploy Mac OS X, when presented with the option to select an operating system for the VM, select Other (32-bit) or Other (64-bit), and deploy the VM as required.

Hardware Specifications

The hardware supported by VMware is constantly expanding and changing with the release of new hardware from various vendors. To obtain the most updated list of supported hardware, visit the VMware Compatibility Guide on the Internet, at: http://www.vmware.com/resources/compatibility/search.php.

As shown in Figure 5.1, VMware provides a web-based compatibility guide that can be accessed to determine if the anticipated hardware has been tested and verified by VMware. This does not mean that the virtualization software will only install on certified hardware; this just means that more reliable results can be obtained by using listed hardware.

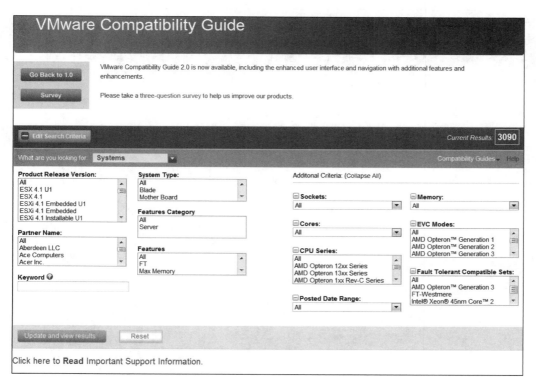

Figure 5.1
The VMware Compatibility Guide.

If desired, the VMware Compatibility Guide can be searched to verify a particular system board or hardware adapter for use with vSphere 5. As shown in Figure 5.2, the search component will allow keywords to be entered, and the results will be displayed at the bottom of the screen. Note that this guide is updated regularly, and it is the best place to confirm hardware compatibility before deployment.

The destination device that is selected can be any of the following: a blank internal or external SCSI disk or one that can be erased, an iSCSI or FC SAN-based LUN, an internal SAS or SATA disk, or a USB key.

If the destination disk for the installation is a SATA device, the installer considers these devices to be remote. The installer will continue with the install, but will not create a scratch partition on these disks.

The scratch partition itself is used by the ESXi hypervisor to contain core dumps and log files, and is a static size of 4GB. In a typical install, the installer will attempt to create this 4GB partition on an internal device; if this is not possible, it will be placed

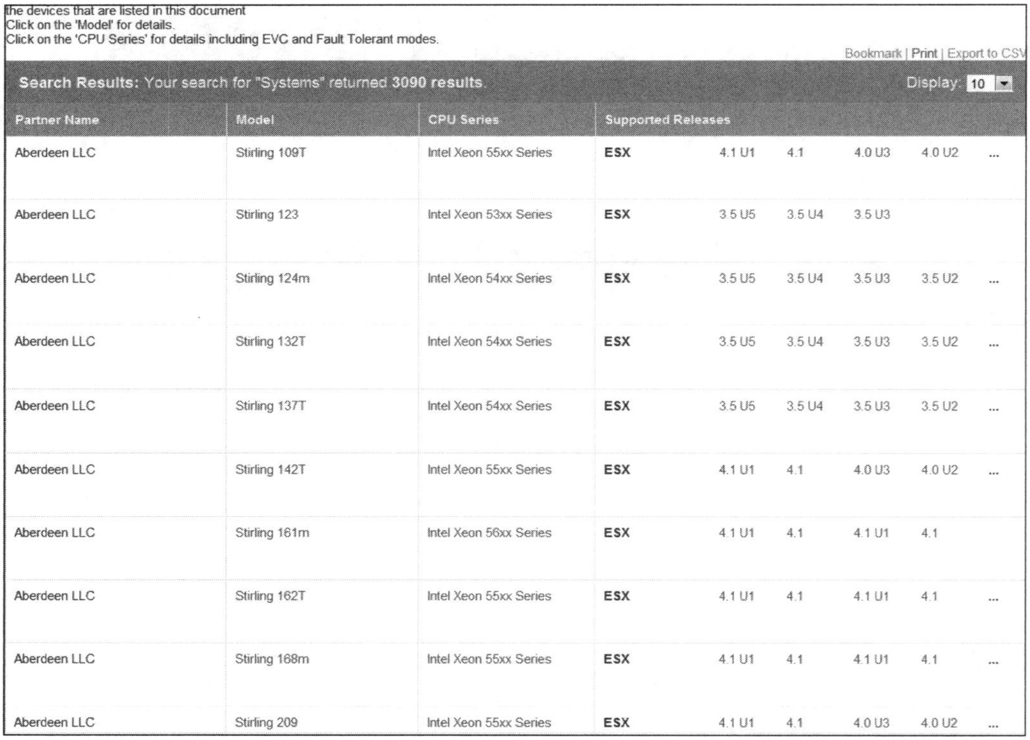

the devices that are listed in this document
Click on the 'Model' for details.
Click on the 'CPU Series' for details including EVC and Fault Tolerant modes.

Bookmark | Print | Export to CSV

Search Results: Your search for "Systems" returned 3090 results.				Display: 10 ▾			
Partner Name	**Model**	**CPU Series**	**Supported Releases**				
Aberdeen LLC	Stirling 109T	Intel Xeon 55xx Series	ESX	4.1 U1	4.1	4.0 U3	4.0 U2 …
Aberdeen LLC	Stirling 123	Intel Xeon 53xx Series	ESX	3.5 U5	3.5 U4	3.5 U3	
Aberdeen LLC	Stirling 124m	Intel Xeon 54xx Series	ESX	3.5 U5	3.5 U4	3.5 U3	3.5 U2 …
Aberdeen LLC	Stirling 132T	Intel Xeon 54xx Series	ESX	3.5 U5	3.5 U4	3.5 U3	3.5 U2 …
Aberdeen LLC	Stirling 137T	Intel Xeon 54xx Series	ESX	3.5 U5	3.5 U4	3.5 U3	3.5 U2 …
Aberdeen LLC	Stirling 142T	Intel Xeon 55xx Series	ESX	4.1 U1	4.1	4.0 U3	4.0 U2 …
Aberdeen LLC	Stirling 161m	Intel Xeon 56xx Series	ESX	4.1 U1	4.1	4.1 U1	4.1
Aberdeen LLC	Stirling 162T	Intel Xeon 55xx Series	ESX	4.1 U1	4.1	4.1 U1	4.1 …
Aberdeen LLC	Stirling 168m	Intel Xeon 55xx Series	ESX	4.1 U1	4.1	4.1 U1	4.1 …
Aberdeen LLC	Stirling 209	Intel Xeon 55xx Series	ESX	4.1 U1	4.1	4.0 U3	4.0 U2 …

Figure 5.2
The VMware Compatibility Guide search results.

within the ESXi RAM space. To manually configure the location for the scratch partition:

1. The administrator should highlight the ESXi server from within the vSphere Client.

2. Select the Configuration tab, and then click on the Advanced Options tab below the Software Options pane.

3. Select ScratchConfig and enter the desired storage location in the ScratchConfig.ConfiguredScratchLocation field.

Support for the UEFI concept is introduced with ESXi 5. UEFI (Unified Extensible Firmware Interface) provides the flexibility to boot a system from a variety of sources, such as fixed disks, CD/DVD drives, or USB keys.

UEFI is a specification that defines a method to isolate an operating system from the underlying physical hardware. This means that control can be passed to a PXE-boot process after the POST sequence has completed, and before the operating system starts. This is the reason that UEFI is categorized as "hardware independent."

The vSphere 5 version of ESXi continues to provide support for guest VMs that have 64-bit operating systems. If the ESXi server is an AMD-based host, a minimum of an E Revision CPU is required, and if the host is Intel based, the VT feature must be enabled in the system BIOS.

Deployment Considerations

When planning the deployment, the first consideration is that the hardware and software requirements are met. It is recommended that the VMware Compatibility Guide be consulted to verify that the planned hardware has been verified and tested for compliance with vSphere.

If the desired hardware does not appear in the guide, this does not mean that the hardware cannot be used; it simply means that the best results will be achieved if the hardware has been tested and verified by your hardware vendor to establish compatibility with vSphere 5.

The pre-virtualization assessment will indicate the amount of hardware resources that will be required to support the planned number of virtual machines; planning is a key factor in the success of the project.

At this point, it must also be remembered that the ESX platform does not exist in vSphere 5, and that any scripts can be edited and reused through the vMA or adapter to work under the PowerShell environment.

Embedded versus Installable ESXi

There are two versions of vSphere 5 ESXi: An embedded installation in which the hypervisor is installed without the use of internal disk storage; and the installable version, which is installed to local disks. Let's take a look at each of these versions and examine their characteristics.

ESXi Embedded

There are two versions of the ESXi operating system, an embedded installation and a storage-based installation. The embedded version is pre-installed using a USB key prior to delivery by the server vendor. As a result, the USB must be first in the boot order for that server. Depending on how the operating system is purchased, this installation can be fully licensed, or can be booted into evaluation mode and a license will need to be installed later.

When ESXi embedded version is installed, the installer first checks the current disk structure, looking for pre-existing data. If a vendor-installed diagnostic partition exists, it will be preserved through the installation, and the operating system files will immediately follow it. First, the installer process will create a 110MB partition, called the vmkcore partition to store core dump information. This is consistent with previous versions. A single 4GB VFAT scratch partition will be created on the boot disk along the vmkcore partition if an existing scratch partition is not found in the local system. At this point, if the installer discovers any blank disks within the system, they are formatted as a VMFS5 partition, creating one large partition per disk.

ESXi Installable

If a new installation is desired, vSphere 5 now utilizes the GPT format, replacing the legacy MS-DOS format that has been the standard until now. The change in the disk support affords increases in reliability and scalability for the operating system.

The installer will evaluate the provided storage and determine whether any vendor-defined diagnostic partitions exist on the disks. If so, the process will preserve these partitions, and move to the next available cluster to begin the installation. If no diagnostic partitions exist, the installation will begin at the first sector of the disk.

Rather than dynamically allocating and preparing the partition table during installation, the installer simply copies the new partition table from the binary image to the local disk. Similar to the embedded installation, the installer automatically creates a 100MB vmkcore partition that is used as a storage location for core dump content. After the host has initially rebooted, the ESXi installer also allocates two additional partitions: a 4GB scratch partition (if one is not already defined) and a VMFS partition on the first disk. On any remaining physical disks, the installer will create a VMFS5 partition and utilize the entire physical disk space.

IMPLEMENTATION AND MANAGEMENT

In the physical world, there are administrators that must remotely access the physical servers in order to fulfill their job role. This access can be in the form of a utility such as the Microsoft Remote Desktop Client (also known as the RDP client), VNC, Dameware, or similar access console.

When you design a virtual infrastructure, you must decide what level of access you are going to grant to these co-workers. Which users want GUI-based management, and which will opt for a CLI-based alternative?

If the choice is a GUI-based access, will you want to deploy a vSphere Client to every desktop, and allow the permissions within vCenter to grant required access, or would the use of the Web Server Client, which provides access to subsets of the vCenter functionality through the use of a web browser, be sufficient for your needs? In most situations, almost all users have some flavor of Internet browser on their device. Opera, Firefox, or maybe IE are all viable candidates.

There are those who are devoted to the command line, and for those administrators, vSphere offers the PowerCLI utility. PowerCLI contains over 230 cmdlets that are defined for use with VMware and virtual machine management. This particular option allows frequently used processes and tasks that are repeated but tedious to be executed through the use of a script. Scripts are extremely handy in that they can be scheduled and run on a specific time frame, removing the requirement that an Administrator manually initiate an operation.

In this same vein, there will be administrators who have executed Perl or Linux-based scripts on ESX hosts in the past. The ESX platform has been deprecated in vSphere 5, but those process and scripts can be updated and modified to execute within the vSphere Management Assistant (vMA). The vMA was released along with vSphere 4.0, and provides a command line alternative for those who want to continue to use scripts or command line syntax to manage their environment.

Now that we have examined the planning of a new environment and the hardware requirements, let's take a look at the methods of installation that are available to deploy the ESXi hosts.

Manual Installation (HDD, SAN, Net, USB)

A manual installation of the ESXi operating system is the default method for small deployments. It is very easy to burn multiple CDs or DVDs and install the servers in a parallel fashion. It is recommended that the administrator document each characteristic of the management network such as the MAC addresses and the bus location of the physical network adapter in use by the management network. These will be very handy if the ESXi OS needs to be reinstalled at a later date, and you do not want to trace existing cabling to determine the correct NIC.

Manual installation also gives administrators who are new to virtualization a "feel" for what is happening during the installation and the parameters that are required during the installation process.

However, in a larger deployment, there may be a requirement to deploy large numbers of servers that make manual deployments an inefficient process. VMware provides two methods to deploy multiple servers: scripting and Auto Deploy.

Scripted Install

Using a scripted install to upgrade an ESX/ESXi host produces a verifiable, reproducible process that can be used to upgrade multiple servers simultaneously. This script will provide all of the information that a user would provide as part of the upgrade process. After the installer is invoked, the installer will look to the script to "fill in all the blanks," and configure the server as defined. The script can be stored locally, in the form of a CD/DVD drive or USB key, or it can also be accessed remotely through HTTP, HTTPS, or NFS.

Scripting an upgrade allows an administrator to create a common script that deploys a standard configuration, and then use a concept called Host Profiles to customize the default installation for a particular environment, or to meet a specific set of standards.

There are several available methods that can be used to implement a scripted upgrade.

- You can define a script for each individual server, with a static IP address, subnet mask, default gateway, FQDN, and network and storage configuration. These scripts can then be archived to facilitate recovery of an individual host.

- You can define a single script that utilizes DHCP to provide a unique IP configuration to each host.

Regardless of the deployment method, you can log on to each ESXi server and make any necessary modifications.

Creating a Script

As part of the standard configuration, there are two sample scripts on the distribution media to give administrators a template to use while creating their scripts. As a part of a fresh installation, the installer will create a sample script named ks.cfg that mirrors the values entered in the Install wizard, and saves it in the /root/folder as a blueprint for future scripts.

Each script will begin with a command section that details the desired configuration parameters for the installation.

The ESXi installer can utilize a standard ks.cfg script that is stored in the /etc/vmware/weasel/ folder; by the way, "weasel" is the name of the installer. This default script can be invoked by selecting the Tab key at the initial installer screen.

The available Boot Options for use with scripted installations are listed below:

- **ks-file.** Specifies the script to be used by the location "file"
- **ks-protocol://sharename.** Specifies a script to be used at the location "protocol://sharename"
- **ks-usb.** Specifies a location that will be searched for a script named ks.cfg
- **ks-usb://location.** Specifies the script to be used found at the location "location"
- **ksdevice-device.** Specifies a network adapter that will be used to locate the installation script
- **nameserver-ip address.** Specifies the DNS server that will be used to access the kickstart script and installation files
- **netdevice-device.** Specifies a network adapter that will be used to locate the installation script
- **netmask-subnet mask.** Defines the subnet mask that will be used by the NIC to access the kickstart script and installation files
- **vlanid-VLAN.** Specifies the defined VLAN on the network adapter

The following commands are deprecated in vSphere 5.

- `auth` or `authconfig`
- `serialnum` or `vmserialnum`
- `bootloader`
- `timezone`
- `esxlocation`

- `virtualdisk`
- `Firewall`
- `zerombr`
- `firewallport`
- `%packages`

Table 5.1 lists the applicable commands for the script.

To use the freshly created script, boot the physical host, and insert the ESXi installation media. When the boot has begun, specify the installation script to be used to configure the host.

Table 5.1   Applicable Commands for the Script

Command	Comments
`accepteula`	Accepts the ESXi licensing agreement
`clearpart`	Will delete any existing partitions on the destination disk
`dryrun`	Verifies that the script contains all the required information
`install`	Indicates that this will be a new installation and defines the location for the installation.
`keyboard`	Defines the keyboard layout for the installation
`network`	Provides static IP addressing information, hostname, and VLAN values
`paranoid`	Displays a warning that will stop the installation if an error occurs
`part` **or** `partition`	Defines a single additional VMFS datatstore
`reboot`	Causes the server to reboot when the installation has completed
`rootpw`	Defines the root password for the server
`upgrade`	Specifies that this is an upgrade from a previous version
`%include` **or** `include`	Defines additional scripts to run as part of the installation
`%pre`	Defines a script to execute prior to the kickstart script
`%post`	Defines a script to execute after the kickstart script
`%firstboot`	Defines a script to execute only during the first boot of the server

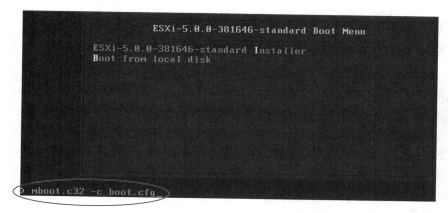

Figure 5.3
Specifying the script to use.

When the host boots from the installation media, it provides the opportunity to specify the script to use as shown in Figure 5.3. This is useful in an environment where each physical ESXi host will have its own script that will define the desired configuration for that host.

To specify the script to be used to configure a new ESXi host:

1. Boot from the ESXi installation CD or DVD

2. Once the installer has loaded and is ready to proceed, press the Tab key.

3. Enter the file name of the desired configuration script.

VMware Auto Deploy

As mentioned earlier, vSphere 5 provides a new deployment and provisioning option: Auto Deploy. Auto Deploy allows you to standardize the deployment of new ESXi servers, and to leverage PXE to deploy ESXi servers without internal storage, which can greatly reduce the initial deployment costs. We can also use the PowerCLI environment to create ESXi installation images using ISO images, extensions, additional drivers, and packages to create a complete installation image. The use of Auto Deploy requires Enterprise Plus licensing to implement.

Installing Auto Deploy

To install the Auto Deploy components:

1. Using the vCenter distribution media, click on the Auto Deploy link and select Install.

2. Provide the administrator credentials.

3. Define the location for the Auto Deploy repository size and location.

Once the installation is complete, open vCenter, and open Auto Deploy from the Home—Administration—Auto Deploy link. When the Auto Deploy window opens, you should be able to view the BIOS DHCP File Name and the EFI File Name. These are used to deploy the ESXi image to physical servers that use the BIOS and EFI hardware sets. Note that the gPXE source is listed, as is the Cache size and the amount of Cache currently allocated to current deployments. Also, the links in the bottom pane provide a method to download the TFTP Boot components, and locate them in the same location as the TFTP server.

Notice in Figure 5.4 that as part of the installation, the administrator is required to specify the default location for the installation and the default location where the Image Profiles and associated files will be stored, and also provide a maximum size for this repository.

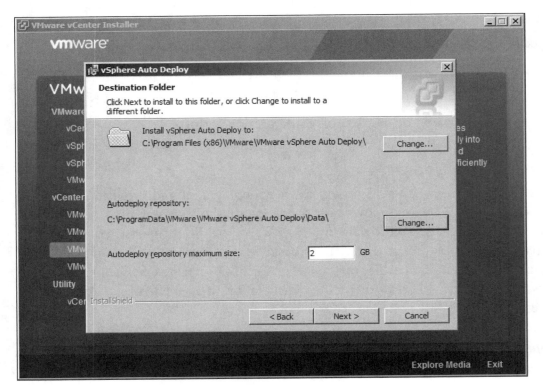

Figure 5.4
Defining the location of the image profiles and image files.

In Figure 5.5, notice the links in the bottom pane provide the link to download the TFTP Boot components, extract them, and locate them in the root directory on the TFTP server. Also, a link is provided to download the log files associated with Auto Deploy processes.

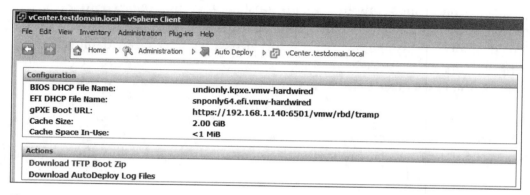

Figure 5.5
Downloading the supporting files.

Auto Deploy Components

Now that we have installed the Auto Deploy components, we must create the images that we want to deploy to our new servers. These images will be a compilation of an ESXi ISO image, plus any additional agents or packages that we want to include, and we can install them in one process. Let's see how this happens.

Image Builder The Auto Deploy environment is created when the vSphere Power-CLI package is downloaded and installed on a local Windows server. As the package is installed, the PowerCLI cmdlets are extracted and the Image Builder server is installed and started.

Software Considerations As a prerequisite, the VMware PowerCLI application must be installed on a computer that is running a version of Microsoft Windows

Server 2003 SP2, XP SP2, Windows Vista, Windows Server 2008, or Windows 7, along with .NET 2.0 and PowerShell 1.0 or 2.0, both of which are free downloads from the Microsoft Technet website.

Image Profiles   An administrator utilizes the Image Builder PowerCLI to define an Image Profile to describe the software that an ESXi host will receive during the imaging process. This Image Profile will consist of ESXi installation parameters and additional packages that will be applied to the host (sometimes referred to as VIB—VMware Installation Bundle). Do not confuse Image Profiles with Host Profiles: Image Profiles apply only to ESXi 5 hosts or hosts that have been deployed using Auto Deploy. Host Profiles apply to hosts managed with a version of vCenter and are used to maintain a consistent configuration.

Requirements for Using Image Profiles   Profiles can be cloned from an existing profile, defined using a custom set of parameters, or modified to add or move VIBs from the profile. Regardless of the method to create the Image Profile, the following requirements exist for all profiles:

- All Image Profiles must have different names and an acceptance level. If the Image Builder PowerCLI is used to modify an Image Profile to add a VIB, Image Builder will verify the package with the associated acceptance level for that package.
- If a VIB is to be removed from a Profile, there must be no dependencies on that VIB within the package.
- Each Image Profile can contain only one occurrence of a specific VIB.

Validation of Image Profiles   Each Image Profile must meet several levels of validation to be usable:

- At a minimum, each Image Profile defined must contain one base VIB and one kernel module that can be used to boot the installation process.
- If there are dependencies between VIBs within a Profile, both VIBs must be present in the image. Dependencies between VIBs are defined within the package's `Depends` property.
- There can be no conflicts between VIBs within the image; these are defined in the package's `Conflicts` property.
- There can be only one version of a VIB within a package. If a new version of a VIB is added to a package, it will replace the older version.

- The Image Builder will evaluate the package after initial creation and after any modifications to verify that no acceptance issues exist.

Acceptance Level Validation   Image Builder performs acceptance level validation each time an Image Profile is created or changed. Image Builder checks the acceptance level of VIBs in the Image Profile against the minimum allowed acceptance level of the profile. The acceptance level of the VIB is also validated each time the signature of a VIB is validated.

You can create a custom Image Profile from scratch or clone an existing profile and add or remove VIBs. A profile must meet the following requirements to be valid:

- Each Image Profile must have a unique name and vendor combination.
- Each Image Profile has an acceptance level. When you add a VIB to an Image Profile with an Image Builder PowerCLI cmdlet, Image Builder checks that the VIB matches the acceptance level defined for the profile.
- You cannot remove VIBs that are required by other VIBs.
- You cannot include two versions of the same VIB in an Image Profile. When you add a new version of a VIB, the new version replaces the existing version of the VIB.

Image Profile Validation   An Image Profile and its VIBs must meet several criteria to be valid.

- Image Profiles must contain at least one base VIB and one bootable kernel module.
- If any VIB in the Image Profile depends on another VIB, that other VIB must also be included in the Image Profile. VIB creators store that information in the SoftwarePackage object's Depends property.
- VIBs must not conflict with each other. VIB creators store that information in the SoftwarePackage object's Conflicts property.
- Two VIBs with the same name, but two different versions, cannot co-exist. When you add a new version of a VIB, the new version replaces the existing version of the VIB.
- No acceptance level validation issues exist.

When you make a change to an Image Profile, Image Builder checks that the change does not invalidate the profile. VMware supports the following acceptance levels:

- **Community Supported.** The Community Supported acceptance level is defined for those VIBs created by groups or individuals who are not part of the VMware partner program.

- **Partner Supported.** The Partner Supported level is defined for any VIBs created by VMware partners, and the partner is responsible for all testing of the VIB.

- **VMware Accepted.** The VMware Accepted level is defined for any VIBs that are created by VMware Partners, and go through testing by VMware. However, all aspects of the software may not be fully tested.

- **VMware Certified.** The VMware Certified acceptance level is defined for those VIBs that are created by VMware partners and these VIBs are subjected to internal levels of testing.

- **Dependency Validation.** When you add or remove a VIB, Image Builder checks that package dependencies are met. Each Software Package object includes a `Depends` property that specifies a list of other VIBs that VIB depends on.

- **Validating an Exported Image.** An option available when using Image Profiles is that of exporting the profile to an ISO. This makes the profile portable in that it can be moved to another location and used there to deploy a new ESXi server, or it can simply be archived locally. When the image is exported, the Image Builder verifies that there are no conflicts by evaluating the `Conflicts` property for the image. The Image Builder validates the package's signature to help reduce the possibility of the package being modified by an unauthorized individual. Finally, the Image Builder will verify if the package is specified as either VMware Certified or VMware Accepted, and that the VIBs contained in the package are in complete compliance with those rules.

Deploying an ESXi Host Using Auto Deploy

The deployment environment must be verified prior to deploying hosts. As part of the deployment, you will be using a PXE boot server of some sort. Connectivity must be tested to verify that each ESXi host can contact the PXE server, and that vCenter can manage each host. Note: care must be taken here to ensure that any VLAN ID assigned to the PXE server must not carry production traffic as well; this can result in delays in the installation process, and also may produce unexpected results. From the Auto Deploy perspective, the DHCP and TFTP servers must be configured and ready to respond to client inquiries. You will need to install the VMware PowerCLI in order to be able to manage the deployment rules and rule sets as needed.

While the new system is being deployed, vCenter places the image for the installation into the host RAM space rather than using a physical disk. As a part of the installation, the licensing information can be provided, or the host can be installed in evaluation mode and the license can be applied at a later date. If desired, the VMware PowerCLI can be utilized to configure Bulk Licensing, licensing each host as it is configured.

The deployment of ESXi hosts is very similar to deploying other operating systems using a PXE device; by default, ESXi hosts are deployed using SSL.

Only hosts that use UEFI firmware are supported for deployment using Auto Deploy.

You will need to define a Host Profile if one does not exist, so that the ability to archive system logs and core dumps from each ESXi host to a Syslog server is configured. We will discuss Host Profiles in more detail in Chapter 13.

Understanding Auto Deploy Boot Operations   When a physical host set up for Auto Deploy is turned on, Auto Deploy uses a PXE boot infrastructure in conjunction with vSphere Host Profiles to provision and customize that host. No state is stored on the host itself; instead, the Auto Deploy server manages state information for each host.

State Information for ESXi Hosts   Auto Deploy stores the information for the ESXi hosts to be provisioned in different locations. Information about the location of Image Profiles and Host Profiles is initially specified in the rules that map machines to Image Profiles and Host Profiles. When a host boots for the first time, the vCenter server system creates a corresponding host object and stores the information in the vCenter database.

Configuring Auto Deploy   As stated earlier, you will need to configure a DHCP server to provide IP addresses to the new servers so they can reach the PXE server, and you will also need to deploy a TFTP server. Microsoft has stopped the availability of a built-in TFTP server with its Windows Server 2008 release due to security concerns. There are several third-party TFTP server packages readily available from the Internet. Keep in mind that this TFTP server can be installed on a physical server or on a VM within the environment.

You will also need to configure the DHCP scope to provide the networking connection information for your PXE server and your TFTP as part of the DHCP process. To do this, edit the scope and add the parameters shown in Figure 5.6.

- Option 66 should be enabled and configured with the IP address of your TFTP server.

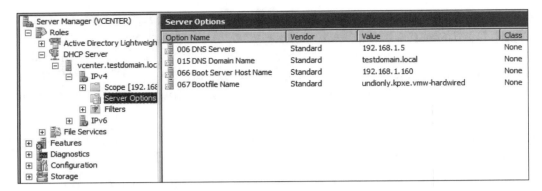

Figure 5.6
DHCP scope options.

■ Option 67 should also be enabled and should contain the value "undionly.kpxe. vmw-hardwired"; this value is found from the Auto Deploy main screen.

Now that we have the supporting cast in place, we can begin to work with the VMware images. This will require the use of PowerCLI to manage our deployment.

The "depot image" must be downloaded from the VMware site and uploaded to the TFTP server. After the VMware image has downloaded successfully, use the following PowerCLI command to add the software depot that will be used to deploy the image files:

```
"Add-ESXSoftwareDepot c:\<folder name>\ESX_Image_file.zip"
```

As shown in Figure 5.7, using the `Get-EsxImageProfile` command will verify that the deployment packages are intact, and will display all images that have been added to the depot.

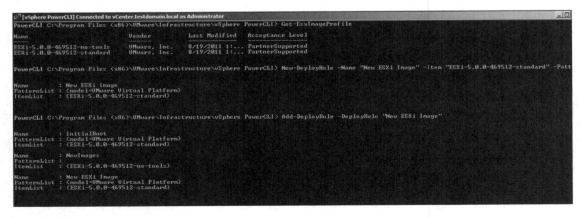

Figure 5.7
Verifying the available ESXi images.

Use the command `-New-DeployRule -Name <your Deploy Rule name> -Item ESXi-5.0.0-469512-standard -Pattern ipv4=192.168.1.100-192.168.1.200` to create a new rule with the name "your Deploy Rule name" for any hosts in the IP range 192.168.1.100 through 192.168.1.200.

You will activate the new Image Profile with `Add-DeployRule <your Deploy Rule name>`.

At this point, you should be able to power on your new hosts, and they will begin to install the new ESXi image.

The First Initialization of an ESXi Host

The first time that a host is provisioned through Auto Deploy, the image package is created using Image Builder, and the profile is assigned to the host. At this point, it is also possible to assign a location in the vCenter inventory to the host.

When the host is booted, verify that the host is configured to perform a PXE boot. This is generally done using the vendor BIOS. If modifications were made to the BIOS boot configuration, reboot the host and it should obtain a DHCP address. Then download the gPXE environment from the configuration location.

The Auto Deploy server will deploy the server according to the rules that have been defined.

If the rule set specifies a Host Profile to be associated with the host, Auto Deploy will apply the Host Profile to complete the installation. If configured in the rule set, Auto Deploy will add the new host to the vCenter server defined in the rule set. At this point, the specified Host Profile is applied.

If a rule exists that mandates input from a user, such as networking parameters, they will be entered at this point. If no input is received, the host will be placed in Maintenance Mode. The host can be brought out of maintenance by applying the Host Profile again, and entering the required information.

Now that the host has been added to the vCenter inventory, vCenter will maintain the parameters for that host in the vCenter database. If necessary, the host can be re-provisioned using the same specifications and profiles.

If it's desired or required to redeploy the server, configure the server to boot from a PXE server. Reboot the server, and if necessary, use the Auto Deploy cmdlets that are included with the VMware PowerCLI package to add, remove, or modify the rules that govern the deployment process. Note that you can also specify a different Host Profile to be applied as part of the installation.

As in the case of the initial install, the host will reboot and the Host Profile will be applied.

DCUI

The DCUI (Direct Console User Interface) is the default management interface provided with ESXi. The DCUI functions as both a management interface and informational interface.

By default, the "root" user has administrative access to the DCUI through the DCUI User role. As a best practice, care should be taken to ensure that this role and its permissions are not edited in any way. Modification of this role could result in no access to the DCUI interface.

To enter the DCUI, you must have network connectivity to the ESXi host.

1. To enter the DCUI, press F2 from the main ESXi screen.

2. Enter the appropriate root-level credentials. The credentials are verified, and the main DCUI interface is presented.

As displayed in Figure 5.8, this option allows you to configure the root password and Lockdown Mode.

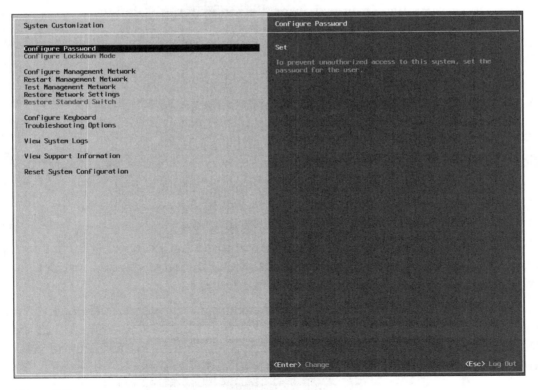

Figure 5.8
Configuring the root password and Lockdown Mode.

Configure Password

This option allows an administrator to change the existing password. Note that when a valid password exists, the term "Set" is displayed in the right column. This is an indicator that a valid password has been defined. If this field is empty when Configure Password is highlighted, this means that no valid password has been defined, and this server is considered an "Open Server."

To change or add a password:

1. Click on Configure Password.

2. Enter the desired password. Note at this point that if a password is already configured, you will be prompted to enter the current password.

Configure Lockdown Mode

This option allows an administrator to reduce the local access to the server console when the server is being managed by a vCenter instance.

When an ESXi host has been added to a vCenter instance, the option exists to configure Lockdown Mode for that host. Lockdown means that all users other than the vpxuser account are denied authentication to the host and are denied permissions to access the ESXi host. The vpxuser account is created by the vCenter agent as the host is added to the vCenter inventory and is the access account for vCenter.

This means that all management of that host is now designed to occur within vCenter. At this point, scripts cannot be executed against the ESXi host; this includes scripts originating from the vSphere CLI, the vMA, or through PowerShell. Once the host is placed in Lockdown Mode you may find that third-party management tools might be unable to gather information from that host as well.

During Lockdown Mode, the root user can still log in to and access the DCUI. The underlying services will continue to run normally, but the individuals who are granted access to those services will be curtailed. These services include SSH, the DCUI, and TSM (local Tech Support Mode).

Lockdown Mode can be configured through the DCUI, when the host is added to vCenter, or by using the vSphere Client.

Note

A directly connected vSphere Client is capable of managing a single ESXi server, while a vSphere Client that is connected to a vCenter instance can manage up to 1,000 ESXi servers from a single management window.

If Lockdown Mode is configured through the DCUI, existing permissions that exist for users and groups are dropped. If it is desired to retain these permissions, you must configure Lockdown Mode through the vSphere Client and the vCenter instance.

To configure Lockdown Mode for this ESXi host:

1. Click on Configure Lockdown Mode.

2. Select the desired mode.

If desired, the administrator can also log on locally to TSM (Technical Support Mode) by using the ALT+F1 key sequence. Once the command shell has opened, enter the following command to verify the status of Lockdown Mode:

```
vim-cmd -U dcui vimsvc/auth/lockdown_is_enabled.
```

This will return a "true" if Lockdown Mode is enabled, or a "false" if disabled.

If you want to enable Lockdown Mode from the command line, use the following command:

```
vim-cmd -U dcui vimsvc/auth/lockdown_mode_enter.
```

If, however, you want to disable Lockdown Mode, use the following command:

```
vim-cmd -U dcui vimsvc/auth/lockdown_mode_exit.
```

Note that when enabling or disabling Lockdown Mode from the command line, vim-cmd will not return a message if the operation was successful.

Configuring the Management Network

This option provides the interface to configure or modify the management network settings. Selecting this option will display the current IPv4 configuration of the interface.

In Figure 5.9, the MAC address of the physical NIC being used by the Management Network can be viewed. In most cases, it is a good idea to document this, as at some future point, it may be necessary to reinstall the ESXi operating system. It is much easier to know the MAC address and select it during the installation, as opposed to choosing the incorrect interface and facing the prospect of troubleshooting the installation.

To view the MAC address of the Management Network interface:

1. Select the Configure Management Network option.

2. The MAC address will be displayed in the right pane.

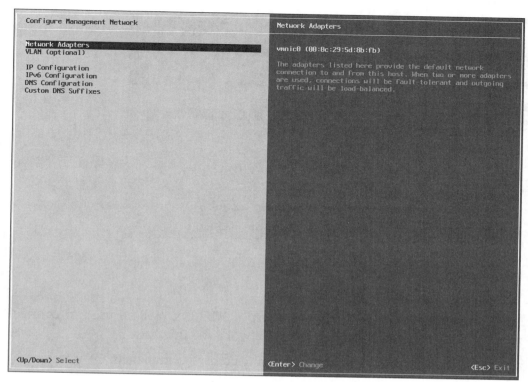

Figure 5.9
Viewing the MAC address of the Management Network adapter.

As shown in Figure 5.10, a VLAN in the range of 1 to 4095 can be assigned for management traffic to the ESXi host, if desired. This will isolate management traffic to only those hosts who are also assigned to the same VLAN number.

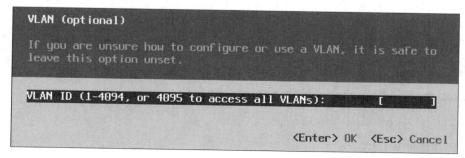

Figure 5.10
Assigning a VLAN.

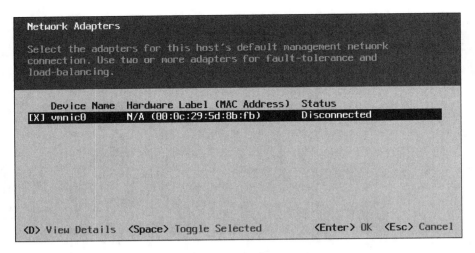

Figure 5.11
Selecting the Management Network adapter.

Figure 5.11 shows the option to select the physical NIC that will be used to connect to the physical network as the Management Network for this host.

To change the physical network adapter that is used as the management interface:

1. Select the Configure Management Network option.

2. Select the Network Adapters link. Note the current NIC, its MAC address, and its connectivity status.

3. Use the space bar to deselect the current NIC and to select the desired network interface.

The VLAN option allows a VLAN to be configured as a means to separate traffic, and it should reflect the current VLAN scheme in the physical network design. Care should be taken here; this will be the VLAN that management traffic will be accepted on, and should an incorrect value be entered, management of the ESXi host may be unavailable on the expected network.

To define the VLAN assignment for the Management Network:

1. Select the Configure Management Network option.

2. Select the VLAN (Optional) link.

3. Enter the VLAN identifier.

The IP parameters of the management interface can be defined as shown in Figure 5.12. Note that the administrator has the option of using either DHCP to provide the correct

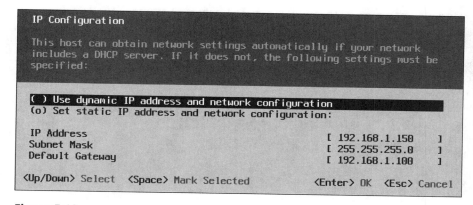

Figure 5.12
The IP configuration of the Management Network.

networking configuration, or the administrator can specify the settings manually. If you plan to use DHCP to configure the networking, consider the use of a reservation in the DHCP pool to reserve an IP address. This will ensure that the server always receives the same IP address when renewing.

To configure the networking parameters for the new ESXi server:

1. Specify whether to use DHCP or static IP configuration.

2. If the choice is made to use static configuration, define the IP address, the subnet mask, and the default gateway for use by the new host.

3. Note that the administrator can simply choose to view the current configuration if desired.

After the networking configuration has been completed, the administrator should also create alias and pointer DNS records for the new host, as the ESXi installer does not automatically create these records for you.

Notice in Figure 5.13 that the DNS Configuration link allows an administrator to configure DNS primary and secondary servers, and the FQDN of the server. This is a good practice; redundant DNS servers provide a level of availability in case one of the servers goes off line.

To configure the DNS servers and FQDN of the new ESXi host:

1. Select DNS Configuration from the Configure Management Network pane.

2. Enter the primary and secondary DNS servers.

3. Enter the desired FQDN of the ESXi server.

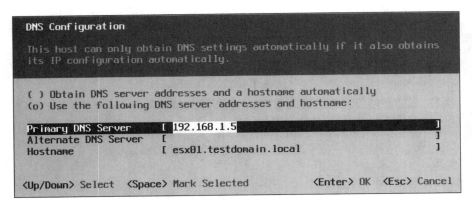

Figure 5.13
The DNS Configuration of the ESXi server.

As a component of the initial configuration, each ESXi host automatically generates a self-signed certificate for the host when the host is restarted. If an administrator changes the DNS configuration for the server at a later time, the administrator will need to regenerate the certificates for the host.

In general, when the hostd service is restarted or is stopped and then started, the `mgmt-vmware` process verifies that the existing certificate files are intact (`rui.crt` and the associated `rui.key`). If these files cannot be located, new certificates are generated.

The administrator can generate new certificate files through the following process:

1. Rename any existing certificate files in the /etc/vmware/ssl folder using the `mv /etc/vmware/ssl/rui.crt /etc/vmware/ssl/old.rui.crt` and `mv /etc/vmware/ssl rui.key /etc/vmware/ssl/old.rui.key` commands.

2. Use the `service mgmt-vmware restart` command to restart the hostd service.

3. Use the `ls -la /etc/.vmware/ssl/rui*` command to verify that the certificate files were created successfully.

Observe in Figure 5.14 that the administrator can also configure alternate DNS domains that can be queried in case there are references to unqualified host names. This option is important if the host name provided for the ESXi host does not contain a domain; "myhost" for example. The ESXi server will look to this field and add the domain name supplied if it attempts to resolve the non-qualified host name.

Using the Restart Management option will cause the existing DHCP information to be discarded, and a new DHCPDiscover packet to be broadcast. In essence, the host

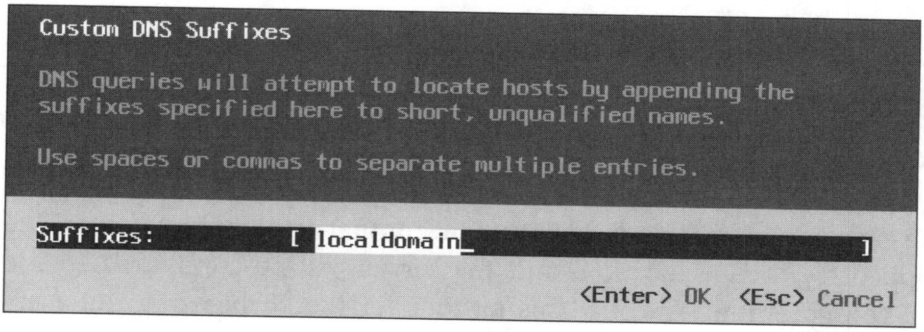

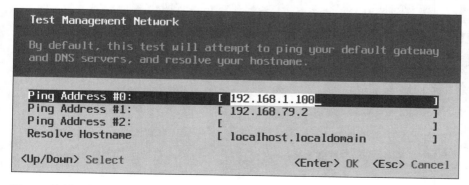

Figure 5.14
Alternate DNS search domains.

will reinitialize the TCP/IP stack. Please note that during the re-initialization, virtual machines may experience a loss of access during this period.

Selecting Test Management Network will allow an administrator to define up to three IP addresses that can be used to verify network connectivity, and DNS can also be evaluated by resolving the host name to an IP address.

As depicted in Figure 5.15, once the networking parameters have been entered, it is a good idea to test this configuration to verify that the IP and networking information is correct and that the host will be reachable across the network. This will also pay dividends if HA clustering is in the plans for this host, as HA heartbeats are primarily sent across the physical network, and if connectivity is interrupted, storage can be used to verify the status of that ESXi host. This will be covered in more detail in Chapter 12.

Figure 5.15
Testing the Management Network.

As seen in Figure 5.16, the Restore Network Factory Settings link will reset the network configuration to the default values. Note that this may also result in a loss of connectivity for a short period of time.

The Configure Keyboard link (shown in Figure 5.17) allows you to configure the default keyboard layout that will be available when managing the server. This is especially useful if the new server will be redeployed in another geographical area. The server can be shipped to its new location, and the server will be configured to use the local keyboard configuration. The available options for the keyboard layout are:

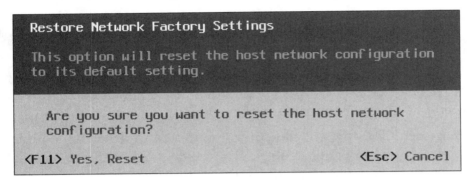

Figure 5.16
Restoring the default network settings.

- Belgian
- Brazilian
- Croatian

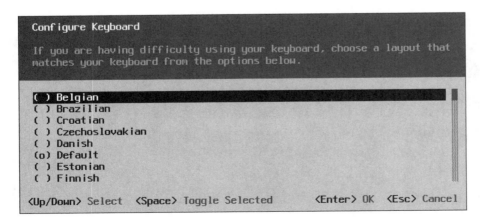

Figure 5.17
Configuring the default keyboard layout.

- Czechoslovakian
- Danish
- Default (English)
- Estonian
- Finnish
- French
- German
- Greek
- Icelandic
- Italian
- Japanese
- Latin American
- Norwegian
- Polish
- Portuguese
- Russian
- Slovenian
- Spanish
- Swedish
- Swiss French
- Swiss German
- Turkish
- Ukranian
- United Kingdom
- US Dvorak

The Troubleshooting Mode Options selection provides access to the tools that are most commonly used as troubleshooting utilities in an ESXi environment.

In Figure 5.18, the ESXi Shell can be either Enabled or Disabled (this is the renamed Tech Support Mode); the SSH option enables or disables SSH access to the ESXi host. Modify ESXi Shell Timeout options allows for the definition of the time interval that

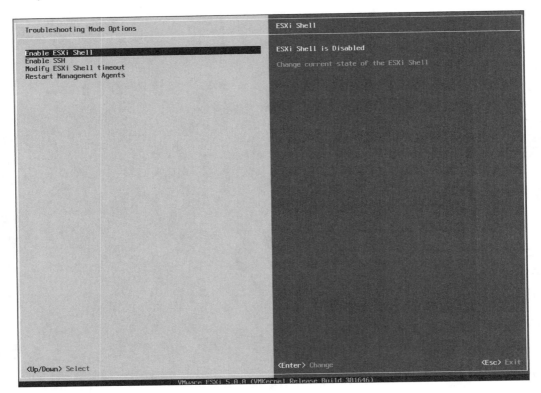

Figure 5.18
Enabling troubleshooting options.

is allowed for an ESXi connection to remain inactive. This can be set from 0 to 1440 minutes (1 day). The Restart Management Agents selection will cause all management agents to immediately restart their services. This may also cause a loss of access by management applications that are currently monitoring this particular host.

The Enable SSH selection either allows or prevents access to the ESXi host from an SSH client.

Modify ESXi Shell Timeout defines the timeframe that SSH sessions are enabled.

To enable the ESXi shell:

1. From the System Customization pane, select Troubleshooting Options.

2. At the Troubleshooting Mode Options pane, highlight Enable ESXi Shell.

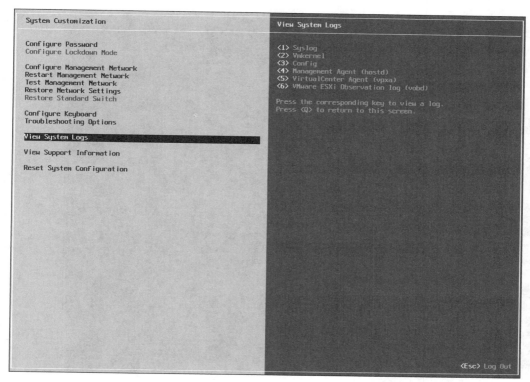

Figure 5.19
The available logs.

The View System Logs link provides an easy way to view current log activity. The administrator has the choice of viewing the contents of the Syslog, the VMkernel log, the hardware configuration through the Config option, information retrieved by the hostd service, the vCenter Agent (vpxa) if the host has been added to a vCenter instance, and the ESXi Observation log.

As shown in Figure 5.19, these logs are chosen simply by pressing the appropriate number. You can return to the menu by pressing "Q" at the log display pane.

Client Access

Now that the ESXi host has completed its installation and initial configuration phases, we can now log in and configure the new virtual environment based on the pre-virtualization assessment that we performed at the outset of our deployment. There are several methods that we can use to connect to and manage our ESXi host(s).

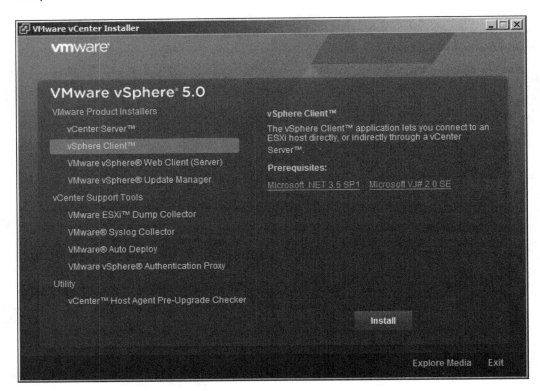

Figure 5.20
Installing the vSphere Client.

The vSphere Client

From the perspective of many vCenter and ESXi administrators, the vSphere Client is the management tool of choice. It provides access to the features of both an individual ESXi host, and those found in vCenter.

The vSphere Client can be installed from the vCenter distribution media.

Figure 5.20 displays the vCenter Installation interface. Before installing the vSphere Client, the Microsoft .NET 3.5 SP1 and VJ# 2.0 SE packages must be installed to provide the necessary framework for the vSphere Client.

As shown in Figure 5.21, the vSphere Client can be used to access the vCenter instance from a stand-alone device on the network, or it can also be installed on the vCenter server itself. If the client is used to access the vCenter from a remote device, the administrator must enter the FQDN or IP address of the vCenter instance and the credentials used to log in to vCenter. If the client is used from the vCenter instance, the administrator can use "localhost" as the host name, but must still provide the correct credentials to successfully log in.

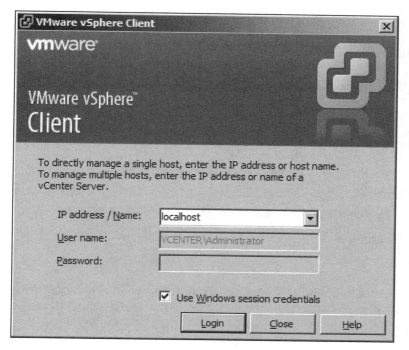

Figure 5.21
Logging in using the vSphere Client.

To install the vSphere Client:

1. Open the vCenter distribution media.

2. Select the vSphere Client from the VMware vCenter Installer menu and select Install.

3. Select the installation language.

4. Accept the EULA.

5. Enter the user information.

6. Select the destination folder.

7. Click Install.

New Web Access

vSphere 5 contains an updated Web Client that can be used to manage the virtual machines by using a web browser. This is a key option, since in many environments it is undesirable or unsecure to deploy a vSphere Client to everyone's desktop or laptop.

Installing the vCenter Web Client

To begin the process, use the vCenter distribution media to install the Web Client server component on the management device, as shown in Figure 5.22.

To install the vSphere Web Client (server):

1. Using the vCenter Installer wizard, select the Web Client, and click Install.

2. Select the installation language.

3. Accept the EULA.

4. Provide the user information.

5. Configure the ports to be used to communicate with the vCenter server.

6. Select the destination folder.

7. Choose Install.

When the installation has completed, the vCenter server must first be registered with the Web Client. To register the vCenter, log in to the vCenter with Administrator-level credentials and enter **https://localhost:9443/admin-app**. At this point, it

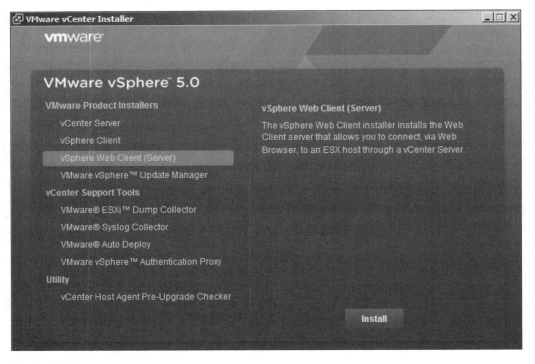

Figure 5.22
Installing the vSphere Web Client.

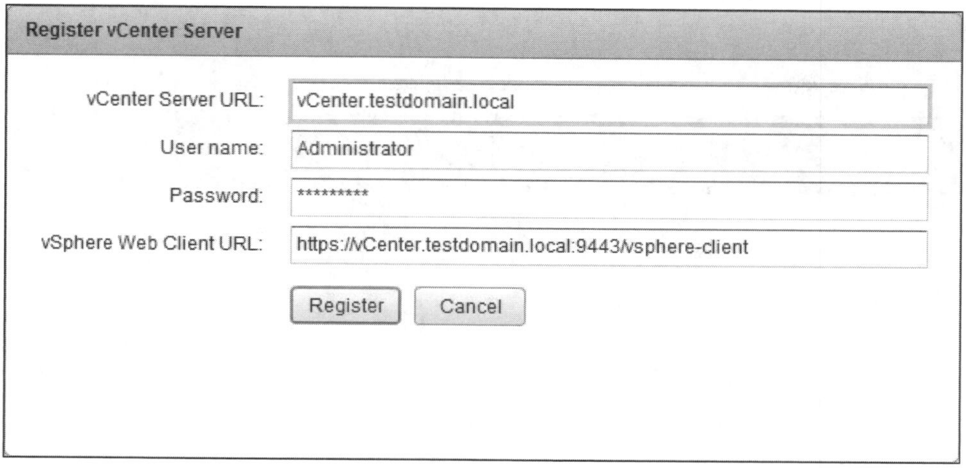

Register vCenter Server

vCenter Server URL:	vCenter.testdomain.local
User name:	Administrator
Password:	*********
vSphere Web Client URL:	https://vCenter.testdomain.local:9443/vsphere-client

[Register]   [Cancel]

Figure 5.23
Registering the vCenter server with the Web Client.

should be mentioned that the default security level may need to be reduced for the web browser in order to access the administrative web page. Alternatively, you can install a certificate that will verify the server identity, and allow you to maintain the default security level of the web browser.

As shown in Figure 5.23, use the Register vCenter link to register the vCenter server. The FQDN of the vCenter server and the administrative-level credentials will need to be provided. The vCenter instance is located and you will need to accept the certificate for the vCenter server. Once these values are entered, the process should complete.

Note that in Figure 5.24 the vCenter instance is listed in the vCenter server URL column, as is the corresponding SSL thumbprint. It is possible to register multiple vCenter server systems with the Web Client, but it is recommended to register only a single vCenter per Web Client, since the Web Client can only connect to a single vCenter instance at a time.

The Web Client Interface

To access the vSphere Web Client, go to https://vCenter.testdomain.local:9443/vsphere-client, where "vCenter.testdomain.local" is the URL of your vCenter instance.

As shown in Figure 5.25, verify the FQDN of the vCenter server is correct, and enter the login credentials.

Figure 5.24
Completing registration for the vCenter server.

After a successful authentication, the Web Client interface is displayed as shown in Figure 5.26. The vCenter instance is displayed in the left column, the ESXi hosts in the vCenter inventory are listed in the center pane, and any detected alarms are displayed in the right column.

In Figure 5.26, the Web Client interface is displayed. On the main screen, a summary of the environment is displayed, from the four main views of vCenter to summaries of physical hosts to recent events and alarms.

The left pane is the inventory pane and displays a summary of the objects in the environment. The Summary pane is in the center of the interface, and the Tasks and Alarms are displayed in the right side of the interface.

Figure 5.27 shows the Web Client Management interface. Note that the different views available are represented by icons identical to those used in the vCenter

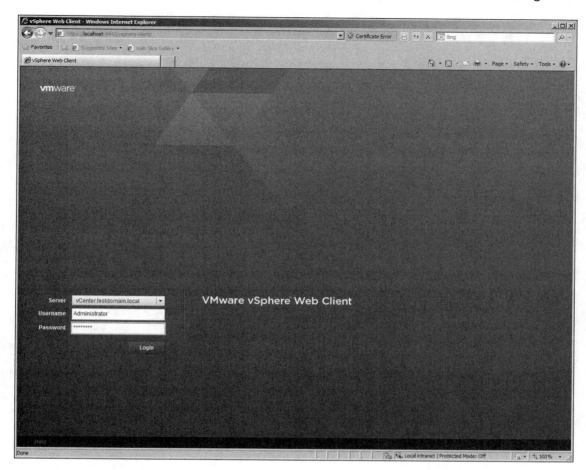

Figure 5.25
Logging in to the Web Client.

interface. Each of the icons references one of the main management views in vCenter (labeled 1–4 in the figure):

1. Hosts and Clusters

2. VMs and Templates

3. Datastores

4. Networking

In the center pane of Figure 5.28, the Summary tab displays the hosts and virtual machines in the vCenter inventory, along with any corresponding notes for those objects.

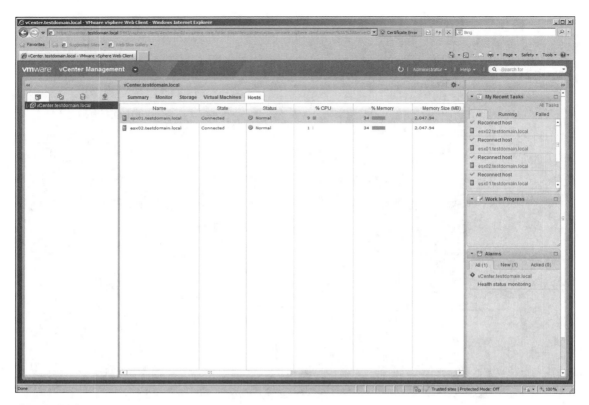

Figure 5.26
The Web Client interface.

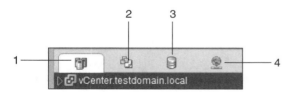

Figure 5.27
The Web Client Management interface.

In this particular example, there are two physical ESXi hosts, there are no VMs currently deployed, and there are no notes provided to document the environment.

Clicking the Monitor tab as depicted in Figure 5.29 displays a list of recent Tasks, Events, and Alarms in the environment. Highlighting one of these events displays a more detailed description at the bottom of the pane.

Figure 5.28
Viewing the Summary pane.

Note that a green "check mark" icon indicates that a process completed successfully, while a red circle with a white "X" indicates a failure while attempting to complete a process.

If you right-click on one of the datastores as depicted in Figure 5.30, you have the option to register a VM in the vCenter inventory from a folder on this datastore, which will add it to the vCenter inventory. VMs can also be removed from the vCenter inventory, which will remove it from visibility in vCenter, but leaves the files intact on the datastore.

Clicking on the Virtual Machines tab displays detailed information about the virtual machines that are in the vCenter inventory.

If you right-click on a particular virtual machine, you are presented with four options: Power, Configuration, Inventory, and Snapshot.

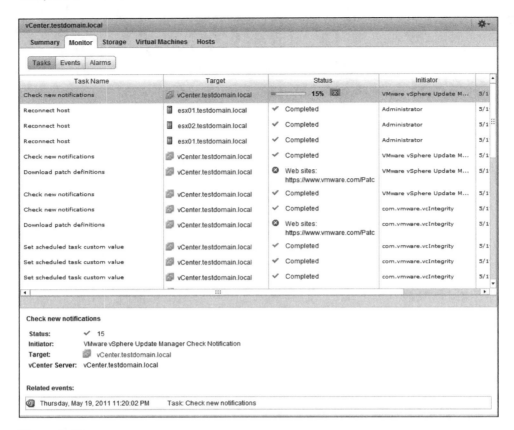

Figure 5.29
Viewing the Monitor tab.

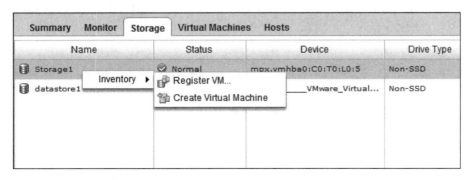

Figure 5.30
Options in the Storage tab.

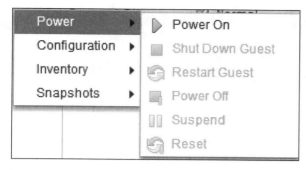

Figure 5.31
Power options in the Virtual Machines tab.

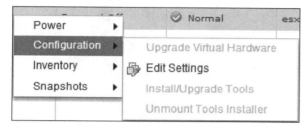

Figure 5.32
Configuration options in the Virtual Machines tab.

In Figure 5.31, the VM Power options are shown. Selecting the Power options allows the administrator to perform the following power-related operations on the virtual machine: Power On, Shut Down Guest, Restart Guest, Power Off, Suspend, and Reset the VM.

As shown in Figure 5.32, selecting the Configuration option allows the Administrator to perform the following tasks: Upgrade Virtual Hardware, Edit Settings, Install/ Upgrade Tools, and Unmount Tools Installer.

As shown in Figure 5.33, selecting the Inventory option allows the Administrator to perform the following tasks: Migrate, Convert to Template, Clone, Rename, Remove, and Delete the VM.

In Figure 5.34, the Snapshots link allows the Administrator to perform the following tasks: Access the Snapshot Manager, Take a Snapshot, and Revert to a Snapshot.

Clicking on the Hosts tab displays the hosts in the vCenter inventory along with their current resource utilization.

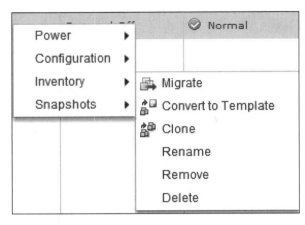

Figure 5.33
Inventory options in the Virtual Machines tab.

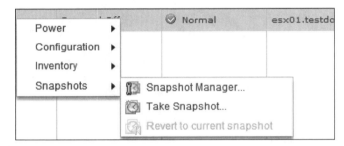

Figure 5.34
VM Snapshot options.

Figure 5.35 shows the options available through the Configuration link. If you right-click on the ESXi host, and choose the Configuration link, you will have the option to place this physical host into Maintenance Mode or to remove the host from Maintenance Mode.

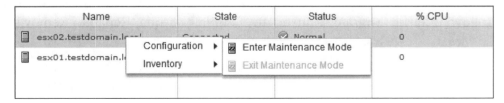

Figure 5.35
The Configuration link.

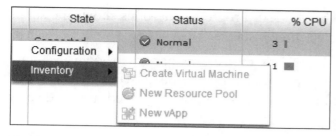

Figure 5.36
The Inventory link.

In Figure 5.36, if the Inventory link is chosen, you have the option to deploy a new VM, Resource Pool, or vApp. This is analogous to right-clicking on a datacenter, folder, or host in vCenter.

As shown in Figure 5.37, on the right side of the Web Client interface is the My Recent Tasks pane. Note that the status of the last four tasks is displayed, along with the completion status in the form of a green check mark for a successful result. To see the currently running tasks, click on the Running link. Similarly, selecting the Failed link will display only those processes that failed.

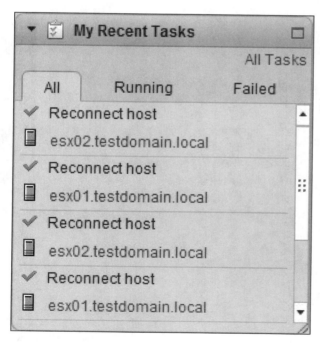

Figure 5.37
The My Recent Tasks pane.

Below the My Recent Tasks pane is the Work in Progress pane. This shows the status of any current operations within the vCenter instance.

At the bottom of the My Recent Tasks pane is the Alarms pane, as shown in Figure 5.38. All current alarms are displayed here, and they can be sorted by clicking the New link to display any new alarms in the environment, or the Acked link to display the alarms that have been acknowledged.

If desired, you can click on a single ESXi host in the left inventory pane, and the parameters for this particular server are accessible in the center management pane. As shown in Figure 5.39, you can use the Summary tab to view an overview of this ESXi host. Note that in the Configuration pane, you can see the version of ESXi that is currently installed; you can also determine whether this host has vMotion enabled or if it is configured for FT.

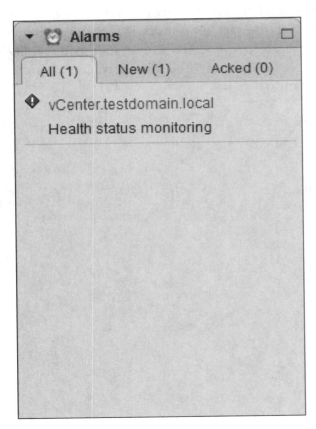

Figure 5.38
The Alarms pane.

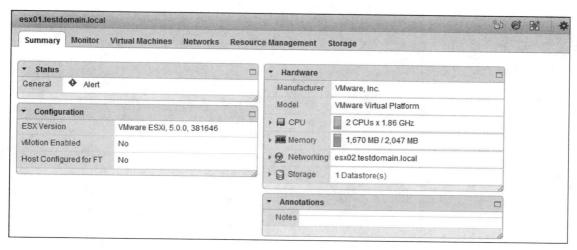

Figure 5.39
Viewing the status of a single ESXi host.

In the Hardware pane, we can view the current hardware configuration of this server: 2 CPUs at 1.86 GHz, 2GB total RAM with 1.67GB free, the FQDN of the server, and we can use the Datastores link to access the current datastores parameters.

As depicted in Figure 5.40, if you click on a specific ESXi host in the inventory, you can view the current tasks and alarms and the individual who initiated these processes by highlighting the Monitor tab, and selecting the Tasks button.

As shown in Figure 5.41, if you click on the Events button, the Web Client will display the details of the most recent events.

If you click on the Performance button, as depicted in Figure 5.42, the Web Client will display a summary of the host's CPU and RAM utilization metrics.

The Alarms button, as shown in Figure 5.43, provides details on the recent alarms, the object reporting the alarm, the type of alarm triggered, and the time and date of the alarm.

As shown in Figure 5.44, the Configuration link displays the current VM inventory for this ESXi server. If you right-click on the VM, and select Configuration, you can upgrade the version of virtual hardware installed in this VM, modify the configuration through the Edit Settings selection, install or upgrade VMware Tools, and unmount the VMware Tools installer from this VM.

Using the Inventory link, as depicted in Figure 5.45, you can vMotion this VM to another host, convert this VM to a template, clone this VM, rename this VM, remove the VM from the inventory, or delete this VM from disk.

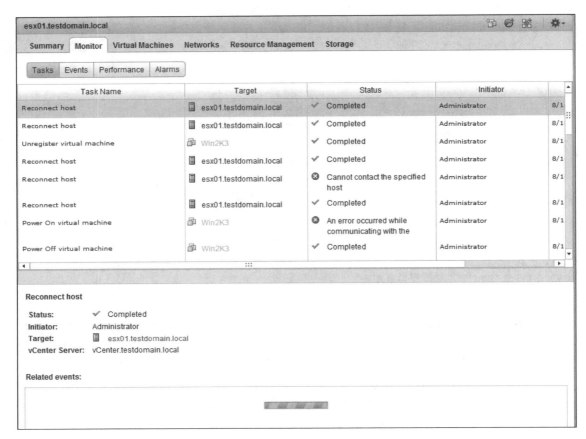

Figure 5.40
Viewing the status of an ESXi host.

The Snapshots link, as depicted in Figure 5.46, allows you to manage snapshots associated with this VM through the use of the Snapshot Manager, Take Shapshot, and Revert to current snapshot.

The Networks link, as shown in Figure 5.47, displays the current network switch configuration associated with this VM.

As shown in Figure 5.48, if you select the Resource Management tab, you can view the current CPU, RAM, and storage resource utilization of this VM.

As shown in Figure 5.49, the Storage link provides access to the Storage configuration of this VM, such as the datastore on which the VM's files are stored, the status of the datastore, the logical path and name of the datastore, the formatted and free space of the datastore, and the format of the datastore.

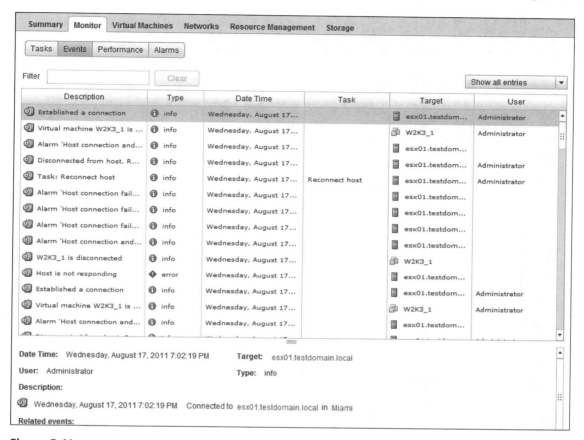

Figure 5.41
The Events pane.

As Figure 5.50 shows, the Management interface also includes a gear-shaped icon that allows you to place an ESXi host into Maintenance Mode, or to remove an ESXi host from Maintenance Mode from the Configuration link.

Figure 5.51 displays the Inventory link accessible from the Management link. As shown, you have the option to create a new virtual machine, resource pool, or vApp.

Configuring the Host via vSphere Client

As in previous releases of VMware virtualization software, physical hosts can be deployed and managed through a GUI-based interface, or the same processes can be accomplished using a CLI environment. The CLI environment provides the ability

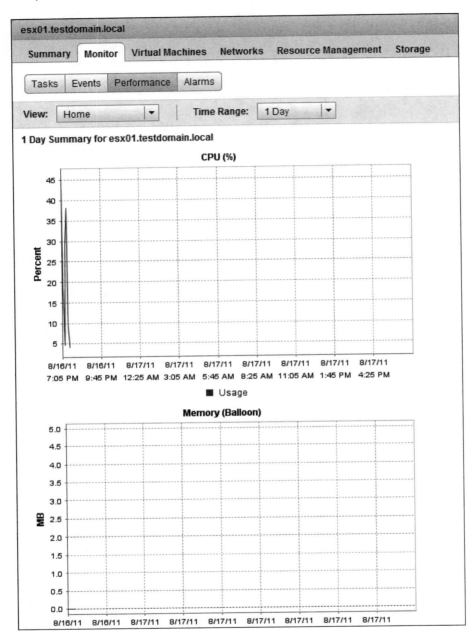

Figure 5.42
The Performance pane.

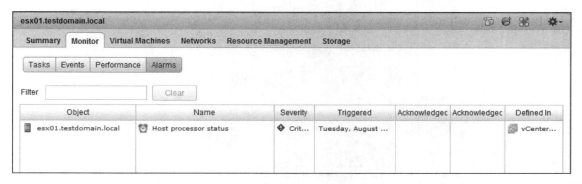

Figure 5.43
The Alarms pane.

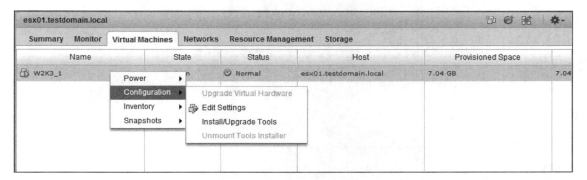

Figure 5.44
The Configuration link.

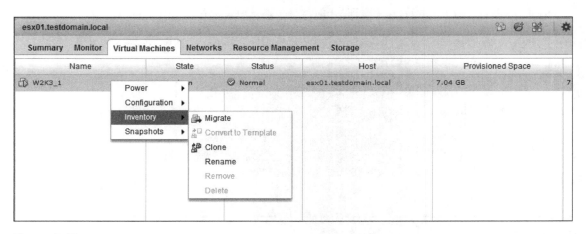

Figure 5.45
The Inventory link.

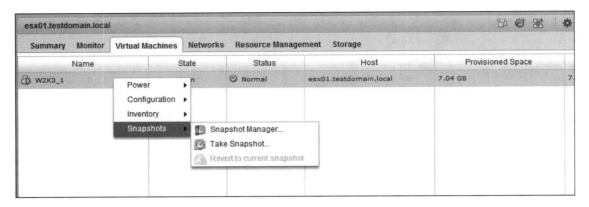

Figure 5.46
The Snapshots link.

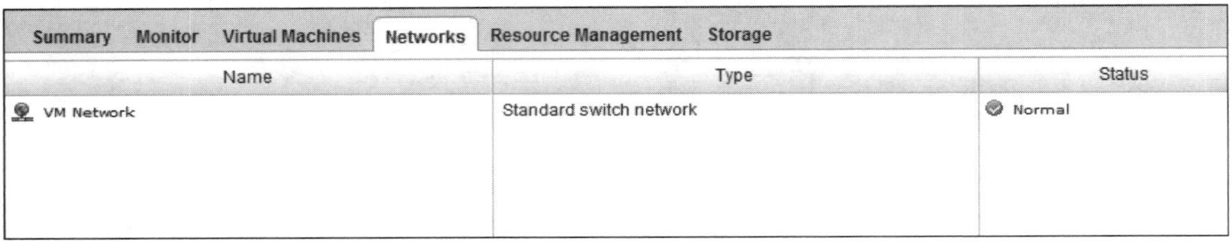

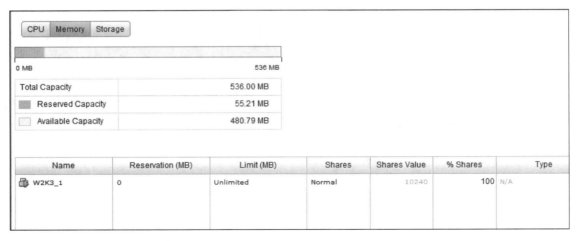

Figure 5.47
The Networks link.

Figure 5.48
The Resource Management tab.

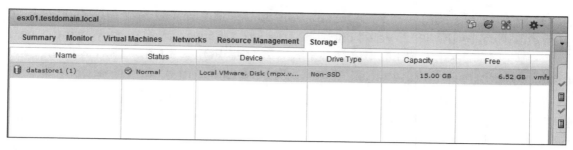

Figure 5.49
The Storage link.

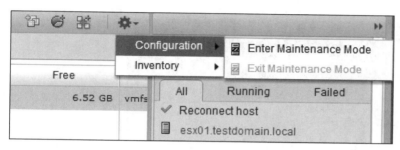

Figure 5.50
The Configuration link.

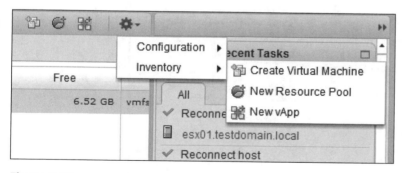

Figure 5.51
The Inventory link.

to script the configuration parameters for the physical host, thereby creating a repeatable, verifiable process.

In this section, we will take a look at configuring an ESXi host using the vSphere Client. Managing the environment through PowerShell will be covered in a later chapter.

After the host has completed the installation phase, administration of the host can be performed using the vSphere Client. The vSphere Client is available by using a web browser and accessing either the IP address or the FQDN of the ESXi host. At the main page, there is a link that allows the vSphere Client to be downloaded.

Figure 5.52 shows the web page that is displayed when pointing a web browser to the ESXi host. Note that on the web page there are links that allow access to the following components:

- The vSphere Client
- The vCenter Installer

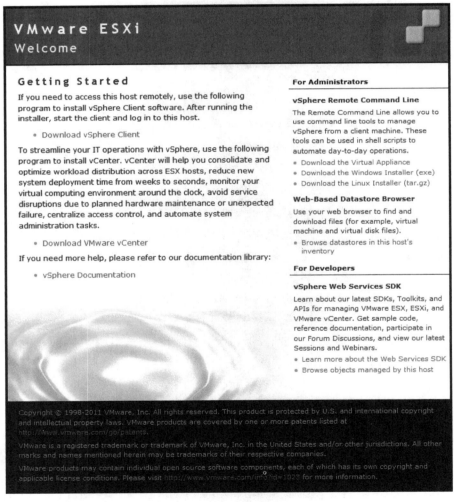

Figure 5.52
Installing the vSphere Client from the vCenter web page.

- vSphere Documentation
- The vSphere Remote Command Line Appliance
- The vSphere Windows Installer for the Remote Command Line
- The Linux Installer for the Remote Command Line

From this page, the administrator can also browse datastores in this ESXi host's inventory, and download the vSphere Web Services Software Developer's Kit (SDK).

Once the vSphere Client has been installed, access the ESXi host interface by entering the FQDN or the IP address of the ESXi host, providing the root credentials. After providing the correct credentials, the management interface can be used to further configure the ESXi host.

As shown in Figure 5.53, the status of the hardware devices in the ESXi host can be easily viewed by highlighting the ESXi host in the inventory pane and selecting

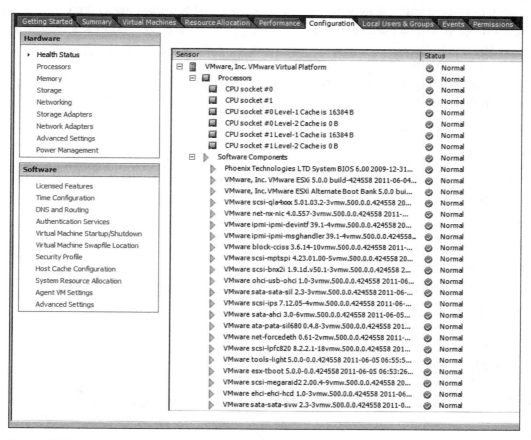

Figure 5.53
Viewing the host health status.

Health Status. Note that any device that displays a red indicator should be immediately investigated.

By highlighting the host in the interface, and selecting the Configuration tab, links then provide access to view the current configuration or to modify options as desired.

Storage Overview

Selecting the Storage link displays the current storage configuration. In the top pane, the current available datastores are displayed. The current characteristics of the highlighted datastore are provided in the viewing panel of Figure 5.54.

The administrator can view the storage for this ESXi host by highlighting the physical ESXi host, and choosing Storage. Note that the datastore named "datastore1" is termed a Local ATA Device. It is a non-SSD device with a maximum presented capacity of 3.00GB, with 2.39GB free. The datastore is formatted as a VMFS partition; the last update occurred at 9:28:48 AM on 8/12/2011. This particular datastore is not enabled for hardware acceleration.

In Figure 5.55, the details for this datastore are displayed. Here, we can view:

1. The datastore file location. This means that we can navigate to the location specified in the file and browse the file structure from the command line.

2. The total capacity, the used space, and the free space available on the volume.

3. The current multipathing policy for the datastore.

4. The formatting information for the volume, including the revision of VMFS and the block size in use.

5. The number and size of all extents that comprise this volume.

Networking Overview

The Networking resources for the host are accessible by selecting the Networking link from the Hardware pane.

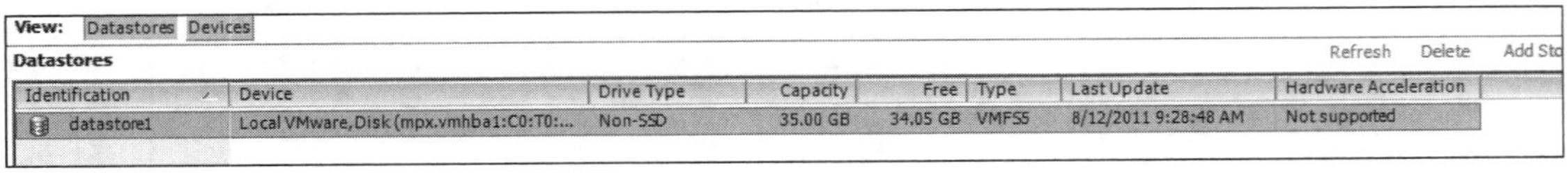

View:	Datastores	Devices							
Datastores							Refresh	Delete	Add Sto
Identification	Device		Drive Type	Capacity	Free	Type	Last Update		Hardware Acceleration
datastore1	Local VMware, Disk (mpx.vmhba1:C0:T0:...		Non-SSD	35.00 GB	34.05 GB	VMFS5	8/12/2011 9:28:48 AM		Not supported

Figure 5.54
Viewing general datastore properties.

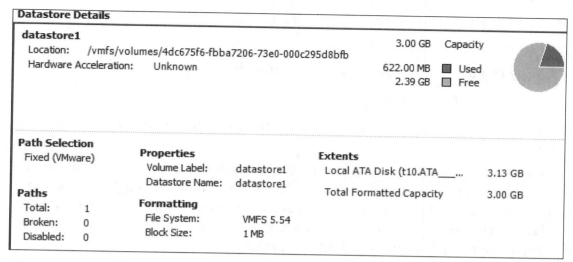

Figure 5.55
Viewing datastore details.

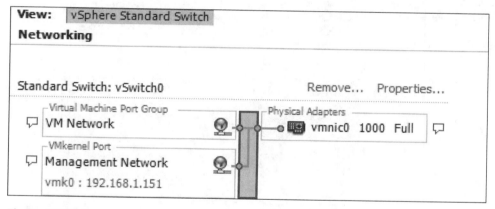

Figure 5.56
Viewing Standard vSwitch properties.

In Figure 5.56, the host only has one standard virtual switch, and it has two port groups: Management Network, with an IP address of 192.168.1.151, and VM Network. The cumulative traffic from these port groups shares the physical network adapter vmnic0.

Note that this pane also provides access to the following functions:

- Refresh the networking view.
- Add additional standard networking.

- Configure the IPv6 properties of the ESXi host.

- Remove the standard vSwitch.

- View or modify the properties of this particular vSwitch.

- View additional networking information.

If you click on the Properties link for this virtual switch, the existing configuration can be viewed or modified.

As shown in Figure 5.57, clicking on the Properties link yields a view of the current configuration of the vSwitch, and the associated port groups. Highlighting one of the entries on the Ports tab displays the characteristics of the object. Here, the vSwitch has been highlighted, and its properties are visible under the Properties pane. Note that these are the default settings for this vSwitch.

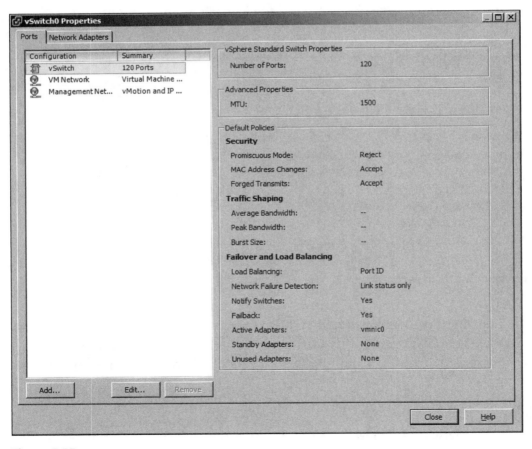

Figure 5.57
Viewing standard vSwitch details.

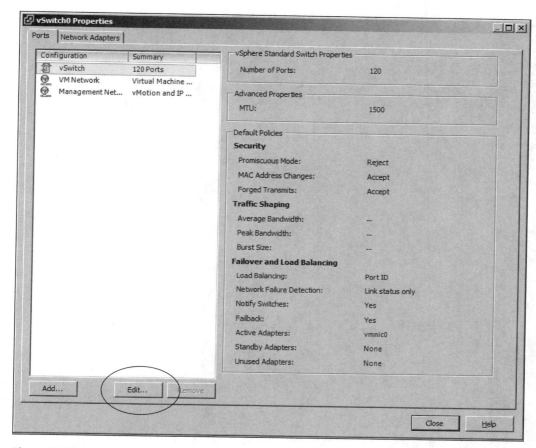

Figure 5.58
Modifying the settings of the vSwitch.

In Figure 5.58, the administrator can click on the Edit button and modify the current configuration this particular vSwitch.

Figure 5.59 shows the options available for this vSwitch. On the General tab, we can change the number of ports available on the switch and we can also change the MTU (Maximum Transmission Unit) supported by this vSwitch. Note that if the number of ports is changed, the ESXi host must be rebooted for the changes to take effect. Note that the administrator has the option to modify the MTU for this standard vSwitch. In previous releases of vSphere, this was accomplished using the `esxcfg-vswitch -m` command from the CLI or the local console.

Selecting the Security tab allows the administrator to change the default security parameters for the virtual switch.

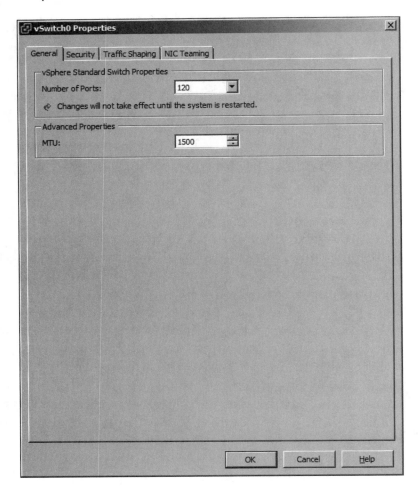

Figure 5.59
Modifying vSwitch properties.

Figure 5.60 shows the current security configuration of this vSwitch. Note that the default configuration is set to Reject Promiscuous Mode, and to Accept both MAC Address Changes and Forged Transmits. We will define these terms further in Chapter 7.

The Traffic Shaping tab allows you to limit the amount of outbound traffic that is permitted to pass through the virtual switch.

In Figure 5.61, the current traffic shaping configuration is displayed. Note that the Average Bandwidth and Peak Bandwidth metrics are in Kbits/sec, whereas the Burst Size is specified in Kbytes/sec.

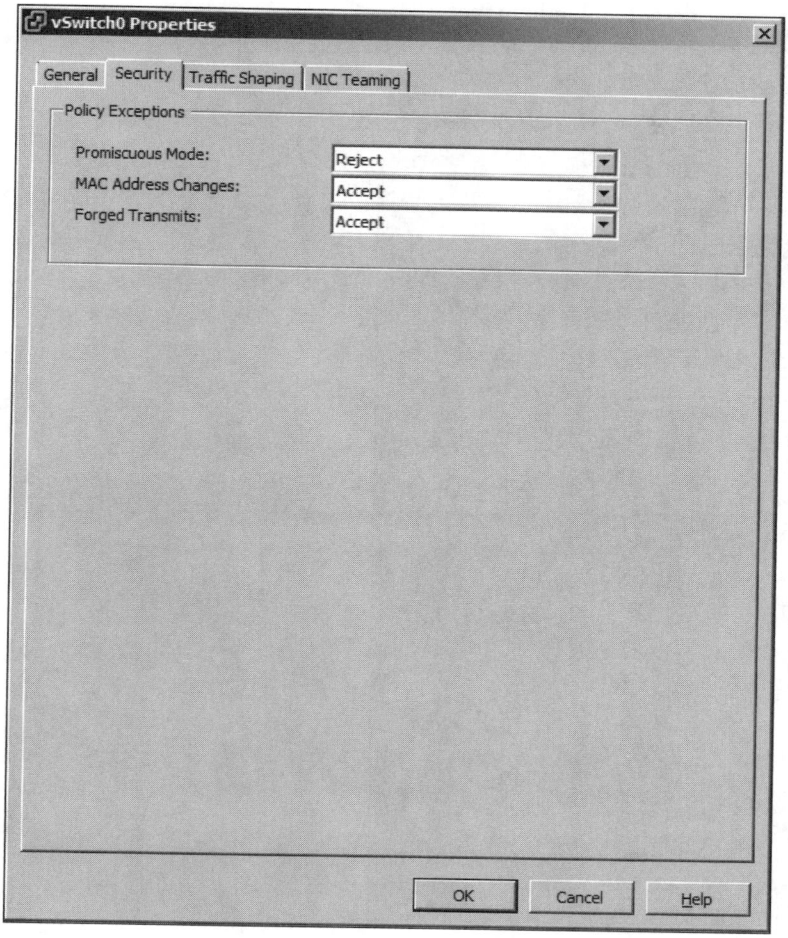

Figure 5.60
Viewing the current Security settings.

The NIC Teaming tab displays the current Policy Exceptions as configured for this virtual switch. These settings include the Load Balancing policy, the Network Failover Detection policy, the Notify Switches policy, and the Failback policy.

If the administrator selects the NIC Teaming tab from the vSwitch properties, the options shown in Figure 5.62 display.

The NIC teaming and failover configuration for the virtual switch is displayed at the bottom of the pane. It also displays the specific details about the adapters. We can specify a failover order, depending on the NICs that are installed, and we can also define a NIC as "Unused" if we do not want to include that particular NIC in the

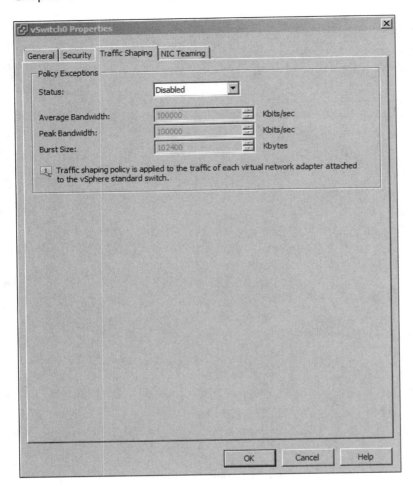

Figure 5.61
Viewing the current Traffic Shaping configuration.

options for this virtual switch. We will cover these options in more detail in the Networking chapter.

NTP Configuration

When the ESXi host is selected in the inventory, click the Configuration tab, and, under Software Settings, click on the Time Configuration link.

Figure 5.63 depicts the NTP configuration interface. In the default configuration, as is depicted in the screenshot, the NTP service is typically in the "Stopped" state, and the time and date that are displayed are those specified during the operating system installation process. If the Properties link is selected, the NTP configuration pane is

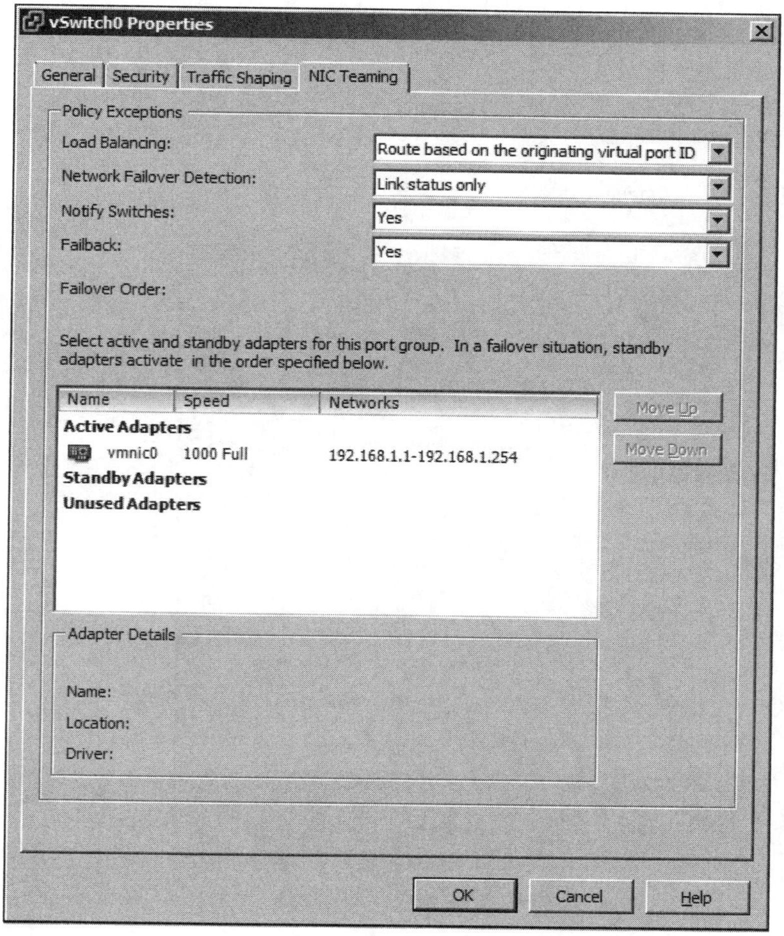

Figure 5.62
Viewing the current NIC Teaming configuration.

presented. Here we can reset the clock and calendar settings to reflect a more accurate timeframe.

To enable and configure NTP:

1. Use the vSphere Client to log in to the ESXi host

2. From the Configuration tab, select the Time Configuration link from the Software Options list.

3. In the upper-right corner, select Properties.

4. At the Time Configuration pop-up, make any necessary changes to the current data and time.

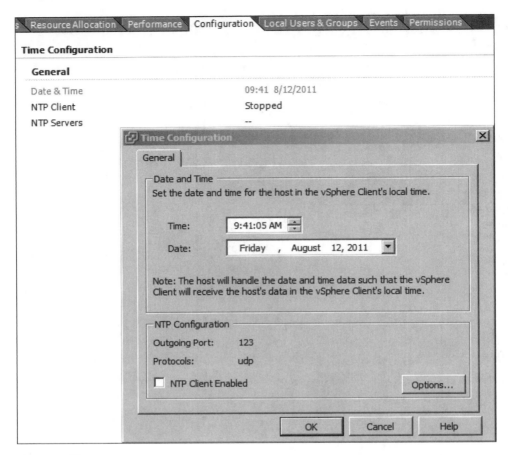

Figure 5.63
Configuring NTP.

5. Select NTP Client Enabled and click on the Options button. This has a two-fold purpose: the NTP client is enabled, and port 123 is opened on the firewall to allow NTP traffic.

The VMware vSphere Authentication Proxy

The administrator has the option to use the vSphere Authentication Proxy or CAM server to join ESXi hosts to the domain, rather than joining the domain directly. The benefit of this would be that if the Authentication Proxy is used, configuration files for ESXi hosts that are deployed using Auto Deploy and PXE-boot ESXi hosts will not contain AD credentials. This enhances domain security while still allowing Auto Deploy to be used to provision ESXi hosts.

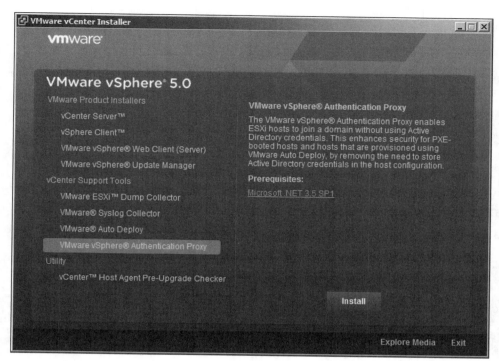

Figure 5.64
Installing the Authentication Proxy.

As depicted in Figure 5.64, the Authentication Proxy is installed from the vCenter distribution media. The vSphere Authentication Proxy can be installed either on the vCenter server or on a stand-alone server in the network. As a prerequisite, the following files must also be installed:

- IIS
- The IIS 6 Metabase Compatibility component
- ISAPI extensions
- IP and Domain extensions

Backing Up an ESXi Host Configuration

If an ESX host must be backed up, a number of backup agents are available from multiple vendors that will enable the backup to be completed. However, since the ESXi platform has no local Linux installation, these agents are incompatible.

The process of backing up the configuration for an ESXi host can be performed from within a vMA or using the PowerCLI by using the vicfg-cfgbackup command.

The syntax is:

```
vicfg-cfgbackup <connection options> -s f:\backup_share
```

where `connection options` represents the FQDN or IP address of the ESXi host to be backed up, and the credentials to be used to perform the backup.

This command will perform the backup and save it to the location defined by `f:\backup_share`.

```
vicfg-cfgbackup <connection options> -s f:\backup_share -q
```

This command will perform the same backup process as the previous command, but will do so without confirmation prompts.

```
vicfg-cfgbackup <connection options> -l f:\backup_share
```

This command will restore the configuration found in the location defined by `f:\backup_share` to the ESXi host listed in the connection options.

```
vicfg-cfgbackup <connection options> -r
```

This command will reset the ESXi host specified in the connection options to the default configuration.

Maintenance Mode

Maintenance Mode can be defined as the state of a physical ESXi host in which no virtual machines can be powered on, nor can any virtual machines vMotion to this host. In fact, all VMs that can be "vMotioned" will be moved to other ESXi hosts. This is the mode that must be used to apply upgrades and patches through Update Manager. Once the patching has completed, the host is returned to an online status, and VMs can then be returned to their original locations.

Maintenance Mode can be a very handy option if a physical hardware component fails in a host. The VMs can be moved to other hosts, maintaining availability while the issue is resolved.

Host Profiles

Host Profiles are a feature that is available with the Enterprise Plus level licensing. They allow an administrator to research and create an ideal ESXi configuration on a "reference host." It is possible to create custom definitions based on:

- Memory Reservation
- Storage

- Networking
- Date and Time
- Firewall
- Security
- Service
- Advanced Configuration Options (Heartbeat and Logging)
- Users and Groups
- Authentication
- Kernel Module
- DCUI Keyboard
- SFCB (Small Footprint CIM Broker)
- Login Banner
- Resource Pool
- SNMP Agent
- Power System
- CIM Indication Subsystem

To create a Host Profile, browse to the Home > Management > Host Profiles path and select Host Profiles.

Figure 5.65 shows the Create Profile wizard. In the Host Profiles interface, select Create Profile. Choose Create Profile from Existing Host, and specify the reference host for this profile. At this point, profiles can be imported from another location. This enables a standardized configuration to be used across multiple locations. Define the name for the profile; this can be a reference to the host name, its function, or its location.

When the Host Profile has been created, you can highlight the profile and select Edit Profile to view the parameters.

As shown in Figure 5.66, when you open the profile, you can modify any of the parameters manually. This allows a profile to remain relevant, even though changes may occur in the physical environment. In this example, we have selected the Physical Network Adapter and in the Configuration Details we can have the vmnic assigned based on the PCI bus discovery process, or we can statically define to vmnic to always be a specific physical NIC.

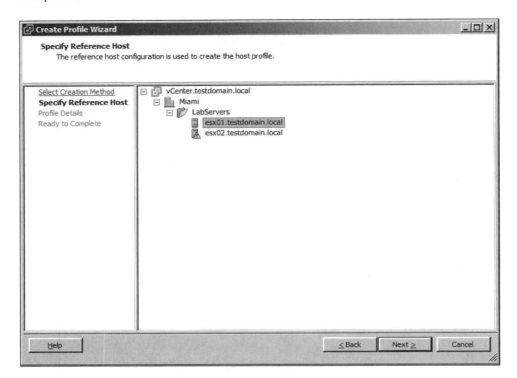

Figure 5.65
Creating a new Host Profile.

When the profile is configured, we can then apply the profile to other ESXi hosts that we want to mirror this configuration.

Figure 5.67 shows the management options for the Host Profile. When we right-click on the Profile, we have the option to Edit the Profile, Enable or Disable Profile Configuration, Clone the Profile, Delete the Profile, Export the Profile, Attach the Profile to a Host or Cluster, Change the Reference Host, and Update the Profile from the Reference Host.

Now that we have the profile edited to reflect the parameters that we want to pass on to the new hosts, we must attach or logically associate the profile with a cluster or individual host.

Figure 5.68 shows the Attach Hosts and Clusters pane. Here you will highlight the chosen host and select Attach. This associates the set of configuration parameters stored in the Host Profile with this particular physical host.

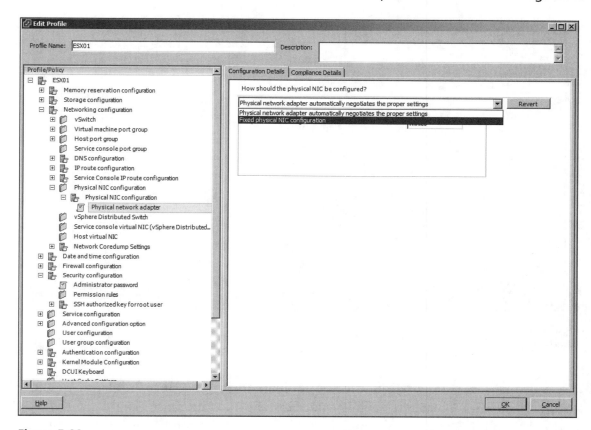

Figure 5.66
Editing an existing Host Profile.

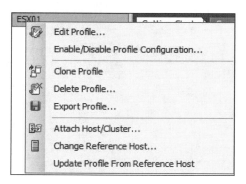

Figure 5.67
Host Profile options.

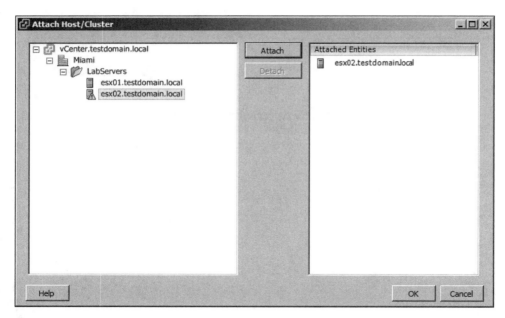

Figure 5.68
Attaching a Host Profile.

The existing host configuration must be compared with this Host Profile, so we move to the Hosts and Cluster tab within the Host Profiles interface. Highlight the host and either select Check Compliance from the links at the top of the pane or you can right-click on the host and select Check Compliance.

Figure 5.69 shows the results of the evaluation. During the analysis of the host, it was discovered that there are inconsistencies with the profile, and those inconsistencies are listed in the Compliance Failures pane, below the host name.

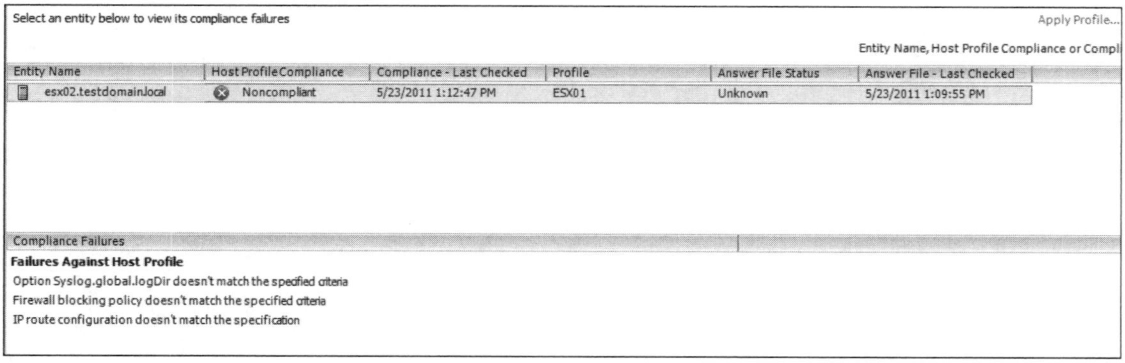

Figure 5.69
Compliance results.

At this point, in order to apply the profile, we must place the host in Maintenance Mode, and then we can apply the profile, bring the host up to compliance, and resume the host from Maintenance Mode. Maintenance Mode will be discussed in Chapter 11.

SECURITY

While we are in the planning phase, we cannot forget about the security of the new environment. We need to decide who will require access to the new environment, and exactly what type of access they need to do their job. This required level of access may be totally different than what the users want.

It may also be useful while planning security to consider if colleagues from other teams or groups will need access. This may take the form of providing access to the networking components to members of the same network team, so they can manage the virtual networks in the same way that they manage the physical networks. This means that they can configure the virtual networking to mesh seamlessly with the physical environment.

Similarly, access to the storage components can be provided to members of the storage team, so they can deploy storage devices as required; this also means that the storage team can access storage-related performance metrics and compare them to the metrics that they obtain from the physical storage. This level of access also allows the SAN to plan their storage much more accurately.

At the same time, we must consider the access needs of the various Servers Administrators. If these administrators have roles and responsibilities on physical servers, doesn't it make sense that they will require the same access when the servers have been virtualized?

When considering the physical servers and desktops that will be hosted in the virtualized environment, we also must consider the security requirements of the new environment. In many cases, there are specific security constraints placed on physical servers due to the nature of the applications or data that they contain.

The virtualized environment should reflect these same concerns. The security of virtual servers should mirror or exceed those placed on physical servers.

Enabling/Disabling Lockdown Mode

As we discussed earlier, we can configure Lockdown Mode in an effort to minimize the access to the local console of the physical host. When the host is added to the vCenter inventory, the vpxuser account is created on the local ESXi host to provide access to the vCenter instance. When Lockdown Mode is enabled in the DCUI, all local console access is denied to improve security, and to prevent someone from modifying the ESXi configuration.

Lockdown Mode also provides access to the vSphere WebServices API exclusively through the vpxuser account. This means that third-party management applications and reporting tools may not function as designed, due to the lack of access to ESXi management objects.

Host Security Considerations

When considering the ESXi host itself, many of the same security concerns apply to each ESXi host as would apply to an Exchange or SQL server. Some basic considerations are:

- Limiting physical access to each server is a primary issue. Many data centers limit access based upon the requirement to present an ID badge or SmartCard to enter the data center. This same concern should be reflected in the provision of access to ESXi servers as well.

- A consideration here would be to configure an NTP server for the environment. This will provide a consistent time frame for all audit logs, security logs, and performance charts. This allows an administrator to compare login and logoff processes within the server, and possibly correlate them to events recorded in the system logs.

- In a general sense, it should be an option that all access to the ESXi host be provided through the vSphere Client. This will reduce the opportunities for operating system administrators to make "unintended modifications" to the server configuration files and cause additional issues.

- Always use a signed certificate to authenticate server-to-server connectivity and client access. This will greatly assist in the effort to reduce and possibly eliminate Main in the Middle attacks.

- If possible, use SSL on the transfer of data from one server to another. This includes the processes of cloning a VM or performing a vMotion between hosts. To enable this, open the vpxd.conf file and add the following line with a text editor: Under the <nfc> heading, add <useSSL>true</useSSL>.

- CIM (Common Information Model) providers are used to expose hardware characteristics to monitoring software and to the vSphere environment. In fact, CIM providers are used to populate the Hardware Status tab for the ESXi host. A best practice here is to create a special account that is used only for CIM provider access and define a corresponding role with limited access. This account can then be used to access the CIM information.

- For many virtualization administrators, SNMP provides an important alerting mechanism that can be used to gather information from a variety of vendors and providers. However, SNMP can also be used to gain unauthorized access to networking and server hardware. IF SNMP is not used, be sure to disable the service locally on the ESXi server. Also, be sure that the SNMP destination addresses are valid, and do not contain extraneous destinations.

Implications of Adding an ESXi Host to a Windows Domain

First, just a quick note on the legalities of adding ESXi hosts to the domain from a licensing perspective. If you license Windows per user, there is no cost to add your ESXi servers to the domain. On the other hand, if you license your domain per connected device, each ESXi server that you add to the domain will need a Windows Client Access License (CAL) to be legal. The reason is that each device that will access a Microsoft server (in this case, a domain controller for authentication) requires a CAL.

Now on to the security implications of adding your ESXi server to the domain. Adding it to the domain will automatically grant the AD group "ESX Admins" full administrative access to the server. Note that the group must be spelled that way, and even if the group is removed from the host, it will automatically come back the next time a host is rebooted. Once the AD group is in place (you or an ADS admin must manually create it), simply add any desired admins to the group and they will thereby gain administrative access to all of the ESXi servers that have joined the domain. You can view this by looking at the Permissions tab when logged directly into the host. You'll see the group listed as *<Domain>*\esx^admins and you'll note that the group has Administrator permissions for the server. Note that it is also possible to add other users and groups from the domain on this Permissions tab as well and you can give them any level of permissions desired. This topic is covered more fully in the ESXi installation chapter, but a quick review here is useful as it may impact authentication from the various automation tools.

Adding the ESXi Host to an AD Domain

By default, the only account that is defined locally is the root account. Three roles are provided to grant access to the ESXi host through the vSphere Client: Administrator, Read-Only, and No Access. While these may be used in a small environment, these roles are local and may not be uniform across all ESXi hosts, resulting in unequal access.

When planning for security, it is beneficial to consider the introduction of AD as a fundamental asset for users and groups. Adding each ESXi host to Active Directory allows the administrator to leverage AD users and groups to grant access based on requirements. Remember, the permissions that a user requires to perform his or her job may differ greatly from the permissions they want to have in vCenter.

If desired, the ESXi host can be added to a local AD domain. This can be used to leverage AD users and groups when providing permissions to this local ESXi host. Navigate to the Configuration tab, and select Authentication Services below Software.

In Figure 5.70, the ESXi host is currently configured to use local authentication, and has no domain membership. This means that users must have a local account in order to log in to the host, regardless of the interface chosen.

If required, you can use the Import Certificate link to add a certificate that will be used to verify the identity of the server when communicating with other hosts.

As shown in Figure 5.71, importing a certificate from either an enterprise CA or a third-party provider allows communication to be encrypted to and from this ESXi server. This is very common in the IT industry; communications are routinely secured with certificates to verify both sender and receiver in the exchange.

To add an enterprise or third-party certificate:

1. Copy the certificate locally to the ESXi server.

2. Using the vSphere Client, log in to the ESXi host.

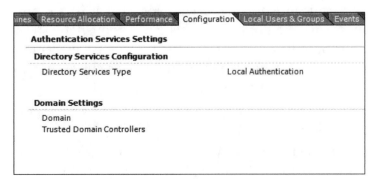

Figure 5.70
Viewing the current authentication.

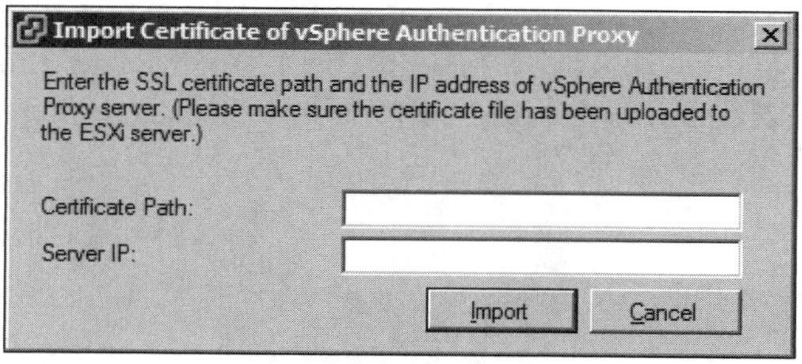

Figure 5.71
Importing a server certificate.

3. From the Configuration tab, select Authentication Services.

4. In the upper-right corner, select Import Certificate.

5. Input the file path to the local certificate and the IP address of the CA in use.

6. Select Import.

The ESXi host may be added to the domain by using the Properties link.

In Figure 5.72, the ESXi host can be added to the domain using the vSphere Client. This provides the administrator with the ability to leverage user and group accounts

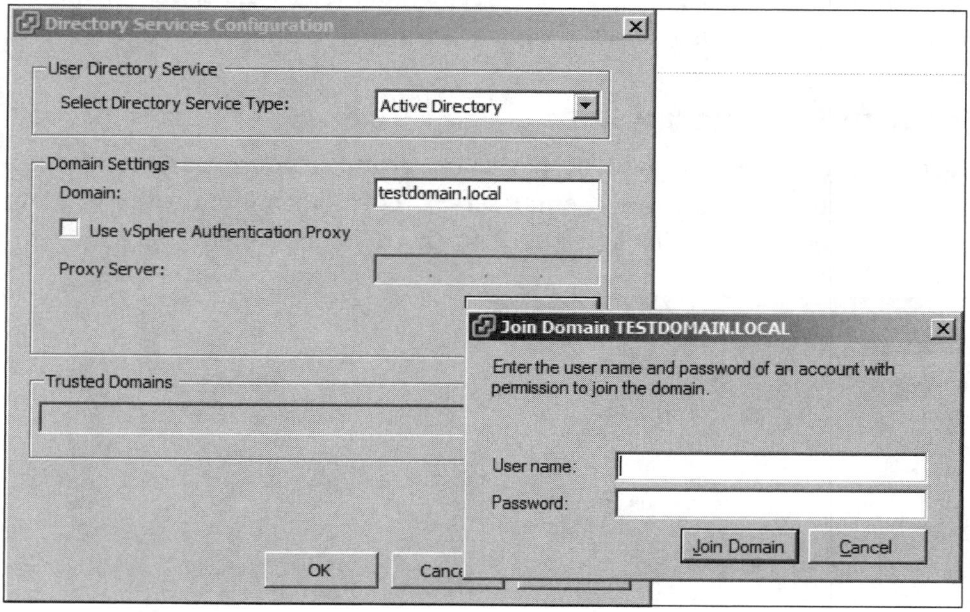

Figure 5.72
Adding the ESXi host to the domain.

that already exist within the local AD to provide access to the ESXi host. Note that the vSphere Authentication Proxy can also be used to join the ESXi host to the domain; the vSphere Authentication proxy will be referred to as the CAM (vSphere Authentication Proxy) server.

To add the ESXi host to AD:

1. Using the vSphere Client, log in to the ESXi host.

2. Select the Configuration tab.

3. Click on the Authentication Services link under Software.

4. In the upper-right corner, select the Properties link.

5. In the Directory Services Configuration pop-up window, change the Directory Services type from Local Authentication to Active Directory.

6. Provide the domain name and click Join Domain.

7. When prompted, provide the necessary domain credentials.

8. If successful, the host will be joined to the domain and the status page will indicate that the host is now using Active Directory as its authentication mechanism, and the domain will be listed under Domain Settings.

As displayed in Figure 5.73, note that after successfully joining the domain, in the Directory Services Configuration section, Active Directory is listed as the configured directory for authentication queries. Also, under Domain Settings, the joined domain is listed.

vCenter Security Considerations

As a best practice, permissions should be based on group accounts defined within AD, rather than local accounts on the vCenter server. Local accounts on the vCenter server create an unnecessary security hole that can be easily exploited.

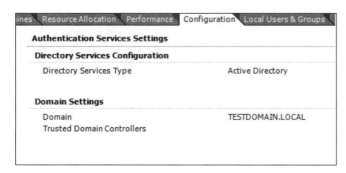

Figure 5.73
Successfully joining the domain.

Similarly, efforts should be made to minimize the number of locally defined accounts on the vCenter server.

When providing access to individual ESXi servers, we can leverage Active Directory as we did with vCenter to provide users and group accounts that can be assigned local access based on business requirements.

As a general rule, access to the root account should be minimized as the root account has administrative access to the ESXi host through SSH clients such as Putty, and the DCUI.

In many situations, you may find yourself managing an environment in which you had no input as to the design, and no role in the implementation. This can be an intimidating thought without any documentation as to the current configuration. If this sounds familiar, you can use the vSphere CLI command `get-vipermission -entity (get-inventory)` to display a summary of current permissions information.

If desired, this same information can be exported in the "csv" format using the `get-vipermission -entity (get-inventory) | export-csv "C:\permissions.csv"` command.

Accountability via User Accounts

In most situations, it is preferable to leverage the AD users and groups functionality through vCenter, rather than providing local accounts for users and administrators. However, there may be a need for local accounts in a small environment where vCenter is not a part of the environment, and local administration of the ESXi host is required.

Consider using individual accounts for administrators rather than providing access to multiple administrators through the root account. It is much easier to determine responsibility for an act when the logs specify exactly who was logged in and who was not.

Consider creating a minimum password length that can be used when logging in to the ESXi host. In its default configuration, ESXi does not mandate a minimum password length. This can be changed using a text editor, such as Notepad, to open the /etc/pam.d/passwd file and modify this line:

```
Password  requisite  /lib/security/$ISA/pam_passwdqc.so  retry=N
min=N0, N1, N2, N3, N4
```

Where:

N = The number of times to allow a user to specify a password of the correct length.

N1 = The number of characters in the password that includes characters from two separate classes.

N2 = The number of words in a passphrase that is used instead of a password. A minimum of 3 words is allowed.

N3 = The number of characters in the password that includes characters from three separate classes.

N4 = The number of characters in the password that includes characters from four separate classes.

New Firewall

In previous releases of the ESXi platform, the ESXi host firewall was based on the Linux iptables concept. In ESXi 5, that has been changed and the current firewall is based upon a set of rules called rulesets that are defined in the service.xml file, located in the /etc/vmware/firewall folder. A ruleset is comprised of a ruleset name, a port number, a direction of traffic, a protocol, and the action for this traffic. If you configure a custom ruleset, you must refresh the firewall to make the new ruleset active. Note that the firewall is designed to block all traffic except "management traffic."

The services that are enabled by default are:

- I/O Redirector (AD)
- Network Login
- NTP Daemon
- vpxa (vCenter Agent)
- Local Security Authentication Service (AD)
- ESXi Shell
- Lbtd (Load Balanced Teaming Daemon)
- SSH
- Direct Console (DCUI)
- CIM Server

The incoming connections permitted by default are:

- CIM SLP (Service Locator Protocol)
- vSphere Client
- SSH Server
- vMotion

- SNMP Server
- CIM Secure Server
- DHCP Client
- Fault Tolerance
- CIM Server
- vSphere Web Access
- DNS Client
- NFC (Network File Copy)

The outgoing connections permitted by default are:

- HBR (Host Based Replication)
- vMotion
- NFC
- DHCP Client
- Fault Tolerance
- CIMSLP
- DNS Client
- VMware vCenter Agent

When considering the ESXi host itself, it is a best practice to only enable those services that are required for a business purpose, and leave all others in a disabled state. Keep in mind also that since ESXi has no built-in firewall, it is a good idea to isolate management traffic related to the ESXi host from other types of network traffic, and also deploy firewalls as appropriate to isolate server-to-server communication.

Figure 5.74 is a sample from the default service.xml file. At the top, there is a line "Known and blessed services." This defines the basic services, their status, the ports that they use, and whether the port is open or closed. For example, you will notice that the first two entries concern the SSH service. The first rule defines the status of inbound traffic:

1. Inbound
2. Using the TCP protocol
3. Using the destination port 22

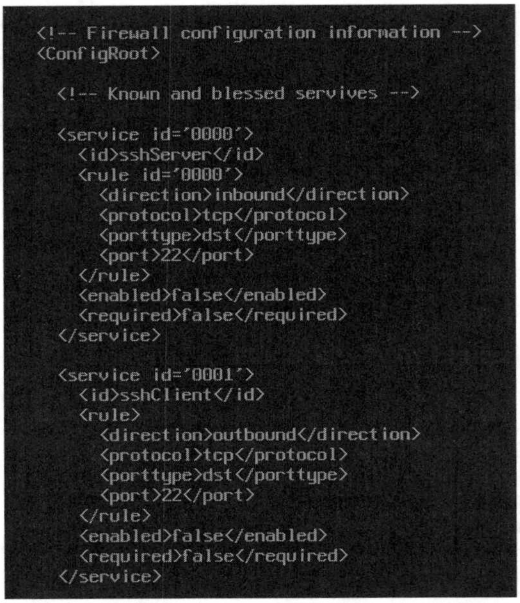

```
<!-- Firewall configuration information -->
<ConfigRoot>

  <!-- Known and blessed servives -->

  <service id='0000'>
    <id>sshServer</id>
    <rule id='0000'>
      <direction>inbound</direction>
      <protocol>tcp</protocol>
      <porttype>dst</porttype>
      <port>22</port>
    </rule>
    <enabled>false</enabled>
    <required>false</required>
  </service>

  <service id='0001'>
    <id>sshClient</id>
    <rule>
      <direction>outbound</direction>
      <protocol>tcp</protocol>
      <porttype>dst</porttype>
      <port>22</port>
    </rule>
    <enabled>false</enabled>
    <required>false</required>
  </service>
```

Figure 5.74
The service.xml file.

The final two lines define the status of the SSH service: currently it is not enabled and it is not required. This is the default status of the SSH service, and you, as the administrator, must modify this to enable bi-directional traffic for use with SSH clients, such as Putty. Also, notice that there is a ruleset for the SSH traffic that defines each type of traffic: inbound and outbound.

If desired, you can manage the firewall status from the command line. Throughout this book, we have tried to show you how to use the command line as an alternative configuration and management tool for your virtual environment. Management of the firewall is no exception.

To query the status of the firewall, you will use the esxcli network firewall get command to retrieve the current status. Note that in Figure 5.75, the default action is to drop traffic that is not explicitly allowed, and the firewall is enabled and loaded. Next, the esxcli network firewall ruleset list command will list the currently defined rulesets. If you look at the top of the list, you will see the default response to SSH traffic.

You can also create custom firewall rules through the command line. This may be required if you are planning to use a management or monitoring utility that uses a non-standard TCP/UDP port to gather information. To create the new rule, you

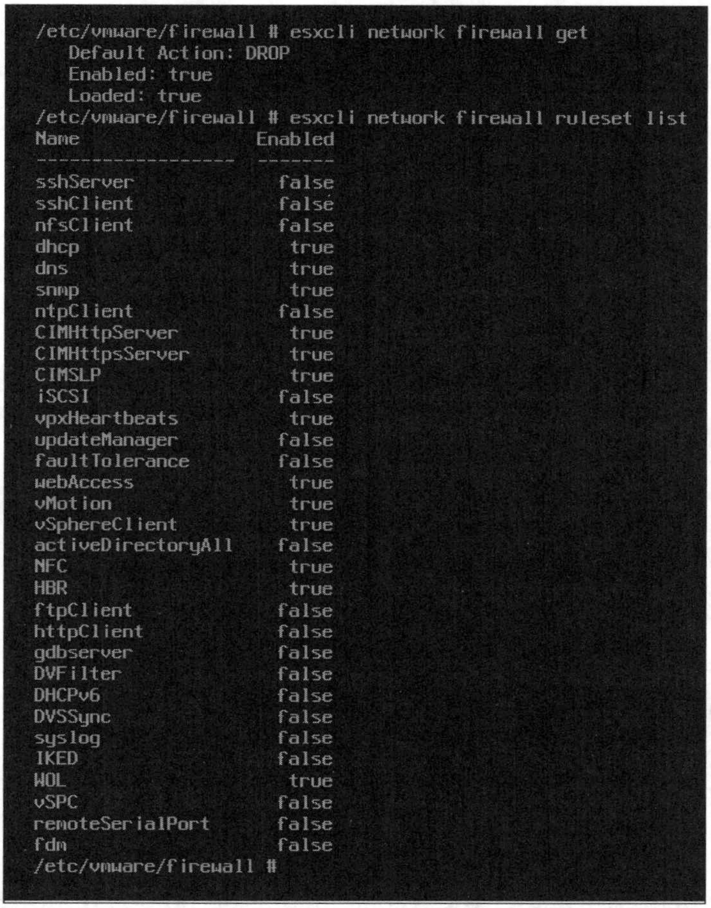

```
/etc/vmware/firewall # esxcli network firewall get
    Default Action: DROP
    Enabled: true
    Loaded: true
/etc/vmware/firewall # esxcli network firewall ruleset list
Name                  Enabled
--------------------  -------
sshServer             false
sshClient             false
nfsClient             false
dhcp                   true
dns                    true
snmp                   true
ntpClient             false
CIMHttpServer          true
CIMHttpsServer         true
CIMSLP                 true
iSCSI                 false
vpxHeartbeats          true
updateManager         false
faultTolerance        false
webAccess              true
vMotion                true
vSphereClient          true
activeDirectoryAll    false
NFC                    true
HBR                    true
ftpClient             false
httpClient            false
gdbserver             false
DVFilter              false
DHCPv6                false
DVSSync               false
syslog                false
IKED                  false
WOL                    true
vSPC                  false
remoteSerialPort      false
fdm                   false
/etc/vmware/firewall #
```

Figure 5.75
Gathering Firewall status through the command line.

should name the rule after the utility, so you will be able to recognize it if you ever desire to remove it at a later time.

To create the new rule, you will create a new .XML file that describes the rule. This file can be created using a text editor. Here is a sample file:

```
<ConfigRoot>
<service id='0100'>
 <id>MonitorApp</id>
 <rule id='0000'>
  <direction>inbound</direction>
  <protocol>tcp</protocol>
  <porttype>dst</porttype>
```

```
<port>1234</port>
 </rule>
   <rule id='0001'>
 <direction>inbound</direction>
 <protocol>tcp</protocol>
 <porttype>src</porttype>
 <port>
  <begin>1235</begin>
  <end>1237</end>
 </port>
 </rule>
<enabled>true</enabled>
<required>true</required>
</service>
```

This text file defines the following parameters for the firewall:

1. The service ID of the service to be used is "0100."

2. The rule name is "MonitorApp."

3. The rule ID is "0000."

4. This rule defines how to handle inbound TCP traffic destined for port 1234.

5. The second rule, rule 0001 defines how to handle inbound TCP traffic from a port range of 1235 to 1237.

6. The line "enabled" defines the service status if the ruleset is applied.

7. Finally, the "required" line defines whether the rule is mandatory and cannot be disabled.

Name the file and save it to the /etc/vmware/firewall folder. Next, we have to refresh the firewall configuration using `esxcli network firewall refresh`. This will cause the kernel to add the new rule to the current list. We can verify the new rule using `esxcli network firewall ruleset list`.

You also have the option to define who can access the new service. `esxcli network firewall ruleset set –allowed-all false –ruleset-id MyRule` will disable all IP access to the new rule. Then, `esxcli network firewall ruleset allowedip add –ip-address-10.0.0.0/16 –ruleset-id Monitor App` will allow the hosts on the 10.0.0.0/16 subnet to access the new rule exclusively.

The firewall can also be configured from the vSphere Client, whether accessing the ESXi host directly or by using vCenter. Using the Configuration tab, select Security

```
Security Profile
  Services
      I/O Redirector (Active Directory Service)
      Network Login Server (Active Directory Service)
      NTP Daemon
      vpxa
      Local Security Authentication Server (Active Directory Service)
      ESXi Shell
      lbtd
      SSH
      Direct Console UI
      CIM Server
  Firewall
  Incoming Connections
      CIM SLP              427 (UDP,TCP)                     All
      vSphere Client       902,443 (TCP)                     All
      SSH Server           22 (TCP)                          All
      vMotion              8000 (TCP)                        All
      SNMP Server          161 (UDP)                         All
      CIM Secure Server    5989 (TCP)                        All
      DHCP Client          68 (UDP)                          All
      Fault Tolerance      8100,8200 (TCP,UDP)               All
      CIM Server           5988 (TCP)                        All
      vSphere Web Access   80 (TCP)                          All
      DNS Client           53 (UDP)                          All
      NFC                  902 (TCP)                         All
  Outgoing Connections
      HBR                  1234,1235,31031,44046 (TCP)       All
      vMotion              8000 (TCP)                        All
      NFC                  902 (TCP)                         All
      DHCP Client          68 (UDP)                          All
      Fault Tolerance      80,8100,8200 (TCP,UDP)            All
      CIM SLP              427 (UDP,TCP)                     All
      DNS Client           53 (UDP)                          All
      VMware vCenter Agent 902 (UDP)                         All
  Lockdown Mode
  When enabled, lockdown mode prevents remote users from logging directly into this host.

      Lockdown Mode:                    Disabled
```

Figure 5.76
The default firewall configuration.

Profile from the Software list. As shown in Figure 5.76, this is the default firewall configuration when viewed through the vSphere Client.

If you click on the Properties link in the upper-right corner of the Services pane, you can view the current status of the services on this ESXi host. Here, you can highlight a service, and, by clicking on the options button, define how this service is to be started and/or stopped. As shown in Figure 5.77, you can:

1. Start the service automatically if any ports are open, and stop the service if ports have been closed. This is the default configuration. In this setting, the service will detect whether the associated port is open, and if so, will try to contact the

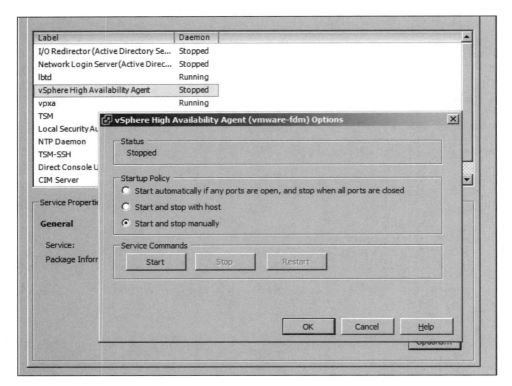

Figure 5.77
Service configuration.

configured server. If a port is closed, that particular service will not contact the
server successfully.

2. Start and stop the service when the ESXi server is started or stopped. As the
host powers on, the services will try to contact the appropriate servers. If the
associated port is closed, the service will continue to try to contact its server,
and if the port is opened at a later time, the service will complete its process.

3. Start and stop the service manually. With this option, the ESXi server does
not evaluate the port status, but instead will retain the service status as
configured by the administrator.

4. Also simply start or stop the service, for example, to test or verify an issue.

Similarly, if you click on the Properties link in the Firewall pane, you can start and
stop the services here are well. As shown in Figure 5.78, if you highlight a service and
click on the Firewall button, you can specify who can access this particular service. In
this graphic, we have defined that only the host with the IP address 192.168.1.225 can

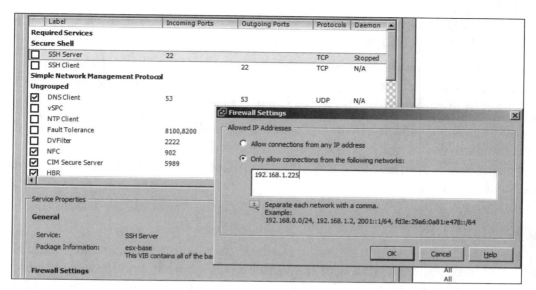

Figure 5.78
Remote access to services.

access this service. Sound familiar? This is the same process that we performed earlier from the command line.

You also have the option to restrict access to an ESXi port to a range of IP addresses, or a specific IP address. In Figure 5.78, if you click on the Properties in the Firewall pane, you can configure what device or devices can access this particular service. Highlight the service and click on Firewall. Select whether to allow connections from any computer or specify particular devices, and click OK.

TROUBLESHOOTING

The task of troubleshooting a virtualized environment involves the examination of standard operating system resources, such as Windows PerfMon, but also includes the necessity to use tools that are designed for specific environments: esxtop for ESX hosts, resxtop for ESXi hosts, performance reporting through vCenter, and SAN-based analysis tools. It can be considered that there is a logical link from the virtual machine through the hardware in the physical host, through the physical network, to the storage device, and the network. Each link in this chain has the potential to cause an issue, so each must be evaluated.

For example, if a virtual machine is experiencing a performance issue, we must examine the operating system's own analysis program to gather relevant information. We then can proceed to vCenter and gather both virtual machine and physical host performance metrics. If necessary, we can also gather metrics from the SAN or the physical network to help resolve the perceived bottleneck.

It is important to understand the data that is available from each of the sources. Remember, we need to see the problem from all perspectives in order to understand the event, and then resolve it in an efficient manner.

Troubleshooting a virtualized environment adds an additional layer of information that must be gathered to fully assess the environment. In addition to the standard information, we must also evaluate how the ESXi host is affected by the issue, or if the ESXi host is causing the issue.

Logging

There are several logging locations that are critical to obtaining an accurate, detailed data set. There are logs associated with the virtual machine itself, and they are located in the VMs folder. Logging can be enabled at the VM level by opening the settings for the VM; selecting VM options; and in the Advanced options, selecting Enable Logging. This is the first tier of logs that provide a complete perspective of the environment.

At this point it bears stating that application logs can be very beneficial when analyzing a virtual machine or when troubleshooting a performance or application issue.

Log Types and Function

The ESXi host has three available logs:

- **vpxa.** This log will exist only if this ESXi host is joined to a vCenter instance. The vpxa log contains data generated by the local vCenter Agent, and is stored in the /var/logs/vmware folder. The default log rotation and maximum log file size can be modified by editing the /etc/opt/vmware/vpxa/vpxa.log file with a text editor.

- **hostd.** These files are generated by the local agent responsible for managing the ESXi host and its VMs. These logs are located in the /var/log/vmware folder. To modify the default log settings for the hostd logs, edit the /etc/vmware/hostd/config.xml file.

- **Messages.** This log contains information generated by the vmkernel and the hostd service. These logs are stored in the /var/log/ "VM name."

Note that each of these files has a maximum size of 5MB and a default log rotation of 10, meaning that a maximum of 10 logs will be retained.

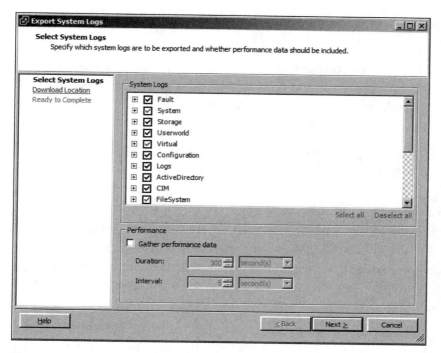

Figure 5.79
Gathering host-based logs.

As shown in Figure 5.79, these logs can be retrieved using the vSphere Client.

To retrieve the logs for an ESXi host:

1. Log in using the vSphere Client.

2. Navigate to the Home > Administration > System Logs path.

3. Click on the Export System Logs link to display the Export System Logs wizard.

An administrator has the option to retrieve all the log content, or to gather only specific log data by selecting or deselecting each category of data. Note that you can also retrieve performance data from the ESXi host as well by:

1. Logging in to the ESXi server using the vSphere client

2. Highlighting the ESXi server

3. Using the Home > Administration > Logs path.

As an alternative, you can create a vCenter log bundle that gathers the local vCenter log files and creates a corresponding .zip file that can be stored in a user-defined location. The path on the vCenter server is Start > Programs > VMware > Generate vCenter Server log bundle. You can also create the log bundle by running the `vm-support` script that is located in the /usr/bin folder.

The vCenter 5 edition of vCenter includes two additional utilities that can assist in the troubleshooting process. The first, the VMware ESXi Dump Collector, can be installed either on a stand-alone physical host or on a vCenter, and provides a centralized collector for core dump information from network-connected ESXi hosts.

The second, the VMware Syslog Collector provides the ability to configure a centralized location for system logs retrieved from connected physical ESXi hosts.

Log Volatility—How to Keep What's Important

The ESXi host utilizes log rotation. This means that when a log reaches 1MB in size, it is archived, and a new log is created. Ultimately, log file 8 is overwritten by log file 7, so the data stored in log 8 is lost. We can save the data in log file 8 by configuring the Syslog service to send the log file to a centralized Syslog server before it is overwritten.

This is configured by highlighting the ESXi host, selecting the Configuration tab, and choosing the Advanced Settings option below Software. The entry that will need to be modified is inside the Syslog link. Using Syslog.RemoteHostname, define the location of the desired Syslog server. If there is no path defined, no data will be forwarded.

If you want to change the default location for the Syslog service to log the messages, this can be configured by highlighting the ESXi host, selecting the Configuration tab, and choosing the Advanced Settings option below Software. The entry that will need to be modified is inside the Syslog link. Using Syslog.LocalDatastorePath, define the location of the desired Syslog server. If no path is defined, the default location is /var/log/messages.

This can also be configured through the command line. Open the/etc/vmware/init/init.d/07.logger file and modify the following line:

```
syslogd - I -s 50000 -b 10 -S -L -O //vmfs/volumes/logfolder/ESXi/messages
```

where

- -s is the maximum file size before the log is rotated
- -b is the number of logs to maintain before rotating
- -S indicates a smaller log output
- -L means to log the files on a local datastore and through the network
- -O is the local destination folder.

The vSphere 5 vCenter Dump Collector

One of the new troubleshooting utilities that is available on the vCenter distribution media is the ESXi Dump Collector. The ESXi Dump Collector can be used to define a central location used to store kernel core dumps that may occur as a result of a hardware failure within the deployment.

To install the Syslog Collector:

1. Open the vCenter distribution media
2. Using the Autorun option, click on VMware Dump Collector
3. Select the language
4. Accept the EULA
5. Define the installation and log repository folders, and specify the maximum size of the dump repository
6. Specify whether this will be a stand-alone installation or if this will be installed on the vCenter server
7. Define the port to be used for the collector
8. Input a network identity for the dump collector
9. Click Install

As shown in Figure 5.80, in order to install the ESXi Dump Collector, highlight the ESXi Dump Collector link and select Install.

At this point, the size of the Dump Collector repository can be defined as well.

This step in the installation wizard is depicted in Figure 5.81.

The administrator can decide whether to install the Dump Collector to a stand-alone computer or to install it locally on the vCenter server. If the stand-alone computer option is selected, the port for Dump Collection can be specified. Note that the default port is 6500.

If the preferred location for the Dump Collector is the vCenter server, the FQDN or IP address of the vCenter server and the administrative credentials must be provided as well. Note that the default port used by the Dump Collector is also specified if the installation will be performed on a vCenter instance.

When the installation has completed, the Dump Collector must be registered with a vCenter instance through the following command:

```
netdumper-register
```

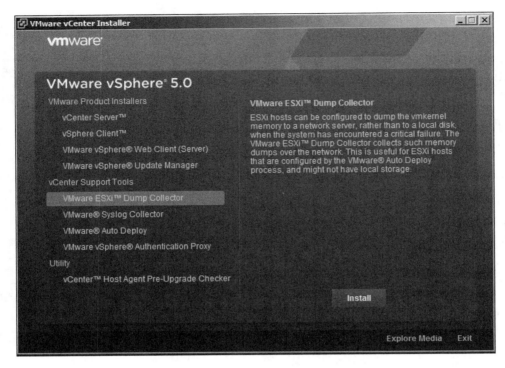

Figure 5.80
Installing the ESXi Dump Collector.

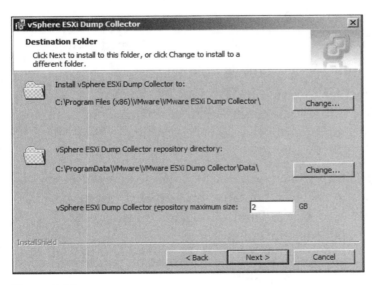

Figure 5.81
Defining the location for the Dump Collector installation files and the Dump Collector repository.

ESXi Syslog Collector

Also on the vCenter distribution media is the ESXi Syslog Collector. This addition to the vCenter installation provides a centralized collection point for Syslog content from multiple ESXi hosts on the network.

To install the Syslog Collector:

1. Open the vCenter distribution media
2. Using the Autorun option, click on VMware Syslog Collector
3. Choose the language
4. Accept the EULA
5. Define the installation and log repository folders, the maximum size of each before rotation, and the number of rotations to keep
6. Specify whether this will be a stand-alone installation or if this will be installed on the vCenter server
7. Define the ports to be used by the collector
8. Input a name for the Syslog server on the network
9. Click Install

In Figure 5.82, you can define the installation folder and default logging repository folder. Here you also specify the logging parameters, such as how large each file is

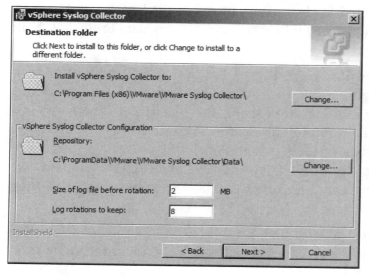

Figure 5.82
Defining locations and logging parameters for the Syslog Collector.

allowed to grow before archiving it and starting a new log, and how many log files to maintain.

As part of the installation, the administrator has the option to change the location for the log folder, and also specify the log size and the log rotation policy.

Like the Dump Collector, the administrator can install this application on a stand-alone device or on the vCenter server itself. This is an option that can reduce the activity on the vCenter server by off-loading the process of log collection to a secondary computer.

After the installation has completed, we need to tell each ESXi server where to send the log information. By default, an ESXi 5 host will write the logging information to a local scratch partition. However, in this case we have installed the Syslog Collector to our vCenter server to provide a centralized location where we can retrieve and review the logs. We can configure the ESXi server to send its logging data to the vCenter server in one of two ways:

The first, is through the vSphere Client:

1. Log in to the ESXi server using the vSphere Client

2. Select the Configuration tab

3. Under the Software Options, select Advanced Options

4. Click on Syslog and highlight the "global" entry

As shown in Figure 5.83, the central log host IP is entered in the Syslog.global.logHost field. In this example, we have configured this host to send its log data to the host with the IP address 192.168.1.140.

We can also use the command line to configure the Syslog Collector from each ESXi server. As shown in Figure 5.84, we can access Technical Support Mode (TSM) and verify the existing configuration using the `esxcli system syslog config get` command. In this example, the default maximum log size of 1024K or 1MB, and the default number of logs to maintain locally is 8. We then enter `esxcli system syslog config set --loghost=192.168.1.140`. Finally, we use `esxcli system syslog reload` to cause the ESXi server to refresh its Syslog configuration.

This will configure the ESXi host to use the host at 192.168.1.140 as its default log server. Keep in mind that this is the same process as using the Security Profile from the vSphere Client.

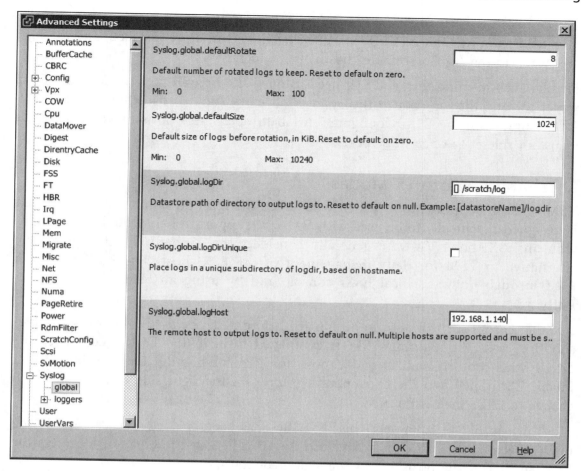

Figure 5.83
GUI configuration of the Syslog Collector.

```
/etc/vmware/firewall # esxcli system syslog config get
    Default Rotation Size: 1024
    Default Rotations: 8
    Log Output: /scratch/log
    Log To Unique Subdirectory: false
    Remote Host: <none>
/etc/vmware/firewall # esxcli system syslog config set --loghost=192.168.1.140
/etc/vmware/firewall # esxcli system syslog config get
    Default Rotation Size: 1024
    Default Rotations: 8
    Log Output: /scratch/log
    Log To Unique Subdirectory: false
    Remote Host: 192.168.1.140
/etc/vmware/firewall # esxcli system syslog reload
/etc/vmware/firewall #
```

Figure 5.84
Command line configuration of the Syslog destination.

This process is exclusively for the Windows-based vCenter. If you are using the vCenter Server Appliance (VCSA), the Syslog Collector is pre-installed, and the logs are stored in the /var/log/remote/"hostname" folder.

Finally, keep in mind that you will need to open the firewall port to allow the ESXi server to send the log data to the Syslog Collector. You can use either the Security Profile link from the ESXi Configuration tab to open these ports or you can create a custom ruleset to open these ports.

Local and Remote TS Modes

TSM or Tech Support Mode has been renamed the ESXi Shell and is an option that is designed specifically to be used with VMware support to help troubleshoot issues with an ESXi host. VMware generally considers the vSphere Client a preferable alternative to TSM for daily management of the ESXi host. The ESXi Shell can used through both the local ESXi console and by using an SSH Client, such as Putty.

In either case, TSM will need to be enabled before it can be used to perform troubleshooting tasks. Configuring TSM is completed through the DCUI. Log in to the DCUI with root credentials and choose the Troubleshooting Options link. Select Enable ESXi Shell and the corresponding entry on the right side of the screen will change to ESXi Shell is Enabled.

As shown in Figure 5.85, once the ESXi Shell has been enabled, you can exit to the main screen for the ESXi host, and use the ALT-F1 key combination to access the ESXi Shell. You will be asked for the root credentials.

Note in Figure 5.86 that using the Alt-F1 key sequence to log in to the ESXi Shell requires root-level credentials.

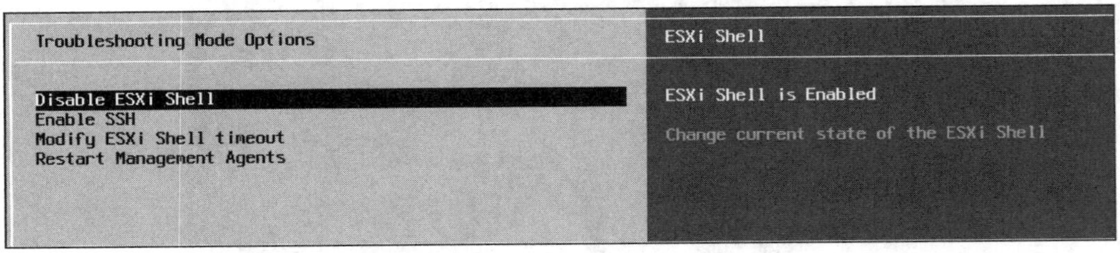

```
Troubleshooting Mode Options          ESXi Shell

Disable ESXi Shell                    ESXi Shell is Enabled
Enable SSH
Modify ESXi Shell timeout             Change current state of the ESXi Shell
Restart Management Agents
```

Figure 5.85
Enabling the ESXi Shell.

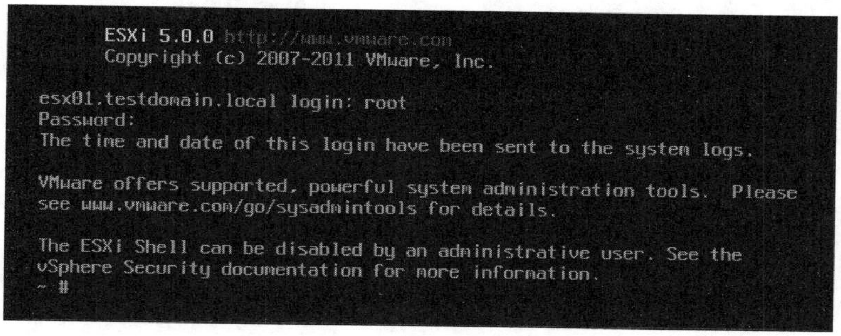

Figure 5.86
Logging in to ESXi Shell.

Remember that although logging in to ESXi Shell can assist in troubleshooting and resolving issues, it is recommended that this utility be used only in conjunction with VMware Technical Support.

SUMMARY

In this chapter we discussed some of the changes to the ESXi 5 platform as compared to the previous releases of ESX/ESXi. We found that ESXi allows us to install the hypervisor entirely in system using Auto Deploy, and that we can now deploy servers with no internal disks. We have looked at the basic configuration of an ESXi server, and how to configure using both the vSphere Client and the new Web Client. We also looked at how to configure the firewall, both through the command line and through the GUI. In the next chapter, we will look at installing vCenter 5, and how it differs from legacy versions.

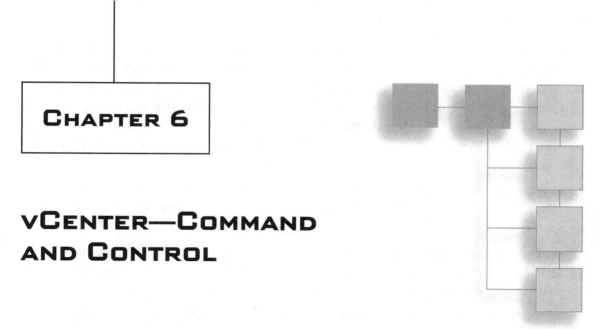

CHAPTER 6

vCENTER—COMMAND AND CONTROL

In previous chapters, we have examined the installation of the ESXi and vCenter servers, the planning of the environment, the networking options that are available when configuring client access for your virtual machines, and we found that there are many ways to automate many of the day-to-day processes involved in managing a virtual environment. In this chapter, we will discuss using vCenter to manage and maintain the virtual environment.

Now that we have a vSphere 5 ESXi host, we need a reliable, easy interface that we can use to manage the host. There are several methods that can be used to manage an ESXi host: directly using the vSphere Client, the Web Client, the vSphere CLI, the vMA, or through vCenter. Managing through the vSphere Client or the vSphere CLI is more of a one-on-one management platform: one client to one ESXi host. While this may be a desirable or acceptable option in many small environments, it does not scale very well if there are a large number of deployed hosts. Additionally, if a host is managed directly through the vSphere host, the enterprise-level features such as vMotion, Storage vMotion, clustering, and access to cloning and templates are all exclusive to vCenter.

PLANNING

When planning the virtualized environment, we first need to determine the number of vCenter instances that will be required to adequately manage the environment. In ESX 3.x, the then-named Virtual Center 2.5 could support a maximum of 200 physical ESX or ESXi servers, and a maximum of 2,000 virtual machines. vSphere 4.0 increased the scalability of vCenter by supporting a maximum of 200 32-bit ESX or

ESXi hosts, 2,000 32-bit powered-on virtual machines, and 3,000 32-bit virtual machines registered in vCenter. If the ESX or ESXi hosts are based on a 64-bit architecture, vCenter supports 300 hosts, 3,000 powered-on virtual machines, and a total of 4,500 64-bit virtual machines registered in a vCenter instance. vSphere 4.1 expanded the host and virtual machines maximums to 1,000 hosts per vCenter instance, 10,000 powered-on virtual machines, and a maximum of 15,000 registered virtual machines.

First, we need to consider: Do we plan to exceed the supported maximums? If so, we may need to plan for more than one vCenter instance, simply based on supported maximums.

Secondly, are the vCenter installations designed to be located in geographically dispersed locations? Perhaps in redundant datacenters located in different time zones to provide more timely support for users and administrators?

If the plan calls for multiple vCenter instances, Linked Mode can provide a single management interface that can display up to 10 different vCenter locations in the same GUI and also provide single sign-on capabilities. Linked Mode can support up to 3,000 physical ESXI hosts, 30,000 simultaneously powered-on virtual machines, and a total of 50,000 registered virtual machines. That provides a high degree of scalability that can meet many enterprise-level demands.

As we will see in this chapter, most of those support maximums have remained in their values from vSphere 4.1, and so provide a high amount of scalability for enterprise deployments. We will also find in Chapter 9 that the capabilities of individual virtual machines has greatly increased from a CPU and memory perspective, and this means that workloads with higher levels of transactions can now be virtualized.

Hardware and Software Requirements

It makes sense that we need to plan the hardware for our ESXi host very accurately if we want to derive the highest levels of performance and scalability. We must decide how many virtual machines will be in the inventory of this ESXi host, and what virtualization components we want to include in this new server. In this section, we will look at the basic hardware and software provisioning that we will need.

Windows-Based

The hardware requirements for the Windows-based version of vCenter are shown in Table 6.1.

The supported operating systems for vCenter 5 are shown in Table 6.2.

Table 6.1   Hardware Requirements

CPU	One Dual-Core 64-bit 2GHz or higher processor. There is no support for any processors based on the Itanium architecture.
RAM	4GB minimum. The Virtual Center Management WebServices requires between 512MB and 4.4GB of RAM, depending on the number of objects in the vCenter inventory.
Disk	4GB. This value will increase if the SQL Server 2008 Express database is used as the database. Note that the disk space required for the vCenter logs is 450MB greater than previous versions.
Network	At least one gigabit physical network adapter is recommended.

Table 6.2   Supported Operating Systems

Operating System	Revision
Microsoft Windows Server 2003	64-bit Microsoft Windows Server 2003 SP2
64-bit Microsoft Windows Server 2003	R2 SP2
Microsoft Windows Server 2008	64-bit Microsoft Windows Server 2008 SP2
64-bit Microsoft Windows Server 2008	R2 SP1

Linux-Based VA

New to vSphere 5 is the addition of the vCenter server appliance. This option allows this appliance to be deployed on a physical ESXi host and can be used to manage the environment. The appliance requires between 7GB and 80GB of free disk space.

The amount of RAM required depends of the number of objects in the vCenter inventory, shown in Table 6.3.

Table 6.3   RAM Requirements

Hosts	Virtual Machines	RAM Required
<100	<1000	8GB
100–400	1000–4000	12GB
>400	>4000	16GB

Table 6.4 vSphere Client Minimum Requirements

CPU	1 500MHz or higher minimum, 1GHz or higher is preferred
RAM	1GB
Network	1GB physical network adapter is preferred

Table 6.5 Supported Operating Systems for vSphere Client

Operating System	Version
Microsoft Windows XP Professional	32-bit Microsoft Windows XP SP3
	64-bit Microsoft Windows XP SP2
Microsoft Windows Server 2003	32- and 64-bit Microsoft Windows Server 2003 SP2
	32- and 64-bit Microsoft Windows Server 2003 R2 SP2
Microsoft Windows Vista	32- and 64-bit Microsoft Windows Vista SP2
Microsoft Windows 7	32- and 64-bit Microsoft Windows 7 SP1
Microsoft Windows Server 2008	32- and 64-bit Microsoft Windows Server 2008 SP2
	32- and 64-bit Microsoft Windows Server 2008 R2 SP1

The vSphere Client minimum requirements are shown in Table 6.4.

The supported operating systems for the vSphere Client are shown in Table 6.5.

The vSphere Client requires 1.5GB of free disk space. These space requirements include the space necessary for the installation of the .NET 2.0 SP2, .NET 3.0 SP2, .NET 3.5 SP1, and the Microsoft Visual J## packages. As a best practice, it is recommended that you uninstall any existing Visual J## components from any devices where the vSphere Client will be installed. This is to reduce the possibility of legacy components conflicting with newly installed packages.

If this is a new installation, and these components are not currently installed, you will require 400MB of free space available on the drive that contains the %temp% folder.

If these components are already installed, the installation requires 300MB of free space on the physical drive that hosts the %temp% folder. The vSphere Client package itself requires 450MB for the installation.

To Be or Not to Be...a VM

When planning to deploy vCenter, the concept of survivability must be addressed. The vCenter instance will become a major management interface for the virtualized environment, so continued accessibility of the application must be ensured. There are basically four methods that can be considered to address the potential loss of vCenter:

- Create a Microsoft Cluster. Since vCenter can be installed on a Microsoft Server ×64 edition, the possibility exists that Microsoft Clustering can be leveraged to provide a level of redundancy. In the case of a failure on the primary node, the clustering service would failover the shared resources, and enable an administrator to verify the ODBC connection and restart vCenter from the passive cluster node. Note that in this option the vCenter database becomes a single point of failure.

- Use the vCenter server Heartbeat option. The vCenter server Heartbeat is an option that can be licensed from VMware and can provide a redundant node hosting a vCenter instance. The advantage offered by the server Heartbeat is that when the package is licensed, the administrator has the option to protect the vCenter instance, the SQL database, or both. Should the option be to protect both vCenter and the database, the primary instance synchronously copies all incoming updates to the primary database to the secondary so both copies are in sync. In this option, the server Heartbeat provides support for long-distance mirroring. Also, protecting both vCenter and the database removes the single point of failure discussed in the Microsoft Cluster option.

- Some administrators may choose to simply use two hardware devices and perform two installations of vCenter. One will be used in production; the second remains in a powered-off state until the primary device experiences a failure. The second instance is then powered on, accesses the database, and resumes operation with a minimum of downtime. Again, is this scenario, the database becomes a single point of failure.

- A fourth valid option is to virtualize vCenter and place it within an HA cluster. This way, if the physical server that is hosting the vCenter VM fails, HA can restart the VM on another physical host. If this option is chosen, it is a good idea to configure the vCenter with a high restart priority, so it will be one of the VMs that are started first. One option here is to create reservations for required resources so that if and when physical resources begin to deplete, we can guarantee sufficient resources to maintain management capabilities, even though peer VMs may be impacted.

A major consideration when deciding to deploy vCenter on a physical device is that the vCenter application will not need to contend for resources such as CPU and RAM as it would if it were virtualized.

The vCenter Database

In order for vCenter to perform its designed functions, it must have a way to collect information about the environment, and use that information to manage each of the physical devices. This information is in the form of FQDN, IP addresses, installed devices, etc.

In VMware, this collection and management of devices is accomplished through the use of a database to store all the environmental characteristics. VMware provides support for databases through several different vendors. The currently supported database options are shown in Table 6.6.

For exact considerations for each of the different databases, refer to Chapter 3 for specifics detailing processes to ensure compatibility.

It is important to note at this point that the vCenter server service is completely dependent on the presence of the associated database. If the vCenter server service loses contact with the database, the service will stop. This means that if you are currently in a vCenter session, the session will freeze, and may require the use of Task Manager to close the process.

If the service has stopped and someone tries to log in, the login attempt will fail as there is no service to perform the authentication. The typical scenario here is the

Table 6.6 Currently Supported Database Options

Vendor	Revisions
IBM	DB2 9.5
IBM	DB2 9.7
Microsoft SQL Server	SQL Server Express 2008 R2
Microsoft SQL Server	SQL Server 2005 32 and 64-bit SP3
Microsoft SQL Server	SQL Server 2008 32 and 64-bit SP1
Microsoft SQL Server	SQL Server 2008 R2
Oracle	10g R2
Oracle	11g

administrator will open the services snap-in on the vCenter server and try to start the vCenter server service. If the database is unavailable, the service will not start, and will time out.

How Do I Size the Database?

It is necessary to ensure that the database is large enough to contain all the information relative to the physical ESXi hosts, the VMs, the virtual infrastructure, and performance data that may be accrued on a daily basis. There are two methods that can be used to determine the database requirements:

The first is to use the VMware vCenter Server 5 Database Sizing Calculator for Microsoft SQL Server. This is a free download from VMware that allows an administrator to determine the expected quantities of physical hosts, clusters, virtual machines, resource pools, datacenters, datastores, and root folders. Then the amounts of resources are estimated, and the Sizing Calculator will estimate the required database size.

In Figure 6.1, estimated values for the individual objects in the proposed environment have been entered, and the estimated database requirements have been displayed, depending on the log level chosen.

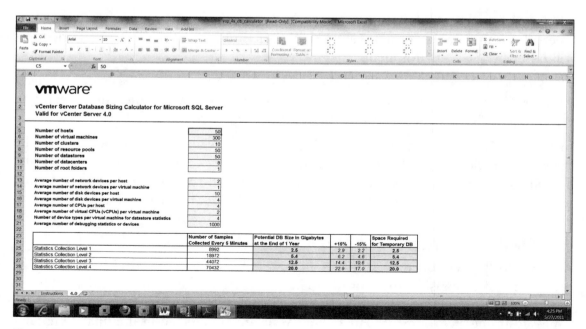

Figure 6.1
The Database Sizing Calculator for SQL Server.

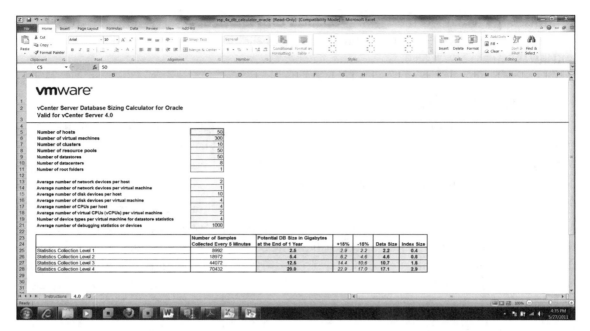

Figure 6.2
The Database Sizing Calculator for Oracle.

While this is a very useful tool, it is entirely dependent on the accuracy of the values entered. Administrators must be very careful to enter the quantities he or she anticipates will be in the final environment.

The second method is to use the VMware vCenter Server 4.× Database Sizing Calculator for Oracle. This free download from VMware provides parallel functionality to the Database Sizing Calculator for Microsoft SQL Server.

In Figure 6.2, the vCenter Server 4.× Database Sizing Calculator for Oracle provides the same functionality as the calculator for SQL Server. As was the case for the Database Sizing Calculator for SQL, the administrator must determine the proposed environment and enter the values in order to accurately size the new database.

How Many vCenter Servers?

As previously mentioned, vCenter is highly scalable, and this decision should be made only after considerable consultation with management and administrators to determine the scope of the project. For example, how many ESXi hosts will be deployed in the environment? How many VMs are anticipated in the final configuration? Are there any plans to implement desktop virtualization? If so, these hosts and VMs must be taken into account as well. Are there any plans to create redundant datacenters for recovery and availability, or are there plans for remote datacenters, perhaps in another time zone or country?

Equally important is the number of ESXi hosts and VMs that are anticipated in the environment over the next 18–24 months. In many situations, virtualization projects are designed and deployed using current utilization, without regard for any future plans for the organization.

Linked Mode

The introduction of Linked Mode with vSphere 4.0 provided the administrator who had the task of managing multiple vCenter instances the opportunity to logically associate the vCenter instances and view all instances from within a single vSphere Client session. Additionally, this process also allows single sign-on authentication, providing the same level of access to each vCenter instance. However, creating a Linked Mode environment does not grant the option to perform vMotion processes between the vCenter instances, or to deploy from template or clone a VM between the instances.

When the Linked Mode is created, either during the installation of vCenter or by using the vCenter Linked Mode Configuration wizard, an ADAM instance is created between the instances. This allows a search to be performed in parallel across all vCenter databases, returning a comprehensive set of search results.

Information relative to licensing, roles, and service status is shared by each of the vCenter servers. This process also requires that the administrator that configures Linked Mode must also have Domain User privileges, and Administrator privileges on both vCenter servers.

Why Implement Multiple vCenters?

The decision to implement multiple vCenter instances can be based on several factors; some are related to hardware or environmental considerations, and others may be related to political pressure. See Table 6.7.

If we follow these maximums, multiple vCenter installations would be required if we plan to exceed 1,000 hosts or 10,000 powered-on VMs. In most deployments, however, the real quantities will be much lower, although there are locations in which there are currently more objects in an environment than would be supported in a single vCenter instance. Also, the decision to deploy additional vCenter instances may be more directly affected by the physical location of datacenters. For example, a company may have regional datacenters in Chicago, Shanghai, Amsterdam, and Johannesburg—none of which exceed the maximums individually. Certainly, the

Table 6.7   vCenter 5 Configuration Maximums Compared with vCenter 4.1

vCenter Server Scalability	vSphere 4	vSphere 5
Maximum hosts per vCenter instance	1000	1000
Maximum number of powered-on VMs	10000	10000
Total number of VMs per vCenter instance	15000	15000
Maximum number of linked vCenter servers	10	10
Maximum number of hosts in Linked Mode	3000	3000
Maximum powered-on VMs in Linked Mode	30000	30000
Total VMs in Linked Mode	50000	50000
Maximum concurrent vSphere client connection	100	100
Maximum number of ESXi hosts per datacenter	400	500

distances alone would prove a design issue simply based on the network bandwidth required. Depending on the distance between sites and the latency of intersite links, it may be beneficial to install local vCenter instances to manage the local environment rather than employing a centralized vCenter that may require WAN access.

Different Geographies   Similarly, there is a growing desire in many organizations to deploy multiple datacenters to improve the accessibility of mission-critical applications. Also of note is the concept of acquisitions and mergers. These can create multiple datacenters, each servicing a separate geographical location. And in this scenario, there may be no desire on the part of management to merge these locations into one central datacenter.

There is also the possibility that this is what is termed a "sunshine shop." A sunshine shop is an organization in which there is a location or an affiliate operating in every area in which the sun is shining around the globe. This type of environment may dictate the use of multiple vCenter instances connected through Linked Mode to create a single, complete management interface that encompasses all locations.

Politics (the 8th Layer of the OSI Model)   When designing a solution, office politics must be considered as well. There are situations where a workgroup or department wants to manage their own servers and desktops rather than delegating this responsibility to others. This may be the result of mandatory security practices that must be enforced on the VMs due to the sensitive nature of the data contained therein.

This could also be the desire to "protect turf": competition between departments and department heads can result in mistrust, and the desire to retain one's own job. If an environment requires 20 administrators and support staff to adequately manage a physical installation, that same environment may require only five staff members to manage that same number of servers when fully virtualized. Self-preservation can be a strong motivator.

Host Cluster Concepts

vCenter contains two types of clusters: DRS and HA clusters. DRS clusters and HA clusters may be combined to enhance the productivity and availability of the VMs, but this is not mandatory.

DRS (Distributed Resource Scheduler) clusters have two main functions. They actively load balance the cluster based on the Administrator's configuration and automatically place new VMs on the most appropriate host.

With the release of vSphere 4.0, DPM was fully supported through the DRS cluster. DPM (Distributed Power Management) allows an administrator to configure the cluster so that VMs will coalesce onto a minimal number of physical ESXi servers when the presented workload drops. This means the empty physical hosts can be placed into a "suspended" state in order to save power and cooling costs.

HA (High Availability) clusters are designed to restart VMs on another physical host in the cluster, in the event of a hardware failure or other loss of functionality, again based on the cluster configuration. vSphere 4.0 introduced the concept of FT (Fault Tolerance). FT basically creates a virtual cluster by defining a VM as the primary, and then creating another VM that is a read-only duplicate of the protected VM on another host in the cluster.

Clustering in the vSphere environment will be detailed in future chapters.

How Many Hosts per Cluster?

The current configuration maximums for DRS and HA Clusters are shown in Table 6.8.

Table 6.8 Current Configuration Maximums for DRS and HA Clusters

Cluster	Physical Hosts	Virtual Machines	VMs/host
HA	32	3000	320
DRS	32	3000	320

As the table indicates, each type of cluster currently supports a maximum of 32 hosts per cluster. This is an increase from the vSphere maximums for DRS clusters of 32 physical hosts, 1280 VMs/cluster, and 256 VMs per physical host.

In a vSphere 4.0 HA Cluster, there was a maximum of 32 physical ESX or ESXi hosts per cluster. If the cluster contained eight or fewer physical hosts, there was a maximum of 100 VMs per host. If the cluster contained fewer than eight physical servers, there was a maximum of 160 VMs per host with the Update 1 package applied. A cluster with more than eight physical hosts had a maximum of 40 VMs per host.

Mix and Match ESX Versions

It is good at this point to remember that both ESX and ESXi hosts can participate in VMware clustering as they support the same functionality. However, in vSphere 5 there are no ESX hosts because the ESX platform has been deprecated. The major concern for clustering is that of CPU compatibility between all physical hosts that comprise a cluster.

From the vMotion perspective, a VM is running within the code set and instruction set of a physical host. When we move that particular VM from the original host to another, it will be presented with the instruction set of the new host. If the instruction and architecture of the new host is not compatible with the previous host, there is a strong possibility that the VM will freeze or "blue screen." This would eliminate the transparency of the vMotion process to the end user.

In preparation to create the cluster, these steps should be considered to reduce the possibility of issues manifesting themselves either during deployment or at a later date.

Utilize the vendor's hardware diagnostic application to determine if there are existing hardware issues that must be addressed prior to cluster creation. These are generally available from the vendor's support website. As an alternative, a third-party diagnostic can also be used, but keep in mind that the vendor's application is written to fully test the vendor's specific hardware, and may be more reliable than a third-party alternative.

During the testing period, be sure to fully test the system memory as a flaky DIMM module can produce intermittent errors, and may prove hard to resolve at a later date. An alternative here is to use a hardware device called a DIMM tester. This diagnostic tool requires the administrator to remove the DIMMs from the system board of the server and install them in the tester. The tester will then proceed to test the DIMMS with different patterns of ones and zeroes to fully validate the memory outside the server.

IMPLEMENTATION AND MANAGEMENT

Using the vCenter application to manage the environment is recommended over using a vSphere Client session to connect to each ESXi host. In many situations, it is far easier to manage multiple hosts using a single management interface, rather than multiple vSphere Client sessions. However, if the vCenter instance is unavailable for some reason, the individual client sessions to each ESXi host become the viable alternative.

Installation Tips

When installing the vCenter platform, there are several considerations that should be evaluated in order to provide a smooth deployment.

- UAC (User Account Control) can interfere with the process of creating a vCenter log bundle. If UAC is enabled, the shortcut to create a vCenter log bundle will fail. Since this is a valuable troubleshooting tool, the administrator may want to disable UAC on the vCenter device.

- If an administrator tries to create a Linked Mode instance, or join an existing Linked Mode instance, the process will fail if UAC is enabled. Again, the administrator may want to disable UAC on the vCenter server.

- If the destination server currently has an ADAM instance that uses the default ports of 389 and 636, the vCenter installation will fail because the installer recognizes that these ports are in use by another application. As a solution, the administrator can disable the ADAM instance during the installation process.

Issues with UAC on W2K8

In general, users will try to log in to their devices using Administrative-level credentials. On one hand, this allows users to update printer drivers or update AV definitions, but it also means that any applications that are executed by these users also execute with those same Administrative-level permissions.

With the release of Windows Vista, Microsoft introduced the concept of UAC (User Account Control). UAC allows all users to log in with standard permissions. This allows users to perform tasks that do not affect critical system resources or processes with no intervention. This also allows any applications that initiate to execute with those same standard-level permissions.

If a user attempts to perform a function that has the potential to directly or indirectly affect the system or its processes, an elevation prompt is displayed. The user is required to provide credentials that match the desired function. If the credentials are sufficient, the program will execute with the elevated permissions; the user continues to function with standard permissions.

This same concept can affect the manner in which vCenter and Linked Mode are installed. If the user or administrator has insufficient privileges to install vCenter, he or she will be required to provide Administrative-level permissions before the installation can complete.

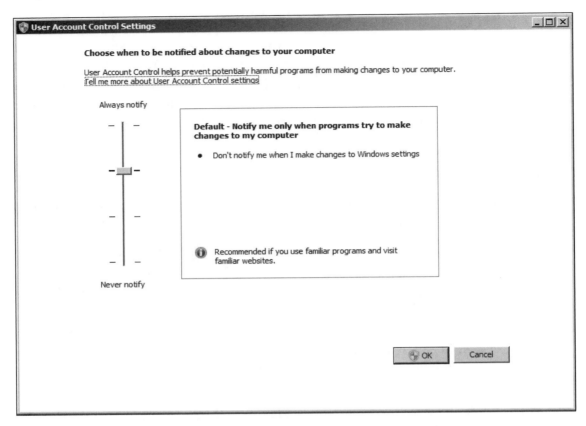

Figure 6.3
The User Account settings.

If you want to disable the UAC, this can be completed in Microsoft Windows Server 2008 by using the Start > Control Panel > User Accounts path, and choosing the System and Security link. From the System and Security pane, select Change User Account Control settings.

In Figure 6.3, the User Account Control settings pane allows the administrator to change the UAC level in order to install applications with the appropriate permission set. In addition, it is possible to manage the UAC configuration through the use of a GPO.

Installing vCenter on Windows

As in previous releases of vCenter and Virtual Center, it is possible to install the vCenter application on a server that is running a copy of Microsoft Windows. One thing to keep in mind here is that vCenter 5 will not install on a 32-bit operating system. The currently supported 64-bit operating systems are listed below:

- Microsoft Windows 2003 R2
- Microsoft Windows 2003 SP2
- Microsoft Windows 2008 R2
- Microsoft Windows 2008 R2 SP1
- Microsoft Windows 2008 SP1
- Microsoft Windows 2008 SP2

vCenter no longer supports a 32-bit DSN, therefore, you will need to use a 64-bit DSN in order to configure the database to be used for vCenter. The supported database revisions and required updates were detailed in Chapter 3.

To install vCenter, download the vCenter installer image and then burn the installation media to a DVD, or, if you going to install vCenter in a VM, attach the .ISO to the CD drive. In either case, use the Autorun feature to allow the installer to initialize. The steps to install vCenter are as follows:

1. When the VMware vCenter Installer screen is displayed, highlight vCenter Server and click the Install button.

2. Choose the language that will be used with vCenter.

3. Review and accept the licensing agreement

4. Enter the customer information and license key. If you decide to use vCenter in Evaluation Mode or if you simply want to add the license later, leave the license key field empty.

5. Select the database that will be used (either Microsoft SQL Server 2008 Express for a small environment or a test deployment) or specify a full instance of a supported database.

6. Specify the account that will connect to the database.

7. Define the destination folder for vCenter and for the Inventory Service.

8. Specify whether this will be a stand-alone instance or whether this new installation will join a Linked Mode configuration.

9. If your environment mandates that special ports be used to connect to this vCenter, you can specify them on the Configure Ports page. If not, you can leave the defaults.

10. If you need to change the default ports for the Inventory Service, specify them on the Configure Ports for Inventory Service page. If not, leave the defaults.

11. Configure the JVM Memory by selecting the radio button that best describes the environment that you anticipate for vCenter.

12. At the Ready to Install page, you can decide to increase the number of Ephemeral ports for vCenter. Ephemeral ports are discussed in Chapter 7.

Installing the vCenter Server Appliance

vSphere 5 brings a new management option to the concept of managing a virtualized environment: VMware has released a new Linux-based vCenter server appliance. The term appliance does not refer to a toaster or a dishwasher, but instead defines a pre-configured virtual machine that is designed to perform a given function. In the case of the vCenter server appliance, that function is the management of a VMware deployment.

Similar to other virtual appliances, the vCenter server appliance can be downloaded from VMware's website, and is imported into the inventory.

As shown in Figure 6.4, the appliance is deployed using the File > Deploy OVF Template link. As part of the Deploy OVF Template wizard, the destination host and

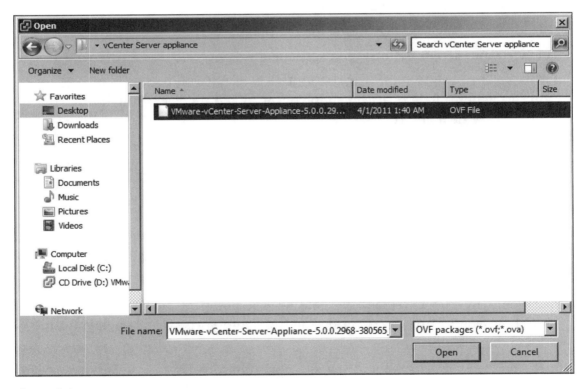

Figure 6.4
Adding the appliance to the vCenter inventory.

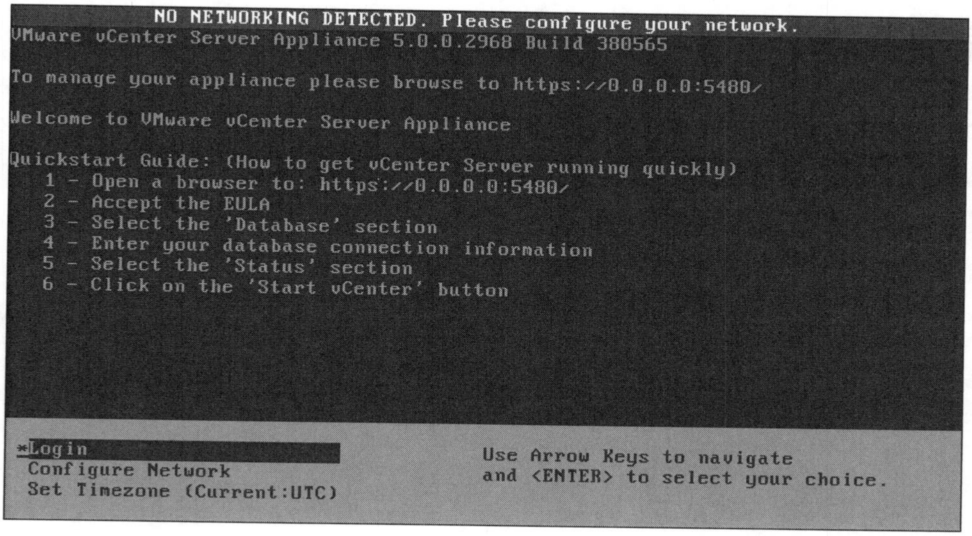

Figure 6.5
The management screen for the vCenter server appliance.

datastore are defined, and a name is specified that will reference the appliance in the inventory. At the completion screen, the administrator has the ability to review the details before completing the process.

After deployment has completed successfully, networking parameters must be assigned to the appliance. By default, the appliance is configured to attempt to obtain a DHCP address, but a static IP is recommended.

As Figure 6.5 shows, after the appliance has been added successfully, you can point a web browser to http://<the IP address of the device>:5480, and the management page will be displayed. Now that connectivity has been established, the appliance can be configured.

From the management screen, select Login from the menu at the bottom of the screen.

As shown in Figure 6.6, you will need to enter the administrator credentials at the login screen and click Login. The default username is *root* and the password is *vmware*. Note also that the vCenter server appliance does not support the use of SQL as a database platform.

Once successfully logged in, you must accept the EULA (does anyone really read these?). After you accept the EULA, the management interface for the appliance is displayed.

Figure 6.6
The Login screen.

Figure 6.7 shows the basic management interface. The appliance is just like the physical vCenter server in that it also requires a database to store the related inventory content. The database is configured as the default of "embedded." Enter the appropriate database information and select Test Settings. The appliance will attempt to log in to the database and establish a session.

In Figure 6.8, the database configuration was successful and the status pane now displays a button to start the vCenter server.

As shown in Figure 6.9, the configuration of the vCenter Appliance is similar to the configuration of the Windows-based vCenter server; you can specify custom port usage for the vCenter services if your environment requires it. This configuration

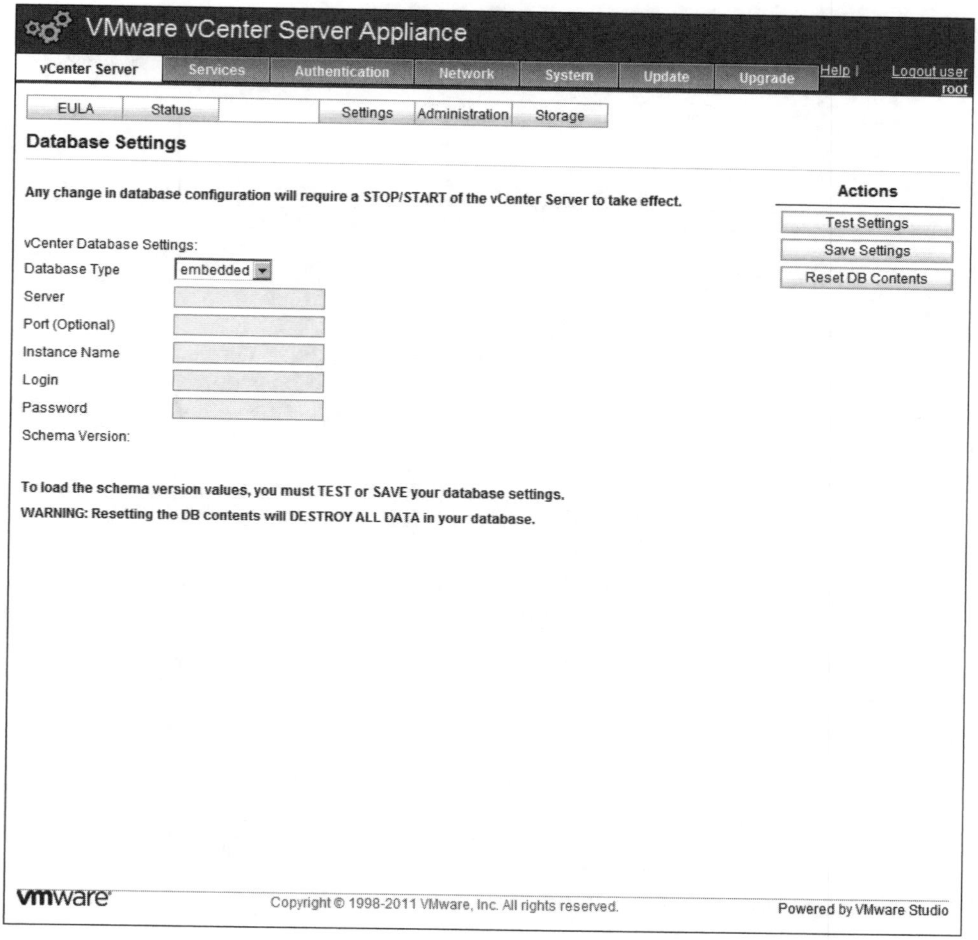

Figure 6.7
The Management interface.

will typically mirror the security approach taken by the network team in dealing with physical devices.

As shown in Figure 6.10, you can change the password associated with the Administrator account by using the Administration button from the main vCenter page. Note here that SSL usage for communication is enabled by default, but you can disable or enable this setting from this page.

Figure 6.11 shows the ability to modify the location used to store the log files and the core files associated with the vCenter instance. Once the locations have been defined,

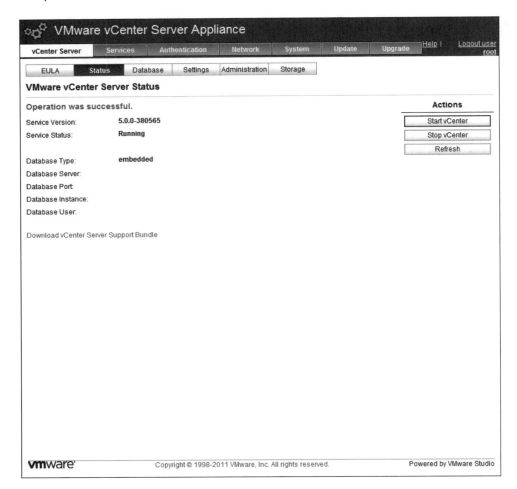

Figure 6.8
Defining the database.

you should always choose to test the configuration, just to verify that the destination is reachable.

As shown in Figure 6.12, the Status button on the Services tab allows the administrator to view the current status of the vCenter services, and stop and/or restart them as needed.

As we discussed earlier, VMware provides the Syslog Collector to maintain the logs from the vCenter server and the individual ESXi hosts in a central location. Figure 6.13 shows

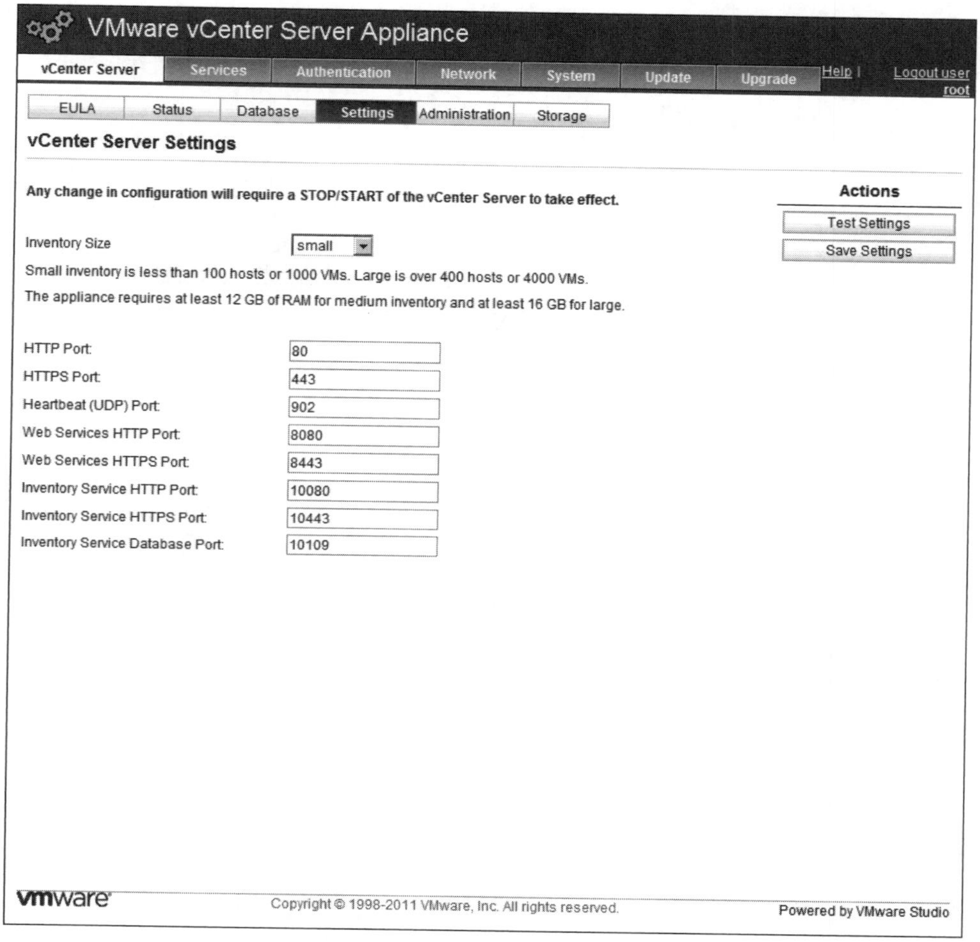

Figure 6.9
Specifying the port usage for vCenter.

the Syslog tab, and the location used to define a custom standard port and a custom SSL port for use by the Syslog server. This information is invaluable when troubleshooting or documenting the virtual deployment.

In Figure 6.14, you have the option to define the port used by the Dump Collector to gather information relative to core dump occurrences. This information is identical to the content gathered from the physical ESXi hosts and includes information such as the modules loaded and their versions, memory content, and CPU state.

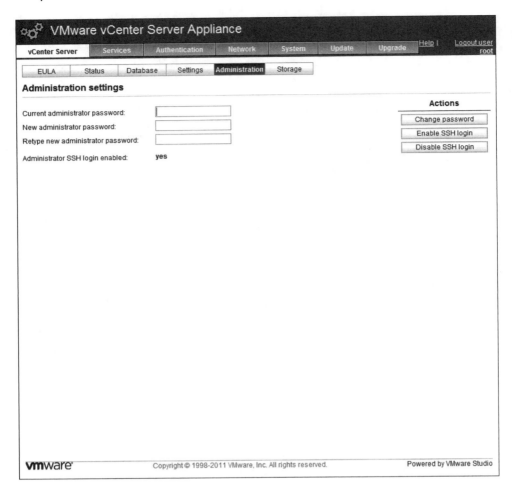

Figure 6.10
Changing the administrator password.

Figure 6.15 shows the options available to modify the server port used by the Auto-Deploy process to communicate with the vCenter server appliance, and the size of the associated AutoDeploy repository. Note that you can test these settings to verify that connectivity is established.

Installing the Extensions

There are additional components that can be installed with vCenter that extend the functionality of the vCenter server. These additional components, or extensions, include Update Manager, Converter, and Guided Consolidation. We will discuss them briefly here, and then detail their capabilities and uses later in the book.

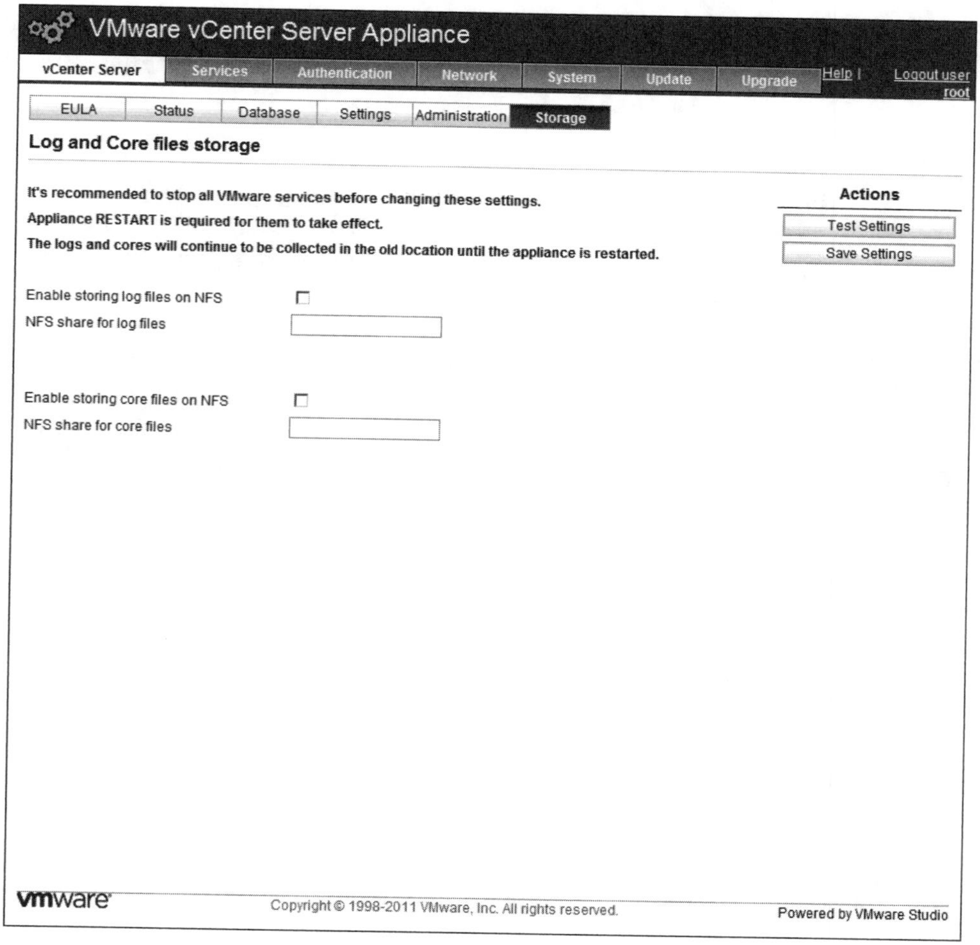

Figure 6.11
Changing the location of the log and core files.

Update Manager

Installing and configuring Update Manager is detailed in Chapter 13.

Adding a Host to vCenter

As mentioned earlier, the administrator has the option to individually manage each of the physical hosts in his or her environment. This is easily accomplished using the vSphere Client, an SSH client such as Putty, or through a scripting mechanism such as the vSphere CLI.

However, in each of these scenarios, the administrator loses the ability to clone a VM, deploy a VM from a pre-configured template, Perform vMotion and Storage

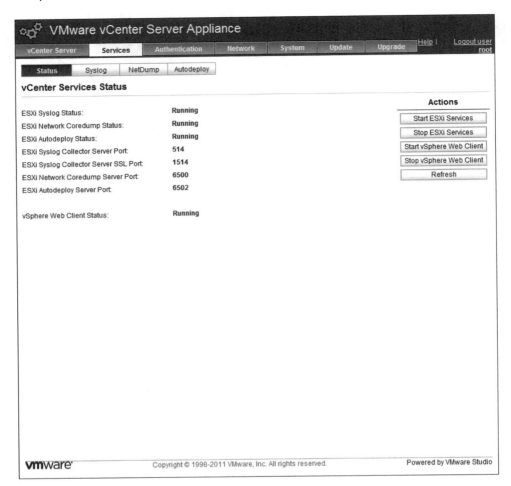

Figure 6.12
Viewing the status of the vCenter services.

vMotion processes, and create and manage a cluster. These are critical components in an enterprise environment, so ESXi hosts should be added to and managed through a vCenter instance.

The process of adding an ESXi host to vCenter requires the root-level credentials for the ESXi host as the vCenter agent is installed locally on the server. The administrator will begin the process by right-clicking on a folder or a datacenter and selecting Add Host.

The Add Host wizard will appear and ask for the IP address or FQDN of the prospective host. The root credentials will also be specified here.

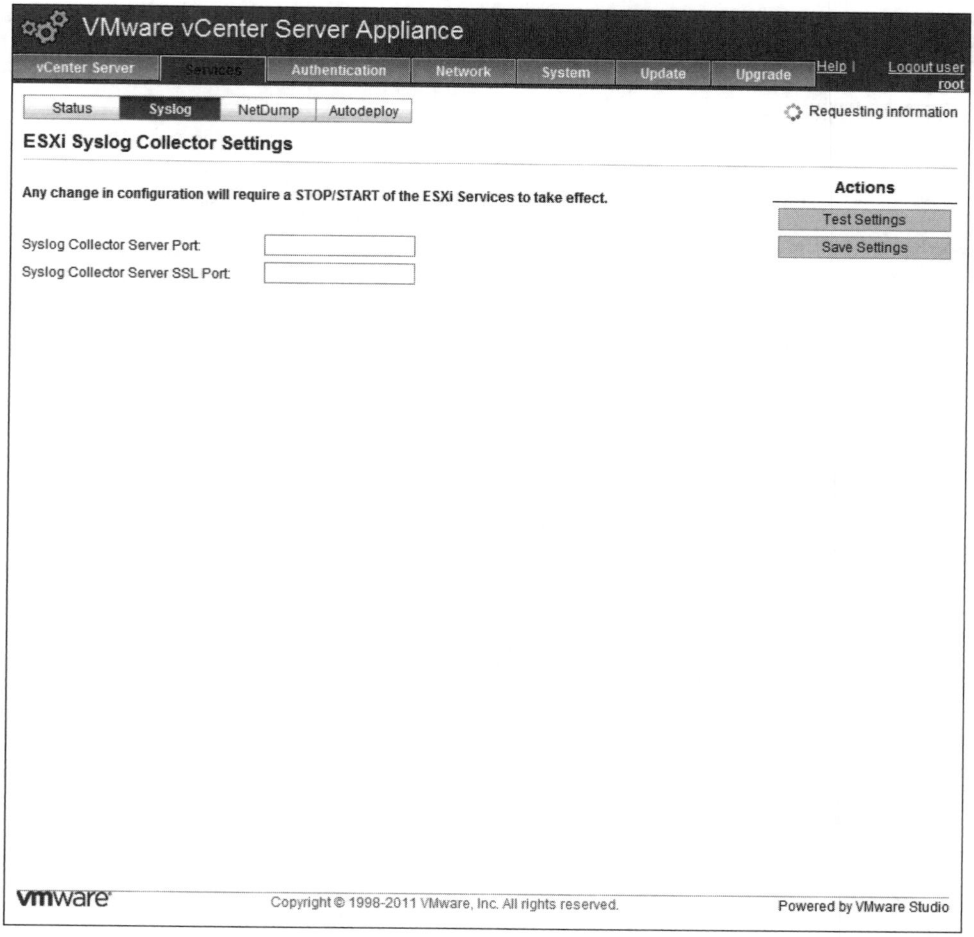

Figure 6.13
Changing the ports used by the Syslog Collector.

As shown in Figure 6.16, the IP address or the FQDN of the new host must be provided, as well as the root-level credentials in order to successfully add the new host to vCenter. Please note at this point that the host should always be added using the FQDN as the addition may fail if the IP address is provided instead.

The vCenter instance will attempt to log in to the ESXi host using the credentials provided. If it is successful, it will install a vCenter agent that will provide a link between vCenter itself and the local hostd service. A user named "vpxuser" will be created and the password will be stored in the /etc/shadow file. This account will be used by vCenter to log in to the local host.

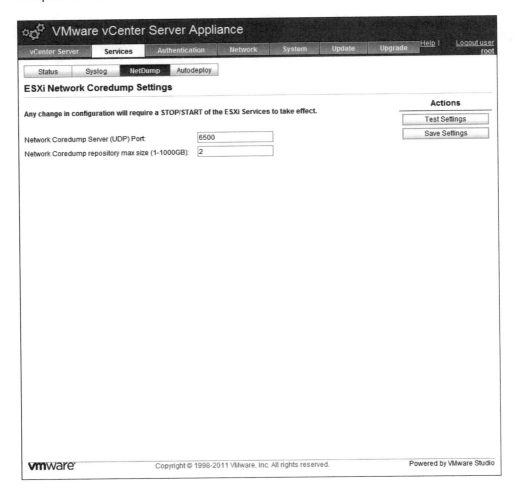

Figure 6.14
Modifying the port used by the Dump Collector.

The vCenter agent will query the hostd server and gather inventory information and send it to vCenter to be added to the vCenter database.

As a best practice, it is a good idea to maintain the accessibility between vCenter and each of the ESXi hosts in the environment. One way to ensure this communication is consistent is to verify that port 902 is open between vCenter and each of the ESXi hosts.

Adding a host to vCenter is a simple task when using the vSphere Client, but what if I want to script this process and have a reproducible, verifiable result? Since the release of vSphere 4.0, VMware has integrated cmdlets into PowerCLI to allow scripts access to many of the most common daily processes. In this example, we will show

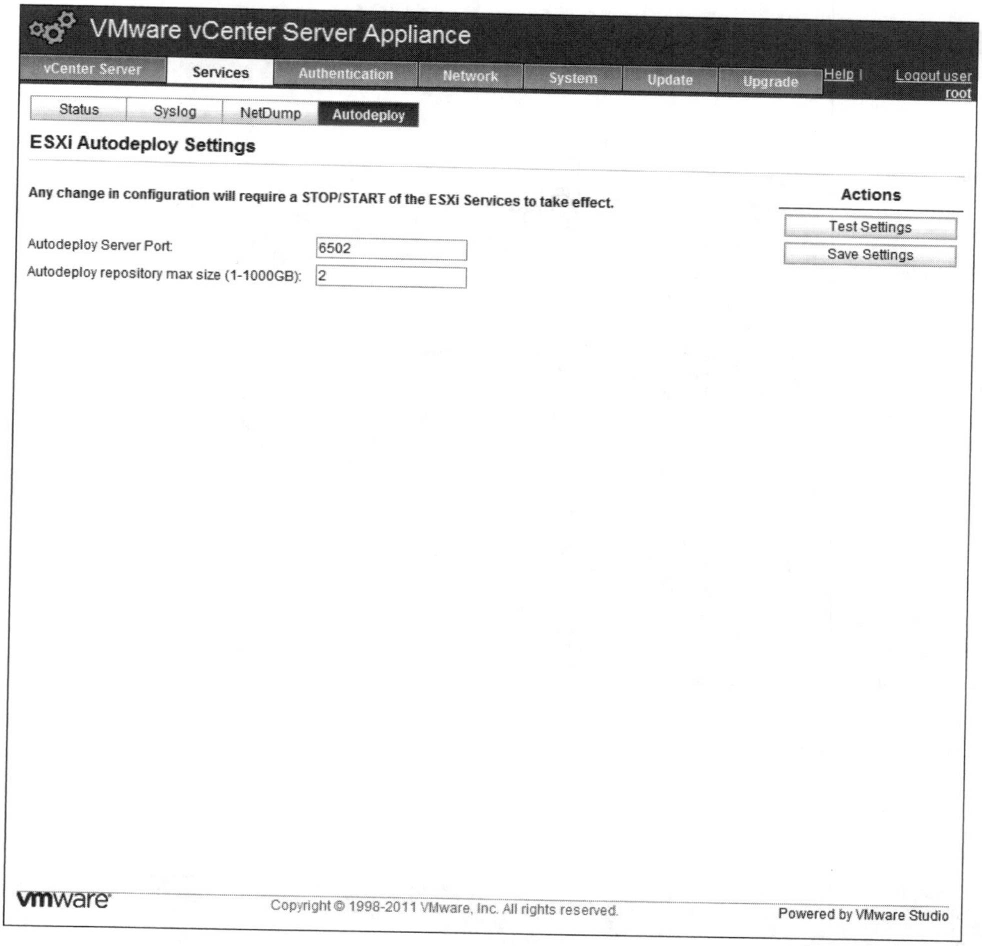

Figure 6.15
Changing the ports used by the AutoDeploy process.

how you can perform the processes of creating a datacenter and a folder in vCenter, and then adding a host to that vCenter instance.

As shown in Figure 6.17, PowerCLI allows us to define the initial objects in vCenter very easily. We can also open a vSphere Client session and watch vCenter as the script executes.

The command syntax is as follows:

1. Use the command `Set-ExecutionPolicy unrestricted` to allow the PowerCLI commands to execute within the PowerCLI environment. The default state is "Restricted," which means that a script must be digitally signed to

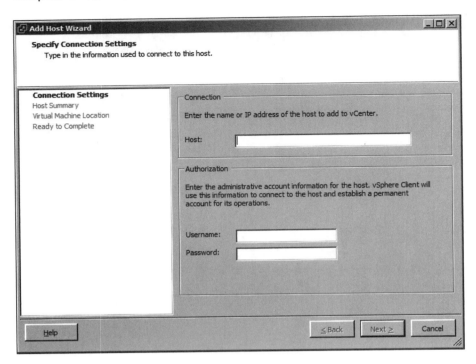

Figure 6.16
Adding the ESXi host to vCenter.

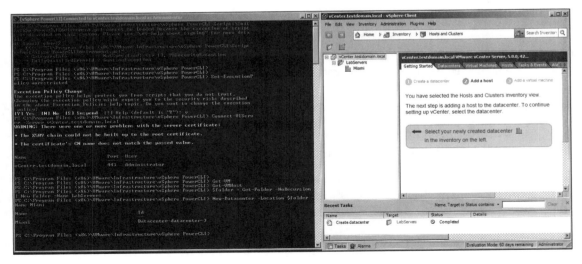

Figure 6.17
Using PowerCLi to create the vCenter enrivonment.

execute. The command is `Set-ExecutionPolicy unrestricted`. Once that command has completed, we can now configure our environment using PowerCLI.

2. Use the command `Connect VIServer --Server vCenter.testdomain.local` to connect to the desired vCenter instance. In this example, we are connecting to `vCenter.testdomain.local`.

3. Using the `Get-VM` command will display any VMs in this vCenter inventory.

4. The command `Get-VMHost` will list the current ESXi hosts in the vCenter inventory.

5. `$folder = Get-Folder --NoRecursion | New-Folder LabServers` will create the folder "LabServers" in the vCenter inventory.

6. We can now define a datacenter that will contain our new ESXi host using `New-Datacenter --Location $folder --Name Miami` to define the new "Miami" datacenter in the LabServers folder.

Figure 6.18 details the addition of the ESXi host to the vCenter inventory.

■ `Add-VMHost --Force --Name esx01.testdomain.local --Location (Get-Datacenter Miami) --User root --Password password` adds the ESXi host "esx01.testdomain.local" to the Miami datacenter with the root credentials supplied. Note the use of the `--Force` option. This causes the host to be added even though it is using a self-signed certificate.

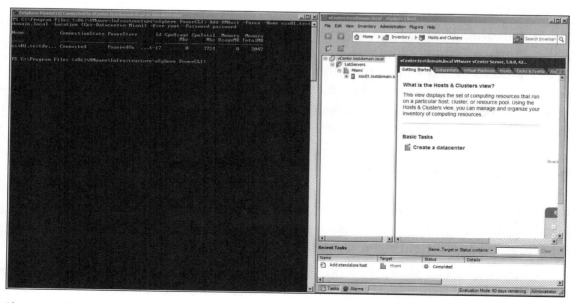

Figure 6.18
Adding the host to vCenter using PowerCLI.

Cluster Configuration

When considering the option of deploying vCenter within an HA cluster, you must also consider the necessity of guaranteeing resources to the vCenter VM so it can be used to manage the environment adequately. Comparing this to installing vCenter on a physical host means that in a VM, the vCenter VM will have to compete for CPU, RAM, network, and disk resources along with other VMs that are running on the same host. So, from a planning perspective, this means placing sufficient CPU and RAM reservations on the vCenter VM so that other VMs on the same host do not impact the performance of vCenter.

If you plan the cluster hardware carefully, the use of an HA cluster to house the vCenter VM can allow the vCenter VM to be restarted if the physical host that is hosting the VM fails. This means maintaining the resource utilization of the cluster to be in the range of 50%–60%. This will help provide enough space to failover the VMs from the failing host. Secondly, this means that the cluster settings should be modified to prioritize the vCenter VM over other VMs so that it will be started first.

We will cover HA clusters in Chapter 12, but these considerations should remain on your "to-do" list if you are planning to virtualize the vCenter instance.

vSphere Client (Reference Back to Hosts)

Managing the ESXi host through the vSphere Client was discussed in Chapter 5.

Licensing

As we stated earlier, the ESXi installation starts with a 60-day evaluation period, in which the virtualization components can be tested and verified before placing them into a production environment. After the 60-day period expires, you will need to address the licensing of your new host(s) and you will need to decide which features fit your particular virtualization plans. In this section we will provide an overview of the current licensing schemes available to you.

How to License Older 3.5(i) Hosts

While vCenter does support the management of ESX and ESXi 3.5 hosts, correct licensing of these hosts requires extra consideration. In ESX/ESXi 3.5 and earlier, licensing was performed using a test-based license file, also known as a .lic file. This file was saved locally on the host, or within the Virtual Center 2.5 Server.

To configure licensing for legacy ESX/ESXi 3.5 hosts that will be upgraded to vSphere 5, the license server component can be downloaded from the VMware website. The license server can be installed on the vCenter server itself, or it can be installed on

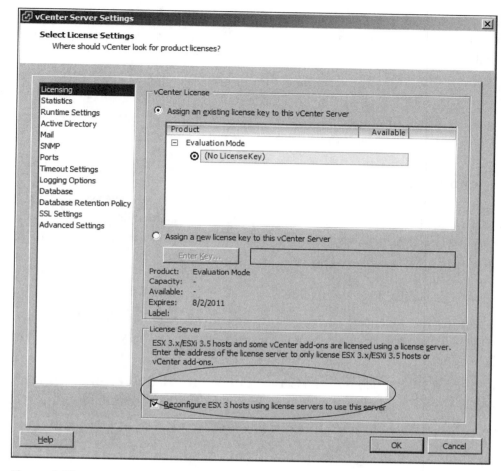

Figure 6.19
Configuring ESX 3.x hosts to use a license server.

another device in the network. Once installed, the legacy ESX/ESXi hosts must be made aware of its location.

As shown in Figure 6.19, the legacy ESX/ESXi 3.x hosts must be configured to reference this server for licensing.

To configure the ESX/ESXi servers to use the license server:

1. Log in to the vCenter using the vSphere Client.

2. Use the Administration > vCenter Server settings icon.

3. Place a check mark in Reconfigure ESX3 hosts using license servers to use this server, and enter the license server name and port number in the box provided.

4. Click OK.

The administrator can add licenses to the vCenter at any time. Remember, both ESXi and vCenter have a 60-day evaluation period, but licensing must be configured to maintain operability.

Starting with vSphere 4.x, VMware changed the manner in which licenses were dispersed. In the ESX/ESXi 3.5 and earlier environments, there was a license file sometimes referred to as a ".lic file" that detailed the purchased options that were available.

How to License vSphere 4.x and 5 Hosts

In vSphere 4.x, the method changed to a 25-digit hexadecimal key, similar to a Microsoft license key. The key can be entered at the physical host level, where each physical server can be presented with the required license key, or the key can be added to vCenter and each ESXI server can be presented with the common license key as it is added. Each ESXi server will "check out" a number of CPUs from the common store as the license key is presented.

To add a license to the vCenter environment, use the Administration drop-down menu from the vCenter toolbar and select vCenter server settings. The top menu selection is Licensing.

As shown in Figure 6.20, the license for vCenter can be provided through entering an existing license key, or by entering a new license key in the provided field.

To add a license for vCenter or a vSphere 5 ESXi host:

1. Log in to the vCenter using the vSphere Client.

2. Use the Administration > vCenter Server settings icon.

3. Click the Enter button.

4. Enter the provided license key for the vCenter instance or the ESXi host(s).

5. Assign a label to describe the license.

6. Click OK.

At any point in the future, additional licenses can be added by using the Home > Administration > Licensing link.

As shown in Figure 6.21, using the Manage vSphere Licenses link will open the Manage vSphere Licenses wizard. Licenses can be added for both vCenter and ESXi hosts. Once the license keys have been entered, the administrator can determine which ESXi hosts, vCenter instances, or devices these licenses apply to.

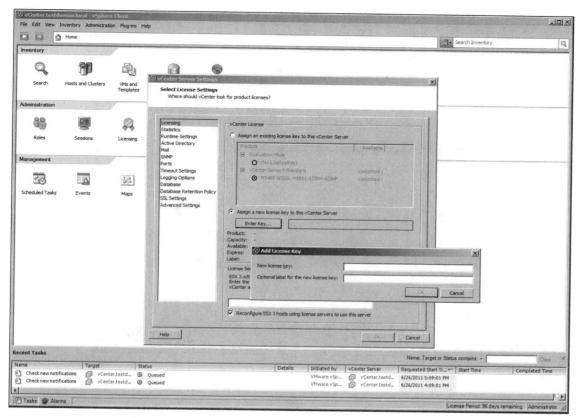

Figure 6.20
The licensing options in vCenter 5.

Backing Up vCenter Server

Since the vCenter server application is an integral component of the datacenter, it makes sense that the data associated with vCenter should be backed up just like any other production-related data.

Caution

A regular database backup should be performed and archived to an offsite location. The ability to recover from a multi-disk failure relies on the availability of an updated backup to restore to the most recent state of the database.

Another option is to use a replication component to move the data from the primary site to a secondary location where it can provide a mirror of the production site, or the data can be backed up at the secondary site, to reduce contention on the production database.

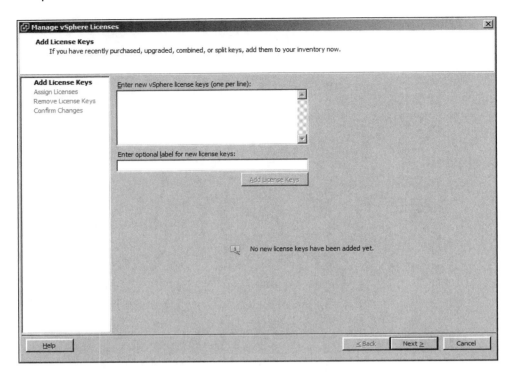

Figure 6.21
Adding licenses to vCenter.

The administrator should consider the frequency of backups that are taken of the vCenter database. Typically, the most recent backup is the method that he or she will use to restore the vCenter database back to a consistent state in the case of a true disaster or hardware failure. A less frequent backup schedule may bring the environment back up at an early time frame, losing valuable performance and troubleshooting data. However, a more frequent backup schedule may result in an impact to the production database, such as a slowdown in the response time of vCenter, or pausing or latency in mouse movement of drop-down menus, etc.

Tips and Tricks

vCenter provides additional options that can make day-to-day management a bit easier in mid-size to enterprise-level deployment. In this section we will take a look at the message of the day and scheduled tasks.

Message of the Day

vCenter provides a MOTD (message of the day) mechanism to update all current users about issues within the environment. This can be very useful if a temporary

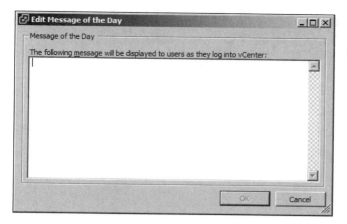

Figure 6.22
Adding a message of the day.

outage or a maintenance period is required to remedy a hardware failure within the deployment.

The message of the day can also be used to display a legal warning to unauthorized access.

A message can be added in vCenter that will immediately be broadcast to all currently connected users. The format is added as shown in Figure 6.22.

To add a message of the day:

1. Using the vCenter toolbar, highlight the Administration drop-down menu and select the Edit Message of the Day link.

2. Enter the desired message.

3. Click OK.

Scheduled Tasks

The Scheduled Tasks feature is used to execute a specific process or task based on a timeframe. To view the status of any scheduled tasks, use the Scheduled Tasks icon that is located in the Management toolbar in vCenter.

The screenshot shown in Figure 6.23 shows that there are currently two scheduled tasks, an administrator-defined description of the task, the last time that the task was executed, and the next scheduled run time.

As shown in Figure 6.24, the administrator has several processes that can be automated through a scheduled task. The available processes are:

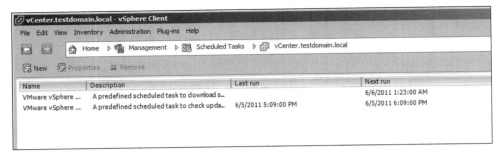

Figure 6.23
View the status of scheduled tasks.

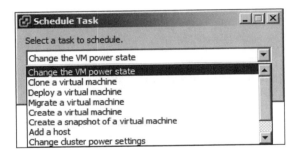

Figure 6.24
The available scheduled tasks in vCenter.

- Change the VM power state
- Clone a virtual machine
- Deploy a virtual machine
- Migrate a virtual machine
- Create a virtual machine
- Create a snapshot of a virtual machine
- Add a host
- Change cluster power settings
- Change resource pool or VM resource settings
- Check compliance for a host profile

To create a scheduled task, use the New link. The available tasks can be displayed by using the drop-down button.

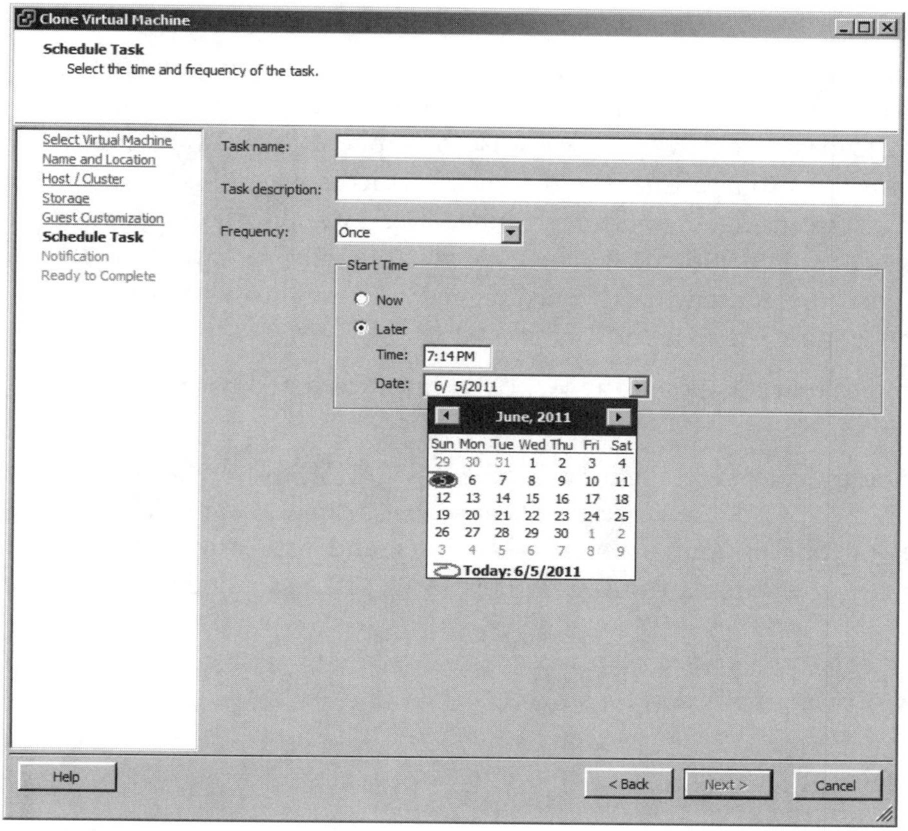

Figure 6.25
Scheduling a new task.

Figure 6.25 shows the scheduling component. The process to be performed is chosen, the parameters for the event are defined, and the timeframe must be specified. Depending on the frequency of the event, the options are:

- Once
- After startup
- Hourly
- Daily
- Weekly
- Monthly

vCMA Fling

Managing the environment through vCenter provides a wealth of scalability and functionality. However, it mandates that the user be connected using the vSphere Client or through a CLI-based tool. With the release of vSphere 5, VMware grants the opportunity to leave the vSphere Client and to access and manage the environment through a mobile device using the vCenter Mobile Access application. This means that you can manage your deployment wherever you can receive a wireless signal. As you would expect, the content has been designed for usability with a small display, and does not require a mouse for functionality.

Please keep in mind that at this point, the vCMA is considered a "Power Tool" and is offered as such.

New in vSphere 5 and depicted in Figure 6.26, the VCMA (VMware vCenter Mobile Access) utilizes a Linux-based appliance that is available from VMware. As an appliance, it will "live" on one of your physical ESXi hosts, and will provide a management alternative to the standard vCenter platform. It has modest hardware requirements:

- 1 CPU
- 512MB RAM
- Approximately 7GB disk space

It is recommended that the ESXi host hosting the appliance have at least 2GB of RAM and 40GB of disk space for best results. Note that the VCMA is designed to access vCenter, but can also be used to directly manage an ESXi host in a limited manner. Since this is a virtual appliance, you can add it to the ESXi host inventory

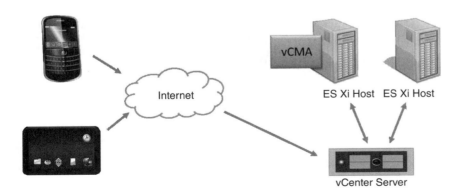

Figure 6.26
The vCMA environment.

using the vSphere Client. Log in to the Windows-based vCenter, and use the File > Deploy OVF Template path to add the vCMA. You will be prompted to provide the ESXi host that will host the VM, the destination datastore, and then the appliance will be added to the specified ESXi host.

Once installed, the administrator can configure the appliance to use any networking scheme desired, but the appliance defaults to DHCP configuration. Keep in mind that the appliance requires IP connectivity to be able to manage devices.

Once you have configured the appliance with the desired networking parameters, the management URL is the same as that for the vCenter server appliance: point your web browser to http://<ip address>:5480 URL and the management page is displayed.

In order to manage through the vCMA, you will need to log in, just as you would if you were using the vCenter or a vSphere Client to manage the environment.

As shown in Figure 6.27, this is the initial management screen for the vCMA. After logging in using "root" as the username, and "vmware" as the password, you can configure the network parameters and the time configuration.

After the network parameters have been configured, the vCMA is ready for access by mobile devices.

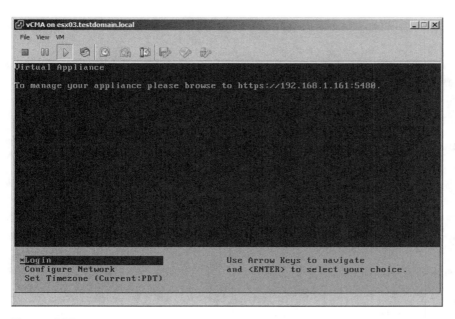

Figure 6.27
Logging in through the vCMA.

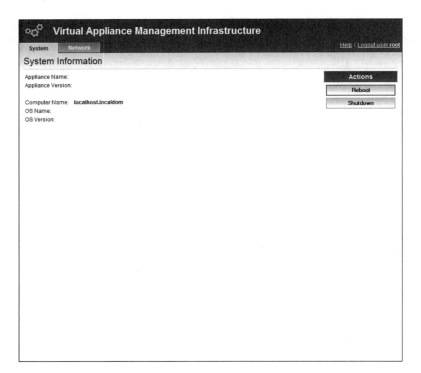

Figure 6.28
The main management screen.

Figure 6.28 shows the default management screen for the vCMA appliance. Note that from this main screen, we can view the name and version of the appliance, which can be useful when considering compatibility with other VMware components.

We can also document and view the Computer Name and OS Version, and from the same screen we can use Actions, Reboot, and Shutdown as well.

Choosing the Network tab provides access to the networking configuration.

As shown in Figure 6.29, the Status tab of the networking screen provides us with the ability to change the networking parameters for the appliance. From this screen, we can view the interface in use; the method of IP address assignment; and the current IP configuration, including the DNS servers.

As shown in Figure 6.30, clicking on the Address button grants the option to configure the appliance to use DHCP or use a static IP address, and to configure the DNS servers.

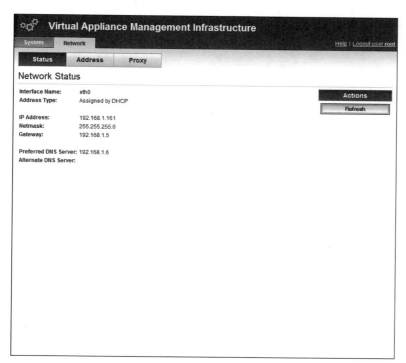

Figure 6.29
The vCMA networking screen.

As depicted in Figure 6.31, you can configure a proxy, if necessary, to allow communication with the vCMA to comply with the existing security configuration for your environment.

After we have configured the vCMA appliance to be accessible, we can log in to the device, as shown in Figure 6.32. You will need to enter your vCenter permissions to log in, just as you would to log in to the Windows-based version. Open a browser and point it to https://<IP address>/sdk, where "<IP address>" is the IP address that was provided during the configuration phase.

As shown in Figure 6.33, once you have logged in to the vCMA, you are presented with a limited subset of the functionality provided by a Windows-based vCenter installation. Note that from this main screen you can search the vCenter database for objects or users, perform a migration process, go to the Hosts and Clusters view, create a scheduled task, investigate Alarms and Events, perform connectivity-related testing through the Tools icon, and configure basic user options by using the Options icon.

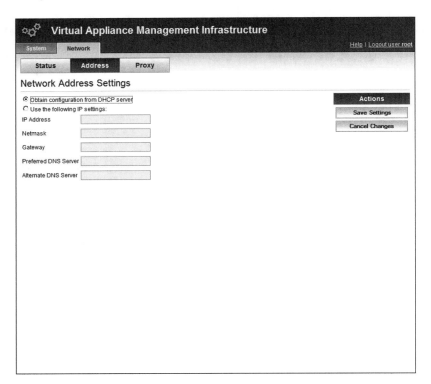

Figure 6.30
Configuring the network interface.

You can choose to search the vCenter database by using the Search icon, as depicted in Figure 6.34. Note that you have the option to search by object type, such as Virtual Machines, Hosts, Folders, Datastores, Networks, or to search for all object types. You can also narrow the search by selecting a particular power state, such as Powered On, Powered Off, Suspended, or you can search for all objects of all power states.

As shown in Figure 6.35, when you select Migrate from the main management interface, the vCenter appliance will query the database and display all virtual machines that are candidates for a migration. This process continues identically to performing a vMotion using the Windows-based vCenter: the destination host and datastore are validated, and the VM will migrate if possible.

When you select the Hosts and Clusters in the main management interface, you can view ESXi host details as shown in Figure 6.36. Note that we can view the basic hardware configuration, the IP address of the vCenter that is managing this ESXi host, the number of VMs currently on this host, its associated datastores and networks, and, at

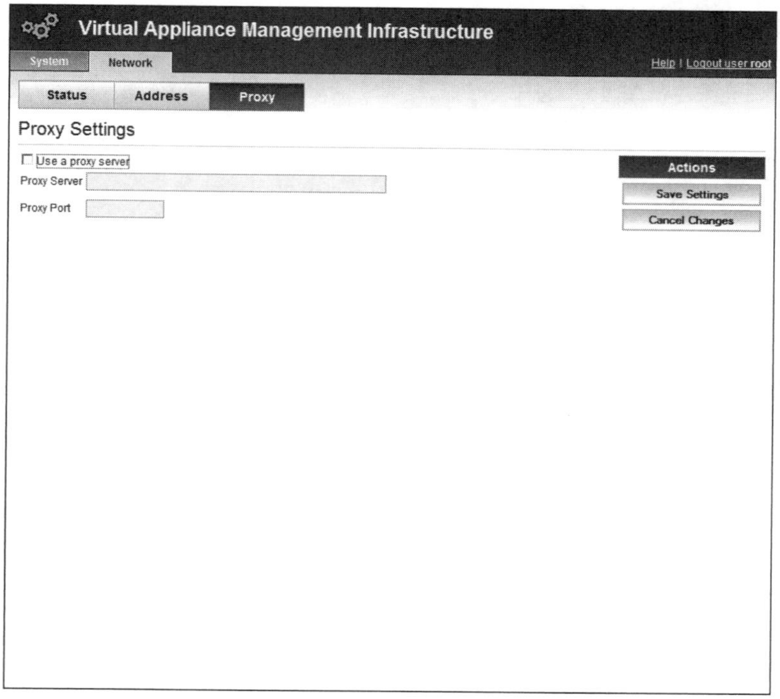

Figure 6.31
Configuring the proxy.

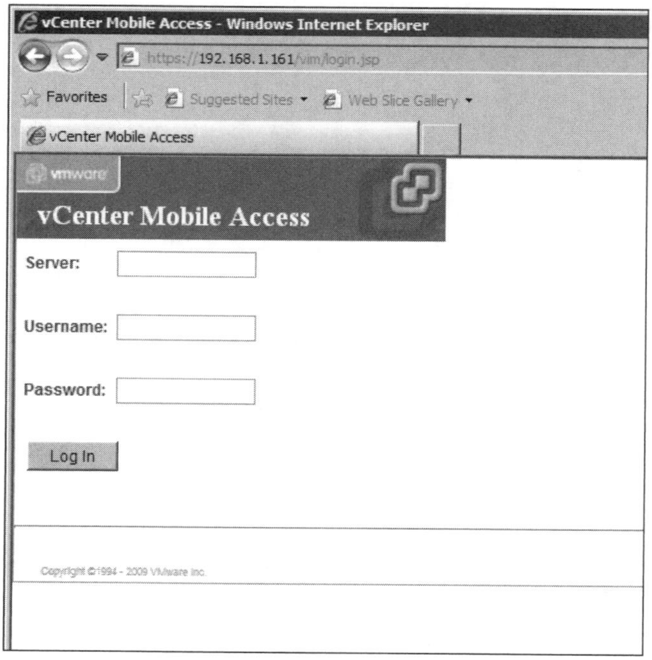

Figure 6.32
The main log-in screen.

Figure 6.33
The vCMA management interface.

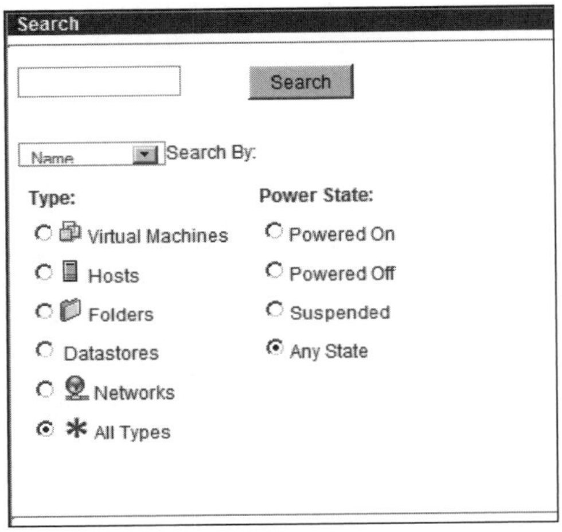

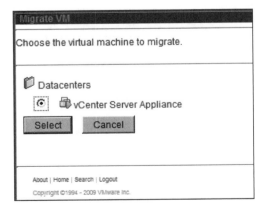

Figure 6.34
The Search interface.

Figure 6.35
Migrating a VM.

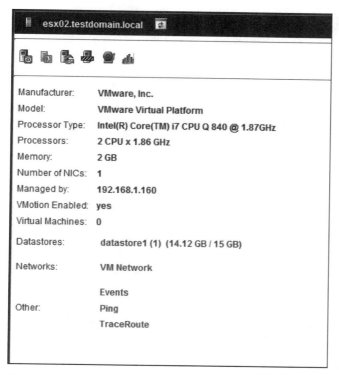

Figure 6.36
ESXi host details.

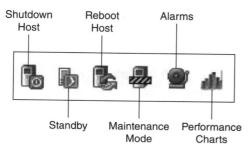

Figure 6.37
The Host toolbar.

the bottom of the screen, we can view recent events, and we can use Ping and TraceRoute to help troubleshoot connectivity issues with this host.

The Host toolbar displayed in Figure 6.37 provides a set of options comparable to one that is accessible by right-clicking on a physical host. From this toolbar you can

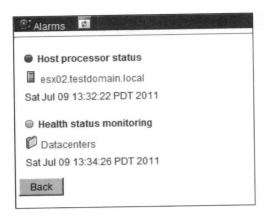

Figure 6.38
The vCenter Alarms icon.

shut down or reboot a host, place a host into standby or Maintenance Mode, and view alarms and performance charts relative to the selected host.

As shown in Figure 6.38, when you select the Alarms icon from the main management interface, any current alarms are displayed along with the object or host that is generating the alarm.

Similar to the vCenter server–based installation, if you choose the Events icon, you are presented with the current events as reported through vCenter. As shown in Figure 6.39, note that, by default, five events are displayed per page, with a brief description of the event and the associated time stamp. At this point it is a good practice to evaluate the log information for any events noted here. The logs will provide a more in-depth description of the events and possibly the surrounding processes that may have led to the event.

As shown in Figure 6.40, selecting the Tools icon will allow you to use Ping or TraceRoute to verify connectivity with an ESXi host or other network destination. You can also send a message from here to let other administrators who may be working in the environment know that you are going to reboot an ESXi host as part of a diagnostic process, or that a host will be entering Maintenance Mode in order to patch the OS.

If you want to change the default number of objects returned through the search feature, the number of events and alarms displayed per page, or the number of scheduled tasks displayed per page, you can use the Options button and customize these values to match your environment.

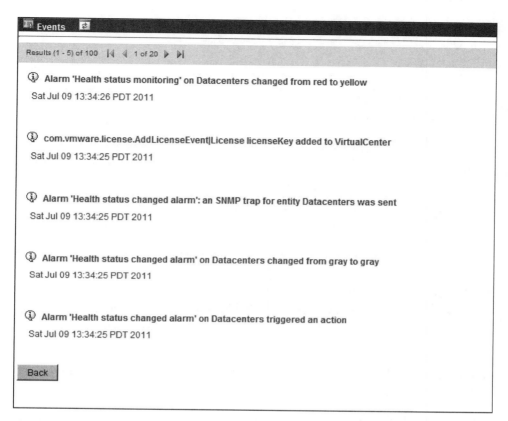

Figure 6.39
Viewing vCenter events.

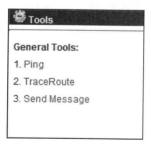

Figure 6.40
The Tools menu.

SECURITY

In many environments, great care is taken to carefully evaluate each server, and the permissions that will be required to allow administrators to perform their jobs, yet not allow excess privileges. This same mindset should be applied at the vCenter

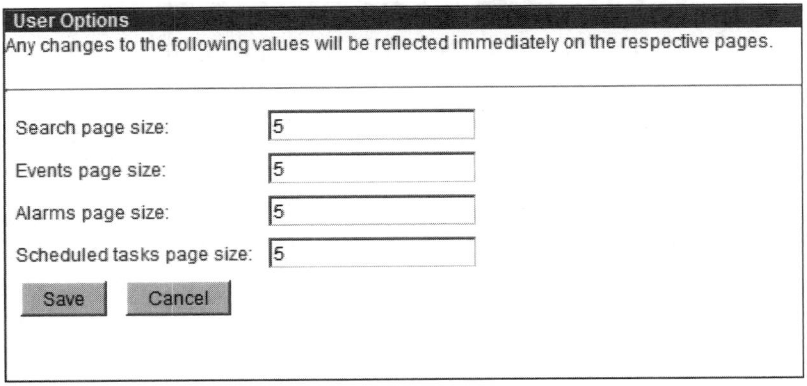

User Options
Any changes to the following values will be reflected immediately on the respective pages.

Search page size: | 5
Events page size: | 5
Alarms page size: | 5
Scheduled tasks page size: | 5

Save   Cancel

Figure 6.41
Setting User Options.

level. When planning a vCenter deployment, it is equally important to provide sufficient access and privileges to allow administrators to perform their jobs.

Roles

There are default roles that exist at the ESXi level and at the vCenter level. The
default roles are:

- **No Access.** Users who have been assigned the "No Access" role do not have
  the ability to see or make changes to the object or its properties. In fact, the
  vCenter tabs that correspond to this object will appear blank to this user. This
  role can be used to block inherited permissions from a parent object. This role
  can be assigned at the ESXi host level and in vCenter.

- **Read Only.** Users with this role can view objects and their properties, but
  cannot make any changes. These users have access to all of the vCenter tabs,
  except the Console tab. This role can be assigned at the ESXi host level and in
  vCenter.

- **Administrator.** This role provides the user with all access and privileges in
  the vCenter environment, unless overridden by an explicit assignment at an
  inventory object. This role can be assigned at the ESXi host level and in
  vCenter.

- **Virtual Machine Power User.** This role grants a user the ability to manage a
  particular VM, including modifying the hardware associated with a VM, taking
  and managing snapshots, etc., but the user has no permissions at the folder or
  datacenter level, and cannot manage hosts, networks, or alarms. This particular

role is usually used at the folder level, granting management access to multiple VMs, and is an option only within the vCenter application.

- **Virtual Machine User.** This user has the ability to use the VM; create a console session; insert or remove media, such as diskettes or CD/DVD; and can change the power state of the VM. The user cannot modify the VM's configuration, and has no privileges outside of the VM. Like the Virtual Machine Power User, this role is typically assigned at the folder level, providing a level of access to all VMs in that folder. This role exists within the vCenter environment only.

- **Resource Pool Administrator.** This set of privileges grants the flexibility to create and modify child resource pools, but provides no access to the parent resource pool. This user can also add VMs to a child resource pool and remove VMs from child resource pools, but provides no access outside the resource pool. This role exists only within the vCenter environment.

- **VMware Consolidated Backup User.** This role provides privileges that allow a user to perform backup and restore processes using the VCB (VMware Consolidated Backup) application. This role applies only within the vCenter platform.

- **Datastore Consumer.** This role allows a user permissions on a per-datastore basis. This privilege is applicable to both NFS and VMFS datastores. This role exists only in vCenter.

- **Network Consumer.** This role, combined with applicable permissions on a VM, allows a user to assign virtual networks to that VM. This role is applicable only within vCenter.

Using the Roles Screen to Check Your Security

After you have begun to deploy your environment, and you have also defined Administrators and other users to both use and manage your ESXi servers and virtual machines, it is a good idea to document the permission that you have assigned. As shown in Figure 6.42, you can click on any object in the left inventory pane, select

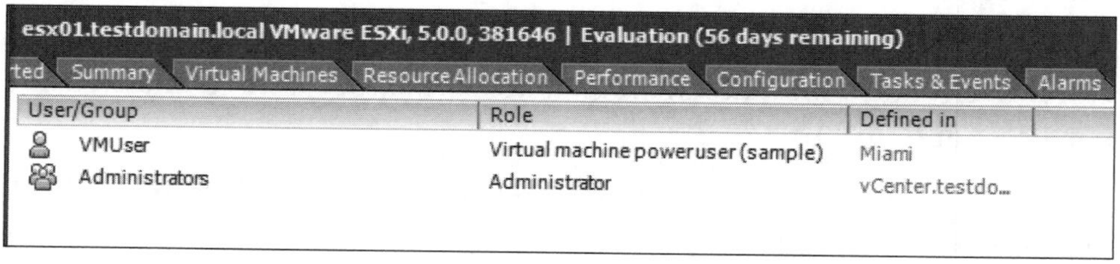

Figure 6.42
Verifying permissions.

the Permissions tab, and view the current permission sets that are assigned to users and groups.

Windows SAM/AD Integration

vCenter does not require the presence of Active Directory for a complete installation, but the use of AD makes the managing of users a much simpler task. By leveraging the currently defined users and groups in Active Directory, the administrator can simply assign the appropriate permissions to those users and groups without the need to define them locally on the vCenter server.

Linux/NIS Integration

For quite a while, Linux and Unix environments have been asking for a version of vCenter that can be integrated into their environments without the use of a Windows Server deployment. In many cases, these companies may not even have a Windows Administrator on staff. As we learned earlier, this request has been answered with the new vCenter server appliance that is built on a SUSE Linux framework. Also with the new appliance comes the ability to leverage existing NIS authentication infrastructure. The vCenter server appliance can be configured to use a NIS server from the Authentication tab.

It is important to note here that this use of NIS does not extend to a Windows-based vCenter installation.

vCenter Security Explained

If a user logs in to a vCenter instance that is installed on a domain member server, the user will receive the assigned permissions that correspond to his or her AD identity. For example, say a user logs in to vCenter for the first time at 10AM; vCenter will contact a DC to verify the user's AD identity, and then cache his or her AD information locally for future reference. By default, this local cache is maintained for 24 hours. That means if the user logs in to vCenter again within that 24-hour period, it will not require another AD query, reducing the network traffic.

Please keep in mind that vCenter cannot function as a replacement for ADUC (Active Directory Users and Computers) in that it cannot be used to manage the AD accounts or users and groups.

If modifications are made to users' passwords, those changes will not be reflected in vCenter until the validation time has expired. To change the validation time in vCenter, use the Administration drop-down menu from the top vCenter toolbar.

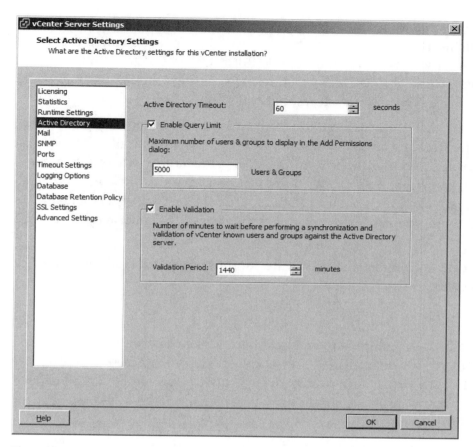

Figure 6.43
Changing the Active Directory configuration for vCenter.

In Figure 6.43, the AD configuration can be modified. Note that there are three variables that can be changed:

- **Active Directory Timeout.** Defines the longest allowed duration for the AD query to execute.

- **Enable Query Limit.** Defines the highest amount of users and groups that will be displayed from the AD query.

- **Enable Validation.** Defines the length of time that vCenter will wait before verifying its local user and group information is correct.

It is always possible to use local users and groups in the granting of permissions, but is recommended to leverage AD as a central point of permissions in the environment.

Permissions versus Privileges

The process of defining levels of access for users within vCenter involves the use of three components: privileges, roles, and objects. Roles are applied to an object in the vCenter inventory. These objects include: datacenters, clusters, hosts, resource pools, folders, VMs, templates, vApps, datastores, networks, and distributed port groups.

A privilege is a task that a user is permitted to perform, such as powering on a VM, connecting to a network, creating a datastore, etc. A role is a group of privileges that can be assigned. An object is a location in the vCenter inventory where the role will be assigned. Roles can either be a direct assignment, meaning that the role is assigned at an object, and any child objects do not inherit the role, or it can be assigned at an upper-level object, and the privileges contained therein will be inherited by all child objects.

Remember that permissions defined in vCenter do not apply if the administrator or user connects directly to the ESXi host.

Why Roles?

The use of roles allows the administrator to configure a set of permissions and assign them to users and groups defined in Active Directory, granting access based on AD memberships. This is a very handy concept in that a set of privileges can be defined once, and effect many users, guaranteeing the level of access desired by the administrator.

In Figure 6.44, a role can be created by navigating to the Administration toolbar and selecting Roles. Using the Add Role link, the administrator can assign any of the pre-defined roles available through vCenter, or a custom set of privileges can be assigned as well.

vCenter Security Considerations

When providing access to the vCenter environment, consideration should be taken to evaluate the actual permissions that a user needs, not the permissions that they desire. In many cases, these are vastly different permission sets. In general, the principle of least privilege should be considered, as a user having insufficient access is generally much safer than the same user with too much access. It is helpful to remember that permissons are inherited from a parent object to child objects by default. For example, a user may be granted Virtual Machine Power User to a folder, but have No Access at a particular VM. You may want to consider creating a spreadsheet that details each user and the permissions that they require. This will come in very handy when troubleshooting user access to vCenter.

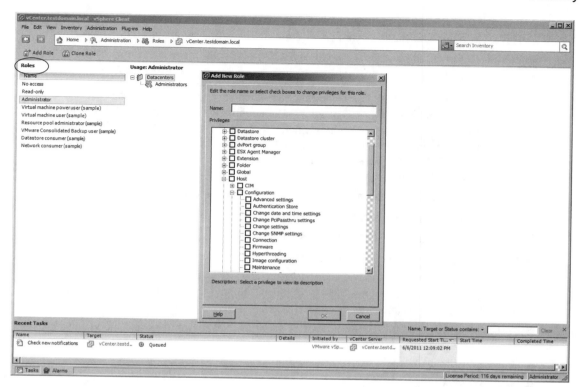

Figure 6.44
Defining a role.

Removing the Administrators Group

There are situations in which the vCenter application is installed on a stand-alone server rather than a domain member. In this situation, the local Administrators group is automatically granted Administrator-level permissions in vCenter. In most cases, this is not a desired outcome. Consider removing this default Administrators group from the vCenter permissions, and add each individual user and grant him the permissions that he requires. This will make management and auditing a simplified endeavor.

As an alternative, the local administrator account can be added to vCenter with the appropriate permissions and can act as a "back door" access point if AD cannot be used as an authentication mechanism.

Windows Firewall Settings

Since vCenter is installed on a Windows-based server, it will utilize the local Windows Firewall rather than defining a separate set of firewall rules that must be enforced. The ports that vCenter utilizes are listed next. It is recommended that these ports remain in an unblocked state during normal operations.

- Port 22 (TCP) is used by vCenter to allow SSH access to vCenter Operations Standard. Port 22 also provides the data path when Converter is converting a Linux-based device.
- Port 25 (TCP) is used by vCenter as part of SMTP-based notifications.
- Port 53 (UDP) vCenter uses port 53 for DNS queries.
- Port 80 (TCP) is used for SRM communication between sites, used to download client plug-ins, and to query vCenter for inventory information. Port 80 is also used by Update Manager to download updates and access patch metadata, communicate with ESXi hosts, and communicate with vCenter. Port 80 is used by DPM to communicate with the iLO or DRAC or each ESXi host. VMware View also utilizes port 80 to upload and download VMs as a part of local mode usage.
- Port 88 (TCP/UDP) is used by vCenter to transmit and receive Kerberos traffic.
- Port 161 (UDP) is used by vCenter for SNMP polling traffic.
- Port 162 (UDP) is used to send SNMP trap information.
- Port 389 (TCP) is used to communicate between vCenter servers participating in Linked Mode.
- Port 443 is used by vCenter and DPM to communicate with the HP iLO for remote management, and to provide web access to the vCenter server.
- Port 445 (TCP) is used by vCenter as part of the authentication of users and the vCenter server.
- Port 623 (UDP) is used by DPM to communicate with IPMI-based hosts.
- Port 636 (TCP) is used to communicate between vCenter servers participating in Linked Mode.
- Port 902 (TCP/UDP) is used to communicate between the vCenter server and each ESXi host.
- Port 903 (TCP) provides console access to the VMs.
- Port 1433 (TCP) is used by the vCenter server to communicate with the SQL database.
- Port 1521 (TCP) is used by the vCenter server to communicate with the Oracle database.
- Port 5989 (TCP) provides a communications link between the vCenter server and each ESXi host.
- Port 8005 (TCP) is used by the vCenter server for internal communications.
- Port 8006 (TCP) is used by the vCenter server for internal communications.
- Port 8080 (TCP) is used by the vCenter Management Web Services.
- Port 8083 (TCP) is used for internal diagnostics purposes by vCenter.
- Port 8085 (TCP) is used for internal diagnostics purposes by vCenter.
- Port 8086 (TCP) is used by the vCenter server for internal communications.
- Port 8087 (TCP) is used for internal diagnostics purposes by vCenter.
- Port 8443 (TCP) is used by the vCenter Management Web Services.
- Port 27000 (TCP) is used by vCenter to provide licensing services to ESX/ESXi 3.x hosts.

- Port 27010 (TCP) is used by vCenter to provide licensing services to ESX/ESXi 3.x hosts.
- Port 60099 (TCP) is used by vCenter to provide inventory information to vCenter add-ons.

SSL Certificates and Host Certificate Checking

Similar to many IT vendors and manufacturers, VMware utilizes the concept of certificates to verify the identity of a device on the network, and to reduce the possibility of an intruder "spoofing" the identity of an internal device in order to gain access to an internal network. By default, all communications between a vCenter server and each ESXi host in its inventory occur through SSL and are encrypted through the use of a certificate.

Entities such as Verisign are termed "pre-trusted" in that they are accepted by default on Windows operating systems. If desired, it is also possible to import a certificate from an internal CA that may already be deployed in an environment. These internal certificates must be pre-trusted by adding it to the local certificate store before VMware can utilize them to encrypt communication. The certificate will need to be added on each device where the vSphere Client will be used to manage the vCenter server.

Each certificate must use an RSA key that uses an encryption length between 512 and 1024 bits, with the recommended key length being 1024 bits. An acceptable certificate has three components: the private key or rui.key file, the rui.crt file (which is the certificate itself) and the PFX. The third component, the PFX (Personal Information Exchange Format), defines the method used to transport the key to the vCenter server or the client device. Microsoft uses PKCS #12 format in its CrytpoAPI implementation.

Note:

- If vCenter is installed on a Windows 2003 x64 server, the default certificate is located on the vCenter server at: C:\Documents and Settings\All Users\Application Data\VMware\VMware VirtualCenter\SSL\.

- If the vCenter instance is installed on a Windows Server 2008 server, the default certificate is located in the C:\Program Data\VMware\VMware VirtualCenter\SSL\ folder.

TROUBLESHOOTING

From a management perspective, the addition of a vCenter server to manage the environment brings a lot of "enterprise-level" tools and capabilities. But at the same time, like any other software management application, things can go out into left field; you may need to investigate and remedy the situation.

vCenter Connectivity Issues

Troubleshooting the vCenter environment begins with determining whether vCenter can be accessed. If the vCenter service has stopped for some reason, there are two ways that this situation will manifest itself:

- Attempts to log in to vCenter will fail.
- If an administrator is in vCenter when the service stops, the screen may turn a "milky" white and the screen will freeze. In some cases, Task Manager may be required in order to exit the vCenter application.

The first step is to verify whether the vCenter service is running. Open Services MMC and verify the status of the VMware services.

In Figure 6.45, the status of the individual services that provide vCenter functionality can be viewed through the Services MMC snap-in. If the vCenter server service status is listed as "Stopped," the first step is to determine whether the service can be restarted. Right-click on the service and select Restart. If the service can be restarted, minimize the Services MMC and attempt to log in. If the login is successful, check the Event Logs from within the Windows server, and check the vCenter logs, particularly the vpxd.log, to analyze the event that caused the service to stop.

If the vCenter service will not restart, the vCenter logs provide the best place to begin the analysis of the problem. For vCenter servers installed on a Windows Server 2003 platform, the logs are located in the c:\Documents and Settings\All Users\Application Data\VMware\VMware Virtual Center \Logs folder. For those installations that use Windows Server 2008 as their framework, the logs are found in the C:\ProgramData \VMware\VMware VirtualCenter\Logs folder. Again, we will be examining the vpxd.log file for additional information.

The vCenter logs are also available from the vCenter database and can be easily exported for troubleshooting purposes. If you are using the Linux-based vCenter

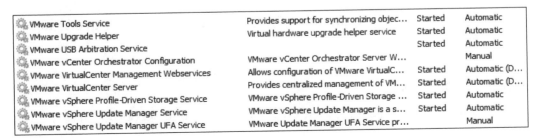

Figure 6.45
Verifying the status of vCenter services.

appliance, the logs can be located at /var/log/vmware/vpx within the file structure of the appliance itself.

There are two mandatory folders that must be present and intact in order for the vCenter server service to start successfully. If this is a vCenter instance that is installed on a Windows Server 2003 server, these folders are:

C:\Documents and Settings\All Users\Application Data\VMware\VMware Virtual-Center\sysprep, and C:\Documents and Settings\All Users\Application Data\ VMware\VMware VirtualCenter\docRoot\diagnostics.

If the base operating system is Windows Server 2008, the mandatory folders are:

C:\ProgramData\VMware\VMware VirtualCenter\sysprep, and C:\ProgramData\ VMware\VMware VirtualCenter\docRoot\diagnostics.

The vCenter server service is intrinsically dependent on the status of the associated vCenter database. If the database becomes inaccessible for any reason, the vCenter server service will stop, and will not restart until the database is accessible again. The first step is to verify that the ODBC connection is configured correctly.

VMware vCenter currently supports databases provided by Microsoft, Oracle, and DB2. The first step is to verify the status of the vCenter database. Check connectivity to the database, the status of the database server services, and whether the database server itself is experiencing hardware issues.

Likely candidates that can also cause problems are:

- If the transaction log or the database fills the underlying disk space
- The sparse file fills up available disk space
- The failure of database backups

In many situations, consideration is given to protecting the vCenter server, and providing a level or recoverability for the server. But it is a design best practice to protect the database through some means of clustering or replication as well.

The database can become unavailable when the default vCenter certificates are upgraded in the environment. In this situation, resetting the vCenter database password is required. From the vCenter server command line, use the vpxd --P new password command, where "new password" refers to the new database password.

The configured ODBC Data Source is defined in the registry under the HKEY_LO-CAL_MACHINE\SOFTWARE\VMware, Inc.\VMware VirtualCenter\DB hive, under the "1" key. An administrator can log in to the vCenter server and use regedit.exe to navigate the registry to this key and verify correct configuration.

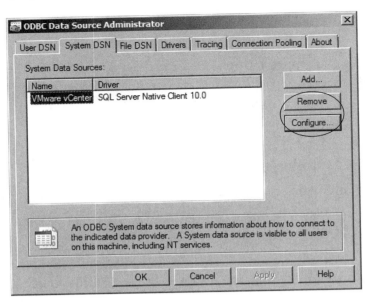

Figure 6.46
Configuring the ODBC data source.

If the current configuration is incorrect, use the Administrative Tools > Data Sources (ODBC) link to modify the configuration.

As shown in Figure 6.46, the Data Sources wizard will allow the administrator to correct any configuration issues that exist with the database connection. To modify the current settings, select the System DSN tab, highlight the currently configured data source, and click on Configure. The wizard will allow the modifications to be completed, and will permit the administrator to test the configuration to verify that the database is configured correctly and that it is accessible. Once the updated configuration has completed, the vCenter server service can now be restarted.

If the vCenter database is using an Oracle instance, the configuration can be verified by opening the tnsnames.ora file located in the C:\Oracle\Oraxx\NETWORK\ADMIN path on the vCenter server. The field containing "xx" refers to the version of Oracle being used; this field will either be a 9i or 10g. The particular field of interest is the "Host =" entry. This value indicates the Oracle instance to be used by vCenter. If this value is incorrect, open the tnsnames.ora file with a text editor such as Notepad, modify the server name to the correct server identity, and save the file. Again, use the ODBC link from the Administrative Tools link, highlight the System DSN, and select Configure. Verify the entries, and use the Test Connection link to verify correct functionality.

If the database configuration is correct, and the vCenter will not start, determine if the required ports are available and not in use by another application. These ports are 80, 443, and 902. If these ports are already in use, the vCenter server service will not start.

The state of the database server plays a major role in the vCenter server service starting correctly. For example, if the database volume or the logs volume has run out of free disk space, the database has a fragmentation problem; or if a scheduled backup has failed, the SQL Server service may stop and this will cause the vCenter server service to stop.

Logging

We've found that VMware provides a wealth of information through log files accessible from the physical ESXi hosts. This is an excellent resource when you are troubleshooting an issue, gathering information about an intermittent problem, or if you are required by law to maintain an archive of host logs.

In this respect, vCenter is very similar to the ESXi host: logging information is easily available, and is an excellent resource for troubleshooting information. If you are using a Windows Server 2008–based vCenter, these files can be found in the C:\ProgramData\VMware\VMware VirtualCenter\Logs folder. If your vCenter is installed on a Windows Server 2003 device, the logs are found in C:\Documents and Settings \All Users\Application Data\VMware\VirtualCenter\logs.

Log Types and Function

vCenter maintains two separate logs; the first is the vpxd log. The vpxd log information is reported by the vpxd service, known as vpxd.exe, and is defined as a service log. By default, there will be a maximum of 10 files, and each will have a maximum size of 5MB. A new vpxd.log is automatically created when the vpxd service is restarted, or when the log file reaches 5MB. In order to reduce the disk space required for these logs, only the two most recent log files are maintained in an uncompressed state.

The second log, the vpxd-profiler log, contains inventory and performance-related information.

Both of these logs can be accessed using the System Logs icon from the vCenter Administration toolbar, or directly through the file system. For a Windows Server 2003 installation of vCenter, the logs are found at c:\Documents and Settings\All Users\Application Data\VMware\VMware Virtual Center\Logs. For a Windows Server 2008 installation, the logs are found at c:\ProgramData\VMware\VMware VirtualCenter\Logs.

Log Bundles (GUI)

In every perfect environment, there will be a problem from time to time. And there may be a time in which you will need to gather a complete group of log files and upload them to VMware via an FTP server. You have the option of locating and copying these yourself and uploading them, or you can use the easy method by using the Generate vCenter Server Log Bundle link from the Start > Programs > VMware folder in Windows programs.

In Figure 6.47, you can use the displayed links to create a standard log bundle or an extended log bundle. The resultant folder that is created will be in the format "vcsupport date time," where date and time are the timestamp when the folder was created. The folder contains details of the vCenter server, the licenses, logs, components, and services.

In Figure 6.48, we can see the files that are gathered through the Generate vCenter server log bundle link.

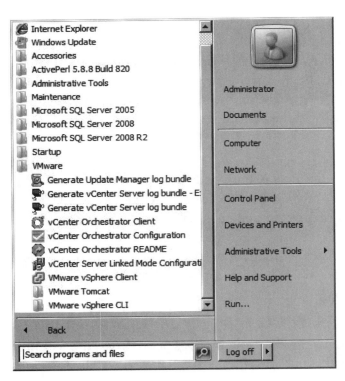

Figure 6.47
Gathering log bundles.

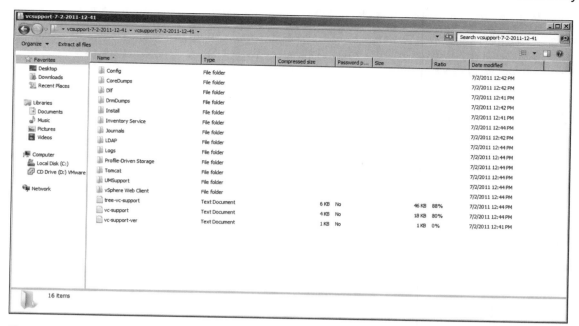

Figure 6.48
The standard log bundle.

Note that the second option in Figure 6.47, the Generate vCenter Server log bundle—Extended link, will generate a set of files that provides operating system details in addition to the vCenter files.

SUMMARY

As we have seen, vCenter provides a centralized graphic interface that simplifies daily management tasks, but the planning behind each of those tasks requires far more time and effort, and ultimately, may be more important that the actual management tasks. We discussed some of the security concerns surrounding vCenter and some tips to help provide a more secure environment. We found that there may be instances in which troubleshooting of the vCenter environment may be required, and we found that a regular backup of the vCenter database is a fundamental step to ensure service with a minimum of data loss.

In the next chapter, we will take a look at providing network access to our virtual machines.

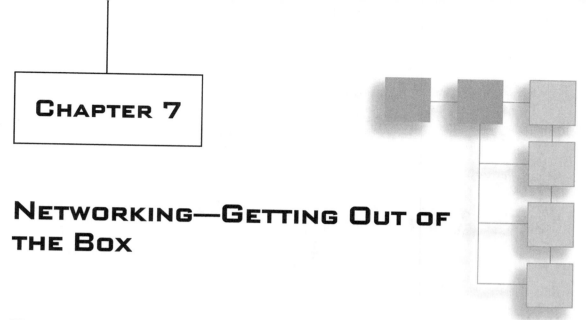

CHAPTER 7

NETWORKING—GETTING OUT OF THE BOX

Have you ever poked around the networking configuration of an ESXi host and wondered about the function of a certain checkbox? Before you learn the hard way, read this chapter. Trust us; you'll save yourself some headaches.

Networking in vSphere is unavoidable; in fact, nearly everything we do in vSphere requires some form of networking. But what if you don't want your VMs on the network? That's fine, but you'll still need some form of networking to manage the ESXi server. So, even if you manage to skirt past shared storage or even performance tuning, you won't escape the perils of networking. But, we will try to make it less painful.

In this chapter we'll explore how VMware incorporates physical networking concepts into vSphere 5. In particular, we will explain what virtual networking is and how it relates to what you may already know about physical networking.

PLANNING

As with our other chapters, planning comes first. It makes things work better and that tends to make people happier. But, to properly plan your virtual network, we first need to explain what virtual networking really is (and isn't) in vSphere 5.

Virtual Networking 101

To understand and use virtual networking, you certainly don't need to be an expert or even understand all the hairy details of TCP/IP subnetting or the OSI model. However, it would be helpful if you were at least familiar with what a physical

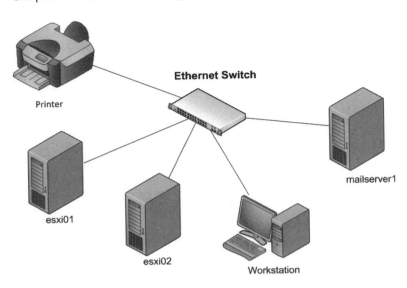

Figure 7.1
Example network diagram.

Ethernet switch looks like and, generally speaking, knew what they do and why we need them.

The Ethernet switch is responsible for passing the communications traffic from one device to another on a network. Network diagrams, such as the one shown in Figure 7.1, typically depict the Ethernet switch at the center of the network because the servers and workstations connect to it to talk to one another.

We have included a brief diagram of the OSI model in Figure 7.2 to help frame our discussion going forward. As you see in the figure, the OSI model is composed of

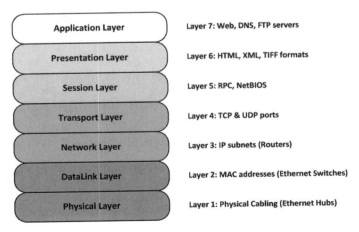

Figure 7.2
OSI diagram.

multiple layers, each with a specific function in networking. In most of our discussions, we will focus on Layer 2 and Layer 3; however, network traffic is comprised of components from all these layers. Refer to The OSI Model sidebar for more information.

In our experience, most would-be vSphere admins already possess more knowledge about networking than they readily admit. Yes, you read that correctly. It's probable that you likely know more about networking than you realize. Considering that even small home networks require some familiarity with IP addresses, if you have worked in IT much in the last few years you probably have what it takes to learn virtual networking.

The OSI Model

Let's review what each of the OSI model layers does for us:

Layer 1 is the Physical layer. Here the electrical or optical signals coming from the network are translated into digital signals that the network equipment can use. This includes physical cabling and connectors, and Ethernet hubs (not switches).

Layer 2 is the Data Link layer, where we can use the Ethernet protocol to frame the digital signals into useful datagrams. At Layer 2 we use Media Access Control (MAC) addresses to uniquely distinguish each host on the network. Each host has a unique MAC address assigned to its virtual or physical network card that allows it to communicate with other hosts. Ethernet switches operate at this layer, breaking up traffic into different broadcast domains.

Layer 3 is the Network layer, where we add the Internet Protocol (IP). Routers operate at this layer, breaking the traffic into different sub-networks called "subnets." At this layer, we direct traffic through a router if the source and destination hosts are in different IP subnets.

Layer 4 is the Transport layer, where we control the connection and state of the communication. Layer 4 is responsible for ensuring the reliability of the data transmission. Typical protocols at this layer include the Transmission Control Protocol (TCP) and User Datagram Protocol (UDP).

Layer 5 is the Session layer, which allows a system on the network to engage in multiple conversations (simplex or duplex) with the same destination without overlapping and confusing the traffic. Example protocols at Layer 5 include Remote Procedure Call (RPC) and NetBIOS.

Layer 6 is the Presentation layer. In this layer we establish a common communication channel for the application sending or receiving the data so that the other layers of the OSI model can interpret the data. Common examples include HTML and XML.

The final layer, Layer 7 is the Application layer. Layer 7 is where we format the request or response into the application-specific format so that the application can use the information it sends/receives. DNS, FTP, HTTP, and Telnet are all protocols that exist at Layer 7.

Virtual networking is really the same networking you've come to love (or hate) without all the hardware. What we mean is that you still have network cards, switches,

MAC addresses, and IP addresses. The difference is that in a virtual environment those devices exist purely as software instead of requiring hardware components like RJ45 ports and printed circuit boards.

Even though everything is virtualized, we still have to adhere to the laws of networking. Guest operating systems such as Microsoft Windows and Linux already know how to handle networking. From a pure compatibility standpoint it makes sense that VMware would want to keep virtual networking as closely aligned to physical networking as possible.

It's Just Software

It may seem a bit odd to think of networking in a pure software form, but in reality much of our physical networking is already software. It's just that the software is embedded in hardware chips. For instance, in addition to the RJ45 connector, a physical network card has a lot of circuitry designed to perform layer 1 and layer 2 networking. The physical network card has circuitry to execute proprietary code and algorithms, which in virtualization we represent with software. The software that operates the virtual network cards behaves similarly (or in some cases even identically) to their physical counterparts. The guest VM sees a network card, but that network card is actually software running in the hypervisor of the ESXi host. That software behaves, for all intents and purpose, like a physical network card so the VM believes it is a real network card. The virtual network card even has a unique MAC address!

The next logical step is to extend the virtualization of networking to include Ethernet switches. Like a physical network card, a physical Ethernet switch controls network traffic using software pre-programed into integrated circuits and other hardware chips. We can once again make this software run in a virtual environment without the hardware, just as we did with the network cards. The key difference here is that we need a mechanism to connect our virtual machines to the virtual switches.

Virtual Connections

With a physical network, we use cables that connect our servers and workstations to the physical ports on our switches. In the virtual world, the virtual network cards of our VMs are not bound to any physical ports, and therefore do not require any cables. Instead, virtual network cards are directly connected to the virtual ports on the virtual switches. Refer to Figure 7.3 for a clearer explanation of how network components are connected in a physical environment versus a virtual environment.

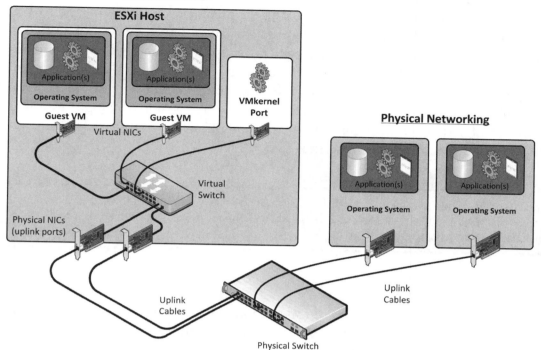

Figure 7.3
Physical connections versus virtual connections.

If you have ever worked with a physical Ethernet switch, you may have already seen or even created a "virtual interface"—that is, a virtual port. Many modern switches allow you to create these virtual ports inside of a physical switch even though the virtual port will never exist in the physical world at all. Often these virtual ports are used for the management of the physical switch; other times they are used for routing traffic, but in order for them to function we must assign them a MAC address and an IP address. In a virtual switch, we also use virtual ports for both management and connectivity to our VMs, but unlike some Layer-3 switches in the physical world, we can't use a virtual switch as a default gateway because it has no routing functionality built into it.

As we said earlier, the virtual switch is composed of virtual ports, but the virtual switch must still address each of these virtual ports somehow. The solution was to program the virtual switch to treat the virtual ports the same way a physical switch handles these ports. That is, give each virtual port a port number on the virtual switch, and allow each port to be managed independently. As you'll see later in this chapter, knowing these virtual port numbers can be useful in troubleshooting or when building advanced networking configurations.

Also, in physical networking, when you run out of physical ports on your switch, you must buy a new switch. In virtual networking we aren't bound to hardware, so you may just increase the number of ports that are available. Remember, a virtual switch is just software; you can increase its capacity by simply adjusting the software parameters. That means that if you add more VMs to your ESXi host, you may run out of virtual ports, but you can just add more and keep going. We don't cascade or chain together virtual switches; we simply increase the number of ports they possess. This is an aspect of virtual networking that we can't duplicate in the physical world (at least not without some help from science fiction).

Tip

Though adding ports to a virtual switch is possible, if you are using Standard Switches it requires a reboot of the host. The size of the VM Port Groups on Distributed Switches on the other hand can be modified without rebooting your hosts.

The Recap

The thing you need to take away from this section is that virtual switches, like virtual network cards, are really just software performing the duties and functions of their physical counterparts. We've taken the hardware shell away from a regular Ethernet switch and moved it into the ESXi server's hypervisor. The virtual switch behaves like a physical switch from the perspective of both the VM and any physical upstream switch it is connected to.

The use of software at the network virtualization layer has been further validated by Cisco with the release of their Nexus switch product line in the previous version of vSphere. The Cisco Nexus 1000V is a software-only switch, meaning you buy it as a virtual appliance, not a physical switch. This just reinforces the fact that you really can have a true network switch without the traditional switch hardware, and yet manage it via traditional command line tools.

Virtual Networking Ports

There are a variety of reasons you might want to add networking to your ESXi server, as a result there are also a variety of port types, all of which you will use. The three types of ports in a virtual switch are:

- **VM Port Group.** Virtual ports configured for the VMs to use.
- **VMkernel Port.** Virtual ports used by the ESXi hypervisor.
- **Uplink Port.** Virtual ports that connect the virtual switch to physical switches.

VM Port Groups

Just as in physical networking, your VMs must also plug into a switch to move their traffic around the network. The VM Port Group, as the name implies, is a group of ports on a virtual switch configured to be used by virtual machines. Only VMs may use these ports. The VMkernel, or hypervisor, has a special type of port that we will talk about next.

So what does a VM Port Group do for us? Well, for starters it is the only means a VM has to communicate on the network. We must assign each of the virtual network cards in our VMs to a VM Port Group.

We refer to these ports as a "port group" because we manage their settings as a group instead of by each individual port. This mirrors a feature we have in physical networking known as a port range. If you wanted to configure several ports on a physical switch to reside in the same VLAN, or to have the same port description, or even the same link and duplex settings, you might configure each port one by one, or you could configure them as a group.

Refer to Figure 7.4 for a comparison of a port group in a physical switch to a port group in a virtual switch.

Physical Switch Port Groups

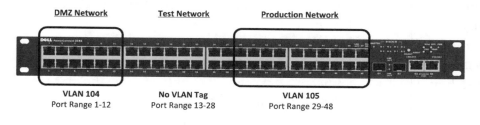

Virtual Switch Port Groups

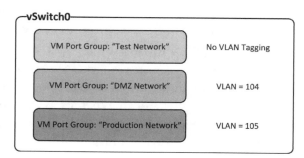

Note:
Port groups are not bound to specific ranges of virtual ports on a standard virtual switch.

Figure 7.4
VM Port Groups.

As we said earlier, in virtual networking we aren't locked in to a specific number of ports in our port groups. It would be a time-consuming mess to require you to configure each and every virtual port on your ESXi server, especially when you take into account that VMs can move between servers thanks to vMotion. You would spend nearly all your day tracking VMs and reconfiguring the various virtual switches. A VM Port Group gives you a centralized management approach. You create the port group, assign it a name, configure its VLAN options or other settings, and then connect the virtual network cards of your VMs into that port group. Each VM that connects to that port group will inherit those port group settings. For instance, you may have configured a port group for your test and development VLAN, which is using VLAN #102. You would configure this port group to tag all the traffic that passes through it with VLAN 102. We show how to do this in the implementation section of this chapter. Also later in this planning section, you will learn that some settings are best implemented at a VM Port Group level rather than configuring the entire virtual switch for a specific setting.

One final note is that it is possible to create multiple VM Port Groups in a virtual switch. Each VM Port Group is typically configured because you want to segregate your traffic into VLANs; however, that isn't the only reason you might create a VM Port Group. There are some planning considerations, such as promiscuous mode, which we'll discuss shortly, that are best implemented in isolated VM Port Groups to maintain higher security for all your VMs.

VMkernel Ports

We've discussed how the VMs connect to the network, but how do the ESXi hosts talk on the network? They aren't VMs, so they can't use the VM Port Groups we just discussed. They can't directly use a physical network card, because those are only used to connect our virtual switches to the physical world. We need a virtual port dedicated to the host. The answer is something called a VMkernel port.

VMkernel ports are special ports that we create in our virtual switches exclusively for use by the ESXi hypervisor, also known as the VMkernel. These ports are different from the VM Port Groups in that we manage each port individually instead of as a group of ports. In addition, unlike the virtual ports used by a VM, each VMkernel port will have its own IP address and MAC address. In many ways, a VMkernel port is equivalent to a virtual interface port on a physical switch; both types of ports are typically used to manage the switch. As we show in Figure 7.5, the end point of a VMkernel port is one or more services running in the hypervisor, not a VM.

When you install ESXi, one VMkernel port is automatically created on the first virtual switch so that you can manage the ESXi host. Though you start off with one

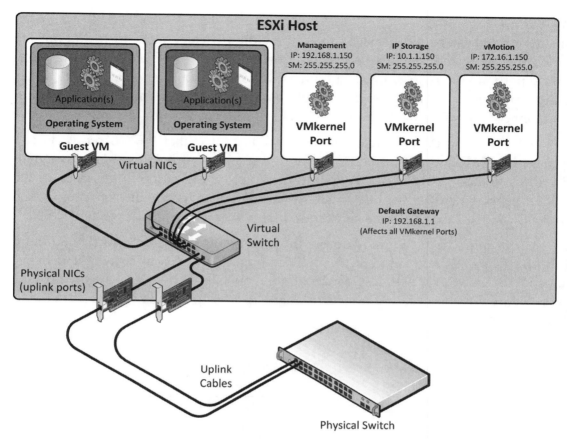

Figure 7.5
VMkernel ports.

port, you can create many different VMkernel ports on a single ESXi host because we can use VMkernel ports for different things. VMkernel ports can be used to gain management access to the host, to allow multiple hosts to communicate with each other for vMotion, to enable VMware's Fault Tolerant (FT) feature, and to enable the host to use IP Storage devices such as iSCSI or NFS mount points.

In addition, VMkernel ports can be multipurpose, serving any combination of these roles. Your network architecture will dictate how many of these ports you will require, as it often involves separate VLANs or even physically separated networks (as is often the case with IP Storage).

Later, in the planning section of this chapter, we will discuss some of the reasons why you might choose to create additional VMkernel ports. We'll also cover some of the advanced configuration settings that may be appropriate if you intend to use iSCSI or NFS.

Uplink Ports

Finally, there must be some means to connect these virtual switches to the outside world. We do this through a special type of virtual port called an "uplink" port. Uplink ports allow us to connect the physical ports on our server's network cards to the virtual switch. This gives our virtual ports a physical interface so that we can then connect the virtual switches to external physical switches in our network.

An important thing to remember about an uplink port is that the VMkernel doesn't leverage the MAC address on the host's physical network card, and we don't assign an IP address to that network card. We're just going to use the electrical interfaces on the physical network card so that our virtual switch can link up to another physical switch. After all, you have to have some sort of physical port to connect to a physical device.

Just keep in mind that we don't address the server's network card directly any more than you would directly address the uplink ports on a physical switch. If it helps, think of the network cards like a telephone—you talk THROUGH them, not TO them. Figure 7.6 shows how the network card is used in relation to the virtual and physical switches.

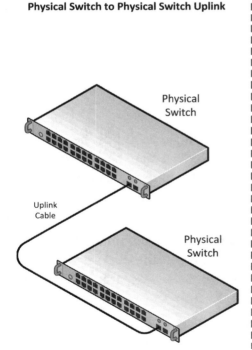
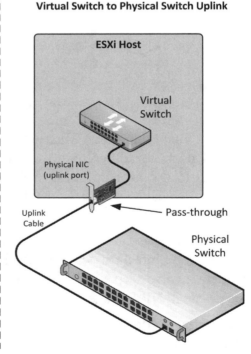

Figure 7.6
Uplink ports.

If you don't believe us, put a packet sniffer on the wire between your ESXi host and your physical switch. All the traffic from the host will originate from virtual MAC addresses generated by ESXi. You won't see the MAC address of your server's physical network card.

Also note that as shown in the diagram, each virtual switch can have multiple uplink ports. That means we can potentially use more than one physical network card when uplinking to a physical switch. That gives us redundancy and some load distribution depending on how you have configured your virtual switches. We'll cover the different outbound load distribution algorithms later in the planning section of this chapter. There are some cases where the defaults aren't ideal, such as when you want your VMs to spread their traffic across more than one network card.

If you intend to use multiple uplink ports on your virtual switches, you should be aware that the uplink ports do not operate like a port channel. That means if you connect two 1Gbps network cards to a single virtual switch, you will not have a single 2Gbps channel; instead, you will have two 1Gbps channels. There is some load distribution as we'll discuss later, but under most circumstances you cannot exceed the bandwidth of a single uplink port per VM.

Also, if you are intending to use VLANs in your virtual switches you will need to configure your uplink ports for VLAN trunking. This isn't something you do in vSphere, but rather something you will do in your physical switches on the ports connected to your ESXi servers—specifically, the ports connected to the virtual switches that you configured to support VLANs.

VLANs

In some instances, creating a separate network would be helpful and perhaps even more secure. For instance, some people prefer to physically separate their IP storage-based networks to prevent anyone else from accessing that storage. Another traditional example would be a DMZ or extranet from which you host web servers and other Internet-facing servers.

The trouble is that it's not always feasible to purchase and install a new switch every time you need a separate network. The solution is to use something called vLANs, or virtual LANs. No, these weren't invented for or even related to virtualization, but we do use them a lot. VLANs have been around in physical networking for a long time as the 802.1Q standard. A VLAN is the logical segmentation of a single physical network into multiple sub-networks.

Each of these sub-networks represents a different broadcast domain, and quite often a different IP subnet. That means your broadcast, multicast, and unicast traffic in one VLAN does not interfere with systems in another VLAN. In fact, if a system in one VLAN needs to communicate with a system in another VLAN, the traffic must pass through a router.

A switch isolates the traffic in VLANs though a method known as "tagging." That means the switch alters the header of each Ethernet frame to include a particular VLAN tag. The VLAN tag is just a numeric field that defines where that frame should be sent. When the switch forwards the frame to a host, the switch removes the VLAN tag from the packet so that the host doesn't realize it is in a VLAN. Only switches or hosts in "VLAN trunking mode" see all the VLANs. VLAN trunking means that we send the host frames with the VLAN tag intact. The host is responsible for reading that tag and responding appropriately. We use this method with ESXi servers to allow the virtual switches to see the VLAN tags. The physical ports that your ESXi servers are plugged into should be configured as VLAN trunk ports so they can service the different VM Port Groups and VMkernel ports with VLANs.

One thing you might have noticed is that by adding VLANs we have begun to share our network bandwidth—meaning that systems on different VLANs are actually competing for bandwidth on the same physical network. Consider the case of five VLANs on a single 1Gbps network. Even if each VLAN is using only 200Mbps of bandwidth, that 1Gbps network is now saturated. However, if we increased the line speed from 1Gbps to 10Gbps, there will be much more bandwidth available to be split across the five VLANs, reducing the contention on the network.

vNetwork Standard or Distributed Switches?

Everything we've discussed so far applies to both types of switches, but there are differences between the two types. The chief difference between the standard and Distributed Switch lies in how we manage them: individually on each host or centrally at the vCenter (respectively). Though a vNetwork Distributed Switch (vDS) has the word "distributed" in its name, it is actually based on a centralized management model. The configuration of a vDS is managed within vCenter's Networking inventory view. vCenter maintains this configuration in the vCenter database, but there is also a cached copy of the configuration located on each of the ESXi hosts that participate in the Distributed Switch. When a configuration change is made in vCenter, the change is propagated out to each ESXi server, as we'll show in a moment.

We said that the configuration of Standard Switches is maintained on each ESXi server. That doesn't mean you have to isolate it from vCenter in order to change the configuration. It means that you have to maintain your switch configuration on each of your hosts separately. That can become a headache, especially if you have many different VM Port Groups and other specialized configuration settings. You would have to recreate all these settings EXACTLY the same way on each of your ESXi hosts.

On the other hand, with a Distributed Switch you will configure those settings one time and in one place. vCenter then distributes this configuration to each of the appropriate ESXi hosts for you, saving you a great deal of time and the risk of human error. Plus, if you did make a mistake and need to make a follow-up change, you can deploy the correction much quicker.

In our experience, Distributed Switches rank pretty high in terms of things people have difficulty understanding. So, to help you better understand this concept, you can think of a Distributed Switch like a physical switch chassis. These are the large Ethernet switches that have multiple blades or cards in front, and that allow you to expand the number of available ports by inserting new "line cards" into the chassis. Figure 7.7 shows an example switch chassis and an illustration of our analogy to the Distributed Switch.

In the figure, you can see the various line cards in the switch chassis. A line card is just a circuit board with physical ports and the logic to forward network traffic between the different ports and other line cards. It is often referred to as the "Data Plane," as shown in the diagram. The line cards typically aren't managed directly. Instead, you connect to the management interface of the chassis, sometimes referred to as the supervisor or controller card. In the diagram this is labeled "Control Plane." Through this controller card, you can configure the ports on the various line cards with different VLANs, speeds, or other settings. The controller card then programs the line cards to respond accordingly. In a Distributed Switch, vCenter is the controller and the individual ESXi servers are the line cards.

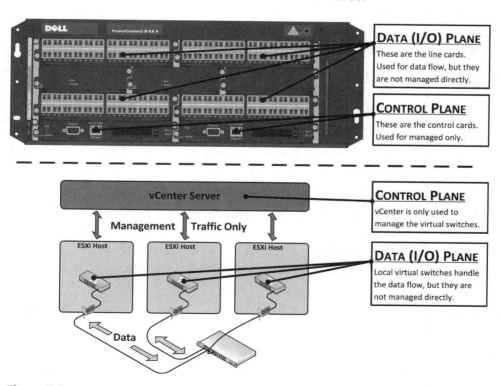

Figure 7.7
Distributed Switch versus switch chassis.

The notable exception to this analogy is that unlike many switch chassis, network traffic on the ESXi servers is NOT sent through the vCenter server. Doing so would create a single point of failure and would require us to bolster vCenter's network connections to handle the bandwidth. Instead, each ESXi server maintains its own layer 2 ARP table for all of its VMs and VMkernel ports. If a VM is moved from one ESXi host to another, its traffic will now originate from the new ESXi host because the VM is no longer executing on the other host. The fact that we are using a Distributed Switch has no bearing on the flow of the network traffic. Traffic from a VM must flow through a switch on the host that is executing that VM. Again, the central difference between a Standard Switch and a Distributed Switch is just in how we manage them.

What Makes a vNetwork Switch Different?

As similar as vNetwork switches are to their Layer 2 physical counterparts, they are also very different in several key ways.

Network Address Discovery

A vNetwork switch on an ESXi server is able to build its MAC address table by directly querying the virtual network cards attached to it. It doesn't need to perform IGMP snooping to figure out multicast group membership, or listen to the unicast traffic to build its ARP table.

Network Loop Prevention

In addition, a vNetwork switch does not require Spanning Tree Protocol to avoid Layer 2 network loops. This is true for a number of reasons. First, the VMkernel ensures that any Ethernet frames entering a vNetwork switch via an uplink port won't be accidentally rebroadcast out of another uplink port. If the frames that entered the switch weren't destined for at least one device connected to that switch, the vNetwork switch drops the frames. This way, the upstream physical switch won't ever see traffic rebound from the ESXi server, and therefore won't block the ESXi server's network ports.

The second reason a vNetwork switch won't cause a network loop is that these switches cannot communicate directly with another, even if they are on the same ESXi host. All traffic between VMs on different vNetwork switches must first traverse an uplink port that is connected to a physical switch. This means that it is impossible for two vNetwork switches to communicate and potentially rebroadcast traffic down multiple network cards, creating a loop.

Link Failure Detection

There are two ways the VMkernel can detect a failed network connection: Link State and Beacon Probing. Link State is actually as simple as it sounds. The VMkernel detects the presence or absence of a link on the NIC. Relying solely on the NIC for link failure notification, Link State will pull a link out of rotation when it detects a failure. While simple, Link State only provides basic failover and will not protect against a failed upstream switch or faulty configuration. For instance, one of your core switches might fail, resulting in your immediate switch losing its connection. In this case your ESXi server retains its link light, but it still can't communicate to other parts of the network because of the upstream switch failure.

Beacon Probing picks up where Link State left off. Beacon Probing broadcasts and listens for proprietary beacon probes over the physical network cards to detect upstream link failures. It combines this with link status to detect a failure and act accordingly. This model is most commonly used when there are stability issues in the physical network that could cause a logical interruption in the traffic that simple link detection couldn't identify.

Note

We explore this topic in more detail in the "Implementation and Management" section of this chapter.

Caution

Beacon Probing should only be used when you have *three or more* uplink ports in the same switch. This is because in a two-port configuration, the host won't know which network card has failed. It could be the NIC that was supposed to send the beacon probe, or it could be the NIC that was supposed to receive the beacon probe. Either could be true.

Enabling Beacon Probing in a two-port configuration may result in one of those ports being deactivated and unusable for network traffic.

In addition to a failover policy, you will also need to deal with a failback policy. The failback policy determines if a NIC is added back into the bundle immediately, or if it is left inactive until the next link failure. This is an important concern if you have a lot of intermittent failures that cause a lot of "flapping" of the network card. Disable this feature if you have that problem, and your failed network card will remain in standby until it is needed due to a failure on another active card.

Fat Pipes

Bottlenecks are everywhere, and they're an ever-present concern in networking. For example, if you cascade two high-speed switches together, the bottleneck becomes the link between them. We typically overcome this problem by using a much higher speed interconnect between the switches, such as using a 10Gbps uplink between two 1Gbps switches. This gives us the additional bandwidth we need to avoid bottlenecks in the traffic flowing between the two switches.

Unfortunately, it isn't always possible to add higher speed links between your switches (maybe they don't support it; maybe it's too expensive). In that case, we often bundle multiple smaller connections together in something commonly referred to as a "fat pipe" configuration. That is, we use a technology known as Link Aggregation Control Protocol (LACP) to bind these smaller links into one larger link. LACP has the ability to dynamically rebalance traffic between the uplinks to maximize the available bandwidth. So in our previous example, if we could use LACP, our two 1Gbps uplinks would yield a single 2Gbps link.

Unfortunately, neither the vNetwork Standard or Distributed Switches support LACP, which means that when you connect multiple uplink ports to a single switch, they behave like individual uplinks instead of one big "fat pipe"; there is no bonding between them. So two 1Gbps uplinks to a vNetwork switch won't behave like a single 2Gbs link—they're two separate 1Gbps channels. You can still use both links, but the traffic won't be evenly balanced across the two uplink ports. This may seem like a weakness, but in many cases we've overcome this limitation by moving to 10Gbps network cards or by adjusting the outbound load balancing options on the switch. Wait, outbound load balancing options? We haven't discussed that yet. Read on...

Third-Party Extensibility

The VMware vNetwork Distributed Switches are very advanced, but if you want to make your vNetwork switch behave even more like a traditional physical switch, you might consider purchasing a third-party virtual switch like the Cisco Nexus 1000V. We aren't trying to advertise for Cisco, mind you. But at the time of this writing, Cisco is the sole provider of software-based virtual switches that can be installed into vSphere.

The Nexus 1000V brings additional features beyond what VMware includes in their virtual switches, such as support for VLAN Trunking Protocol (VTP). Many of these features are intended for enterprise networks, but there are also features that could benefit even small businesses, such as LACP (mentioned above in the Fat Pipes section).

The third-party extensibility means that over time there may be more venders who participate in the virtual switch marketplace. The more venders that participate, the more options network administrators will have when it comes to integrating their virtual networks with the physical ones.

NIC Teaming

In vSphere 5, there are several things you can do with your physical network cards to enhance redundancy and balance your network traffic load. By teaming two or more network cards you can prevent a single point of failure and help distribute the load of your network traffic across multiple ports. In vSphere, we configure these settings as NIC teaming policies at both the vNetwork switch level and port group level (as an override to the vNetwork switch settings). While mostly unchanged from ESX 3.5, the concepts are still important to cover.

Load balancing gives the vSphere administrator the ability to distribute virtual machine traffic across multiple NICs. As you'll see soon, by default, a VM only uses one outbound network adapter at a time. Redistributing traffic becomes useful in situations where you need to provide the virtual machine more bandwidth than a single NIC would allow. Remember, vSphere doesn't support LACP to create "fat pipes," but we can support static port channel configurations with some load balancing options so that we can at least spill into a second network card with a little configuration change. There are five types of load balancing policies that can be set in vSphere. Each of these is unique and has some advantages depending on your deployment. They are as follows:

- Route based on originating switch port ID
- Route based on source MAC hash
- Route based on IP hash
- Route based on physical NIC load (load-based teaming)
- Explicit Failover Order

Note

"Route based on physical NIC load" is only available in the Distributed Switches.

Port ID–Based Load Balancing

The first of these, also the default policy, is "route based on originating switch port ID." This policy will route traffic out to the network based on the original port it entered the switch. You might recall we said that even switches have port numbers. This is one of those cases where the port number is put to good use. Each VM or even VMkernel port is given a number. That number is placed into an algorithm to determine the assigned outbound network card (uplink port). The assigned uplink port doesn't change unless that port fails or the VM is removed from the switch (via vMotion or otherwise).

Using this method, the hypervisor does not inspect the traffic as it flows through the switch to determine which outbound network card to use. That means that every packet is forwarded quickly and there is less overhead in the hypervisor. Again, this is the default option and it works well for most situations, but it means each VM or VMkernel port will use EXACTLY ONE outbound network card.

Source MAC Address–Based Load Balancing

The second policy was actually the default in ESX 2.x, "route based on the source VM's MAC address." With MAC address–based routing, the ESXi host will form an association based on the MAC address of the source VM to a particular outbound uplink port on the switch. Note that we said source VM, not source and destination. Since it is very unlikely you will change a VM's MAC address (at least not very often), you will also not likely change uplink ports very often. Hence, this method, like port ID–based routing, will only leverage a single uplink port per VM or VMkernel port.

IP Hash–Based Load Balancing

The third policy, "route based on IP hash," is the only policy that can split traffic from a single VM or VMkernel port across multiple outbound uplink ports. That means that a VM could potentially use two or more uplink ports if you route based on the IP hash policy. The hypervisor does this by inspecting the traffic and creating a hash value from the source and destination IP addresses of each packet. That hash value is used to determine which uplink port should be used to send the data.

As new pairs of IP addresses are found, new hash values are generated. This means that a conversation between one VM and one client will always use the same outbound uplink port. However, if the VM begins talking to a different client, the IP address hash will change and a new uplink port may be chosen; thereby distributing the VM's traffic across multiple network cards.

The key problem with this method is that most switches will not accept traffic from the same MAC address to flow from two different ports. It would regard this as a loop or some other configuration problem. The solution is to create a port channel of the network ports connected to the switch. That is, any network card bound to the switch must be in the same port channel on the upstream physical switch. The port channel configuration tells the physical switch that it's okay to accept traffic for the same MAC address on different ports.

Caution

If your ESXi servers will have vNetwork Switches connected to multiple upstream physical switches, you should be careful when selecting IP hash–based routing. In order to use the IP hash–based routing, you must create a port channel that includes all the uplink ports in that vNetwork Switch. If those ports are spread across two physical switches, you must have the ability to create a port channel that spans the physical switches.

Some manufactures support this behavior, while others do not. Check with your networking vender to be sure you can do this before enabling IP hash–based routing.

Load-Based Teaming

This algorithm is only available on the vNetwork Distributed Switches, but it isn't new. This feature, first released in vSphere 4.1, allows the VMkernel to shift temporarily some of the outbound network traffic from an overwhelmed uplink adapter to a lesser-used one. The load isn't truly rebalanced, but it does prevent a bottleneck on a single over-worked network card from creating a problem for all the VMs on that ESXi host.

Due to the behavior of load-based teaming, you must also configure your upstream physical switches in a port channel arrangement. This is the same requirement we have when using the IP hash algorithm, and it is required because a VM's MAC address may be presented to the upstream switch on multiple physical ports. Remember, switches typically only allow a given MAC address to send and receive from a single port on the switch. If a MAC address may be seen by the physical switch on more than one port, those ports must be configured in a port channel arrangement, or else the switch may reject the traffic from the alternate network card.

Explicit Failover

The fifth and final policy type isn't exactly a load balancing option, but it is in the same configuration window so we'll include it here. It is called Explicit Failover Order, and its job is to dictate exactly which network cards are used for that particular switch, port group, or VMkernel port. The most common use for this option is when configuring IP Storage on a single switch with multiple VMkernel ports (for multipathing).

In general, the default option, port ID–based routing, is sufficient. This is especially true if you are already using 10Gbps networking, but it even applies at lower speeds because the typical VM won't saturate a 1Gbps link during normal operations. If you have an exceptional VM, you can either consider upgrading to 10Gbps networking or use IP hash–based routing to distribute the traffic a bit more.

Design Considerations

We've assembled a collection of questions that we're often asked both during class and when on consulting engagements. In many cases our answer starts with "well, it depends." We won't try to answer your question; we want to teach you how to figure out the answer on your own. To that end, here are the most common design questions we are asked:

- How many network cards do I need?
- How many vNetwork switches do I need?
- How many VM Port Groups do I need?
- How many VMkernel ports do I need?
- I want to use iSCSI/NFS; do I need 10 Gigabit networking?
- Do I have to use VLANs?
- Do I need to use jumbo frames?
- Do I need a dedicated VLAN for my backup traffic?
- Which virtual network card should I use?
- Should VMkernel ports be on Distributed Switches?
- Which outbound NIC teaming option should I use?

How Many Network Cards Do I Need?

This answer is heavily based on the speed of the network adapter. If you're talking about 1Gbps, you may require several network cards to prevent a bottleneck. However, if you're talking about 10Gbps, you might be able to get by with just two (more if your traffic is particularly heavy). It will really depend on what you intend to put on the network and how much traffic growth you anticipate.

High Throughput VMs are systems that send large quantities of data on the network. This isn't necessarily a high volume of packets, but rather each packet is stuffed full of information. A very busy file server is a prime example of a server that may send a lot of data as people upload and download their data files.

The next factors depend on the type of traffic. You may wish to dedicate network cards to your iSCSI or vMotion networks because those networks require very low latency connections. If that traffic has to wait due to a congested network port, you will experience delays that could impact your VMs. It may be appropriate in your environment to bundle the traffic into a single virtual switch, but you should still provide additional network adapters so that you have multiple paths to the physical network.

In consideration of these points, here are some driving factors that may influence you to include additional network adapters in your design:

- **High Throughput VMs.** Systems that send/receive a lot of network traffic.
- **Production Network.** The regular network your servers and clients use.
- **vMotion Network.** Burst communication during vMotion.
- **FT Logging Network.** Heavy communication, and it requires very low latency.
- **IP Storage.** A dedicated iSCSI and/or NFS storage network.

How Many vNetwork Switches Do I Need?

How many physically separated networks do you have? By physically separated, we mean the switches are completely isolated from one another and in no way are uplinked. Each physically separated network should have a separate vNetwork switch (Standard or Distributed) to make the configuration easier to maintain—and to avoid accidental network cross-talk. A few examples follow:

- **Extranet/DMZ.** If not in a VLAN, a DMZ is often completely isolated.
- **Production Network.** The regular network your servers and clients use.
- **Management Network.** A secure network used exclusively for your management interfaces.
- **IP Storage.** iSCSI and NFS storage network.

How Many VM Port Groups Do I Need?

That depends on how many logical networks you will need. If the network has a strict requirement that nothing else may share its segment, you will need a separate VM Port Group and either a separate physical switch or a separate VLAN. Here are some examples:

- **Extranet/DMZ.** Public-facing, high-security area.
- **Core.** Production network, private-facing, but very limited access.
- **Production Network.** The regular network your servers and clients use.
- **Test/Isolation.** VMs that may share duplicate IPs of production systems.

How Many VMkernel Ports Do I Need?

Are you planning to use vMotion? Fault Tolerance (FT)? iSCSI/NFS Storage? If so, you should have a VMkernel port for each. That means a separate IP address too!

You will have one VMkernel port by default. It is created at install-time for management of the ESXi server.

I Want to Use iSCSI/NFS; Do I Need 10 Gigabit Networking?

The short answer is "no," but before you breathe a sigh of relief you need to consider a couple of points. 10Gbps networking is extremely advantageous in storage solutions because it allows the VMkernel to burst beyond the bandwidth of a single 1Gbps connection (you guessed it, transferring the storage data faster will improve storage performance). Also, the VMkernel CANNOT bond multiple 1Gbps network cards to create a single port channel with a speed higher than 1Gbps (these bonded connections are often called "fat pipes"). This means that if you have multiple 1Gbps connections, we have to use each connection separately. In virtual machine networking, this can be a significant problem, but in storage networking we have a solution: storage multipathing.

Storage multipathing enables the VMkernel to split up its storage traffic across the individual 1Gbps (or even 10Gbps) connections to achieve a higher throughput. This can increase your storage performance even when the VMkernel is under a moderate storage I/O load because we no longer have a bottleneck on a single network adapter!

Note

While 10Gbps networking is not required for iSCSI or NFS, it *is* required for Fibre Channel over Ethernet (FCoE).

Do I Have to Use VLANs?

No, VLANs are not *required* for virtualization, but they certainly help in many ways (not the least of which is cost). If you need to isolate your network traffic, you have the option to use dedicated physical switches or VLANs. If you either don't need separated traffic or you have a surplus of network cards and switches, you can skip the VLANs.

Do I Need to Use Jumbo Frames?

This one we'll explain a bit more because it has a pretty clear answer. If you will be using iSCSI or NFS datastores, you should consider enabling jumbo frames in your virtual and physical network switches. If you're not sure what a jumbo frame is, you can refer to the sidebar on jumbo frames for a brief explanation. In short, a jumbo frame is an Ethernet frame that is larger than normal. We typically accomplish this by increasing the Maximum Transmission Unit (MTU) size from 1500 bytes to

9000 bytes. Although any size larger than 1500 bytes can be considered a jumbo frame.

This is important because the size of a storage-based packet is actually larger than the size of an Ethernet frame. That means the ESXi host will need to break apart, or fragment, the storage packets to make them fit inside the network frames. By increasing the Ethernet frame size, we can reduce the amount of fragmentation required to transport your storage networking data. That equates to less overhead in the VMkernel, increased storage performance, and reduced network overhead.

Just remember to check with both your storage array and networking venders to verify that your equipment can support jumbo frames.

Jumbo Frames

The term "jumbo frames" refers to a technique used in networking that allows a host system to send Ethernet frames that are much larger than normal. A normal Ethernet frame has a Maximum Transmission Unit (MTU) of 1500. This means it can carry a payload of data up to 1500 bytes in size. A jumbo frame, however, has an MTU of 9000, meaning it can carry a payload of up to 9000 bytes in size; a 6x increase! That larger frame size doesn't really make the data move faster, but it does help with efficiency. Consider this analogy:

You work at a construction site where workers are digging a very large hole for a new building. They have a pile of dirt that is getting larger and larger and they want to move the dirt as efficiently as possible to another building site on the other side of the city. You are given two vehicles to choose from: a small truck like a light pickup truck, or a very large earth-moving truck such as a dump truck. Assume that both trucks will move at the same speed, but the cargo capacity of the dump truck is 6x that of the pickup truck. You only have one vehicle to use, and you assume that someone else will load either vehicle for you (after all, we're IT people). Which truck would you choose?

Our instinctive response was "the dump truck" because it can haul more in one trip, but there is a problem. Not all roads are equipped for such a large vehicle; some small bridges just can't handle trucks of this size.

This echoes the situation with jumbo frames. They can carry more, but not all of our network switches (the bridges) can support these larger Ethernet frames. They substantially reduce the amount of traffic on the network though (the driving across town), because we can put more data into each frame. Before deciding to use jumbo frames, you should consult with your networking vender to determine if your equipment supports this technology (and how to enable it if it does support it!).

Do I Need a Dedicated VLAN for My Backup Traffic?

That depends on whether your backup software will use agents within the individual VMs or if you will leverage one of the image-based backup tools such as VMware's Data Recovery product. In a physical environment, some companies prefer to segregate their daily/nightly backup traffic into a separate network to reduce traffic on the production network. In a virtualized environment you can certainly do this as well, but there are more ways to accomplish backups that don't apply to physical machines.

If you do intend to use agent-based backups in your VMs, you should consult your backup software vendor to determine whether they support a separate network for backups. If so, you can certainly do it in a virtual environment. Just add a second virtual network adapter to each of your VMs, and then attach the second network adapter to a dedicated VM Port Group.

Which Virtual Network Card Should I Use?

We said earlier in this chapter that VMs have virtual network cards. Like physical network cards, virtual network cards come in different models and types. In fact, with most of the major releases of vSphere we have seen a new version of virtual network card.

It's best to use the latest version of the VMXNet adapter because that is VMware's paravirtualized adapter. That means it has some advanced abilities that the other emulated cards do not have, such as making HyperCalls to the hypervisor. That's right, your virtual network card is talking to your hypervisor—and it's a good thing! Paravirtualized adapters generally grant us better performance because the hypervisor and the guest can communicate together directly.

There are many more network adapter types, but we'll cover these in more detail in Chapter 9 when we discuss virtual machines.

Should VMkernel Ports Be on Distributed Switches?

This is a tricky subject because there isn't anything inherently wrong with placing VMkernel ports on a Distributed Switch, yet if you ask two people their thoughts on the matter you are likely to get three opinions…. Note that we said "opinions."

From a technical perspective, you can certainly do this. Just bear in mind that if you choose to place your VMkernel ports in a Standard Switch and your VMs in a Distributed Switch, you'll need additional network cards because you cannot share network cards between the two types of switches. If you intend to place the VMkernel ports in a Distributed Switch, you should keep in mind that if vCenter goes down you might be unable to modify the VMkernel port settings. Okay, so that's a bit obscure and altogether unlikely, but it is a technical reason not to do this.

The truth is that you can migrate your VMkernel ports to a Distributed Switch with great success. Just be sure that you have architected the rest of your virtualization environment properly (reducing your single points of failure, etc.).

Which Outbound NIC Teaming Option Should I Use?

That depends on the type of traffic that exists in this virtual switch or port group. As we discussed earlier, you have five different load balancing options for your outbound network traffic, and each has its specific advantages and weaknesses. The default, "route based on the originating port ID," involves the least amount of overhead for the VMkernel, and still provides fault tolerance if you have multiple uplink adapters bound to the virtual switch. If you are using vNetwork Standard Switches, the default mode may be your best bet, but if you are using Distributed Switches you may want to consider the load-based teaming option "route based on physical NIC load" because it will help prevent bottlenecks at your network adapters.

The "route based on source MAC hash" method is actually a carryover from the ESX 2.x days, but it may be beneficial if you have a VM that actually has two MAC addresses on the same vNIC. How is that possible? Consider for a moment that you have two (or more) VMs that leverage Microsoft's Network Load Balancing (NLB) to distribute inbound network traffic evenly between them. In this case the VMs have a virtual MAC address shared between them and their own MAC address for all other traffic. Routing based on the source MAC hash could permit the traffic to flow out multiple network adapters, and it doesn't require any special upstream configuration on your physical switch unless you place your NLB VMs on different ESXi hosts. The "route based on IP hash" method can be used if you have a VM (or group of VMs) that regularly communicates with a wide variety of clients on your network. As you read earlier, the IP hash method allows each unique IP conversation (the source and destination pairing) to potentially use a different uplink adapter when leaving the virtual switch. It does this at the expense of overhead; the VMkernel must inspect the traffic to determine the routing. If the majority of the VMs in your VM Port Group will take advantage of the distributed traffic, feel free to use the IP hash method. Otherwise, stick with the default or use load-based teaming. Don't forget, if you choose to use IP hash your physical switch must be configured to use 802.3ad for the ports connected to the ESXi host.

Lastly, we have the Explicit Path Failover option. This is really intended for cases where you want to manually direct the outbound traffic over specific network adapters. You can also use this method in your software iSCSI configuration to force a VMkernel port to use a particular network adapter.

IMPLEMENTATION AND MANAGEMENT

After all that talk, you must be ready to dig in and start playing! This section covers the various means to put all that planning into motion, as well as explaining some of the more obscure settings found in the vSphere Client.

We'll start with some general network settings that are common between both the Standard and the Distributed Switches. Thereafter, we'll dig into the settings for each switch type, because while they share similar features, the features are often implemented in slightly different ways.

General Network Settings

There are some network settings that are common among Standard and Distributed Switches, or even unrelated to either. We'll go over those first:

- Enabling IPv6
- Changing VLAN IDs
- Changing the network bindings for software iSCSI
- Configuring NIC Teaming/Failover
- Network failover detection
- Switch notification and failback
- Traffic shaping

Enabling IPv6

Though the adoption of IPv6 has been slow, there are many organizations that make use of it. You can use IPv6 addresses within your VMs without any special configuration because the virtual switches are Layer 2 devices. However, before you can assign an IPv6 address to the VMkernel ports on your ESXi host, you must first enable the protocol within the hypervisor; IPv6 is disabled by default.

Caution

This change affects the entire ESXi host, not just a single switch or virtual port type, and it requires a REBOOT of the ESXi host to take effect.

You can enable IPv6 in the DCUI screen on the ESXi server, from within the vSphere Client, and from the command line. All the methods require a reboot to effect the change. To enable IPv6 from within the vSphere Client, follow these steps:

1. In the vSphere Client, select the host you wish to modify, and then click on its Configuration tab.

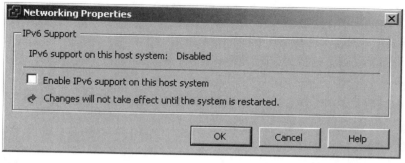

Figure 7.8
Enabling IPv6.

2. On the Configuration tab, click on the Networking link.

3. Click the Properties link in the upper-right corner next to the Add Networking link as shown in Figure 7.8.

4. Click the Enable IPv6 checkbox, and then click OK.

5. Restart your ESXi host.

Changing VLAN IDs

If you begin your virtualization project without VLANs and later decide to create them, you will need to edit the port configuration to include the new VLAN IDs. You might also do this if you mess up and have to change VLAN IDs because you typed it wrong when you created the port (that never happens, right?).

Caution

If you change the VLAN ID of your management network, you may lose connectivity to your ESXi server. Before changing the VLAN ID of this port, ensure that you have local console or remote KVM access to your server. Alternatively, you could create a second VMkernel management port for this host on another LAN/VLAN that you are not adjusting.

You can configure VLAN IDs on VM Port Groups and on each VMkernel port that you create. Don't forget about the default VMkernel port on your ESXi server. That one can be configured in the vSphere Client as well as the DCUI directly on

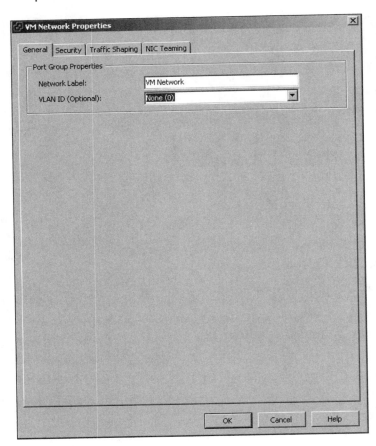

Figure 7.9
Adjusting VLAN settings on a port group.

the ESXi host. We'll now show how to change the VLAN ID on both a VM Port Group (Figure 7.9) and a VMkernel port (Figure 7.10) on a Standard Virtual Switch using the vSphere Client.

1. In the vSphere Client, select the host you wish to modify, and then click on its Configuration tab.

2. On the Configuration tab, click on the Networking link.

3. Locate the Standard Virtual Switch that contains the port group you wish to modify, and then click the Properties link to the right of its name.

4. Select the port group or VMkernel port from the list, and then click Edit.

5. Change the field labeled VLAN ID to the desired VLAN number, as shown in Figures 7.9 and 7.10.

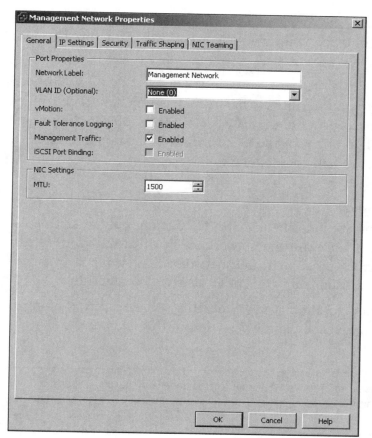

Figure 7.10
Adjusting VLAN settings on a VMkernel port.

6. Click OK to save the changes to the port or port group.

7. Click Close to dismiss the virtual switch properties dialog box.

Changing VMkernel iSCSI Network Card Bindings

Another cool feature VMware introduced in vSphere 5 is the ability to change the network bindings of the iSCSI software initiator from within the vSphere Client. Like many other advanced functions, in previous versions of vSphere this feature was reserved for those fluent with the command line.

These network bindings determine which VMkernel port(s) will be used to transmit data on the iSCSI storage network. This is important if you intend to load balance your traffic or have a failover system in place. To make use of the iSCSI bindings, you must first create the VMkernel port, and then select it from the list of available network adapters in the Software iSCSI adapter's configuration page. Configuring multiple network adapters will provide failover in the event one of the uplink ports were to fail.

If you edit the properties for a VMkernel port, you can easily see if the port has been dedicated to iSCSI traffic, but you are unable to change that setting here. The configuration is actually done on the properties of the iSCSI software adapter in the storage configuration section. The configuration for the iSCSI software initiator is covered in more detail in Chapter 6 when we talk about storage.

Configuring NIC Teaming/Failover

As we discussed in the planning section, the default NIC teaming option isn't necessarily ideal for every situation. If you want the network traffic of each of your virtual machines to be distributed across more than one network card, you may want to consider using either load-based teams or the IP hash distribution algorithm.

You can change the teaming configuration at any time. It is non-disruptive as long as you meet the requirements noted in the planning section of this chapter.

Caution

Do NOT enable IP hash unless you can create an Ethernet port channel for the uplink ports on your physical switch. Otherwise, the physical switch will block all but one of your uplink ports (creating, not eliminating, a bottleneck).

Teaming is configured using the vSphere Client, but you can configure it in two places: at the switch level, and you can override the settings at the VM Port Group level.

1. In the vSphere Client, select the host you wish to modify, and then click on its Configuration tab.

2. On the Configuration tab, click on the Networking link.

3. Locate the Standard Virtual Switch that you wish to modify, and then click the Properties link to the right of its name.

4. Select the switch name at the top of the list, and then click Edit.

5. Click the NIC Teaming tab, and then select the appropriate option from the Load Balancing drop-down list, as shown in Figure 7.11.

6. Click OK to save the changes to the switch configuration.

7. Click Close to dismiss the virtual switch properties dialog box.

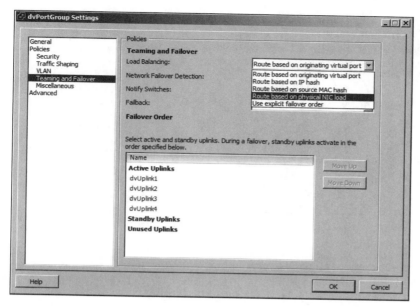

Figure 7.11
NIC teaming options.

Network Failover Detection

Has your ESXi host ever lost the ability to communicate on the network, even though it didn't lose its link light? Perhaps there was a routing issue, or perhaps an upstream switch suddenly failed. Whatever the case, your server was properly configured and connected to the network, but still couldn't communicate.

VMware instituted a solution for this problem, but it requires that you have at least *three* network cards active in the same virtual switch. The solution is referred to as beaconing because the VMkernel sends out proprietary "beacon" packets on the network and then listens for them on other adapters connected to the same virtual switch. If a beacon packet isn't received on the other adapters, the VMkernel knows something went wrong with the port that was supposed to have sent the beacon packet.

Notice again that we said three adapters. The use of link detection with beaconing requires that you have more than two adapters connected to the same virtual switch, because we get into trouble if you enable beaconing when you only have two uplink adapters in the virtual switch. Why? Refer to Figure 7.12 for a hint. If you have at least three uplink adapters, the VMkernel can easily distinguish which adapter is not responding because it will be the one that didn't receive any beacon packets from the other uplink adapters. Plus, the other uplink adapters won't receive any

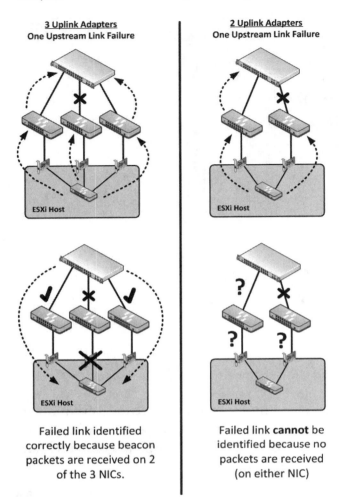

Figure 7.12
Link detection and beacon probing.

beacon packets from the faulty adapter. Consider what would happen if you only have two uplink adapters. The VMkernel won't know which adapter is at fault because the problem could be either adapter: neither adapter receives its peer's beacon packets, yet both adapters sent the beacon packets to their respective upstream physical switch.

Note

Beaconing is only used to determine if an online link has an upstream fault. The VMkernel will only send out beacon packets if the adapter's link light is on.

If you don't have three or more network adapters bound to the same virtual switch, don't despair, there is still standard link detection, known as "Link State only." While this isn't going to help you detect upstream switch failures, it will detect if someone unplugs/disables your network ports.

"Link State only" is enabled by default. If you wish to enable beacon probing as well, follow these steps.

1. In the vSphere Client, select the host you wish to modify, and then click on its Configuration tab.

2. On the Configuration tab, click on the Networking link.

3. Locate the Standard Virtual Switch that you wish to modify, and then click the Properties link to the right of its name.

4. Select the switch name at the top of the list, and then click Edit.

5. Click the NIC Teaming tab, and then select the Beacon Probing option from the Network Failover Detection drop-down list.

6. Click OK to save the changes to the switch configuration.

7. Click Close to dismiss the virtual switch properties dialog box.

Switch Notification

If a failover or load balancing event forces a VM to use a different network adapter, we need a way to tell the upstream physical switch that we've made a change. If we don't tell the switch what changed, it will continue sending data down the wrong port, creating a potential network outage for the affected VM.

Fortunately, VMware gives us the ability to notify the upstream switch via a Reverse Attribute Resolution Protocol (RARP) packet. This tells the upstream switch that the MAC address assigned to that VM has moved to a new port, and that the switch should begin sending data down that port instead. The net effect is that our convergence time is dramatically reduced, and the VM doesn't suffer an outage due to switch confusion.

The default configuration is to allow the virtual switch to notify the upstream physical switch of this change. Under almost all circumstances, this is a good thing; however, there are exceptions. One well-known exception is when you have two or more VMs configured to use Microsoft's Network Load Balancer (NLB) in unicast mode. That is, when the VMs are sharing the same network address, we don't want the virtual switch to initiate any sort of RARP notification because in doing so it would disrupt the traffic and cause the NLB team to fail.

Traffic Shaping

If you have a VM that is sending a lot of unwanted traffic on your network, you have a couple choices. One is to solve the problem by stopping the unwanted traffic. If that doesn't work, or is just undesirable, you could enable traffic shaping. One example that comes to mind is a Windows update server; though later versions of this product have introduced a built-in rate filter, earlier versions consumed a tremendous amount of network bandwidth at the expense of other systems. Traffic shaping can help curb that effect by throttling a virtual machine's network activity.

You can adjust the traffic-shaping properties of a switch at any time and the effects are implemented in real time, so be careful when making your selections. Also, in a vNetwork Standard Switch, you can only curtail the outbound traffic for your virtual machines. If you also desire the ability to restrict how much traffic actually reaches your VM's network cards, you must upgrade to a vNetwork Distributed Switch. The inbound traffic shaping doesn't prevent network traffic from entering your ESXi server, but it does prevent the traffic from reaching the VMs. This is done by rate limiting the virtual ports on the Distributed Switch. If you want or need to reduce the amount of traffic entering the physical network adapters of the ESXi host, you should invest in a third-party hardware device that would sit in-line with the ESXi host and the upstream switch.

Traffic shaping is controlled by three values: Average Bandwidth, Peak Bandwidth, and Burst Size. These three values work together to determine how much traffic a particular virtual network adapter can send. Note that we said virtual network adapter, and not Virtual Machine. That's because a VM may have more than one virtual network card, and each may be subject to a different traffic-shaping policy if connected to different port groups.

We'll use a car analogy to help clarify how these terms work together:

The Peak Bandwidth is the speed limit, but unlike in real life, you can't break this one. The Average Bandwidth is your "cruising speed." Yes, that is BELOW the speed limit in this case. Again, we're not talking about real life here. The burst size is a bit more complex so we'll extend the analogy a bit.

Think of the burst size like a turbo boost. (We have these in racing games for those of you without a hot rod in your garage.) The turbo boost is basically a small reservoir of power (the Burst Size) that you can use for emergencies. Normally you drive at cruising speed (the Average Bandwidth), but if you want to pass someone, you hit the turbo and race the engine until the reservoir is empty (again, that Burst Size). There is still a speed limit (the Peak Bandwidth) that you cannot exceed no matter what you do.

The faster you go (the VM's actual bandwidth), the sooner you exhaust that turbo boost reservoir (the Burst Size). When you do, you must return to normal cruising speed (again, the Average Bandwidth) until the reservoir has had enough time to recharge. That recharge period is dictated by how long you were above the average. In the case of our traffic-shaping algorithm, once your adapter is at or below the average bandwidth value, you may resume transmitting; in the mean time, the VM is momentarily blocked from sending.

So, hopefully you can see that there are use cases for this feature, but they aren't to simulate a WAN connection. Nowhere have we mentioned anything about simulating latency. That's because traffic shaping doesn't simulate latency. It is used to keep a rowdy VM in check, so that it doesn't consume all the available bandwidth on your 10Gbps network!

Okay, enough analogies. To control traffic shaping you must edit the VM Port Group or virtual switch as shown in Figure 7.13. The settings placed on the VM Port Group

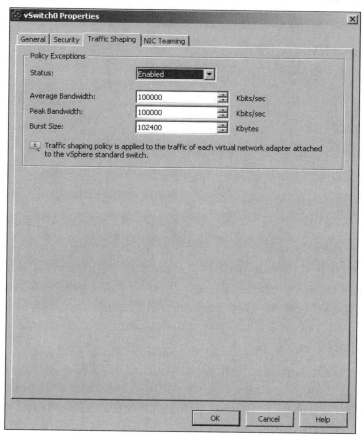

Figure 7.13
Traffic shaping.

will override what you configure at the virtual switch so that you can get granular with a specific group of VMs or virtual network cards. Note that the Peak Bandwidth and Average Bandwidth are controlled in Kilobits per second, whereas the Burst Size is controlled in Kilobytes. That is because the burst size is an amount, not a rate.

Caution

> These bandwidth values are configured in KILObits per second, not MEGAbits per second. Be sure that you add enough zeros to the end of these values or your VMs won't have enough bandwidth to communicate!

vNetwork Standard Switches

The vNetwork Standard Switch is available on every ESXi host. During the installation process of ESXi, one Standard Switch is created for you to manage the host and to provide connectivity for your first VMs. You can choose to either reconfigure this switch to meet your needs or you can create additional switches.

Here are some settings that are specific to the vNetwork Standard Switches:

- Creating a new vNetwork Standard Switch
- Creating VM Port Groups
- Creating VMkernel ports
- Adding/Removing uplink ports
- Adjusting the number of switch ports
- Adjusting the MTU size
- Switch discovery protocols

Creating a New vNetwork Standard Switch

There are many reasons why you might create a new Standard Switch. Here is one example: Perhaps you have a physical network dedicated to your iSCSI or NFS traffic, and you need to connect your ESXi host to this network. You can't share uplink ports between physically separated networks, so you must dedicate one or more physical network cards (uplink ports) to the job.

The easiest way to do this is to create a separate switch for your iSCSI/NFS VMkernel ports, and then assign the dedicated network cards on the ESXi host as uplink ports for that new switch. It sounds harder than it is, and you can do this at anytime. It will not interrupt your running VMs as long as you don't take active uplink ports away from other switches.

Use these steps to create a Standard Switch from within the vSphere Client. You can connect either directly to an ESXi host or to vCenter to perform these tasks.

1. In the vSphere Client, select the host you wish to modify, and then click on its Configuration tab.

2. On the Configuration tab, click on the Networking link.

3. Click the Add Networking link in the upper-right corner next to the Properties link.

4. In the Add Networking wizard, select Virtual Machine as the connection type to add, and then click Next.

5. Select "Create a vSphere Standard Switch" and pick an available network adapter from the list of vmnics, as shown in Figure 7.14, and then click Next.

6. In the Port Group Properties box, enter a name for the first port group created. Note that this is not the name of the virtual switch (which are numbered 0, 1, 2, 3...), but rather the name of the first port group inside of that switch.

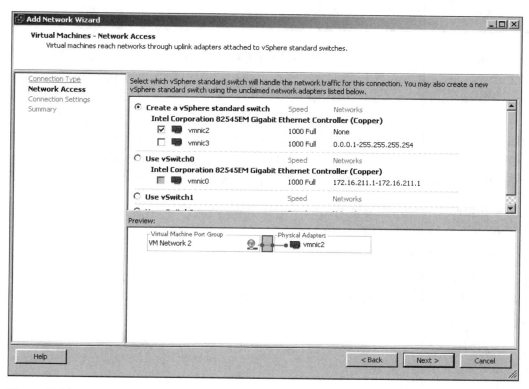

Figure 7.14
Creating a Standard Switch.

7. If VLANs are in use, enter the appropriate ID number.

8. Click Next, and then Click Finish to complete the wizard.

Alternatively, you can use either scripts or command line tools to create a vNetwork Standard Switch. If you are using the vCLI or VMA, the syntax is:

```
vicfg-vswitch -a <switch_name>
```

If you are using PowerCLI the cmdlet is `New-VirtualSwitch`.

Creating VM Port Groups

One VM Port Group is created for you during the ESXi installation, but you may wish to create another VM Port Group if you have multiple VLANs or special port security needs.

Tip

> You need to name your VM Port Groups identically among your hosts, or you will be unable to use vMotion to migrate VMs between your hosts. You can use Host Profiles (discussed in Chapter 13) to simplify this task.

You can create VM Port Groups in the vSphere Client or from the command line. In cases where you are manipulating a large number of hosts, you may opt for the command line approach or write a script.

If you intend to place the VM Port Group in its own virtual switch, just follow the instructions in the previous section on creating a Standard Virtual Switch because it automatically creates a port group for you. However, if you would like to add a new port group to an existing Standard Virtual Switch, follow these steps.

1. In the vSphere Client, select the host you wish to modify, and then click on its Configuration tab.

2. On the Configuration tab, click on the Networking link.

3. Locate the Standard Virtual Switch where you intend to create the port group, and then click the Properties link to the right of its name.

4. Click Add to start the Add Network wizard.

5. In the Add Networking wizard, select Virtual Machine as the connection type to add, and then click Next.

6. In the Port Group Properties box, enter a name for the port group, and if VLANs are in use, enter the appropriate ID number.

7. Click Next, and then Click Finish to complete the wizard.

8. Click Close to dismiss the virtual switch properties dialog box.

You can also use either scripts or command line tools to create a VM Port Group in a vNetwork Standard Switch. If you are using the vCLI or VMA, the syntax is:

```
vicfg-vswitch -A <port_group_name> <switch_name>
```

If you are using PowerCLI the cmdlet is `New-VirtualPortGroup`.

Caution

These instructions are for Standard Switches only! We explain how to create a port group in a Distributed Switch later in this chapter. Also note that these commands are case sensitive. There is a big difference between upper- and lowercase letters here!

Tip

For more information on how to use the vCLI or PowerCLI commands, refer to Chapter 4.

Creating VMkernel Ports

Like the VM Port Group, one VMkernel port is created at install-time, but if you intend to use vMotion, IP Storage, or VMware's FT feature, you will likely want additional VMkernel Ports to keep the traffic separate.

Much like a VM port Group, you can create VMkernel ports in the vSphere Client or from the command line.

1. In the vSphere Client, select the host you wish to modify, and then click on its Configuration tab.

2. On the Configuration tab, click on the Networking link.

3. Locate the Standard Virtual Switch where you intend to create the VMkernel port, and then click the Properties link to the right of its name.

4. Click Add to start the Add Network wizard.

5. In the Add Networking wizard, select VMkernel as the connection type to add, and then click Next.

6. In the Port Group Properties box, enter a name for the VMkernel port, and if VLANs are in use, enter the appropriate ID number. Refer to Figure 7.15 for an example.

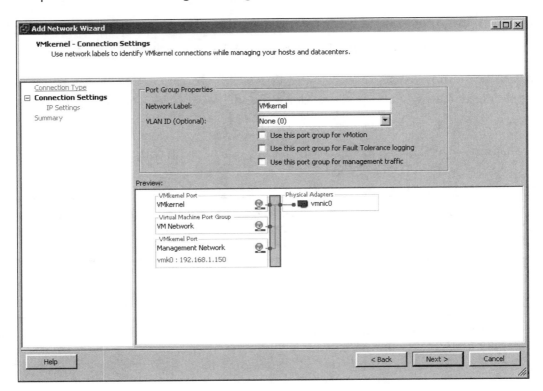

Figure 7.15
Creating a VMkernel port.

7. If the VMkernel port will be used for vMotion or the Fault Tolerance features, select the appropriate checkbox.

8. If the VMkernel port will be used as a redundant management port for the ESXi host, select the last checkbox.

9. Click Next and enter an IP address and subnet mask for the VMkernel port. You can also change or add the default gateway.

10. Click Next, and then Click Finish to complete the wizard.

11. Click Close to dismiss the virtual switch properties dialog box.

You can also use either scripts or command line tools to create a VMkernel port in a vNetwork Standard Switch. If you are using the vCLI or VMA, the syntax is:

```
vicfg-vmknic -a --ip <IP address> -n <subnet mask> "VMkernel_port_name"
```

If you are using PowerCLI the cmdlet is `New-VMHostNetworkAdapter`.

Adding/Removing Uplink Ports

You can create a new switch with only one uplink port, but if you want any degree of redundancy in your virtual networking, you should ensure that you have at least two uplink ports per switch. You can add and remove uplink ports at anytime, and the result is non-disruptive as long as you don't remove the last uplink adapter in your switch.

You add uplink ports via the vSphere Client, but you can also do this via the command line.

1. In the vSphere Client, select the host you wish to modify, and then click on its Configuration tab.

2. On the Configuration tab, click on the Networking link.

3. Locate the Standard Virtual Switch that you wish to modify, and then click the Properties link to the right of its name.

4. Click the Network Adapters tab, and then click Add.

5. In the Add Adapter wizard, select an appropriate network from the list, as shown in Figure 7.16, and then click Next.

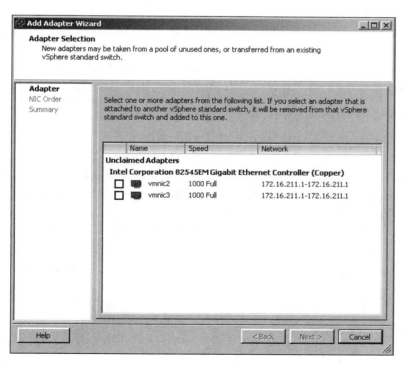

Figure 7.16
Adding uplink ports to a Standard Switch.

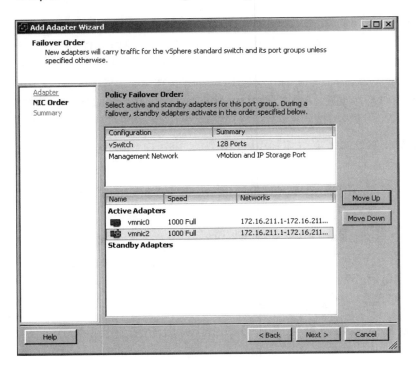

Figure 7.17
Adding uplink ports to a Standard Switch (continued).

6. If the new adapter's failover order is acceptable, click Next; otherwise, move it up or down in the list, as shown in Figure 7.17, and then click Next.

7. Click Finish to save the changes to the switch configuration.

8. Click Close to dismiss the virtual switch properties dialog box.

Tip

After you have changed the number of uplink ports, you may wish to edit the NIC Teaming/Failover options for the switch to properly balance the outbound traffic.

To add uplink adapters from the vCLI, you may use either the `vicfg-vswitch` command or the `esxcli` command. Here is the syntax for the `esxcli` command:

```
esxcli network vswitch standard uplink add --uplink-name=vmnic2 vswitch-name=vSwitch0
```

Adjusting the Number of Switch Ports

The default number of ports in a vNetwork Standard Switch is 120, but if you have more than 120 VMs on your server, you may need to increase this setting. It is uncommon to need to decrease the number of ports, but this can also be done. The number of ports is based on a doubling number of 32, 64, 128, 256, 512, 1024, 2048, and 4096; however, each has 8 ports subtracted from it to provide ports for future uplink ports. Therefore, the numbers of ports available to you are: 24, 56, 120, 248, 504, 1016, 2040, and 4088. Again, the default is 120 ports. You can see the total number of switch ports (including the eight ports reserved) from the vCLI using the `vicfg-vswitch -l` command.

Caution

This is a disruptive configuration change and requires a reboot to take effect. If you have vMotion enabled, you can migrate your VMs off the ESXi host to avoid taking VM downtime.

You change the number of switch ports using the vSphere Client or a script.

1. In the vSphere Client, select the host you wish to modify, and then click on its Configuration tab.

2. On the Configuration tab, click on the Networking link.

3. Locate the Standard Virtual Switch that you wish to modify, and then click the Properties link to the right of its name.

4. Select the switch name at the top of the list, and then click Edit.

5. Select the appropriate number of ports from the drop-down list, as shown in Figure 7.18.

6. Click OK to save the changes to the switch configuration.

7. Click Close to dismiss the virtual switch properties dialog box.

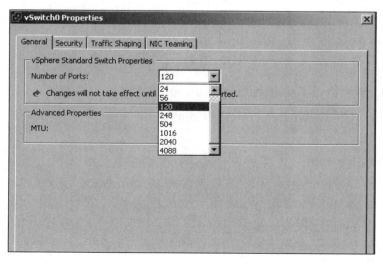

Figure 7.18
Setting the number of ports on a Standard Switch.

Adjusting the MTU Size

If you intend to use software iSCSI or NFS connections for your storage, you should consider changing your MTU use to allow for jumbo frames. As we discussed in the planning section of this chapter, it will improve the efficiency of your storage network, which may translate into better performance.

Tip

You should also consider increasing the MTU size on your VMotion and FT Logging VMkernel ports and port groups to improve the efficiency and performance of your VM migrations.

Caution

You can make this change at any time, but you must have end-to-end support in your physical network for jumbo frames before you enable this feature in vSphere. Otherwise, your traffic may be interrupted or completely blocked by the incompatible physical switches.

In previous versions of vSphere this could only be performed via the command line for vNetwork Standard Switches. VMware has changed the GUI to allow us to change the MTU size right from the vSphere Client!

1. In the vSphere Client, select the host you wish to modify, and then click on its Configuration tab.

2. On the Configuration tab, click on the Networking link.

3. Locate the Standard Virtual Switch that you wish to modify, and then click the Properties link to the right of its name.

4. Select the switch name at the top of the list, and then click Edit.

5. Enter the appropriate MTU value in the MTU field, as shown in Figure 7.19.

6. Click OK to save the changes to the switch configuration.

7. Click Close to dismiss the virtual switch properties dialog box.

Switch Discovery Protocols

Suppose that you want to know what port your ESXi server is connected to on the upstream physical switch. You could consult your documentation…. Ah right, no documentation. Well then, you could call someone to check for you. Oh, it's after-hours and no one is around. If only you had configured your system to accept CDP, the Cisco Discovery Protocol.

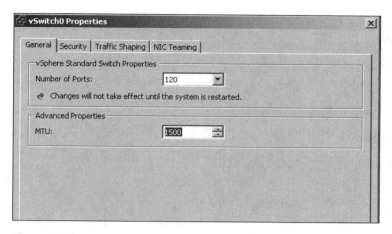

Figure 7.19
Setting the MTU size on a Standard Switch.

CDP is a Cisco tool used to discover other switches in your environment, and potentially collect information from them. This requires your equipment to support CDP, and your network administrator must have it enabled on the devices. If you meet all those criteria, read on.

In vSphere 5, CDP is enabled by default, and configured to "listen" for CDP information from its upstream physical switches. In this mode the virtual switch does not advertise any of its information to its peer physical switches, but you can change that behavior. These options are available in the GUI if you are using a Distributed Switch; however, if you are using a Standard Switch, you must use the command line. This means you will either use the vSphere Management Assistant (vMA) or the actual ESXi command line. The commands used in our example reflect the syntax used at the ESXi command line via SSH.

To set CDP to both advertise and listen, use the mode both as shown in our example (note that the virtual switch name is case sensitive):

```
esxcfg-vswitch -B both vSwitch0
```

If you want to check your work, or just verify the current settings, use the lowercase b argument as shown in this example:

```
esxcfg-vswitch -b vSwitch0
```

This will return the value currently set on the switch.

Tip

The Standard Switches only support CDP, but the Distributed Switches now support LLDP and CDP!

vNetwork Distributed Switches

Distributed Switches have a lot more features than their Standard counterparts. We discussed some of these differences in the planning section of this chapter, but now we're going to cover the details of how to implement some of those features.

- Creating a new vNetwork Distributed Switch
- Upgrading a Distributed Switch
- Enrolling an ESXi Host into a Distributed Switch
- Creating VM Port Groups
- Creating VMkernel ports
- Adding/Removing uplink ports
- Adjusting the number of ports in a VM Port Group
- Port Binding
- Adjusting the MTU size
- Switch Discovery Protocols
- Changing VLAN options
- Network I/O Control
- Network resource pools
- NetFlow
- Port mirroring

Creating a New vNetwork Distributed Switch

This is one set of steps that you won't likely follow very often. Not because Distributed Switches aren't used often, but because you only create them one time and in one place. Each Distributed Switch is created in the Networking section of the vSphere Client's inventory views. You don't create a Distributed Switch on each ESXi host.

Unlike their less-sophisticated cousins, the vNetwork Standard Switches, the Distributed Switches are created one time in vCenter, and then you "enroll" your ESXi hosts into them. That is the act of telling the ESXi host that it should retrieve its network configuration from the vCenter server. It downloads the configuration, keeps a cached copy for safe-keeping, and then behaves as vCenter tells it to; complete with VM Port Groups and VMkernel ports.

When you create a Distributed Switch, you will be prompted to indicate which version you would like. The choices are version 4.0, 4.1, and 5.0. Pick the highest option supported in your environment to enable the most features. The highest option is determined by your lowest version of vSphere that will participate in this particular Distributed Switch. So, if all the hosts in this switch will be 4.1 or later, and you are certain no 4.0 hosts will need to use this switch, pick 4.1. Just be aware that some of the features described here may not work unless you are able to choose the 5.0 option.

To create a vNetwork Distributed Switch, follow these steps. We'll then go through the various configuration options to tune the switch to your liking.

1. In the vSphere Client, select the Networking Inventory view.

2. Right-click the datacenter that will contain the Distributed Switch, and then select "New vSphere Distributed Switch" from the context menu.

3. In the Create vSphere Distributed Switch wizard, select the appropriate version of the Distributed Switch. If you are uncertain, and you have no legacy vSphere 4.x hosts, choose version 5.0. Click Next.

4. Enter a name for the Distributed Switch. This should describe the physical network that the Distributed Switch will connect to. For example, you might use "Extranet" or "Internal Network." This is NOT the name of a VLAN or subnetwork. Click Next.

5. On the next screen, shown in Figure 7.20, select the host(s) you would like to enroll into the Distributed Switch, and then select the network adapters from each host. You can edit the settings for the host as shown in the figure to change the number of virtual switch ports available per ESXi host. When you're done, click Next.

6. On the next screen, you can opt to allow the wizard to create a default Distributed Port Group for you, or you can deselect the option and create it manually after the wizard completes.

7. Click Finish to complete the wizard.

Upgrading a Distributed Switch

If you are upgrading from vSphere 4 and you already have a Distributed Switch in your environment, you may wish to upgrade it to version 5 to take advantage of the new features like Port Mirroring, QoS, and NetFlow. The process to upgrade the switch is very straightforward, and all the work can be done with just a few clicks of your mouse. To upgrade the switch follow these steps:

1. Before you begin, ensure that all the hosts enrolled into the Distributed Switch are running at least vSphere 5. Once you upgrade the switch, older vSphere 4 hosts will be unable to use it.

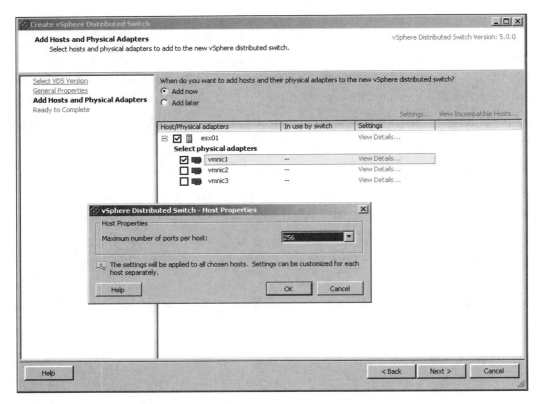

Figure 7.20
Creating a Distributed Switch.

2. In the vSphere Client, select the Networking Inventory view.

3. In the hierarchy on the left, select the Distributed Switch you wish to upgrade.

4. Click on the Distributed Switch's Summary tab. An Upgrade link next to the Distributed Switch's version should appear.

5. Click the Upgrade link, and then follow the steps in the Upgrade wizard to select the new version for this Distributed Switch.

Caution

While we can easily upgrade a Distributed Switch to a later version, there is no option to downgrade a Distributed Switch to an older version. This means that once you have upgraded, you won't be able to add older vSphere 4 hosts to the Distributed Switch.

Enrolling an ESXi Host into a Distributed Switch

During the creation of your Distributed Switch you are given the option to "enroll" ESXi hosts into its configuration. This allows the ESXi host to download its configuration data and then act upon it, configuring itself according to the vCenter administrator's design. The enrollment process installs an agent on the ESXi server that communicates with vCenter to retrieve configuration changes and updates.

To enroll an ESXi host, perform the following steps:

1. In the vSphere Client, select the Networking Inventory view.

2. Right-click the Distributed Switch you wish to modify, and then select "Add Host" from the context menu.

3. The next screen will look like the figure from the last exercise, shown in Figure 7.20. Here again, select the host(s) you would like to enroll into the Distributed Switch, and then select the network adapters from each host. When you're done, click Next.

4. The next screen will prompt you to migrate any existing VMkernel ports to the Distributed Switch as shown in Figure 7.21. You may choose to migrate all,

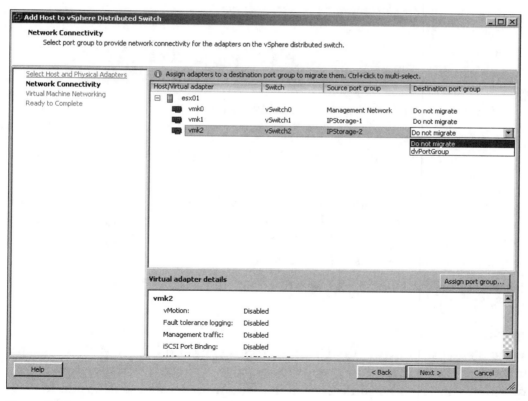

Figure 7.21
Enrolling an ESXi server in a Distributed Switch—migrating VMkernel ports.

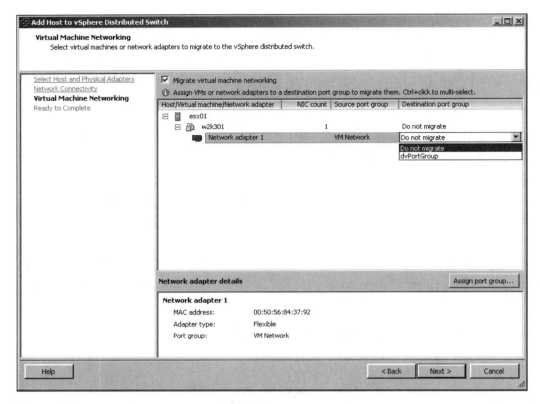

Figure 7.22
Enrolling an ESXi server in a Distributed Switch—migrating VM networking.

some, or none of the VMkernel ports to existing Distributed Port Groups. When you are finished, click Next.

5. Next you will have the option to migrate your VMs to the Distributed Port Groups on the Distributed Switch, as shown in Figure 7.22. Again, you may choose one, some, or none of the VMs to migrate to the Distributed Port Groups. When you are finished, click Next.

6. Click Finish on the summary screen to complete the wizard.

Creating VM Port Groups

Just like the Standard Switches, the Distributed Switches also have VM Port Groups. You will need to create these port groups in the Networking view of the vCenter server's inventory pane. Another difference is that you must create a port group for any VMkernel ports you wish to add to the Distributed Switches. So, for example, if you wanted to place your vMotion network on your Distributed Switch, you must first

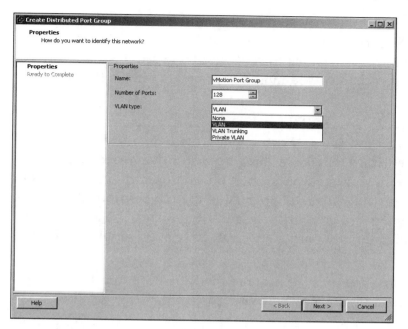

Figure 7.23
Creating a VM Port Group in a Distributed Switch.

create a port group for those VMkernel ports before you attempt to migrate or create the ports on the individual ESXi servers.

As we said, the creation of the ports is much the same as in the Standard Switches; however, you start the process in a different place.

1. In the vSphere Client, select the Networking Inventory view.

2. Right-click the Distributed Switch you wish to modify, and then select "New Port Group" from the context menu.

3. In the Create Distributed Port Group wizard, shown in Figure 7.23, enter a descriptive name for the new port group. If the port group is based on a VLAN, select the appropriate entry from the VLAN Type list and then enter the VLAN information. When you're done, click Next.

4. On the summary screen, click Finish to complete the wizard.

Creating VMkernel Ports

VMkernel ports are something in a Distributed Switch environment that we must still create locally. There is no central method to create these ports because each port is unique to its host. Remember, a VMkernel port is the network connection to the hypervisor on an ESXi server, and that port will have its own unique MAC address and IP address. While it is possible to configure these settings via Host Profiles as discussed earlier in this chapter, you must still provide a unique IP address for each ESXi host.

There are actually two ways to create VMkernel ports. You can either create a new port from scratch, or you can migrate an existing one from a Standard Switch. Both options are available in the wizard that we're going to walk through next. The migration method is commonly used when you start your environment in a vNetwork Standard Switch environment and then later upgrade to use the Distributed Switches. Also, all management adapters are created by default on a Standard Switch, so you must either manually migrate the ports, or create a clever script to do this automatically.

To create the VMkernel ports, you must navigate to the ESXi host, not the Networking view as we did when creating the VM Port Groups.

1. In the vSphere Client, select the host you wish to modify, and then click on its Configuration tab.

2. On the Configuration tab, click on the Networking link.

3. At the top of the configuration window, select the vSphere Distributed Switch toggle button to change the view to the Distributed Switch configuration pane.

4. Click the Manage Virtual Adapters link.

5. In the Manage Virtual Adapters wizard, select the Add link as shown in Figure 7.24.

6. The next window will ask if you want to create a new VMkernel port, or migrate an existing one. Click on "New virtual adapter" and then click Next.

7. Next you must choose VMkernel (it's your only option). Click Next.

8. The screen shown in Figure 7.25 asks you to select the port group to add the VMkernel port to. You may also designate the port for vMotion, the Fault Tolerance feature, or management. Click Next when you have made your selections.

9. Enter an IP address and subnet mask for the VMkernel port. You can also change or add the default gateway.

10. Click Next, and then Click Finish to complete the wizard.

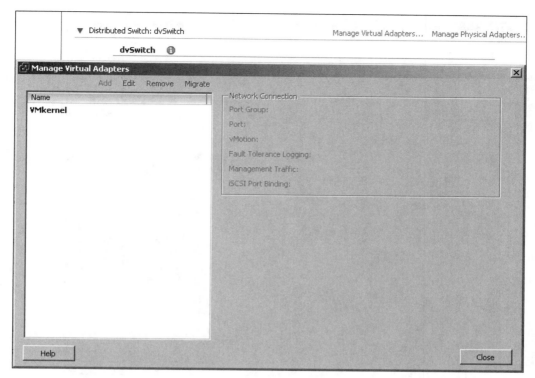

Figure 7.24
Working with VMkernel ports in a Distributed Switch.

To migrate a VMkernel port to a Distributed Switch, you will complete the same first steps, but we deviate at step 6:

1. In the vSphere Client, select the host you wish to modify, and then click on its Configuration tab.

2. On the Configuration tab, click on the Networking link.

3. At the top of the configuration window, select the vSphere Distributed Switch toggle button to change the view to the Distributed Switch configuration pane.

4. Click the Manage Virtual Adapters link.

5. In the Manage Virtual Adapters wizard, select the Add link as shown in Figure 7.24.

6. The next window will ask if you want to create a new VMkernel port, or migrate an existing one. Click on "Migrate existing virtual adapter" and then click Next.

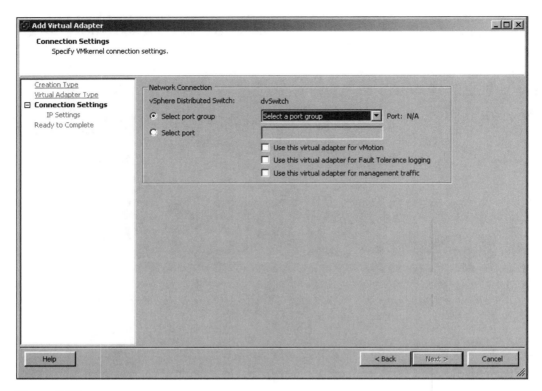

Figure 7.25
Creating a new VMkernel port in a Distributed Switch.

7. The screen, shown in Figure 7.26, asks you to select a port group to migrate each of the existing VMkernel ports to. Click Next when you have made your selections.

8. Click Finish to complete the wizard.

Adding/Removing Uplink Ports

Just like the vNetwork Standard Switches, a Distributed Switch can support multiple network adapters as uplink ports. The method to include those ports is very different; however, the behavior is much the same. Again, like the creation of a VMkernel port, the uplink ports must be modified on each individual ESXi host.

You may wish to increase the number of ports if you add a network adapter to your ESXi server, or if you were migrating from a mixed environment of Standard and Distributed Switches. Whatever the reason, here's how you do it.

1. In the vSphere Client, select the host you wish to modify, and then click on its Configuration tab.

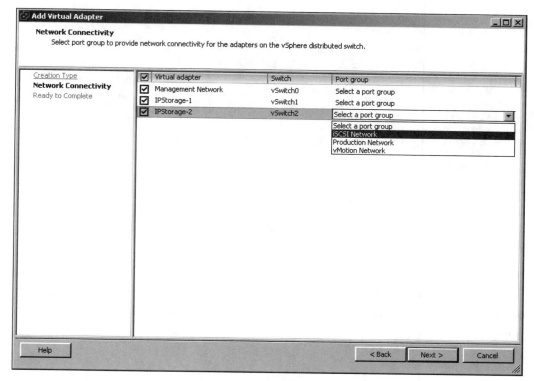

Figure 7.26
Migrating VMkernel ports to a Distributed Switch.

2. On the Configuration tab, click on the Networking link.

3. At the top of the configuration window, select the vSphere Distributed Switch toggle button to change the view to the Distributed Switch configuration pane.

4. Click the Manage Physical Adapters link.

5. In the Manage Physical Adapters wizard, select the Click to Add NIC link as shown in Figure 7.27. Alternatively, you can click the Remove link to remove a network adapter.

6. The next window, shown in Figure 7.28, will ask you to select a network adapter. Choose one from the Unclaimed Adapters section and then click OK.

7. Click OK to dismiss the Manage Physical Adapters wizard.

Adjusting the Number of Ports in a VM Port Group

Another difference in the switch architecture of a Distributed Switch is the way that the virtual ports are allocated. In a Standard Switch we configure the maximum number of switch ports on the switch itself. In a Distributed Switch, the number of

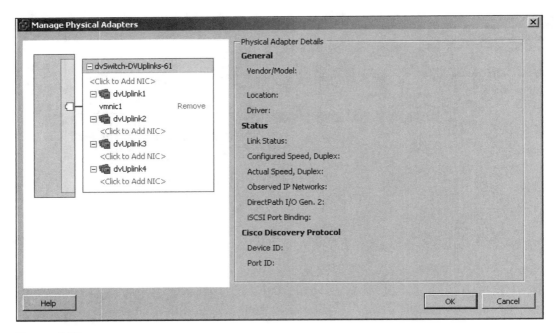

Figure 7.27
Working with uplinks in a Distributed Switch.

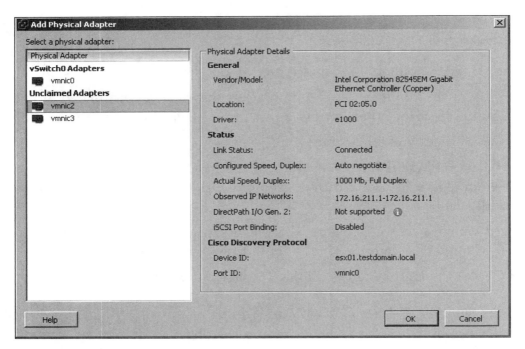

Figure 7.28
Adding a new uplink to a Distributed Switch.

ports on the entire switch may change as we add/remove hosts from the pool, so instead we configure the maximum number of ports available on each port group.

Also, unlike a Standard Switch, the number of available ports is unaffected by the number of uplink adapters, so eight ports aren't automatically reserved from the pool. The number of ports can be adjusted on the fly without forcing a reboot or even Maintenance Mode. That means you can start small and move up as needed.

For these steps, we have to go back to the Networking Inventory view because we are going to modify the properties of a Distributed Port Group, and those are maintained in vCenter, not the hosts.

1. In the vSphere Client, select the Networking Inventory view.

2. Expand the Distributed Switch containing the port group you wish to modify, and then select the port group.

3. Right-click on the port group and choose "Edit the settings" from the context menu.

4. In the port group settings screen, as shown in Figure 7.29, adjust the number of ports listed, and then click OK.

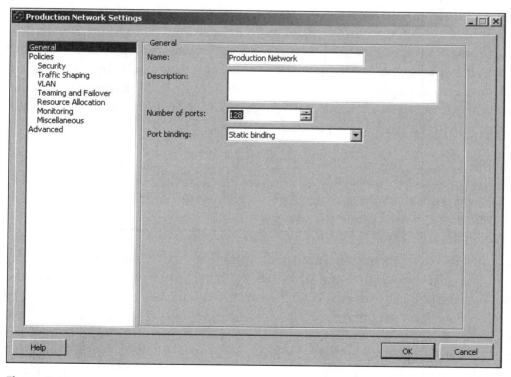

Figure 7.29
Adjusting the port count in a Distributed Switch.

Port Binding

In a Distributed Switch we can also adjust the mode of the virtual ports in the VM Port Groups. By mode, we mean the behavior of the port if the VM attached to it is powered on or off. There are three modes available to us, and each has a specific use case.

- Static Binding (the default)
- Dynamic Binding
- Ephemeral Binding

In the first mode, Static Binding, the virtual switch behaves just like a physical switch from a connection point of view. If you plug a VM into a static port, that VM retains its connection to the port even when it is powered off. In addition, if you configure a VM Port Group to use static binding you must also specify the number of available ports in that port group. When the number of ports has been exhausted, no more connections will be permitted to that port group. This behavior mimics a physical switch because when you power off your workstation, the physical switch doesn't spit out the LAN cable from its port, and your physical switch has a limit to the number of ports that it can provide to your workstations. If you run out of ports, you can't connect to the switch (this goes for physical and virtual switches in this case). It's the most straightforward port binding option because you can configure the number of available ports to match the number of available IP addresses in your IP subnet. For example, if you know you have only 128 IP addresses available for your VMs, you can restrict the VM Port Group to 128 ports. vCenter will prohibit the 129th VM from connecting to the VM Port Group.

Note

By default, VM Port Groups use the static port binding mode, and they are assigned 128 ports. This ensures that no more than 128 VMs or VMkernel ports may be connected to this port group at any one time (powered on or off).

But what if you do have a variable number of VMs that may connect to a particular subnet? You can use the second mode, called Dynamic Binding. In this mode the switch does spit out the cable of the VM when it powers off. Go back to our previous example. We know that we only have 128 IP addresses available, but now we have 200 virtual desktop VMs. We could assign those 200 VMs to a port group configured in dynamic port binding mode, set to 128 ports. vCenter will allow you to assign all 200 VMs to that port group even though the port group doesn't have enough ports. The catch is that vCenter won't allow you to power on more than 128 of those VMs at any one time. Why would you do that? Well, if you have a virtual desktop infrastructure (VDI) you might overprovision your switches because not all your desktops will be active simultaneously. This can be used to restrict the number of machines that ask the DHCP server for addresses because the extra machines won't be connected.

Now, if all of this is too complex and you just want to go back to the way a Standard Switch works, you can. The third and final mode is called Ephemeral Binding. This mode is very special in that there is no limit to the number of ports you can have in the port group because each port is created on demand when a VM joins a VM Port Group, and then destroyed immediately after a VM disconnects from that VM Port Group. This is very similar to how some Wireless Access Points (WAPs) work. Ports are created and destroyed as needed, and the maximum number of available ports is really based on how much bandwidth the switch can deliver, as opposed to a predefined number of ports. In addition, ephemeral mode is the only mode of VM Port Group that can be modified if vCenter is down. Again, this is because the virtual switches on each ESXi host are not required to check with vCenter to determine if enough ports are available (they are unlimited). A common use for this uncommonly used mode is for vCenter's network adapters. If vCenter is down and you wish to move a VM to another VLAN, a static or dynamic VM Port Group will not permit you to alter the VM's network bindings. If the VM Port Group were in ephemeral mode however, you could use the vSphere Client to directly connect to the ESXi host and change the binding for that VM.

You can see the port binding mode setting in Figure 7.29, listed below the number of ports in the port group. Again, this is made on each VM Port Group on a Distributed Switch, and the default is Static Binding.

Adjusting the MTU Size

The MTU size discussion has been covered again and again, but we must cover it one more time. The same principles apply whether it is in a Distributed Switch or a Standard Switch, but the implementation varies slightly. In a Distributed Switch you must go to the Networking view of the vCenter inventory, and then edit the properties for the Distributed Switch. You'll find the MTU setting under the Advanced properties as shown in Figure 7.30.

Tip

Remember, if you have created VMkernel ports in your Distributed Switch, you must change both the Distributed Switch containing the VMkernel port AND the VMkernel port itself on the ESXi host.

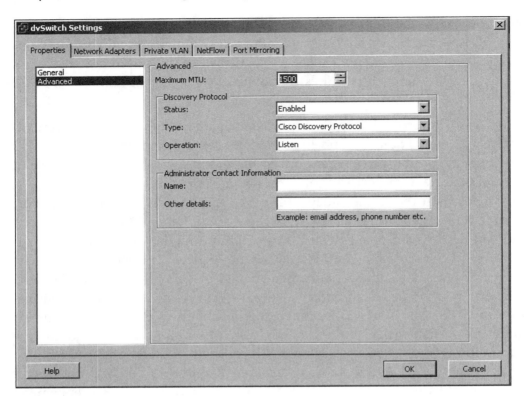

Figure 7.30
Adjusting the MTU value of a Distributed Switch.

Switch Discovery Protocols

Here's something new with vSphere 5. We can now use Link Layer Discovery Protocol (LLDP) in addition to CDP to provide network discovery information to the vSphere administrators. This will come as a relief to those organizations that do not support CDP and still want the troubleshooting advantage of network discovery. LLDP is a vender-neutral discovery protocol that enables network administrators to learn about other LLDP-enabled devices on the network. It is most useful in troubleshooting situations.

LLDP or CDP can be enabled at the Distributed Switch in the Networking view of the vSphere inventory. This is also a feature only available in the 5.0 or later versions of the vNetwork Distributed Switch. Refer to Figure 7.30 under the Discovery Protocol section for an example.

Changing VLAN Options

We've already covered how to change the VLAN ID, so what's all this about? Well, we can support a few different modes of VLANs in a virtual switch.

The first mode is just Off; no VLAN tagging at all. This is the default, and you use it when you either don't require VLAN tagging on a particular port group or the physical switch is tagging the traffic instead of relying on the ESXi server to tag it.

The second mode is called VLAN tagging. That is the popular one where the switch tags the traffic according to a particular VLAN ID. The upstream switch then reads the tag and sends the data to the appropriate VLAN.

The third mode is called VLAN trunking. This is the mode you would use if you wanted a VM to handle its own VLAN tagging. It also is the mode you want if you intend to use an intrusion detection device or other network sniffer, because in VLAN trunking mode the virtual switch sends traffic for all VLANs, not just a specific one. Coupled with promiscuous mode, your VM will be able to see every packet for every VLAN exposed to it. That's right, exposed to it. We can restrict which VLANs are presented, so you can still block access to your really sensitive VLANs.

The fourth mode is called Private VLANs, or PVLANs. We won't go into much detail on it here because we discuss it in greater depth in the security section of this chapter, but the premise is simple: transparent firewall. Through PVLANs you can restrict the flow of traffic between hosts in the same IP subnet in the same VLAN without the use of a firewall. The switch keeps the traffic apart based on rules you configure.

Network I/O Control

Network I/O Control was first released in vSphere 4.1 as a means to control the traffic of the VMkernel, but why would you want to do that? The VMkernel probably knows what's best for your VMs, right? While most of the time that's probably true, there are a couple occasions when we need to help the VMkernel by defining some rules.

To put this into perspective, think of your virtual switches as very busy streets. In our example the streets have only two lanes (inbound and outbound), and all the traffic must queue in one of these lines regardless of its importance. This is what your network looks like without Network I/O Control. The VMkernel is unable to adjust the traffic, so your only means to prioritize traffic is to give it a dedicated uplink adapter, which can be impossible if you can't add network adapters to your ESXi host.

Of course if there isn't much traffic on the streets, you don't have much contention, but during rush hour a bottleneck on a network adapter can affect everyone. Your VMs will fight for the same network bandwidth that the VMkernel is using for iSCSI and NFS storage connections. The result can be a dramatic slowdown for both the VMs and the VMkernel (which may indirectly affect the VMs again); it's a nasty cycle.

Now that you're hopefully getting the picture, let's turn on Network I/O Control to add some order to this chaos. Enabling Network I/O Control has the same effect as earmarking special lanes on each street for high-occupancy vehicles (potentially the storage or vMotion traffic). This allows us to control how much bandwidth the VMkernel can use so that a congestion caused by storage doesn't impact your VMs (as much).

In reality, Network I/O Control doesn't carve up your network into dedicated lanes, but it does give us the ability to rate-limit certain traffic and set shares to define the relative priority of other types of traffic. In addition in vSphere 5.0, this control has been extended to the individual VMs allowing us to leverage Quality of Service (QoS) tagging using the 802.1p standard. Going back to our analogy, this would be equivalent to allowing certain vehicles to be seen as more important even though they drive in the normal lanes of traffic (lights and sirens, anyone?).

In addition, vSphere 5 gives us new Network Resource Pools that allow vSphere administrators to group VMs by their relative network priority. We'll talk more about how (and why) you use these in the next section, but first we need to talk about how to enable Network I/O Control.

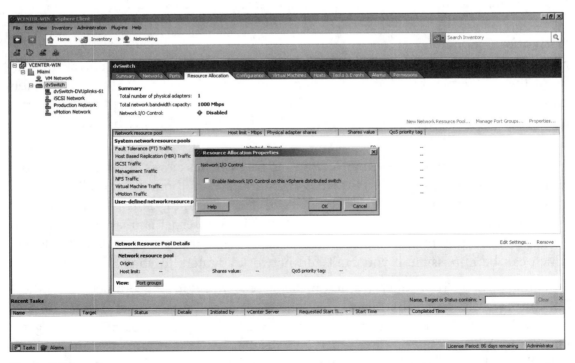

Figure 7.31
Enabling Network I/O Control.

For these steps, we have to go back to the Networking Inventory view because we are going to modify the properties of a Distributed Switch.

1. In the vSphere Client, select the Networking Inventory view.

2. Select the Distributed Switch you wish to modify, and then click its Resource Allocation tab.

3. Click the Properties link on the far right of the screen (you may have to scroll to the right to see it).

4. Select the box for Enable Network I/O Control, and then click OK.

Network Resource Pools

As we just mentioned, through the use of the new Network Resource Pools, vSphere 5 gives more control to the vSphere administrator by allowing him/her to control the maximum bandwidth and relative priority of a group of VMs. These Network Resource Pools are configured in a very similar manner to the traditional DRS Resource Pools that we will describe later in Chapter 10.

All of this customization and prioritization is great, but what happens to the traffic after it leaves the ESXi host? In vSphere 4 we had the ability to prioritize traffic too, but once it left the virtual switch the physical switches had no idea the traffic was special. This is where vSphere 5 comes in. One of the new features of Distributed Switches in vSphere 5 is the ability to leverage Quality of Service (QoS) tags that the physical switches can see and understand.

Caution

QoS tags aren't a "virtualization thing." They've been around for a long time in the networking world, but not all switches support them. Check with your switch vender to see if your switches support QoS tags before enabling them in vSphere 5.

In addition to setting limits and shares, Network Resource Pools also give us the ability to add QoS tags to traffic sent by VMs. QoS tags aren't supposed to be used for every piece of traffic in your network. That would be similar to every vehicle using flashing red and blue lights and sirens; if everything is priority 1, nothing is priority 1. You might configure QoS tags if you have a particular VM or group of VMs that require very high (or perhaps low) priority on the network. vSphere 5 uses the industry standard Priority Code Point (PCP) numbers specified in the 802.1p standard in the settings of the Network Resource Pools. This field is referred to as the QoS priority tag. The levels range from "0 (None)" to "7" as shown in Table 7.1.

Table 7.1   QoS Priority Tags

PCP Tag	Network Priority	Function/Example
1	0 (Lowest)	Background Traffic
0 (None)	1	Normal Traffic
2	2	Critical Traffic
3	3	Storage Traffic
4	4	Video Traffic
5	5	Voice Traffic
6	6	Internetwork Control
7	7 (Highest)	Network Control

The settings on a Network Resource Pool operate much like a port profile in a physical switch in that it doesn't affect the entire switch. Instead, the Network Resource Pool allows us to control the traffic of VMs connected to a specific VM Port Group.

Here is how you create a Network Resource Pool and then modify its QoS settings.

1. In the vSphere Client, select the Networking Inventory view.

2. Select the Distributed Switch you wish to modify, and then click its Resource Allocation tab.

3. Click the New Network Resource Pool link on the far right of the screen (you may have to scroll to the right to see it).

4. In the Network Resource Pool Settings window, enter a name and description for the pool.

5. In that same window, configure the Physical Adapter shares and QoS priority tag under the resource allocation section.

6. When you have finished modifying the settings, click OK to create the pool.

Now we need to assign the pool to a port group on the Distributed Switch:

1. In the vSphere Client, select the Networking Inventory view.

2. Right-click the Distributed Port Group you wish to assign to the new resource, and then choose Edit Settings.

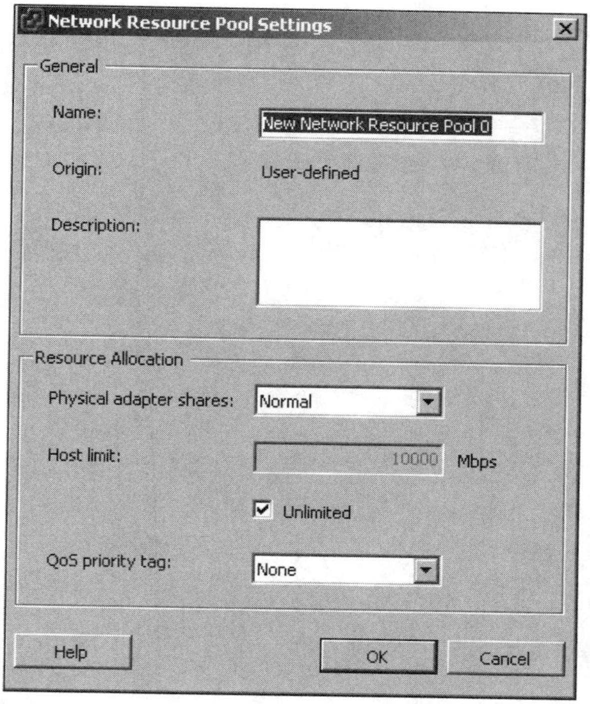

Figure 7.32
Creating a Network Resource Pool.

3. Click the Resource Allocation section under Policies, as shown in Figure 7.33.

4. Select the appropriate Network Resource Pool from the drop-down list and then click OK.

NetFlow

A new feature in vSphere 5 is the support for NetFlow in the vNetwork Distributed Switches. NetFlow is a troubleshooting and analysis tool that allows network administrators to determine how much traffic is being sent from one device to another.

Of course, we can accomplish protocol analysis using a number of tools, but NetFlow simplifies the process by collecting statistics of specific communication dialogs between the devices. We don't have to use a network sniffer to collect every packet. NetFlow gathers these statistics and forwards the data to a NetFlow Collector device.

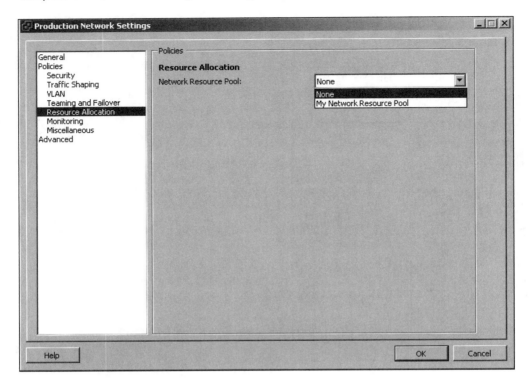

Figure 7.33
Assigning a Network Resource Pool.

Note

A NetFlow collector can be any server or device that you set up on your network to collect and analyze the protocol statistics and messages sent to it by your network switches. Look for tools such as Scrutinizer, Flowd, IPFlow, and the Cisco NetFlow Collector.

For years NetFlow has been available on physical switches, and in vSphere 4.0 it was even supported in the Cisco Nexus 1000V, but this is the first time we have been able to use NetFlow in a virtual switch provided by VMware. This gives network administrators the ability to see not only the traffic flows between physical hosts on our network, but now we can see the traffic patterns all the way up to the VMs within the ESXi hosts in our networks. That makes a huge difference when trying to troubleshoot unusually large volumes of traffic without the introduction of a packet sniffer. We'll discuss some uses for NetFlow later in the Troubleshooting section of this chapter.

There are two types of traffic flows: Internal and External. In the case of a vNetwork Distributed Switch, the internal flows involve traffic where both the source and destination VMs reside on the same ESXi host, and are connected to the same virtual switch. External flows involve VMs on different ESXi hosts or even other physical devices such as workstations. The difference being that an internal flow doesn't leave the virtual switch, whereas an external one does.

These flows are collected and then forwarded to the NetFlow collector for analysis. The collector may be a dedicated server, workstation, or even appliance with the collector software installed and running.

You must first configure the NetFlow collector information in the properties of the Distributed Switch as shown in Figure 7.34. Then you must enable NetFlow on the port group or specific port in the Distributed Switch.

1. In the vSphere Client, select the Networking Inventory view.

2. Right-click the Distributed Switch you wish to modify, and then choose Edit Settings from the context menu.

3. In the Distributed Switch settings window, click the NetFlow tab as shown in Figure 7.34.

4. Enter the IP address and port number of your NetFlow collector system.

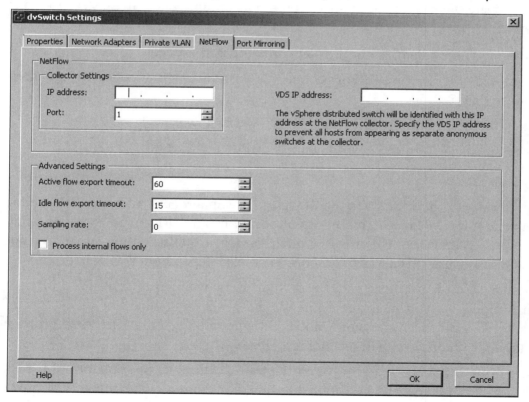

Figure 7.34
NetFlow configuration on the Distributed Switch.

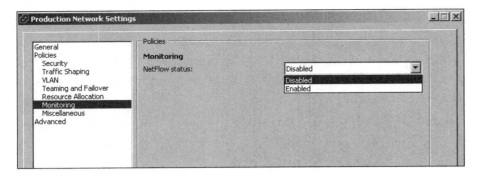

Figure 7.35
NetFlow configuration on the Distributed Port Group.

5. Enter an IP address in the VDS field to identify your Distributed Switch to the NetFlow collector system.

6. Click OK to commit the changes to the Distributed Switch.

Even though we have configured the NetFlow collector settings on the switch, we still need to activate the NetFlow monitoring on a port group. Follow these steps to make that happen:

1. In the vSphere Client, select the Networking Inventory view.

2. Right-click the Distributed Port Group you wish to assign to configure, and then choose Edit Settings.

3. Click the Monitoring section under Policies, as shown in Figure 7.35.

4. Select Enabled from the drop-down list and then click OK.

Port Mirroring

Port Mirroring is a new (and very cool) feature in vSphere 5. It allows us to monitor the network traffic of one or more virtual ports on our Distributed Switches using tools such as WireShark. This is most often used in troubleshooting situations, but tools such as Intrusion Detection Systems (IDS) also depend on Port Mirroring.

But, wait a second; if you're scratching your head wondering if you're having a moment of déjà vu, you might be right. We did cover something like this earlier in the chapter. It's called promiscuous mode, but compared to Port Mirroring, promiscuous mode is crude cave man technology. Here's why.

Port Mirroring is the ability to mirror all the traffic coming in or going out of particular virtual ports on a virtual Distributed Switch. For those of you familiar with physical networking, Cisco-compatible devices refer to this as SPAN, and you'll see in a minute it's actually closer to RSPAN.

So how does Port Mirroring differ from promiscuous mode, and what's all the hype about? Well for one thing, you can't configure promiscuous mode to forward the monitored traffic to a particular port on the virtual switch. Instead, promiscuous mode simply repeats the traffic it receives to any virtual adapter that has entered promiscuous mode, making your virtual switch more like a virtual hub.

For those of you not old enough to appreciate the simplicity of an Ethernet hub, let me explain. A hub performs no packet inspection; it just repeats the traffic it receives without regard for MAC addresses or any other identification. This is why in past years when we wanted to "sniff" the network using a product like WireShark (then called Ethereal), we would connect all the devices we wanted to monitor, including the sniffer, to a regular old Ethernet hub. In doing so, everything connected to that Ethernet hub would see the same traffic, allowing us to monitor the traffic into and out of the target machines.

When we activate promiscuous mode on a virtual switch, we are allowing the virtual switch to temporarily behave like an Ethernet hub. This can present a security risk because any other VM attached to that port group can also enter promiscuous mode, permitting it to monitor the traffic.

Port Mirroring, on the other hand, is completely configured by you at the Distributed Switch level. There is no blanket promiscuous mode that could allow another VM to suddenly start sniffing the network traffic. You must configure which virtual port(s) to monitor (the source ports), and then you must specify which port(s) will receive those mirrored packets (the destination ports).

So how do we know which ports to monitor and which ports to send the data to? There has to be a list of VMs to port numbers somewhere, right? There is. If you click on the Distributed Virtual Switch in the Networking Inventory view, you can see the various Distributed Port Groups. Select one of these port groups and click on the Ports tab to see a complete list of the virtual port numbers and all the VMs and VMkernel ports assigned to those ports. By default, those port numbers won't change unless you remove the VM from the Distributed Switch because, and we're going to dust off your memory here, the default port binding mode is Static. If you had changed the port binding mode on your Distributed Switch to Dynamic Binding, these port assignments may change every time you power off/on your VM.

When you select your source ports to monitor, you must choose to monitor ingress or egress traffic (or both). Remember, we are mirroring from the perspective of the virtual port, not the VM, so ingress and egress take on that same perspective. Ingress is traffic flowing into the port, meaning the VM sent it. Egress traffic is flowing out of the port, meaning it is headed to the VM. It may seem counter intuitive from a VM perspective, but remember this is a networking tool, not a server tool. Port

Mirroring follows the same terminology used on physical switches when monitoring ports using SPAN/RSPAN.

The next step is to select your destination ports. In promiscuous mode we could have multiple devices sniffing the network simultaneously (sometimes this was even desirable). In Port Mirroring, we can do that too, but we have much more control. To do it you configure multiple destinations in your Port Mirroring session. Why would we want that? You might have two IDS systems in your DMZ, or you might need to send traffic inspection data to two different types of protocol analyzers (one for low-level stuff, and one for application-level stuff). Whatever your reason may be, you can do it. Just enter the virtual port IDs of the destination ports when you create the Port Mirroring session and you're done.

But wait, there's more! Port Mirroring can also work with protocol analyzers on the physical network. That's something that promiscuous mode can't do for us. When you were configuring the destination ports for your Port Mirroring session, you might have noticed that you can add uplink ports to the list of destinations as well. After all, an uplink port is technically just a port on a Distributed Switch. And if you remember, an uplink port on a Distributed Virtual Switch is actually a physical network adapter on the ESXi host. That means that you can connect your protocol analyzer to that NIC port on the server, or better yet, you can tie that port into your physical Ethernet network to remotely monitor the traffic from your desk. Okay, so that last part might have been a bit unclear, so let us explain.

There is a technique in physical networks, known on Cisco-compatible devices as RSPAN, that allows Port Mirroring sessions to span multiple Ethernet switches. Traditionally, this traffic is encapsulated into a dedicated VLAN so that the integrity of the session is preserved end to end. In doing so, any VLAN tags that were present in the Port Mirroring session may also be preserved for inspection and analysis. With Port Mirroring on a Distributed Virtual Switch, we can do just that. We can use the uplink ports on our Distributed Switches to mirror the traffic to ports on our physical network. We can also encapsulate the traffic in a VLAN, as shown in Figure 7.36.

One important aspect of Port Mirroring is that it can be a bandwidth hog. Remember, you are *mirroring* the traffic. That means you are sending every bit and byte of data twice. If the target that you are monitoring suddenly downloads a 10GB file, you will mirror the download of that 10GB file. If you are monitoring locally, that may not be a deal breaker, but if you intend to mirror this traffic across the physical network, you may want to slim the traffic down a bit.

So how can we make the mirror not a mirror? By retaining and forwarding only the header information for each packet. If you are interested in analyzing packet flows or

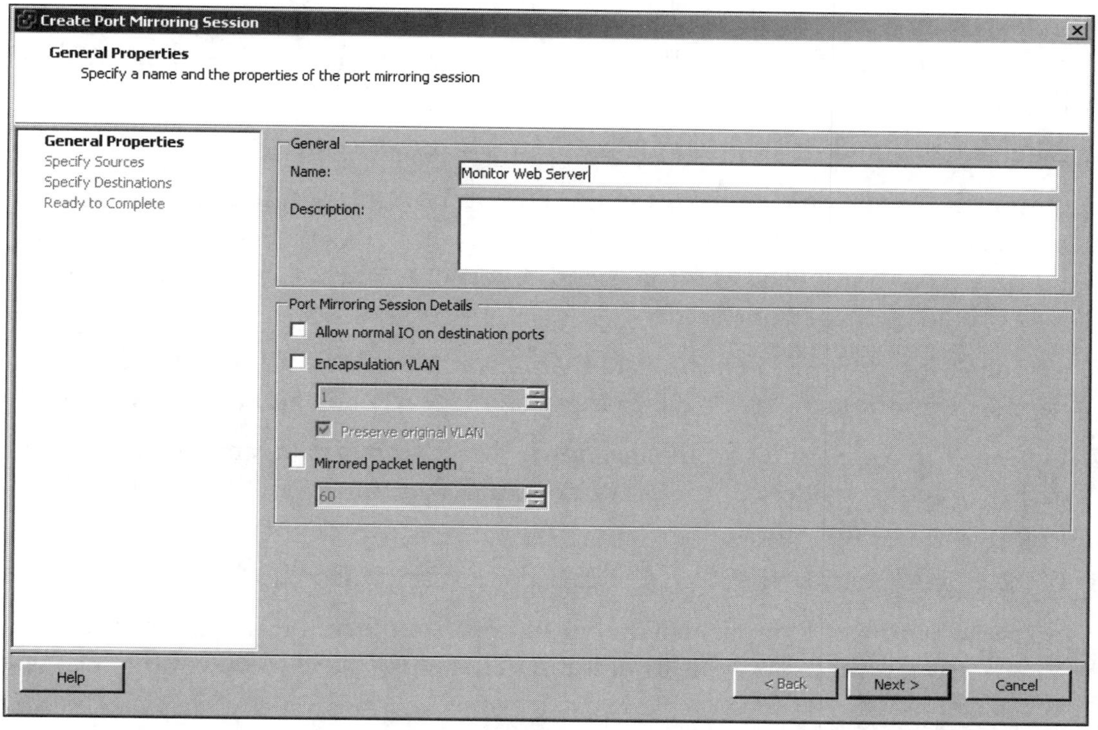

Figure 7.36
Creating a Port Mirroring session.

you are searching for typical communications issues, you can usually find the source of the trouble in the headers. Those headers are typically less than 60 bytes long on a packet that may be 1500 bytes long. You can adjust this setting by selecting the "Mirrored packet length" property in the GUI when you configure Port Mirroring.

In our example of the 10GB download, if you had been grabbing only the headers of the traffic, you wouldn't even care that they started the download because you wouldn't mirror 10GB of data. The mirror would only transfer the beginning of each packet, which works out to about 4% of the traffic.

So now that we've covered the various reasons for creating a Port Mirror, let's show you how to configure one in your environment. You'll be working with a Distributed Virtual Switch, so you'll need to switch back to the Networking Inventory view.

1. In the vSphere Client, select the Networking Inventory view.

2. Right-click the Distributed Switch you wish to modify, and then choose Edit Settings from the context menu.

3. In the Distributed Switch settings window, click the Port Mirroring tab and then click Add to start the Create Port Mirroring Session wizard as we illustrated in Figure 7.36.

4. Enter a name and description for the Port Mirror session.

5. Optional: If you want to allow the destination port to continue to function normally (sending and receiving traffic), check the box labeled "Allow Normal IO on destination ports." This is useful if you don't have a dedicated virtual network adapter for your sniffer.

6. Optional: If you need to encapsulate the mirrored traffic into a VLAN (as we described in our text), check the Encapsulation VLAN box and enter a VLAN ID.

7. Optional: If you would like to slim down the mirrored data, and would like to gather only the headers of the network traffic, you can restrict the packet length to 60 (or a custom length).

8. Click Next to specify the source virtual ports (the ports being monitored).

9. As shown in Figure 7.37, enter the virtual port numbers on the Distributed Virtual Switch that you want to monitor. They don't have to be contiguous, but

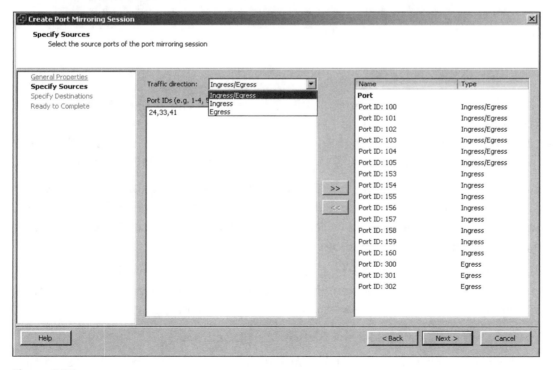

Figure 7.37
Port mirroring sources.

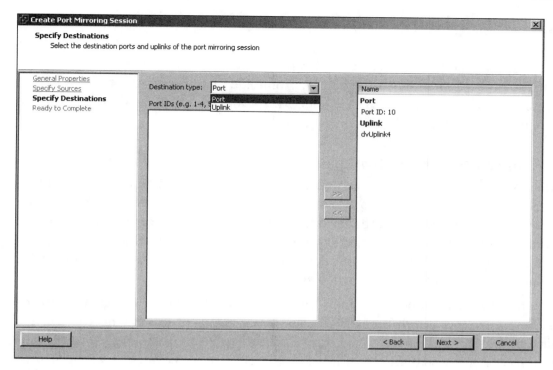

Figure 7.38
Port mirroring destinations.

they do need to be accurate. You may select Ingress, Egress, or both directions. Refer back to the text of this section for a better explanation on this step. Click Next when you are done adding ports.

10. The next step is to specify the destination(s) of the Port Mirror session, as shown in Figure 7.38. You can choose another port on the Distributed Switch, or you can pick one of the uplink ports (physical network adapters) on an ESXi host. You can add multiple destinations. Click Next when you are finished.

11. The next screen is a summary and confirmation screen. If you are satisfied with the configuration, check the box labeled "Enable this Port Mirroring session," and then click Finish.

SECURITY

There are a number of ways that we can secure our virtual networks in vSphere 5. That's not to say that virtual networking is insecure by default. On the contrary, in some cases we will need to disable some of the built-in security features to allow us to troubleshoot our virtual machines. In this section, we will explore just a few of these methods. Entire books could be written on virtual network security; after all, virtual networking has just as many facets as physical networking when it comes to security.

Virtual Networking Permissions in vCenter

As you have seen in our chapter on vCenter, there are a number of places where we can apply permissions in the vCenter hierarchy. One of those areas is, of course, virtual networking. Depending on your environment, you may wish to increase or decrease that security. You might wonder why you would ever want to decrease your network security. Well, read on and we'll tell you.

Protecting You from Yourself

vCenter is a marvelous tool. You can get as granular or as broad with your security as you need. By default, only users assigned the "administrator" role can do anything within vCenter. Typically, we see that organizations create additional roles and assign these non-administrative users to special roles restricted to job functions. The separation of roles does two things, it protects you from the "good intentions" of your helpdesk, and it protects them from their own curiosity.

The granular security model within vCenter allows us to restrict things at a broad-stroke level, such as creating new virtual switches and port groups, or you can get detailed and even block specific ports on a Distributed Port Group. Part of the advantage to these security settings is that it helps protect us from picking the wrong setting, or to move a VM into the wrong port group. It's easy to do because all these settings are software based. In a traditional physical network, it is more complex to accidently unplug a server and move it to another physical switch.

We can help reduce the accidents in a virtual environment by not granting administrative rights to every user. For example, if you don't give your helpdesk the right to assign a VM to your high-security DMZ Port Group, the helpdesk users can't select the DMZ Port Group from the list when editing a VM, thereby preventing them from exposing your production VMs to the Internet.

This is a perfect case for creating non-administrative user accounts for vCenter access. Even the best vCenter administrators make mistakes. Maybe it was an errant right-click, or maybe there was lag in an RDP session; whatever the case, when you click on the wrong thing you'll wish you had created a non-administrative user account.

Just How Granular Can We Get?

The flip side of this security model is that all this granularity means there are a lot of privileges in vCenter. As a result, it isn't always clear which privileges are required to perform a specific action. If you look at the role configuration in vCenter there are a lot of privileges that pertain to networking. To help clear up some of the confusion we've included Table 7.2, illustrating the various options and their descriptions.

Table 7.2   vCenter Networking Privileges

Privilege Name	Privilege Description
dvPort group	
Create	Create a Distributed Port Group
Delete	Delete a Distributed Port Group
Modify	Modify the configuration of a Distributed Port Group
Policy Operation	Set the policy of a Distributed Port Group
Scope Operation	Set the scope of a Distributed Port Group
Host, Configuration	
Network Configuration	Modify the ESXi host's network configuration
Security profile and firewall	Modify the ESXi host's security and firewall settings
Network	
Assign network	Assign a network to a VM, VMkernel NIC, or physical NIC
Configure	Configure a network (Standard Port Group)
Move network	Move a network (Standard Port Group)
Remove	Remove a network (Standard Port Group)
vSphere Distributed Switch	
Create	Create a Distributed Switch
Delete	Delete a Distributed Switch
Host operation	Change the host membership of a Distributed Switch
Modify	Modify the configuration of a Distributed Switch
Move	Move a Distributed Switch into another folder
Network I/O Control operation	Add or update Network I/O Control resource pools
Policy operation	Change the policy of a Distributed Switch
Port configuration operation	Modify the configuration of a port in a Distributed Switch
Port setting operation	Change the setting of a port in a Distributed Switch
VSPAN operation	Change the Port Mirroring configuration of a Distributed Switch

As you can see, there are many settings, and they affect several different objects from Distributed Port Groups to the ESXi hosts. It's a good idea to know what these settings do and where to apply them to gain the desired effect. That's right, you have to apply the roles on the right object to get the desired effect. Keep reading to learn where we apply these roles to get the best effect.

What Can We Secure?

A role is just a collection of privileges; it doesn't specify where the privilege applies because that's your job. You must assign that role on an object in the vCenter hierarchy to grant the privileges contained in the role. Of course, you could always apply the role at the top of the vCenter hierarchy, but that would give the user(s) a broad range of control that most organizations wouldn't want or need. It's better to assign a user/group that role on a specific object such as a Distributed Virtual Switch or a Distributed Port Group. This way, you retain control over the "who, what, and where" as it pertains to security permissions.

In our previous example, we had a high-security DMZ network that we didn't want anyone to accidently assign to a VM. We could create a helpdesk role that allows the assignment of network adapters, but we would only assign the role to the appropriate Distributed Virtual Switches instead of every switch under the Networking Inventory view. That way, the helpdesk isn't granted access to the DMZ network, and therefore can't assign any VMs to it.

In addition to restricting whether a vCenter user can connect a VM to the network, we can also restrict the ability to reconfigure a virtual switch or port group. This may not seem like a big security threat, but if you keep reading, you'll see that there are some settings that could present a threat if changed from their defaults.

Virtual Switch Security Settings

You may recall from our planning section that there are a couple settings on a virtual switch that can alter its behavior from a security standpoint. Some of these options are used for troubleshooting, while others are configured to allow legacy applications to function properly. Be sure that you understand each option and the ramifications of enabling/disabling each before adjusting your configuration. If in doubt, create a dedicated VM Port Group to experiment with your settings before enacting them in production.

Promiscuous Mode

We've talked about Port Mirroring as a tool to mirror traffic from one adapter to another so that you can monitor or troubleshoot a particular VM. Port Mirroring is a new feature in vSphere 5, but we've had something similar in vSphere for a long time. It's called promiscuous mode.

Promiscuous mode is a setting on network card drivers (physical or virtual) that allows the Ethernet adapter to accept Ethernet frames that were not specifically addressed to the adapter's MAC address. You'll remember from our discussion on Port Mirroring that this differs greatly from the default behavior of an Ethernet adapter. Normally an Ethernet adapter will discard these packets. When we tell an adapter to enter promiscuous mode, we are bypassing that discard operation and sending *every* frame up to the operating system for processing.

Why would we do that? Well, if you wanted to analyze your network traffic, you might do it. But there are other reasons. Intrusion Detection Systems (IDS) require this functionality because they are constantly inspecting the contents of the data on the network. Without promiscuous mode, an IDS doesn't function.

There are also less-than-noble uses of promiscuous mode. For example, there are a number of network attacks that employ promiscuous mode to gain access to security keys or other sensitive data. Even encrypted traffic can become susceptible to these attacks because if you collect enough data, a brute force attack may just work. For this reason, promiscuous mode is disabled by default on a virtual switch.

In a Standard or Distributed Virtual Switch, we can activate promiscuous mode on VM Port Group by allowing promiscuous mode in the security policies. This means that instead of activating just a single port for mirroring, you are allowing any VM connected to that port group to enter promiscuous mode.

Whether good or bad, it is also possible to configure an entire Standard Virtual Switch to use promiscuous mode. From a security standpoint, we suggest avoiding this practice because it would allow any VM on that switch to inspect your network traffic. Instead, create a port group dedicated to your network sniffers and IDS machines. Place that port group into promiscuous mode, but leave promiscuous mode disabled on your regular port groups.

Caution

Just because you can easily permit promiscuous mode, doesn't mean your virtual switch or port group policies should allow this. There is a reason VMware has promiscuous mode disabled by default; it's called "security." You likely don't want every VM in your network to be able to sniff your network traffic. Instead, create a dedicated port group for your sniffers, even if the ports groups will share the same VLAN ID.

MAC Address Changes and Forged Transmits

If you remember our discussion in the planning chapter on MAC addresses, you'll recall that each Ethernet adapter, whether virtual or physical, must have a unique MAC address assigned to it. In a physical server, the MAC address comes from the physical Ethernet card. In a virtual environment, ESXi must generate the MAC addresses for us.

The trick with creating MAC addresses for VMs is that we must still follow the industry standards for physical hardware or we'll run the risk of having a duplicate addresses on the physical network (which will not work). If you're curious about how MAC addresses are formed, refer to the following sidebar for more information.

As we said, MAC addresses assigned to virtual network adapters are automatically generated by ESXi, and under most circumstances these addresses do not need to be changed. However, there are a few cases where you may need to change from the VMware-generated MAC address.

One such example comes after migrating a physical license server to a virtual machine. Occasionally vendors bind their licenses to a specific MAC address on the license server. By virtualizing the server, you changed its network adapter, and therefore have changed its MAC address. This typically invalidated your license. In this case, you can either request a new license file from the vendor or allow the VM to change its own MAC address. But how can you do that?

It's not really that difficult. If you do find yourself in the situation where you must change a VM's MAC address, don't start with the hardware, virtual or physical. That won't help. In a physical world, to change the MAC address, we change the physical network adapter. In a virtual world, the VM's MAC address isn't encoded into any hardware; it's written to the VM's configuration file. Fortunately, editing the configuration is easy in vSphere 5.

We have an alternate means to change the MAC address as well. If you are running Microsoft Windows Server, for example, you can edit the advanced settings of the network card's device driver. Under Network Address, you can enter a custom MAC address that is not bound to the VMware prescribed pattern. Note that anything you type in this field overrides whatever value is present in the virtual hardware. This way, you can re-enter the MAC address of that old network card you needed and run your software.

There's still one catch though. The virtual switch is just software, so it has full advantage of knowing everything the hypervisor knows. In other words, it knows what that VM's MAC address is supposed to be. If you change the MAC address from a VMware-sanctioned address to a custom address, you may need to modify your virtual switch configuration, and that leads us right back to the point of this section: MAC address changes and forged transmits.

If anyone were permitted to change the MAC address of their VM, you could easily have chaos on your hands. Duplicate MAC addresses can create either denial of service (DoS) attacks or impersonation attacks. Both physical and virtual switches will permit the changing of your MAC address by default, but it isn't something that you want to necessarily leave enabled for every VM in your datacenter.

Like we suggested in the promiscuous section before, you might consider creating a separate port group for the handful of VMs that require the ability to change their MAC addresses from the VMware default. Then you can disable the ability for all the other port groups on your virtual switches. The two values that permit VMs to change their MAC addresses are called "Change MAC Addresses" and "Forged Transmits." By default, both are enabled on every virtual switch and port group.

The "Change MAC Addresses" setting tells the virtual switch to allow a VM to receive traffic destined for a MAC address other than the VMware-approved address in its configuration file. This is only half of the configuration required to allow a VM to change its MAC address.

The other half is called "Forged Transmits." This setting allows a VM to alter the source MAC address on packets that it sends on the network. If this setting is enabled, the virtual switch will forward the packet even though it knows the source address has been forged by the VM.

As we said before though, this is another feature that would be best isolated into its own port group. The setting is enabled by default so that a virtual switch behaves like a physical switch, but as you've just learned, the defaults aren't always the most secure setting.

MAC Addresses

A MAC address is a unique address assigned to every Ethernet adapter created, whether physical or virtual. In the case of a physical adapter, the manufacturer encodes the unique MAC address into the firmware on the card. In the case of a virtual adapter, VMware generates the address and stores it in the VM's configuration file.

MAC addresses are 48-bit numbers written as six octets in hexadecimal format. Traditionally, each octet is separated by a colon such as AA:BB:CC:DD:EE:FF. The number is composed of two equal parts. The first three octets, in our example AA:BB:CC, represent the vender's unique ID number. The remaining three octets, in our example DD:EE:FF, are the card's unique ID number. Together they were intended to create a globally unique ID that was theoretically non-repeating. We say "theoretically," because as you'll read in the troubleshooting section of this chapter, we do occasionally run into conflicts.

Each network card hardware manufacturer must use its assigned ID(s) for any network cards it creates. The vendor is then required to keep a log of which unique addresses have been assigned, and they must not assign the same MAC address to any two cards. Given that each half of a MAC address is three bytes long, that means that each range has 16.7 million unique values in it. You can probably imagine there are a lot more than 16.7 million network cards made by the same vendor, so most of the vendors have more than one range assigned for their use.

VMware is also a manufacturer of network cards. Now, these aren't physical cards, but nonetheless they are network adapters; therefore, they must each have a unique MAC address. VMware has been assigned several ranges, but the most common range used is 00:50:56:xx:yy:zz, where the xx:yy:zz values are intended to be unique per ESXi host. The MAC address ranges assigned to VMware are as follows:

- 00:05:69:00:00:00 – 00:05:69:FF:FF:FF
- 00:0C:29:00:00:00 – 00:0C:29:FF:FF:FF
- 00:1C:14:00:00:00 – 00:1C:14:FF:FF:FF
- 00:50:56:00:00:00 – 00:50:56:FF:FF:FF

Port Blocking

Port Blocking is the ability to administratively shut down individual ports in a Distributed Port Group. Though it may be one of the most granular means to secure a virtual network, it is also very effective because you can stop a VM from communicating on the network in response to large volumes of traffic coming from or going to that port. Coupled with analysis tools such as NetFlow and the vSphere APIs, you could script the ability to shut down a port in response to traffic thresholds. Of course, shutting down a port isn't a long-term solution, but having this ability would be a real boon in the midst of a denial of service attack stemming from a compromised VM.

Note

Port Blocking is only available for port groups in vNetwork Distributed Switches.

Private VLANs

Has this ever happened to you? You manage a group of Internet-facing servers. Perhaps they're in a DMZ or extranet. You have a firewall inspecting and filtering the traffic, yet somehow an attacker has breeched your security and has taken control of one of the servers. The worst part is that the attacker is now going from server to server breaching the rest of your security because you no longer have any network firewall control—they're inside! Within minutes, they have breached the security of every single device in the subnet, and you're in reaction mode trying to contain the mess.

Stop. There was a way to prevent this, and it didn't involve more firewalls, or even creating a dedicated VLAN or IP subnet for each device in your DMZ. The solution is called a Private VLAN (PVLAN), and it is supported on a number of network devices, including the Distributed Switches in vSphere 5.

A PVLAN is not a virtualization concept, but it does work very well in virtualized environments. A PVLAN is a technique used in physical networks to subdivide a VLAN into different security zones. Through the use of PVLANs you could have prevented this situation in our example from spreading because machines in an isolated PVLAN are unable to communicate with one another, even if they are on the same subnet. Here's how it works.

A PVLAN has three different security modes: promiscuous, community, and isolated. The promiscuous mode is identical to a standard VLAN; everyone can talk to everything. It is typical to place routers and IDS/sniffers in the promiscuous mode because those devices must be able to communicate with all the devices in the subnet. There is only one promiscuous PVLAN ID because it is a big group. Creating multiple promiscuous zones wouldn't accomplish anything because they can see everything anyway.

The next mode is called community. Devices in the same community PVLAN are able to communicate with each other. This differs from the promiscuous mode because we can create multiple community PVLANs, each separate from the others. As we mentioned above, the devices in the promiscuous VLAN are able to communicate freely with anyone, and that still applies to community members. Remember, your router is typically in the promiscuous PVLAN; if you have a VM in a community VLAN, you likely want devices in it to talk to the router.

The final mode is called isolated, and that is exactly what it does: isolates. The devices within an isolated PVLAN are unable to communicate with anything other than the devices in the promiscuous PVLAN (again, the router and maybe an IDS or sniffer). Think back to the DMZ hacking example at the start of this section. If we had configured that DMZ using an isolated PVLAN, the attackers would have breached one server and then stopped. They wouldn't even have been able to ping any other device on the subnet (other than the router).

So why does this matter? PVLANs are a great way to separate your traffic in a DMZ because you can do so without expending costly IP subnets and creating a million virtual IP interfaces on your firewall. In a PVLAN configuration, your router is placed into the promiscuous PVLAN and you place everything else into the isolated PVLAN. If you happen to have a group of servers that must communicate with each other, like an application server and its database server, you can create a community

PVLAN just for that group. Each group you have like this should be assigned its own community PVLAN. This way, you have created isolation areas that will help keep attackers at bay even if they knock down your front line defenses.

To implement PVLANs, first of all, you must have a vNetwork Distributed Switch because PVLANs are only supported in the Distributed Switches. The next step is to define the various PVLANs you will need. Before you get too far, consult with your network administrator of your physical network. In order to use PVLANs in a virtual environment, the upstream physical switches must support, and be configured to use, PVLANs. If you forget this step, you'll figure it out while reading our troubleshooting PVLANs section later in the chapter.

You must have the PVLAN IDs defined in advance before you can proceed. These IDs must be entered into the Distributed Virtual Switch, as shown in Figure 7.39, specifying the mode (promiscuous, community, or isolated) for each PVLAN ID. Later you will assign these PVLAN IDs to Distributed Port Groups.

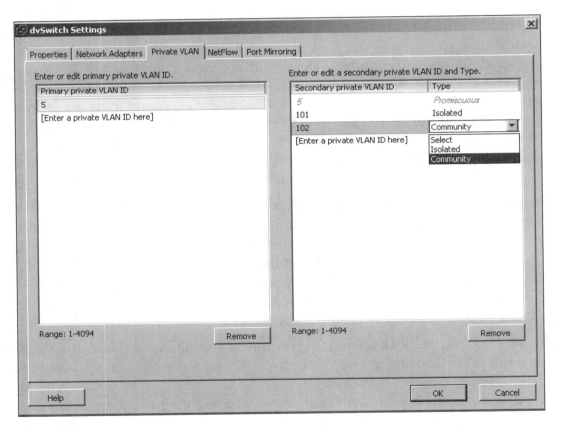

Figure 7.39
Private VLAN switch configuration.

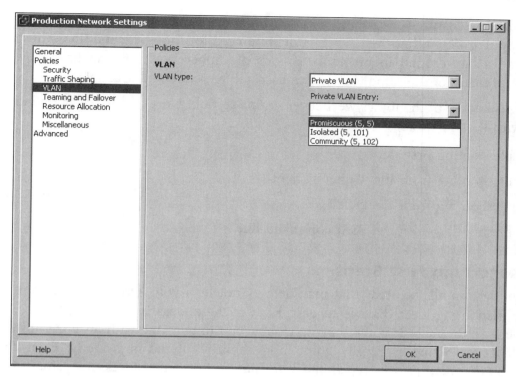

Figure 7.40
Private VLAN Port Group configuration.

The next major step is to create new Distributed Port Groups for each PVLAN ID. You must then edit the settings of the port group to specify its associated PVLAN ID, as shown in Figure 7.40. Note that each port group will have a unique PVLAN ID, much like when you assign a traditional VLAN to a port group. You cannot have multiple VLAN/PVLAN IDs in a single port group.

Once you have built the port groups and assigned the PVLAN IDs, you are done. Add your VMs to the appropriate port groups, and test the connectivity. If you have difficulties, ensure that your network administrator has placed your router or default gateway in the promiscuous PVLAN.

TROUBLESHOOTING

Who needs a network troubleshooting section anyway? Networks just work, right? Right.... Well then we'll just call this a reference. This section is a compilation of the things we've used in the field when working with virtual networking, some of which might be useful for you when working with vSphere 5.

Some of the new features in vSphere 5 help bring more troubleshooting information into the vSphere Client, but there is still a definite need for the command line. Those of you with a background in previous versions of vSphere will have an advantage here because many of the same tools we've used for years are still available.

Here's a breakdown of the topics we'll cover in this section. Note that we recommend starting with the "First Steps" section.

- Troubleshooting first steps
- Troubleshooting from the vSphere Client
- Troubleshooting from the DCUI
- Troubleshooting from the ESXi command line

Troubleshooting First Steps

Before we dig into all the areas that may or may not help you, here are some common troubleshooting ideas that we suggest. Each of these ideas is listed here because we've seen it in the field. If you're having trouble communicating with an ESXi host, or your VMs are acting erratically, something is likely entered improperly. Even if you are 100% sure that you typed the information correctly, check it again. It's okay; we'll say that the mystical network gnomes snuck in and changed it on you.

Here's a breakdown of what we're going to cover:

- IP address, subnet mask, and the default gateway
- The DNS, hostname, and domain name values
- Check the MTU values on everything
- Create a port channel if using IP hash load balancing
- Private VLAN issues?
- Did you pick the wrong network card?
- Lockdown mode
- ESXi firewall trouble

IP Address, Subnet Mask, and the Default Gateway

These are things we can easily mistype; especially the subnet mask. If you happen to be working in an environment as a consultant, you may not be aware that your client uses an obscure subnet mask like 255.255.192.0 instead of something more traditional. Verify and then check your settings. Also, the default gateway can catch you off guard. Typos in this field are *not* checked against your IP and subnet. The DCUI assumes you know what you're doing. It is entirely possible to enter a gateway that is on the wrong IP subnet (which just won't work).

The DNS, Hostname, and Domain Name Values

In the DCUI there are entries for the DNS servers and the Fully Qualified Domain Name (FQDN) of the ESXi server. There isn't a dedicated field for the host name and another for the domain name. Why are we stressing this? Because all too often we see people enter only the short name into the field for the FQDN, or they leave it set to something like localhost.localdomain because they forgot to change it. This could easily impact things like VMware's High Availability and Fault Tolerance features, not to mention your ability to connect to the host from within vCenter. Also, double-check that the DNS servers you're using are actually accessible from your ESXi host (think firewall).

Caution

No version of vSphere (past or present) performs Dynamic DNS (DDNS), so you must manually enter your ESXi host names into your DNS server(s).

Check the MTU Values on Everything

Even if you aren't planning to use jumbo frames, you might want to check that your MTU values are configured properly. You or someone else may have accidently changed the values from 1500 to a value that isn't supported on your physical network. If you are intending to use jumbo frames, you need to verify that every physical network component that you will use can support the higher MTU values. Also determine what that MTU value should be; it may not be 9000 depending on your vendor's support for jumbo frames. On the virtualization side, use the command line and/or vSphere Client to determine the MTU values on your virtual switches and the VMkernel ports.

Create a Port Channel if Using IP Hash Load Balancing

If you are using the IP hash or load-based teaming algorithms for outbound network load balancing, you must ensure that your uplink ports are configured in a port channel on the upstream physical switch. A port channel is often referred to as 802.3ad. If you have not configured a port channel, and you are using one of these algorithms, you may notice all of your traffic flowing out of only one network card because the upstream switch has blocked the other ports.

Private VLAN Issues?

So you set up Private VLANs in your virtual switches and now something doesn't feel quite right. Maybe you have unexpected traffic in your PVLANs, or perhaps communication just isn't flowing. Whatever the case, we'll try to help you figure out the source.

The first thing you have to check is whether you have enabled and configured your Private VLANs in your physical switches. Before any PVLAN configuration will work in a virtual world, you must configure it in the physical world. Why? The reason actually involves how we encapsulate VLAN and PVLAN traffic. The encapsulation is really just tags that we insert into the header of each Ethernet frame. This works well enough when PVLANs aren't involved. The trouble is that when switches (virtual or physical) are configured to use PVLANs, the switches actually reuse the same VLAN header location of each Ethernet frame to store a combined PVLAN/VLAN value. If your switch doesn't know that you have enabled PVLAN tagging in your virtual switches, the physical switch will interpret the PVLAN/VLAN combo tag as a standard VLAN tag. This can cause all sorts of unexpected security issues as well as excess traffic in the wrong VLANs. Read below for some examples.

Here are some symptoms that indicate you have misconfigured (or not configured) your physical switches for Private VLANs:

- Workstations in other parts of your network that happen to share the same VLAN ID as one of your PVLANs are suddenly able to see the PVLAN traffic (applies to all PVLAN modes).

- All the VMs on a single ESXi host respect the PVLAN boundaries, yet VMs on different hosts are unable to see each other, or can see far too much (applies to community or promiscuous PVLAN modes only).

- VMs on the same ESXi host, but in different Distributed Switches are unable to communicate in the PVLANs (applies to community or promiscuous PVLAN modes only).

Did You Pick the Wrong Network Card?

It happens. You get a new server in the rack, not realizing that the vmnics are enumerated in a different order from your previous servers, and now you can't connect to it. The physical Ethernet adapters in an ESXi server are enumerated based on the bus ID of the card. Some manufacturers change the bus IDs of their PCI slots between models of their servers, so be careful when making assumptions about which NIC will end up becoming vmnic0.

If you happen to know the MAC address of your network cards, you could sort out the problem easily because the MAC address is listed in the DCUI. But if you're like the rest of us, you didn't record that info when you installed the server. In that case, you could unplug the adapters to see which ports show as "connected" in the DCUI. Once you have the management network connected, you can use the vSphere Client to determine which IP ranges the ESXi host sees on each adapter. This information is listed on the properties of each physical network adapter in the Network Adapters section of the ESXi host's Configuration tab.

In the event you can't find the right management network, but you do have remote access (or local access) to the server's console, you can use the command line to help. Refer to the "Troubleshooting from the Command Line" section in this chapter for a command entitled `esxcfg-info`. With the `-n` parameter it will give you a nice listing with the "network hint" you were looking for.

Lockdown Mode

It was designed to keep out attackers or would-be rogue administrators, but you've enabled lockdown mode and managed to lock yourself out of your ESXi host. Not to worry, you can fix the problem easy enough; you just need local access to the host or some form of out-of-band remote access that will give you remote control of the keyboard and monitor. You need to get to the DCUI. The second from the top option in the DCUI will allow you to disable (or enable) lockdown mode.

You are also prompted to enable lockdown mode when you add an ESXi host to vCenter. If you choose to enable lockdown mode, be aware that it will prevent you from accessing the ESXi host directly over the network; only vCenter will have the authority to control that host.

ESXi Firewall Trouble

So you were "experimenting" and somehow found a creative way to modify the ESXi firewall, and now you can't communicate with your ESXi host. No worries, there's a backdoor, but you need to have direct access to the console of the ESXi host. From the command line you can temporarily disable the ESXi firewall so that you can use the vSphere Client to reconfigure the security properly this time. Refer to the "Troubleshooting from the Command Line" section in this chapter for a command entitled `esxcli`. There is a parameter that will disable the firewall module to give you access again. Just remember to enable it again when you're done.

Troubleshooting with the vSphere Client

Most of your network connectivity troubleshooting won't happen in the vSphere Client, but there are a few elements that we wanted to highlight.

Viewing VMkernel Routing Table Settings

A cool feature VMware introduced in vSphere 5 is the ability to see the routing table for VMkernel ports. Historically, you had to use SSH or log on locally to the ESXi server to see this information. We can now access it from within the GUI of the vSphere Client.

To find it, edit the settings of your virtual switch and select the VMkernel port. Now click on "View Routing Table…." A pop-up window will display showing the routes assigned to the VMkernel interfaces. You cannot edit the routes from this interface, but it can be helpful to at least see if a default gateway was entered.

Checking the Network Hints

Another great feature is the ability to see which IP ranges each physical network card detects. This feature has been around for a while, but for those unfamiliar with it we'll explain. The network cards in an ESXi server listen for broadcast, unicast, and multicast traffic that needs to be forwarded to the virtual switch. The VMkernel keeps a running list of any IP addresses that it finds in the SOURCE field of broadcast packets. This list will only contain the IP addresses of hosts or devices on the same physical segment/VLAN as that network card. The process is called snooping, not sniffing, because the VMkernel isn't inspecting the traffic. It's just collecting statistics about who is sending traffic so that we know what IP address ranges are in use on that segment.

You can see this information if you go the Configuration tab of any ESXi host, then click on the Network Adapters tab. There is a column labeled "Observed IP address ranges," with one entry per network card. Note that sometimes this list can be a bit misleading if you have multiple IP subnets in the same broadcast domain. The list may be accurate, but the range will always show the smallest number found and the largest number found. Therefore, if you had two different IP ranges (say 10.1.1.0/24 and 192.168.1.0/24) on the same physical network or VLAN, the VMkernel would report that the observed IP ranges for that card were 10.1.1.1–192.168.1.255. It doesn't hurt anything if the numbers are invalid; so if the range looks funny, don't worry about it. This is just present to help you figure out which network adapter is connected to a given LAN segment.

Checking the MTU Values

We've mentioned the MTU values a lot because they tend to cause issues if misconfigured. You can see the MTU values on the VMkernel ports and on the virtual switches. This is true even for the Standard Virtual Switches now in vSphere 5.

To view the MTU for a switch, go to the Configuration tab of an ESXi host, and then click on the Networking section. Click on the Properties link next to your Standard

Virtual Switch. When selecting the virtual switch entry, the information will change to show the current MTU value for that switch. To view the MTU for a VMkernel port, in that same window, select the VMkernel port. In both cases, the MTU will be shown on the right side of the window.

Troubleshooting with the DCUI

The DCUI should really be your starting point for troubleshooting operations that go beyond the vSphere Client. There are a number of tools VMware has provided within the DCUI to enable you to repair basic networking issues. We've listed some of those tasks here:

Testing the Management Network

When you first log in to the DCUI, you are presented with a list of options, as shown in Figure 7.41.

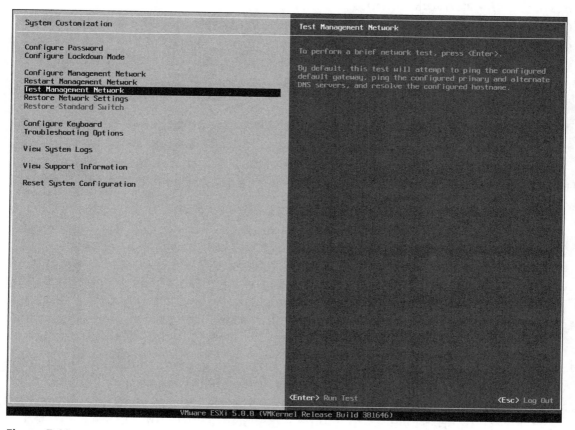

Figure 7.41
ESXi DCUI.

If you are having trouble with connectivity, one of the first things you should try is "Test Management Network." This option does three things. First, it pings the IP address of the management interface's default gateway. Next, it pings your DNS servers. Finally, it uses those DNS servers to resolve the ESXi hostname you entered in the DCUI. If all of these things pass, you can be certain that your ESXi server is seeing the network.

Editing the Management Interface

If the test of the management network didn't succeed, you should consider editing the management network's IP configuration. Perhaps there was a typo, or maybe an address has changed since you built this server. Whatever the case, enter the correct information and then save the settings. When finished, retry the test on the main DCUI menu to confirm your settings are working.

Restoring the Network Settings

On occasion, a host's network configuration becomes so messed up that the only sensible thing to do is start over. But before you wipe out the entire ESXi host, log on to the DCUI and review your options. You have the ability to revert the management network configuration to the default configuration right from the DCUI, and without rebuilding your ESXi server!

This option should be one of your last resorts because it will revert the IP address of your server back to DHCP and recreate a standard network switch with vmnic0 attached to it. If you had a custom configuration, you may have some work to do to get things back in order. For that reason, we recommend doing this when the server can be taken offline.

Adding a vmnic to vSwitch0

Right along with the above advice, there are times when we accidently click on the wrong option and make our ESXi hosts inaccessible. For example, if you were editing your network configuration settings, you might have meant to click on the vmnic1 entry, but instead clicked on vmnic0 and now your management network is offline and the host is disconnected from vCenter.

The solution is simple, but likely painful. You need to get to the DCUI to reattach the vmnic to the management interface. Just open the DCUI and select Configure Management Network, and then select Network Adapters. From that screen, you can select the appropriate vmnic to bind to the management interface. The effect is immediate, so you can log out of the DCUI and return to the vSphere GUI.

Troubleshooting with the ESXi Command Line

Though VMware did attempt to bring more information into the GUI in vSphere 5, you will likely spend more of your troubleshooting time at the command prompt, especially if you accidentally disable or delete your ESXi host's management interface. The command prompt has been greatly improved since previous versions, in that there are more tools. In many ways, the ESXi command prompt feels more like the service console of the old vSphere 4 ESX servers.

Note

You can run many of these commands from within the VMA. That is, if you didn't accidentally disable your ESXi host's management interface.

By no means is this list exhaustive. There are many command line tools. We are highlighting some of the more commonly used tools.

- General commands
- `esxcfg-vswitch`
- `esxcfg-vmknic`
- `esxcfg-route`
- `esxcfg-info`
- `esxcli network`

General Commands

Just because we're working with a hypervisor doesn't mean we can forget about using traditional TCP/IP commands. Sometimes the simplest troubleshooting method involves simply using `ping` or `traceroute` to locate a problem before delving into the mysteries of the `esxcfg` commands.

Here are some of the common tools that are available from the ESXi command line:

- `ping`
- `ping6`
- `traceroute`
- `nslookup`
- `vmkping`

Note

Commands sent to the `ping` command are actually redirected to the `vmkping` command. We no longer need two different `ping` commands because VMware removed the Service Console from vSphere 5; therefore, all `ping` commands are technically running from the VMkernel anyway!

esxcfg-vswitch

As the name implies, the `esxcfg-vswitch` command is used to control virtual switches. With it you can list, create, delete, or modify the various Standard Virtual Switches on your ESXi host. There are even some options to control port groups on Distributed Switches.

So why include it here in the troubleshooting section? Because you may accidentally remove vSwitch0 or make a modification to the switch configuration, which makes the ESXi host inaccessible. If so, you can use this subset of the command syntax and a couple examples to get you started. The command is much more robust than this, and you can always type `esxcfg-vswitch -help` to get a full listing.

```
esxcfg-vswitch [options] [vswitch[:ports]]
  -a|--add              Add a virtual switch.
  -d|--delete           Delete a virtual switch.
  -l|--list             List the virtual switches.
  -L|--link=pnic        Add an uplink for the vswitch.
  -U|--unlink=pnic      Remove an uplink from the vswitch.
  -A|--add-pg=name      Add a portgroup to a Standard virtual switch.
  -D|--del-pg=name      Delete a portgroup from a Standard virtual switch.
  -B|--set-cdp          Change the CDP status for a virtual switch.
  -m|--mtu=MTU          Change the MTU of the vswitch.
```

esxcfg-vmknic

The `esxcfg-vmknic` command is used to work with VMkernel ports on the ESXi host. While you can edit the IP address information of the management ports via the DCUI, you are restricted to editing only one of those ports. If you had two or more management ports, this command would help you get the IP addresses straightened out.

We'll forego adding the command syntax here because the output would be several pages long. Suffice it to say there are a lot of options and you can use this command to manipulate VMkernel ports on both Standard and Distributed Virtual Switches.

esxcfg-route

This command is similar to the "route" command on a Windows machine. There isn't much to say about it other than it can be helpful if you have multiple VMkernel ports on different IP subnets. Instead of using just one gateway, you could have multiple routes configured. Another use of the command is to see what your default gateway is set to. In fact, that is what it outputs if you type in the command without any arguments.

esxcfg-info

Probably the most informative tool you'll find on the ESXi console is the esxcfg-info command. Aptly named, this tool provides information on a large number of areas including networking, storage, and resources to name just a few.

The command has only one argument, which determines the category of information that is given. The output is hierarchical and is best read using the less command so that you can page up and page down. If you forget the less command you'll have to speed read at a rate of about 50 pages per second.

In the beginning of this troubleshooting section, we mentioned this command because it will help you determine information about your physical network cards. In particular, it will tell you about the observed network ranges that the ESXi host sees on the physical network adapters. In the output of the command, it refers to these ranges as a "Network Hint."

The syntax for the esxcfg-info command is:

```
Usage: esxcfg-info mode
 -a, --all          Show all information
 -w, --hardware     Show only hardware information
 -r, --resource     Show only resource information
 -s, --storage      Show only storage information
 -n, --network      Show only network information
 -y, --system       Show only system information
 -o, --advopt       Show the advanced options
 -u, --hwuuid       Show the hardware uuid
 -b, --bootuuid     Show the boot partition uuid
 -e, --boottype     Show the boot type (VMVisor Only)
 -c, --cmdline      Show the vmkernel command line
 -F, --format       Display the information in a different format
                    You may use "xml" and "perl"
 -h, --help         Show this help message.
```

As we said though, you'll want to run the command using the `less` command to allow a bit of page control. To get a useable output focused on your network configuration, type this:

```
esxcfg-info -n | less
```

You could also pipe the output to a file and use it for documentation, though admittedly it would be like finding a needle in a haystack if you needed to use it.

esxcli Network

The `esxcli` command is based on various namespaces that can be chained together to configure different values on the ESXi host. This is the command we mentioned earlier that can be used to temporarily disable the ESXi firewall. There are a great many things you can do with this command, including list the virtual switches and VMkernel ports, show the ARP table for specific adapters, and enable or disable IPv6 support. Here are some useful examples:

Show the ARP cache information:

```
esxcli network ip neighbor list
```

Disable the ESXi firewall:

```
esxcli network firewall set --enabled false
```

Show all the VMkernel ports:

```
esxcli network ip interface list
```

SUMMARY

As you have seen, networking is a deep subject and VMware did much to improve the virtual networking in vSphere 5. The major feature changes focused heavily on the Distributed Switches (Port Mirroring, LLDP support, load-based teaming, and NetFlow), but VMware also simplified our Standard Switches by incorporating many of the commonly used "advanced" settings into the GUI. As you will see in our next chapter, there are some aspects of networking that interrelate with storage (iSCSI/NFS). Also, you will see why vSphere 5 is being hailed as the storage-centric release of vSphere. Compared to the changes in networking, VMware has nearly redefined how storage is handled in virtualization.

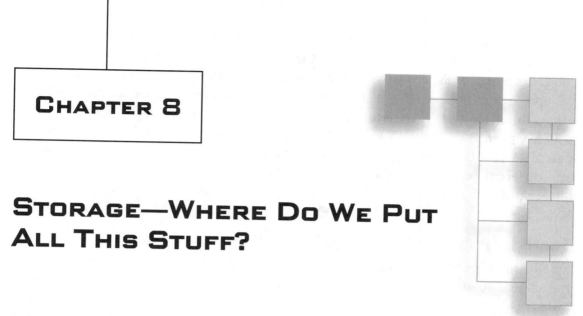

CHAPTER 8

STORAGE—WHERE DO WE PUT ALL THIS STUFF?

Just one thing stands between you and building VMs—storage. At this point you have a functioning server, controlled by vCenter, and you have networking, both for the management and use of the server as well as for VMs to use, but you have no place to actually put any VMs. We discussed networking before storage because you will need to leverage networking to use NAS, iSCSI, or FCoE; if you're using directly connected storage or Fibre Channel, then networking is not needed to access storage (but of course is still required for management and other internal purposes).

Storage is a vast topic with many options and optimizations—that's why this is one of the longest chapters of the book. Storage can be very simple (such as internal drives in a server) to very complex (such as a Storage Area Network [SAN] leveraging iSCSI and/or Fibre Channel). This book does not purport to replace any kind of SAN training from either VMware or your SAN vendor, but it does provide a good basis to get started.

Ready? Let's dive in!

PLANNING

Many questions about storage need to be answered before anything is implemented. Among the most important, with lots of implications for the entire deployment, is the choice between shared and local storage, closely followed by the type of storage (iSCSI, Fibre Channel, or NFS) that will be used. We'll start with those two subjects and then look at the types of SAN arrays that can be used (if local storage isn't used), compare and contrast hardware versus software iSCSI and NFS versus VMFS datastore types (more on datastores in a moment), and then look at using virtual disks (VMDK is the VMware term; they are analogous to the VHD format that Microsoft uses) versus native disks (called RDMs—Raw Device Mappings by VMware). We'll look at some sizing issues and limitations, and then take a brief look at VAAI—an API by VMware to make storage more efficient—which was introduced with vSphere 4.1. If all that wasn't enough, there is also the new VSA (vSphere Storage Appliance) feature that can turn local storage from several different servers into shared storage—like a very simple SAN. Wow! That's a lot of stuff—and those are just the planning issues! Let's get started.

Shared versus Local Storage

One of the biggest design choices you need to make in any vSphere deployment is the choice to use either local (inside or directly connected to the server—often called DAS—Direct Attach Storage) or shared storage (either NAS [Network Attached Storage] or SAN [Storage Area Network]). Many of the features we will discuss later in this book require the use of shared storage (such as vMotion, DRS, and HA). In general, all but the smallest of implementations will use shared storage.

Let's begin by looking at the advantages and disadvantages of local storage in Table 8.1.

Table 8.1   Local Storage

Advantages	Disadvantages
Inexpensive	Minimal expandability
Moves with the server—no special cards, cables, etc., required in most cases	Can't use any features requiring shared storage (unless the VSA feature is implemented—see the Planning and Implementation sections in this chapter for more details)
Simple	
Typically where ESXi is installed (though boot from SAN is also possible)	
Can create VM clusters (such as Microsoft Clusters [MSCS]) for testing	Limited to all nodes of the VM cluster residing on one node

Table 8.2 Shared Storage

Advantages	Disadvantages
Expandability: add more space, spindles, etc., on the fly	More complex (from mildly to very, depending on the design, protocol(s) used, vendor, etc.)
Usually simpler recovery in the event of a failure	Expensive
No Single Point of Failure (NSPoF) for enterprise storage implementations	Even more expensive and complex, but better availability
Access to all features requiring shared storage	
Centralized management of storage	
Ability to create VM clusters across physical hosts	
Potential to use native storage data replication (snapshots, clones, mirroring between arrays, etc.) for better availability, DR (for example, for use with Site Recovery Manager—discussed in Chapter 15), etc.	

Now let's do the same for shared storage, shown in Table 8.2.

With all the advantages of shared storage, why would anyone choose local storage? In a word, cost. Shared storage costs at a minimum a few thousand dollars, and often tens to hundreds of thousands of dollars, with high-end configurations extending into the millions. Still, for all but the smallest implementations, shared storage (or the VSA, which creates shared storage out of local storage) should be deployed.

What Types of Storage Can Be Used?

Most implementations of vSphere will involve DAS as the location for the actual installation of ESXi itself, unless either ESXi Embedded, which is a form of DAS (it is just preinstalled) or boot from SAN is used. Boot from SAN is most common on diskless blade servers, but can be used to make recovery from a server failure simpler by reassigning the boot LUN to a standby blade and booting the new blade—no further configuration of ESXi is required. Alternatively, Auto Deploy (covered in Chapter 5) can be used to boot from the network (PXE boot) with no local or SAN storage required for ESXi itself.

Most, if not all, VMs will thus reside on some form of shared storage. But which type? If you have already deployed shared storage in some form, you can leverage that. If you haven't, however, you have several supported options from which to choose. While a thorough discussion of all of the types and the advantages and disadvantages of one vendor's implementation versus another's is beyond the scope of this book, a brief overview of each of the major technologies' characteristics may prove helpful. Let's start with the simplest and work up to the most complex (although this is a bit subjective, as most of the complexity occurs within each vendor's management system for their products).

Network Attached Storage (NAS)

NAS implementations can range from the simple (a server with Windows or Linux sharing some files) to the complex (a dedicated array that handles many terabytes of data and costs hundreds of thousands of dollars). In any case, to be used with ESXi, it must support NFS (Network File System), the Linux/UNIX method of sharing files. ESXi does not support CIFS (Common Internet File System), also known as SMB (Server Message Block), the native file sharing method used by Windows. A Windows server can be made to work with ESXi by installing and configuring Services for UNIX (SFU), but the configuration of that depends on the version of Windows and is beyond the scope of this book.

To use NFS, the NFS server or storage array must support NFS version 3 (not 2 or 4) over TCP (not UDP). If your device supports it, you can use it; if not, you can't. It's that simple.

NAS presents storage as files—without any direct access to the disk. This isn't a problem, but it does preclude the use of a few features in vSphere, such as Boot from SAN and RDMs (Raw Device Mappings—more on this later in the chapter). The maximum size of an NFS volume is whatever the storage vendor supports; there are no maximum volume sizes like there are for block-based storage.

iSCSI

iSCSI runs the SCSI command set over TCP over IP (hence the "I" part of the name) over Ethernet. On the network, it travels in packets as shown in Figure 8.1.

TCP/IP was designed to withstand nuclear war, unreliable networks, and so on, and thus has a fair amount of overhead compared to other protocols (such as Fibre Channel). However, it works over standard Ethernet networks and does not require (although supports) dedicated HBA (Host Bus Adapter) cards, which reduces the

Figure 8.1
iSCSI packet format.

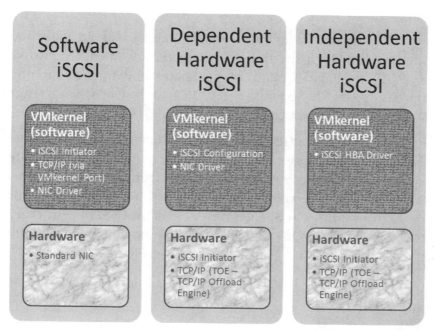

Figure 8.2
iSCSI initiator types.

cost to implement this storage choice, at the cost of consuming more CPU cycles, reducing the cycles left to run VMs (though typically not drastically).

vSphere supports three kinds of iSCSI adapters: Software, Dependent Hardware, and Independent Hardware (also known as iSCSI HBAs), as shown in Figure 8.2.

Software iSCSI is the cheapest, costing nothing more than a standard NIC (or several NICs if desired), while both Independent Hardware and Dependent Hardware iSCSI manage most, if not all, of the iSCSI tasks in hardware, increasing the cost of the card, but lowering the CPU load. Dependent Hardware iSCSI cards tend to be dramatically cheaper than Independent Hardware cards, with the primary difference where the actual iSCSI and network configuration is performed—with the former it is in vSphere; with the latter it is in the card's BIOS.

iSCSI works at the block level on disk, so almost every feature available in vSphere can be used with iSCSI, including Boot from SAN. This is becoming more and more popular due to the relatively low cost and well understood components, as well as the lack of required special cards, cables, switches, etc. It is also popular because there are no distance limitations (imposed by the protocol at least—there may be some limitations for performance reasons) between the initiator (the ESXi server) and the target (the storage array or server).

Fibre Channel (FC)

Often considered the "gold standard" in storage, Fibre Channel was standardized back in 1989 and was designed for high-speed, high-reliability, low-latency networks (just the opposite of TCP/IP), so it lacks many of the space- and time-consuming checks that TCP/IP imposes. Today, FC operates at 1, 2, 4, and 8Gbps (with faster speeds up to 16Gbps available, but not yet commonly deployed).

In Fibre Channel, HBAs connect to Fibre Channel switches, which connect to storage arrays. Typically, two HBAs are in each server, with each HBA connecting to a separate FC switch, and the array connecting to both switches (typically from both Storage Processors—SPs, which are basically blade servers that are dedicated to and optimized for storage). This provides a network with No Single Point of Failure (NSPoF). In other words, any switch, cable, port, HBA, or SP can fail and a redundant path will still move data between the HBA and the array. This is illustrated in Figure 8.3.

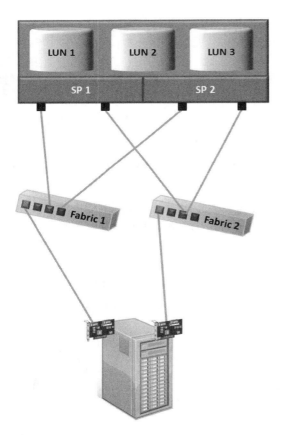

Figure 8.3
FC connectivity.

Just as we use a MAC address in networking, we use World Wide Names (WWNs) in FC. In fact, we have two WWNs—World Wide Port Names (WWPNs) and World Wide Node Names (WWNNs). Every device has at least one WWNN (typically each array has one and each HBA [not necessarily HBA port] has one). Every port on every device has a WWPN. A device's address is thus the WWNN:WWPN. One difference between a WWN and a MAC address is that a MAC address is 48 bits, whereas a WWN is 64 bits, thus the WWNN:WWPN address is 128 bits.

There are two important tasks when using FC that must be completed by a SAN administrator before you can use FC storage (at least from the SAN perspective; you obviously need the drivers installed in ESXi as well). You must zone the SAN and mask the LUNs.

Zoning Zoning is somewhat like a VLAN in networking in that if two devices are in the same zone, they can see each other, but if they are not, they can't. Note that unlike a VLAN, no special configuration is needed for this (other than the zone configuration on the FC switches). Also, every device in a zone will let every other device in the zone know of its presence, so nothing special is required to know what initiators and targets are available (unlike with iSCSI). Without properly configured zoning, the host has no physical path to the array, and thus will not be able to use any of the array's resources.

LUN Masking LUN masking is not necessarily unique to FC; it may also be used with iSCSI. LUN masking is the process of defining which LUNs are visible to which servers; it is typically done on the array. The process varies from vendor to vendor (and sometimes from product to product). Without masking configured, there may be a path to the array, but no resources will be available to the host.

Note

LUN masking without zoning and zoning without LUN masking is useless because no storage will be available to the host.

Fibre Channel over Ethernet (FCoE)

In the last few years, a variant of FC has been introduced called Fibre Channel over Ethernet (FCoE). It replaces Fibre Channel cables and switches at Layers 1 and 2 in the networking stack (as described in Chapter 7) with Ethernet cables and switches. It also replaces a FC HBA with a FCoE CNA (Converged Network Adapter), which basically is a standard NIC and an FC HBA in one card that typically looks like two devices to the OS (ESXi in our case). Hardware FCoE has been supported since vSphere 4.

Support for software FCoE is new in vSphere 5. Software FCoE is similar to dependent hardware iSCSI. It is a NIC/HBA with FCoE support that is configured via the vSphere Client. In the latter type, instead of an FCoE HBA driver for the CNA, a software FCoE driver is used instead. It is usually a 10Gb NIC with some extra code that looks at the incoming data in Layer 3 and decides if it is standard networking traffic, in which case it is sent up the stack as a standard TCP/IP packet and to the NIC driver in ESXi. If it is FCoE traffic, it is sent as FC data to the FCoE driver in ESXi. FCoE was approved as a standard by the T11 FCoE committee at ANSI.

While vSphere has supported FCoE since version 4.0, only in the last year or so have companies started to produce CNAs and FCoE modules on their respective arrays. The advantage of this system is that you get the standards (and cost savings) of Ethernet versus the less well understood (by the masses) and expensive Fibre Channel, while at the same time you get the performance and low overhead of Fibre Channel at the upper layers (compared to TCP/IP). Many people see this as the future of FC with ever-increasing Ethernet speeds (10Gb is standard today; 40Gb and 100Gb are on the horizon), whereas others see the future of FC staying with the traditional FC mechanisms at Layers 1 and 2, with 16Gb FC commercially available now and 32Gb FC in the labs.

From a requirements standpoint, note that the Ethernet Fabric must be an Enhanced Ethernet Fabric. Enhanced Ethernet is three interrelated standards that provide for lossless data transfer and congestion control, making Ethernet suitable for the demands that storage makes without incurring the penalties of handling errors and lost packets at higher levels of the OSI model. The three standards are:

- Priority-based Flow Control (PFC), which is covered by the IEEE standard 802.1Qbb. This protocol standard looks at the classes of service defined in 802.1p and provides flow control for each class independently, with the goal of zero packet loss in congested networks. For this to work properly, the following two standards must also be implemented.

- Congestion Notification, which is defined in IEEE 802.1Qau, provides end-to-end congestion management at Layer 2. By handling congestion at Layer 2, it is designed to respond to congestion more quickly than the current mechanism of managing this at Layer 4 (via TCP). It does this by working with higher level protocols to lower the packet transmission rates to keep packets from being dropped.

- Enhanced Transmission Selection (ETS), defined in IEEE 802.1Qaz, provides the basic management structure for assigning bandwidth to the various classes of service defined in 802.1p.

Table 8.3 VMware Classification of SAN Types

SAN Vendor	VMware	Why
Active-Passive	Active-Passive	One SP does all of the work and the other is used only if the first SP fails.
Active-Active	Active-Passive	Both SPs are active, but for different LUNs; i.e., for any one LUN, only one SP can access it at a time.[*]
Active-Active	Active-Active	Both SPs are active and both SPs can access any LUN at any time.

* ALUA (Asymmetrical Logical Unit Access), a SCSI standard implemented by some SAN vendors, is a gray area. ALUA allows one SP to own the LUN, but provides access to the other SP in some situations (such as the failure of a backend [SP to disk] cable on one SP with front-end [SP to host] access only available on the other SP). Some call this pseudo active-active and others call this asymmetric active-active, and depending on the SAN vendor's implementation with vSphere, it may be considered either active-active or active-passive.

These standards require networking infrastructure components and software and/or drivers at the server level that implement them for the process to work. Most major network, storage, and HBA vendors are working to make their products compliant with these standards, but the standards are still in the draft stages and subject to change as of the writing of this book.

Array Types: Active-Active or Active-Passive

When you purchase a storage array (or use one you already have), ask the vendor (or your SAN administrator) whether the type of array is active-active or active-passive. VMware defines this a little differently than many SAN vendors do. Table 8.3 compares what a SAN vendor may say about their array versus the VMware definition.

Why does this matter? Read on for our review of multipathing and you'll find out!

Multipathing

Multipathing takes advantage of the redundant connections described previously to physically provide NSPoF and extends that to the software so that there is NSPoF end to end. Figure 8.4 illustrates the pieces involved and each is described next.

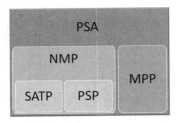

Figure 8.4
Multipathing support in the VMKernel.

Let's begin by defining each component and describe the role of each, then the I/O flow from VM to storage will be described at the end of this section. One quick note before we do so: this section contains many acronyms; they will be spelled out in the section in which they are described, not necessarily the first time they are used.

PSA (Pluggable Storage Architecture)

The PSA (Pluggable Storage Architecture) is the layer inside of the VMkernel that is responsible for all storage I/O, both from the VMs and from the VMkernel itself (such as Storage vMotion). The PSA is a framework, as illustrated in Figure 8.4, with many subcomponents responsible for the various functions required to actually read and write data. The PSA (and its various subcomponents) is responsible for the following:

■ Loading (and unloading, though that rarely ever happens) any MPPs as well as NMP.

■ Routing I/O requests to the appropriate MPP that manages the device the I/O is destined for.

■ Queuing any I/O for the logical devices, including managing how much bandwidth any given VM will get and how the available bandwidth is divided between the VMs.

■ Queuing for the physical HBAs.

■ Discovery (and removal if a path fails or the storage infrastructure is modified) of all physical paths, primarily via the SATP in NMP.

■ Statistics for the logical devices (used by the VMs) as well as physical devices (HBAs and LUNs). These are reported using the standard Performance tab in the vSphere Client, as well as via resxtop using either the vCLI or the vMA. Performance monitoring is covered in Chapter 10.

As you can see, the PSA has a lot of responsibilities and coordinates the various components to keep I/O moving smoothly.

MPP (MultiPathing Plugin)/NMP (Native MultiPathing)

Just inside the PSA are any MPPs (MultiPathing Plugins) that have been installed as well as NMP (Native MultiPathing), which is always there. MPPs, such as EMC's PowerPath/VE and Dell's EqualLogic Multipathing Enhancement Module (MEM, another name for an MPP), are never there by default and must be installed to be used. Conceptually they do the same thing, though third-party vendors usually add additional functionality beyond the basics that are a part of NMP to take advantage of advanced device capabilities as well as to provide other multipathing options. For example, PowerPath/VE provides seven load balancing options versus the three that are part of NMP.

All LUNs are owned by NMP until an MPP is installed, which will add some rules to the system claiming some LUNs for itself (usually based on the brand of storage attached) and taking them away from NMP. Any given LUN may only be owned by one MPP (or NMP) at a time.

The responsibilities of an MPP or NMP include the following:

- Claiming the physical paths for the specific MPP or NMP, and if NMP, associating it with the correct SATP. These paths can also be dynamically unclaimed as long as there is no I/O to the device when the `unclaim` command is issued.

- Registering and deregistering logical devices for use by upper-level components, such as datastores. The purpose of the logical devices is to hide the details of the path being used from the device from higher layers.

- Linking the physical path options to the logical devices; in the case of NMP, the selection of a specific path for a given I/O is the responsibility of the PSP. Likewise, for NMP, the SATP handles any I/O failures (or new I/O paths discovered), failing over to other paths (such as when an HBA or SP fails), and adding and removing paths as needed for the PSP to use. The duties and responsibilities of both the SATP and the PSP layers will be described in detail later in this section.

- Handling all other management tasks required by the VMkernel, such as aborting I/O, management of SCSI reservations for logical devices, etc.

The specifics of how a given MPP works is up to that vendor and can be found in that vendor's documentation. NMP provides two subcomponents that help further divide up its responsibilities, SATPs and PSPs.

SATPs (Storage Array Type Plugins)

vSphere comes with many SATPs (Storage Array Type Plugins) out of the box and additional SATPs can be added by adding third-party SATPs later. The purpose of the SATP is to provide the link between the generic I/O components of the rest of the PSA and the specific capabilities, error handling, etc., of each vendor's array. Many vendors have multiple SATPs for the different arrays they sell.

The primary responsibilities of the SATP layer are as follows:

- Determine and monitor the health of each physical path to the LUN and report that to NMP, which in turn shares the information with the PSP for path selection.

- If a path that has failed has been repaired, report the newly available path to NMP.

- Conversely, if a path fails, take appropriate action (retry and then if that fails, mark the path as failed and handle any necessary failover with the array, such as to a different SP if the original SP fails).

Note that while the SATP is constantly monitoring the states of the LUNs, it only reports changes to NMP.

PSPs (Path Selection Plugins)

PSPs (Path Selection Plugins) provide the various load balancing options. The PSP selects the physical path any given I/O will take. There are two PSPs that provide availability only (Fixed and MRU) and one that provides both scalability and availability (RR). Note that RR is usually not the default—it must typically be selected for a given datastore (more on how to do that in the implementation section). This has key performance implications, as both MRU and Fixed (by default—it is configurable for Fixed) pick the first path seen and all I/O goes down that path. This can lead to a bottleneck on that path (HBA, storage port on the array, and/or SP). Most vendors recommend that RR be selected to better balance the load, but be sure to refer to your vendor's documentation before selecting it for their best practices.

Let's look in a little more detail at each of the three PSPs.

Fixed Fixed is the default (and recommended) PSP for most active-active arrays (but VMware does not recommend using it for arrays that support ALUA, though some vendors do). This policy defaults to using the first path to a LUN that it sees, but a preferred path can be specified if desired (and you really should do this), allowing manual load balancing across paths (assuming you monitor and adjust the preferred paths to the different LUNs based on the I/O to each). If this path fails, any other random path (that is still functioning) will be chosen and used, but once the failed path is restored, the PSP will resume using it (automatic failback). This works great in active-active scenarios, but in active-passive scenarios may lead to path thrashing (where the LUN path goes to the preferred, fails over, fails back, and repeats the cycle) in certain circumstances.

Nevertheless, it can be used with active-passive arrays to get some basic load balancing as just described. If you chose to do so with this type of array, it is recommended that you change them back to MRU after they are set for the aforementioned reason (unless the array vendor recommends otherwise). The only problem with this plan is that the paths you set are not retained after a reboot, so this process must be repeated with each reboot (or scripted to run with each reboot), or a different PSP mechanism should be selected.

MRU (Most Recently Used) MRU (Most Recently Used) is the default for most active-passive arrays. With this mechanism, the first working path found to a LUN will be used and will continue to be used until a failure occurs, at which time it will select another path. Once it fails over, it will continue to use that path until a failure occurs on that path, at which point it will select another path at random from the list of paths again. In other words, it has an automatic failover policy, but no automatic failback (unlike fixed).

RR (Round Robin) Round Robin (RR) is the third PSP that comes with ESXi's NMP. With this policy, a fixed number of packets (1,000 by default) is sent down the first available path, then that same number down the second path, and so on through all available (active) paths. It then goes back to the first path and the process repeats. Note that this is a simple load balancing mechanism; it does not take into account latencies, number of outstanding packets, etc., but rather just a fixed number of packets per path. It will use all active paths on an active-passive array and all paths (that haven't failed) on an active-active array. In vSphere 5 it is the default for some arrays, but most still default to either MRU or Fixed. As mentioned previously, you should check with your storage vendor to determine what their best practice is for the PSP, and then use it.

Note

You can change the number of I/Os sent down each path if desired. There is a lot of debate on the value and cost of doing this, but the general consensus is that it is a good idea for large and/or sequential I/O, but for other types of I/O, the results are less clear. Experiment in your environment to see if the change will help. The syntax to do so is as follows:

```
esxcli nmp roundrobin setconfig --device=naa.<device naa> --iops 1 --type iops
```

This will send one I/O down a path before switching to the next available path. Other values may also be used if desired; benchmark in your environment to determine the optimum value.

Multipathing I/O Flow with NMP

So how do these components work together to provide multipathing in NMP? The process from an I/O in a VM to the array (when NMP is used) is as follows:

1. The VM sends an I/O request through its virtual SCSI controller.

2. The VMkernel receives the request and passes it to the PSA to be handled.

3. The PSA selects the correct MPP for the I/O, based on the configured claim rules. By default, all I/O goes to NMP.

4. NMP passes the I/O to the PSP specified for the datastore.

5. The PSP looks at the policy for the datastore and selects the matching physical path (for MRU and fixed, it will usually be the same LUN for every I/O to the datastore unless a failure has occurred, whereas for RR the system looks at the number of packets that have been sent and decides to continue with the same path or rotate to the next path in the list).

6. At this point, there are two possible scenarios:

    a. If the I/O is successful, it is complete and NMP reports the successful completion up the stack. The response is sent back to the VM when it arrives from the storage device.

    b. If the I/O fails (due to things such as a path failure, a failed HBA, cable, switch port, or SP), the following process is undertaken:

        i. NMP determines the SATP that owns the device and reports the error to it.

        ii. The appropriate SATP interprets the error and takes appropriate corrective action (marking the path dead, selecting a new path, activating a formerly passive path as part of trespassing LUNs to the other controller, etc.)

        iii. Once SATP has updated the available path list, it is sent back to the PSP, which will look at the new list of available paths and retry the I/O based on configured policies as described in Step 5 above.

If other MPPs have been installed and a LUN is claimed by one of them, the PSA still receives the I/O. It just passes the I/O to the correct MPP and the I/O is handled within the MPP however the vendor has created it and the user configured it.

NFS versus VMFS

Now that we have covered the types of storage, you may be wondering which one you should choose. The short answer is, it really doesn't matter. You probably want to stay away from DAS in all but the smallest environments as you automatically lose access to all of the features that require shared storage (such as DRS, vMotion, and HA, all of which will be discussed later in the book), though shared storage will almost always cost more. The only exception to this recommendation is if you are using the VSA—vSphere Storage Appliance (described below).

At this point, you still have two choices—use VMFS or NFS—so which should you choose? Shared Storage of either type will work similarly, although there are a few differences. VMFS is used with block-based storage, while NFS is file based. Your storage arrays may support both; if not, your choice has already been made.

Advantages and Disadvantages of NFS

Let's start with the negative and then we'll conclude on a positive note. The things that are not available with NFS are:

- You can't boot ESXi servers from NFS—it requires a block-based storage device.

- You can't use RDMs (Raw Device Mappings—discussed below), which also means you can't use applications that require them (such as Microsoft Clustering).

- Load balancing is based on network throughput, and due to the way that 802.3ad works, you are limited to the capacity of a single link for a single conversation (and all NFS I/O to a single datastore goes through a single TCP session). iSCSI and FC have the load balancing Round Robin option previously described (plus whatever an MPP may provide).

On the other hand, some things are better with NFS, including the following:

- NFS allows (and has allowed) for large volumes—at least as large as 16TB and some up to 256TB, depending on the vendor. This can provide a high number of VMs per datastore.

- No command queue limits, meaning that you can throw a large amount of I/O at the NFS-based SAN and the limitations show up at either the bandwidth level to the array or at the array level, not at the number of outstanding I/Os that can be queued on the host.

- No SCSI reservation capability, so no overhead for SCSI reservations. SCSI reservations are used when creating and deleting VMs, taking a VM snapshot, allocating space in thin provisioning, etc. The impact of these reservations is generally quite small, especially if the VM is thick provisioned (more on that later in this chapter).

In the end, it's up to you to determine your budget, technical expertise with various storage technologies, any requirements from the applications you are deploying, and the existing infrastructure (if any) that you can leverage. Just keep in mind that if you are considering any technology that runs over the Ethernet network (everything except DAS and FC), you really should be considering a 10GbE infrastructure, at least for storage, and probably for the entire environment.

VMFS 3 versus VMFS 5

One of the small changes with large consequences in vSphere 5 is the new file system that was introduced, VMFS-5. VMFS is the Virtual Machine File System and is (and has been) VMware's native file system for all block-oriented (i.e., non-NFS) storage types.

VMFS-3 was a major improvement from VMFS-2 that was used in ESX 2, introducing a directory file structure among other changes. VMFS-3 (with minor modifications) was used in both ESX(i) 3 and 4, but had a maximum LUN size of 2TB. The maximum LUN size was 2TB in VMFS-3 because VMware used the traditional MBR (Master Boot Record) disk format that had been used for the last 25+ years.

With VMFS-3 you also had to select your block size, where your options were 1, 2, 4, or 8MB. The block size refers to how much storage space on disk is allocated at a time (files on the virtual disks can be smaller, however). A 1MB block size was the most efficient in many cases, but imposed a maximum file size (and hence maximum virtual disk size) of 256GB. If you chose the larger block sizes, the maximum file size would raise with it, so a 2MB block size equated to a 512GB disk, 4MB supported a 1TB disk, and 8MB up to a 2TB disk (technically 2TB minus 512 bytes). For those not familiar with virtual disks, they are stored in files with a .vmdk extension, with (normally) one file per virtual disk, each a configurable size that the guest OS would see as a native SCSI disk.

VMFS-5 uses the newer GPT (GUID Partition Table) format (that can be used in Windows and other operating systems as well). This allows datastores up to 64TB to be created from a single LUN (the maximum datastore size was and is still 64TB, no matter how many LUNs comprise it).

In a new VMFS-5 datastore, the block size is always 1MB, but the maximum file size is 2TB. With a 1MB block size, you may be wondering how space efficient it is for the many small files (configuration files, log files, etc.) that are created. VMFS-5 optimizes that as well. If the file size is ≤ 1KB, the file itself is stored in the file descriptor directly (part of the metadata maintained by every datastore for every file). If the file is still small, but larger than 1KB, VMFS-5 will use sub-block allocation where a 1MB block is broken down into 128 8KB sub-blocks and files will be placed in those smaller chunks of space instead. VMFS-5 also increased the number of sub-blocks available to 32,000 and the maximum number of files to approximately 100,000 (up from around 30,000).

Note

> Sub-block allocation was also available in VMFS-3, but there were a limited number of them and they were 64KB each instead of 8KB.

Perhaps you've been using VMware for years and have many old datastores that are VMFS-3. What should you do with them? The simplest answer is that VMFS-3 datastores can be upgraded non-disruptively to VMFS-5 with no data loss, although on upgrade, the block size will be maintained. In addition, the old-style 64KB sub-block allocation size will be used and the maximum number of files will remain at approximately 30,000. It will also continue to use the MBR format until the volume is grown above 2TB, at which point it will seamlessly change to the new GPT format (with no downtime to VMs). For all these reasons, VMware's best practice if space is available is to create a new VMFS-5 datastore and then migrate the VMs to the new datastore (Storage vMotion is an easy, non-disruptive way to do so) and then delete the now empty datastore and repeat the process until everything is migrated. This way, you can take advantage of the 1MB block size and large LUN size right away.

RDM versus VMDK

All disks appear to any VM as SCSI disks (unless an IDE driver was installed, then a disk would appear as an IDE drive; that capability was added in Hardware Version 7, introduced with vSphere 4). It doesn't matter if the disk is located on local SCSI storage, local SATA storage, on an FC SAN, an iSCSI SAN, or an NAS device; to the VM it is a local SCSI disk. Most of the time, you will create a virtual disk (or multiple virtual disks if the circumstances require) for each of your VMs; as previously mentioned, these disks have a .vmdk extension in the file system. This works fine in the majority of cases, but there may be times when you want to dedicate a disk to a particular VM. VMware says there are three (and a new fourth reason in vSphere 5) good reasons to use an RDM (Raw Device Mapping), namely:

- If you are converting a physical server to a VM and there is too much data to copy over as part of the process (you can always use Storage vMotion later to convert from an RDM to a .vmdk file if desired).

- To take advantage of disks bigger than 2TB. Recall that the largest .vmdk file that can be created is 2TB (technically 2TB – 512 bytes), and that has been the case for years; vSphere 5 (with a VM set to use Hardware Version 8, also introduced with version 5—more on this in Chapter 9) can use RDMs up to 64TB (in physical compatibility mode only; the virtual compatibility maximum is still 2TB), which is 32 times the size of the largest .vmdk.

- If you are creating a Microsoft Cluster system (MSCS), where a dedicated disk must be used for cluster operations; this is recommended for all clusters and required if one or more physical hosts are part of the cluster with one or more virtual machines.

- If you want to access the disk on the SAN directly; for example, to take SAN-based snapshots or clones (not to be confused with the ability to take a snapshot or clone of a VM using native VMware tools).

Vendors sometimes suggest that performance is another good reason to use RDMs, but based on VMware's testing, .vmdk files perform as well as RDMs and can provide better consolidation ratios as multiple .vmdks can live on a single datastore, whereas RDMs are dedicated to a single VM.

Okay, now that we have discussed when to use an RDM or a .vmdk, you may be wondering what an RDM is. An RDM is simply a pointer (on a VMFS datastore) that dedicates a LUN to a VM. Figure 8.5 shows the difference between a .vmdk file and an RDM.

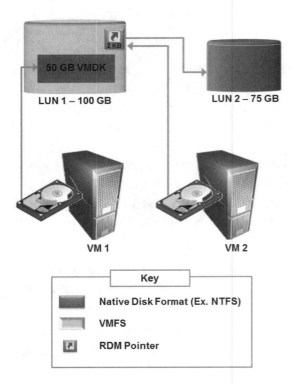

Figure 8.5
RDM versus .vmdk.

A couple of quick tips on using RDMs. First, make sure that they are assigned to all of the nodes that might run the VM so that the VM can be vMotioned from one host to another. Second, they can be used in two compatibility modes: physical and virtual. Let's discuss those two modes now.

Virtual Compatibility Mode

Virtual Compatibility mode provides compatibility with the standard .vmdk file, and thus the things you can do with a .vmdk (such as take a vSphere snapshot of it) can be done with RDMs in virtual compatibility mode. Relative to the use cases previously described, this mode makes sense for the first use case described above, in which there is a lot of data (but less than 2TB) on an existing disk that you don't want to spend the time and/or disk space to copy to a .vmdk file. We rarely use this type of RDM as it doesn't bring many advantages.

Physical Compatibility Mode

The other option is Physical Compatibility mode; it can be used for all of the aforementioned use cases, and is required for use cases two through four for the following reasons:

- It is the only way to access a single disk in a VM that is > 2TB without doing iSCSI directly inside the VM.

- Microsoft Clusters with physical hosts require the same view of storage between all nodes and this is the only disk format that looks the same to a physical host as a VM.

- SCSI commands are typically virtualized before sending them to the SAN, which is a good thing unless you actually want the SCSI command to reach the SAN, such as when storage-based snapshots will be used.

This mode is the primary reason that RDMs exist today.

Clustered Storage (MSCS)

VMware supports Microsoft Clustering (MSCS) in vSphere and has for many versions, but there are specific storage and vSphere configuration requirements. One great source of what is and what is not supported can be found at this KB article: http://kb.vmware.com/kb/1037959. It lists the supported configurations for shared disk clustering (where two or more nodes share a common disk—the traditional method of doing MS clustering) as well as non-shared disk configurations that many newer Microsoft applications (such as Exchange) use. It is probably best to start here and review what is supported before creating a cluster.

Once you have determined that the cluster you want to deploy is supported and that any limitations (such as not being able to vMotion the VMs or not supporting the storage you want to use) are not going to be show-stoppers for your deployment, it is time to refer to the authoritative work on clustering from VMware: the *Setup for Failover Clustering and Microsoft Cluster Service* that VMware maintains, which can be found here: http://pubs.vmware.com/vsphere-50/topic/com.vmware.ICbase/PDF/vsphere-esxi-vcenter-server-50-mscs-guide.pdf.

First, you must determine which scenario best fits your objectives:

- **Clustering within a box.** This approach uses two VMs on the same physical ESXi server when creating the cluster. This approach provides protection for OS level outages (like blue screens or to patch one node at a time) and application outages (such as a service that locks up or stops unexpectedly), but does not provide any protection against physical hardware issues as both VMs are on the same server. This is commonly used in testing environments as all of the clustering features can be tested and debugged with less hardware required. In fact, this design can even be implemented using local storage on the ESXi host.

- **Clustering across boxes.** This approach is similar to the one just described, but requires two physical hosts and shared storage to work. It provides protection from OS, application, and hardware issues. This is commonly used in production where the great majority of the environment has already been virtualized and administrators are comfortable with virtualizing mission-critical applications. It provides for better consolidation ratios than using physical servers as multiple clusters can be run on the same physical hosts.

- **Physical to Virtual (P2V) Cluster.** This approach uses a physical server for the production node of the cluster but a VM on an ESXi host as the standby node for the cluster. This allows multiple clusters to have the standby node for each cluster on a single server, reducing the equipment by approximately half, with the assumption that you will not be experiencing multiple cluster failures at once, so the ESXi host will probably not be over utilized most of the time. This approach is often adopted by administrators new to virtualization who want to gain experience with virtualizing mission-critical applications while not "betting the farm" initially.

There are some specific requirements that must be met to configure any of the aforementioned cluster types, as listed in the clustering guide mentioned above. The most important of them are reviewed here:

- **Supported Operating Systems.** Windows 2003 SP2 and Windows 2008 R2.

- **Disk Format.** Eager Zero thick provisioned if a .vmdk (only supported in the cluster within a box scenario), a virtual compatibility mode RDM (for clusters involving VMs running Windows 2003 only), or a physical compatibility mode RDM if a P2V cluster or a cluster across boxes approach is taken.

- **Number of nodes supported.** Two nodes only (for shared disk clusters; non-shared disk clusters are only limited by OS or application limits).

Tip

Many of the above limitations and configuration requirements can be avoided if you use Software iSCSI within a VM instead of configuring the shared storage at the ESXi level. In that case, no special support from VMware is required; simply configure the OS per Microsoft recommendations and best practices.

Finally, there are some significant limitations when creating a virtual (or P2V) MSCS cluster; key among them are the lack of support for any of the following:

- The use of iSCSI, FCoE, or NFS storage for .vmdk files (RDMs must be used).

- The use of vSphere FT (discussed in Chapter 12).

- vMotion to migrate any MSCS VM to another physical host.

- NMP with Round Robin multipathing policy (it works with the other two policies). Note that other vendors using third-party MPPs may support the use of Round Robin in a cluster however.

- Memory overcommitment, where VMs are given more RAM than the physical server has available. This is common and leads to better consolidation ratios, but because MSCS is very time sensitive and swapping pages to disk may cause delays in running the VM as pages are swapped back into memory, it is not supported.

Tip

For all of the foregoing reasons, many people will use VMware technologies such as HA in conjunction with Application Monitoring instead of building a shared disk cluster (these technologies will be explained in Chapter 12). Creating a highly available design without using MSCS, such as using a DAG (Database Availability Group) in Exchange or database mirroring in SQL are also very common. Refer to VMware's best practices documents for the applications you are considering deploying for a thorough discussion of the issues and advantages/disadvantages of each option.

We have found that while there are use cases for MSCS, those are declining and the steps to implement the various types of clusters are somewhat lengthy, so for directions on implementation we'll refer you to the clustering guide listed earlier in this section.

VAAI (vStorage APIs for Array Integration)

VMware introduced VAAI, the vStorage APIs for Array Integration, in version 4.1 to allow closer integration between iSCSI or FC storage arrays (or even local storage, though this was less common) and ESX(i) 4.1. Specifically, VAAI allowed the following tasks to take place within the array instead of being driven by the host, consuming CPU cycles and bandwidth going to and from the array:

- Locking at the storage level instead of the LUN level allows the locking needed to create, start, stop, or snapshot a VM; clone a template; and vMotion a VM, etc., to be handled by the array instead of the host. It also increases the granularity of the lock, such that only the required blocks are locked, not the entire datastore. This potentially allows ten times the number of VMs to reside on the same datastore. VMware calls this "Atomic Test & Set" (ATS).

- Hardware accelerated zeroing allows the array to write zeros to blocks on disk instead on having the host write gigabytes of zeros. This is especially true with Eager Zeroed disks potentially reducing the I/O between the host and the array for these tasks by 90 percent. VMware calls this "Zero Blocks/Write Same."

- Hardware-accelerated copy is used when a VM is cloned, deployed from a template, or Storage vMotioned to another datastore (inside the same array). Normally, the host reads the old data then writes the new data, but this requires a lot of bandwidth and some CPU cycles to manage. With this approach, all of the I/O is internal to the array and thus reduces the load on the SAN or network dramatically (potentially up to ten times), besides allowing the array to optimize the copy process. VMware calls this "Clone Blocks/Full Copy/XCOPY."

A few requirements and caveats should be mentioned in conjunction with this feature:

- Enterprise or Enterprise Plus versions of vSphere 4.1 or later are required.

- vCenter is also required.

- It only works with VMFS datastores and RDMs (in 4.1).

- No extra software is required on the host (beyond the base vSphere and vCenter), but array vendors must also enable the support on the arrays. This usually involves updating the software that runs the array.

- It does not work in any of the following scenarios:
  - When the source and destination datastores use different block sizes.
  - When the source is an RDM and the destination is a .vmdk.

- When multiple arrays are involved (in any number of datastores).

- When cloning a VM with vSphere snapshots, as the host must figure out which blocks from which of the snapshot components are required to create a new VM based on the current source VM state (snapshots are discussed in Chapter 9).

For a great article on the specifics of this feature, how to see if you have it, how to manually enable or disable it (it is enabled by default), etc., please refer to VMware KB article 1021976, which can be found at: http://kb.vmware.com/kb/1021976.

vSphere 5 adds a couple of new features to those just described, namely:

- Support for NAS devices, so that the features described above will also now work with supported NAS devices.

- Support for thin-provisioned storage at the storage level (for block storage only—not for NFS), allowing monitoring of physical space utilization in the UI. Thin provisioned space was supported before, but vSphere had no idea about actual space consumption on the array. vSphere 5 also adds the ability to reclaim unused space on the LUN, making a thin-provisioned LUN physically smaller (logically it doesn't change size) when the space a VM consumes shrinks (such as when snapshots are deleted, a VM is Storage vMotioned to another datastore on another LUN, or an entire VM is deleted).

vSphere Storage Appliance (VSA)

The vSphere Storage Appliance (VSA) is yet another new feature in vSphere 5. It is designed to provide shared storage for the SMB (Small and Medium Businesses) market, while at the same time providing high availability for that storage to ensure that VMs can keep running, even in the event of a failure of any component in the system. This is a huge benefit for this market, where the price of a SAN may be cost prohibitive (a simple, small iSCSI SAN can easily cost tens of thousands of dollars, and a larger implementation or a Fibre Channel SAN can easily be in the hundreds of thousands), yet a small NAS server may not meet the performance requirements of the VMs.

Caution

This is one area that requires careful planning, as the number of nodes in the cluster and the storage available on each node in the cluster can't be changed after installation, so read this section then plan carefully.

Let's begin with a tour of VSA's purpose and capabilities, and then we'll cover the architecture and components. After that, we'll review the requirements to implement VSA and continue on to review storage capacity calculations. We'll conclude this section with how failures are handled.

Purpose and Capabilities

The purpose of the VSA is to provide shared storage for all of the vSphere features that require shared storage (such as DRS, HA, and vMotion) without the cost of purchasing an expensive SAN or NAS configuration. At the same time, simple shared storage has no resiliency, so a failure of a NAS server (for example) could render unavailable all of the VMs at a company. To prevent this, the storage that the VSA creates and manages is all replicated (synchronously) to another host, such that if anything fails, the redundancy features will allow uninterrupted (or possibly briefly interrupted with automatic failover, depending on what failed) access to those VMs.

We'll discuss the specific requirements shortly, but at a high level, local storage on two or three hosts is configured and replicated between them and then shared to vSphere as NFS storage, providing "shared" storage on what is actually local storage.

The system can tolerate the loss of any of the following:

- One physical NIC.

- One physical switch (if two redundant switches are implemented—this is not required, but for better availability is recommended).

- One physical host (which would obviously take a physical NIC out as well, but that situation is still okay).

- One VSA Cluster member (which could be the physical host; just the VA that makes the host part of a VSA cluster; or in a two-node cluster only, the loss of the VSA Cluster service).

Architecture and Components

The components of the system are illustrated in Figure 8.6.

Let's review the purpose of each component:

- **ESXi 5.0 Hosts.** The basis for everything vSphere, including a VSA cluster. Currently a VSA cluster can contain only two or three nodes.

- **vCenter 5.0.** The configuration and management service for the entire vSphere environment, as well as the VSA cluster.

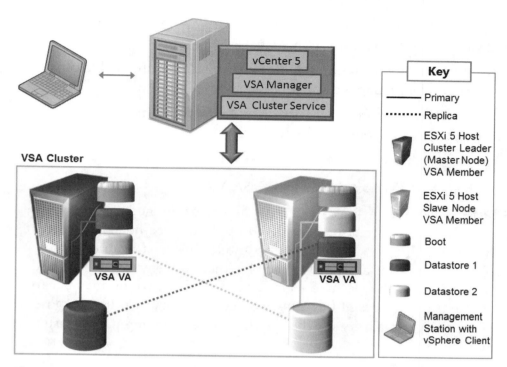

Figure 8.6
VSA cluster architecture.

- **vSphere Client 5.0.** GUI to manage the entire environment as well as the VSA cluster (via the VSA Manager tab, accessible after VSA has been installed, the extension added to vSphere, and the associated plugin loaded into the vSphere Client instance(s) that will be managing the cluster).

- **VSA Manager.** An extension to vCenter (implemented as a Windows service that is installed on the vCenter server) that allows the following tasks to be undertaken:

  - Deploy the VSA Appliance (VSA VA) on two or three ESXi servers to create the VSA cluster.

  - Make the datastores created by each VSA VA accessible to the cluster.

  - Manage, monitor, and troubleshoot the cluster.

- **VSA Appliance.** A VA that runs SUSE 11 SP1. There can be only one VSA Appliance running on any given ESXi host at a time (and if a functioning ESXi host has a failed VSA VA, the node is considered down as far as the cluster is concerned). It provides the underlying functionality to do the following:

- Manage all of the communications between the VSA members and between an individual member and the VSA Manager.

- Manage the local storage on each ESXi host (calculating the usable capacity and managing the redundancy on each node).

- Take the local datastore and export it (over the network, not shown here but discussed later) for the other nodes to access.

- Manage any hardware of software failures within the cluster.

■ **VSA Member.** An ESXi host running the VSA VA.

■ **VSA Cluster Service.** In a VSA cluster, a majority of the nodes must be functioning for the cluster to be considered up. In a three-node cluster, that means two of the three nodes, but in a two-node cluster, it is an exact 50-50 split, and thus not a majority. To solve this problem, the VSA cluster service is installed on the vCenter server and is simply a voting member to make the majority—it doesn't have any storage or serve any other purpose except establishing a majority for the purpose of determining if the cluster is functioning.

■ **VSA Cluster Leader.** One of the VSA VAs is elected the cluster leader, which is responsible for communicating with the VSA Manager to report the status of the cluster. It is also referred to as the Master Node, while all other nodes in the cluster are Slave Nodes.

Requirements

To help understand the requirements and how things need to be configured (except for the datastores, which are created as part of the installation process), refer to Figure 8.7. Note that this diagram shows the two-switch configuration. If a single switch were used instead, the same number of physical NICs would be required; they would just all go to the same physical switch.

To create a VSA cluster, a number of requirements must be met as outlined in the following sections (one for each major component).

ESXi Host Only some servers, RAID controllers, and disks are supported for use in a VSA cluster; check with the latest VSA documentation for that list. Using other hardware may work but is not supported by VMware.

All of the ESXi hosts in the cluster must have the same hardware configuration (except possibly for the size of the storage available on each node; it is recommended that this also be the same—for more information see the Usable Cluster Capacity

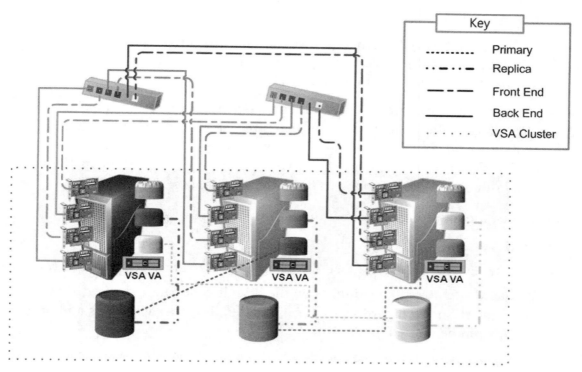

Figure 8.7
VSA cluster datastore and network configuration.

section below). Beyond the basic requirements for any ESXi installation, the following hardware requirements must be met for use as a VSA Cluster Member:

- **RAM.** 6GB minimum, 24GB recommended, 72GB maximum supported (and tested by VMware).

Caution

Memory over commitment is not supported in a VSA cluster because the high I/O rates involved during swapping can make the cluster unstable if I/Os take too long to complete. To prevent this, set a reservation on each VM equal to the memory assigned to the VM. In addition, if HA is implemented, vCenter will automatically set aside half the memory in a two-node cluster or a third of the memory in a three-node cluster to allow VMs to properly restart. (See Chapter 12 for details on HA.)

- **NICs.** A minimum of four 1GbE are required (on one to four physical cards). The supported options are:
  - Four single-port NICs.
  - Two single-port NICs and one dual-port NIC.

- Two dual-port NICs.

- One quad-port NIC (although this does not provide physical card level redundancy and thus creates a potential single point of failure, which could cause the entire server to be unavailable).

■ **Storage.** Eight or more drives of the same type (SAS or SATA), model, and speed. Ideally, they should all be of the same capacity as well. A minimum of 180GB per node is required and a maximum of 64TB is supported. Note that these disks must be in a hardware RAID 5, 6, or 10 configuration, as JBOD (Just a Bunch of Disks) configurations are not supported.

In addition, the following software requirements must also be met:

■ **ESXi Version.** 5.0 (or higher).

■ **License.** Evaluation mode (good for 60 days) or Essentials Plus or higher.

■ **Virtual Switch Configuration.** Only the default configuration (created at installation) on a standard vSwitch can be used; no other vSwitches and/or Port Groups can be created.

■ **Management IP.** It must be a static IP on the same subnet as the vCenter server.

■ **Virtual Machines.** No virtual machines deployed when the cluster is created.

■ **HA Cluster Membership.** None of the nodes can be part of an HA cluster that contains any nodes outside of the VSA cluster.

vCenter   There are no special requirements for vCenter beyond the standard vCenter requirements, with the exception that if you deploy vCenter as a VM, it should not be on any of the nodes in the VSA cluster. This means that you can deploy it on the free ESXi version, on a physical host, or on another vSphere server outside the VSA cluster.

Network   A minimum of one gigabit Ethernet switch that supports IEEE 802.1q VLAN tagging are required. Two VLANs are recommended, one for front-end (VM to client) traffic and one for backend (VSA cluster communication, disk replication, etc.) traffic.

In addition, you will need the following static IP addresses (all on the same subnet as the vCenter server, with the exception of the backend IP addresses, which can be on a private subnet):

■ vCenter IP (one per vCenter).

■ ESXi Management IP (one per node in the cluster).

- VSA Cluster IP (one per VSA cluster, owned by the VSA Cluster Leader; one of the other nodes can get the IP if the cluster leader fails and it is elected the new Cluster Leader).

- VSA Cluster Service IP (one per VSA cluster in a two-node cluster only; not used in a three-node cluster).

- VSA Management IP (one per node in the cluster).

- NFS IP (one per node in the cluster; for the shared storage created by the VSA VA).

- VSA Backend IP (one per node in the cluster—it can be a private IP if desired).

- Feature IP address (one per node in the cluster, used for vMotion, HA, etc.).

After the VSA installation has completed (and a couple of VMs created), the networking configuration illustrated in Figure 8.8 will be created. On the left-hand side of the diagram is the virtual configuration; on the right is the physical configuration. This configuration is per host, and thus would be repeated on each node in the cluster.

The network has two major components, one on each vSwitch. Each vSwitch has two physical NICs (or more if you have more than four physical NICs) that provide failover for the vSwitch.

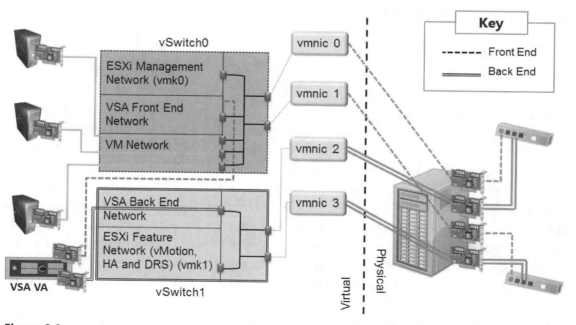

Figure 8.8
VSA cluster network configuration.

The front-end vSwitch contains the following:

- The ESXi Management port (vmk0) created at installation.
- The VSA front-end network, which is used for the following:
  - Communication between each cluster member and the VSA Manager.
  - Communication between each cluster member and the VSA Cluster Service (in a two-node cluster only).
  - Communication between the ESXi servers and the exported NFS volumes.
- The VM Network created at installation to which all of the VMs will be connected. Three VMs have been created for this example to illustrate where they fit in the design.

The backend vSwitch contains the following components:

- The VSA backend network, which is used for the following:
  - Replication of the datastore between the primary and replica node (for each datastore).
  - Cluster communication between each of the cluster nodes
- The ESXi "Feature network" (vmk1) for use by vMotion, HA, and/or DRS.

The VSA VA is connected to both the frontend and backend VSA networks.

Usable Cluster Capacity

Note that the usable capacity of the cluster depends on three variables: the number of hosts in the cluster (two or three), the RAID level used on each node (5, 6, or 10), and the raw storage capacity on each node. The usable capacity with RAID 10 will be one quarter of the raw capacity (after removing the space for the boot volume) due to the overhead of using RAID 10 (which cuts the space in half) and then mirroring that data to another host (which cuts it in half again). The usable capacity with RAID 5 with eight disks would be 7/16 (approximately 44%) of the raw capacity. This is due to the loss of one drive to parity (leaving 7/8 of the capacity) and then the overhead of mirroring the data to another server (7/8 * 1/2 = 7/16). With RAID 6, two drives are lost to parity, leaving 3/8 (about 38%) of the space usable instead. The numbers will vary with the number of disks in the RAID group. If the servers have different amounts of raw capacity on each, the system will use the value of the smallest server, thus VMware recommends that all of the servers have the same capacity, as the extra capacity on the larger nodes will be wasted. Let's look at a couple of examples to help illustrate the usable space in a cluster (again assuming the boot volumes already exist in a separate boot drive). Note that these calculations are approximate as VSA automatically reserves at least 20GB for VM swap files.

Two-Node Cluster, Same Disk Space on Each Server   Disk capacity of each node: 10TB

Total space in the cluster (raw): 20TB (10TB * 2 nodes)

Usable space in the cluster (RAID 10): 20TB / 4 = 5TB

Usable space in the cluster (eight drive RAID 5): 20 TB * 44% = 8.8 TB

Three-Node Cluster, Different Disk Space on Each Server   Disk capacity of Node 1: 10TB

Disk capacity of Node 2: 12TB

Disk capacity of Node 3: 8TB

Total space in the cluster (raw): 24TB (8TB * 3 nodes; 2TB wasted on Node 1 and 4TB wasted on Node 2)

Usable space in the cluster: 24TB / 4 = 6TB

Usable space in the cluster (eight drive RAID 6): 24TB * 38% = 9TB

Handling Node Failures

Now that we've reviewed the requirements and architecture, we're ready to discuss how various node failures are handled. Refer to Figure 8.9 for the standard configuration and the normal operational state of a three-node cluster.

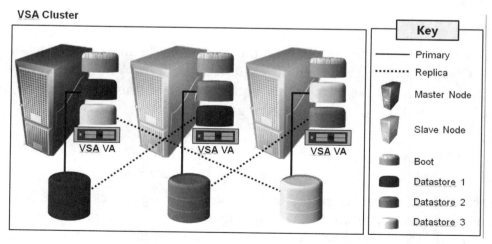

Figure 8.9
VSA cluster configuration—initial.

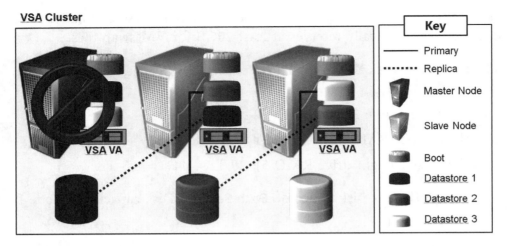

Figure 8.10
VSA cluster configuration—failure.

In this design, data is synchronously replicated between each of the copies of the datastores—the primary to its replica, but only the primary copy is accessible by the ESXi servers (in an active-passive fashion).

In the event of any of the failures described above (in the example shown in Figure 8.10 the host has failed, specifically the host that was the Cluster Leader, sometimes referred to as the Master Node), a failover process is instituted to provide failover of the datastore without causing downtime to the VMs that rely on that datastore.

The process is as follows:

1. Since the Cluster Leader failed, the first thing that must be done is an election of a new Cluster Leader. This node now interfaces with the VSA Manager to report cluster status. If one of the other nodes had failed, this step would be skipped. In Figure 8.11, the node on the right was elected as the new cluster leader.

2. The primary replica of the datastore that is now offline is replaced by its replica and will service all of the I/O. This is illustrated in Figure 8.11.

3. Once the failure has been corrected and the server brought back online, VSA will automatically resynchronize the changes that occurred during the failure back to the original node for protection when the next failure occurs, as shown in Figure 8.12.

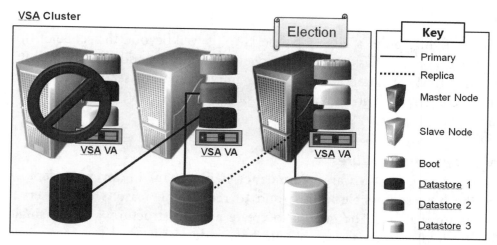

Figure 8.11
VSA cluster configuration—after failover.

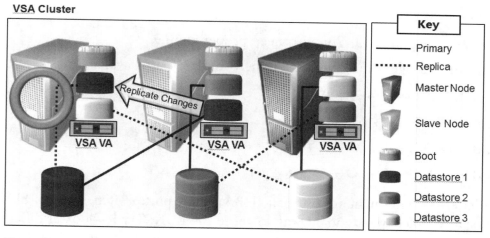

Figure 8.12
VSA cluster configuration—recovery.

IMPLEMENTATION AND MANAGEMENT

As you can see from the preceding section, there are many great storage technologies available that can help all sizes of businesses to take advantage of whatever storage they have available. Many of these technologies require careful planning to implement properly. Now that you have done that planning, you're ready to begin implementing. Let's get started!

FC Arrays

The setup and configuration of a Fibre Channel SAN is well beyond the scope of this book (or any other VMware class); it is the purview of storage vendors, such as EMC, Hitachi, Dell, and IBM, to name a few. For the implementation section, we're just going to hit a couple of high points that you should review with your SAN administrator.

Redundancy of the Infrastructure

First, while not required by VMware, redundancy is important in any SAN deployment to give the highest possible uptime and to reduce the reasons that a server would appear as unavailable. The goal is to create an infrastructure with no single point of failure (NSPoF); to do so, you should have redundant:

■ HBAs in the servers

■ Fibre Channel Switches

■ Storage Processors (SPs)

This is illustrated in Figure 8.13. You also need proper zoning.

You can see from this figure that there are four redundant paths available:

■ Path 1: A + C + F + H + L + P + R

■ Path 2: A + C + F + J + N + Q + S

■ Path 3: B + D + G + I + M + P + R

■ Path 4: B + D + G + K + O + Q + S

Thus, if any lettered component were to fail (HBA, cable, port, switch, or even SP), there would be a completely redundant way to get to the LUN. Try it—look at different letters, block one out as if it failed, and see if you can still get to the LUN, then verify that it really works that way in your infrastructure and fix any deficiencies found.

FC Zoning

Most SAN vendors will have a best practice when it comes to zoning their array to servers; typically this is implemented as either Single Initiator, Single Target or as Single Initiator, Multiple Target zoning. In the former, one HBA port is placed in a zone with one SP port. Using the information in Figure 8.13, four zones will be required per server (one for each possible path). In the latter configuration, one HBA port is placed in a zone with all of the SP ports that HBA can see. Using the same figure,

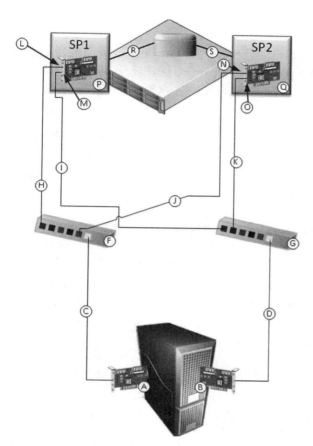

Figure 8.13
Redundant infrastructure.

two zones will be required per server, one that contains HBA A and thus encompasses paths 1 and 2, and another that contains HBA B and contains paths 3 and 4.

Software FCoE Configuration

Similarly to the FC configuration just described, FCoE configuration is beyond the scope of this book. The only area that we want to address is how to set up and configure software FCoE. VMware suggests that you disable Spanning Tree Protocol (STP) on all switch ports used by FCoE because having it enabled may delay the FCoE Initialization Protocol (FIP) that discovers and initializes targets in an FCoE environment. VMware also suggests that you enable (and set to Auto) Priority-based Flow Control. The process to do so is also beyond the scope of this book, but your network and/or storage administrator should know how to complete these tasks.

The process to set up software FCoE is as follows:

1. Create a VMkernel port on a new standard vSwitch connected to the desired FCoE-enabled NIC. Note that the VLAN and Priority are discovered during FCoE initialization and aren't configured via the vSphere Client. The steps to do so were discussed in Chapter 7.

   ■ Be sure to use an isolated VLAN ID as FCoE requires a separate VLAN to work properly.

   ■ Each VMkernel port requires its own unique IP address, no matter what it is used for.

2. Repeat Step 1 as needed for multiple NICs. Each vmnic supports a maximum of one FCoE initiator (even if the physical NIC has multiple ports—each port is seen as a separate vmnic). Each vmnic can be on its own standard vSwitch or you can combine multiple FCoE vmnics on the same vSwitch (each with its own VMkernel port of course) as long as you configure only one active vmnic per VMkernel port and make all other vmnics unused (via a custom failover order in the VMkernel port configuration).

Note

ESXi 5.0 supports a maximum of four FCoE ports per host.

There must be a 1:1 relationship between VMkernel ports and the CNAs that will be used with FCoE. In other words, if you have two CNAs, you will need two VMkernel ports.

Caution

Be careful not to change the vSwitches or VMkernel ports after FCoE is set up and configured or you may cause problems with connectivity to your datastores.

3. Add a software FCoE adapter by selecting your host from the Configuration tab, selecting Storage Adapters, then clicking the Add link (at the top of the page), and then selecting Add Software FCoE Adapter. You will also need to specify the Physical NIC (CNA) used with this software FCoE adapter.

4. Repeat Step 3 as needed (you should have as many FCoE software adapters as you have VMkernel ports created in Steps 1 and 2).

iSCSI Arrays

Many VMware implementations use iSCSI, either alone or in combination with Fibre Channel and/or NAS. As with the previous discussion on Fibre Channel, we are not going to cover how to set up and configure an iSCSI array. Nor will we address how to install a hardware HBA. As for configuring redundancy, the previous Redundancy section in the Fibre Channel section just covered also applies to iSCSI and thus won't be covered again here either. What we will discuss is how to configure software and dependent hardware iSCSI and the other areas related to that configuration.

Configuring Dependent Hardware iSCSI

Recall from the planning section that dependent hardware iSCSI handles iSCSI in hardware, but depends on the vSphere Client for the actual configuration. There are a couple of quick notes to be aware of before we get started with this:

- Relative to performance monitoring, the NIC may show little or no activity even when being pounded with iSCSI traffic because the iSCSI traffic bypasses the networking stack. Monitor the vmhba instead (or in conjunction with if you use the card for both standard networking as well as iSCSI traffic) for a better understanding of the traffic through the card.

- If you use a third-party switch, such as the Nexus 1000V, be sure to disable automatic pinning and configure manual pinning instead. Pinning is the process of associating a physical NIC with a vmnic and as the capabilities of the different NICs in the system may be different (some supporting hardware iSCSI and others that don't), manual pinning ensures that the VMkernel port stays associated with the correct physical NIC.

Before you can use dependent hardware iSCSI, you need to verify that it shows up in the list of storage adapters (if not, it may need to be licensed first—consult with your server or storage vendor on this) and then determine the name of the vmnic associated with it. To do so:

1. Select your host, go to the Configuration tab, and select Storage Adapters.

2. For each dependent hardware iSCSI adapter listed, select it, click Properties, and do the following:
   a. View the default iSCSI name; it can be changed by clicking the Configure button, but rarely is, so we'll not discuss that. You may need the name for configuring the iSCSI target to allow access to it, however, so make a note of it.
   b. Click the Network Configuration tab and then click the Add button to view the associated vmnic. Make a note of this as it will be required when configuring networking for iSCSI.
   c. Close out of any open dialog boxes.

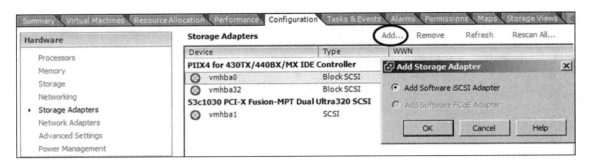

Figure 8.14
Add iSCSI adapter.

Configuring the Software iSCSI Initiator

The process to set up the software iSCSI adapter is as follows:

1. Add a software iSCSI adapter by selecting your host, going to the Configuration tab, selecting Storage Adapters, then clicking the Add link (at the top of the page), and then Add Software iSCSI Adapter (see Figure 8.14). You will be notified that a new vmhba will be created (it will always be vmhba32 or higher).

Note

Unlike the software FCoE adapter, you are allowed only one software iSCSI adapter, and once added, it cannot be removed (though it can be disabled).

2. Once it appears, select it (the vmhba line, not the iSCSI Software Adapter heading), as shown in Figure 8.15. Notice that it is enabled by default (previously it was always there but had to be enabled) and that your host has an iqn associated with it already. The iqn will be in the format: iqn.1998-01.com.vmware:<host name>-<random digits>. It can be modified if desired, but *must* be unique on the network or iSCSI will not work properly. It can be changed by displaying the properties and clicking the Configure button, but since it's rarely changed, we'll not discuss that here. You may need the name for configuring the iSCSI target to allow access to it, however, so make a note of the iqn in the Properties area.

Configuring the Network for Either Dependent Hardware or Software iSCSI

Both dependent hardware and software iSCSI use VMkernel ports to move the necessary traffic between the host and the iSCSI target(s). At a high level, this means that you will need to create a VMkernel port for each NIC that will be used with iSCSI

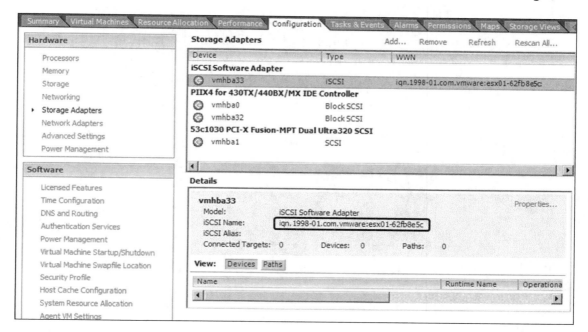

Figure 8.15
Properties of an installed iSCSI adapter.

and associate that VMkernel port with iSCSI, similarly to how software FCoE was configured. There are two methods to do so:

- Put each VMkernel port on a separate vSwitch (or a Distributed vSwitch [DVS] if preferred). A two-node configuration is illustrated in Figure 8.16.

Caution

When using this approach, you need to use different IP subnets for each VMkernel port or you may experience connectivity issues and/or iSCSI LUNs may not be discovered properly.

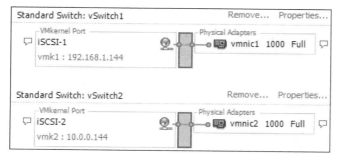

Figure 8.16
Separate vSwitches.

■ Place all of the VMkernel ports on the same vSwitch (or DVS), and then configure each VMkernel port to use a single NIC only. This is illustrated in Figure 8.17, with the VMkernel port configuration for iSCSI-1 shown in Figure 8.18 and the VMkernel port configuration for iSCSI-2 shown in Figure 8.19.

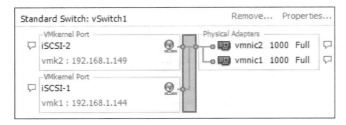

Figure 8.17
One vSwitch.

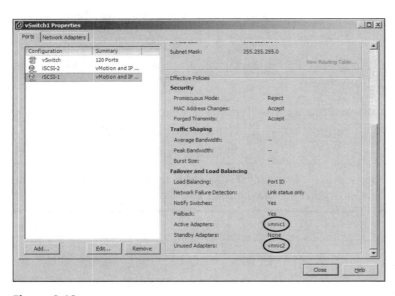

Figure 8.18
One Switch-iSCSI-1.

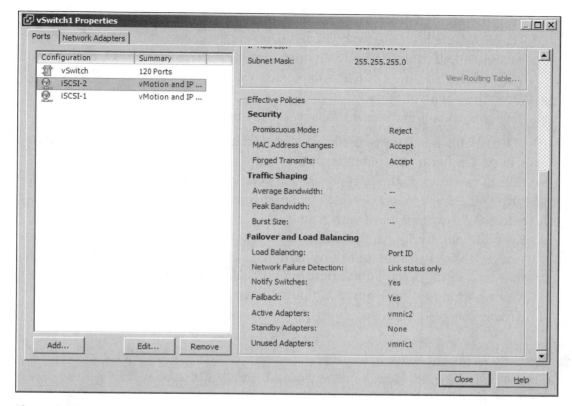

Figure 8.19
One Switch-iSCSI-2.

The procedure to configure networking on the vSwitch is as follows:

1. Create a VMkernel port on a standard vSwitch (or a DVS if preferred) connected to the iSCSI NIC. The steps to do so were discussed in Chapter 7.

2. Repeat Step 1 as needed for multiple iSCSI NICs. Each vmnic needs to be associated with a single VMkernel port. This can be done by creating separate switches or using a single switch as just discussed.

3. If a single standard vSwitch is used, associate each VMkernel port with its associated vmnic in this manner:
   a. Display the properties of the vSwitch.
   b. Select the desired VMkernel port.
   c. Click Edit.
   d. Select the NIC Teaming tab.
   e. Check the Override switch failover order checkbox.

   f. Keep the one NIC that needs to be associated with this VMkernel port in the Active Adapters section and move all of the others to the Unused Adapters section by selecting each NIC in turn and click the Move Down button until it is anywhere in the Unused Adapters section.

   g. Close the open windows.

   h. Repeat Steps a–g until each VMkernel port is associated with a single NIC.

4. If a Distributed vSwitch is used, associate each VMkernel Port Group with its associated vmnic in this manner:

   a. Edit the settings of the port group that contains the related VMkernel port (be sure that each VMkernel port [per host] is in a separate port group).

   b. Select the Teaming and Failover link.

   c. Keep the one dvUplink that needs to be associated with this port group in the Active Uplinks section and move all of the others to the Unused Uplinks section by selecting each uplink in turn and clicking the Move Down button until it is anywhere in the Unused Uplinks section.

   d. Repeat Steps a–c until each port group is associated with a single uplink.

Caution

Be careful not to change the vSwitches or VMkernel ports after iSCSI is set up and configured or you may cause problems with connectivity to your datastores.

This method requires the VMkernel and target IP addresses to be on the same network as routing is not supported when manually configuring multipathing in this way.

Software iSCSI Adapter Association with VMkernel Ports

Software iSCSI requires an additional configuration step, namely associating the software iSCSI adapter with the VMkernel ports.

Note

If you skip this step, ESXi will pick one of the possible VMkernel ports and use it exclusively, so it will work, but you will not have any multipathing capabilities.

This process is the same for either type of vSwitch, and is as follows:

1. Configure the software iSCSI adapter by selecting your host, going to the Configuration tab, selecting Storage Adapters, and then selecting the vmhba adapter.

2. In the Details window, click the Properties link.

3. Select the Network Configuration tab.

4. Click Add.

5. You should see each of the VMkernel ports that you want to use for iSCSI. If you don't see one or more of them, one of the configuration steps above was probably not done properly (for example, a VMkernel port that has access to multiple physical NICs will not be displayed). Select a VMkernel port that will be used with iSCSI and click OK.

6. Repeat Steps 4 and 5 until all VMkernel ports that will be used with iSCSI have been added.

7. Verify that the Port Group Policy for each port shows Compliant, then click Close when finished.

8. You'll be notified that you need to do a rescan of the software iSCSI adapter to see any configuration changes. Unless you have already configured targets, nothing will change either way, so you can click either Yes or No. However, if you have previously configured targets, be sure to click Yes.

CHAP

CHAP (the Challenge Handshake Authentication Protocol) is an optional part of iSCSI that can be used by the array to verify the identity of the host (and optionally the other way around as well). It does *not* encrypt any data. While this can be used in iSCSI implementations, often it is not. It is a security option to further increase the security (although only marginally), and thus will be discussed in the Security portion of this chapter.

Static versus Dynamic Target Discovery

In iSCSI (as with SCSI and Fibre Channel), there are initiators and targets. If you are familiar with the client-server model of networking, your ESXi host (specifically each port on each HBA or NIC as the case may be) is the client (which in storage we call the initiator—the one that starts the conversation), and the storage array is the server (which we call the target—the other end of the conversation with the ESXi host). Targets are the ports on the storage processors (NICs or HBAs) that the host can connect with. If you have two ports on each storage processor (SP) and two SPs, you have a total of four possible targets. The number of available targets with Fibre Channel depends on proper zoning as previously described. In Figure 8.13, those targets are letters L, M, N, and O. For the sake of discussion in this section, let's assume that the following IP addresses are associated with these letters:

- L: 192.168.1.200
- M: 192.168.1.201

- N: 192.168.1.202

- O: 192.168.1.203

With Fibre Channel, targets will automatically be discovered based on the zones the initiators and targets are in. iSCSI has a bigger issue in this regard, as it uses IP and there are literally billions of IP addresses potentially available. To make the problem manageable, there are two methods of target discovery available in iSCSI, namely:

- **Static.** This technique configures targets by typing in the IP address of each port that you want the initiator to see, and it will use what is explicitly configured. Thus, if you used the IP of 192.168.1.201, that would be the only IP address that iSCSI was aware of, unless you also manually added the .200, .202, and .203 IPs.

- **Dynamic.** This option is designed to be easier to use; simply type in the IP of any of the targets on an array (for example, 192.168.1.201 from the previous scenario), and the array will return the other targets that are available on the array (in our example .200, .202, and .203). These targets will then automatically be configured and used.

Note

Not all arrays return all possible target IPs; some arrays only return the peer SP's IP, so entering the IP for port L would return the IP for port N and the same for M and O.

Some arrays use TPGS (Target Port Group Support) to determine the characteristics of groups of ports (such as all the ports on an SP) and then route the I/O to the port currently offering the best performance. This is useful for performance as well as for load balancing. In this case, only one IP address is typically used (or one per SP).

With the target information from your SAN administrator, you're ready to configure your host to use those targets (remember that if you've implemented CHAP, you'll need that information as well).

To set up targets, do the following:

1. Select your host, go to the Configuration tab, select Storage Adapters, and then select the vmhba adapter.

2. In the Details pane, click the Properties link.

3. Select either the Dynamic Discovery or the Static Discovery tab as desired.

4. Click Add.

5. Type the IP address (or FQDN, though FQDNs are rarely used as administrators don't want to advertise the IPs of storage arrays and they are often on physically separate subnets) and port (TCP port 3260 is the default) of the desired target. If you are adding static targets, you'll also need to enter the iSCSI target name.

6. Click OK.

7. The system will take a little while to add the new target; wait for it to complete.

8. Repeat Steps 4–6 as needed to add additional targets.

Tip

After you add targets on the Dynamic Discovery tab, the actual targets will appear on the Static Discovery tab.

9. Click Close when finished.

10. You'll be notified that you need to do a rescan of the software iSCSI adapter to see any configuration changes; click Yes.

11. Verify that the connected targets appear (both the count in the Details pane, as well as the actual targets themselves below that).

Tip

If all of the targets you expect don't appear, click the Rescan All link at the top of the page and see if additional targets are found; it may take a few refreshes to get them all. If they don't all appear, you may need to work with your network and/or SAN administrators to make sure the configuration is correct.

Jumbo Frames

Jumbo frames are recommended whenever IP-based storage is used to maximize the data portion of a packet versus the overhead. This was described in Chapter 7 in detail; refer to that chapter for proper configuration.

Connecting to an NAS Device

Up to this point, we have discussed how to connect to various forms of block-based storage; let's turn our attention to NAS-based storage. This kind of storage is actually fairly easy to connect to. The only requirement (setup step) is to create a VMkernel port on a standard vSwitch (or a DVS if preferred) connected to the NIC that has access to the network segment that the NAS device(s) is/are connected to. VMware recommends for best performance that if both iSCSI and NAS are used that separate NICs (and physical switches if possible or at least separate VLANs) be used, which of course implies distinct VMkernel ports. The steps to create VMkernel ports were discussed in Chapter 7 and won't be reviewed here.

One quick note on NFS volumes: by default, VMware will only mount a maximum of eight NFS volumes to any one server; this can be changed by setting the advanced parameter NFS.MaxVolumes to a different setting; the range is 8 to 256 (previous versions had a limit of 64).

It is also important to note that many storage vendors have their own best practices that should be followed; this is just as true for NAS as it is for any of the block storage vendors.

Datastores

Now that you have access to one or more kinds of block-based storage (FC, FCoE, iSCSI, or local SCSI, SATA, SAS, or RAID storage) or to NAS storage, we can look at creating, managing, and deleting datastores on block storage. Then we'll cover datastores on NAS storage, and we'll conclude this section with a few tasks that are the same for both kinds of storage.

Datastores are where all of the VMs will exist, including virtual disks, configuration files, etc.

Block-Based Storage Tasks

This section will review the various tasks that are unique to block-based storage. Before we begin with the specifics of how to create and use this kind of datastore, let's look at a couple of key questions that should be addressed before they are created.

Block Sizes   The first of these is the question of block size. Block size refers to the smallest amount of space that can be allocated at a time. The value we are discussing here is at the VMFS level—the guest OS may (and almost always does) have a smaller block size, but the guest OS block size has reference to how the space within a VMFS block is subdivided. If it needs another VMFS block, the system will automatically allocate (if necessary) the space.

As described in the planning section of this chapter, with VMFS-5, the block size is always 1MB; if you choose to create a VMFS-3 datastore (for compatibility with vSphere 4, for example), you need to specify the block size. Setting the block size also sets the maximum file size, which effectively sets the largest virtual disk (.vmdk) you can create, per Table 8.4.

Table 8.4 Maximum File Size versus Block Size

Block Size	Maximum File Size
1MB	256GB
2MB	512GB
4MB	1TB
8MB	2TB – 512 bytes

LUN Sizes   When it comes to LUN sizes, 2TB is the maximum size supported (technically it is 2 TB minus 512 bytes) when VMFS-3 is used. With VMFS-5, the maximum LUN size is 64TB. In any case, the maximum file (and thus .vmdk) size is 2TB. While these are the stated maximums, in many cases you will want to use substantially smaller LUNs as having a lot of VMs on a single LUN may cause more I/O than the physical disks can handle, causing performance issues.

Thick versus Thin Provisioning   One of the big decisions that must be made in creating a VM is whether to thick or thin provision a VM (from a vSphere perspective, regardless of what is done at the storage level). Let's begin with a brief overview of the terms involved and understand the implications of each option from a utilization perspective. Figure 8.20 shows the differences graphically. Note that the left side of the graphic represents the physical storage configuration with two LUNs, and the right side shows the VMs and their associated .vmdk files. In the middle are two datastores, one of which has only thick provisioned .vmdk files and the other with only thin provisioned virtual disks, though in practice they can be mixed and matched on the same datastore if desired. We didn't simply to illustrate the different concepts as succinctly as possible. The datastore disk usage alarms are set on all datastores by default, but are only shown on the top datastore to save space and reduce clutter in the diagram. Finally, it is important to note that the over allocated space is thin provisioned and may or may not exceed the free space available; in our example, it does exceed the free space and if all the VMs wanted to use all the space they thought they had, we'd be out of disk space and would run into an error condition.

The terms shown in Figure 8.20 are defined in Table 8.5.

When you thin provision, space is allocated on demand and then that space is zeroed out, and then the VM's I/O is executed.

Table 8.5 Provisioning Terminology

Term	Applies To	Definition
Capacity	Datastore	The physical size of the LUN.
Provisioned Space	Datastore	The space currently in use on the datastore (LUN).
Free Space	Datastore	Free space left on the datastore; it is Capacity minus Provisioned Space.
Datastore Disk Usage	Datastore Alarm	There are two default alarms, warning and alert set at 75% and 85%. (These can be modified if desired. Alarms are covered in Chapter 10.)
Provisioned Storage	VM	The amount of space given to the VM (the total size of all the virtual disks) plus the size of the VMkernel swap file (by default the amount of RAM assigned to the VM—more on this in Chapter 10).
Not-Shared Storage	VM	The physical disk space used by the VM (if thick provisioned, it will be the size of the virtual disks). It is the space unique to this VM; unless linked clones are used (VMware View can do this, for example) it will be the same as Used Storage.
Used Storage	VM	The physical disk space used by the VM (including any shared space if linked clones are in use).

This is illustrated in Figures 8.21 and 8.22. In Figure 8.21, you'll notice that some blocks are in use by VM1 (P, S, F, dark C, and K), some by VM2 (B, J, I, S, T, light C, and F), and the rest are free blocks on the disk (illustrated as numbers to show that they have previous content in them). Note that a data point may take up an entire block (for example, P, S, or T), others may have multiple data points in a single block (for example J and I), while for others there may be room left over for future data (as illustrated by the 0 in the blocks with F or K). Note that the data for a VM may be physically fragmented on disk. There is no mechanism to determine fragmentation or to defragment a disk at this point; the only solution to perceived fragmentation is to Storage vMotion the VM to another datastore, where the system will allocate contiguous blocks if possible or at least minimize the number of fragments. Figure 8.21 also shows that block Z is ready to be written by VM1.

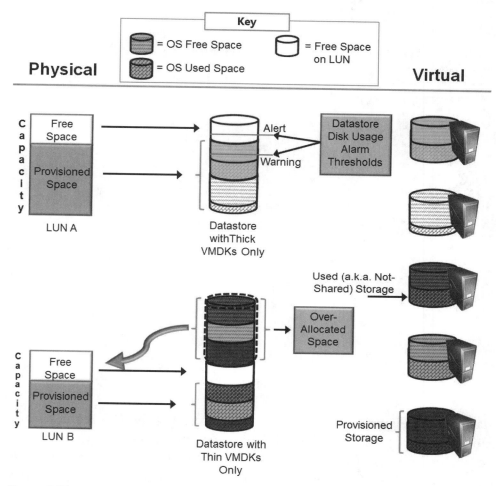

Figure 8.20
Thick vs. Thin Provisioning overview.

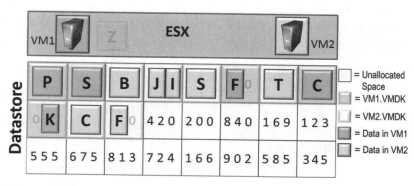

Figure 8.21
Thin provisioning.

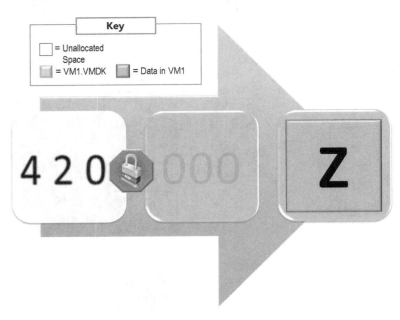

Figure 8.22
Thin provisioning 2.

Figure 8.22 starts where Figure 8.21 leaves off—from receiving the I/O request from the VM to actually writing it on disk. The VMkernel gets the request to write an I/O, and then picks a block on disk (in this example, it is 420). The system will lock the LUN (or a portion of it if VAAI is supported) and add that block to the LUN list for the VM, then unlock whatever it just locked; this locking period is very short, typically a few milliseconds. Next, vSphere will write all zeros to the block to reset any old data that may have still been on the block. Finally, the system will process the I/O request to the newly initialized block, in this example writing Z. At that point, the I/O will be acknowledged back to the VM.

This is the cheapest way to go from a storage capacity perspective, but it does have slightly higher overhead (and thus a small negative performance impact as just described). Nevertheless, this is very popular today because of the potential storage savings and the ability to overcommit disk space (much like CPU and memory can be overcommitted for VMs on a physical host).

With thick (called Thick Provision, Lazy Zeroed in the vSphere Client) provisioning (the default type of storage allocation, as it has been in all previous versions), the disk space is allocated when the virtual disk is created, but to make that process occur quickly, the space is not zeroed out until it is first accessed, at which time zeros will be written to the block, and then the actual I/O is completed. This has less of a performance penalty than thin provisioning, but there is still a slight penalty. This process is shown in Figures 8.23 and 8.24.

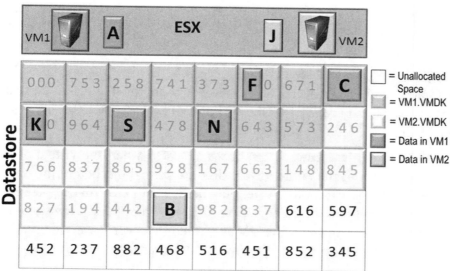

Figure 8.23
Lazy Zero thick provisioning 1.

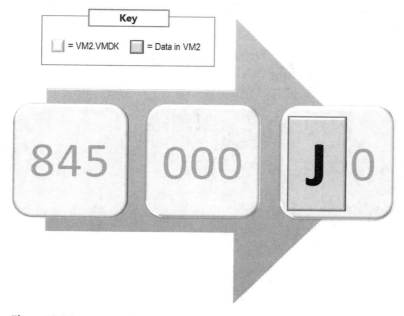

Figure 8.24
Lazy Zero thick provisioning 2.

In Figure 8.23, the space for VM1 and VM2 is preallocated (and will be contiguous if possible), thus all of VM1's space happens to be at the start of the datastore; VM2's space is in the middle; and free space is at the end (in our example, it does not physically need to be allocated this way). Some of that space contains data used by the VM (similar to the situation described in Figure 8.21), while some contains old data (possibly from previous VMs that have been deleted). Figure 8.24 depicts the point where VM2 is ready to write data point "J."

In Figure 8.24, you'll notice one less step than Figure 8.22 as the space is already allocated. The old (stale) data (845) needs to be zeroed, then the J written, but as the J didn't consume all of the space in the block (the VMFS block, not the file system block), the rest of the VMFS block contains zeros.

Finally, with Eager Zero thick provisioning, the space is allocated when the virtual disk is created, and then the contents of the entire virtual disk are zeroed out before the disk can be used. This takes the longest time to create, but there is no performance penalty when it is used. We recommend choosing Eager Zeroed disks when thick provisioning as we'd rather pay the cost of zeroing when the VM is created (and when we are usually not under any kind of time restriction to get the VM built) rather than pay an ongoing cost with every I/O to a new block. This process is illustrated in Figures 8.25 and 8.26.

Figure 8.25 is much like Figure 8.23 except all of the space has already been zeroed; VM2 is ready to write data C. Figure 8.26 has one less step than Figure 8.24 as the block has already been zeroed, so all that needs to happen is to write C to the block and then acknowledge the I/O to the VM.

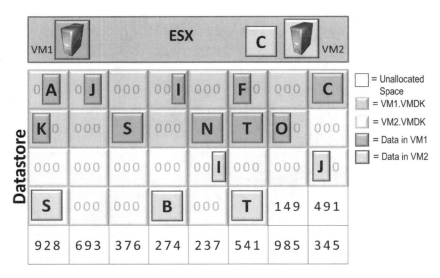

Figure 8.25
Eager Zero thick provisioning 1.

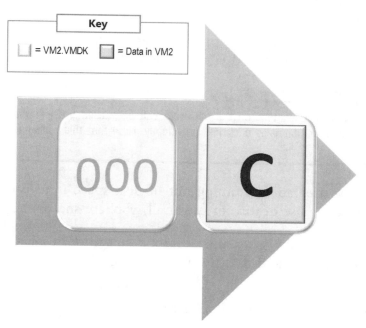

Figure 8.26
Eager Zero thick provisioning 2.

Note

If you have a VAAI-compatible array, vCenter will utilize the zero block feature to have the array write gigabytes of zeros; if not, the host will do so at the cost of SAN bandwidth and CPU utilization on the ESXi host. The host-based approach will also take longer to complete due to the extra communication needed.

To summarize, let's compare and contrast the three options (note that the performance difference is fairly small among the three options). See Table 8.6.

If a datastore is overcommitted, it is especially important to keep an eye on free space (or use the alarms previously mentioned) to ensure that you never run out of

Table 8.6 Provisioning Operations and Implications

	Thin	Lazy Thick	Eager Thick
Space Allocated	On demand	At Creation	At Creation
Space Zeroed	On demand	On demand	At Creation
Performance	Good	Better	Best

available disk space. When you run low, you'll need to either move some of the VMs to another datastore (using Storage vMotion for example, as described later in this chapter) or make the datastore bigger (as described later in this section).

Caution

If you run out of disk space on the datastore, *All VMs* on the datastore will be paused (frozen) until space is made available and the administrator unfreezes *each VM* individually. Note that this will affect thick and thin VMs.

The two best ways to minimize worries about running out of disk space is to use thick provisioning and to minimize the use of (or not use at all) vSphere snapshots.

Creating   Now that you understand all the issues and decisions that must be made to create a datastore, it is time to get started; it is fairly simple, as follows:

1. Select the host (or any one of them if multiple hosts have access to a shared LUN that will become a datastore) in Hosts and Clusters view.

2. Select the Configuration tab, then click the Storage link.

3. Click the Add Storage link in the top-right side of the screen as shown in Figure 8.27.

4. Select Disk/LUN and click Next.

5. Select the desired LUN; the system will only display LUNs that are not in use by other datastores or are assigned as RDMs.

6. Click Next.

7. Select the datastore format VMFS-3 (for compatibility with ESX(i) 3 and 4) or VMFS-5 (to take advantage of the new features, but compatible with ESXi 5 only) and click Next.

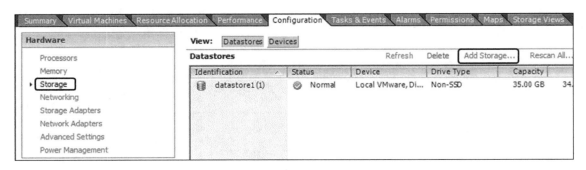

Figure 8.27
List of datastores with the Storage link selected.

8. You will be shown any existing partitions (for new LUNs you will see the message "The hard disk is blank"). Click Next.

Caution

If the disk contains existing data and you continue, the existing data will be permanently lost, so be very sure this is what you mean to do or you may cause an RGE—a Résumé Generating Event!

9. Give the datastore a descriptive name and click Next.

10. By default, all the available space on the LUN will be used; if you want to use less (and rarely will this be the case), click the Custom space setting radio button and then enter the desired size for the datastore.

11. If you selected the VMFS-3 option, you'll also be prompted to enter the block size on this screen.

12. Click Next.

13. The system will display a summary of what is currently on the disk and what will be done; review it then click Finish.

Growing   Over time, as more VMs are created, or thin provisioned VMs consume more space, you may find that your datastores are getting full. Several methods of resolving this problem have been previously described; for our purposes, we'll look at how to grow a datastore. There are fundamentally two approaches: work with your SAN administrator to expand an existing LUN using native SAN tools, or work with the SAN administrator to provision another LUN and expand the datastore on to another LUN. Let's look at each.

Adding Extents   The ability to add an extent (another LUN) to a datastore has been available for several versions of vSphere. To increase the datastore size using this method:

1. Select the datastore you want to add an extent to by either:
   a. In Hosts and Clusters view, select a host with access to the datastore, go to its Configuration tab, click the Storage link, then click on the datastore.
   b. In Datastores and Datastore Clusters view, select the datastore and then click the Configuration tab.

2. Click the Properties link just above the Datastore details pane, as shown in Figure 8.28.

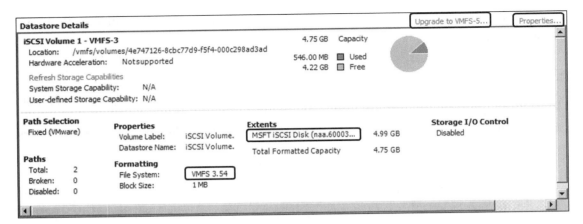

Figure 8.28
Datastore properties −1 extent. VMFS version 3.

3. In the <datastore name> Properties dialog box, click the Increase button. This will bring up the Increase Datastore Capacity wizard, which is used for both adding extents and growing the volume.

4. As shown in Figure 8.29, the Expandable column indicates whether an LUN can be added as a new extent (Expandable is *No*) or if the free space on the LUN can

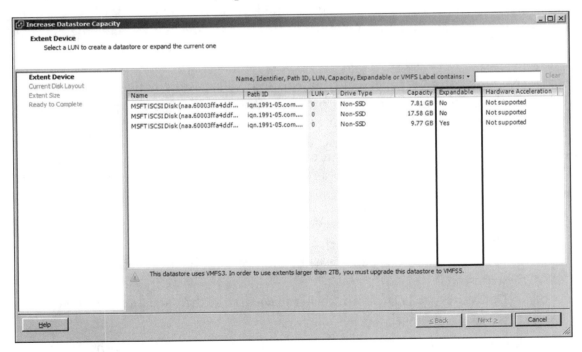

Figure 8.29
Increase Datastore Capacity.

be used to grow the size of the datastore on the same LUN (Expandable is *Yes*). For this task, be sure to choose a LUN where expandable is No.

Caution

When selecting LUNs, it is best to choose LUNs of the same type (Fibre Channel, iSCSI, etc.), often from the same array. It is always bad to mix local and shared storage, as you have no control over which LUN(s) in the datastore a VM will reside on.

5. Click Next.

6. The existing data (if any) will be displayed; review it to make sure you selected the correct LUN and click Next.

7. On the Extent Size page of the wizard, you can choose to use all of the space on the LUN or just a portion of it, similarly to when you created the datastore in the first place. You will usually want to use the entire space, so leave "Maximum available space" selected and click Next.

8. A summary of what will happen will be displayed; click Finish to add the extent and finish the process.

Figure 8.30 shows the extents that make up the datastore, and the space contributed by each, while Figure 8.28 (Datastore properties) shows an example of a single extent datastore.

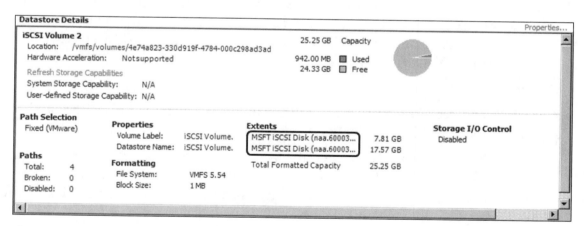

Figure 8.30
Datastore Details −2 extents.

Caution

Be careful to provide redundancy on your LUNs that make up a datastore, as the failure of any of the LUNs will cause any VMs that have any data on those LUNs to stop working. Be especially careful with the first LUN (the one you originally created the datastore on) as it contains all of the metadata for the entire datastore—losing it will cause the loss of all VMs on that datastore.

Volume Grow   The ability to utilize space in an existing LUN, either because you did not use all the space initially or more often because the SAN administrator made the SAN volume larger, is a great way to grow the size of the datastore without causing a dependency on multiple LUNs. This feature was introduced with vSphere 4. To increase the datastore size use this method:

1. Select the datastore you want to add an extent to with one of these options:
   a. In Hosts and Clusters view, select a host with access to the datastore, go to its Configuration tab, click the Storage link, and then click on the datastore.
   b. In Datastores and Datastore Clusters view, select the datastore and then click the Configuration tab.

2. Click the Properties link just above the Datastore details pane, as shown in Figure 8.28.

3. In the <datastore name> Properties dialog box, click the Increase button. This will bring up the Increase Datastore Capacity wizard, which is used for both adding extents and growing the volume.

4. As shown in Figure 8.29 (Increase Datastore Capacity), the Expandable column indicates whether an LUN can be added as a new extent (Expandable is No) or if the free space on the LUN can be used to grow the size of the datastore on the same LUN (Expandable is Yes). For this task, be sure to choose a LUN where expandable is Yes.

5. Click Next.

6. You should see Free Space listed with a note that "Free space will be used to expand the VMFS volume"; click Next.

7. On the Extent Size page of the wizard, you can choose to use all of the space on the LUN or just a portion of it, similarly to when you created the datastore in the first place. You will usually want to use the entire space, so leave "Maximum available space" selected and click Next.

8. A summary of what will happen will be displayed; click Finish to add the extent and finish the process.

Converting from VMFS-3 to VMFS-5   If you have existing VMFS-3 datastores, you can either create a new VMFS-5 datastore and use Storage vMotion to move the VMs to the new datastore or upgrade the existing datastore to VMFS-5 as described in the planning section. We'll discuss Storage vMotion later in this chapter; to upgrade the datastore to VMFS-5, do the following:

1. Select the datastore you want to convert to VMFS-5 using either option:
   a. In Hosts and Clusters view, select a host with access to the datastore, go to its Configuration tab, click the Storage link, and then click on the datastore.
   b. In Datastores and Datastore Clusters view, select the datastore and then click the Configuration tab.

2. Click the Upgrade to VMFS-5 link just above the Datastore details pane as shown in Figure 8.28.

3. The system will inform you that all of the hosts that access the datastore must support VMFS-5 (i.e., be vSphere 5 or later), then show a green checkmark if they meet that criteria; click OK to upgrade.

4. The system will upgrade the datastore. When complete, note in the Datastore Details pane that the version is now 5.xx (the GA version is 5.54). Also note that the block size configured when the volume was created is the same.

Creating an NFS-Based Datastore

Up to this point in this section, we have been looking at ways to create datastores based on block-based storage. In this section, we'll review how to create an NFS-based datastore. While the functionality of both datastore types is similar, the creation process is quite different. To create an NAS-based datastore:

1. Select the host that will have access to the NFS share in Hosts and Clusters view.

2. Select the Configuration tab, then the Storage link.

3. Click the Add Storage link in the top-right side of the screen, as shown in Figure 8.27.

4. Select Network File System and click Next.

5. Enter the following parameters in the dialog box shown in Figure 8.31:
   a. **Server.** Enter the name or IP address or FQDN of the NAS server. In most cases, an IP address is used as administrators don't want to place all of the company's data on a network share that is available to users and then advertise the existence of that server to increase security.
   b. **Folder.** The name of the NFS export (or share to use Windows terminology) to be accessed in standard Linux/UNIX format (forward, not backward slashes between directories).
   c. **Datastore Name.** The name of the datastore.

Caution

If you want the datastore accessible by multiple hosts as a form of shared storage, for use by vMotion or HA for example, be sure to use the same information for all three inputs just described; if not, they will be treated as different datastores on the different hosts, even though they point to the same location, preventing features that require shared storage from working for the VMs located on those datastores. This is also shown in the dialog box in Figure 8.31 as well.

d. **Mount NFS read only.** Tells VMware that the datastore should be mounted read-only, preventing VMs from running on the datastore or other data being placed on it. You may wonder why you would create a datastore that you can't write to. The answer is because you have other forms of storage that you use for your VMs and want the NFS datastore simply for access to ISO files, for example, that you upload directly to the NFS share from another system. We use these types of datastores often to provide shared storage on less expensive storage when iSCSI or Fibre Channel SANs are used for VMs to store ISOs so that vMotion and other shared storage features will work.

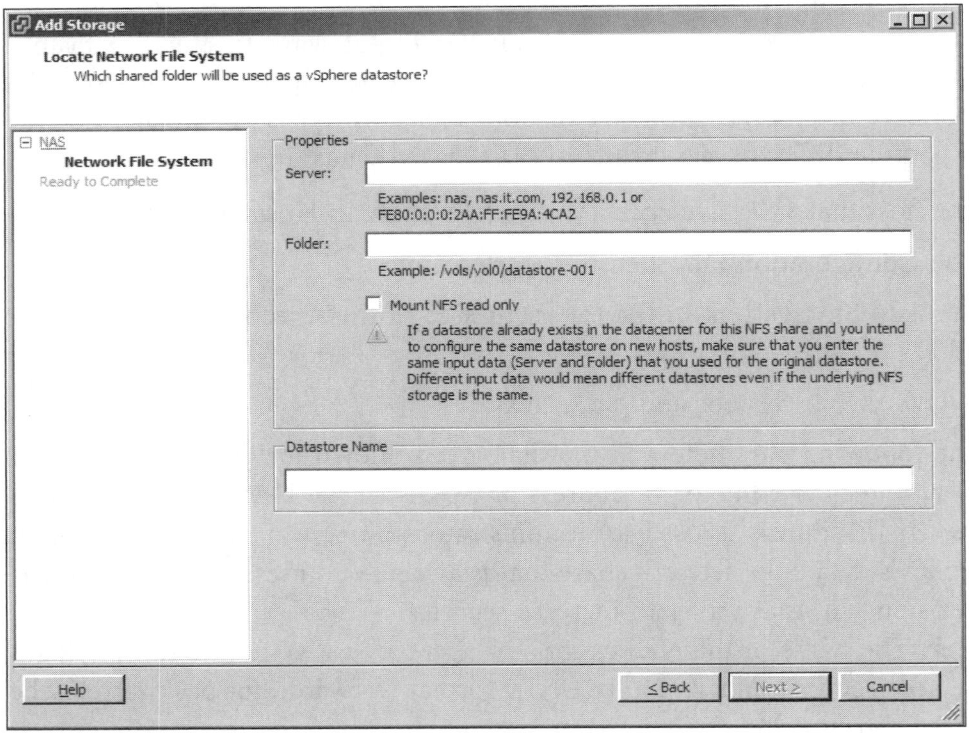

Figure 8.31
NAS datastore details.

6. Click Next.

7. The system will summarize your entries; click Finish to create the datastore.

Tip

If the process fails, verify the entries made and the configuration of the VMkernel port; often the VMkernel port was not created or is on the wrong switch or subnet.

8. Repeat the above procedure for each host that needs access to the same NFS export—there is no way to do it once and automatically update other servers as there is for block-based storage.

Common Tasks for Both Block and NAS Storage

Up to this point in this section, we have been looking at ways to create datastores based on either block- or NAS-based storage. In this final portion of the datastores section, we'll review tasks that are common to both types.

Renaming   If you have an existing datastore that you want to rename, you can do so non-disruptively to VMs (powered on or powered off) by doing the following:

1. Select the datastore you want to rename using either option:
   a. In Hosts and Clusters view, select a host with access to the datastore, go to its Configuration tab, click the Storage link, and then click on the datastore.
   b. In Datastores and Datastore Clusters view, select the datastore.

2. Right-click the datastore name and select Rename.

3. Type the new name and hit <Enter>.

Unmounting and Mounting   New in vSphere 5 (for block-based storage anyway— NAS mounts have always been unmountable) you can take datastores that you no longer want to have accessed by one or more hosts, and unmount the datastore from it/them. You might do this for maintenance activities, before deleting a datastore to be sure it is unused, or to stop using an NFS mount that has been transitioned to another server or simply another export. Unmounting, unlike deleting, does not remove any content and access could be added back in the future if desired. To unmount a datastore, follow these steps:

1. Select the datastore you want to unmount by either:
   a. In Hosts and Clusters view, select a host with access to the datastore, go to its Configuration tab, click the Storage link, and then click on the datastore.
   b. In Datastores and Datastore Clusters view, select the datastore.

2. Right-click the datastore name and select Unmount. One of two things will happen at this point, depending on whether you are trying to unmount a VMFS datastore or an NFS datastore.

c. For a VMFS datastore:

    i. If the datastore is accessible by multiple hosts, select the host or hosts that should lose access (by default all hosts with access will lose it) and click Next. This step is skipped if it is only available to a single host.

    ii. The system will display the prerequisites that must be met to unmount the datastore, as shown in Figure 8.32.

    iii. If all prerequisites have been met and it is associated with a single host only, click OK and the volume will be unmounted; if not follow these steps to complete the wizard:

        1. Click Next (if the prerequisites were not met, click Cancel and correct any missing items).

        2. The system will display a confirmation dialog box; click Finish to complete the task.

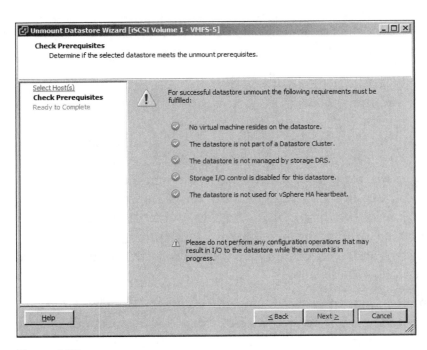

Figure 8.32
Unmount datastore prerequisites.

d. For an NFS datastore:

    i. If the datastore is accessible by multiple hosts, select the host or hosts that should lose access (by default all hosts with access will lose it) and click Next. This step is skipped if it is only available to a single host.

    ii. If it was accessible by a single host, a dialog box will be displayed indicating that the data will be inaccessible; click Yes to unmount it. If it was accessible by multiple hosts, click Finish to remove it from all hosts.

Once unmounted, a VMFS datastore will appear grayed out, while an NFS datastore will disappear from the list of datastores (from a single host or if it was removed from all hosts; if it was removed from only some hosts, it will continue to be displayed in Datastores and Datastore Clusters view).

To restore access in the future for a VMFS datastore, repeat Steps 1 and 2, selecting Mount instead of Unmount in step 2 to get access back (all other steps will be skipped as there are no prerequisites or confirmation required to mount a volume). To restore access to an NFS datastore, simply create a new NFS datastore as previously described.

Deleting   If you have a datastore that you no longer need, you can delete it easily. Deleting means two different things, depending on whether the datastore being deleted is NAS or block based. If it is block based, the LUN or LUNs that the datastore was based on will be made available for other uses, such as a new datastore based on a subset of the LUNs originally used, or as a RDM. It can also be used if you want to decommission the underlying LUN(s) in the event you are retiring your SAN or making other storage changes. On the other hand, if you select a NAS-based datastore, deleting it is functionally and practically the same as unmounting it—the datastore access is removed, but the data remains on the NFS share.

To do delete a VMFS datastore, follow these steps:

1. Select the datastore you want to delete using one of these options:
   a. In Hosts and Clusters view, select a host with access to the datastore, go to its Configuration tab, click the Storage link, and then click on the datastore.
   b. In Datastores and Datastore Clusters view, select the datastore and then click the Configuration tab.

2. Right-click the datastore and select Delete (in Hosts and Clusters view you could also click the Delete link above the datastore list).

3. A dialog box will be displayed indicating that the data will be permanently deleted; click Yes to delete it (all servers that had access to it will automatically do a rescan and remove it from the list of datastores on that host).

Caution

Any time that VMware uses the word "Permanently," it is indicating that there is no undo available, and that data loss may result—deleting the wrong datastore could have disastrous consequences!

Deleting an NFS datastore is different because the datastore will not really be deleted, just unmounted. The only way you can "Delete" an NFS datastore is to select it in Hosts and Clusters view, as described in Step 1a and then click the Delete link (which will provide the same warning described above under unmounting an NFS datastore).

Rescanning and Refreshing

As mentioned previously, one of the great advantages of using a SAN or NFS storage array is that you can dynamically change the LUNs and/or their size that are presented to a server. This is technically possible with local storage as well, but many controllers do not permit drives to be added dynamically, and even if they do, the server must be rebooted to add it to a RAID volume or to create a new RAID volume. Unfortunately, most operating systems (including VMware and Windows) are not always looking for these changes, but rather take a static look when the OS is booted only. The good news is that it takes only a few clicks to update the OS with any changes that have occurred on the storage side. To update a host with changes to LUNs and/or VMFS volumes, simply:

1. Select the host in Host and Clusters view.

2. Select the Configuration tab, then the Storage Adapters link.

3. Click the Rescan All link in the top-right side of the screen.

4. You can choose to look for changes on the storage arrays (the Scan for New Storage Devices option) and/or changes to VMFS (the Scan for New VMFS Volumes option). By default, both are checked, and usually you'll want to stay with the default. Click OK to initiate the scan.

Note

Even though the options state New, they will detect new, changed, and removed LUNs and volumes.

5. Wait for the tasks to complete in the Recent Tasks pane, then confirm that the new storage and/or LUN size is reported on the expected HBA. If you don't see it, verify that you are looking on the correct HBA; you may also try rescanning again to see if it is found after a second scan. After the space has been recognized, you can grow the datastore as previously described.

On the other hand, NFS datastores will not reflect updated space as rescans are done, because rescans focus on changes to LUNs and VMFS volumes. To update the information for an NFS volume (and some information on a VMFS volume that would also be reported with a rescan), use the Refresh option instead. To do so:

1. Select the host in Host and Clusters view.

2. Select the Configuration tab, then the Storage link.

3. Click the Refresh link at the top, toward the middle of the screen.

4. Wait for the task to complete in the Recent Tasks pane and then confirm that the NFS volume size is reported correctly. If you don't see it, wait a minute or so for the information to update; you may also try refreshing again to see if it is updated after a second refresh.

One of the great features of vSphere is that if a change is found on a shared datastore, initiating a rescan on one host will automatically start one on the other hosts connected to the same shared datastore. Likewise, a refresh that updates the size of an NFS volume will automatically update the available space on all hosts connected to the same datastore.

SSD Usage

Prior to vSphere 5, SSD storage was usable locally or over the SAN, but vSphere didn't treat an SSD drive any differently than any other kind of disk. Now the vSphere Client has a new column listing the disk type (SSD, non-SSD [everything else—SAS, SATA, or Fibre Channel], or unknown) when datastores or LUNs are listed (such as on the Storage and Storage Adapters links on the Configuration tab).

Why is this important? Because SSD drives are capable of much higher I/O rates (primarily in IOPS; to a much lesser degree in terms of bandwidth) than non-SSD drives and we can leverage these extra capabilities to increase performance for several scenarios, including the obvious one of running a disk-intensive VM on faster storage for better performance, but also as swap space for hosts that are memory limited, where the host will move pages from the VM to disk to save physical RAM for other VMs that need it. By swapping to SSD disks, the penalty of swapping to disk, which can dramatically reduce the VM's performance, can be reduced over slower disk types (though in most cases it is cheaper to add RAM to a server than to buy an enterprise class SSD that can cost tens of thousands of dollars).

In addition, VMs can make standard SCSI or IDE queries to the virtual disks that make it up to determine if the disk type is SSD, as long as the following criteria are met:

- The VM is on an ESXi 5 or higher host.

- The VM is configured with Hardware Version 8 (introduced with ESXi 5.0).

- The .vmdk file is located on a VMFS-5 volume (not a VMFS-3 volume).

- If the datastore is shared across multiple hosts, all hosts must recognize the datastore as residing on SSD drives.

Usually, SSD drives are automatically detected and reported correctly, but it is possible to manually mark or unmark a device as being SSD based, as well as informing vSphere that a specific device is local or remote (again, this is usually automatically detected, but in some cases it may not do so). Any changes must be made using the command line, but as this will probably rarely be done in practice, we will refer you to the Storage Guide in Chapter 15, entitled "Solid State Disk Enablement," for the exact procedures.

Storage vMotion

Storage vMotion is a great feature that was introduced with ESX 3.5, and it has come a long way since then. The purpose of this feature is to allow a live running VM to be migrated from one storage location to another with no discernible downtime for the user. This section is a little longer than most in the implementation section because we need to discuss what it is and why it is used, but it really requires very little planning and thus doesn't belong in the planning section.

To get a better feel for the product and what it can do as well as how it has changed over the versions, refer to the sidebar: A Brief History of Storage vMotion.

A Brief History of Storage vMotion

Storage vMotion has come a long way since it was first released, becoming faster, more powerful, and easier to use. The major features and improvements over the years are as follows:

- **3.5: First version.** Command line only (no supported GUI was available, but some third-party options were created and available). Used standard snapshot and vMotion capabilities to get the job done. A snapshot was taken, freezing the original data for copying and directing all new writes to the snapshot instead of the original disk. The snapshot files could get very large, requiring large amounts of disk space for the process to work and taking a long time to commit all the changes once the process completed. After copying was complete, a self vMotion (a vMotion on the same host) took place, creating a second VM that pointed to the copied data, then transferred control to it, whereupon the changes in the snapshot were committed to the "new" VM and the original data was deleted. This required twice the memory and CPU during the copy process. Storage vMotion could not be used with VMs that had snapshots due to this architecture.

- **4.x:** Change Block Tracking (CBT) was introduced as a feature of VMs to denote when blocks had changed for backup purposes and for use with Storage vMotion. CBT kept a bitmap table that tracked which blocks had changed. Storage vMotion would copy the data, noting changes in the table as they occurred, then iteratively repeat the process, copying the blocks that had changed since the last pass until the two copies were the same. This could cause problems in very I/O-intensive workloads where the data change rate was higher than the system could keep up with. Once the two copies were the same, Fast Suspend/Resume was employed, which paused the VM, changed the pointers to the new copy of the data, and then resumed the VM, getting rid of the need for double the memory and CPU during the process—much faster than the first approach. A GUI was also added, making it simple to use the feature. This version was still incompatible with snapshots (and linked clones which are used with VMware View).

- **5.x:** A new mirroring mechanism is used so that after a block is copied, if it is changed before the copy process completes, the change will be synchronously mirrored to the destination datastore. This means one complete pass across the source disk is all that is required and the extra disk space used during the process is minimal. The process completes faster, even under heavy I/O loads and even if the destination datastore is slower than the source datastore. It now works properly with linked clones and snapshots.

Use Cases

Let's begin our discussion of Storage vMotion with a discussion of some use cases—why do people use it? There are many reasons, some of which we have previously mentioned in this chapter, as well as elsewhere in the book. Some common reasons include:

- Moving a VM from one disk type or RAID type to another. Many times people place VMs on datastores with no thought to performance, and then they start experiencing performance issues, while other times development starts on slow, inexpensive storage (such as RAID 5 on SATA or 10K RPM SAS drives) and then moves to faster drives and/or RAID levels as the VM is placed into production.

- Moving a VM on an overloaded datastore to another datastore. This could be because the source datastore is running low on capacity or because the I/O load on the datastore is too high, causing performance issues.

- Moving all the VMs on a storage array to its replacement when the array comes off lease. In the physical world, this would almost always require some down time to switch over, but with Storage vMotion, all that is required is that you create new datastores on the new array and then migrate the VMs from the old to the new array. Once all the VMs have been relocated, the original datastores can be decommissioned, the original LUNs deleted, and the array reset in preparation for returning it to the vendor.

- Moving VMs from local, internal storage to a shared storage array as the company grows.

- Moving from one type of storage to another, including local to Fibre Channel, iSCSI to NAS, or FCoE to local. There are no restrictions on what type of datastore the source and destination datastores need to be—any type can be migrated to any other type.

All of these options (and more) allow users to properly place VMs without incurring any down time or performing the storage maintenance tasks at strange hours, such as on weekends.

How It Works

So how does Storage vMotion work? As shown in Figure 8.33, there are several steps to the process (the figure shows the process a third of the way through):

1. The basically static files (configuration, log, etc.) are copied from the source datastore to the destination datastore. This includes all the files but the virtual disks (and any snapshots of them). This is illustrated as the folder being copied from the source to the destination datastore.

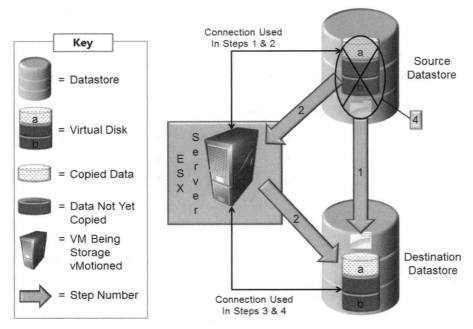

Figure 8.33
Storage vMotion.

2. The data is copied from the source virtual disk(s) on the source datastore(s) to the copies made on the destination datastore(s). In the figure, data is copied from a single datastore to a single datastore. One pass is made across each disk. The basic copying I/O can be completed by the VMkernel itself or it can leverage VAAI if the source and destination datastores are on the same array and the array supports VAAI. As shown in Figure 8.33, the I/O is going through the VMkernel, not VAAI; in addition, letters a and b are block writes that take place during the process, as follows:

a. The "a" represents a block on the virtual disk that had already been copied to the destination. In this case, the data is mirrored (synchronously written) to the destination disk so that the two disks are kept in sync. At the end of the pass, the two disks are identical. The mirroring process is handled by a separate driver in the VMkernel from the one that is used by the basic copying process (or VAAI).

b. The "b" represents a block that has not been copied yet. In that case, nothing needs to be done on the destination side, as it has not been copied already, so the I/O goes to the source disk only.

3. Once all disks have been copied, the server conducts a Fast Suspend/Resume operation, where the pointers for the VM are changed from the source disks on the source datastore (the arrow at the top of the diagram) to the destination disks on the destination datastore (the arrow at the bottom; at this point the top arrow is removed). This does involve downtime, but typically it is less than a second and well within the TCP retry time frame, so any packets lost during the process are simply retransmitted from the client to the VM that was just migrated and the client has no idea that the datastore was just changed.

4. Once the VM is running on the destination datastore, there is no need for the source files on the source datastore, so they are deleted—Storage vMotion is always a move, never a copy. This is illustrated by the oval with an X through it. Use the Clone VM functionality in vCenter if you want to copy instead of move the VM.

Prerequisites

Storage vMotion does not have many prerequisites, especially in vSphere 5, but there are a few, namely:

■ Both the source and destination datastore must be accessible by the ESXi host that the VM is running on because the VM is not changing hosts.

■ The VM can use virtual disks and/or RDMs.

■ If you want to change the host and the datastore in one step, you must either power off or suspend the VM. You can, however, perform a Storage vMotion from local storage to shared storage first and then initiate a standard vMotion from one host to another, potentially even running a second Storage vMotion to relocate the VM on storage local to the new host.

Using Storage vMotion

So how do we actually migrate the VM from one location to another? It is actually a very simple process. All migrations (cold, suspend, Storage vMotion, or standard vMotion) begin with the same initial step, with the wizard steps varying depending on which option is selected. The process is as follows:

1. Right-click on the VM you want to move (creating and using VMs will be discussed in the next chapter) and select Migrate as shown in Figure 8.34. "Change host" is a standard vMotion (discussed in Chapter 10), "Change datastore" is

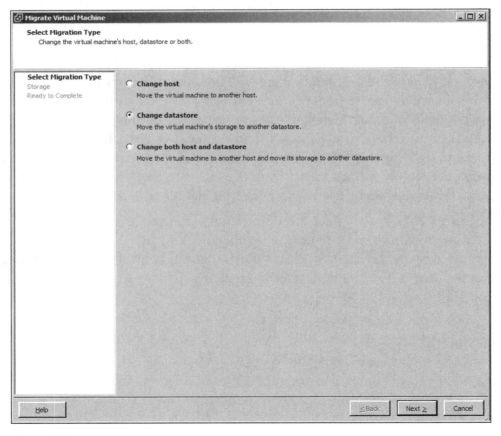

Figure 8.34
Migrate Virtual Machine wizard.

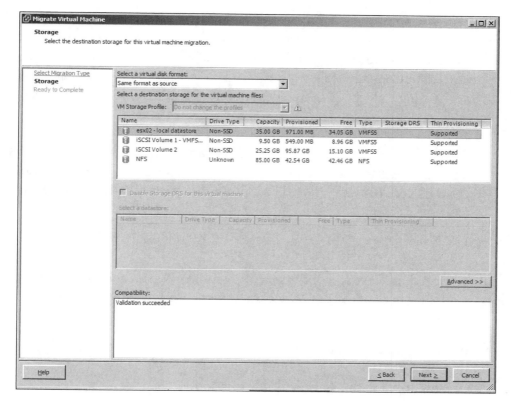

Figure 8.35
Storage options.

Storage vMotion, and "Change both host and datastore" is used for cold or suspend migrations and will be unavailable if the VM is powered on.

2. Select Change datastore and click Next.

3. Select the destination datastore and disk type (shown in Figure 8.35) per the following options:

   a. Select the destination disk format (thin or eager or lazy zeroed thick), or leave it the same as the default option.

   b. If you have defined storage profiles, you can select a different profile from the list (this will be discussed later in Chapter 11). Selecting a different profile will display datastores that are compliant with that profile as well as those that aren't, indicating which datastores fall into each category.

   c. Select the destination datastore. Note the destination free space and make sure sufficient space is available for the VM. If you want the entire VM relocated to a single datastore, this is all you need to do—continue to step d. On the other hand, if you want the VM to be split across multiple datastores (for example, a database drive on one datastore and a log drive on a different datastore with the VM configuration, log, and other files on a third datastore), click the Advanced button and follow these steps for each entry (Configuration file [which includes all the files except the virtual hard drives] and each hard disk individually):

    i. Select the destination datastore. You can choose [Current Location] to leave that file where it is or click Browse to select an alternate location. If you select Browse, you will be presented with a list of other datastores to choose from.

    ii. For virtual disks only, you can specify a storage profile if desired, which works as previously described.

    iii. Click either Next to continue with Step 4 or Basic to return to the simple version where all of the VM components are relocated to a single datastore.

    d. Optionally, you can disable Storage DRS for the VM if it was configured; Storage DRS is covered in Chapter 11.

    e. Click Next to view the summary information.

4. Review the information for accuracy then click Finish to complete the process. Look in the Recent Tasks pane for progress information. The larger the virtual disks, the longer the process will take.

Storage DRS (Load Balancing)

While Storage DRS is related to storage (obviously) it is really a feature that is designed for resource optimization relative to Storage, and as such, is discussed in Chapter 11, DRS Cluster Configuration.

Multipathing

Multipathing was discussed in the Planning section of this chapter. The purpose of this section is to see how those multipathing concepts can be applied to viewing and configuring the multipathing options. In many cases, there is little that needs to be done (except perhaps setting the policy and/or a preferred path for a datastore). In this section we'll discuss how to determine which multipathing plugin (MPP) is claiming a given datastore or device, the claim rules that determine which SATP owns a given LUN, and how to set a PSP for a datastore (or change the default so that all future LUNs using a specified SATP automatically default to the PSP you desire).

Caution

It is important to note that all of the MPP configuration that will be viewed and configured is done so on a host-by-host basis, and thus must be configured on each host if a change is to be made.

MPP/NMP

Before you can configure anything relative to multipathing, you need to know which MPP has claimed the LUN; we'll only be discussing VMware's NMP in this book as all others are third-party products with their own documentation, training courses, books, etc.

To determine which MPP has claimed an LUN, do the following:

1. Go to Hosts and Clusters view and select a host with access to your chosen LUN.

2. Select the Storage Adapters link on the Configuration tab.

3. Select the HBA that owns the LUN(s) in question in the top half of the dialog box.

4. View the Owner column; the LUNs shown in Figure 8.36 (and discussed in this book) are owned by NMP.

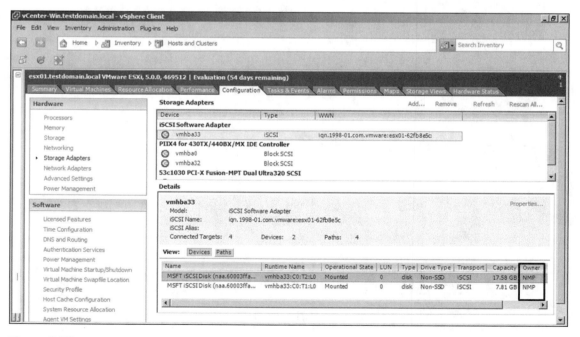

Figure 8.36
Viewing the owner of a LUN.

SATPs

First, you may wonder which SATP (Storage Array Type Plugin) has claimed a specific LUN. Unfortunately, this is a little harder question than it first seems. You'd think this would be displayed as an LUN property in the Storage Adapters view or listed under one of the Storage Views options, but you'd be wrong. Finding the associated SATP using the GUI is a little convoluted; to do so:

1. Select the host that is connected to the LUN you want to determine the SATP for.

2. Go to Configuration > Storage.

3. Select the datastore that uses the LUN from the list of datastores and click the Properties link (just above the datastore details).

4. Select the extent of the datastore built on the desired LUN from the Extents list (which unfortunately lists the extent's NAA address and capacity, but not run time name or other identifying characteristic—you may need to look in Storage Adapters to determine the correct NAA address and then come back here and try again. We told you this was a little convoluted!). This is illustrated in Figure 8.37.

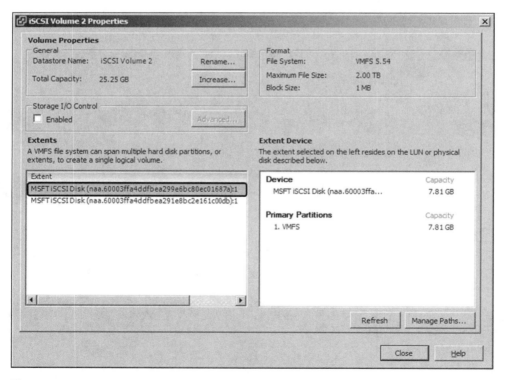

Figure 8.37
Extents list.

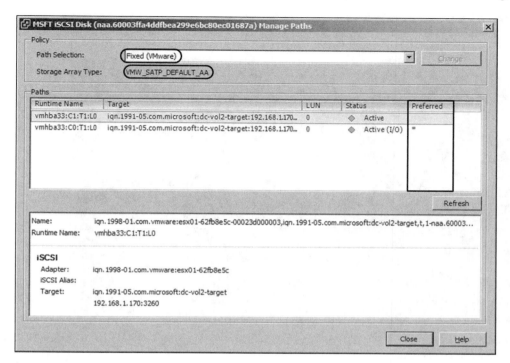

Figure 8.38
Manage paths dialog box showing the SATP for a LUN.

5. With the correct extent selected, click the Manage Paths button. This displays the Manage Paths dialog box for the LUN, as shown in Figure 8.38.

6. The SATP is listed next to Storage Array Type. Note that this is a read-only value in the GUI. In the example, it is VMW_SATP_DEFAULT_AA.

7. Close all open dialog boxes when finished.

On the other hand, you can find it from the command line by using this command (assuming you're connected to the proper ESXi server using Fast Pass, or add the appropriate options to the command as described in Chapter 4):

```
esxcli storage nmp device list
```

The output of this command will show all the LUNs connected to the host, the SATP and PSP associated with each, the working (active) path(s), etc. This is illustrated in Figure 8.39 (the command is at the bottom of the window, and the results are several screens long).

Much simpler and easier, right? Sometimes the command line is a lot easier for some tasks.

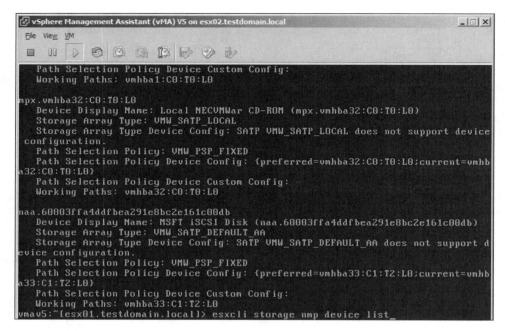

Figure 8.39
NMP device list from the CLI.

Next you may want to determine which SATPs are installed on the host. The only way to find that out is at the command line; you can do so with this command:

```
esxcli storage nmp satp list
```

The output of this command is shown in Figure 8.40.

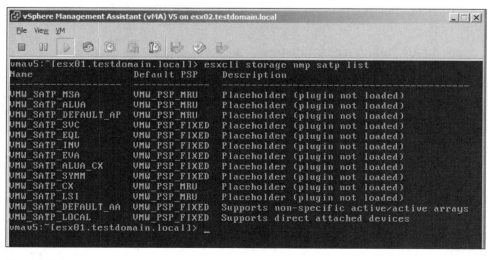

Figure 8.40
List of SATPs installed on the host.

Note in Figure 8.40 that all of the available SATPs are listed, but many are not loaded (as shown in the description), while the SATPs that are currently used, based on the storage environment of the ESXi server the command is run on, will have a description for the SATP. Other than searching on the Internet, this is really the only way to determine which SATP is being used in a human-friendly format, not just an SATP name.

To change the default PSP for an SATP, you have to use the command line as explained later in this chapter.

You may be wondering how the system determines which SATP to use for a particular LUN. It does this via SATP claim rules. You can view them with this command:

```
esxcli storage nmp satp rule list
```

You can see the output in Figure 8.41. Note that each entry is several lines long and there are a lot of rules (we've shown just the first one here to give you an idea—you may want to pipe the results out to "more" to view them all). You can view the name, array, or device it is associated with, transport protocol, default PSP, and description among other things. You'll note that some devices are no longer supported but have a rule description of "[Legacy Product, Not supported in this release]".

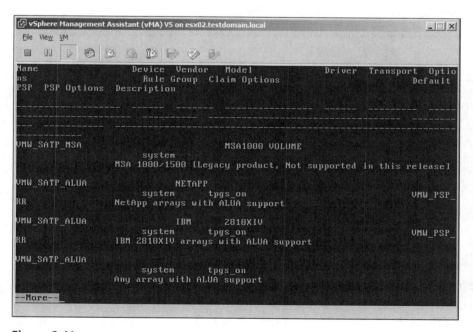

Figure 8.41
SATP claim rule list.

Managing Long Output

Many of the commands in this section (and indeed throughout the book) generate output that may be multiple screens long. A standard feature of Linux/UNIX is the ability to take the output of one command and use it as the input of another; this is known as piping. In the context of long outputs, there are three useful options: `more`, `less`, and redirecting the output to a file.

`More` has fewer features than `less` (hence the popular saying in Linux-land "less is more") in that `more` allows you to scroll forward through the output a line or a screen at a time. `Less` also allows you to scroll backward and do pattern matching to search for text in the output. The `man` (short for manual) command provides documentation on most commands as well as listing the options of each.

Sending the output to a file is a useful way to view and edit the contents in a text editor such as vi or nano, as well as saving the output as a form of documentation for the environment.

To pipe the output of one command into a second command, use the | (vertical bar) character. To redirect the output of a command to a file, use the > (greater than) character.

A couple of examples of how to do so. First, to pipe the SATP list output to `more` (`less` could be used as well), use this syntax:

```
esxcli storage nmp satp rule list | more
```

On the other hand, to redirect the output to a file named SATPlist in the /root directory instead, use this command:

```
esxcli storage nmp satp rule list > /root/SATPlist
```

PSPs

Just as with SATPs, PSPs (Path Selection Policies) can be viewed from both the GUI and command line, but unlike SATPs, PSPs can also be changed from both locations and a default PSP for an SATP can be configured (though only via the command line). To view or change the PSP for a datastore from the GUI:

1. Select the host that is connected to the LUN for which you want to determine the PSP.

2. Go to Configuration > Storage.

3. Select the datastore that uses the LUN from the list of datastores and click the Properties link (just above the datastore details).

4. Select the extent of the datastore built on the desired LUN from the Extents list (which unfortunately lists the extent's NAA address and capacity, but not run time name or other identifying characteristic—you may need to look in Storage Adapters to determine the correct NAA address and then come back here and try again). This is illustrated in Figure 8.37.

5. With the correct extent selected, click the Manage Paths button. This displays the Manage Paths dialog box for the LUN, as shown in Figure 8.38.

6. The PSP is listed in the Path Selection drop-down list. Select a new one if desired from that list (check with your storage vendor for their recommended PSP and only change them if you understand the change and are following your vendor's directions on the subject). In the example, it is Fixed (VMware).

7. If you set the policy to Fixed, you should also set a preferred path—by default, the system will select the first path it finds, causing lots of I/O on that path and none on the other possible paths. To do so, right-click on the preferred path in the list and select Preferred.

8. Close all open dialog boxes when finished.

Note

Remember that this setting is per host, per extent in each datastore, and thus if you want to have consistency, you may need to repeat this many times on many hosts.

Command Line Manipulation   That is a lot of work if you have a lot of datastores and hosts; isn't there an easier way? How about a simple PowerCLI script? To use this script, just connect to the ESXi server on which you want to change the policy and run this command (which will update all the datastores with a LUN type of disk—you may need to specify some filters if you only want to change the policy on some LUNs):

```
Get-ScsiLun -VmHost (Get-VmHost) -LunType disk | Set-ScsiLun -MultipathPolicy "<Policy>"
```

Note that in that command, the policy must be enclosed in quotation marks, and <Policy> is one of the following:

- RoundRobin
- Fixed
- MostRecentlyUsed

This command can also be used to set a preferred path if the policy is fixed, but you'd want to apply a filter to the datastores or all the datastores would have the same fixed path, which would defeat the purpose (from a load balancing perspective), but this command works great for the other two options.

The command could be used with the For-Each command to loop through a cluster or even through all ESXi hosts in all of vCenter to make the change on multiple servers with one command.

To view the list of installed PSPs on the ESXi host, connect to the host using the vMA or vCLI and run this command:

```
esxcli storage nmp psp list
```

But isn't this the hard way to see the list of PSPs? Couldn't you just look in the GUI? Well, yes, but if you want to set the default PSP for an SATP, you need to know the internal name, not necessarily the name in the GUI, and this is a simple way to view them all.

Setting a Default PSP for an SATP   You may want to change the PSP for the datastores and the above script can help do that, but it only affects existing datastores, not new ones you create. This is okay, but you probably don't want to run the script each time a new datastore is created. There is a simple solution that will change the default PSP for all new datastores (though not for existing ones). This can easily be achieved with a simple `esxcli` command on each host (or use the ability to target multiple hosts as described in Chapter 4 to do many at once). The command is as follows:

```
esxcli storage nmp satp set –satp <SATP name> --default-psp <PSP name>
```

You can get the list of SATPs and PSPs as described above for use here. The <> characters are not part of the syntax and just indicate that you need to replace them with the appropriate option.

SECURITY

In this section, we'll look at some of the security implications of storage. Many of them are usually handled at the storage array by the SAN administrator and thus will only be briefly touched on here. The biggest topic is CHAP, which can be used with iSCSI.

Zoning

Zoning is used in a Fibre Channel environment to connect server HBAs (initiators) to array ports (targets). VMware generally recommends a Single Initiator, Single Target or a Single Initiator, Multiple Target zoning scheme. Check with your storage vendor for their best practices in a VMware environment and discuss them with your storage administrator. Zoning is implemented at the Fibre Channel switch level.

Note

> Zoning is a security issue and a practical matter that must be implemented to make Fibre Channel work properly and thus was covered in both the "Planning" and "Implementation and Management" sections of this chapter.

LUN Masking

LUN masking is the process of associating certain LUNs with a specific server or group of servers and is used in most Fibre Channel, iSCSI, and FCoE environments on the storage array itself. LUN masking can also be achieved at the host level using the MASK_PATH plugin (described in the troubleshooting section), but we *never* recommend its use unless there are no other alternatives. It can be difficult to troubleshoot why a LUN does not appear when the storage admin says the LUN is properly assigned. Due to most, if not all, LUN masking taking place on the storage array and the variety of ways that this can be accomplished, we will not discuss this further here, but rather refer you to your SAN administrator. The only cautionary point we'd suggest you pass on to your SAN administrator is that vSphere strongly prefers the same host LUN number on each node that will share access to the same LUN.

CHAP (iSCSI)

CHAP (the Challenge Handshake Authentication Protocol) is the lowest level of security that a target or initiator must support to state that they support iSCSI. VMware supports CHAP, though many administrators choose not to implement it, especially if the storage devices and iSCSI initiators are located on a dedicated, isolated network. If CHAP is desired in the network, you will need to work with your SAN administrator to make sure it is set up the same on the array as it is on your hosts. In this section, we'll review the available options and the configuration details for each.

Options

vSphere 5 supports CHAP for all types of iSCSI initiators, though the support depends on the type of adapter, per Table 8.7.

What do the CHAP options mean? We'll get to unidirectional versus bidirectional and per-target CHAP in just a little bit. First, let's understand the other options; refer to Table 8.8 below for a brief description of each option.

There are a few more important concepts that need to be considered when implementing CHAP. First, it does not encrypt any data; just the handshake process (basically a simple form of identity confirmation) is protected so as to not be in plain text. Second, CHAP uses something called a "CHAP secret" that must be the same on both sides to work. The secret is basically a password that both sides know in advance, so when the password is put through the algorithm and sent to the other side and the same calculation done, they will match. This implies that both sides

Table 8.7 CHAP Options Available By iSCSI Adapter Type

CHAP Option	Software iSCSI	Dependent Hardware iSCSI	Independent Hardware iSCSI
Do not use CHAP	X	X	X
Do not use CHAP unless required by target	X	X	
Use CHAP unless prohibited by target	X	X	X
Use CHAP	X	X	
Unidirectional	X	X	X
Bidirectional (Requires Use CHAP)	X	X	
Per-target CHAP	X	X	

Table 8.8 CHAP Option Descriptions

CHAP Option	Description
Do not use CHAP	CHAP will not be used; if currently enabled, it will be disabled, though any existing connections will remain active until the host is rebooted, the sessions are terminated via the command line, or the storage array forces a logout.
Do not use CHAP unless required by target	CHAP will be used only if the target (array) requires it, but otherwise will not.*
Use CHAP unless prohibited by target	CHAP will always be used unless the target refuses.*
Use CHAP	CHAP will always be used; if the target won't or can't, the LUN will not be accessible to vSphere.

*Note that in these two scenarios, the result of "unless required" or "unless prohibited" can vary based on the storage vendor's implementation of the protocol and the outcome may not be what was expected. Check with the vendor for expected behavior.

have been configured with the same CHAP secret. The CHAP name is technically limited to 511 characters, and the secret is limited to 255 characters, though some vendors may have smaller maximums. In practice, this is rarely an issue as no one wants to type perfectly several hundred characters on the array and each host.

vSphere 4 and 5 support unidirectional and bidirectional CHAP and allow for individual settings per iSCSI target as well as per initiator. Let's look at these options.

Unidirectional

In unidirectional CHAP, the target (array) authenticates the initiator (ESXi host) only. If CHAP is used, this tends to be the most common configuration. To configure CHAP at the initiator level (which is the most common approach), do the following:

1. Select the host on which you want to configure CHAP.
2. Go to Configuration > Storage Adapters.
3. Select the HBA to be configured and click the Properties link (in the Details pane).
4. Click the CHAP button.
5. In the Select Option drop-down list, select from the options described Table 8.8.
6. For all options except "Do not use CHAP," specify the CHAP secret in the text box and then either:
   a. Check the "Use initiator name" to set the CHAP name equal to the initiator name.
   b. Type the CHAP name that is used on the target (they must match).
7. Click OK and close out of any open dialog boxes.

Bidirectional

In bidirectional CHAP, the target (array) authenticates the initiator (ESXi host) and the initiator (host) authenticates the target (array) so that both sides have some degree of confidence that they are talking to the intended host or array. The configuration is similar to unidirectional, except there are two different CHAP configurations in the dialog box; the process is as follows:

1. Select the host on which you want to configure CHAP.
2. Go to Configuration > Storage Adapters.
3. Select the HBA to be configured and click the Properties link (in the Details pane).
4. Click the CHAP button.
5. In the Select Option drop-down list, select Use CHAP.

6. Specify the CHAP secret in the text box and then either:
   a. Check the "Use initiator name" to set the CHAP name equal to the initiator name.
   b. Type the CHAP name that is used on the target (they must match).

7. In the Mutual CHAP (bottom portion) of the dialog box, select Use CHAP and then repeat Step 6 in the Mutual CHAP text boxes for CHAP name and secret.

8. Click OK and close out of any open dialog boxes.

Per-Target

vSphere 4 and 5 support per-target CHAP where different secrets can be used for each target if desired. This is a little more secure, but requires more configuration. To configure this, do the following:

1. Select the host on which you want to configure CHAP.

2. Go to Configuration > Storage Adapters.

3. Select the HBA to be configured and click the Properties link (in the Details pane).

4. Select the desired target on either the Dynamic Discovery or Static Discovery tabs.

5. Click the Settings button.

6. Click the CHAP button.

7. Uncheck the Inherit from Parent checkbox in the CHAP and/or Mutual CHAP sections of the dialog box and fill in the details below for that section or both sections.

8. In the Select Option drop-down list in the CHAP section of the dialog box, make a selection from the options described in Table 8.8 (if you want to use Mutual CHAP, you must select Use CHAP).

9. For all options except "Do not use CHAP," specify the CHAP secret in the text box and then either:
   a. Check the "Use initiator name" to set the CHAP name equal to the initiator name.
   b. Type the CHAP name that is used on the target (they must match).

10. If bidirectional CHAP is desired, in the Mutual CHAP (bottom portion) of the dialog box, select Use CHAP and then repeat Step 9 in the Mutual CHAP text boxes for CHAP name and secret.

11. Click OK and close out of any open dialog boxes.

NFS IP Security

There are a few security issues relative to using NFS with vSphere. The first is that VMware does not support any form of encryption between the NFS device and the ESXi server, so all data transferred is in plain text. All of the company's IP (Intellectual Property) that is stored in VMs on NFS is thus vulnerable during network I/O. Second, the vSphere server accesses the NFS shares using root as the user name; this must be enabled on the NFS server. Using root to access NFS shares is generally not a good security practice, but this is how vSphere is configured. To minimize both of these threats and to maximize performance, a dedicated switch (or at least VLAN) just for NFS traffic is recommended.

Datastore Permissions

Proper permissions are required to access and configure storage and datastores. Permissions were described in Chapter 6 and will not be discussed in depth here other than to verify they are set correctly. The documentation lists the specific privilege(s) required to complete any given task.

TROUBLESHOOTING

That brings us to the final portion of the chapter—troubleshooting. Hopefully you have taken careful note of the procedures, tips, and notes listed in this chapter and read and planned your storage environment, as this will minimize issues. However, issues will still arise. We'll look at one of the bigger issues related to storage—performance—as well as why LUNs may be missing.

Performance Issues

One of the biggest common complaints in vSphere is poor performance. This is typically caused by poor planning (or no planning at all). Nowhere is this more prevalent than in storage. People often assume that RAID 5 is the best because it is the cheapest, or that the biggest, slowest drives (usually the cheapest per gigabyte) should be used. In fact, if performance is the primary characteristic considered, RAID 10 on fast 15K SAS or Fibre Channel (or better yet SSD) drives should be considered. But how do you know if storage performance is "good enough"? We'll cover latency and bandwidth and throughput issues first.

We'll cover performance monitoring in Chapter 10, but for our purposes in this section, we want to point out some parameters that should be monitored and threshold values that if exceeded may indicate performance issues.

How to Check Latency

The Overview and Advanced buttons are found on the Performance tab for hosts and VMs. On the Overview screen, look at Disk (ms) for the Highest Latency statistic. That value should be as low as possible, ideally never crossing 20 ms, and certainly not be above 50 ms. Remember that this is the maximum latency seen during the reporting period on the graph. If the value seems high, go to the Advanced button and select Disk from the Switch to drop-down menu. Click Chart Options and look at the following values:

- **Physical device read latency.** Average latency per read (time from when the I/O leaves the HBA until the response is received).

- **Physical device write latency.** Average latency per write (time from when the I/O leaves the HBA until the response is received).

- **Physical device command latency.** Average of the physical device read and write latency values divided by the I/Os observed. This value should be < 20 ms (and ideally < 15ms to allow time for the other components to add a little latency and still ensure that the total latency to the client is < 20 ms).

- **Kernel read latency.** Average amount of time spent in the VMkernel processing through the I/O stack layers and waiting in a queue to be processed by an HBA for a read. Typically < 2 ms.

- **Kernel write latency.** Average amount of time spent in the VMkernel processing through the I/O stack layers and waiting in a queue to be processed by an HBA for a write. Typically < 2 ms.

- **Kernel command latency.** Average of the read and write kernel latency values divided by the I/Os observed. This value should be < 2 ms.

How to Check Bandwidth and Throughput

Before we start checking bandwidth (a measure of the amount moved per unit time, usually measured in KB per second or MB per second) or throughput (the number of I/Os per unit time, usually expressed as IOPS [I/O Operations Per Second]), we should discuss what to expect from a typical drive (note that Table 8.9 assumes 4–8 KB I/Os; if the values are smaller, you can get more IOPS but less bandwidth, and if larger you will get more bandwidth but fewer IOPS—they are inversely proportional).

Note that for the best possible bandwidth, sequential reads or writes are required. Any randomization adds seek time to the drive heads, and seek time is wasted time.

Table 8.9 Typical Bandwidth and Throughput Values by Drive Type

Drive Speed and Type	Bandwidth (MB/s)	Throughput (IOPS)
5400 RPM SATA	6–7	50
7200 RPM SATA	7–8	60–80
10K RPM SAS/Fibre Channel	10	130
15K RPM SAS/Fibre Channel	12	180
SSD	Varies	6,000+

On the Performance tab for hosts and VMs, click the Overview button. Find the Disk (KBps) for the Usage statistic, which will give you an indication of bandwidth. That value should be as high as possible. Compare values to Table 8.9 for a rough idea of your performance (per spindle) versus industry averages. Obviously the value will increase with more spindles on the storage side and potentially decrease as additional datastores are created on the same physical spindles, depending on the load of each datastore. For more detailed information, click the Advanced button and select Disk from the Switch to drop-down menu. Click Chart Options and look at the following values:

- Bandwidth:
  - Read rate: Average amount of I/O read (in KBps).
  - Write rate: Average amount of I/O written (in KBps).
  - Usage: Summation of Read and Write rate values.

- Throughput:
  - Average read requests per second: Average number of reads per second.
  - Average write requests per second: Average number of writes per second.
  - Average commands issued per second: Sum of the average reads and writes per second.

For a high-level overview, the usage and average commands values are sufficient; to make more informed changes to your environment, you'll need to know the read: write ratio, which is also reported in the above statistics.

A detailed performance analysis and recommendations are beyond the scope of this book, but there are many great articles that cover these topics.

Path Thrashing

Another possible reason you may be getting less performance than you expect is what is known as path thrashing. Path thrashing happens as the system selects different paths (often through different storage processors on the array) causing the backend storage array to move the LUN between storage processors so that it is where the server is looking for it. This happens most often on active-passive arrays and on mis-configured (or malfunctioning) ALUA arrays. These issues can't be truly diagnosed using vSphere tools alone—you'll need to work with your SAN administrator if you suspect problems to determine what the underlying cause is and to determine the best corrective action to take.

NFS Optimizations

If you are going to use NFS as your primary datastore type, you may want to use multiple datastores for better aggregate bandwidth (see the planning section for details on this in the VMFS versus NFS section). There are a couple of parameters that may need to be adjusted for best performance. They can be set in the vSphere Client by selecting your host (and this is done on a host-by-host basis, so you'll need to do this for all of your current and future hosts, or consider using Host Profiles to automate this process; Host Profiles are covered in Chapter 13) and selecting the Configuration tab. Under Software, select the Advanced Settings link. From there select the following:

- *NFS* to select the NFS-related parameters, then select:
  - *NFS.MaxVolumes*: Specifies the maximum number of NFS volumes that may be mounted to this host. The default is (and always has been) 8, but may be set to 32 (ESX 3.x), 64 (4.x), or 256 (5). More volumes means more TCP sessions and that can provide better aggregate throughput.

- *Net* to set networking-related parameters. The values recommended here are good general values and are usually not very high considering the amount of RAM in a typical server, but if you are very tight on RAM and/or don't use many NFS volumes, you may leave these values at their defaults. Note that changing either of the values requires a reboot of the ESXi server to take effect.
  - *Net.tcpipHeapSize*: The initial (minimum) size of the heap (in MB) used for all networking I/O (including NFS traffic). The default is 0, meaning allocate on demand, but large NFS vendors typically suggest setting this value to 30 (32 is the maximum).

- **_Net.tcpipHeapMax_**: The maximum size of the heap (just discussed; in MB), with a default (in V 5) of 64MB, and a range of 32–128. Many NFS vendors recommend that this value be set to 120. Remember that this is a maximum, so it will not grow above the size parameter just described unless there is a need for it.

Can't See Your LUN? (Zone/Masking)

If an LUN is not visible that you think should be, consult with your SAN administrator and verify that the zoning and masking have been configured properly (as discussed previously). If those check out properly, the LUN may have been masked out at the host level. The only way to determine if this is the actual issue is to run a series of command line commands and then another sequence if the LUN has indeed been masked. We've found this to be fairly rare (or nonexistent if you listened to our earlier recommendations) so we won't discuss this here but rather will refer you to the following sections of the vSphere 5 storage guide:

- List Multipathing Claim Rules for the Host
- Mask Paths
- Unmask Paths

SUMMARY

Wow! Who knew that there was so much to storage? Unfortunately, most vSphere administrators don't know or understand storage well and this causes issues throughout the environment. Now that you do have a better grasp on them, however, we're ready to move on to the next section and discuss virtual machines.

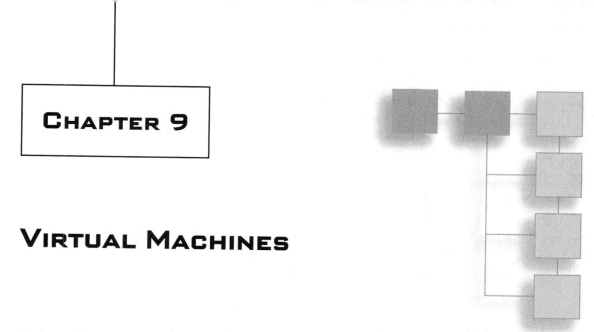

CHAPTER 9

VIRTUAL MACHINES

We've talked about Virtual Machines (VMs) throughout this book, but we haven't really discussed what they are or even what they can do for us. Much like a physical computer, a virtual machine can be customized with different hardware and software. You can add memory, CPUs, hard drives, network cards, and even sound cards. You install your operating system, applications, and even control the VM like a normal server. But, here is where the similarities come to an end. With a VM, we can not only control all of these things, but we can control how the VM is permitted to use its virtual hardware. We can take point-in-time snapshots of the VM, allowing us to undo major changes to the VM's software. And, we can create image files of our VMs for disaster recovery purposes. VMs are very versatile, and in some cases rival the abilities of physical machines.

In this chapter we'll explore the do's and don'ts of virtual machines, dig a little deeper into how they function, and finally wrap things up with the details of editing a VM's configuration files manually (something you hopefully never have to do, but it will serve as a great reference just in case).

PLANNING

It is deceptively easy to create and run a VM, but deep down you know there must be more to it than right-clicking and choosing "Create New Virtual Machine." There is, and by following some of the advice we've included in this chapter you'll soon see just how powerful a VM can become. Plus, we're going to introduce some resource management concepts that will help you in the next chapter when we dig into performance optimization.

What Is a VM?

VMs are virtual, not magical (though some would argue that at times). VMs are the end product of turning hardware into software, and then allowing multiple instances of the software to run on a single physical machine. There are many facets to a VM, but first we need to explain what a VM is before we can tell you how to use it properly.

What Does a VM Look Like?

There are two ways to look at a VM: one is from the end-user's perspective; the other is from the hypervisor's perspective. Users of VMs often do not even realize that they are connected to a VM, nor do they care. The VM functions just like any other server they use, and as long as it remains available the end user neither experiences a difference nor expresses concern about virtualization. To further this thought, if you connect to a file server that happens to be a VM, you won't see a difference in your mapped drive or in your data. If you want to know whether the machine is virtual or physical, you really need to connect to the server's console and look at its hardware. VMs don't advertise they are virtual any more than a physical box advertises that it is physical. If you want to know whether a server is a VM or a physical machine, you must look a bit deeper.

The key to the difference lies in the drivers. For example, when you look in Device Manager on a virtualized Windows machine, most of the hardware looks very familiar. There are devices that look like Intel chipsets or LSILogic SCSI cards, and there are generic devices like the CPU and system resources. But, if you look a little closer, you will also find devices such as VMware Hard Drive or VMXNet, which you won't find on a physical server. In addition, you'll often find a service running on the VM with the name "VMware Tools." These special drivers and the service you found are actually part of the virtualization process. In particular, this software is what allows the operating system to use the virtual hardware that the VMware hypervisor (VMkernel) presents to the VM.

Where Do VMs Reside?

To properly explain this, we have to go back and explain how a VM appears to the hypervisor. The ESXi hypervisor manages each VM as something known as a "world." We'll cover the concept of "worlds" in depth later in the Troubleshooting section of this chapter, but what you need to understand now is that each world is composed of processes and memory consumed by the VM. These processes represent a number of things, but most importantly they represent the virtual processors in your VM. So, the more vCPUs you assign to a VM, the more processes the VM's world will possess. The memory is, as you may have guessed, the RAM assigned to your VM. The more you grant to your VM, the larger the pool of RAM will be that the hypervisor assigns to the VM's world.

However, a VM is much more than just processes and memory. There are also disk and network resources to consider. In Chapter 7 we discussed how virtual networking operates, and in Chapter 8 we discussed how the disk subsystems function. You learned that VMs are not required to have network cards, but many do. The same thing is true for hard disks. VMs aren't required to have a hard drive; you might choose to make your VM boot from CD-ROM or from the network. But, regardless of whether your VM has a hard disk, the VM will still use disk resources for a variety of purposes. The hypervisor uses files for things that need storage, such as the configuration of the VM, the contents of any hard drives, and the VMkernel swap file (you'll learn about this file in the next chapter).

As you might guess, each file has a specific purpose, and when it comes to troubleshooting you would do well to memorize them. All of these files are collected together and stored in folders in datastores either on local or shared storage. For a refresher on datastores, refer to Chapter 8. Table 9.1 lists some of the files that a VM might possess. In this list you can substitute [vmname] for the name of your VM.

Table 9.1 Virtual Machine Files

File Type	File Purpose	Text-based
[vmname].vmx	The VM's Configuration file.	Yes
[vmname].vmdk	The disk metadata file(s) for the VM.	Yes
[vmname]-flat.vmdk	The binary content of the disk file(s).	No
[vmname].nvram	The non-volatile RAM configuration.	No
vmware.log	The most recent startup log file for the VM.	Yes
vmware-#.log	Incrementally older startup logs for the VM (by default, 6 are kept).	Yes
[vmname]-######.vmdk	The metadata files for each disk in a snapshot.	Yes
[vmname]-######-delta.vmdk	The binary content of the disks in a snapshot.	No

As you can see, a VM is a collection of files, but it is a finite list of files. For example, the VM's hard drives are represented by binary files called VMDK files. They are very similar to the binary files that you might get if you created a disk-image of a physical computer's hard drive. Having a guest VM's hard drive represented by a single, large file makes the VM much more portable and doesn't represent a significant performance difference from accessing a hard disk directly.

Each hard drive is composed of two files: the actual binary data file and a metadata descriptor file. The descriptor is a very small text file that defines the geometry of the virtual disk as well as indicating to the hypervisor where to find the binary data file. The binary data files end with the extension "-flat.vmdk," whereas the metadata descriptor file just ends in ".vmdk." The "-flat" term signifies that this file is a large binary data file that should not be edited or directly opened.

As we said earlier, a VM is composed of many different pieces of virtual hardware, so there must be a file that lists all of this configuration data. That file ends with the extension ".vmx," and it happens to be human readable. Inside, it contains value pairs much like an .ini or .conf file. These values control the behavior of the VM, and the file can be edited as you will see in the Troubleshooting section of this chapter.

Just as a physical machine has a BIOS or CMOS pre-boot setup menu, a VM must also maintain some sort of system configuration data. In a physical server this configuration data is stored in non-volatile RAM (NVRAM) in a dedicated chip on the system board. Non-volatile RAM retains its data when the power to the server is removed (intentionally or by accident), as opposed to normal RAM that is reset when the server loses power. Typically, NVRAM is kept intact with a small amount of power from a battery installed on the server's system board. Because a VM doesn't have physical chips or system boards, that system configuration data must be stored in a file. The hypervisor handles this by creating a file aptly named with the extension ".nvram." This file isn't human readable, and shouldn't be edited or deleted. If you delete this file, the VM will behave as though someone reset its CMOS configuration back to factory defaults, or as if its NVRAM battery died.

During the startup of each VM, the hypervisor creates and rotates text-based log files that may be useful during troubleshooting. The log files rotate every time the VM is powered on. By default, six (6) log files are kept, the newest being the one named "vmware.log," the oldest being the log with the highest number. These files contain any and all event information pertaining to the power-on and subsequent operation of the virtual hardware. In a sense, you can think of these files as your VM's system event log, much like you would get from one of the newer servers with an Intelligent Platform Management Interface (IPMI) remote server management board.

What Is Virtual Hardware?

Virtual hardware is software. Specifically, it is software that is emulating the behavior of physical hardware devices such as network cards, system boards, SCSI cards, and more. VMware can do this because physical hardware is already largely composed of software embedded into chips. If you think about it, a physical PCI card isn't just a collection of copper and silicon; it consists of software/firmware embedded into chips, which performs specific actions. We can duplicate that behavior in a pure software environment, and therefore present the look, feel, and behavior of hardware to a guest operating system running within a virtual machine.

Does that mean our physical ESXi hosts must match the hardware in our VMs? Not at all. The physical hardware has little to do with the virtual hardware installed in your guest VM. The ESXi hypervisor is a resource abstraction layer that insulates the VM from the physical hardware in the host server. That means we can use any physical network adapter on VMware's Hardware Compatibility List (HCL), and the hypervisor will translate our virtual hardware requests into physical commands. The guest and host can in fact have very different hardware.

All VMs have virtual hardware, but you can define the specific complement of hardware per VM by editing the VM's settings. For instance, you might wish to add an extra network card, or perhaps you would like to change the type of SCSI adapter. You are the administrator; therefore, you get to choose what hardware exists in your VM. Now, that being said, there are restrictions. You must choose hardware from the list provided by VMware, and this list doesn't include every piece of hardware known to man.

Instead, VMware has created several pieces of virtual hardware to emulate the behavior of the more common physical hardware devices. For example, you may add an Intel-based e1000 network card, but you won't find an option to add a 3Com card because VMware didn't write a virtual device that behaves like a 3Com NIC.

Why no 3Com adapters? Because the majority of guest operating systems have a built-in driver for one of the other provided emulated adapters. In cases where the guest operating system doesn't provide native support for the e1000 adapter, VMware also provides a legacy 10/100Mbps adapter that emulates an AMD PCNet32 NIC (the "Flexible" adapter) as well as a more advanced e1000e adapter that emulates a PCIe Intel 82574L card.

Paravirtual Adapters

Virtual hardware isn't just about emulation. In addition to the emulation of physical devices, VMware also wrote their own paravirtualized virtual adapters. These adapters aren't based on any physical hardware equivalent, so they don't have the same limitations as the emulated devices. The paravirtual devices can actually perform better because they are software applications running in the hypervisor and they are aware of and interact with the hypervisor. In comparison, the emulated devices run as applications in the hypervisor, but do not communicate or adjust their behavior based on feedback from the hypervisor. That means that when the ESXi host becomes very busy, the paravirtual adapters can actually modify their operation to speed up or slow down to allow the guest VM to take advantage of the ESXi hosts conditions. The emulated devices can't do this because they have to mimic the behavior of physical cards, which have no awareness of hypervisors and assume that they have full access to the underlying hardware resources.

That's a lot to digest, but the short version is that the paravirtualized adapters that VMware provides, such as VMXNET, VMXNET 2, VMXNET 3, and the SCSI Paravirtual adapters, perform better when the host is under load. Table 9.2 shows the various network adapters we can add to the VMs.

Note

Use the VMXNET 3 network adapter whenever possible because it offers much better performance and functionality than any of the other virtual hardware options (emulated or paravirtual).

Table 9.2　Virtual Network Adapters

Adapter Name	Emulated/ Paravirtual	Hardware Version Required	Notes
Flexible	Emulated	4	Emulates the AMD 79C970 PCnet32 (10Mbps)
e1000	Emulated	7	Emulates the Intel 82545EM (PCI-x)
e1000e	Emulated	8	Emulates the Intel 82574L (PCI-e)
VMXNET	Paravirtual	3	VMware's original paravirtual NIC
VMXNET 2 (Enhanced)	Paravirtual	4	Expanded the VMXNET adapter's functionality
VMXNET 3	Paravirtual	7	VMware's best performing network adapter

Note

For more up-to-date information, refer to VMware's Knowledge Base article number 1001805. This article explains the use cases and functionality of each network adapter type.

So why does VMware provide so many different makes/models of SCSI and network cards? For one thing, guest operating systems typically do not include any native driver support for VMware's paravirtual VMXNET adapters, so if you want network connectivity before you install the VMware Tools, you'll need to use the emulated devices. VMware has to provide several models of emulated network adapters because some of the older guest operating systems do not support the newer cards, and vice versa. You need to match your guest operating systems with an appropriate adapter, but remember: the emulated adapters are there as a stopgap measure during the initial installation process. You should replace them with the VMXNET adapters once the VMware Tools have been installed in your guest operating system.

Supported Guest OSs

That brings us to the guest operating systems discussion. VMware endeavors to support every major x86 operating system on the market. This can be seen in Table 9.3. This is the list of officially supported guest operating systems with vSphere 5, but

Table 9.3 Supported Guest Operating Systems

Microsoft Platforms	Linux Platforms	Other Platforms
Microsoft Windows 8 Server (64-bit)	Red Hat Enterprise Linux 6 (64-bit)	Apple Mac OS X 10.7 (64-bit)
Microsoft Windows Server 2008 R2 (64-bit)	Red Hat Enterprise Linux 6 (32-bit)	Apple Mac OS X 10.7 (32-bit)
Microsoft Windows Server 2008 (64-bit)	Red Hat Enterprise Linux 5 (64-bit)	Apple Mac OS X 10.6 (64-bit)
Microsoft Windows Server 2008 (32-bit)	Red Hat Enterprise Linux 5 (32-bit)	Apple Mac OS X 10.6 (32-bit)
Microsoft Windows Server 2003 (64-bit)	Red Hat Enterprise Linux 4 (64-bit)	Apple Mac OS X 10.5 (64-bit)
Microsoft Windows Server 2003 (32-bit)	Red Hat Enterprise Linux 4 (32-bit)	Apple Mac OS X 10.5 (32-bit)
Microsoft Windows Server 2003 Datacenter (64-bit)	Red Hat Enterprise Linux 3 (64-bit)	FreeBSD (64-bit)

(Continued)

Table 9.3 Supported Guest Operating Systems (*Continued*)

Microsoft Platforms	Linux Platforms	Other Platforms
Microsoft Windows Server 2003 Datacenter (32-bit)	Red Hat Enterprise Linux 3 (32-bit)	FreeBSD (32-bit)
Microsoft Windows Server 2003 Standard (64-bit)	Red Hat Enterprise Linux 2.1	IBM OS/2
Microsoft Windows Server 2003 Standard (32-bit)	Novell SUSE Linux Enterprise 11 (64-bit)	Novell NetWare 6.x
Microsoft Windows Server 2003 Web Edition (32-bit)	Novell SUSE Linux Enterprise 11 (32-bit)	Novell NetWare 5.1
Microsoft Windows Small Business Server 2003	Novell SUSE Linux Enterprise 10 (64-bit)	Oracle Solaris 11 (64-bit)
Microsoft Windows 8 (64-bit)	Novell SUSE Linux Enterprise 10 (32-bit)	Oracle Solaris 10 (64-bit)
Microsoft Windows 8 (32-bit)	Novell SUSE Linux Enterprise 8/9 (64-bit)	Oracle Solaris 10 (32-bit)
Microsoft Windows 7 (64-bit)	Novell SUSE Linux Enterprise 8/9 (32-bit)	Sun Microsystems Solaris 9 (experimental)
Microsoft Windows 7 (32-bit)	CentOS 4/5/6 (64-bit)	Sun Microsystems Solaris 8 (experimental)
Microsoft Windows Vista (64-bit)	CentOS 4/5/6 (32-bit)	SCO OpenServer 6
Microsoft Windows Vista (32-bit)	Debian GNU/Linux 6 (64-bit)	SCO OpenServer 5
Microsoft Windows XP Professional (64-bit)	Debian GNU/Linux 6 (32-bit)	SCO UnixWare 7
Microsoft Windows XP Professional (32-bit)	Debian GNU/Linux 5 (64-bit)	Serenity Systems eComStation 2
Microsoft Windows 2000	Debian GNU/Linux 5 (32-bit)	Serenity Systems eComStation 1
Microsoft Windows 2000 Server	Debian GNU/Linux 4 (64-bit)	Other (64-bit)

(Continued)

Table 9.3 Supported Guest Operating Systems (*Continued*)

Microsoft Platforms	Linux Platforms	Other Platforms
Microsoft Windows 2000 Professional	Debian GNU/Linux 4 (32-bit)	Other (32-bit)
Microsoft Windows NT 4.0	Asianux 4 (64-bit)	VMware ESXi 5.x
Microsoft Windows Me	Asianux 4 (32-bit)	VMware ESX 4.x
Microsoft Windows 98	Asianux 3 (64-bit)	
Microsoft Windows 95	Asianux 3 (32-bit)	
Microsoft Windows 3.1	Novel Open Enterprise Server	
Microsoft MS-DOS	Oracle Linux 4/5/6 (64-bit)	
	Oracle Linux 4/5/6 (32-bit)	
	Ubuntu Linux (64-bit)	
	Ubuntu Linux (32-bit)	
	Other 2.6.x Linux (64-bit)	
	Other 2.6.x Linux (32-bit)	
	Other 2.4.x Linux (64-bit)	
	Other 2.4.x Linux (32-bit)	
	Other Linux (64-bit)	
	Other Linux (32-bit)	

note the category of "Other 32-bit" and "Other 64-bit." That means you can give pretty much any ×86–×64 operating system a try, but if it doesn't work you can't blame VMware.

We'd also like to point out that even though you see an operating system listed, that doesn't mean it will magically be installed when you select it in the vSphere Client. You still have to install the operating system yourself, and you still have to license the software appropriately. We'll cover how to start the installation process in the Implementation and Management section of this chapter.

Caution

Don't forget to license your guest operating systems and applications! Also, check with your vendor(s) to see if they have special rules pertaining to the use of their software in a virtualized environment.

Just How Large Can You Make a VM?

If you ever want to know just how large (or small) your VM can be, check VMware's website for a document called "Configuration Maximums." This document shows the largest (or smallest) configuration settings possible within the ESXi hypervisor, and serves as the standard for VM "speed limits." The document is updated every time VMware releases a new version of vSphere. This includes updates and service packs, so it's worthy of your time to download this document before applying any major updates/upgrades. The changes just might surprise you.

Table 9.4 is a sampling of the Configuration Maximums document as it pertains to VMs running on the initial release of vSphere 5. Keep in mind that these figures can change with every release of vSphere (including service packs), and they always assume you have the most expensive license level available (Enterprise Plus in this release).

Changes to VMs in vSphere 5

We won't dig into all the details in this little section, but we wanted to provide a synopsis of what changed as far as VMs are concerned in the latest edition of

Table 9.4 VM Configuration Maximums

Virtual Machine Attribute	Maximum Value
Virtual CPUs (vCPUs) per VM	32
RAM per VM	1TB
Virtual Network adapters per VM	10
Virtual SCSI adapters per VM	4
Virtual SCSI targets per VM	60
Virtual Disk Size (VMDK)	2TB minus 512 bytes
Virtual Disk Size (RDM—virtual compatibility mode)	2TB minus 512 bytes
Virtual Disk Size (RDM—physical compatibility mode)	64TB

vSphere. This can be a handy chart for you to cross-reference as you're reading this and other chapters. This is by no means an exhaustive list, but it gives you an idea of the major functionality changes in VM Hardware Version 8.

- Increased the maximum number of vCPUs per VM to 32 (it was 8).

- Increased the maximum amount of RAM to 1TB (it was 255GB).

- Introduced support for High Definition audio, 3D Video graphics, and multi-monitor support for VMs.

- Introduced booting the VM from EFI as an alternative to the BIOS boot method.

- Introduced support for Mac OS X Server on supported Apple hardware.

- Virtual CPUs can now be carved up into virtual sockets and cores for the VM.

- Expanded VM hardware support, including client-connected USB devices, smart card readers, and USB 3.0 devices.

- Introduced VMDirect Path I/O version 2 for expanded direct hardware access from within a VM.

How Do We Get VMs?

So you want a VM, but you don't understand how to get it. Well, there are a number of ways to get VMs; some methods are easier than others. We're going to discuss each method in detail later in the Implementation and Management section of this chapter, but from an overview perspective, here are your options:

- Create a new VM from scratch (via wizard).

- Create a clone of an existing VM.

- Deploy a VM from a template.

- Import a VM from an .OVF file.

- Convert a physical server to a VM (commonly referred to as "P2V").

- Convert an existing VM to a different VM format (referred to as "V2V").

- Manually import a VM from another ESXi server (using VMX files).

As you can see, there is no shortage of means to procure VMs. In fact, the number of these possibilities is one of the major advantages to virtualization: versatility.

Standardization and Change Control

With the relative ease of VM deployment comes great responsibility. In practice we've learned that the ease of VM deployment brings with it anything but great responsibility. If you shortchange your planning meetings, you'll spend that time and more in the management of your environment. For example, if you give your helpdesk the ability to deploy VMs, but don't explain how the VMs should be named, you'll end up with an administrative nightmare. Likewise, if you don't explain proper change management procedures, your future troubleshooting time goes from minutes to days because you will have to play detective while you're playing IT Administrator.

The key to avoiding all of this trouble is to establish naming conventions and standards for everything. If you have multiple datastores, you need a document that explains what each datastore can be used for. If you have multiple clusters, you must explain the function of each cluster. Documentation isn't just about recording what exists; it is also a guide for operations.

Another avenue is the changes that occur from one server deployment to the next. In a physical environment this is quite common because each server must be loaded individually. In a virtual environment we have an advantage; we can create templates. You'll learn more about templates in an upcoming section, but templates allow us to deploy VMs from a standard image. This ensures that each VM is created using the same configuration settings because they are essentially copies of one another.

Finally, you can set up alerts to notify you if someone creates a VM. Why? What if you are responsible for licensing? If you receive an e-mail whenever someone creates a VM you can create a spreadsheet to use when you true up your license agreements. You might consider coupling this alert with one that detects VM deletions though. That way you can eliminate temporary VM creations from your list.

As a recap, here are a few things you can do to reduce your future headaches:

- Create a standard for VM and host names.
- Track and log IP addresses as they are used.
- Create templates from VMs to ensure consistent initial configurations.
- Configure alerts when people create/delete VMs.

What Does Building a VM Entail?

If you don't have a VM and you want one, you can either download it from someone else, or you can create your own. Creating your own is easy, but you need some software and a bit of time. Though it is definitely a more involved approach, it's a great way to start your virtualization project because you gain maximum control over how each VM is constructed. Plus, copying off someone else is cheating, right? Let's do it the hard way first, and then we'll get into the shortcuts.

We're going to go through the planning elements of creating a VM. In this section we'll cover:

- Virtual hardware versions
- 32-bit versus 64-bit
- VM file location
- Adapter types and paravirtualization
- Audio/visual aspects
- VMkernel swap space
- vNUMA
- Installing your guest operating system
- VMware Tools
- Installing third-party applications
- Start order (vApps)
- Security permissions

Virtual Hardware Versions

You'll recall from earlier in this chapter that all VMs have virtual hardware. This hardware represents all the features that the hypervisor can provide to a particular VM. Over the years the ESXi Hypervisor has increased in capabilities and complexities, and the virtual hardware presented to the VMs has also changed accordingly. For example, early versions of the virtual hardware didn't support things such as VM DirectPath I/O or the newer paravirtualized SCSI adapters. These were features added when vSphere 4 was released (Virtual Hardware version 7). The latest version, Hardware version 8, includes things such as the EFI boot firmware and VM Direct-Path I/O with vMotion.

The version numbers are listed in Table 9.5, along with the hypervisor support for each.

When you create a VM you must tell the wizard which hardware version you want to use. This is a lot like picking the model of the server you want to buy in the store.

Table 9.5 VM Hardware Versions

Version	Initial Support	Functionality in vSphere 5
3	ESX 2.x	Run only (may be upgraded to virtual hardware 8)
4	ESX 3.x	Edit and Run
7	vSphere 4.x	Create, Edit, and Run
8	vSphere 5.x	Create, Edit, and Run

The later the model number, the more features you will receive. Also, like models of servers, some of the older hardware just won't work with the newer software. As you can see in Table 9.5, the older versions of the virtual hardware are able to run on vSphere 5, but the hypervisor can't create new VMs using the old versions.

If your environment is brand new, or if you've upgraded all your ESXi hosts to vSphere 5, you should choose Virtual Hardware version 8 because it will give you all the latest VM functionality and it has much higher resource limits than the previous versions. If, however, you still have vSphere 4.× hosts in your environment, you may wish to create a version 7 VM. A VM created with version 7 hardware may not have all the functionality available in vSphere 5, but that VM will be able to execute on your vSphere 4 hosts. VMs created with hardware version 8 (the latest version) will not run on previous versions of vSphere.

Caution

Be careful when selecting your VM's hardware version. Only ESXi 5.0 hosts or later can power on VMs with hardware version 8. If you have legacy vSphere 4 hosts, create your VM with hardware version 7.

32-bit versus 64-bit OS

Your next major decision is actually linked to your choice of operating system. You need to determine whether a 32-bit VM will suffice, or if you need to use a 64-bit VM. If your workload is light and won't require more than 4GB of RAM or 64-bit applications, you can choose a 32-bit Operating System. There is a bit more overhead involved in the hypervisor to handle 64-bit VMs, so there is still a valid use for 32-bit VMs.

Note

There is no direct option to change the VM's processors from 32-bit to 64-bit; that function is controlled indirectly by the hypervisor, and is based on the guest operating system you installed.

The hypervisor will present a 64-bit virtual CPU to a 64-bit guest and a 32-bit vCPU to a 32-bit guest. You can also change this selection by powering off the VM and editing its settings, as you'll see later in the Implementation and Management section of this chapter.

Caution

If you intend to use the new EFI firmware (instead of the BIOS firmware) for your VM, you should choose a 64-bit operating system, as many 32-bit operating systems do not support booting from EFI firmware.

VM File Location

As you create your VM, you'll be asked where you will keep the VM's files. This is an important decision because it doesn't just affect your organizational structure. The wizard is asking where you want to store all the configuration files, swap files, the hard disks of the VMs (VMDK files), and any Raw Device Mappings (RDMs). VMs can use a lot of space, but more importantly, they can use a lot of I/O bandwidth. Before you can choose an appropriate datastore, you really need to know two key pieces of information.

First, get some sense of the I/O bandwidth required for this VM. If it's a file server, application server, or database server it will use disk I/O. Your job is to monitor the performance on the existing server (if it's physical), or make an educated guess based on similar machines.

The second piece of information is the capacity and capabilities of each datastore. Keep in mind that it is possible to place two or more datastores on the same underlying disk array, so you must identify whether this datastore will share its performance with another datastore. You'll have to analyze the I/O requirements of your new VM, and then compare that information to the storage capabilities to determine where best to store the new VM.

For example, if you are creating a series of database servers, you may be tempted to group them all together because that would make the administration easier (or so you believe). The trouble is that a database server can be quite active and intense on the disk systems. Depending on the capabilities of your storage system and the demands of your applications, you may wish to break up the individual files onto separate datastores that are located on different disk arrays. It is typical of high-performance VMs to require dedicated sets of physical hard drives for I/O purposes.

Note

For a discussion on RDMs vs. VMDKs and their respective size limits, refer back to Chapter 8, " Storage."

Remember that you don't have to use an RDM to prevent other VMs from using a particular datastore. You can simply choose to only place one VM on a given datastore if you like. Now, if you have a lot of vSphere administrators in your organization, you might need to hold an all-staff meeting to explain this, but it can be done. If your co-workers listen as well as a three-year-old, you can even set up permissions on the various datastores to prevent the accidental misuse of the storage areas.

Adapter Types and Paravirtualization (SCSI/Network)

If you remember back again to our discussion about virtual hardware, we talked about something called paravirtualization. Paravirtualization means that the guest operating system is aware that it is virtualized. That knowledge can result in better performance for the guest when the host is under heavy use, or even when the guest just needs to utilize every ounce of performance it can get. The hypervisor and the guest can coordinate how resources are used and make more effective use of them.

The trouble is that to make an operating system aware that it's virtualized, we'd have to somehow modify its kernel and then enable the kernel to communicate directly with the ESXi hypervisor. In open-source projects such as Linux, modifying the kernel is possible; it's not easy, but it is possible. However, in cases such as Windows, Solaris, or even Mac OS X, we don't have the ability to easily modify the kernel of the operating system.

The solution is a sort of middle ground. While we can't easily modify the kernel of the guest operating system, we can install drivers into a guest that run with extremely high privileges. These drivers are written by VMware and have the ability to perform the necessary hypercalls to allow the paravirtualization to operate.

One of the choices you'll have is to use paravirtualized drivers in your VM. These drivers are available for both storage and networking. On the storage side, there is only one adapter that provides the paravirtualized advantages, and it is called the "Paravirtual SCSI adapter." On the networking side, the paravirtual adapters include "VMXNET," "VMXNET 2 (Enhanced)," and "VMXNET 3." These adapters tend to perform better when the guest has a moderate to heavy I/O load.

The Paravirtual SCSI adapter in vSphere 5 has been upgraded and is now suitable for all types of virtual disks, but it is particularly useful for data volumes that see moderate to heavy I/O load, such as the transaction logs or database files of a database server. It takes a bit of reconfiguration, but the Paravirtual SCSI adapter can even be used for the system drive of your VM. Historically, you had to use one of the standard SCSI or SAS adapters for the system drive; however, as of vSphere 4.1 the paravirtual SCSI adapter is supported even for these drives. In the Implementation and Management section we'll go over how to install a paravirtual SCSI adapter, and explain how the SCSI ID of your virtual hard disk comes into play.

Similarly on the networking side, the VMXNET adapters are the more advanced paravirtual devices. When you first build your VM, the VMXNET device will not be included. Instead, you will be given the "Flexible," "e1000," or now the "e1000e" adapter. These devices emulate physical network cards so that your guest operating system can load one of its pre-installed drivers. Though the VMXNET cards perform significantly better than the emulated physical cards, the VM Creation wizard won't automatically add a VMXNET card to your VM because guest operating systems do not have a built-in driver for the VMXNET virtual hardware devices. Like the Paravirtual SCSI adapter, we can only use these paravirtual devices after we have installed the VMware Tools inside your guest VM.

Audio Visual Aspects

In the past, Virtual Machines were never intended to be graphics workstations or advanced CAD stations; they had modest video performance and we were often satisfied just to have sound. All that changed in vSphere 5. Thanks in part to the advances in the VMware workstation product line, we now have the ability to add a virtual 3D video adapter and a high-definition (HD) audio adapter to our VMs. While this isn't likely to help you when it comes to servers, you might consider using this in your VMware View implementations where you might have a few advanced users who need a little extra video performance.

By adding the new video adapters, you can enable the Windows Aero interface as well as enable some 3D modeling applications within your virtual desktops. Coupled with the high-definition audio adapter, these new cards can be used to deliver HD streaming audio and video to your end users. The system also allows for multiple monitors, and the vSphere Client finally has a video memory calculator in the settings of each VM.

VMkernel Swap Space

Swap space? You mean the pagefile right? Well, in this case, no. VMkernel swap space refers to a temporary file on the ESXi host's disks that may be used by VMs instead of using the actual RAM in the ESXi host. We'll cover this swap stuff in much greater depth when we get to Chapter 10, "Resource Optimization," but it bears mentioning now because you can specify the swap file location when creating your new VM.

In vSphere 5, the ESXi host can store these VMkernel swap files on Solid State Disks (SSDs). A little background is in order so that you can appreciate the significance of this new feature. Whenever a VM is powered on, the hypervisor on your ESXi host automatically creates a temporary file that is used as swap space for your VM. This swap space is often equal to the size of your VM's RAM, but it isn't directly addressable by your VM. That means that if you have a VM with 8GB of RAM allocated to it, it might very well have an 8GB temporary file out on one of your datastores.

The swap space is used by the hypervisor as temporary space when the ESXi host begins to run out of physical memory. As you might guess, temporary files are nowhere near as fast as physical memory, so the use of VMkernel swap space is no trivial matter. VMware found that we could decrease the pain of relying on this temporary space by allowing the use of SSDs for the swap space instead of regular hard drives. Considering that SSD drives are often an order of magnitude faster than traditional storage drives, utilizing them for your VMkernel swap files can have a very positive impact on your resource management plans.

Caution

By default, the VMkernel swap file for each VM is located on the datastore that contains all your other VM files. If you are using a SAN, your VM might be using your SAN as memory when your ESXi host becomes overloaded (not a good thing).

vNUMA

This is a topic that we'll revisit in the next chapter, but we'll introduce it now while we're talking about VM capabilities. NUMA, or Non-Uniform Memory Access, is a means to divide a physical server's bus and RAM into discrete nodes of equal size. One or more processors can be included in a NUMA node, and these processors are supposed to access only memory within their node. This is referred to as accessing memory "local" to the node. The NUMA architecture makes accessing this "local" memory faster than traditional systems, but it comes at a price. Accessing memory from a "foreign" node (a memory range outside of the "local" node) takes more time and should be avoided.

Generally NUMA is a good thing because it does speed up the memory access for applications that are NUMA aware or that can completely fit their memory into a single NUMA node. The trouble comes in when you have an application (or VM) that uses more memory than is available in a single NUMA node. In this case, part of the memory will be quick, while the rest will be a bit sluggish.

VMware recognized this issue and developed vNUMA, a means for VMs to become aware of the underlying NUMA architecture so they will stay in a single NUMA node whenever possible. vNUMA is a new feature of vSphere 5, and should help in situations where a large VM has been assigned more RAM than what each NUMA node on the underlying hardware possesses. The underlying NUMA architecture will be presented to the guest operating system so that it can appropriately handle the memory address ranges to minimize the impact of crossing NUMA nodes.

Installing Your Guest Operating System

During the VM creation process, the wizard prompts you to select the guest operating system that you're planning to install. While it would be great if the wizard would go ahead and install the operating system for us, that isn't one of its features. Instead the wizard uses this information to prepare the virtual hardware so *we* can install the selected Operating System.

The first step is locating the necessary installation media. This might come in actual CD/DVD form, but the most common form is an ISO image because they are very portable and operate identical to a CD/DVD disc. In many cases, vSphere administrators create a dedicated datastore on their shared storage to hold their various ISO images. Keeping these images on shared storage allows multiple ESXi hosts to use the same ISO image, reducing the storage requirements.

Note

Be sure to store your ISOs on shared storage, but if possible place them on a datastore that will not be used by any VMs. Having non-VM files on a datastore will prevent Storage DRS from properly evacuating datastores.

When you install the first instance of a particular guest operating system, you might consider being fairly generic in your configuration so that you can create copies of the VM later. When we say that you should be "generic" in your configuration, we just mean that you should only include customizations to the operating system that you would want deployed with each subsequent copy of this VM. That could include things like service packs, updates, or even settings that align the VM to your organization's standards. Ideally you'll avoid configuring the VM with any name or static IP address that you might later use in production, and which would potentially cause a conflict if you deployed a copy of this VM later.

Once you've figured out what you want to install, the next major step in the process is to actually install the operating system. But how do we do that in a VM? It's not like we can walk up to the console of the ESXi server and see the VM's operating system. Instead, we use the VM Console within the vSphere Client. It gives us access to the direct video feed, the keyboard, and the mouse of the VM; much like you might have seen when using an IP KVM or a remote access board such as HP's iLO, Dell's DRAC, or IBM's RSA. Using this console view, we can even access the BIOS or EFI firmware of the VM, and then configure it to boot from the operating system's installation media (which again, should be an ISO on shared storage if possible).

So now we've started the installation process of your guest operating system, but what do we do if the installer doesn't find an appropriate storage adapter or device to use? Well, what did you do in the days of physical servers when the operating system installer didn't find your local storage device(s)? Use a driver disk. In a VM it is no different; you'll need to download either the LSILogic or BusLogic drivers for your operating system from VMware (or potentially another source on the Internet). You can then use the virtual floppy drive to supply the driver to the guest operating system installer.

Upon successful installation of your guest operating system, the single most important thing you can do is update the drivers. Now, these aren't just any drivers; they are the drivers that VMware provides for all of their virtual hardware. Unlike a physical server, we don't have to go out to the Internet to track down all these drivers one by one. VMware provides them all in a nice bundle for us, and we install them when we install the VMware Tools package.

VMware Tools

As we mentioned above, we don't need to fetch any special drivers for the virtual hardware because VMware includes all the drivers we need in a single package called VMware Tools. These drivers are customized to the guest operating system you are running, and they include support for all the virtual hardware devices you could add to your VM.

But how does VMware know what drivers to provide? After all, we could have installed any one of 90+ different guest operating systems. Think back to the VM Creation wizard. You told the ESXi server or vCenter what guest operating system you were planning to install. VMware doesn't have any magic that can read minds, so if you selected Windows 2008 R2, but then decided to install RedHat Linux 6, the VMware Tools package is going to supply the wrong drivers.

The VMware Tools package not only adds drivers to your VM, it also adds a few pieces of much-needed software. One of which is the heartbeat service that allows the hypervisor to communicate directly with the guest operating system through an in-band channel. That means the hypervisor doesn't need to use the regular network to communicate with your VM. This is pretty cool stuff because it means we don't need to use the management network to communicate with a VM. Think about it. What if your VM was only connected to a protected network without any access to your ESXi host's management network? How would the ESXi hypervisor be able to communicate with the guest operating system within your VM? The VMware Tools service solves this problem.

One of the more important tasks VMware Tools provides for us is the ability to gracefully shut down your VM as opposed to simply pulling its virtual power cable. The in-band communications channel allows the hypervisor to make calls to the guest operating system to shut down the server properly, avoiding data loss. And again, it does this without using the management network.

Another task is the time synchronization. Guests inherently lose track of time. It's not really their fault though because nearly every operating system uses CPU "ticks" as a method to keep track of time. Since a VM isn't guaranteed 100% access to a CPU, some of these ticks can be lost, which allows the guest operating system to drift backward in time. The VMware Tools has a time synchronization function that sweeps the VM's clock forward to match the ESXi host's internal clock. Of course, this requires that your ESXi host have the correct time, or none of this will help your VM.

Also, you should avoid using the VMware Tools time synchronization when your guest operating system is already using NTP or another form of network time synchronization. This typically applies to any computer in a Microsoft Windows Active Directory domain because their clocks are already synchronized with an appropriate server (the Domain Controller). This is because the VMware Tools service only sweeps the guest VM's clock forward; it doesn't actually perform synchronization. That means that if a guest VM's clock is ahead of the ESXi host's clock, no adjustment is made, despite the fact that the guest's clock is incorrect.

Caution

> You should avoid using the VMware Tools time synchronization if your guest operating system is already using NTP or another form of network time synchronization.

Another important function of the VMware Tools service is the special memory management driver that is often referred to as the "balloon driver." We'll cover the purpose for this driver later in Chapter 10 when we discuss resource optimization and how the hypervisor can reclaim memory politely from a VM. If the VMware

Tools are not installed, the hypervisor resorts to a much more brash method of randomly pulling pages of RAM away from the VM instead of allowing the guest operating system to choose which pages will be written to virtual memory (disk).

So how often should you install or update the VMware Tools package? The answer is simple: anytime the vSphere Client directs you to do so. When you upgrade an ESXi host, that host will have a new version of the VMware Tools installed on it. These tools should then be installed/updated in each VM running on that ESXi host. Keep in mind though; an update or install of VMware Tools typically forces a reboot of the guest operating system, so it is best to do this during one of your scheduled maintenance windows.

What if my maintenance window is in the middle of the night? No problem, you can use the VMware Update Manager, discussed in Chapter 13, to automate the updates to both VMware Tools and the VM Hardware (if required). The process is typically straightforward and error free, but we recommend you test this process first on non-production VMs until you get the hang of it.

Caution

Automated or interactive updates to the VMware Tools package will generally force a reboot of your VM.

Installing Third-Party Applications

If you've gotten this far, stop and smell the roses; or at least stop and clone this VM. Up until this point we have only performed tasks that comprise a base image of your guest operating system. You've installed the OS, tweaked the settings to match your organizations standards, and you've updated the drivers and installed the VMware Tools package. This VM is ready to be cloned. Why? Because the next step is to install third-party applications. If these applications don't install properly, or you want a VM without these applications installed, you would need to repeat the entire build-a-VM process, and let's face it, it wasn't quick or easy.

You should refer to the Implementation and Management section of this chapter for details and the do's and don'ts of creating a clone or a template from this VM. Once you're done, we'll be right here ready for you.

Now, we're assuming you've created a clone of this VM or that you have some form of backup. Once you're ready, install your applications just as you would if the server were physical. In some cases you can install these applications via RDP or SSH access to the VM; however, if you need direct console access, open up the vSphere Client.

If your third-party applications are designed to directly interact with or manage the server's physical hardware, you may not need them anymore. The VMs don't monitor the hardware of the ESXi host; that is vCenter's job. If you remember back to Chapter 5, each ESXi server now has a CIM agent that sends hardware health information back to the vCenter server and/or the vSphere Client.

You may wish to separate out the guest operating system virtual disks from the virtual disks where you will install your third-party applications. This is commonly done because a data disk is often easier to expand than a system disk in most operating systems. If you wish to do this, add a second virtual hard drive to your VM, and then format it accordingly in your guest operating system. Remember, we can increase the size of these virtual hard disks, but we can't shrink them; so keep the size reasonable.

Finally, you should ensure that the application you are installing has a method to back up its data. If the application uses databases or other open files, the data might not get backed up cleanly if you use traditional VM snapshots or other image-based backups. Check with your vender to ensure you are using the best backup method possible. If all else fails, treat the VM like it was a physical server and use an agent within the VM to ensure a quiesced backup.

Start Order (vApps)

If you are building a series of VMs that will have interdependencies, you may need a solution to control their start order. Going back to VMware's early versions of ESX we have had the ability to control the startup and shutdown order of VMs on a single ESX(i) host. But what happens when the VMs are scattered across several ESXi hosts? The solution involves something called a vApp to contain the VMs as though they were a package. vApps give you the ability to control the exact startup and shutdown order of a set of VMs even if they are scattered throughout a large cluster of ESXi hosts.

vApps leverage vCenter to maintain this start/stop order. We'll cover vApps in more detail later in the Implementation and Management section of this chapter.

Security Permissions

Okay, you've created a VM, installed your applications, made everything pretty, and now I bet you'd like to keep it that way. So how do we keep other people from messing up your handiwork? There are two ways, and both are required to do this right. We'll cover the basics now, but you can find much more information later in the Security section of this chapter.

First, you need to secure the VM in vCenter. This is equivalent to the physical security aspects that you might see in a datacenter. You need to ensure that access to a VM's settings, files, and power operations are kept secured. If an attacker can get to the VM's console or settings within the vSphere Client, it's only a matter of time before he gains access to the software within the VM.

The second step is to secure the guest OS. This is the same you've (hopefully) done for years. You must configure the security within your guest OS and its applications appropriately to avoid the more traditional attacks we face in a datacenter. This also includes the configuration of firewalls (software- and hardware-based), virus protection, and spyware removal. Yes, we still have to install antivirus in our VMs, though as you'll see later, vSphere gives us a few options that we don't have in the physical world.

Virtual Assembly Line

After all that, there has to be a simpler way to reproduce these VMs. Fortunately there is, and it isn't all that different from what we've used for years when deploying physical workstations. Bring on the clones!

Cold-Cloning and Hot-Cloning

Cloning is a great way to mass-produce VMs with minimal effort on the part of the vSphere Administrator. Cloning is exactly what it sounds like, a copy process that results in an exact clone of the original VM's disks. You might wish to clone a VM before you make any major changes to its applications or operating system, or you may just clone VMs for safe keeping—like a backup. Whatever your reason, you need to understand the limitations of cloning because they might surprise you.

First of all, there are two ways to clone a VM. The source VM can either be powered on or powered off. In some cases you may not have the luxury of powering off your VM prior to creating a clone. Perhaps you need to test a particular service pack, but you can't take the source VM down for maintenance. You could create a "hot clone" of that VM by initiating a clone operation while it is still powered on. There are some caveats to be aware of though.

Note that earlier we said the clone results in an exact copy of the source VM's "disks." While you can clone a VM that is running, the clone process only looks at the VM's virtual disks, not the memory and CPU processes that were running on the source VM. This means that the resulting clone operation will ignore these running CPU and memory spaces, producing a VM that, when powered on, appears to have been shut down abruptly. This might not be desirable, especially if you have database programs that were running at the time of the clone operation.

Alternatively, you can shut down the source VM, and then perform the clone operation. This is referred to as "cold cloning" because in this case the source VM was powered off. Because the source VM was powered off, it had no running processes or memory. This means the resulting clone is a perfect match to the source because we only needed to copy the disks to have a match. Without a doubt, this is the preferred method of cloning because it produces the most consistent results. Of course, the downside is that the source VM must be powered off.

Later in the Implementation and Management section of this chapter we'll explain the semantics of cloning a VM and how you can get started. Here are just a handful of situations where clones (hot or cold) are particularly useful:

- Long-term testing of application updates and service packs.
- Creating an isolated platform for data restorations during legal discovery.
- To preserve the state of a VM for forensic analysis after a security breach.
- Cold backups of VMs for archival or disaster recovery purposes.

Note

You can use the Guest Customization wizard during the clone process to change the destination VM's host name, IP address, and/or license keys.

With vSphere 5, you can also customize the guest operating system during the clone operation. This is the same function we use when deploying VMs from a template. Guest Customization is the ability to change things in the destination VM such as the hostname, IP address, license keys, and SID (for Microsoft Windows-based VMs). During the clone, the source VM is never modified, so following the Guest Customization routine the resulting VM becomes unique and could possibly co-exist with the source VM. This feature would be used in cases in which you create a single VM that serves as a "golden master" that is periodically cloned to create identical VMs from a single source.

We'll talk more about the Guest Customization process later in this chapter, but first let's discuss templates.

Templates

Templates are very similar to clones, but they offer a slight twist that makes them very popular with vSphere administrators. A template often starts life as a clone of another VM, but it is a clone that you leave powered off in a read-only state. You can still update clones, but it requires the administrator take an extra step to help prevent accidental updates of the template. This way, you can use the template as your source for any new VMs that require the operating system installed in that template. We call this process "deploying from a template."

Earlier in this chapter we suggested that you should clone your VM just before installing your third-party applications. If you followed our advice, you've already performed 99% of the requirements for a VM template. The remaining step is to either convert this VM to a template, or clone it to a template.

For instance, say that you wanted to create a new web server VM. You go through all the steps of building a VM, including the installation of your guest OS, all your hot-fixes, service packs, and organizational tweaks. You wrap things up with the installation of VMware Tools, and shut down the VM. Stop there. Don't join the system to your domain or designate a permanent name/IP for it. At this point you have a great launching point for future VMs that require this operating system. Once you have created your clone to a template, you may proceed with installing your third-party applications, keeping that original template safe for future use.

Note

Refer to the Implementation and Management section of this chapter for details on how to properly clone, convert, update, and deploy from your templates. We also discuss the Guest Customization wizard.

Exporting Your VMs

Imagine that you maintain multiple locations around the world, or even just your country. Each site is connected via a typical WAN link; none have the bandwidth you'd like, and the latency isn't exactly great either. Each of these locations has a virtual infrastructure already in place, but they lack your expertise. Your boss has tasked you with deploying your custom templates to these other locations, and you have to figure out how to do it.

There are a couple of options. You could attempt to deploy VMs across the WAN link. Now, that might not make you very popular with your network support group, but it could be done if you give it sufficient time and money. Alternatively, you could export your templates to an Open Virtualization Format (OVF) file. OVF files are an industry standard maintained by dmtf.org, to provide a common language format for VM descriptor files. That's a mouthful, but it means that you can use OVF files to exchange VMs between sites because each site will be able to understand and import these files into their inventories.

The process goes something like this: You first create and customize a VM or a template to your liking; next you export this VM or template in OVF format; next you copy this OVF-formatted template to some portable storage; finally, you send that storage device to your remote site where the OVF file is imported into their vCenter or ESXi host. We'll cover the semantics of all this later in the Implementation and Management section of this chapter, but let's explore what these OVF files can do for you.

By exporting a template to a common format like OVF, you can move that template to another vCenter or just another site connected to the same vCenter. The OVF file is basically metadata that tells the other host how to create an appropriate VM configuration file (VMX) and how to organize the VM's virtual hard disk files. In some cases you can even move OVF files between virtualization venders (VMware, Microsoft, Citrix, etc.). The details of this fall well outside the scope of this book, but if this is something you need, search for it and be amazed.

There are two formats you may choose from: OVF or OVA (Open Virtual Appliance). Whereas OVF files are metadata files that accompany the original virtual disk files, an OVA file is a single-file compilation designed for deployment on portable media (like a USB drive). OVA files are massive, but they contain everything you need in one file as opposed to dozens, making them a bit more portable from a library or inventory sense.

One final, yet very important parting note about exporting VMs is the security aspects surrounding their storage and deployment. Neither the OVF nor the OVA formats include an encryption option for the contents of the VM. If you intend to transport or store your exported VMs using USB hard drives or any other portable media, you need to seriously consider encrypting the entire drive to avoid losing your organization's data. You need to treat these OVF and OVA files as though they were servers in your organization; you likely wouldn't want them to fall into the wrong hands.

Note

One popular encryption tool comes from TrueCrypt.org, an open-source encryption provider. They have a number of means to encrypt drives, which can help reduce the number of Résumé Generating Events in your future.

VM Backups

You've created a very nice VM, loaded all your applications and data, and then someone accidentally deletes the thing. Hopefully you had a backup. But wait, how exactly do we back up VMs? Are they the same as physical machines? Should our disaster recovery plans be adjusted if we use VMs? Are there VMs we should back up more or less frequently? What are RPOs and RTOs?

These are all very common questions, but fortunately we can help. VMs can be backed up like physical machines using all the traditional tricks of the trade. You can use the operating system's built-in tools, you can use your third-party software to extract your databases and files, you can install agents in the VM to back it up, and you may even be able to leverage your SAN's snapshot tools. But VMs also have a few additional options that physical machines do not have. The leading advantage is that we can grab the VM's virtual disk files and make an image-based backup of the VM. This method even trumps the traditional bare-metal restores that you can do with physical servers.

Before we get too far, we need to define two very important terms: RPO (Recovery Point Objective) and RTO (Recovery Time Objective). An RPO is the point to which you must restore your system. In many cases, your RPO is last night's backup, or about 24 hours. The Recovery Point is last night when the backup ran; the Objective part just means that getting last night's data is your goal. An RPO implicitly determines the amount of data that you can lose. If you have an RPO of 24 hours, you are saying that you can only lose 24 hours of data, and your backup routine must make certain you don't exceed this window of data loss.

RTOs on the other hand indicate how long it will take you to restore your data to the level of the RPO. For example, if your RPO was last night's backup and your RTO is 4 hours, you believe you can restore the server from last night's backup in less than 4 hours. Hopefully your backup tapes are good and that the backup job ran correctly. RTOs are typically measured from the moment of the system failure, including all the other troubleshooting steps you perform while the system is offline, so be sure to give yourself time. A 4-hour RTO is extremely aggressive for most systems unless you have VMs with image-based backups.

That brings us to how VM backups have changed, and what technologies exist to help us get these image-based backups while still maintaining our ability to restore individual files for the average user-created disaster (such as "oops, I deleted my home directory!").

vStorage APIs

The vStorage APIs aren't really new, but they are wonderful. VMware released them several years ago to replace the aging VMware Consolidated Backup (VCB) framework that allowed developers and administrators alike to perform LAN-free backups of VMs. A LAN-free backup is one where the backup of the VM doesn't occur over your production or management network. Instead, a LAN-free backup leverages the storage network to allow the backup server (known as the "proxy host") to directly access the VMware datastores and then back up the VM's data.

The vStorage APIs expanded on this functionality to allow VMs to serve as the backup server. Now you can virtualize even your backup server and still create image-based backups of your VMs. The backup server VM uses a feature referred to as "Hot-Add" to quickly add another VM's virtual hard disk, and then back up that virtual hard disk as though it was locally attached storage.

If you're following along closely you might be scratching your head a bit. How can you mount a disk on one VM when it is still in use by another VM? The answer is called "snapshots," and we'll cover those later in this chapter. For now, you need to understand that snapshots allow us to free up the target VM's virtual hard disks long enough to back up the data. Once the backup is complete, the backup server uses the vStorage APIs to remove the snapshot on the target VM, but during the backup process, the target VM operates normally aside from a bit more disk latency while the backup occurs in the background.

Either the old-school proxy host method or the newer Hot-Add method will achieve the same goal: an image-based backup and a file-based backup of the VM. That's right, in addition to creating an image that can be restored for disaster recovery purposes, the vStorage APIs also allow the backup server to perform a file-based backup on the virtual hard disk (in a single backup operation nonetheless!). That means you can achieve your disaster recovery RPOs and RTOs using the same backup process that you'll use to provide the run-of-the-mill file restores, and it all can happen without bogging down your production network!

VMware's VDR

Like many software providers, VMware also created their own backup software to help protect your VMs. VMware's solution is called VMware Data Recovery or VDR for short. It is a virtual appliance that you may download from VMware's website if you obtain the appropriate licensing. The VDR appliance is a 64-bit VM and it must run on one of the hosts listed in your vCenter inventory. This is because the VDR connects to vCenter to exchange information about the VMs residing in the cluster and on the various datastores.

When VMware upgraded vSphere to version 5, they also re-released and upgraded VDR to version 2.0. The new version appears to solve some of the issues that plagued the earlier releases of VDR. Here are a few noteworthy items:

- The VDR Appliance is now a fully 64-bit appliance (future scalability potential).

- New automated e-mail reporting with detailed log reports.

- New destination-based maintenance windows allow background processing to run when no backup jobs are running.

- Individual backup jobs may be suspended to prepare for maintenance windows.

- Windows pagefiles and Linux swap partitions are automatically excluded from backup jobs.

- Several reported performance improvements and bug fixes since VDR version 1.2.1.

One very large caveat of the VDR appliance that yet remains in version 2.0 is its limited capacity. VMware designed VDR for Small to Medium Business (SMB) customers who otherwise might not have a VM-based backup solution. The limitation again is based on capacity. Each VDR appliance is hard-coded to back up a maximum of 100 VMs, and/or a maximum of 2TB of de-duplicated data (whichever comes first). Each vCenter server can host up to 10 VDR appliances though, so you could magnify these maximums by 10 if you have the resources (or need) to back up 1,000 VMs and 20TB of de-duplicated data.

Because it is a VM, the VDR appliance uses the Hot-Add methodology described above to back up the VMs. This means that it also leverages snapshots to perform its back ups. Refer to the section on Snapshots in this chapter for an example script that you can run to see if your back up software removed the snapshots that it created. It's more important than you might think.

In summary, VDR isn't for everyone, but it has a lot of merit for software that is included free in all but the one of the vSphere license levels (vSphere Essentials). Try it out. If it doesn't serve your purpose, you can always buy a third-party package. Whatever you do though, make sure that you get an image-based back up for your VMs so that your disaster recovery RPOs and RTOs are minimized.

Tip

Alternatively, you can export your VM as an OVF or OVA file and move it to portable storage for off-site back up. Refer to our section on Exporting VMs to OVF/OVA Files later in this chapter in the Implementation and Management section.

Agent-Based Backups

What if I'm just testing the waters of virtualization; must I use the aforementioned solutions, or can I continue to use agents? You can definitely continue the way you always have, and in some cases you might want to couple both an agent-based solution and an image-based solution to give you more options.

As back up software progresses, it seems that more venders are attempting to incorporate the vStorage APIs into their existing products. This really gives you the best of both worlds, as you'll get a great back up image for disaster recovery, and you'll have the ability to restore individual files or databases with relative ease.

In some cases, back up software administrators use a dedicated LAN or VLAN for back up traffic. While it isn't required when using virtual machines, it can help isolate and secure your back up traffic in some cases. Of course we think the best plan is to avoid using a back up solution that sends data over the network altogether, but if that isn't in your plans, you might consider the network segmentation approach. Unfortunately, this would require adding multiple virtual network adapters to each VM, and then creating a new vSwitch or VM Port Group for the traffic. It can add a lot of administrative overhead to your project, so only do this if you really need that level of separation and you can't leverage the vStorage APIs for a LAN-free back up.

Direct Hardware Access

What happens if we encounter one of those near-mythical VMs that can overpower the built-in VMware virtual hardware? Don't give up; look at ways to give that VM some real physical hardware. It is possible, but there are a ton of caveats and limitations that go along with this privilege, so don't plan to do this for every VM.

VMware has a number of means to map physical hardware directly into a VM, but the method depends more on the hardware than on your purposes. For instance, if the device is USB-based, the connection is relatively simple; whereas if the device is a PCI card, we'll have to make quite a few configuration changes to both the ESXi host and the VM.

Also keep in mind that regardless of what we say here, understand that giving a VM access to physical hardware should not be your first reaction. That really defeats one of the main goals of virtualization: flexibility and independence from hardware-bound configurations. Instead, try to find a way to address the need within the bounds of the virtual hardware. If the problem is that the application in the VM is too demanding on the storage or network I/O, try to figure out why before just throwing hardware at the problem. Perhaps there is a way to reduce the I/O or spread it out across multiple VMs in a pool configuration. Again, adding physical hardware to a VM shouldn't be your first reaction.

Here's a rundown of the various means we have to get the job done:

- USB
- NPIV
- vSphere DirectPath I/O
- Serial and parallel ports
- Smart card readers

USB

We've had the ability to add USB devices to VMs for some time, but it's only been since the release of vSphere 4.1 that we could easily map a USB device to a VM running on ESX/ESXi (and then vMotion the VM!). Now vSphere 5 adds limited support for USB 3.0 devices in select Linux guest operating systems. We can add a client-attached USB 3.0 device if the operating system has a driver for the xHCI USB controller that comes with Virtual Hardware version 8.

Note

At the time of this writing, USB 3.0 devices are only supported in Linux VMs because there are no Windows drivers for the xHCI USB controllers.

If you intend to upgrade your Windows VMs to Virtual Hardware version 8, and you wish to provide those VMs with USB support, you may need to edit the VM's settings to remove the xHCI USB controller and add in the legacy EHCI+UHCI USB controller. This will again permit the Windows VM to use USB 1.1 and 2.0 devices because Windows has a driver for the EHCI+UHCI USB controllers.

One final note regarding the use of USB 3.0 devices: Keep in mind that the devices must be presented from a workstation running the vSphere Client, and not from the ESXi host directly. Also, a 1Gbps network is actually a bottleneck for USB 3.0 devices because the maximum speed of USB 3.0 is 5Gbps. Therefore, unless you are connected to the ESXi host via a 10Gbps network, you won't be able to achieve the full speed of the device.

So, why would you need to map a USB device to a VM? Have you ever had software that requires a USB dongle for licensing? Your needs could also include adding temporary hard drives, thumb drives, scanners, cameras, etc. You might even use this on your virtual desktops for things like Smartcard Readers.

NPIV

Unfortunately, NPIV doesn't stand for "No Problem If Virtualized." It's an acronym for N-Port ID Virtualization, which is a mechanism that several Fibre Channel venders support to allow a physical Fibre Channel HBA to support multiple World-Wide Name (WWN) values. If you're not a Fibre Channel expert, that's functionally equivalent to allowing a network card to have more than one MAC address assigned to it. It can be challenging, but if your Fibre Channel switches and HBAs support NPIV, it can be very handy when introducing fine-grain security on the LUNs of your Fibre Channel SAN.

Caution

NPIV isn't supported on every Fibre Channel HBA or switch. Make sure your vender supports it, and that you understand how to configure your Fibre Channel switch and zones before attempting this.

For example, if you want to provide a VM access to a LUN directly on an SAN, you can choose to use Raw Device Mapping (RDM). This gives the VM access to the storage, but the SAN doesn't really know which VM is using the storage. The SAN only sees the WWN from the ESXi host. If you wanted to allow the SAN to identify the initiator as the VM, you could enable NPIV to provide the VM with its own WWN, and then have that VM access the RDM using that WWN. You must also configure the SAN to present that LUN to both the WWN of the ESXi server and the WWN of the VM in order for the NPIV to function properly.

Note

vMotion is possible for VMs using RDMs with NPIV as long as you ensure that the underlying LUN has been presented to the WWNs of each ESXi host and the VM.

Also keep in mind that because NPIV leverages RDMs, you are still bound to the same volume size limits on RDMs found in the VMware vSphere Configuration Maximums document on VMware's website. The real advantage comes from the increased visibility on the storage side as to which VM is using which LUN on the SAN arrays, which could lead to greater visibility for charge-back or show-back purposes.

Note

RDMs in *virtual* compatibility mode are limited to 2TB, whereas RDMs in *physical* compatibility mode can be up to 64TB if the VM's system files are stored on a VMFS version 5.0 datastore.

vSphere DirectPath I/O

There are times when even NPIV or in-guest iSCSI initiators just won't support the extreme levels of I/O that some applications can dish out. vSphere DirectPath I/O allows a VM to bypass the hypervisor on an ESXi host to directly access a PCI device for I/O purposes. This bypass has some inherent limitations because your VM is going around the hypervisor to use the hardware. The biggest limitation is that with this feature enabled, vMotion is disabled for most VMs. That means you can't move the VM to another host while the VM is powered on.

DirectPath I/O was first released in Virtual Hardware version 7 in vSphere 4.0. In vSphere 5's Virtual Hardware 8, VMware updated DirectPath I/O to allow vMotion operations if the underlying ESXi host's hardware is based on a supported Cisco UCS system. Also, the VM must only be leveraging DirectPath I/O to get a high-speed network adapter. In all other cases, vMotions are still not possible once you have enabled DirectPath I/O.

DirectPath I/O was designed to solve high-performance I/O problems for VMs. It is used exclusively for storage and network I/O devices, not as a means to add things like fax boards or other custom PCI devices. Though some people have been successful doing so, VMware doesn't support DirectPath I/O for this purpose.

Note

> Before you can use DirectPath I/O, you must ensure that the host has enabled either the Intel VT-d or AMD IOMMU features in its BIOS.

DirectPath I/O is a multi-step process. Be sure you have installed the latest version of the VMware Tools before starting any of this process. First, enable the Intel VT-d or AMD IOMMU features in the BIOS of your ESXi host. Next, configure the ESXi host to allow the target PCI card to be "reserved" by a VM. Then you configure the VM in a powered-off state, to use the PCI card. The last step is configuring the appropriate drivers in the guest operating system.

Again, DirectPath I/O isn't something that every VM should have because it can impose some severe limitations on the features of the VM.

Serial and Parallel Ports

Despite all the more advanced USB devices, serial and parallel devices still exist. If you have such a device, you're in luck because vSphere 5 supports both serial and parallel port connections in VMs. Both port types may be either directly connected to the corresponding physical port on the ESXi server or the I/O can be directed to a file on the ESXi host. The virtual serial port can be configured to allow VM-to-VM serial port connection over Named Pipes.

Tip

A VM with a serial or parallel port connected to an ESXi host will not be eligible for vMotion to another host. A better solution: use the vSphere APIs to create a proxy for a vSphere Virtual Serial Port Concentrator.

In vSphere 4.1, VMware released an API that allows a VM's virtual serial ports to connect to a centralized network proxy service to enable the VM to use vMotion while it maintains a network serial port connection. This technique is very similar to the technology used in the USB arbitrator service, where a VM may vMotion from host to host as long as the USB target is online and available. The virtual serial port connections leverage telnet sessions to maintain the communications between the VM's virtual serial port and the proxy, and from the proxy to the serial device.

Refer to the vSphere Web Services SDK documentation for more information on how to build the proxy for the Virtual Serial Port Concentrator.

Smart Card Readers

If your organization uses smart cards for authentication, and you are using VMware View or another virtual desktop infrastructure product, you may really appreciate this feature. In vSphere 5 we can map a client-side smart card reader to a VM to enable the two-factor authentication to pass back to the VM where the user can be properly authenticated. It is possible to attach the smart card reader to multiple VMs from a single workstation.

To attach a smart card reader in a VM, you must have the vSphere Client installed on the workstation where the smart card reader is connected. The smart card reader operates as a pass-through device, so if the workstation reboots, the smart card reader's connection back to the VM is lost. Therefore, you may consider dedicating a workstation for VMs that require smart card authentication.

Special Use Cases

We covered the run-of-the-mill VMs, but what if you're not building something so bland? What if you have a project that isn't as cut and dry as building a new VM from scratch, or deploying one from a nicely created template? Read on, you're not alone.

Physical to Virtual Conversions (P2V)

Though virtualization has been around for a while, there are plenty of physical systems out there, many of which are just begging to be virtualized. A Physical to Virtual (P2V) conversion is the process of copying a physical machine's hard disks to an ESXi host in the form of new, virtual hard disks. A VM is created during the process to host these virtual disk files, and the operator of the P2V is given the chance to fully customize the VM to either match the source or another design. The P2V operation is key to many datacenter consolidations and is one of the most effective tools a vSphere administrator has when working with odd, undocumented physical systems that need to be virtualized. Albeit the process is a bit more complex or we wouldn't have dedicated a chapter to it, but why reinvent the wheel? Just copy it into a VM and be done with it.

Note

We've dedicated all of Chapter 14 to these P2V (and V2V) conversions. We just mention it here for completeness, and for those of you who like to skip around while reading these tomes of technical wonder.

Virtual Desktop Infrastructure (VDI)

In VDI, we create VMs for use as personal virtual desktops for the users. These desktops are often assigned to users much in the same way they are assigned workstations or laptop computers. Each user may have a different complement of applications loaded so that he can perform his normal day-to-day tasks. Some of these applications may include Microsoft Office, CRM applications, or a custom line of business software. The possibilities seem endless, but are they?

Until vSphere 5 was released, applications that required high-end audio or 3D video just didn't run well (or at all). These applications were always a stumbling block for VDI. Now, with Virtual Hardware Version 8 in vSphere 5, we can include new devices such as the HD Audio adapter and the 3D video card to help increase the performance of these demanding applications that previously struggled to run or perhaps even didn't run when virtualized. It's opening the door for more use cases of VDI, but there are still limits.

For one, virtual desktops can consume large amounts of resources if managed improperly. The typical pain points include excessive disk I/O during logon/logoff operations, or intense CPU/memory usage because of a wild application or web plugin. Again, vSphere 5 has come to our rescue, but even now it is still limited. vSphere gives us the tools such as enabling Network I/O control to achieve true QoS down to the VM level, or using Storage I/O control to balance overtaxed datastores. The key is to keep the VMs managed completely, throughout their entire life cycle.

That brings us to deployment and operations. VDI takes on many flavors. Up until now we haven't mentioned one vender or another because you can run XenDesktop on a vSphere 5 infrastructure just as easily as you can run VMware's View 5.0 product. The key to success is to know which product fits your project, and then exploiting every advantage you can from that product.

We aren't going to dig in too deep here on how to implement VDI. It's a topic that deserves a book (or more) just to itself. We just wanted to give you a taste of VDI and toss out some ideas that might help you along in your projects.

Resource-Intensive VMs

When vSphere was still in its infancy, we used to say that there are some VMs that were either too important or just too powerful to be virtualized. While this may still be true, the numbers of these special physical servers are dwindling, thanks to the improved limits and capabilities available in vSphere 5. For instance, one of the more limiting features for large VMs has always been RAM and CPU. With the increase to 32 vCPUs per VM and a new memory cap of 1TB, we've opened the door for some rather large contenders. Now it becomes your job to determine if your Tier-1 VMs are really virtualization candidates based on things like network and disk I/O performance. That's a factor that VMware can help with, but it ultimately comes down to how you've architected the rest of your datacenter, and how willing you are to analyze the data.

Given all these high limits, it seems like we should be able to virtualize anything. While it might be possible, there is often quite a bit of configuration required both within the application and at the VM level in vCenter before the application really performs well. Large and powerful VMs expand upon the typical rules of VM construction. You still have to build the VM, install the operating system, assign resources, and configure settings. The difference is that you will be assigning a lot more resources, and potentially tweaking even more settings.

For one, adding more vCPUs or more RAM to a VM isn't necessarily going to make it run faster. As you'll see in the next chapter, performance is a 4-fold equation between CPU, RAM, network, and disks. That last one, "disks," is often the most overlooked of the bunch. Keep in mind that if you add an excessive amount of RAM to a VM, you will need to support that RAM in three places: once in RAM, once in the VM's pagefile or swap partition, and once in the VMkernel swap file. This means that if you have given a VM 50GB of RAM, you will likely use 100GB of disk space just to support the memory.

So in summary, our recommendations are to first analyze what the exact requirements are for your VMs. Don't over allocate resources in an attempt to save time or effort because you might inadvertently tip the scale and begin expending resources just to keep status quo. And finally, know what level of data protection and high availability is appropriate for these VMs. They are likely too large to back up using a traditional method, and they are likely too important to leave unprotected. Size it right, and save yourself a lot of time in the end.

vCenter as a VM

vCenter is one of several applications that tend to evoke a philosophical debate when the question is raised whether or not to virtualize it. But why? In the past there were all sorts of reasons not to virtualize vCenter; remarkably performance rarely made the top of the list. With the advances in vSphere, such as host-based affinity rules, and the cached copies of license configuration data, virtualizing vCenter is no longer taboo. Remember, VMware released a pure VM-based vCenter in vSphere 5, the Linux-based vApp. That should tell you something about VMware's level of confidence in virtualizing vCenter.

There are a few drawbacks, most involve playing hide and go seek with vCenter if the datacenter is completely powered down, but we do need to consider what would happen if vCenter didn't come back online. Remember our discussion on clones? You might consider creating a clone of your vCenter VM (and then exporting the clone to an OVF file for safekeeping). Also keep a good copy of your vCenter database somewhere that isn't virtualized just in case you have to recover things quickly. Considering that most of the administration features of vSphere require the vCenter server to be online, you might also ensure that the ESXi server hosting vCenter is properly configured for high availability.

Sizing concerns and other performance-based optimizations tend to change quickly, but one static comment we can make is that you don't want to deprive vCenter of RAM. The more hosts you add, the more RAM vCenter will consume. If you intend to co-locate your database engine on the vCenter VM, you will also need to add some RAM so that the database engine doesn't consume everything. In fact, make sure that you place a limit on the RAM that SQL, Oracle, or DB2 can use if you intend to co-locate the database and vCenter services.

Overall, virtualizing vCenter is not a problem as long as you plan for the obvious and predictable failures that will occur in your datacenter. If you go into this believing that vCenter will never crash, or that your datacenter will never have a UPS-related accident, you're asking for trouble. Create a plan, restrict vCenter to exist on only a couple different ESXi hosts, and ensure that it has sufficient power to succeed, and so will you.

IMPLEMENTATION AND MANAGEMENT

In the Planning section we discussed *why* you might do certain tasks. This section focuses on *how* to perform the steps necessary to build and maintain vSphere 5 environments. In this section we'll cover the following topics:

- Creating a VM
- Controlling a VM
- Modifying a VM
- Snapshots
- Migrating VMs
- Using vApps
- Working with OVF files
- Nested Virtualizaton—ESXi as a VM

Creating a VM

As we discussed in the Planning section, there are several ways to create VMs, and each method has its purpose. Methods such as the VM Creation wizard involve more effort than deploying a VM from a template, but the wizard offers us more control over the resulting VM.

We need to first address the tasks required to create a VM, and then we'll move into how to clone and template the VM so that your deployments are a bit quicker in the future. In this section we'll cover:

- Using the VM Creation wizard
- Working with VM clones
- Creating a template
- Deploying from a template
- Working with the Windows Customization Resources
- Customizing the guest operating system
- Updating a template
- Importing a Virtual Appliance (VA)

Using the VM Creation Wizard

You can start the VM Creation wizard in a number of ways, but they all hinge around selecting an appropriate container for the VM. So what constitutes a valid container for VMs? You can select an ESXi host, a folder, a resource pool, a datacenter, or a cluster. Once you have selected one of these containers, choose File > New > Virtual Machine. Alternatively, you can press Ctrl+N, or right-click on the container and then choose New Virtual Machine.

Regardless of how you launch the wizard, you will be prompted with the same options. The first choice is whether to use the Typical or Custom wizard. Again, both paths lead to the same result: a VM. The difference is that the "typical" version of the wizard assumes many facts about your future VM, whereas, the "custom" wizard allows you to tweak many more settings as can be seen in Table 9.6.

Tip

In most cases you'll want to use the "custom" wizard, because it is a one-stop shop for the majority of the settings you need to adjust in a new VM.

Working with VM Clones

We covered a few use cases for clones earlier in our Planning section, but as a recap, clones are great when used to keep a back up copy of a VM (for testing or forensic

Table 9.6   VM Creation Wizards

VM Setting/Option	Typical	Custom
VM Name and Location in the Folder Hierarchy	X	X
Storage Location and Storage Profile	X	X
Guest Operating System	X	X
Network Cards (Quantity, Adapter Type, VM Port Group)	X	X
Virtual Disk (Size and Type: Thin, Thick)	X	X
Edit the VM's Settings Before Completion	X	X
VM Hardware Version (7 or 8)		X
Virtual CPU Sockets vs. Cores		X
RAM Size		X
SCSI Controller type (SCSI, SAS, Paravirtual)		X
Disk Creation Selection (New, Existing, RDM, None)		X
Advanced Disk Options (SCSI ID, Independent mode)		X

analysis). They can also be used to deploy a VM, but we recommend that you use templates for this.

Remember, clones can be made of VMs that are either powered on or powered off, but there are risks when cloning a powered-on VM. The clone operation doesn't capture the running processes and memory, and a running VM will likely have open files that may not be saved properly. When the clone of the VM is powered on, its guest operating system believes it was shut down improperly. This is what we refer to as a "crash-consistent" state because the applications and data are only as consistent as they would be if the VM had suddenly crashed. We have no way to know how much data (if any) was lost due to the crash. This is the reason we try to avoid operations that could leave our VMs in a crash-consistent state. The safest plan is to clone a VM that is powered off.

Caution

Hot clones, or clones of powered-on VMs, are risky because they will have open files that may not get copied properly during the clone. Instead, power off the VM before cloning it to get a perfect copy.

To start the clone process, select the VM you wish to clone and select Inventory > Virtual Machine > Clone from the vSphere Client menu. Alternatively, right-click on the source VM and select Clone to start the Clone VM wizard. The wizard will present you with several options before the clone process begins. These options are a bit more limited than the VM Creation wizard because we are duplicating a VM, including nearly all of the VM's settings. Here are the wizard options for creating a clone from a VM (running or powered off):

1. VM name and location in the folder hierarchy

2. Virtual disk (type: thin, thick, same as source)

3. Storage location and Storage Profile

4. Customize the guest operating system

5. Edit the VM's settings before completion

During the wizard, you can choose to place the destination VM's files in the same datastore or separate each virtual disk onto different datastores. You might want to separate the virtual disks if the VM has strict disk I/O requirements which necessitate that certain virtual disks are located on a dedicated datastore.

If you choose, you may initiate the Guest Customization wizard during the clone operation. As we discussed in the Planning section, this wizard leverages Sysprep in Windows and Perl scripts in Linux to make the resulting clone less like a clone and more like a unique VM. The cloning process automatically generates a new MAC address for the new VM, but it doesn't modify the guest operating system at all. That is the job of the Guest Customization wizard, and you can run it to modify the clone's network settings with or without modifying the hostname. This is particularly useful when cloning a VM to a test network for development work.

Tip

When cloning a VM you can also change the destination disk type. This is useful if you clone a VM with thick provisioned disks because you can convert the clone's disks to thin provisioned disks (to save disk space).

Creating a Template

After you've created a VM, you can make clones of it to expedite the deployment of future VMs. But what if you wanted to protect the source copy so that no one can accidentally power it on or change its settings? The simple solution is to convert the source VM to a template. This is one of the two methods to create templates. The other is to clone an existing VM to a template. The difference is that when you convert a VM to a template, the source VM becomes the template. When you clone a VM to a template, the source VM remains a VM, but the clone becomes the template; you have two copies of that VM now.

Tip

When you create a template it is bound to a particular ESXi host. If you shut down that host for maintenance, you should first migrate the template to another host.

To convert a VM to a template, follow this two-step process:

1. Power off the source VM. While you can clone a powered-on VM, you cannot convert a powered-on VM to a template.

2. Select the VM from the hierarchy and choose Inventory > Virtual Machine > Template > Convert to Template from the vSphere Client menu.

Note

If you are in the Hosts and Clusters view when you convert a VM to a template, the VM will seem to disappear from vCenter. Look under the VMs and Templates view to find it. Templates do not appear in the hierarchy in the Hosts and Clusters view.

To clone a VM to a template, the process is a bit more involved, but not by much:

1. Launch the Clone Virtual Machine to Template wizard by selecting the VM from the hierarchy and choosing Inventory > Virtual Machine > Template > Clone to Template from the vSphere Client menu.

2. Enter the name of the template and choose its location in the folder hierarchy.

3. Select the ESXi host or cluster where the template will be stored.

4. Select an appropriate virtual disk type: thin, thick, or keep the same format as the source.

5. Choose the Datastore and Storage Profile (if applicable).

6. Confirm the settings for the template and wait for the clone to complete. When completed, the template will be listed in the inventory in the VMs and Templates view in vCenter.

Caution

You can clone a powered-on VM to a template, but we don't advise it. A powered-on VM will have open files that may not clone well, making your future VMs unstable. If possible, power off the VM before making a template.

Deploying a Template

After you've created a template, we can put it to work. The deployment process is very similar to the cloning wizard. At the end you will be given the chance to customize your guest operating system as we discussed in the Planning section. Here are the steps to deploying a VM from a template:

1. Launch the Deploy Template wizard by selecting the VM from the hierarchy and choosing Inventory > Template > Deploy Virtual Machine from this Template from the vSphere Client menu.

2. Enter the name of the VM and choose its location in the folder hierarchy.

3. Select the ESXi host or cluster where the VM will be stored.

4. Select an appropriate virtual disk type: thin, thick, or keep the same format as the source.

5. Choose the Datastore and Storage Profile (if applicable).

6. Choose whether to power on the VM after deployment (typically you should power on the VM to allow the Guest Customization wizard to run).

7. Select whether or not to customize the guest OS. Note this option is only available for Windows 2003/2000/XP if Sysprep (the "Windows customization resources") has been installed on vCenter.

8. Confirm the settings for the VM and wait for the clone to complete.

Tip

If you are customizing a Windows Guest OS, be sure to let the system complete its multiple reboot cycles. If you attempt to log on to Windows too soon, you will interrupt the cycle, causing the Ctrl+Alt+Del to Log on screen to reappear in a loop. If this happens, just reboot the VM and leave it alone for 5 minutes so that Sysprep can initialize and finish its process.

Working with the Windows Customization Resources

If you've deployed a template or cloned a VM, you've seen the prompts for the Guest Customization wizard. If you were deploying an older version of Windows, such as 2003, XP, or 2000, you may have even been blocked from initiating Guest Customization with a message that vCenter couldn't locate the "Windows Customization Resources." What was it looking for, and why is it not included in vCenter?

The Guest Customization wizard makes use of a piece of software known as Sysprep for early versions of Windows (2003 Server and earlier). The Sysprep software is distributed on the Windows installation media by Microsoft, and does not include a redistributable license. This means that VMware can't bundle it with their vCenter software, but you can download it and install it yourself.

Note that each version of Windows has a different Sysprep file, and there are 32-bit and 64-bit versions of the software. Though they all bear the same name "sysprep.exe," don't be fooled; they are in fact different files and mixing them up will cause the customization to fail. Because Sysprep is a Microsoft Windows tool, it is not needed to customize any Linux VMs. Also note that Sysprep is not required to customize Windows Vista, 7, 8, or Server 2008 (and later) because the mini-setup routines are built in to the OS.

VMware has created a comprehensive Knowledge Base article that lists the location of each Sysprep version on Microsoft's website. The article also explains where to extract each of the packages (remember, they have the same Sysprep.exe filename, so each version has a unique path). The VMware KB Article is 1005593, and can be found here: http://kb.vmware.com/kb/1005593.

When you have downloaded the correct Sysprep files, you must transfer them to the vCenter server. If you run vCenter server on Windows, you must copy them to one of the following folders (depending on the version of Windows):

For Windows 2008 and later:

`%ALLUSERSPROFILE%\VMware\VMware VirtualCenter\Sysprep\`

For Windows 2003 and earlier:

`%ALLUSERSPROFILE%\Application Data\VMware\VMware VirtualCenter\Sysprep\`

If you are using the vCenter Appliance (vCA), you must copy the files to this folder (using an appropriate SCP application such as WinSCP):

`/etc/vmware-vpx/sysprep/`

Note that the Sysprep files must be extracted from the appropriate deploy.cab file and placed in the correct subdirectory based on the following chart in Table 9.7. The variable <Sysprep_folder_path> represents the folder paths identified above for your version of vCenter server.

Table 9.7 Sysprep Downloads and Paths in vCenter

Windows Version	Sysprep Subdirectory	Sysprep Version
Windows 2000 Server SP4 with Update Rollup 1—Download at: http://www.microsoft.com/downloads/details.aspx?FamilyID=0c4bfb06-2824-4d2b-abc1-0e2223133afb	<sysprep_folder_path>\2k	5.0.2195.2104
Windows XP Pro SP2 http://www.microsoft.com/downloads/details.aspx?FamilyId=3E90DC91-AC56-4665-949B-BEDA3080E0F6	<sysprep_folder_path>\xp	5.1.2600.2180
Windows 2003 Server SP1—Download at: http://www.microsoft.com/downloads/details.aspx?familyid=A34EDCF2-EBFD-4F99-BBC4-E93154C332D6	<sysprep_folder_path>\svr2003	5.2.3790.1830 (srv03_sp1_rtm.050324-1447)
Windows 2003 Server SP2—Download at: http://www.microsoft.com/downloads/details.aspx?FamilyID=93f20bb1-97aa-4356-8b43-9584b7e72556	<sysprep_folder_path>\svr2003	5.2.3790.3959 (srv03_sp2_rtm.070216-1710)

(Continued)

Table 9.7 Sysprep Downloads and Paths in vCenter (*Continued*)

Windows Version	Sysprep Subdirectory	Sysprep Version
Windows 2003 Server R2—Download at: http://www.micro-soft.com/downloads/details.aspx?FamilyID=93f20bb1-97aa-4356-8b43-9584b7e72556&displaylang=en	<sysprep_folder_path>\svr2003	5.2.3790.3959 (srv03_sp2_rtm.070216-1710)
Windows 2003 x64—Download at: http://www.microsoft.com/downloads/details.aspx?familyid=C2684C95-6864-4091-BC9A-52AEC5491AF7&displaylang=en	<sysprep_folder_path>\svr2003-64	5.2.3790.3959 (srv03_sp2_rtm.070216-1710)
Windows XP x64—Download at: http://www.microsoft.com/downloads/details.aspx?familyid=C2684C95-6864-4091-BC9A-52AEC5491AF7&displaylang=en	<sysprep_folder_path>\xp-64	5.2.3790.3959 (srv03_sp2_rtm.070216-1710)
Windows XP Pro SP3—Download at: http://www.microsoft.com/downloads/details.aspx?familyid=673a1019-8e3e-4be0-ac31-70dd21b5afa7&displaylang=en	<sysprep_folder_path>\xp	5.1.2600.5512
Windows Vista—Built-in	Not Applicable	Not Applicable
Windows Server 2008—Built-in	Not Applicable	Not Applicable
Windows Server 2008 R2—Built-in	Not Applicable	Not Applicable
Windows 7—Built-in	Not Applicable	Not Applicable
Windows 8—Built-in	Not Applicable	Not Applicable

Customizing the Guest Operating System

We talked about Guest Customization briefly in the Planning section, but there are a few things we left out for the sake of brevity. For one, how does the Guest Customization process work? And what are the requirements for the customization process to succeed? And finally, after we've customized one VM, can we save the customization details for later use?

We'll start with how the Guest Customization process works. Guest Customization currently only works with Windows and Linux VMs, and the process works differently depending on which OS you are running. In Windows VMs, we use either the built-in mini-setup routine or Sysprep (depending on the version of Windows). In Linux VMs we use Perl and Shell scripts to perform the modifications.

Starting with Windows Vista, and proceeding into Windows 7 and Server 2008, Microsoft built into the OS a mini-setup routine which, among other things, allows us to rename the VM, change its IP address, and enter a new license key. The inclusion of this software has simplified the Guest Customization process because for these operating systems, we do not require any additional software. However, for Windows 2003, XP, and earlier editions of Windows, we must download and install the Sysprep tools for each operating system and version that we intend to deploy. There are actually different versions of Sysprep for each version of Windows, and in some cases there are different versions of Sysprep for a 32-bit versus 64-bit OS. It is critical that you acquire the correct version and install it in the appropriate location before running the Guest Customization wizard for these operating systems.

Linux VMs don't use Sysprep; instead, we need to run some custom shell scripts that call a variety of Perl scripts to complete the Guest Customization process. We are chiefly interested in changing the hostname and IP address of the VM, but we can also change things like the time zone of the VM. Note that not all distributions of Linux are supported, and that list changes between service packs and updates. Check the VMware vSphere Compatibility Matrixes document on the VMware website for the most current support information.

In either case, the VM that served as our "source," whether it was a template or just a VM, must have the VMware Tools installed before the Guest Customization process will work. Another caveat is that the guest operating system must be installed on a SCSI virtual disk and that disk must be set to the SCSI ID 0:0 in the properties of the VM. This isn't something that typically causes issues, but you might have trouble if you intend to deploy an IDE-based VM, or you have changed the SCSI ID of your system disk for some reason.

The Guest Customization process is a wizard that asks you to enter details about the new VM that you are creating. It stores this information in an XML file, which is then adjusted to work as an answer file for Sysprep or an input file for the Linux Perl scripts (depending on the operating system being customized). Once you've answered all the questions, you will be prompted to save this customization specification to the library. This will allow you to re-use these details later, such as the license key, network settings, Active Directory Domain settings, etc. The real benefit takes a second to realize.

We'll use a typical Windows example here. You could have a Windows Domain administrator create the customization specification, enter the appropriate license key and credentials to join the domain, and then allow a different set of users to use these specifications to deploy VMs. This would allow the other group of users without the proper domain credentials to deploy VMs into the domain as long as they use this specification.

So that leads us into the reusability of the customization specifications. When you complete your first deployment using the Guest Customization wizard, you will be prompted to save the customization specification to the library. This is the vCenter server's database, and this means that you could later access, edit, and reuse the customization specification you just created. You can store many of these customization specifications because you may have several different use cases. For example, you may have more than one Windows domain, or perhaps you have some machines where you don't want to alter the domain membership, but you still need the hostname and IP address changed. Whatever your reason, you can store many different versions of these specs and call on them as needed. To edit them, just look at the dashboard that vCenter displays when you first log on; you may need to click "Home" to get there, but the icon you are looking for is called "Customization Specification Manager."

Updating a Template

What makes a template so unique? If you remember back to our Planning section, you can't edit or power on a template. So how do you update them?

To make any sort of changes to a template, whether in the guest operating system or in the VM settings, you must first convert the template back to a VM. This is a simple process, but it exists so that you don't accidentally change a template. Also, you can apply security permissions to this ability so that no one can make unauthorized changes to your templates.

To convert a template back to a VM, follow these steps:

1. Launch the Convert to Virtual Machine wizard by selecting the template from the hierarchy and choosing Inventory > Template > Convert to Virtual Machine from the vSphere Client menu.

2. Select the ESXi host or cluster where the template will be stored.

3. Select the resource pool for the VM (if applicable).

4. Confirm the settings for the VM and wait for the conversion to complete (typically under 5 seconds).

One other method involves cloning a template. For example, say you have put a lot of work into a particular VM, converted it to a template, and now there is a new service pack available. Before you change your template, clone it to a new template. This way, if the service pack goes badly, you haven't affected your main template. Also, you may want a template that didn't have that service pack installed. We've all seen those legacy applications where a vender refuses to support an app if you dare keep your server up to date with the times. Cloning a template solves that problem because you can deploy VMs from a cloned template prior to the installation of the new service pack.

The template clone process works much the same way you would clone a VM. The chief differences are that you are not prompted to customize the guest operating system, and the resulting VM is a template.

Importing a Virtual Appliance (VA)

We had mentioned the idea of pre-build VMs earlier in this book. You can find a complete marketplace of these VMs on VMware's website, but you don't have to leave the vSphere Client to get there. Just click on File > Browse VA Marketplace in the vSphere Client menu to spawn a wizard with the web browser window that immediately navigates to the VA Marketplace, as shown in Figure 9.1.

Controlling a VM

VMs don't really have much self-control. We have to tell them when to start, stop, reboot, and hold still for snapshots. This section is all about how to manipulate the controls of a VM. That is, how to power it on/off, access the VM's console, and work with the VMware Tools.

In the paragraphs that follow we'll refer to various parts of Figure 9.2. It will help you connect the dots when you're working in the interface later.

Power Buttons and Effects

If you've opened the vSphere Client, you've undoubtedly seen the famed "VCR Buttons," the Start, Stop, and Pause icons, in the toolbar. We're not really sure who invented the icons, but for some reason a sideways triangle automatically means

Figure 9.1
Importing a VM from the VA Marketplace.

Play, two vertical lines means Pause (or suspend), and the little red square means Stop. These are illustrated as point #1 in Figure 9.2.

These power buttons can operate in two fashions: graceful or abrupt. If you have the VMware Tools installed (and running) in your VM, the buttons will attempt to gracefully shut down or reboot your VM. However, if the VMware Tools service isn't present or running, the power buttons will unplug the VM's virtual power cord—stopping it dead in its tracks. Most servers don't react well to that sort of power operation, so ensure that the VMware Tools are installed. You'll be happy you did.

Console Access

If you want to see what is on the VM's virtual monitor, you must open the VM's console. The first step is to select the VM from the inventory. From here you can either launch the console as an independent window, or you can view it in the tabbed interface under the label "Console." These are illustrated in Figure 9.2 as point #2. Note that it has two arrows, one pointing to the Console window button, the other pointing to the Console tab.

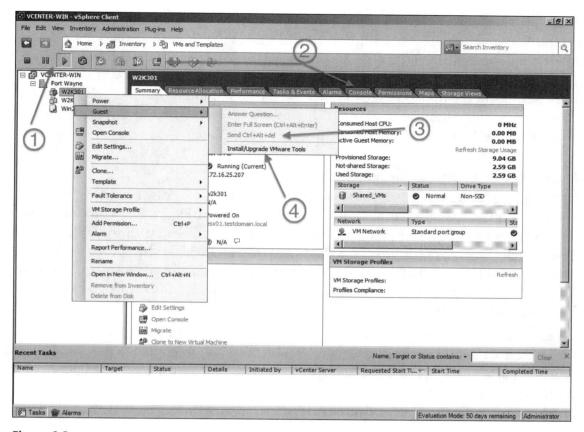

Figure 9.2
Controlling a VM in the vSphere Client.

This view is particularly helpful when a VM gives us that pretty blue (or purple) screen of death. It can also be helpful during the initial installation process for a VM before RDP or SSH access has been enabled.

Sending Ctrl+Alt+Del and Releasing the Mouse

Once you've installed Windows in a VM on ESXi, you will need to log on. Typically, this requires you to press Ctrl+Alt+Del to reach the logon screen. If you're running the vSphere Client from Windows, pressing this key combination will pop up your own security box. While the vSphere Client will pass this right to the VM, it will also reprimand you and advise you to instead press Ctrl+Alt+Insert. This new key combination is detected by vSphere Client and passed to the guest as the standard Ctrl+Alt+Del. Alternatively, you can just right-click the VM in the vSphere Client and select Send Ctrl+Alt +Del from the context menu, as illustrated by point #3 in Figure 9.2.

Another cute trick is the locked-up mouse pointer. If you ever lose control of your mouse while working on a VM, don't panic. You've just learned one of the more interesting side effects of the VM console. If you haven't installed the VMware Tools in your VM yet, your mouse becomes the property of that VM as soon as you click inside of the console window. To get your mouse back, simply press the magic key combination of Ctrl+Alt. This breaks the keyboard and mouse control away from the VM and gives it back to your workstation.

Installing and Updating the VMware Tools

We keep preaching about the importance of the VMware Tools, but where are they and how do you install them? Have a look at point #4 in Figure 9.2. You don't have to download anything from VMware; the VMware Tools come with the ESXi server. You install them by selecting the VM and then choosing Inventory > Virtual Machine > Guest > Install/Upgrade VMware Tools from the menu of the vSphere Client. As you can also see from the figure, this is another option available from a VM's right-click context menu.

When you first initiate the installation of the VMware Tools you will need to open the console or another remote access method to the VM to complete the installation process. Each guest operating system may have a different set of instructions for completing the installation of the VMware Tools. In most cases, the VM will need to reboot when the tools have been installed.

Tip

> For more detailed information, you can reference VMware's Guest OS installation guide here (be aware, this link may change): http://www.vmware.com/pdf/GuestOS_guide.pdf.

Upgrading the VMware Tools is equally important. We approach the upgrade the same way we start the initial installation of VMware Tools. When you click Install/ Upgrade VMware Tools, a dialog is displayed like the one shown in Figure 9.3.

The automated mode is the preferred method when you know that you can reboot the VM at any time. Once the installation has completed, the VM will automatically (but gracefully) reboot to effect the changes. This is disruptive, and if you're not expecting it, it can be embarrassing. As you can see in the figure, there is another option: Interactive mode. The Interactive mode will allow you to operate the wizard from within the guest operating system. This is useful when you don't want the guest to automatically reboot after the installation. We caution you against leaving a VM with a partially installed VMware Tools package. Your mileage may vary, but you're likely to experience instability issues with the memory management driver and you

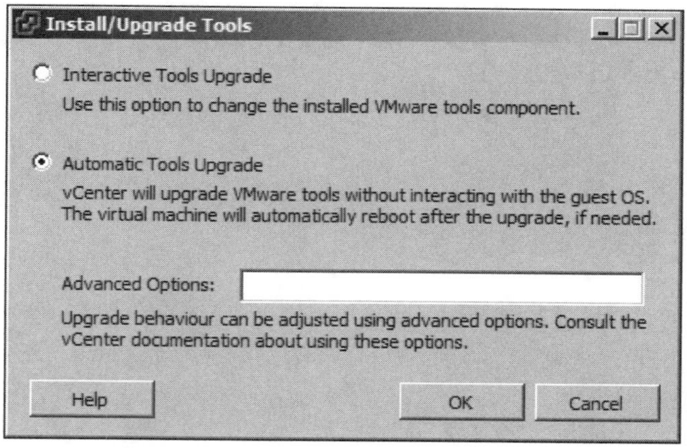

Figure 9.3
Upgrading the VMware Tools.

could have VM heartbeat issues because the VMware Tools service hasn't been 100% updated.

The best plan is to update the VMware Tools when you know that the VM can be rebooted. If the only maintenance window is inopportune, consider using Update Manager to install the updates. Update Manager can also be used to upgrade the Virtual Hardware to version 8, and you can schedule the updates to occur in your non-peak time.

Modifying a VM

Perhaps you want to add new hardware to your VM, or perhaps you just want to give your VM a little resource boost. Whatever the case, you'll do all this and more by editing the settings of your VM. This is typically performed in the vSphere Client; however, many of these tasks can also be performed via the web interface and through vCLI/PowerCLI scripting.

Here's what we'll cover in this section:

- Adding hardware
- Adding a Raw Device Mapping (RDM)
- Hot-Add RAM and CPUs
- Options and Advanced Options
- Resources

- Increasing a VMDK file's size
- Converting a thin disk to thick (and vice versa)
- Renaming a VM
- Viewing a VM's files
- Removing a VM from inventory
- Registering a VM into inventory
- Deleting a VM from disk

Adding Hardware

There are several different types of hardware that we can add to a VM. As we discussed in the Planning section, most hardware changes will require the VM to be powered off, but there are a few, such as network adapters and hard disks, that can be added at anytime. In Figure 9.4 you can see the Add Hardware wizard of a VM that is powered on. Note that most of the categories are marked as "unavailable" because the VM is running.

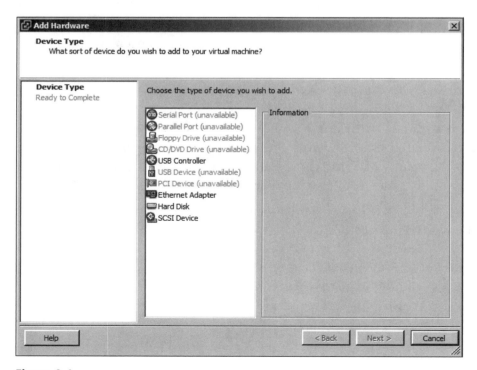

Figure 9.4
Adding hardware to a running VM.

Adding a Raw Device Mapping (RDM)

As you saw in Figure 9.4, a virtual hard disk is one of the devices we can add. We don't have to choose to create or add an existing VMDK file though. We can opt to use an RDM if an LUN has been properly presented to the ESXi server. Unlike adding a VMDK file, there are actually several steps to adding an RDM.

1. Present the LUN to your ESXi server(s). This is the LUN that you want to assign to the VM as an RDM. Ensure that each ESXi host server sees the LUN as the same ID number.

2. Rescan the ESXi server's storage adapters as we discussed in Chapter 8. You need to ensure that your ESXi server can actually see the LUN that you created and assigned.

3. Verify that the new LUN is listed in the list of storage devices under your adapter configuration. Again, please refer back to Chapter 8 for details on where to find the storage adapters.

4. Select the VM where you intend to assign this new LUN, and then select Inventory > Virtual Machine > Edit Settings to open the properties of the VM.

5. On the first tab (Hardware), click Add, and then select the Hard Disk entry.

6. Select Raw Device Mappings. If this option is gray, your ESXi server can't see any unassigned LUNs. Go back and start over at step #1 and verify that the new LUN has been assigned to this ESXi server properly.

7. Select the LUN that you wish to assign to this VM. Be absolutely certain you select the correct LUN. Use the LUN ID, disk size, and the NAA ID number as cross-reference guides.

8. Select the datastore for the metadata descriptor for this RDM. The file is very small; typically you will select Store with Virtual Machine unless you have very custom requirements. This metadata file is referenced infrequently so the performance of the chosen datastore shouldn't be a significant factor.

9. Select the Compatibility mode for the RDM. Choose Virtual unless you are planning to use this LUN for things like Microsoft Cluster services, or any other software package that must have a true block mapping. Virtual compatibility mode gives you the greatest flexibility because snapshots are enabled when using this mode.

10. Choose the SCSI ID for this disk. If you change the first number to something other than 0, you will also add a SCSI controller to the VM, which can be changed later. If you had selected Virtual Compatibility mode on the previous

screen, you may also mark this RDM to be ineligible for snapshots (Persistent Independent mode).

11. Confirm the selections you have made and commit your changes to the VM. The process typically takes less than 5 seconds to complete.

Note

For a review on the differences between an RDM and a VMDK, or between the Virtual and Physical compatibility modes of an RDM, please refer to Chapter 8.

Hot-Add RAM and CPUs

Some hardware can be added while the VM is running, but this isn't a privilege for all editions of vSphere. This functionality isn't required by everyone, so VMware includes the Hot-Add functionality in the Enterprise license or higher. In addition to adding hard disks, you may be able to add virtual CPUs and RAM to a VM. This is highly dependent on the guest operating system of the VM, but if the OS supports this behavior, you can enable the feature with the flip of a couple switches, as shown in Figure 9.5. Don't get carried away just yet though, there are a few caveats we need to cover first.

Not all operating systems support the Hot-Add of RAM/CPU, and even fewer support the removal of RAM/CPUs. Check with the vender of your operating system first. Second, you need to be running at least Virtual Hardware version 7, and your VMware Tools should be up to date. Third, just because you can add the hardware while the OS is running doesn't mean you'll be able to use it. Again, check with your vender before proceeding. Fourth, the Fault Tolerance (FT) feature in vSphere 4 or 5 will not work if your VM is configured for Hot-Add CPUs/RAM.

Caution

Check with the vendor of your operating system before adjusting any of these settings. Just because the vSphere Client will allow you to do it, this is no guarantee everything will work properly. Oh, and check your back ups before doing this too.

Options and Advanced Options

The options are plentiful in a VM. We would love to cover each and every one of these options for you, but frankly that is what the vSphere documentation is for. Instead, we're going to cover the options we feel are the most valuable, or the most commonly used.

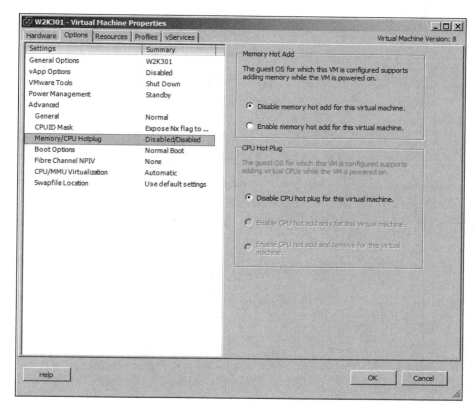

Figure 9.5
Hot-Adding RAM or CPUs to a running VM.

In Figure 9.6 we show the basic options of a VM, including the name, path, and guest operating system selection. Most of these options are only changeable when the VM is powered off (as shown in the figure), but the name of the VM is shown here and it may be changed at any time. Directly below the name, however, is the folder path, which is an informational (read-only) field. Note that all the VMs virtual disks may or may not be in this folder because you can adjust the placement of virtual disks now dynamically via Storage Policies and Storage DRS. Also, we'll make a couple of references back to this figure soon, so don't let it slip your mind just yet.

In Figure 9.7 we show the VMware Tools options that are adjustable from the vSphere Client. Note that you can change the function of the VCR buttons from a graceful shutdown/reboot to a forced power-off operation. You can also configure the guest to run a set of scripts during its power operations. We've used these options in the past to run a script within the guest VM to release its DHCP address. This is particularly useful in Virtual Desktop environments.

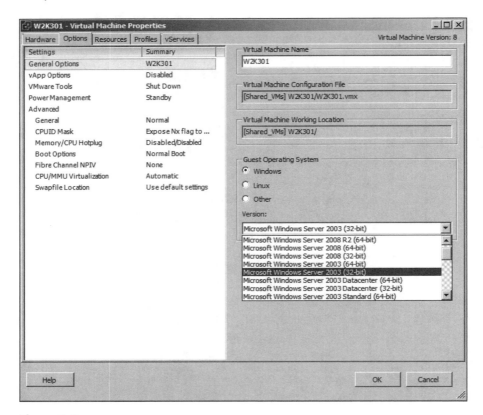

Figure 9.6
General options for a VM.

Finally, pay special attention to the two options at the bottom of the list because they can get you into trouble. "Check and upgrade Tools during power cycling" might seem like a great idea at first, but it can actually cause you a great deal of stress. That option forces the guest VM to update its VMware Tools the next time it is reset or powered on (a power cycle operation, not a soft reboot). If you had checked this box and the VM were to crash in such a way that it must be reset (blue/purple screen of death), on the next boot cycle that VM will upgrade its virtual hardware drivers and services. This might cloud the water a bit when trying to troubleshoot why the VM crashed because the upgrade will replace a lot of system files that could have been the cause of the crash. We find it safer to just update the VMware Tools on a scheduled basis using Update Manager.

The last option is for the guest time synchronization. If you recall back to our Planning section, you'll remember that we don't want our VMs to synchronize against the ESXi server unless there are no Network Time Protocol (NTP) servers available for the VM. This setting is available both in the vSphere Client, as you can see from

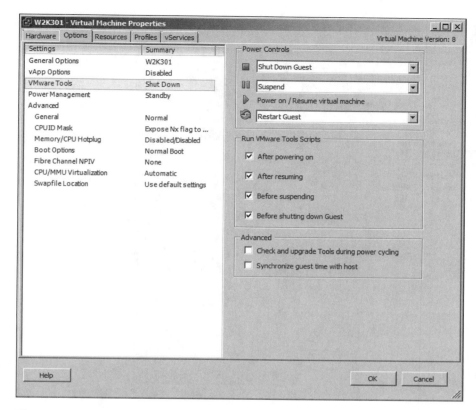

Figure 9.7
VMware Tools options for a VM.

Figure 9.7, as well as within the guest VM. The setting of this box is mirrored to the value in the guest so that you only have to go to one location (either here or the VM) to change this setting. Again, we recommend both of these boxes remain unchecked unless you are certain you need to use these features.

Moving into the Advanced options, we need to first declare a point that VMware drives home for a very good reason: Advanced Options rarely need to be changed! These options fundamentally change the behavior of the VM either by allowing Hot-Add CPUs, NPIV components, or adjusting the VM's CPUID masks. Any of these things can cause a troubleshooting nightmare, so only change these options if you are certain you need to.

We're not going to steer you into traffic, but we are going to show a couple of these advanced options because we feel their benefits outweigh the risks. Take a look at Figure 9.8. At the top of the window in the figure you can see the boot Firmware configuration. In Virtual Hardware version 8 we now have the ability to choose EFI

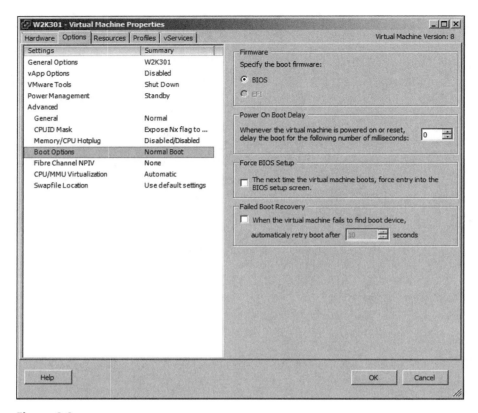

Figure 9.8
Advanced boot options for a VM.

instead of BIOS. Just be careful choosing EFI because not all guest operating systems support it.

Next in line we have the boot delay. Have you ever tried to enter the BIOS setup of a VM? If you've done it, you either have cat-like reflexes or you've previously seen the screen shown in Figure 9.8. We can insert a delay during the VM's boot cycle so that we can enter the BIOS setup as needed. Of course the value is in milliseconds, because that's how we live our lives in IT. Just make sure you put something in there like 5,000 or 6,000 to give yourself 5 or 6 seconds to hit the right key.

The other nice option is the one-time check box that forces the VM to enter the BIOS setup. This box will automatically clear itself after boot, so the VM doesn't end up in an infinite loop. It's a great alternative to the power-on delay if you don't want your VMs waiting that extra 5 seconds.

The last option here is the Failed Boot Recovery. This is useful during initial OS installs as well as PXE boot scenarios. We don't see a lot of demand for this option normally, but it is nice to know that we can prevent the VM from sitting at a blank screen if we forgot to mount a bootable ISO.

Resources

Moving right along, we change tabs now to look at the Resources options of our VM, as shown in Figure 9.9. There are four sections here, and they loosely correspond to CPU, RAM, disk, and CPU. Yes, we mentioned CPU twice. The first entry for CPU usage controls the resources used by the VMs. We'll go into much more depth on this topic in our next chapter. The second CPU entry, labeled "Advanced CPU" is just that, advanced. Under this section you can configure CPU affinity or Hyper-threaded Core Sharing. Under normal circumstances, you will adjust neither of these settings. The CPU affinity is great for labs and testing the behavior of a VM under stress, but it has little use in common practice. It can also be useful in extreme computing environments where it becomes helpful to "pin" a VM to a particular CPU core to maximize resource efficiency.

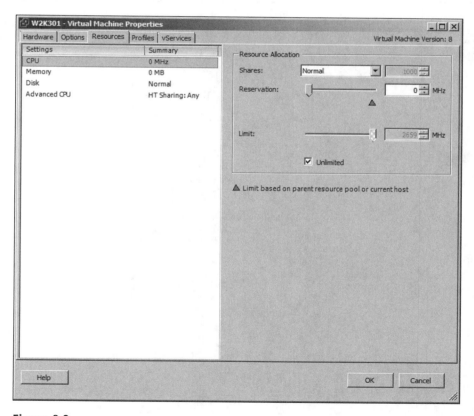

Figure 9.9
Resource options for a VM.

Increasing a VMDK File's Size

If you have ever run out of disk space in the middle of a critical process, you'll appreciate this next section. We can actually expand a virtual disk by adjusting the settings of a VM. To do so, let's go back to the Hardware tab in the VM's properties, and then select the appropriate hard disk as shown in Figure 9.10.

In the figure, we have circled the area that describes what format this virtual disk uses, the current size of the virtual disk, and the maximum size the virtual disk can become (typically the free space on that datastore). The disk size value can be increased, but not decreased. There is no officially supported method of shrinking a VMDK aside from using VMware Converter to migrate to a new VM.

Note

A VMDK file can be increased, but not decreased. There is no officially supported method of shrinking a VMDK, and all unofficial methods are incredibly risky. If you must shrink a VM's disks, use VMware Converter to migrate to an entirely new VM with smaller virtual disks. Just remember that the VMDK must be at least as big as the data within the VMDK (otherwise we would call this vMagician).

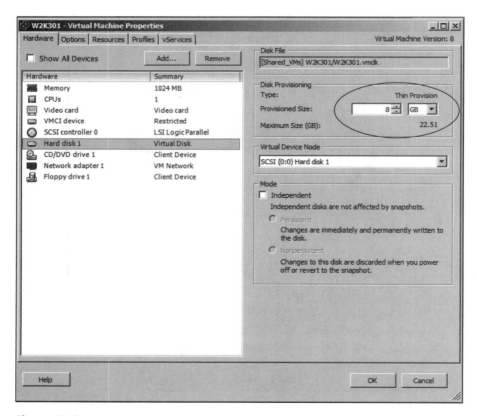

Figure 9.10
Increasing a VMDK file's size.

In the early versions of ESX you could also increase a VMDK file, but the VM had to be powered off. In vSphere 4 and 5 the disk increase can be performed when the VM is running. Now that doesn't mean that your guest operating system will automatically learn about the additional space. Some guest operating systems routinely analyze their SCSI buses and will detect the additional space; others must be told to do so. In Windows, for example, you may need to tell the Disk Management tool to rescan, as shown in Figure 9.11.

Prior to the rescan, the system recognized Disk 0 as having 8GB of total space. After we adjusted the VM settings to increase the VMDK to 16GB and performed the rescan, we were shown the new 8GB of unallocated space at the end of Disk 0, as shown in Figure 9.12.

Now it is up to you to make use of that space. Notice that Windows didn't automatically assume control of the unallocated space. You must now expand the volume into the new unallocated space using either a native or third-party tool within the guest operating system; vSphere's job was done as soon as the virtual disk was expanded.

Converting a Thin Disk to Thick (and Vice Versa)

Another problem that we see from time to time is when administrators have been deploying all their VMs using thin provisioning. Over time this can lead to

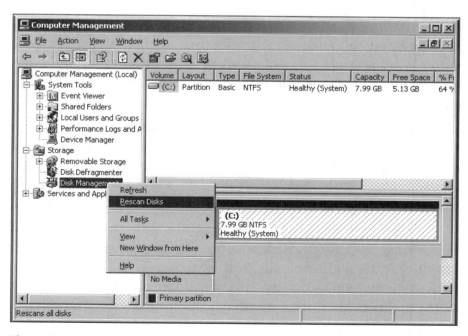

Figure 9.11
Rescanning in Windows Disk Management.

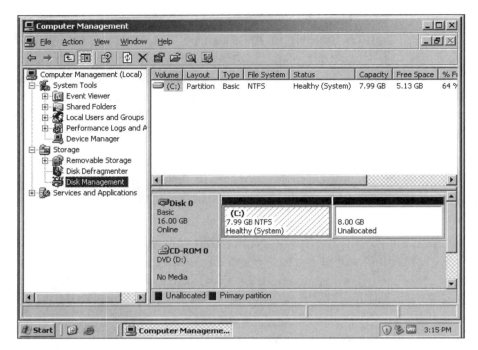

Figure 9.12
Unallocated space in Windows Disk Management.

over-allocation issues and other performance-related problems. So how can we convert a VM from thin provisioning to one of the thick provisioning formats? It's easier than you might think. We can leverage a tool called Storage vMotion to do the job. We'll cover Storage vMotion shortly, but we wanted to include a mention of it here because it is a common question.

If you aren't licensed to use Storage vMotion, there is a manual method to inflate a thin provisioned VMDK, but the VM must be powered off. There is no supported manual mode of migrating from thick to thin provisioning aside from Storage vMotion. That doesn't mean you can't hack the files, but that's not something we recommend trying on a production VM. Stick to Storage vMotion or use VMware Converter if you aren't licensed for Storage vMotion.

To manually inflate a VMDK file, open the datastore browser and navigate to the VM's folder. Right-click on the VMDK file and choose "Inflate" as shown in Figure 9.13. This process will take some time depending on the size of the virtual disk. The datastore browser will be covered in this chapter when we talk about how to find a VM's files.

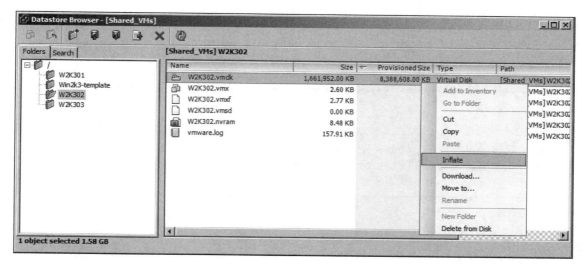

Figure 9.13
Inflating a thin provisioned VMDK file.

Note

Refer to Chapter 8 for a discussion on the differences between Eager Zero thick provisioned, Lazy Zero thick provisioned, and thin provisioning.

Renaming a VM

There are times when it becomes necessary to change the name of a VM. Perhaps you typed it wrong initially, or maybe the VM was renamed in the guest operating system. If you need to rename a VM, it is fairly easy. You can right-click on the VM and rename it, or you can edit the settings as shown back in Figure 9.6.

That takes care of the name of the VM, but it left out a couple of things. First and foremost, did we change the hostname or computer name of the guest operating system within the VM? No, we didn't. The guest operating system is completely unaware of our little name change, which is probably a good thing. If we want to change the VM's hostname, we need to do so from within the VM console or another remote access means.

But that brings up a good point. If we change the hostname of a VM, and we change the name of the VM in the vSphere Client, what happens to all the various files and folders that make up the VM? Unfortunately, nothing. The files and folder names remain unchanged, which can become very confusing later after you have forgotten what the original name of the VM was. If you ever want to check though, it's easy. Refer back to Figure 9.6 and you'll see just under the name of the VM a complete path listing. That path listing will remain accurate even if you rename the VM. That way you can find the files for the VM, even if you renamed it a year ago.

Caution

We don't recommend that you manually rename your VM's files or folder path unless you are an expert (or you like troubleshooting), because there are many files that need to be changed, including the contents of the VM's VMX file. Be careful, you have been warned!

Note

In previous editions of vSphere it was possible to use Storage vMotion to correct the name of all the various VM files after a VM had been renamed. In vSphere 5 that function no longer works, but we hear they're working on a solution.

Tip

Though it works best if you to shut down the VM, you can solve the renaming problem by cloning the VM. The cloning process will take care of the name changes, but be aware that the cloning process changes the MAC address of the new VM!

Viewing a VM's Files

With all the talk of files and renaming, there has to be a way to find these files and show them in browser view. Fortunately there is; it's called the datastore browser, and we've snapped a picture of it in Figure 9.14. To get to this view, just right-click on any datastore and select Browse Datastore from the context menu.

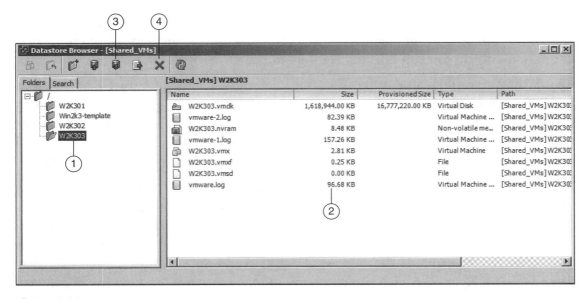

Figure 9.14
vSphere Client's datastore browser.

To make the rest of this section a little easier to read we annotated Figure 9.14 with numbers and defined those sections of the figure.

- Point #1 shows the folder hierarchy, much like a Windows Explorer view.
- Point #2 shows the VM files and any subfolders.
- Point #3 shows the upload and download buttons to transfer files in and out of the datastore (ISOs, Logs, VMDKs, etc.).
- Point #4 shows the delete and refresh buttons; be careful with that delete button, there is no undo or undelete.

As you can see, the folder view is handy, but there's a catch. It masks some of the details about our files. For one, look at the VMDK file shown in Figure 9.15. Notice anything funny about it? Back in the beginning of this chapter we explained that there are actually several different types of VMDK files, and that the small, human-readable metadata file was the one that ends with a .vmdk extension. The large binary file ends with a -flat.vmdk extension.

In the datastore browser, the VMDK file is shown as a single large file, but that is a simplification for the user interface only. There still is a metadata file, and you can prove it. Open an SSH connection to your ESXi server and list the contents of the directory containing your VM's VMDK files as shown in Figure 9.15. At point #1 you can see the large binary "flat" file listed separately from the smaller metadata file at point #2.

Caution

Be careful working in the datastore browser or the direct file system of an ESXi host. There is no undo or undelete option!

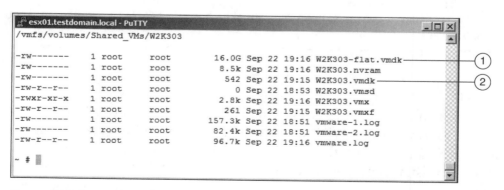

Figure 9.15
A VM's directory contents shown from the command line.

Removing a VM from Inventory

That final cautionary note brings us to the removal and deletion of a VM. Like the datastore browser, there is no undo or undelete for VMs. Once you delete them from disk, they are gone forever.

VMware included a second type of removal process that just removes the VM from the vCenter or ESXi host's inventory view. This mode is a bit more forgiving because it doesn't actually delete the VM (in case you want to get it back). However, like most nice features, there are two problems we have when people use it.

The first problem is that removing a VM from inventory doesn't clean up that old disk space. While this wasn't a huge problem for vSphere 4, in vSphere 5 we have something referred to as Storage DRS. If you've been reading along you may recall us mentioning a few times that extra files on a datastore will cause Storage DRS to fail when "evacuating" a datastore. Plus, even if you're not using Storage DRS, all those files and folders are still taking up valuable storage space in your datastores. Unfortunately, this makes it very easy to forget to go back and clean up afterward.

The second problem is that there is no pop-up box that tells you where to find the VM once you have removed it from inventory. Now, this won't be a big deal if you have never renamed your VM because the folder name will still likely be the same as the VM's name. Unfortunately, if the VM has ever been renamed you may have trouble locating it because, as you read earlier, renaming a VM does not rename its folders and files. Also, as of this writing, in vSphere 5 Storage vMotion no longer corrects the name of a VM's files/folders. In other words, you could be playing hide and go seek with a VM if you failed to record its folder path before you removed it from inventory.

Tip

Be sure to check (and write down) the exact path of your VM before you remove it from inventory. The path may be different than you think. Also check the path of each virtual disk file because they may not all be grouped together!

Registering a VM

Registering a VM is another way of saying: "add a VM to the inventory." We're a bit ambiguous when we say "inventory" because you can add a VM to either vCenter's inventory or an ESXi server's inventory (for instance, if it isn't part of a vCenter environment). While this isn't some sort of means to create a VM, it could be considered a manual deployment method because you can use this method to add VMs that were created on other ESXi servers. It's not the most ideal way to deploy VMs because it takes so much manual interaction, but it works well when moving a VM between vCenters or unrelated ESXi servers.

To register a VM into the inventory of vCenter or another ESXi host, you must first launch the datastore browser and navigate to the folder containing the VM's VMX file (the configuration file for the VM). If you refer back to Figure 9.13, you'll see the menu system for the datastore browser. If you notice, there is an entry in the context menu labeled Add to Inventory. This option is disabled in our figure because we've right-clicked on a VMDK file. If you were to instead right-click on the VM's VMX file (also shown in the figure), the Add to Inventory option would be enabled. This is also true for the VMTX files for templates. Though the VMTX file's icon looks a bit different, it's really just a VMX file that was renamed when the VM was converted to a template.

A really practical use case for this feature is moving VMs between vCenter installations. If you have multiple vCenters connected together in a single site (say you have a large implementation of VMware View), you'll learn fast that you can't migrate VMs between the vCenter installations even if they are in linked mode. You must remove the VMs from one vCenter and then register them in the new vCenter to make the transfer.

Another great use is when you have removed a VM from the inventory instead of deleting it. As we mentioned above, there isn't an undo option for deleting VMs, but this makes for a great workaround. If you noted the path to the VMX file of the VM, you can open the datastore browser, navigate to the file, and add the VM back into the inventory.

Deleting a VM from Disk

If you're 100% sure that the VM you have selected needs to be permanently removed from vCenter, you can select Delete from Disk instead of Remove from Inventory. This is a dangerous option because, while it does ask for confirmation, it is a typical "are you sure?" type of dialog box. There isn't any special protection method to keep you from accidentally deleting the wrong VM.

This feature really will delete the VM and all of its associated files from the datastore. By the way, there is no "undo" feature, unless you include finding your back up tapes and restoring the VM (provided you had a back up). Be careful.

Snapshots

We've all had those moments when we wished we could undo something we just did. In computer games we use saved games, in books we use bookmarks, and in VMs we use snapshots. A snapshot is a clever system that allows us to save the state of a VM before we do something risky, so that we can revert back to that state if things don't work out. Let's explore this a bit further.

What Is a snapshot, and What Is It Not?

First and foremost: *a snapshot is NOT a back up*, nor is it a replication or recovery technology. You may leverage snapshots in your back up process, but you should never rely on snapshots alone as your back up method because having multiple snapshots on a VM will decrease its disk performance. Snapshots, in general, are best used for quick tests that could produce unexpected results (such as a service pack installation). You shouldn't leave a snapshot on a VM for longer than absolutely necessary. Ideally, if you can safely remove the snapshot that same day, do so; it will prevent your disk I/O from suffering unnecessarily.

How Does a Snapshot Work?

There are a number of analogies to help explain how snapshots work, but the easiest one that we have found involves relating them to bookmarks in books (like the kind you're reading now). For instance, let this book represent a VM that you are upgrading. The upgrade can be anything from an OS service pack to a new application (you choose, this example works for almost anything). In order to make this work, we'll need you to help us out. Go find a couple of bookmarks that you can use to mark the pages in this book. Really any bookmarks will do—even scraps of paper will work for this exercise.

Now, before we get too far you should really bookmark your place in this book because you'll be flipping pages back and forth in a minute. After all, we don't want to lose you. By bookmarking your page, you've just created your first pretend snapshot—congratulations! Before you install service packs or updates, you might want to create a snapshot so that you can get back to where you started if things go wrong. In this case, the bookmark you've just placed represents a snapshot.

Next, we want you to skip ahead a few pages to represent the installation of a service pack, and then insert another bookmark on that page. Go on; we'll wait.

Now, if you did exactly what we asked you wouldn't be reading this section because we never told you to revert back to this snapshot. But that's okay; you made a great point for us. The fact that you could come back to this section proves that snapshots (bookmarks) work! You were able to swap back to this page without losing any of the work you had just performed. Snapshots behave the same way: you can navigate between them, but you can't have more than one active snapshot at a time; much like you can't really read from two different pages of a book simultaneously (try it, you can't do it). Let's explore this a bit further by explaining what is happening under the hood.

Creating Snapshots: Cold and Hot

When you create a snapshot, you have several options. You can create the snapshot with the VM powered on or off. If the VM is powered off (cold) you'll have a very consistent snapshot because all the VM's files were closed properly. If you want to create a snapshot of a VM that is powered on (hot), we won't stop you, but understand that there are some drawbacks. First, if you take a snapshot of a running VM, we need to preserve the state of that VM or else the VM will think it crashed if we revert back to the snapshot in the future. Why? Because it was running and it had active memory, processes, and open files. When you create the snapshot, you only protect the disk in its current state (with the files still open). Without a means to close these open files, the VM will think that it crashed when we resume that snapshot because those open files may be missing some data (corrupt). Remember our discussion earlier regarding crash-consistent clones? This is another case where we must be careful or data loss could result.

Since this isn't a very ideal situation, we can also capture the VM's RAM and execution state much like when we suspend a VM or hibernate a physical machine. The state is automatically replayed when the snapshot is reactivated later, meaning that the VM doesn't even realize that anything happened to it—aside from the fact that it just travelled in time. The downside is that in order to keep the operating system from experiencing a crash when you revert back to it later, we must create a very large file in your datastore; a file the size of the VM's RAM!

On the other hand, what if you don't care if the operating system crashes? There are actually several (almost legit) cases where this could be the case. For one, if you are pressed for time you may not want to take the time to save the RAM to disk. The process takes some time, especially for VMs with many GB of memory. Or, maybe you have a test VM and you just like troubleshooting broken operating systems. Whatever the case, if you want to see how your VM behaves after a sudden crash, deselect the option "Snapshot the virtual machine's memory" shown in Figure 9.16.

Navigating the Snapshot Manager Hierarchy

Let's go back to our bookmark analogy. You already proved for us that you can move around the book from one bookmark to another, but what happened when you switched places? You couldn't read from the page that you moved away from, and you began reading from the page that you moved to. This too is like the snapshot

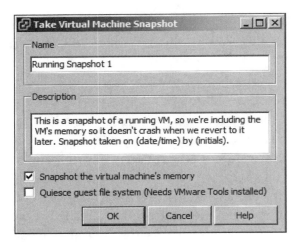

Figure 9.16
Creating a snapshot of a VM.

hierarchy. When you move from one snapshot to another, you stop making changes to one "delta" VMDK file and you create a new delta file. These delta files are where ESXi keeps the changes that you're making to the VM because we don't want to contaminate any other VMDK file or another snapshot's file. You can have many snapshots attached to a VM, but only one snapshot can be active at any one time.

Note

> You can see these delta files in the datastore browser that we discussed earlier in this chapter. If you ever see a VMDK file with "delta" in its name, it means that VM has a snapshot.

You can freely move from one snapshot to another in the Snapshot Manager for your VM. First select the snapshot you wish to move to, and then click the Go to button shown in Figure 9.17.

Committing or Deleting Snapshots

So everything worked out as you had hoped and now you want to delete a snapshot. Depending on where you're located in the snapshot hierarchy, clicking the Delete button shown in Figure 9.17 will produce different results.

If you haven't moved to a previous snapshot, you are at the bottom of the snapshot hierarchy. This would be the case if everything worked out perfectly with your service pack or application installation; you didn't need to go back to a previous point in time. In this case, any snapshot that exists would be before your current position in time. This would be like looking at this book and seeing bookmarks in the previous chapters. If you were to grab one of those bookmarks and remove it, you didn't

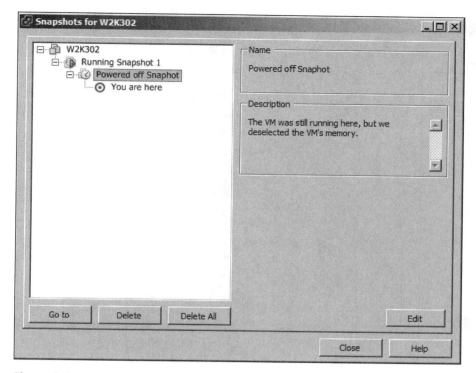

Figure 9.17
Reverting to a VM snapshot.

change your place in the book, nor have you lost your place in the book. The same behavior happens with snapshots: the snapshot is removed, but the data is "committed" to the disks (no changes occur to the state of your VM). But what if you had reverted back to an earlier snapshot. We've shown an example of this in Figure 9.18.

Prior to taking that screenshot, we selected the snapshot labeled "Running Snapshot 1," and then we clicked the Go to button. This moved our "You are here" pointer above the "Powered off Snapshot," as you can see in the figure. In this case, if we select "Running Snapshot 1" and then click the Delete button, the delta files in "Running Snapshot 1" will be committed to the underlying VM's permanent disks. If we select and delete "Powered off Snapshot" however, the delta files associated with the "Powered off Snapshot" would be deleted and not committed (because it is below our "You are here" pointer in the hierarchy).

Caution

Be careful when deleting snapshots. The position of the "You are here" pointer determines whether the data is committed to the VM's disks or deleted permanently.

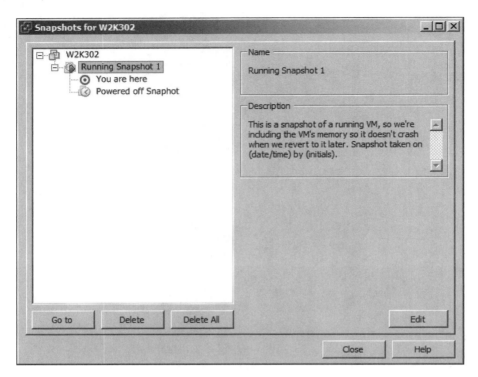

Figure 9.18
Deleting a VM snapshot.

There is another button in the Snapshot Manager that you no doubt saw: Delete All This button will remove all the snapshots, committing to disk those snapshots above your pointer, and permanently deleting the snapshots below the "You are here" pointer. Use extreme caution with this option because it cannot be stopped. If you have some very large snapshots, this operation may take hours to complete. If you interrupt the process (such as by powering off the ESXi host or the SAN), you will likely have a very corrupted VM. Instead, allow the process to complete. If you are uncertain, call VMware for assistance before making any rash decisions.

There is also a new feature in vSphere 5 that allows us to reconcile our list of snapshots in the event that the snapshot database becomes inconsistent with the actual delta VMDK files in the datastore. We'll talk about this a bit more in the Troubleshooting section of this chapter.

Migrating VMs

Can you think of a time when you had to perform maintenance on a physical server or SAN during the middle of production hours? Wouldn't it have been nice if you could have performed that maintenance without experiencing any downtime on

Table 9.8 VM Migration Methods

Migration Method	VM Power State(s)	Purpose
vMotion	Powered On	Change host
Suspended Migration	Suspended	Change host and/or datastore
Cold Migration	Powered Off	Change host and/or datastore
Storage vMotion	Any	Change datastore

your production systems? If your production workloads are virtualized and you have licensed vMotion and Storage vMotion, you can do just that—migrate your VMs to another host or datastore without taking downtime.

There are a number of ways to migrate a VM from one host or datastore to another, and each method has a purpose. For example, we can migrate a powered-off VM fairly easily from one host to another because it is really just a bunch of files; no processes or memory are being used. Once CPU instructions or RAM are active, we have some limitations on how and when we can migrate the VMs or their storage. See Table 9.8 for a bit of clarification on which options are available to us, and then reference the following sections to learn more about how these migrations are performed.

What's Changed in Version 5

Before we dig into the details of each migration method, here's a synopsis of the changes that occurred to VM migrations in vSphere 5 as compared to vSphere 4.x. These features require both ESXi hosts (source and target) to be running vSphere 5.

- **vMotion.** Stun During Page Send (SDPS) enables very active VMs with lots of vRAM to migrate between hosts.
- **vMotion.** Metro vMotion doubles the latency tolerance from 5ms to 10ms.
- **vMotion.** ESXi can use multiple VMkernel NICs to migrate VMs between hosts.
- **Storage vMotion.** Uses mirroring instead of snapshots to copy the disks.
- **Storage vMotion.** VMs with snapshots can be migrated now.

The Stun During Page Send (SDPS) function of vMotion in vSphere 5 allows us to vMotion VMs that were otherwise either too large or too active to migrate when using previous versions of vSphere. If you're not already familiar, read below to understand the vMotion migration process. This feature allows the ESXi host to slow down the VM's vCPUs to reduce the VM's memory change rate; meaning there will be fewer pages of memory that get changed during the vMotion RAM copy process. This means that VMs with very large allocations of vRAM, or VMs that change their memory pages at a very rapid rate, can now vMotion successfully. This has also allowed vMotion operations to succeed when the LAN speeds aren't ideal or have latency has high as 10ms. This feature, referred to as Metro vMotion, may allow VMs to migrate between replicated datacenters if the WAN connection remains under 10ms during the vMotion operations.

Note

SDPS can be disabled via advanced options on the VM if you would prefer the vMotion to fail rather than momentarily slow down the VM's processors.

In addition to the above change, the ESXi hosts can now use multiple NICs to perform vMotion operations. This is very similar to the behavior we had in vSphere 4 when we used multiple NICs for software iSCSI connections. You actually bind the vmnics to the VMkernel ports in the same way. If present, multiple NICs will even be used for single-VM vMotion operations. This is very valuable when performing multiple simultaneous vMotion operations as the additional bandwidth will help evacuate your ESXi hosts quicker in the event of urgent system maintenance.

Storage vMotion has undergone a complete overhaul in vSphere 5. In previous versions, Storage vMotion leveraged snapshots to release and then copy the VMDK files of the VMs. In vSphere 5, the ESXi hosts use a mirroring driver to transfer the virtual disk files from one datastore to another. This has served two functions. First, because we no longer issue a snapshot on the VM's files, Storage vMotion has a reduced impact on the performance of the VM. The operation now creates the files on the target datastore and then mirrors every write operation between the source and target until the target datastore has a complete copy of the virtual disk.

The second advantage of the mirroring technique is that we can migrate VMs that have active snapshots. Previously this was impossible because Storage vMotion used snapshots to unlock and then copy the VMDK files from one datastore to another. Now we can use the mirroring driver to migrate the snapshot delta files when we migrate the regular virtual disk files.

vMotion

vMotion is one of the quintessential features of vSphere. Cloud computing would be very different indeed without the ability to migrate running VMs between physical servers.

As vSphere Administrators we've had vMotion at our disposal for years, but what exactly does it do and how does it do it? You likely already know that vMotion is a tool that allows us to migrate a running VM from one ESXi host to another (without the VM crashing or becoming unavailable).

In order for vMotion to work, the VM and the ESXi hosts must meet several prerequisites:

- Both the source and target ESXi hosts must be connected to shared storage, and the VM we intend to move must be located on one of the shared storage volumes.

- The ESXi hosts must have the exact same CPU type or use Enhanced vMotion Compatibility (EVC) to smooth out the differences—this is discussed in Chapter 11.

- The ESXi hosts must have a dedicated network channel for the vMotion traffic that connects at 1 Gigabit or 10 Gigabit speeds.

- The VM must not have CPU Affinity configured—pinning the VM's vCPUs to a particular physical processor core.

- The VM must only have connections to disks, ISOs, networks, CD-ROMs, floppys, or other resources that are shared and available on both ESXi hosts.

The process involves a few steps that we'll detail below:

1. The ESXi servers are verified for compatibility (see above for the list of prerequisites).

2. The destination ESXi host creates a shadow VM to contain the memory pages from the VM we are migrating.

3. The source ESXi host begins tracking changes to the VM's memory pages, and then copies the pages to the destination host. This process may take multiple passes to completely copy all the VM's pages.

4. As the VM's final memory pages are synchronized between the two ESXi hosts, the VM may be briefly stunned or slowed to allow the source ESXi server to complete the memory transfer.

5. The execution state of the VM is passed from the source ESXi host to the destination, and the VM is then resumed on the destination ESXi host.

6. The destination ESXi host sends a notification to its upstream physical switch to alert the network that the VM has moved.

As you can see from the list above, there isn't any part where the VM's virtual disks are transferred or even affected. The vMotion process is all about moving the execution state of the VM from one host to another. That's why there is a prerequisite that the hosts share storage volumes—we don't move the virtual disks.

Storage vMotion

Despite the fact that vMotion and Storage vMotion share a name, they really have little in common. Storage vMotion allows us to relocate a VM's virtual disks from one datastore to another without taking that VM offline. In previous versions of vSphere, Storage vMotion accomplished this by taking a snapshot of the VM to release the VM's lock on its VMDK files. In vSphere 5, the ESXi host leverages a storage mirroring driver to allow the VM to continue accessing whatever virtual disks it possesses, while in the background the ESXi host copies the data to the target datastore. The mirroring driver allows us to finally migrate a VM that has an active snapshot, as well as improving the performance of our disk migrations.

Note

We discussed Storage vMotion in much more detail in Chapter 8.

Storage vMotion has been incorporated into vSphere's storage automation and load balancing feature called Storage DRS—covered in detail in Chapter 11. Storage DRS leverages Storage vMotion in much the same way that regular DRS leverages vMotion. Storage DRS can automatically migrate a VM's virtual disks from one datastore to another for performance or maintenance reasons.

Tip

In previous versions of vSphere, Storage vMotion was often used to correct mismatched filenames resulting from renaming a VM.

In vSphere 5, Storage vMotion does not automatically rename a VM's files during the migration. This may be corrected in future versions or service packs. In the meantime, you can clone a VM if you must rename it and have its files/folders match.

Suspended Migration

A suspended VM isn't actively using any memory or processes, but once it resumes it certainly will use these resources. This means that we have the same limitations on host-to-host migrations that are present with vMotion migrations because we have to be careful of where we migrate the VM. If we were to migrate the VM to an incompatible host, the VM would crash as soon as it were resumed.

The migration wizard will automatically sense whether the VM is running, suspended, or powered off. It will only present options that are relevant to VM. If there is a risk that the VM would crash, the wizard won't allow you to migrate the VM to that host.

Unlike the vMotion operation above, in a Suspended Migration, the ESXi hosts are permitted to relocate the VM's virtual disks. If desired, you can perform a Storage vMotion at the same time that you perform a host migration.

Cold Migration

As we mentioned earlier, if your VM isn't powered on, you can easily move a VM from one host to another. This is because the VM doesn't have any active processes that are running on a CPU, and it is the way that our CPUs interpret these instructions that cause us grief when trying to migrate a VM between dissimilar CPU types.

The wizard we use to migrate VMs in a powered-off state is the same as the one used during vMotion or Storage vMotion operations. The difference is that the wizard doesn't have to validate the remote ESXi host's CPU type because our VM is powered off. The process is also simplified because we don't have to copy any RAM from host to host. We are essentially unregistering and then registering the VM onto the target host. You might recall our discussion on registering a VM earlier in this chapter.

As with the Suspended Migration, during a Cold Migration the ESXi hosts are permitted to relocate the VM's virtual disks. If desired, you can perform a Storage vMotion at the same time that you perform a host migration.

Using vApps

Can you think of a time when you would have liked to group your VMs together? Maybe it was because you needed synchronized startup/shutdown, or perhaps it was because you wanted to export the VMs as a bundle. vApps are a means to bundle your VMs in such a way that you can do both of these things and more. You can think of a vApp as a bag of VMs. There can be one or many VMs inside a vApp, but typically the function or purpose of these VMs is intertwined.

As with so many vSphere features, the concept behind vApps originated in the early versions of VMware workstation in a function known as VM Teams. The concept of teaming VMs together made even more sense at a server level because we have so many different VMs that depend on one another. The team concept allows the VMs to start up and shut down in a prescribed order so that your applications function properly when they start.

Earlier in the Planning section of this chapter we discussed how the start order concept works and why it might be helpful. Here we will explore how to create, delete, modify, and export them.

Creating and Deleting vApps

If your hosts are in a cluster, and you wish to create a vApp, you must first enable DRS. Once you have DRS enabled on your cluster, creating a vApp involves a simple, two-step wizard, which asks you the name of the vApp and the resources that you intend to assign to it. You can create vApps inside clusters, hosts, resource pools, and even other vApps! The creation process doesn't add VMs to the vApp, nor does it configure everything for you. To add VMs, drag and drop whatever VMs you want into the vApp. Once the VMs that you want have been included, edit the vApp settings to configure the fine details such as the start order or resource management.

Note

For more information on how to enable and configure DRS, refer to Chapter 11.

Caution

Exercise caution when removing a vApp. Doing so will also remove any VMs that were contained within the vApp!

If you no longer need a particular vApp, you can delete it. To delete a vApp, right-click on it and choose either Remove from Inventory or Delete from Disk. It's the same options you have when removing a VM; it also has the same impact. If you choose Remove from Inventory, all the VMs within the vApp are removed from the host/vCenter's inventory. Likewise is true for Delete from Disk, so be careful!

Editing Start Order

There are a number of options we can fine-tune. One of these options is the VM start order, as you can see in Figure 9.19. We discussed the start order problem earlier in the Planning section of this chapter. As a refresher, you can control the start order of multiple VMs via a vApp even if those VMs are located on different ESXi hosts. To alter the start order of the VMs in your vApp, select one from the list as shown in Figure 9.19, and then click on the up or down arrow to position it in an appropriate group. The groups at the top start up first and shut down last.

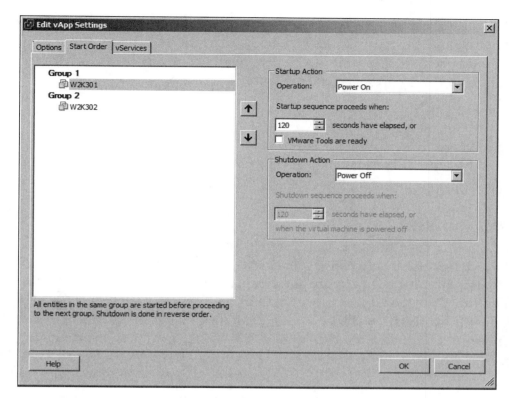

Figure 9.19
vApp Options—VM start order.

Editing the Configuration

In addition to adjusting the start order for a group of VMs, you may also adjust advanced settings such as IP network pools (for fenced networks) and the resource consumption of the vApp much like a mini-resource pool. We'll discuss resource pools in greater detail in the next chapter, but they are a means to control how much CPU and memory a group of VMs is permitted to use. In this case, you would be limiting, reserving, or prioritizing the resource consumption for the VMs within this vApp.

Exporting vApps to OVF files

In the next section, we'll cover the intricacies of OVF files. These are the files that allow us to move VMs between virtualization platforms. You can export vApps in the same way we export VMs. The difference is that when you export a vApp, you will get an OVF file that includes each VM in the vApp, so be careful, you might get a very large collection of files if you export a vApp!

Also, if you intend to deploy your own vApps, you may be interested in a program that VMware provides known as VMware Studio. This application allows you to edit OVF files to customize your vApps. It can be particularly handy if you are a software developer looking to deploy a multi-tier application as a vApp.

Working with OVF/OVA Files

Part of the advantage to virtualization is the portability of VMs. We discussed the OVF and OVA formats in the Planning section of this chapter, so now we'll focus on how to export and then import VMs using this format.

Exporting VMs to OVF/OVA Files

If you want to keep a copy of some VMs on cold storage, you can do so using the OVF files that we discussed earlier in the templates section of this chapter. vCenter uses the OVF format when you export any template or powered-off VM in your inventory. You run the export process from within the vSphere Client, and the files are brought to the workstation where you are running the vSphere Client. That means that if you are accessing vCenter over a WAN link, you'll be exporting that VM across a WAN link, so be careful!

Caution

> The OVF Export process copies the VM to your local workstation. Make sure you're connected to vCenter via a high-speed LAN connection before exporting a VM or template!

Nearly every command in the toolbar can be found on the right-click context menu of a VM. The notable exception is Export to OVF Template, which can only be found by selecting the VM from the hierarchy and then selecting File > Export > Export OVF Template from the vSphere Client Window as shown circled in Figure 9.20.

These OVF files can be copied to USB storage for safekeeping, or perhaps you might copy them to an encrypted portable drive for transfer to an offsite recovery facility. Just keep in mind that an OVF file isn't a back up; it's a disaster recovery image. Recovering individual files from within an OVF file isn't an easy task. You should plan to have some other software to allow your administrators to perform file-level restores.

Importing VMs from OVF/OVA Files

If you have already exported a VM to an OVF or OVA file, the process of bringing it back into vCenter is fairly easy. This process can also be used for any OVF or OVA

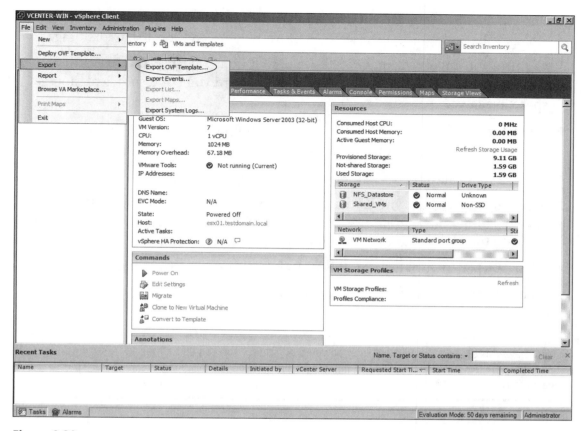

Figure 9.20
Exporting a VM to an OVF/OVA file.

file that you might find online or that you may receive from partner organizations. Many venders now deploy their software in pre-packaged Virtual Applications (VAs), which use OVF/OVA files instead of mailing out physical hardware or even software. This cuts down on their costs, and reduces the time to delivery on their products, which coincidently helps the customer because the savings can be passed right down the line.

We're going to assume for our example that you have just exported some VMs from one of your remote locations and you have securely transported them to your organization's main datacenter. You now would like to import the VMs into an isolated test environment so that you have a copy of their servers to review. This example can be adjusted as you see fit; the instructions are all nearly the same.

1. Launch the wizard by choosing File > Deploy OVF Template from the vSphere Client menu.

2. Enter the source path or URL for the OVF/OVA file. This may be on local storage, shared storage, or a web URL (we recommend local/shared storage).

3. Confirm the details of the OVF/OVA description. Pay special attention to the disk format and size configuration and ensure you have sufficient storage space available.

4. Enter the name of the VM and choose its location in the folder hierarchy.

5. Select the ESXi host or cluster where the VM will be stored.

6. Choose the Datastore and Storage Profile (if applicable).

7. Select an appropriate virtual disk type: Lazy Zeroed thick provision (the "normal" thick formatted disk), Eager Zeroed thick provision (if you intend to use this VM for VMware's FT solution), or thin provision.

8. Choose whether to power on the VM after deployment (optional).

9. Confirm the settings for the VM and wait for the import to complete.

Tip

You may wish to leave the imported VM powered off so that you can edit all the VM's settings prior to it powering on for the first time. Check things like the network connections, reservations, shares, limits, connected CD-ROM drives, etc.; anything that may block the VM from booting properly.

Caution

Be careful if the OVF/OVA file that you are importing came from another site where the source VM is still active. Powering up this VM on your production network may cause duplicate name/IP address conflicts. Ensure the other VM is powered off, or this VM's network adapter is properly isolated or disconnected before proceeding.

Nested Virtualization

A book on vSphere wouldn't be complete without addressing one of the more incredible features of the software: nested virtualization. That is, virtualizing ESXi within ESXi.

This isn't really something new with vSphere 5, but it has been improved. Also, we're certainly not advocating that you virtualize your production ESXi servers. This technique is for lab studies; in particular, it is for those of us who learn best by doing and seeing. Creating a mini-lab of ESXi servers, complete with a vCenter server and an iSCSI software SAN, will prove very helpful in understanding vSphere. You may never actually use the lab, but the process of building it will stick with you, and the lessons you learn along the way will be worth much more than what the lab could offer anyway.

ESXi runs very well as a VM; in fact, many of the sample images shown in this book were taken from screen shots of ESXi running in a VM on either VMware Workstation or VMware Fusion. The only real catch is that ESXi has some hefty requirements. For one, you must allocate two vCPUs and 2GB of RAM. The disk and network is fairly minor. Next, you'll need a vCenter server. This could be the vCenter server appliance or a Windows VM. Either way you'll need another 2GB of RAM and another 2 vCPUs to make it work properly. Finally, you'll need some sort of shared storage if you intend to experiment with vMotion in your test lab. Yes, you can actually vMotion a nested VM between two virtual ESXi servers. It's the stuff we live for…well, it is if you don't get out much. In our virtual labs we use things like Open-Filer or FreeNAS. They can both be easily installed as a VM and can both serve as iSCSI and NFS targets.

Note

Remember, the goal of this exercise is to learn in a trial-by-fire situation. You will learn more if you have to research things to get it working. We're not providing a step by step because you could write a small book on this topic.

This is a very advanced topic, and not one that everyone will undertake. When you finally achieve the satisfaction of performing a vMotion of a nested VM between two virtual ESXi hosts, you'll see what we mean: it's the journey not the destination. You'll likely never use the lab once you've constructed it other than to amaze your significant other (who will hopefully at least pretend to be amazed).

Here are a few ways that you can virtualize ESXi 5.0:

- Running ESXi in VMware ESXi
- Running ESXi in VMware Server
- Running ESXi in VMware Workstation (Windows or Linux)
- Running ESXi in VMware Fusion (Mac)

SECURITY

Security doesn't cease to be a problem in a virtual environment. On the contrary, there are at least as many concerns to consider when designing your virtual infrastructure. We still experience physical security issues, operating system vulnerabilities, and patch management requirements.

VM Console Access

While you might not think of it as a security vulnerability, a VM's console (the redirected video, keyboard, and mouse access) is actually shared by multiple vSphere administrators. If multiple administrators open the VM console window (or tab) of the same VM, they will all see the same thing: shared video, mouse movement, and keystrokes. This has many positive uses, including shadowing a session for troubleshooting or education purposed, but it can also be used to spy on someone. Fortunately, VMware added a notification bar in the vSphere Client that informs you if multiple administrators are simultaneously viewing a VM's console. If you see this banner, you have an observer!

For security purposes you can restrict the ability to share a VM's console. This is controlled on a per-VM basis by adding a line to the VMX configuration file or by adding this parameter to the advanced settings list in your VM:

```
RemoteDisplay.maxConnections=1
```

The VM must be powered off before you can add this setting. It will allow you to have one remote console session in the vSphere Client. Any subsequent sessions will be blocked until the first one has been closed.

Access Control

A VM has the same security problems that plague physical machines; you must secure them from logical attack, but you must also protect them from physical theft and damage. It might seem odd to think of a VM in this way, but a VM is constructed of files, and those files can be stolen or modified in such a way that the VM becomes compromised.

Permissions

There are a number of ways to secure your VMs, but one of the most effective methods is to keep it simple and just secure the VM using vCenter or ESXi permissions. Create a proper folder structure or hierarchy and then use roles to prevent accidents. There are a vast number of permissions in vCenter that focus on accessing, cloning, modifying, and deleting VMs. You can choose to make your permissions very granular or keep things simple. Do what makes sense for your organization, but whatever you do, document it so that you don't lose VMs.

Caution

Remember, you can grant users and groups the "no access" role on a VM. Doing so removes the affected VM(s) from the hierarchy for any of those users. That makes it rather difficult to fix the permissions problem.

Note

For more information on permissions and security in vCenter, refer to Chapter 6.

VM versus OS Security

Just because you lock down vCenter doesn't mean that someone can't get to your VMs from RDP or SSH. You must also take into consideration all the patches, security updates, and lock down settings that apply to your guest operating systems. vCenter has no ability to guard your VM from attacks that originate on your network, so you would do well to invest in some security analysis software to periodically scan your VMs for vulnerabilities that are unrelated to VMware and virtualization.

VM Storage Concerns, NFS versus VMFS Access to VMDKs

Another area that often goes overlooked is the actual storage devices where we place our VMs and their data files. If you store these files on VMFS volumes, you make it difficult (but certainly not impossible) for someone to view and download your VMDK files. That is only because most operating systems have no driver support for VMFS volumes. If you had instead stored your VMs on NFS storage, you need to be aware that the underlying filesystem may be readable by other operating systems—certainly by the OS that is serving up the NFS Datastore(s). This may allow an administrator of those systems to create unauthorized back ups of your VMs' files.

Change Control

Change control processes typically result in excessive bureaucracy, but they serve a purpose—to keep your systems online and secure. Though it may not seem security related, implementing a form of change control can prevent a lot of problems that lead to security vulnerabilities. For one, a strict change control process could potentially prevent someone from registering an insecure VM in vCenter. It also may prevent someone from implementing a change that would grant inexperienced users access to the VMs in vCenter.

Another option is to use VM templates to control the initial configuration of VMs. If you create a VM and then customize it according to your organization's needs, you can convert that VM to a template to avoid someone else changing the configuration. Add security permissions to the equation and you can guarantee that only a select number of users can actually convert the template back to a VM to modify it. This makes change control easy for initial VM deployments, but it does nothing for changes that occur to the configuration of vCenter or the ESXi hosts.

Note

Occasionally we find applications that can streamline or at least help you streamline the process. Two such applications are VMware's Configuration Manager and Update Manager (both referenced in Chapter 13).

Change control can also help avoid, or at least reduce, VM sprawl. What is VM sprawl? This is when organizations make deploying VMs so easy that nearly any power user or junior administrator can make VMs appear on the fly. The method to this madness varies by organization, but the result is almost always the same: an administrative and security nightmare.

It is just as important to control the creation and deletion of VMs as it is to control the changes within these VMs. VM sprawl has become such a problem that there are companies dedicated to VM life cycle management software. VMware originally had their own variety: vCenter Lifecycle Manager. That product was discontinued in 2010 and its functionality (and so much more) was integrated into VMware vCloud Director.

VM Alerts from a Security Perspective

We'll talk more about alerts and the various types of triggers and actions when we discuss Resource Optimization in Chapter 10, but you can also use alerts to notify you about VM security events. For example, you could configure an alert to e-mail you any time a VM is created or deleted in vCenter. This way, you can keep a running tally of the number and type of VMs so that you can "true-up" your guest operating system licensing as needed.

Here is a partial list of example events that pertain to security threats. Notice that some of the events pertain to a situation in motion, while others pertain to the results of an action.

- Creating VM
- VM created
- VM registered
- Deploying VM
- VM being cloned

- Guest OS shutdown
- Guest reboot
- VM powered off
- VM powered on
- VM starting
- VM resetting
- VM stopping
- VM renamed
- VM reconfigured
- VM MAC changed
- VM remote console connected
- VM remote console disconnected

As you can see, VMware has included many alerts in vSphere 5. It's up to you to identify the ones that are most applicable to your organization, and then configure the alert actions properly.

Note

For more information on alarms, refer to Chapter 10.

VMSafe API

VMSafe is an API that allows security software developers to write applications that can monitor the CPU, memory, network, and disk access of VMs from a hypervisor point of view. The monitoring application leverages the VMSafe APIs to communicate with the hypervisor to gather and analyze information about the I/O of the VM. Because the monitor works at the hypervisor level, VMSafe could detect and report on the presence of rootkits and other stealth malware that traditional scanning tools may find undetectable.

Note

VMSafe is deployed in Virtual Appliances because the APIs require direct access to the ESXi hypervisor.

TROUBLESHOOTING

VMs virtually never have trouble. Sorry, we had to say it. But the truth is VMs are likely the number one source of our troubleshooting time because they are also the most diverse and the least constant factor in our infrastructures. We're going to cover a series of areas that we feel will help you isolate problems and potentially even solve them.

- Diagnostics
- CPU misbehavior
- vMotion issues
- Manually copying/moving a VM
- Editing a VMX file
- Other troubleshooting tips

Diagnostics

There are a number of places we can look when a VM isn't behaving quite the way we expect. If the VM is not powering on, we can look at the VM's log files. If its performance is a bit off, we can review the charts in vCenter. Here are a couple of topics we feel will help you troubleshoot some basic VM problems.

VM Log Files

A VM creates a new log file every time it is power cycled. These log files contain information pertaining to the boot cycle as well as events affecting the VM's virtual hardware. Each VM by default has six (6) log files that it stores in the datastore alongside its configuration and virtual disk files. The most current log file is named vmware.log, and this log file is rotated when the VM is powered on. Older logs have a number appended to them, with the highest number representing the oldest log.

Caution

If you are having difficulties booting a VM, don't continue to cycle its power or you may overwrite useful logs showing a previously successful boot cycle. Remember, by default only 6 logs are kept, and a new log is rotated every time the VM is power cycled.

These logs, like the VMX files, are Unicode files. That is the native format used on Linux, Unix, and Mac operating systems, but if you are viewing these files on a

Windows workstation, you will need to use an editor such as WordPad instead of Notepad. The log files can be located and downloaded using the datastore browser in the vSphere Client.

Performance Less Than Ideal?

We've devoted the next chapter in this book to performance issues, but a little can be said for the basics. Where do we look when we think there is a performance problem?

The first place is to check out the trending information in vCenter. This can be found in the vSphere Client under the Performance tab on any VM. The performance charts can give you an immediate indication as to whether the problem you are noticing is something new or something that's been happening for a while.

The next place to look is in the VM itself. Digging around vCenter isn't necessarily the answer because there are very few configuration options on a VM that would cause a sudden change in the VM's performance. You'll read about the options in Chapter 10.

If you've done your due diligence, the final place you should be digging is the tasks and events that pertain to the VM in question. You're looking for anything that would indicate someone changed a setting on purpose or on accident. This is another case where change management comes into play. Tracking any change, even those that seem inconsequential, can help when troubleshooting performance-related issues.

Can't Power On/Off the VM?

If you have a VM that will not power on or off, you can typically find the root cause in the VM's own log files. As you read above, these are found in the VM's directory on its home datastore. You'll want to review the logs before you've cycled the VM's power too often. Remember, by default, only six logs are kept.

If you still don't find anything useful in the VM's logs, you can check out the ESXi server's hostd.log file. This file is contained in the /var/log/vmware/ directory on the ESXi server. The hostd.log file includes event information relevant to the management of VMs, including failures that would prevent VMs from initializing.

Console Access and Shadowing

If you can't use RDP or SSH to connect to the VM, how do we troubleshoot issues? Use the VM console. We discussed the console earlier in this chapter, and you might recall that it is a redirection from the VM's virtual video card, keyboard, and mouse.

We can use this console to log on to the VM, watch it boot, and access any local-only operating system commands for troubleshooting (such as single user mode in Linux, or recovery mode in Windows).

Also, another use for the console is actually educational. We have used the console screen of a VM to shadow power users to help them complete a task. In addition, because the console is shared and every click and key press is visible anywhere the console is accessed we have used this screen to shadow users for security purposes.

Note

Be aware that vCenter notifies all users of the VM's console if another connection is opened or closed. This is supposed to discourage unauthorized shadowing because both parties are suddenly aware of each other.

CPU Misbehavior

There are times when a VM's CPU doesn't behave or perform quite the way you would expect. Here are a couple of common situations when the VM and the host report very different values for the VM's CPU utilization (either too high or too low).

- HAL/Kernel mismatch after a P2V
- Resource limits on the VM's CPU
- High "CPU Ready" values on a VM

HAL/Kernel Mismatch

If your VM is reporting very low CPU utilization within the guest operating system, yet vCenter is reporting the VM's CPU usage at nearly 100%, you could have a HAL/Kernel mismatch with the number of vCPUs assigned to the VM. We see this often after physical to virtual conversions when an administrator reduces the resulting VM to a single vCPU, but the source physical server had multiple CPUs or cores. If the source system had multiple CPUs, it likely had a Symmetric Multiprocessing (SMP) kernel loaded. When you migrated the physical server to a VM, that SMP HAL or Kernel remained loaded and is causing the system to use additional processor cycles at the virtual hardware level.

The solution is to either change the HAL or Kernel in the guest operating system to a uniprocessor version, or upgrade the VM to at least 2 vCPUs.

Note

Not all operating systems react the same way. This has not been an issue in 64-bit Windows 2008, but it did affect Windows 2003 and earlier versions of Windows.

Resource Limits on the VM's CPU

The opposite can also be true. For instance, you notice that your VM is indicating a very high CPU utilization within the guest operating system, yet vCenter reports that the VM is using a negligible amount of physical CPU resources. This can be caused by excessive contention on the ESXi host, but if the host isn't busy, check the VM for a CPU limit. In this case, the VM is using 100% of the resources it has been provided, so both vCenter and the VM are correct.

CPU limits are discussed more in Chapter 10, but remember, a CPU limit is divided by the number of vCPUs. Therefore, if a VM is granted a 1GHz limit, but it has 2 vCPUs, the effective limit for that VM is 500MHz—making your VM run unexpectedly slow.

High "CPU Ready" Values on a VM

If the ESXi host is under heavy contention, the guest operating system may report excessively high CPU usage, yet vCenter declares the usage to be minimal. The contention can be checked easily by viewing the CPU Ready counter in the performance charts in vCenter. We'll talk more about CPU Ready in Chapter 10, but this counter represents the amount of time a VM's vCPUs are sitting in a "ready to execute" mode when the underlying physical CPUs on the ESXi host were too busy. A high CPU Ready value indicates that the VM had processing work to perform, but it couldn't do the job because the host didn't have enough unused processors available.

vMotion Issues

vMotion is a great tool, but to get all the nice features it has a lot of requirements. These requirements tend to cause us trouble, so we have provided a bit of insight into solving a few of the more common issues with vMotion.

Affinity Rules

Some VMs just shouldn't be allowed to play together. Others can't live apart from one another. VMware created the vMotion affinity and anti-affinity rules for just this purpose. These rules either force vCenter to migrate multiple VMs together (affinity) or they force vCenter to never place two or more VMs on the same ESXi host (anti-affinity). Together these rules are very powerful and allow us to prevent undesirable situations like having your only two Domain Controllers on the same ESXi host (from a recovery perspective), or placing your two heaviest SQL Database servers on the same ESXi host (performance). There is yet another affinity rule that can force a VM to stay on a specific host or we can tell it to stay away from a specific host. These are called host-based affinity rules.

These rules will be discussed in more detail when we talk about DRS clustering in Chapter 11. We are including this here because if you experience difficulties with VMs running together (or apart), you may wish to consider configuring these rules. Also, it is possible for these rules to create a bit of confusion if you don't realize that they exist or that someone else had created them. Again, these rules are configured in the DRS settings of your ESXi host cluster.

CPUID Masking and EVC

If you are having trouble migrating a VM from host to host using vMotion, but you are able to migrate it cold (powered off), you may have incompatible CPUs. Of course there could be any number of problems, but fortunately the vCenter error messages are usually pretty specific when it encounters a problem relating to CPU mismatch.

In this case you have a couple of options: mask each VM's vCPU to allow the VMs to migrate, or you can use something called Enhanced vMotion Compatibility (EVC). Masking a CPU's features doesn't do nearly the harm that it sounds like. What you are doing is restricting the guest VM from leveraging certain CPU instructions that are not present on the other ESXi host's physical CPU. This allows vMotion to migrate your VM to the other host because there is no risk that your VM is using those "missing" instructions.

To edit the CPUID Masking settings per VM, first power off the VM. These settings cannot be changed while the VM is powered on. Next, right-click the VM and select Edit Settings. From here, choose the Options tab, select CPUID Masking, and finally click the Advanced button. This will display a dialog box like the one shown in Figure 9.21. This page will allow you to mask individual bits of the CPUID mask.

Editing the CPUID for each and every VM in your cluster may not be desirable, so VMware created EVC to help. EVC will be discussed in more detail in Chapter 11, but it essentially does the CPUID masking on a host level, and you don't have to mess with the individual ID bits.

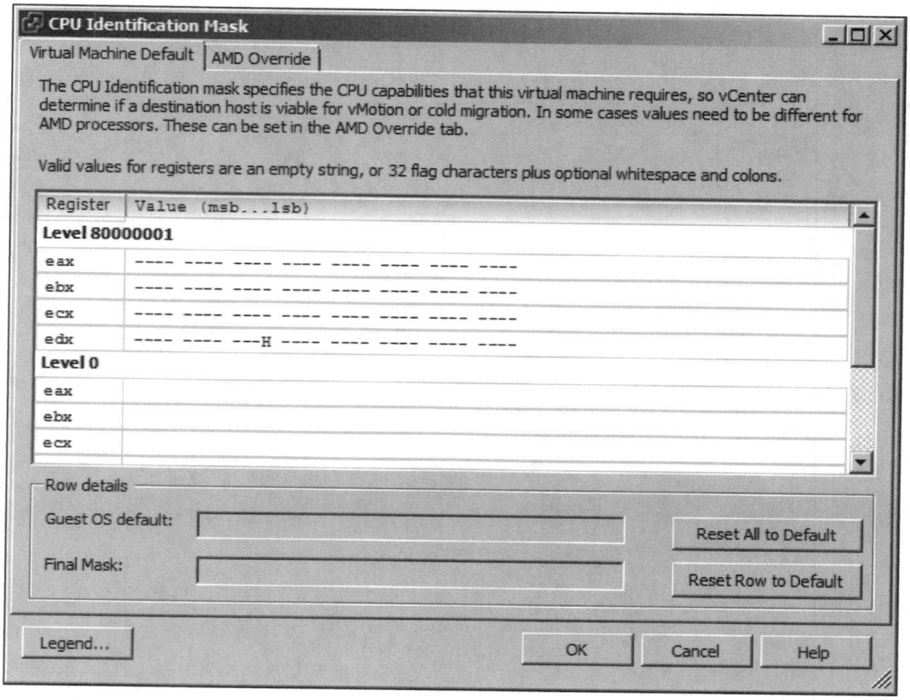

Figure 9.21
Adjusting the CPUID mask of a VM.

Disks Not Available on All Hosts

A common source of trouble with vMotion migrations is shared storage, or the lack thereof. Both the source and the destination ESXi host must have access to every datastore or RDM that the VM is connected to. This includes things like datastores used as ISO repositories.

The vMotion wizard also checks any snapshots present on the VM for connections to non-shared resources. For instance, say that your VM has a snapshot that was taken several weeks ago (not a good practice, and you'll soon see why). That VM may have been connected to a temporary datastore containing ISOs for a particular application/service pack installation. If the snapshot was taken when the VM was connected to that datastore, that connection will remain a requirement for any vMotion migrations. If that datastore is no longer available, you will not be able to migrate that VM until you remove the offending snapshot.

Maps Can Help

If you aren't able to vMotion a VM from one host to another, you can also check the vMotion maps. These maps are generated based on all the available information,

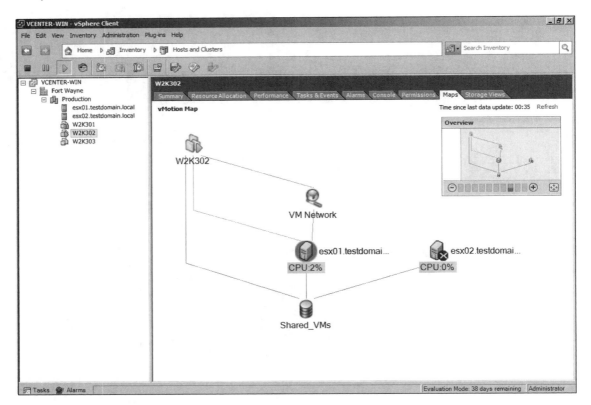

Figure 9.22
vMotion maps.

including connections to networks and disks in snapshots. To access a vMotion map for a VM, first select the VM in the hierarchy and then select the Maps tab, as shown in Figure 9.22.

You can see at a glance the resources that are required by this VM, and which hosts are suitable destinations. Note that if the VM is not permitted to migrate to a particular host (due to resource dependency or host misconfiguration), a small red X icon will appear next to the name of the ESXi host, as shown next to server ESX02 in the figure.

Manually Copying/Moving a VM

Sometimes it's necessary to move a VM from one vCenter environment to another. Because we can't vMotion between vCenter environments we have to find another method to move the VMs. That method is most often to power off and unregister the VM from the source vCenter, move the VM's files, and then register the VM in the destination vCenter. This of course requires a bit of downtime for the VM, but it gets the job accomplished.

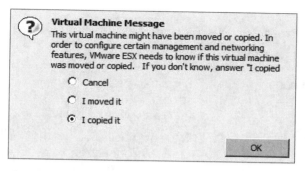

Figure 9.23
VM moved or copied.

There are a number of cases when you might do this, but moving a VM's files has the potential to change the MAC address of the network card(s) within the VM. Why? Because the MAC address is generated based on the UUID of the VM, which is in turn generated based on a hash of the directory path where the VMX file is located. If you move or copy a VM from one place to another you will be prompted by vCenter or ESXi (or even VMware Workstation/Fusion for that matter) as to whether you moved or copied the VM, as shown in Figure 9.23.

If you select "I copied it," the hypervisor will regenerate the UUID based on the new folder path of the VM. This also means that you will likely get a new MAC address on any network cards you may have had in this VM. If, on the other hand, you select "I moved it," the VM will remain unchanged and a notation will appear in the VMX file indicating that the UUID is no longer directly linked to the hash of the VM's folder path.

Advanced Configuration Parameters

VMs have many settings, but as you've learned, some of these settings aren't exposed in the GUI. We can always edit the VMX file and add in the parameters, but there is an easier way: we can use the vSphere Client. VMware allows us to add advanced configuration parameters to a VM's configuration file by entering the parameters into a list box when the VM is powered off.

To get there, edit the settings of a powered-off VM (yes, it must be powered off), and then click on the Options tab. You'll see a lot of different options, many of which we have already discussed. Click on the General entry in the Advanced Options section of the hierarchy. You should now see a button labeled Configuration Parameters. If the VM is powered on, this box will be disabled.

Table 9.9 Common Advanced Configuration Parameters

Parameter Name	Value (example)	Purpose
keyboard.typematicMinDelay	2000000	Reduce repeating keystrokes in the VM console (microseconds of delay)
RemoteDisplay.maxConnections	1	Prevent more than 1 simultaneous connection to a VM's console
isolation.tools.copy.disable	true	Disables copying text from the VM console
isolation.tools.paste.disable	true	Disables pasting text into the VM console
isolation.tools.setGUIOptions.enable	false	Disables the copy/paste functions in the GUI

When you open the configuration parameters dialog, you can edit existing parameters or add new ones. To add a parameter that isn't listed, click Add Row and then enter the exact name of the parameter and its corresponding value. When you close this window the vSphere Client will save your changes to the VM's VMX file. The changes will take effect the next time you power on the VM. In Table 9.9 we have a short list of some of the more common parameters and a brief description of their purpose.

Caution

Be extra careful when entering parameters into this box. If you type something wrong, the best-case scenario is that nothing will happen; the worst-case scenario is that something entirely unexpected happens instead.

Editing a VMX File

As you've seen by now, VMs have many different configuration settings. Some of the more basic settings are exposed as general options in the vSphere Client, whereas others must be manually entered into the advanced options section. While these options lead to greater versatility, they can also lead to configuration issues, especially if you have been "experimenting."

Let's say that you have a particular VM that you have adjusted a bit too much, and now vCenter is reporting an error when you attempt to power on the VM. If you've looked through the VM's logs you may have noticed errors that tell you about configuration mismatches or bad parameters. You could either dig through each and every configuration dialog box in the vSphere Client, or you could go to the source where the configuration is stored—the VM's VMX file.

Caution

Of course, we have to include the disclaimer that you should never experiment on a production machine. Be aware there is a point where VMware may not be able to help you if you alter the configuration too much.

If you recall back to earlier in this chapter, the VMX file is where we store all the configuration values for the VM. This includes things like the virtual hardware settings as well as things like connected ISOs and the version of the guest operating system.

The VMX file is stored in a folder on the datastore with the rest of the VM's files. You can also check the settings of the VM in the vSphere Client to determine where that folder resides. We showed this in Figure 9.6 earlier in this chapter when we were discussing the options of a VM.

To view the VMX file, you simply need to locate it in the datastore browser and download it. The VM doesn't need to be powered off. However, if you wish to make changes to the VMX file, the procedure is a bit different. See below:

1. Locate the VM's VMX file in the datastore browser.
2. Right-click on the VMX file, and then choose Download to save the file locally on your workstation.
3. Create a back up copy of the original VMX file (in case your creativity fails you).
4. Edit the VMX files according to your needs in any Unicode-compliant editor (i.e., WordPad, not Notepad).
5. Save the file, retaining the Unicode format.
6. Shut down the VM in vCenter.
7. Remove the VM from inventory (do not choose Delete from Disk).
8. Using the datastore browser, upload the modified VMX file to the VM's folder.
9. Using the datastore browser, register the VM by right-clicking the VMX file and choosing Add to Inventory.
10. Power on the VM (if desired).

Other Troubleshooting Tips

Here are a couple more tips we have for you when troubleshooting or working with VMs that aren't quite behaving the way you expected. Just remember, when in doubt troubleshoot the problem as though the VM were a physical box. Virtualization, or the configuration of the VM, may end up being the culprit, but in our experience most problems originate from misbehaving applications.

Network Port Mirroring

If you can't seem to figure out what your VM is doing on the network, but it seems to be doing an awful lot of something, you can leverage the new network Port Mirroring feature of vSphere 5's Distributed Switches.

Note

Port Mirroring is discussed in greater detail in Chapter 7.

A common use case for this feature is to monitor all the traffic coming from and going to a particular VM. For instance, you could use this to analyze the network traffic of a web server that is having trouble with Kerberos single-sign-in. The data in the traffic may be of greater help than the event log entries.

To use network Port Mirroring you will need to have a network sniffer application installed in another VM or physical machine if you mirror the port traffic to a specific vmnic (Ethernet card) in the ESXi server.

VM Won't Boot Due to Driver Problems

Another common problem with VMs stems from driver issues after replacing virtual hardware. For instance, if you edit a Windows XP virtual machine, you will notice that most of these VMs use the BusLogic SCSI card for their virtual disks. This is because Windows XP has a built-in driver for the emulated BusLogic SCSI adapter. As we discussed earlier in the chapter, having that built-in driver allowed Windows XP to install without need of third-party drivers. If you were to change this SCSI card to the VMware Paravirtual SCSI card before you install the VMware Tools, the Windows XP VM will likely not boot because it doesn't have a driver for the Paravirtual SCSI card.

Fortunately, the problem is simple enough to fix: just remove the new hardware and put back the original virtual hardware. Then try to remember to not change things that are required by the VM to boot properly. For instance, don't change the boot

SCSI controller of a VM unless you are absolutely certain that you have an appropriate driver in the guest operating system.

Performance Problems

We didn't want to leave out performance problems in our list of VM troubleshooting, but the next chapter is entirely dedicated to performance-related issues. In it you will learn about resource controls as well as some of the ways we can help a VM get the resources it needs.

SUMMARY

This chapter covered a lot of ground. We started by talking about planning and building your first VM. We then moved into how to maintain a VM, including how to export it to an OVF file or back it up using the vStorage APIs. Hopefully you remember the golden rule of snapshots: they aren't a back up method! We wrapped things up with some of the more advanced features of a VM, but we left something out: how can we tune a VM for performance?

In our next chapter you will learn how resource optimization plays a role in VM performance, and how best to configure your vSphere infrastructure to support your VMs.

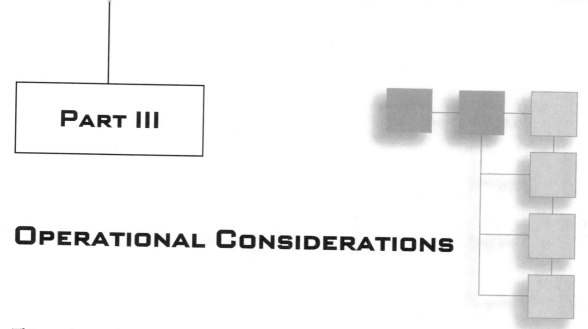

PART III

OPERATIONAL CONSIDERATIONS

This section is focused on the usability of vSphere and how you can tune it to your needs. We start by exploring how to make the most of your resources, both at the VM and host level. We then proceed to the ins and outs of clustering and High Availability (HA), and then round things out by discussing configuration management and converting physical servers to VMs.

As usual, we must give you insight into the planning or theory side of things. These sections are highly focused on the conceptual aspects of vSphere instead of the task-level procedures.

In the Implementation and Management sections of each chapter we explain how to implement what we discussed in the Planning section, as well as covering topics that are focused on the management aspects of vSphere.

Finally, we cover the troubleshooting topics. These can range in depth from basic concepts to specific case examples. We don't attempt to re-create the VMware knowledge base, but rather we provide the insight on how to troubleshoot certain situations.

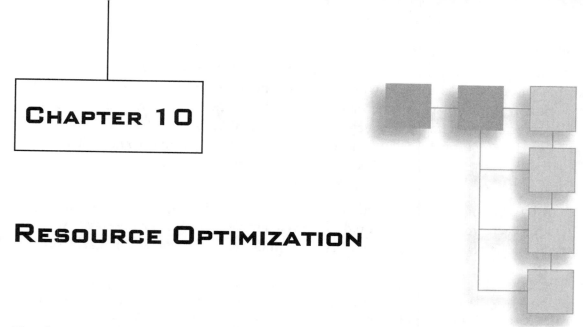

CHAPTER 10

RESOURCE OPTIMIZATION

The key to avoiding performance problems in any environment is designing an infrastructure that is appropriately sized, but yet is flexible and scalable enough to adapt when your workloads increase. Of course that's easier said than done, and figuring out what an "appropriate size" is can be the most difficult aspect of planning. For that reason we've put this chapter together to help you understand how the ESXi hypervisor can help us with resource optimization.

PLANNING

We're going to start by teaching you how to accurately measure your "needs" instead of your "wants." We have a term for this: resource responsibility. There is actually a downside to allocating too many resources to a VM, especially if the VM can't utilize them effectively. We'll explain more about that later, but first we need to teach you how to analyze the resource demand of what you already have.

Analyzing Your Workloads

We use the term "workload" because a workload could be a VM, it could be a physical machine that is slated to become a VM, or it could be a physical box (not slated for conversion) that is sharing resources with your virtualization environment. Unfortunately, that too counts because the resource sharing directly impacts how well your VMs will perform.

What Should We Gather?

We need to gather resource statistics about these workloads. The statistics will come from a variety of sources, ranging from the operating system to the underlying network and storage devices. The objective is to build the most complete picture possible, depicting both how and when the server uses its resources. This data will then be analyzed to look for hot spots and lulls where resource sharing would either be prohibitive or beneficial. Also, this data will help us ensure that each workload can perform at its best, even when the ESXi servers fall under heavy load.

Start by creating a chart showing the allocated RAM, CPUs, disks, and network adapters for each workload. This could take on a simple form for now because we're just trying to get started (baby steps). Try something like what you see in Table 10.1.

Note

> Remember, you need to grab the stats from all your VMs and any physical server that is either slated to become a VM or that is sharing storage resources with the virtualization infrastructure.

Benchmark and Create a Baseline

Table 10.1 will serve as a reference point later when we look at reallocating resources. Next, we need to begin gathering statistics to determine the utilization of the server. For this, you will need to connect to each server and use performance monitoring tools such as PerfMon, IOStats, VMStats, and the Linux/Unix "top" command. It goes well beyond the scope of this book to advise you on the specific statistics that you will need to gather because each of your virtual workloads will differ. It's safe to say that you will need to gather statistics such as the CPU utilization, available memory, network utilization, and disk latency/utilization. Refer to the Troubleshooting section of this chapter for counters that you can monitor within vCenter and with tools such as esxtop.

Caution

> Measuring performance stats in a VM is tricky because a VM is typically unaware of the overhead that the hypervisor incurs on its behalf. Also, VMs don't track time perfectly, especially when the ESXi host is under excessive CPU load. These factors can skew your results.

The statistics you gather from VMs is often questionable because a VM leverages the CPU to determine the time component of its performance statistics. If the ESXi host is overburdened, you may get very odd results, potentially showing substantially lower or higher utilization values than what actually occurred. If you have access to vCenter, you may want to compare your VM-based performance statistics with the performance data available in vCenter.

Table 10.1 Workload Chart

Workload	CPUs	CPU Speed	RAM	NICs	Disks	Disk Capacity (Total)	Disk Used (Total)	Datastore/ Array	VM/ Physical
Mailserver01	4	2.0GHz	8GB	1	3	120GB	45GB	Email01	Virtual
Mailserver02	4	2.0GHz	8GB	1	3	120GB	75GB	Email02	Virtual
DC-DNS01	2	2.0GHz	2GB	1	1	40GB	25GB	DC01	Physical
DC-DNS02	2	2.0GHz	2GB	1	1	40GB	25GB	SharedVMs	Virtual
FileServer01	2	2.0GHz	4GB	1	4	450GB	300GB	Data01	Virtual
AppServer01	4	2.5GHz	4GB	1	2	50GB	35GB	SharedVMs	Virtual
AppServer02	4	2.5GHz	8GB	1	2	100GB	50GB	SharedVMs	Virtual
Database01	8	3.0GHz	16GB	1	4	250GB	175GB	DB01	Physical

You will use this data as a baseline for calculating how a VM uses its allocated resources. It is important to create this baseline because over time the numbers will change. If you conduct this benchmarking routine on a quarterly basis, you can compare the new numbers to past baselines to see how your environment is expanding or contracting.

Trend the Performance for a While

You will need to gather performance data for several days, if not weeks, before you know the true values. Servers are like people in that they too have good days and bad days. You want to know what the average workweek looks like for each server, including its downtime, backup windows, and peak production hours.

The best plan is to set up a logging function to collect the performance data at set sample rates, such as once every five minutes. Let the collectors run for a week or so, monitoring them periodically to ensure they are still running. The data collected by the monitoring application should then be analyzed, looking for averages, high and low watermarks, and periods of extreme activity.

Note

You may be surprised to learn that your peak utilization on some servers actually occurs during off-hours when your data backup runs. Many backup programs cause a tremendous amount of I/O that is often incorrectly excluded from performance benchmarks. You need to account for everything, including backups!

Collect the Data

Now that you've gathered the data, we need to put it all together. If you're really creative you might be able to adapt our previous chart (Table 10.1) to hold this data, but it would be better to just create a new one. You need to gather the summary information for each CPU/core, disk, and network adapter. The disks are particularly important as you'll see later because they happen to be the one resource that is very difficult to dynamically scale up if you undersized it.

Note

In the next few sections we'll be reviewing the summarized data often, so you should compose it in such a way that you can easily refer back to the raw data if there are questions. An Excel spreadsheet with a worksheet for each server seems to work pretty well.

Define Minimum Acceptable Performance Levels

Based on what you can see in your data, you should be able to determine a minimum level of acceptable performance for each server. This assumes of course that your server performance was acceptable while you were monitoring the servers. If not, you will need to start over or adjust the performance data with a handicap of sorts (inflating or deflating some of the numbers).

For example, if you look at the data for one of your e-mail servers (mailserver1) and notice the average CPU utilization during the monitoring exercise was 38%, then your minimum acceptable level is 38%. But what does that tell you? Unless you can compare the percentage to an allocated amount, it doesn't say a lot. Refer back to Table 10.1, which breaks down how many CPUs each server had and what type of CPU they were. If we say that mailserver1 had 4 CPUs, each at 2.0GHz, 38% utilization means that your server was consuming 3.04GHz of processing power on average (2Ghz × 4 CPUs × 0.38 = 3.04GHz). Do this for each of your servers and place the numbers in your spreadsheet. These percentages will be used later when we talk about reservations in VMs.

Right-Sizing Your VMs

There's a very fine line between being conservative with your resources and starving a VM of what it needs. While you should be responsible with your resources, if you fail to give a VM sufficient CPU or memory, that VM will begin to tax other resources or even slow down other systems that depend on it.

All servers use RAM; you know this. As a server runs low on physical memory, what does it do? Old memory pages are swapped out to disk so the new memory pages can be stored in RAM. It's called virtual memory, and we've done this for years, but until virtualization entered the equation, the expense was always isolated to a single machine. What expense you ask? Disk I/O and CPU cycles. Every time you swap pages out of physical RAM to a swap partition or pagefile, the disk is used to write those pages (and potentially read in others) and the CPU is called on to make all this happen.

The expense can be quite large, especially if the RAM was significantly undersized. Also, if you don't supply your VMs with appropriately performing disks, you may use your CPU excessively to handle retries or cause other VMs to wait unnecessarily on the "slow guy." Learning the resource demands of the workloads within your server will go a long way to avoiding this problem.

CPU Sizing Considerations

We'll start the sizing discussions by looking at our CPUs. While it might seem easier to just assign every VM two CPUs, many VMs can't or won't take advantage of the second processor. Not using an assigned resource may not seem so bad until you learn that contrary to popular belief, unused virtual resources actually *do* consume real physical resources. In the case of CPUs, an unused virtual CPU forces the hypervisor to execute a CPU Halt instruction on that core. Without digging into the technical nuances of the CPU Scheduler, this effectively idles one CPU instead of allowing another VM to use it. Therefore, there really can be a downside to adding too many CPUs to a VM.

How Many vCPUs Do We Really Need?

Do we need more than one vCPU in a VM? Here are some factors that will help you make that decision:

- Is the workload multi-processor-aware and is it able to take advantage of multiple simultaneous threads of execution?
- Does the application vendor recommend multiple processors? If so, determine whether you can scale-out instead of scale-up. (See definition below.)
- If the VM is assigned multiple CPUs, are all the processors active and balanced?
- If the VM has only one CPU assigned to it, is the CPU saturated (above 80% average utilization)?
- Verify the guest operating system can support the additional processors; many have limits.

We mentioned the idea of scaling-out as opposed to scaling-up. Scaling-up is the idea of adding CPUs or RAM to a VM in an effort to bolster the performance of that VM's applications. The rationale for doing this is typically an application cannot be distributed across multiple nodes, and therefore the only means to increase its performance is to enlarge the capabilities of the underlying VM.

On the other hand, scaling-out is the idea of adding more servers, and then distributing or separating the workload across those servers. This effectively spreads the load across multiple VMs, so that we can in turn spread those VMs across multiple servers. Scaling-out can theoretically provide you more performance increases, but it requires an application specifically designed to run as a team on multiple servers.

Is HyperThreading a Good Thing?

In the early days of ESX, enabling HyperThreading on your host was frowned upon due to performance issues. Today, however, with the advances in CPU architecture, the leading practice is to enable HyperThreading to take advantage of the multiple execution queues. If you're not quite sure what HyperThreading does, you're not alone. A common misconception is that HyperThreading somehow doubles the performance of a CPU. That isn't far from the truth, but it's not the performance per se; it's the efficiency.

HyperThreading enables two pathways to a single point of execution. That may sound complex, but it's something that we deal with in real life all the time. Picture a doctor's office with two exam rooms and only one doctor. The doctor's support staff can place a patient in each room, prepping the patients just in advance of the doctor's visit. As the doctor moves from room to room, the support staff can remove the old patient from the room and then prepare a new patient. This keeps the doctor as close to 100% utilized as possible. Likewise, HyperThreading allows us to increase the utilization and efficiency of the CPU by scheduling two processes onto the same CPU core. While it doesn't make the CPU run twice as fast, it does allow the CPU core to get more work done in a given time span.

So why then can you disable HyperThreading in the BIOS? If it were really so great, wouldn't everyone want HyperThreading enabled all the time? HyperThreading has its uses, but there are cases where it might be better to pay the extra money and get a CPU with more cores. To explain, we'll continue the analogy of our doctor's office. Our good doctor sees a great many patients each day. Some have minor, easy-to-diagnose ailments, while others have complex, time-consuming problems. As you might guess, the easy problems take less time, so the doctor can breeze through these without trouble. On the other hand, the complex problems take longer to diagnose, and they tend to require special diagnostic equipment that everyone in the doctor's office must share. If every patient had a complex problem, this shared equipment might cause a bottleneck and actually decrease the doctor's efficiency.

How is all of this relevant? Much of a HyperThreaded core is shared between the two logical processors. For instance, both logical processors use and share access to the cache and Floating Point Unit, but some of those components can only be used by one logical processor at a time. That means that if you have two threads of execution that require access to the Floating Point Unit, one thread will have to wait on the other. If this happens infrequently you might not even notice, but if it happens often you may see a performance impact.

CPU instructions are similar to the patients' problems in our analogy in that some instructions are very basic, while others require much more complex processing. If you have an environment where all the processes generate complex instructions, you might be better off having a dedicated CPU core instead of sharing one with another process. Complex processes include anything in the area of mathematical modeling, High Performance Computing (HPC) applications, or even cryptography.

Caution

You can disable HyperThreading on a per-VM basis by adjusting the HyperThreaded Core Sharing option in your VM's properties. This dedicates a physical core to your VM's vCPU, which may create additional CPU contention on the ESXi host because you are reducing the number of logical processors available to other VMs.

If you have HyperThreading enabled on your ESXi host, but you have a particular VM that doesn't respond well to sharing its processor core with other VMs, you don't have to disable HyperThreading on the host to fix your problem. Instead, you can disable HyperThreading at the VM level. To do so, edit the VM and open the Resources tab. On the left, select the entry labeled "Advanced CPU." At the top of this window you can adjust the "HyperThreaded Core Sharing" option to allow or prevent the VM from sharing a HyperThreaded core with another VM. There are actually three modes to this option: Any, None, and Internal. The default mode is "Any," which means that the VM will participate in HyperThreading. We describe each mode in the list below.

■ **Any.** HyperThreading is enabled. The VM will share HyperThreaded cores with any other VM. This is the default.

■ **None.** HyperThreading is disabled for this VM. The VM will not share any physical cores with any other vCPUs.

■ **Internal.** HyperThreading is enabled, but if more than one vCPU is scheduled on the same physical core, both vCPUs must belong to this VM. If the VM has only one vCPU, this option behaves like the "None" option.

Note

You can adjust these settings while the VM is running or when it is powered off. Also, these settings will not prevent your VM from migrating to another ESXi host via vMotion.

Cores versus Sockets

In vSphere 5 we can tell a VM that it has a certain number of sockets or cores. For example, if we have a dual-processor VM, we can tell it that it has two CPU sockets, or that it has a single socket with two CPU cores. From an execution standpoint it doesn't make much of a difference because the hypervisor will ultimately decide whether the VM executes on one or two physical sockets. The notation is purely cosmetic.

So why is this useful? Some software is licensed by socket instead of core. Specifying that the dual-CPU VM really has two *cores* instead of two *sockets* could make all the difference in the world for your software licenses.

The Effects of NUMA

As we discussed in Chapter 9, with the addition of vNUMA in vSphere 5, our VMs are now aware of the NUMA architecture of the underlying ESXi host. If possible, you should construct your cluster of similarly configured ESXi hosts because VMs only identify the underlying physical NUMA architecture when they first power on. Once a VM is powered on, it will not adjust its memory configuration even if migrated to a new host via vMotion, which may result in poor performance if the VM is migrated to a host with a different NUMA architecture.

CPU Affinity

CPU Affinity is a feature, controlled at the VM level, which allows us to assign a VM's vCPUs to a specific physical CPU core on the ESXi host. This means that the CPU scheduler in the ESXi hypervisor is forced to keep that VM on a given core, even if another core is available. It sounds like it would be awfully limiting, so why would we ever want to use this?

It turns out that processes may perform better if they are allowed to execute on the same core time after time. This is due to the process being able to populate the local CPU cache with all of its memory pages, thereby making all of its memory calls that much faster. To equate this to the real world, imagine the difference in your own productivity if you are given a dedicated cubicle or office as opposed to being bounced around from desk to desk, never having a permanent place to store your stuff. Now there are advantages to the bouncing around model: you are very flexible and can execute anywhere. If we lock a VM to a specific CPU it is like guaranteeing you a particular desk in a particular building; it isn't easy to move you because that desk isn't in the other building. Think vMotion. If we configure a VM to use CPU affinity, we may be able to get a bit more productivity out of it, but we won't have the ability to migrate the VM to another host using vMotion.

The most likely case where you would use this feature is in high-performance computing (HPC) applications where there are a lot of complex, memory-intensive instructions running on the CPU. Moving these processes from one core to another is very expensive in terms of CPU and memory resources. Just remember though, if you configure the CPU affinity rules, you can't use vMotion.

RAM Sizing Considerations

Memory isn't exactly cheap, but it is a whole lot cheaper than disk IOPS (not to be confused with disk space, check Chapter 8 for more information on this topic). Why make that comparison? As you run out of RAM, your VM will undoubtedly begin to use disk space, which means you burn disk I/O accessing that virtual memory.

How Much Should We Give to the VM?

There is no magic number, but a good guideline is to take the software vendor's recommendation and see how it performs in the wild. If you notice that even under heavy load the system is never paging to disk or even leveraging all of the RAM, you might be able to reduce it. On the other hand, you may notice that even with all the memory the vendor recommended, the VM's peak commit charge is well into the virtual memory.

It's a balancing act, and one that you must measure per VM to avoid over/under-allocating RAM. In our earlier exercises we had you create a spreadsheet showing the amount of RAM used by your workloads. Look at the Peak Commit Charge. That is the amount of RAM that was used by the system during its heaviest load. If that number exceeds the physical memory by a large margin, you may need to increase the RAM. We say "may" because you have to see how often the memory utilization is that high. If it happens once a month for 15 minutes, you can leave the RAM where it is; but if it's happening several times per day, you should increase the RAM.

Will the VM Use the RAM?

Before adding more RAM to a VM, you have to be certain that the VM can actually use the new memory. For instance, if you have a 32-bit VM, adding more than 4GB of memory may be a waste because the memory address space of a 32-bit process is limited to 4096MB. That's not to say that there aren't ways around this limit, but it takes special configurations that not all applications can support.

Even if your VM is a 64-bit operating system, there is no guarantee that the application you are supporting is 64-bit. There are many applications that appear to be 64-bit when the core services are still 32-bit and cannot address more than 4GB of RAM. Check with the vendor, or just install the application in a lab and see how it performs. You can usually tell in Windows or in Linux whether the application image is 32-bit or 64-bit, and how much memory that application is addressing.

The Hidden Costs of vRAM

Until vSphere 5, there wasn't a huge reason to not give your VMs a lot of RAM. Now with the introduction of vRAM licensing, administrators may be inclined to starve

VMs of RAM to cut their licensing costs. This can have a significant effect on the speed of your VM because, as we noted above, your VM will start to page to disk, which taxes everything else.

The introduction of vRAM licensing may give you pause about allocating additional RAM, but if your VM requires the additional memory you will pay for it one way or another. The additional vRAM will likely be cheaper than the cost of the wasted IOPS on the SAN or the wasted CPU cycles on the ESXi host.

Now to go the other direction: allocating too much RAM to a VM. Whenever you allocate RAM to a VM, that VM must have the ability to page the memory to disk…twice. Why twice? The VM has an operating system that is programmed to use virtual memory. All memory it sees typically is eligible for swapping as virtual memory. Now of course you can configure that behavior, but by default you will allocate the total amount of RAM as either a pagefile or a swap partition on the disk (and in many cases it is 1.5 to 2.0 times the size of the RAM).

But we said twice didn't we? The second allocation comes from the hypervisor. ESXi automatically creates a VMkernel swap file equal to the size of the allocated RAM every time the VM is powered on. This file is typically stored with the VM's virtual disk files on the SAN. And just like the operating system within the VM, this VMkernel swap file can also be customized by assigning something known as a reservation to the VM. We'll talk more about reservations later in the chapter—we like to tease.

So take a VM that has been given 64GB of RAM. Depending on the operating system we'll need a VMDK file that is at least 64GB in size just for the swap partition or pagefile. In addition, we must store a 64GB file on disk so that the VMkernel can swap the memory out to disk should the ESXi server come under heavy memory load. This means that we have at least 128GB of disk space locked up just because we decided to allocate a bunch of RAM to a VM. It may go without saying, but make sure you are allocating RAM for the right reason, and that the VM will actually use the additional RAM before you allocate it—your disks will thank you.

Disk Considerations

We spent a lot of time in the storage chapter (Chapter 8) discussing how to use storage in vSphere, and the impact of the various storage choices. Storage is one of the easily overlooked aspects of virtualization because most people equate storage to disk space instead of disk performance. We're not going to rehash the entire storage chapter, but we wanted to summarize the aspects that are relevant to performance.

How Much I/O Does the VM Need?

Look back at the benchmark that you created. We had to record both the IOPS and throughput of the disks because each number matters. You will need to check the charts to see what your workloads were using during peak and non-peak hours. Don't forget to include the backup window in your equation because if you can't get your data out of the VM, you're just asking for a résumé-generating event.

Also, looking at averages might seem logical; however, consider the effects of using an average. If you size your storage arrays to provide only enough IOPS for the average, you will find that the storage will constantly be overworked. In addition, tasks that once completed in seconds may take minutes to complete because they are waiting on disk responses (or timing out). The most appropriate solution is to size the backend array at the 95th percentile; meaning you take all your samples and exclude the top 5% of the numbers. This way, you eliminate a lot of the bursts, but you retain your peak data transfers, which typically occur during backups and batch processing times.

How Much I/O Can Your Array Deliver?

This is where you want to interview your storage engineers or storage vendor(s). You need to know how to best allocate your disks so that you can achieve those IOPS that you calculated in the previous step. Be careful when talking to vendors that cite charts and graphs in the hundreds of thousands of IOPS. While it is possible that you can obtain these numbers, keep in mind that their marketing department was paid to make their product look awesome, even if the circumstances were a bit skewed in their favor. Try to get a vendor to loan you an array to see how it will perform in your environment. Just keep in mind that arrays are designed to deliver a specific amount of performance. If you exhaust that level of performance, adding features like deduplication or thin provisioning isn't likely to help; you need to add more disks or cache to solve performance problems.

IOPS, MBPS, Latency

When seeking a storage solution, pay special attention to the I/O Operations Per Second (IOPS) and Megabits per second (Mbps) figures. Any vendor can provide terabytes of storage; it's when they can provide the capacity alongside the performance that attracts attention. The storage command latency numbers are also very important, but these numbers are derived from how heavily utilized your storage array is.

To put latency into perspective, think about the last time you ran the `ping` command on your network. The system responded, telling you how long the round-trip took in milliseconds. Longer delays equate to slower performance. Likewise, in a storage network we measure the latency of packets going to and from the storage arrays. As the storage array or the storage network become more congested, the latencies increase. We typically consider latency figures above 20ms to be troublesome, but if possible we want those numbers down around 5ms–10ms. These numbers can be found either within your guest operating system, vCenter's performance monitors, or in your storage array performance monitor (if you have such a tool).

VMs, Datastores, LUNs, Arrays, and Disks

You may remember this, but we need to frame the discussion for the rest of this chapter for those folks who skip around in the book. Arrays are constructed of disks in your storage device. Your storage device may consist of a single tray of disks composed into a single disk array, or you may have multiple trays of disks with disk arrays configured all throughout the trays. These arrays are then carved into LUNs, which are in turn presented to the ESXi hosts. The ESXi host formats these LUNs using VMFS, calls it a datastore, and then we store VM files within that datastore.

At any given time, your performance depends on the utilization of the underlying disks. If you have a lot of VMs sharing the same physical disks, your performance may be negatively impacted. Understanding which VMs are allocated to each array of disks may help you prevent accidents like placing two very disk-intensive database servers into the same datastore. Unfortunately, ESXi can only detect the LUN to datastore to VM mapping. We can't use ESXi or vCenter to determine how you have configured the underlying disk arrays, so you must rely on your SAN Administrator, documentation, and configuration software. Keep a map showing the relationship between disks, arrays, LUNs, and datastores so that you can avoid problematic placement of VMs.

Disk Subsystem Type (FC, iSCSI, FCoE, NAS, Local)

ESXi supports storage systems using Fibre Channel, iSCSI, Fibre Channel over Ethernet (FCoE), NFS, and direct attached disks (local). Each architecture presents a medium to communicate to the backend disks, but those disks can also be of a variety of types and speeds. For instance, it is entirely possible for you to have a Fibre Channel storage array that uses SATA disks, or an iSCSI array that leverages solid-state disks (SSD). You have to understand the network and the disk type to determine your disk throughput.

A Fibre Channel network may transmit at speeds up to 2, 4, 8, or even 16Gbps; however, if you are using SAS disks that only communicate at 6Gbps or 3Gbps, the bottleneck is moved from the SAN to the disks. Work with your storage vendor to determine the composition and configuration of your storage array to see where your bottlenecks are located. You will always have a bottleneck somewhere; you just want that bottleneck to be as least restrictive as possible.

Spindle Count Is Important, but so Is Cache

Spindle count refers to the number of disks in a storage array. The more disks you have in an array, the higher the I/O throughput (IOPS and Mbps). In addition to adding disks to arrays, you can also increase your performance by increasing the cache sizes. There are two main locations to do this: at the storage controller and at the hard disks.

As I/O requests come from ESXi servers, the storage controller fetches the result from the hard disks in the backend arrays. If there were no cache in the system, each and every I/O request would need to come directly from the disks, resulting in a very slow access time. By inserting cache at the disk level, each hard drive can cache certain highly requested data areas so that it can respond at least one order of magnitude faster than if the result had to come from the spindle itself. We can then add cache at the storage controller level to allow whole I/O requests from ESXi host to remain in cache, improving the overall I/O throughput because we are essentially transferring data out of memory instead of spinning disks.

Cache is very advantageous, but priced per gigabyte, it is typically much more expensive than the hard drives. A middle-of-the-road solution that has been gaining popularity recently involves the use of SSD drives as a form of caching in the storage array. These disks, while priced higher than spinning disks, are substantially cheaper than cache of an equivalent size. The SSD disks create a sort of buffer zone that can dramatically improve the I/O performance of even older storage arrays. Check with your storage vendor to see if your storage array can support this technology.

Partition Alignment

While partition alignment is nearly a thing of the past, it still bears mentioning. In older operating systems such as Windows 2003 Server and earlier, the guest's file systems needed to be aligned to the underlying physical disk block map. Partitions that are improperly aligned incur additional read/write operations because the data is stored in overlapping regions of the disks.

To put it in perspective, look at the different bars represented in Figure 10.1. These regions form a hierarchy starting at the guest operating system's sector mapping and

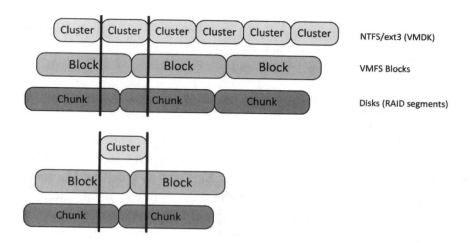

Partition Misalignment
One cluster requires multiple read operations

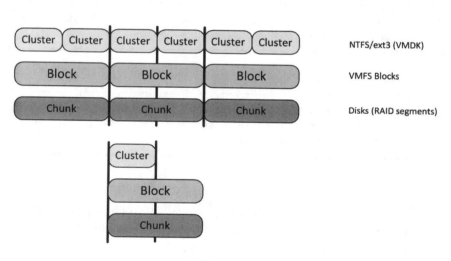

Partition Aligned
One cluster requires one read operation

Figure 10.1
Partition alignment versus misalignment.

flow down the storage stack until we finally reach the RAID segment size on the underlying physical hard disks. As you can see from the figure, a series of misalignments will cause the VMkernel to request additional blocks from the storage system. This extra work comes at a price: wasted I/O operations Per Second (IOPS).

Fortunately there are tools that help you correct the partition alignment in your guest operating systems, and unless you created your VMFS volumes via the CLI, they are aligned properly in vSphere 5. Also, most recent operating systems (such as Microsoft Windows 2008) take the disks' geometry into consideration when creating their file systems; therefore, they aren't typically impacted by the misalignment problem. The trouble is that most organizations still have older software that does experience the misalignment problem. To fix partition misalignment we must use third-party tools. One such tool is vOptimizer by Quest Software, and it is free.

Snapshots—The Disk I/O Thief

We mentioned this in Chapter 9 when we discussed snapshots. Leaving a snapshot on a disk is a sure way to waste disk I/O because the snapshot is constantly growing in size instead of just updating an already-established VMDK file. This problem is nearly mitigated if your storage array supports the advanced vSphere APIs for Array Integration (VAAI) features that allow updates without imposing a SCSI reservation against the LUN. For everyone else, a growing snapshot will cause contention on your datastore very quickly because every time the file grows (and it does so in 16MB increments) the ESXi host must expand the snapshot file, which imposes a momentary SCSI reservation on the entire LUN. This is highly disruptive in an I/O intense datastore, and can significantly detract from the number of IOPS you can achieve on the LUN. Check with your storage vendor to see if your array supports the VAAI features in vSphere 5.

Expensive RDMs for Those of Us without Self-Control

If you're just not into sharing disk I/O, you can avoid the matter entirely by allocating Raw Device Mappings (RDM) to your VMs. Now, we're not suggesting you do this for all your VMs because the administrative effort may be a bit taxing, but it is a viable option for your more disk-intensive VMs.

By allocating an RDM to a VM, you are guaranteeing that no other administrator or VM can access and therefore consume I/O on your VM's LUN. The LUN is dedicated to one VM, and unless you intend to run a cluster server environment, no other VM will be configured to use that RDM—thereby guaranteeing your VM a set amount of disk I/O performance at the expense that no other VM may use that storage area.

All this goes right out the window if you have carved up this LUN out of a shared array of disks because the array is what determines the performance, not the LUN. In order for this to work, you must dedicate a set of physical disks to the array, which will have only one LUN, which will be given to the VM as an RDM. No exceptions.

Storage I/O Control for the Rest of You

Now the rest of you that can't afford to dedicate disks to a VM might be wondering how else to guarantee disk performance. The answer is Storage I/O Control. You saw how Storage I/O Control and storage policies could create an automated system back in Chapter 8. The storage policies dictate what level of storage each datastore possesses, whether it is fast, expensive storage, or slower archive storage. By leveraging the Storage I/O Control configuration, you can dictate the performance of your VM, and allow vSphere to use things like storage DRS to migrate your VMs from disks to disk to maintain that performance level.

Note

Of course all of this assumes that you have configured your disks with that one array to one LUN mindset, or that you calculated for the shared performance aspects when you carved up the storage. Remember, storage isn't just about disk space; you need to consider IOPS and Mbps too!

Using SSD Drives for Swap Space

If you know that you will be using the VMkernel swap files often, or if you know that your Guest VMs are constantly paging to virtual memory on disk, you may want to consider using SSD drives in your storage array. SSD drives are quick, but make no mistake, they are not a suitable substitute for RAM. You should still architect your solution to make use of RAM whenever possible.

vSphere 5 allows you to designate an SSD-backed datastore as the VMkernel swap area for your ESXi hosts. This just means that if the VMkernel must swap out to disk, the penalty to the VM isn't as severe; it doesn't mean the VM will be happy. Read more on VMkernel swapping later in this chapter to see why VMkernel swapping is a last resort, and not something we want to do often.

Alternatively, you can configure an SSD-backed datastore for your VMs to use as their pagefile and swap drive area. This requires a bit more configuration because you will need to add an extra virtual disk to the VMs, and then place this new disk on the SSD-backed datastore. Now, when the guest operating system pages to its swap area, the penalty is greatly reduced. Considering that paging to disk is something that guest operating systems do all throughout the day, this might noticeably improve your performance if you can't afford to increase the VM's physical RAM levels.

Note

We discuss the use of SSD drives in more detail in Chapter 8.

Network Considerations

With storage out of the way, now we need to focus on networking. You hopefully were gathering the networking statistics we requested at the beginning of the chapter; you're going to need them.

How Much Network Bandwidth Do You Need?

Look back at the collection of performance data that you gathered from your workloads. You should have been pulling statistics from the various network cards such as Kb/second and packets/second. These two numbers will tell you how much traffic you are sending and receiving on your network cards. Like every other statistic, you must also consider the time frame of the traffic because there will likely be periods of peaks and lulls throughout the day/week.

Like storage networking, using an average isn't likely to help you much because your average will include all those lull periods, which can make your bursts look miniscule on the chart. Instead, go for the 95th percentile figure again in terms of both bandwidth (Kb/s) and I/O traffic (packets/second).

1Gbps or 10Gbps

If you look at your chart of servers, you'll likely see the same thing that everyone else sees: the average bandwidth requirement of most of your servers is staggeringly low.

So why then do we continue to suggest using 10Gbps networking? The reason is burst bandwidth.

During your backups or other peak times, you may notice that your bandwidth needs skyrocket. In some cases you may even saturate the bandwidth of a single 1Gbps NIC. As you read in Chapter 7, when we discussed virtual networking, ESXi doesn't have the ability to combine multiple 1Gbps NICs into a single "fat pipe." That means if you routinely saturate a 1Gbps NIC you will need to go to the next size up, 10Gbps.

How Many NICs Are in the ESXi Host

Once you have a good grasp as to how much network bandwidth you need for your workloads, you need to determine how many NICs per ESXi server you need to support that bandwidth. At this point, we can't complicate it too much. It comes down to math; add the numbers and divide by the size of the NIC. Of course, if you plan to use 10Gbps NICs in the server, you will require fewer cards than if you go with 1Gbps NICs, but you can't forget about redundancy. Don't restrict yourself too heavily. You need to ensure adequate bandwidth for your VMs even if you lose a port on a switch, or an NIC goes bad.

vSwitches and Bus Speeds

Here's another topic we mentioned in Chapter 7 involving the speed of a link between two VMs on the same vSwitch (on the same ESXi host). If you have two VMs that are in constant communication over the network, you may consider pinning them to the same ESXi host, or using a DRS rule to keep the VMs together during vMotion migrations. The reason is simple: the link speed between two hosts on the same vSwitch isn't 1Gbps or 10Gbps; it's memory bus speeds. That's substantially faster than any physical networking speed on the market.

The best part is that there is nothing you need to configure on the VMs to take advantage of this. As long as the VMs are in the same subnet and connected to the same vSwitch, the transmissions move at bus speed.

Dedicated Network Cards

In Chapter 9 we talked about VMs and the use of dedicated hardware using a technology called VM DirectPath I/O. If you have a VM that requires so much bandwidth that it can't tolerate sharing an NIC, you may need to dedicate a physical NIC to the VM. Keep in mind though, dedicating hardware to a VM usually results in that VM being a prisoner to a host; you can't use vMotion to migrate it around the cluster. If at all possible, try to find another option by investigating just why the VM needs direct access to an NIC.

Network I/O Control

Much like Storage I/O Control does for SANs, Network I/O Control gives us the ability to shape the bandwidth sharing of our VMs on the Ethernet networks. For more information on Network I/O Control and packet shaping, refer back to Chapter 7.

VLANs Don't Solve Saturation Problems

At the risk of sounding obvious, we should state that while VLANs provide great separation of networking, they don't solve oversaturation issues; in fact, they can make matters worse. A VLAN is just a subdivision of a LAN, meaning that if you take a 1Gbps network and divide it into VLANs, you don't get multiple, dedicated 1Gbps VLANs; you get a shared 1Gbps network carved into VLANs. If you are adding networks because you have saturated the performance of one VLAN, adding more VLANs is not going to help. You will need to add additional physical LANs with dedicated bandwidth. This can entail adding additional physical NICs as well as physical switches, depending on the severity of the network saturation.

High Availability Considerations

When managing High Availability (HA) clusters, you want to design the system to withstand at least one ESXi host failure without impacting the performance of the cluster. This is often referred to as n+1 sizing because you typically add one or more extra nodes to the cluster to allow for failures or maintenance windows.

Sizing a cluster for n+1 nodes is easy on paper; you just add an extra server to the configuration. But it can be challenging when making a case financially or operationally. The most responsible approach is to calculate the financial or operational impact of losing a node in your cluster. If losing a node means that you suffer tangible losses financially, you can use those numbers to justify the additional expense of the server.

In Chapter 12 we will explore the high availability aspects of vSphere 5 in more detail. In that chapter we will discuss admission control and how it impacts the availability of your cluster. In a nutshell, vCenter will limit the number of VMs that you can power on in a given cluster if you configure that cluster to reserve capacity for failover situations.

Ideally, you should be able to take two nodes down in your cluster and still operate without impact. We say two nodes because it's possible to suffer a failure on one node while you are performing maintenance on another node. If you have sized your cluster to withstand this loss, your performance and Service Level Agreements (SLAs) will be unaffected.

Contention

All this planning has a purpose: to avoid the ill effects of contention. But, what is contention and why is it bad? When more than one VM competes for the same resource at the same time, such as the CPU or disk I/O, we say that there is contention on that resource. The key here is time. We may be able to deliver the resource to both VMs, but not at the same time. In many cases, we resolve the problem of scarcity of resources by time division; meaning that each VM is given a set amount of time to use that resource before the resource is yielded to another VM. Because the VMs must take turns, each VM is also deprived of the resource for a set amount of time, thereby reducing the VM's performance. So, contention can, and often does, lead to poor performance for VMs.

But some contention isn't necessarily a bad thing. If your ESXi host has no contention at all, it also means that you likely have resources that are going to waste (or you have superhuman powers of resource optimization). Resource sharing is part of the reason that virtualization is so popular. Applications and operating systems tend to demand more resources than they actually use. Allowing other VMs to use these underutilized resources allows us to consolidate our servers. The trick is to keep the contention to a minimum, or at least architect the resource allocation so the more important VMs are given priority during periods of heavy contention.

In the next few sections we are going to introduce how the VMkernel helps us minimize contention and avoid situations where one VM could cause another VM to fail. The control methods include things such as adjustments to the individual VMs, the memory management techniques of the hypervisor, and even large-scale management using things called Resource Pools.

How Can We Curb Contention?

VMware has many built-in tools to help us mitigate the effects of contention and to allow us greater control over our resource allocation. Many of these settings can be adjusted while the VM is running, allowing us to fine-tune or even correct the performance of a running VM without forcing it to reboot.

Reservations

In virtualized systems, VMs typically compete for resources. The problem is that not all VMs are the same, and some VMs are justifiably more important than others. For instance, in a Microsoft Windows infrastructure the domain controllers serve an important role. If they are unable to operate because other VMs are starving them of resources, the impact will be felt on many systems. For these cases, we need a means to guarantee resources to certain VMs. That guarantee is known as a reservation.

Reservations can be configured on each VM to guarantee a minimum amount of CPU, RAM, or disk I/O to the VM. For instance, configuring a CPU reservation for a VM will modify something referred to as its resource entitlement. As the reservation increases, so does the VM's entitlement to that resource. The hypervisor uses these entitlement values to determine how the physical host's resources will be allocated to the VMs.

Setting reservations has a downside though. Reserved resources are earmarked for a particular VM, and typically will not be given out to other VMs. This can restrict the amount of available RAM or CPU bandwidth on the host. Fortunately, some reservations are more lenient than others. For example, RAM and CPU reservations behave slightly different from one another. A RAM reservation is granted as soon as the VM initializes its memory, and it won't forfeit that hold on the memory until it is powered off. Fortunately, some guest operating systems, such as Linux, do not initialize their RAM when they first boot, so you may have VMs that do not consume their entire RAM reservations. Unfortunately, Windows does initialize its memory on boot, so be cautious when assigning large memory reservations to these VMs.

A CPU reservation, on the other hand, is quite a bit more flexible. While moving pages in and out of RAM takes a lot of time, executing CPU instructions is typically a fast, and therefore easily queued, operation. An idle VM with a CPU reservation may elect not to use its cycles if it has no work to perform. If CPU reservations behaved like RAM reservations, the reserved CPU cycles would go to waste if not consumed. To keep the CPU efficiency as high as possible, the hypervisor allows other VMs to temporarily use those CPU cycles. Again, the logic being that the VM borrowing CPU cycles can be temporarily queued should the VM with the reservation suddenly request to use the CPU.

Note

The default reservation for CPU or memory on a VM or resource pool is zero! If you don't specify a reservation, your VM may be completely starved of resources during periods of extreme resource contention (such as a host failover event).

Despite seeming rather negative, RAM reservations have a very bright side. You'll soon read about how the hypervisor handles extreme shortages of physical RAM on ESXi hosts. While it doesn't happen often if your system is adequately sized, the hypervisor can strip a VM of all its non-reserved pages of memory. That means without a reservation of memory, the VMkernel can take every last byte of RAM away from a VM, forcing it to use disk-based virtual memory instead. As you might guess, VMs run horribly slow and may fail to function properly if you they are swapped out to disk for too long.

A nice side effect of a reservation is the effect that it has on the VM's VMkernel swap file—the file used for virtual memory during host-level resource emergencies. The VMkernel swap file is reduced by the size of the memory reservation; meaning that if your VM had 8GB of RAM allocated to it, it would normally have an 8GB VMkernel swap file. If you add a 2GB memory reservation, that VMkernel swap file is reduced to 6GB because the other 2GB must always come from physical RAM. This side effect is most beneficial when you must allocate hundreds of GB of RAM to VMs. The resulting disk space for the VMkernel swap files would be incredible without the use of reservations.

Caution

CPU-based reservations are special because the reservation value is divided by the total number of vCPUs (cores and sockets) assigned to the VM. So if you have a VM with four vCPUs and you assign it a reservation of 1,000MHz, the effective reservation per vCPU is only 250MHz. Knowing this, you may want to increase the reservation so that the effective speed guarantee per vCPU is appropriate.

Limits

Limits artificially cap the CPU, RAM, and/or disk I/O of a VM. We want to stress the word "artificially" because adding a limit doesn't change what the guest operating system sees. If you have allocated 8GB of RAM to a VM, and then later assign a limit of 4GB of RAM to that same VM, the guest operating system still sees 8GB of RAM even though only half of that memory will ever be located in real physical memory on the ESXi host. The other half will come from the VM swap file (virtual memory).

Note

Setting a limit does not change the amount of CPU or RAM that the guest operating system sees. If you allocate 8GB of RAM to a VM, the guest operating system will see 8GB of RAM even if you set a limit. The limit just restricts the amount of physical RAM the VM can address; the rest comes from disk (virtual memory).

Setting a limit also places an extra burden on the hypervisor because it must manage the VM utilization and de-schedule it from the CPU or remove it from RAM when it exceeds a specific threshold. Limits can be a great tool to demonstrate what would happen to your VM if the ESXi host were to fall under extreme contention, but limits aren't great at curbing resource contention.

For example, to use a limit to curb contention, you would need to place a limit on every other VM on your ESXi host. This is a complex process, and one that is further complicated if you place your host into a cluster, and then use vMotion to distribute your VMs across different ESXi servers. Tracking where you have placed these limits isn't difficult, but explaining why you intentionally degraded another VM's performance on an otherwise unrestricted system might be challenging. Don't use them on individual VMs unless you enjoy troubleshooting and have excess time on your hands.

Later we will talk about resource pools. Limits may help you in certain circumstances with resource pools, but again they should be used with caution.

Caution

Like the CPU reservation noted above, CPU limits are also affected by the number of vCPUs assigned to the VM. If you place a 1,000MHz limit on a 4-vCPU VM, the effective maximum speed of that VM will be 250MHz per CPU. That is nearly Pentium 1 speeds! Be careful!

Shares

Instead of using limits, a better way to control the unreserved capacity of your ESXi hosts is to set shares. Shares allow us to assign relative priority levels to each of the VMs so that your most important VMs can use the unclaimed resources. By default, all VMs are assigned an equal number of shares, so they compete equally unless you adjust the number of shares or you group the VMs into resource pools. We're assuming that your VMs aren't all of equal importance, so you'll likely want to know how shares work so that you can prioritize things properly.

Alone, one share has no value because shares don't equate to megabytes of RAM or even MHz of CPU power. Instead, shares are used in a proportional system where the hypervisor compares the total number of shares assigned to a resource in one VM to the total number of shares issued to that same resource in other peer-level VMs. The part about the "peer-level" will come in later. For now, you need to understand that the VM with the most shares is going to be allowed to use the resource more often than the other VMs.

Remember, we said this is a proportional system, not a voting system. That means that if a VM has proportionately more shares than another, it will get proportionately more access to the resource. Ultimately, the system of shares defines the amount of time the VM can spend on the physical CPU and the amount of memory allocated to VM during periods of extreme contention on the ESXi host.

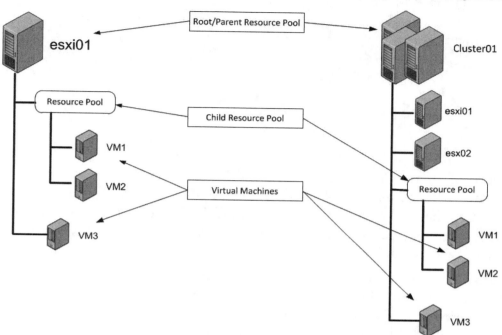

Figure 10.2
The root resource pool.

We said we'd come back to that peer-level part of the shares. Each ESXi host or cluster of hosts can represent something known as a root resource pool. The root resource pool is the top of the resource hierarchy, and from it we can define additional child resource pools or place VMs directly at the root. See Figure 10.2 for an illustration of the root resource pool in relation to child resource pools and VMs configured at the same peer level.

Now that you see how the hierarchy can be organized, we should explain how the ratios of shares work. Remember, it's proportional so the individual values aren't as significant as the ratios of shares between the VMs and resource pools.

There are three predefined resource share levels for memory and CPU usage on VMs and resource pools: High, Normal, and Low. Table 10.2 shows the share values for each object and resource by priority level. Hopefully you also see the 4-2-1 ratios between high, normal, and low priority. You can also add a custom share value if you want to override the predefined share levels, but we recommend sticking to the predefined values unless you are certain.

Table 10.2 Share Values

Object	Resource	High Priority	Normal Priority	Low Priority
VM	CPU	2,000 per vCPU	1,000 per vCPU	500 per vCPU
VM	Memory	20 per MB RAM	10 per MB RAM	5 per MB RAM
Resource Pool	CPU	8,000	4,000	2,000
Resource Pool	Memory	327,680	163,840	81,920

At each level of the resource hierarchy, the total active shares will be compared to the shares of the VM or resource pool to determine the resource entitlement. Notice that we said "active shares." VMs that are powered off do not consume resources; therefore, their shares can be excluded from the equation. All other VMs, even those seemingly idle, will be included.

Referring back to Figure 10.2, VM3 is presently competing at a peer-level with the resource pool. Assuming the resource pool and the VM were both configured with a "normal" priority of shares, VM3 would have 1000 shares to the resource pool's 4000 shares. If the host were to fall under contention, this distribution would give the resource pool approximately 4/5 of the CPU's time, whereas the VM would only get 1/5 (5000 total shares were issued).

If we were to shut down VM3, the resource allocation would change, resulting in the resource pool gaining all the resources, as shown in Figure 10.3.

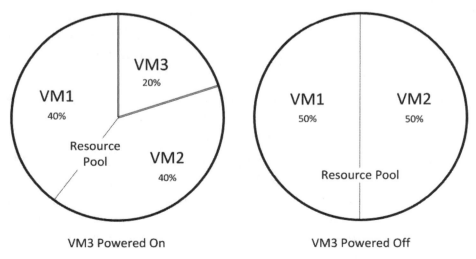

Figure 10.3
Resource allocation changes.

Be sure that you have allocated your shares fairly and in accordance to your service level agreements or you may have development and standby VMs taking resource priority during times of contention on your ESXi host.

Note

One important thing to remember: All of this priority manipulation with shares is only relevant during times of resource contention, but don't let that fool you into neglecting to configure your shares. Your host can experience contention at the least expected times, and you need to be prepared!

Tip

For a much more in-depth look at how vSphere 5 manages its resources, including the precise technical behavior of reservations, shares, and limits, check out the book entitled, *vSphere 5 Clustering Technical Deepdive*, by Duncan Epping and Frank Denneman.

Policy-Based Storage

Now with vSphere 5 we can also define the appropriate class of storage for our VMs. We discussed this in Chapter 8, but if you'll recall, policy-based storage allows us to group our storage devices into similar pools that can be automatically or manually used to keep the I/O of our VMs in-line with our users' expectations. By properly defining your storage resources into these pools, and then creating appropriate storage policies, you can ensure that your VMs are kept on storage that meets or exceeds your demands.

How Does the Hypervisor Help with Contention?

Part of the advantage of vSphere is its ability to oversubscribe access to an ESXi host's resources. Through the use of certain controls, we can oversubscribe the ESXi host's resources without worrying about the host crashing if more than one VM were to suddenly request access to the same resources. In addition to the reservations, limits, and shares, the hypervisor has a number of tools at its disposal to help avoid resource contention and improve the overall efficiency of the ESXi host. Some of these tools are dedicated for the CPU, while others are focused on RAM, network, or disk resources.

CPU Scheduler

The CPU scheduler is responsible for allocating time to a VM's vCPUs, and, if necessary, shifting it from one logical processor to another. Remember, each vCPU in a VM is just a process that we're scheduling on either a core or hyperthread of a physical

CPU in the host system. One of the CPU scheduler's jobs is to move these processes around to make the most efficient use of the physical CPUs in the ESXi host.

There are times when the CPU scheduler may also force some VMs to stop executing so that other VMs may have a turn. The goal is to make sure that the right VM gets time on the CPU. To figure out which VM is the right VM, the hypervisor uses reservations, shares, and limits to calculate a VM's resource entitlement. In the absence of contention, resource entitlement isn't much of an issue because every VM is provided all the resources they request. However, when the ESXi host falls under contention, the hypervisor must allocate resources based on each VM's effective resource entitlement.

For example, under contention, a VM with a large reservation will be granted more time on the physical CPUs of the host than a VM with a smaller reservation. The other VMs without reservations are left fighting over the remaining resources. As you read above, this is where shares come into place because the CPU scheduler uses the relative number of shares to calculate the resource entitlement of each running VM to determine which VM is scheduled on a physical CPU, and which VMs must wait.

As the vSphere administrator, you can control the behavior of the CPU scheduler by adjusting the reservations, shares, and limits of the VMs. While we hope a host never experiences long-term contention for its resources, the reality is that a moderately used ESXi host can experience short-term bursts of contention throughout the day. This can be caused by other host failures or even VM boot storms, where many VMs suddenly power on or demand 100% of the CPU. Configuring the VMs' shares and reservations appropriately will go a long way to avoid problems in these situations.

Memory—Deduplication

While not really a true fighter of contention, Transparent Memory Page Sharing (TMPS) allows the hypervisor to deduplicate the RAM of the ESXi host. This indirectly helps us with contention because the deduplication process removes excess memory pages, essentially creating free space in RAM. The TMPS process runs periodically in the background on the ESXi host, groveling the host's memory space looking for duplicate pages in RAM. When it finds duplication, it removes the duplicate pages and replaces them with pointers to a single copy of the source memory page.

Note

The TMPS process is far more beneficial on hosts where the VMs are all homogenous and very similar in configuration because there will be a much higher ratio of duplicate to unique pages in RAM.

Memory—Ballooning

There are some situations where the ESXi host's memory will quickly start to deplete. Typically this is caused by several VMs attempting to power on with memory reservations, such as the case after another host suddenly fails. If the cluster was configured for High Availability (HA), the VMs on the failed host will be started on the remaining hosts, occasionally creating a temporary resource shortage.

There are four memory states in an ESXi server: high, soft, hard, and low. In previous versions of ESX, these states corresponded to decreasing hard coded values starting at 6% of the host's total physical memory. In vSphere 5, VMware restructured the system to use a tiered system based on the "minfree" memory value of the ESXi host. This is a good thing because under the old rules, the ESXi server might start reclaiming RAM when it really wasn't in danger of running out. For example, 6% of available memory on a host with 1TB of RAM equates to just over 61GB of free memory available. That's still a lot of free memory! So instead, the new tier-based system is calculated based on the amount of physical RAM in your ESXi host, and again you can determine the threshold by examining the "minfree" value using esxtop on your ESXi host.

Tip

The "minfree" value of the ESXi host's memory can be seen in esxtop. This is the point at which the hypervisor will begin reclaiming memory from VMs due to memory contention.

The first action the hypervisor will take is called "ballooning." It allows the hypervisor to reclaim some of the RAM that a VM is using by inflating a special driver in the guest operating system known as the "balloon driver." The balloon driver isn't magical; it's really just a driver that is installed with the VMware Tools package. It typically runs in the background of the guest operating system, and like any other application, it can request RAM from the operating system.

If the balloon driver asks the guest operating system for RAM, the guest operating system will first surrender any free memory available, and then begin swapping lesser used services to the guest's pagefile or swap partition. This enables the guest operating system to effectively choose which pages of RAM will be written to disk, maintaining the more active pages in physical RAM (if possible). Later you will see that we have another method to reclaim physical RAM from a VM that isn't so polite; we call it VMkernel swap. The balloon driver mechanism is considered the nice-guy approach because the hypervisor allows the guest operating system to choose which pages of RAM are inactive and that can be safely written to disk. The VMkernel swap method doesn't ask the VM; it just takes the physical RAM away.

Note

By default, the hypervisor can attempt to reclaim up to 65% of the guest's RAM using the balloon driver method; however, this figure can be adjusted in the advanced options of the ESXi host.

Memory—Compression

If the server is still in need of more physical RAM after the ballooning process has commenced, the hypervisor can resort to something known as memory compression to reclaim a bit more memory before we resort to stealing RAM from unsuspecting VMs.

Unlike the ballooning and VMkernel swap methods, the memory compression process doesn't scavenge the memory of each VM individually. Instead, the hypervisor evaluates the entire memory space of the ESXi host as a whole and then begins searching for areas of RAM that can be compressed at a 2:1 ratio (or more). The compression process uses the gzip algorithm, but it doesn't create a gzip file on disk. The compressed pages are stored in RAM, which dramatically reduces the impact of compressing/decompressing these memory pages. Once the VMkernel is no longer under memory contention, the pages can be expanded and restored to their original state.

Memory—VMkernel Swap

If the VMkernel is still unable to reclaim enough RAM using ballooning or compression, it will react with drastic measures, taking physical RAM away from VMs and substituting virtual memory (disk-based memory) in its place. This virtual memory is referred to as "VM swap" space, and it results in a dramatic slowdown for the access of the guest's memory.

The VMkernel swap takes the form of a file in each VM's home directory. The file is created each time the VM is powered on, and it equals the size of the allocated RAM of the VM minus any reservations configured for that VM. The reservation, if you recall, must be fulfilled using physical RAM, therefore that portion of the guest's memory will never be swapped to the VMkernel swap space. Consider this a nice side effect of setting a reservation; the VMkernel swap file size is reduced on disk, saving you some disk space.

As you know, disk-based memory is not fast; in fact, it is downright slow, but using the VMkernel swap space prevents the ESXi host from crashing. At this point the hypervisor evaluates which VMs have the lowest priority (as determined by their shares), and then it begins swapping the RAM randomly to disk. The random part is actually an attempt to reduce the impact of the swapping process because by randomly swapping pages, we spread the impact across the entire VM, not just a single application.

Regardless of how the memory is swapped, a VM that is actively using VMkernel swap space will not perform well. This is the main reason we suggest using shares to accurately identify which VMs are the lowest priority, and it is why we recommend configuring at least some level of memory reservation for your production VMs. You want to avoid swapping to disk whenever possible.

Storage—Multipathing

We discussed storage multipathing in Chapter 8. While you might not immediately consider multipathing a form of performance management, there is one mode that can help us balance the load. That mode is referred to as Round Robin, and it enables the VMkernel to distribute storage traffic across multiple HBAs in an attempt to spread the load across the various pathways to the shared storage device(s).

Note

> If you have an active-active SAN, you may wish to consider using the Round Robin path selection policy (PSP).

Storage I/O Control

Storage I/O Control was also discussed in Chapter 8, and as you'll recall it gives us the ability to refine how each of the VMs uses the storage network. The hypervisor can restrict the storage communications of certain VMs in favor of more important VMs. You decide the importance of the VMs by configuring the shares, just as we do with memory or CPU resources.

Network—Multipathing

Like storage multipathing, network multipathing may not seem like a performance consideration, but it can be if you have vNetwork Distributed Switches. As we discussed in Chapter 7, the Distributed Switches allow for outbound load redistribution if the network cards become saturated. This doesn't happen for the Standard Switches, which can limit your network performance if your VMs are very active on the network.

Network I/O Control

As we noted in Chapter 7, Network I/O Control was dramatically improved in vSphere 5. It now includes QoS tagging, which finally gives us the ability to designate individual VMs into different classes of service that are respected and adhered to in the physical network. Prior to vSphere 5, we could force the hypervisor to prioritize certain traffic, but once it left the ESXi server, the physical network had no visibility as to how the traffic should be handled. Not all VMs should be configured for QoS tagging, but it is nice to have for those high-priority VMs, such as call center managers and other network-intensive servers.

Macromanagement of Resources—Resource Pools

While you can set reservations and shares at a per-VM level, using a resource pool allows you to define these settings for a group of VMs. The advantage is that you can move VMs in and out of the pool, without maintaining the resources on each VM. In addition, resource pools can be used to allocate resources to a business function or business group rather than a specific application or server. This allows you, as the administrator of the entire cluster, to define how much CPU or memory should be devoted to a particular group of applications or even a group of other administrators.

Resource pools can be created either on a cluster or an individual host. If you opt to create the resource pool at the cluster level, you must license DRS, which is bundled with the vSphere Enterprise license. You may, however, create resource pools on each individual host if the hosts are not yet in a cluster. If you create your resource pools at the host-level, you will need to place the VM into the appropriate resource pool if you move a VM from one host to another.

Reservations and Shares

Like VMs, resource pools can have reservations, shares, and limits. The key difference is that resource pools are containers for other resource pools and VMs. Resources are allocated to a resource pool in much the same way we allocate resources to a VM, but we typically allocate more resources to the resource pools because these pools will supply their resources to any VMs or child resource pools they contain.

For example, when you allocate a reservation to a resource pool, any VM that powers on will attempt to fulfill its own reservation by deducting RAM or CPU from the resource pools reservation allotment. When the resource pool's allotment has been depleted, no further VMs may power on that require a reservation. To avoid running out of RAM in the resource pool, you need to review the list of VMs you wish to add to the pool, and then size their reservations in accordance with the size of the resource pool.

In addition to serving as a bank account for VMs' reservations, the resource pools also compete for the leftover resources using the same share-based system that VMs use. Here, the difference is that resource pools are granted a much larger starting value than the average VM. By default, a VM is granted 2000 shares when configured at "Normal" level, whereas a similarly configured resource pool is configured with 4000 shares. This doubling is required because resource pools typically contain more than one VM and therefore shouldn't be evaluated equally with other VMs.

Of course, you can override the share configuration, and in many cases you may need to if you place VMs next to (instead of inside) resource pools in your cluster or on your ESXi host.

Expandable Reservation

So what happens if you attempt to power on a VM that requests a larger reservation than the resource pool can satisfy? The same thing that happens if you try to take more money out of the bank than you have in your bank account; you are both denied. Now we know what you're thinking. You have overdraft protection on your bank accounts. If you accidentally draw too much money from an account, the bank will grant you a temporary loan to cover your deficit. Resource pools can do this too, but like overdraft protection, you must enable it before it will work.

The protection mechanism on resource pools is called an expandable reservation. If enabled, it will attempt to fulfill the reservation of the powering on VM by using resources from its parent resource pool. If the resource pool was already the top-most resource pool, it will draft those resources from the "root resource pool," which is the cluster or the ESXi host depending on your configuration.

Expandable reservations can continue up the chain until the root resource pool is queried. At this point there is nowhere else to go, so if there are either insufficient resources at the parent pool or the parent pool has expandable reservations disabled, the VM will not be permitted to power on.

Note

> The hypervisor will also check the unreserved capacity on the host/cluster if an administrator attempts to increase a VM's reservation, or if the administrator attempts to create another child resource pool with a new reservation.

Limits on Pools

Yes, it is possible to configure limits on resource pools, but we strongly caution you against this practice. Perhaps even more than with VMs, assigning a limit to a resource pool can create unexpected results. Just as with reservations, a limit is shared by all the VMs within a resource pool. If you assign a limit to a resource pool, the collective resource consumption of all the VMs in that pool must not exceed the limit at any one time.

For example, you have a resource pool that contains 10 VMs, each with a single vCPU. All 10 VMs are test/development servers used only during the day. During the evening hours you would like to ensure that these VMs consume as few resources as possible, while remaining powered on and accessible to your remote management tools. You decide to create a scheduled task in vCenter that adds a 10GHz CPU limit on this pool during the evening hours, and another task that removes this limit for the daytime hours. During the day the servers behave as expected; however, at night the collective use of all the servers may not exceed 10GHz of processing power. If the servers attempt to exceed this threshold, the CPU scheduler will withhold CPU time from the VMs to maintain the limit established on the resource pool.

Caution

This is just an example. We aren't suggesting you create such a rule or task in your own environment because despite the resilience of vCenter, a failed scheduled task could leave your environment in a highly restricted state if the limit were not removed during the daytime hours.

Alarms

Alarms probably require the least planning of any of the topics discussed in this section. Most of the work will be covered in the Implementation and Management section, but from a planning perspective we tend to focus on two things: what should be monitored, and what we want vCenter to do if it finds a problem.

vSphere 5 contains a list of over 50 predefined alarms, so the first part of this exercise may be pretty easy; just review the list. The catch is that, by default, vCenter doesn't do much when it finds a problem. Sure, it will flag the troublesome entry in the inventory, but vCenter won't send you an e-mail unless you configure it to do so.

That brings us to the second planning consideration: defining what vCenter should do when it finds a problem. There are a number of actions vCenter can take, such as sending e-mail, text messages [via e-mail], SNMP traps, or even running a script to respond in a programmatic way. In order to send SNMP traps, you'll also need a trap receiver (the destination the trap should be sent to), and to send e-mail you will need an SMTP server that accepts anonymous SMTP. The configuration of these options will be described in the following section.

Implementation and Management

By now you should have a good idea of what resource controls you'd like to implement in your environment. This section is going to review some of the more hands-on or practical situations, whereas the first section of this chapter was largely focused on theory.

We've organized this section into the following main topics:

- Managing VM resources
- Managing resource pools
- VM optimizations
- Host optimizations
- Mitigating contention
- Understanding performance data in vCenter
- Alarms

Managing VM Resources

You can adjust the resource settings of a VM by right-clicking on it and selecting "Edit settings." This will display the same properties screen we discussed in Chapter 9, but if you click on the Resource tab as shown in Figure 10.4, you will have the option to

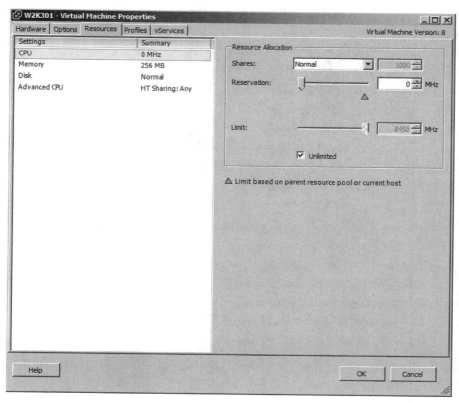

Figure 10.4
VM CPU resources.

fine-tune the amount of memory, CPU, or even disk resources that are allocated to the VM. As we discussed in the Planning section of this chapter, adjusting the values on the Resource tab doesn't change what the guest operating system sees. It adjusts how much of each resource is guaranteed to the VM versus restricted or delivered on a best-effort basis.

Note in Figure 10.4 that on the left side of this window you can toggle between CPU, RAM, Disk, and the Advanced CPU configurations. The first three options allow us to adjust reservations, shares, and/or limits on the resources, whereas the Advanced CPU option controls CPU affinity as we discussed in Chapter 9.

CPUs and Memory

The adjustments for CPU and memory are very similar so we'll cover them together so you don't have to read the same information twice. The difference between the CPU and memory is one little check box shown in Figure 10.5, "Reserve all guest memory

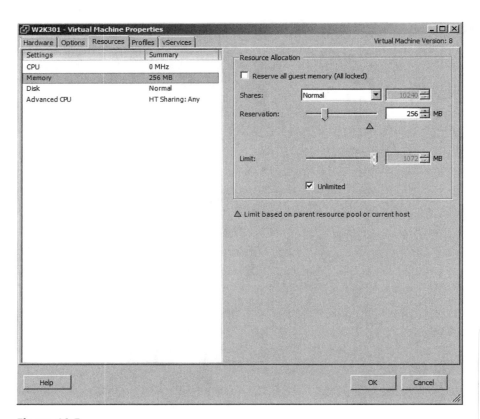

Figure 10.5
VM RAM resources.

(All locked)." As it sounds, this option reserves 100% of the VM's RAM and sets the limit to unlimited. Compare the two screen shots and you'll see what we mean. That option doesn't appear on the CPU resources page.

If you don't select the option to reserve 100% of the RAM, you can adjust the reservation or limit by dragging the slider or entering a value in the text boxes. Note that you can't reserve more RAM than you allocated to the VM, nor can you set a limit greater than what you allocated to the VM. The vSphere Client will help you determine the maximum size of a reservation (CPU or RAM) that you can configure. It does this by displaying a little triangle under the reservation line. You can't configure a reservation beyond this point because the physical ESXi host either doesn't have enough unreserved resources remaining or the resource pool containing the VM doesn't have sufficient capacity.

Also take note of the checkbox labeled "Unlimited." You should check the Unlimited box whenever possible rather than just dragging the slider to the maximum value. Under most circumstances it won't make too much of a difference; however, if you don't select unlimited you can get a nasty surprise if you add a vCPU or upgrade the underlying physical CPUs because the resource limit won't automatically scale with the changes you implemented. Checking the Unlimited box ensures that the VM is never limited, regardless of the number of vCPUs you add or the number of times you upgrade the physical CPUs of the ESXi host.

Disk

Take a look at the disk options in Figure 10.6. In comparison to the CPUs and RAM, the disk options appear insignificant, but don't be fooled. The configuration page appears different because VMware had to show different options. In this list you can control the resource settings for each individual virtual disk that a VM uses. That means that you can fine-tune the transaction log disk of a database server, or you can place an I/O limit on an overactive data warehouse disk.

Like the other selections, you can adjust the limits and shares, but notice there are no reservations. So how do we guarantee a specific level of disk performance to our VMs if we can't use reservations? Remember the discussion of VM storage profiles in Chapter 8? We can control which storage profile is assigned to each VM. The storage profiles are tied to different classes of storage, which in turn are (hopefully) designed to guarantee a set amount of disk I/O for your VMs. The storage profile selection has a dedicated tab on the settings page of each VM as shown in Figure 10.7. Again, notice that you can control the storage profile for each virtual disk so that you can fine-tune the settings for your VM.

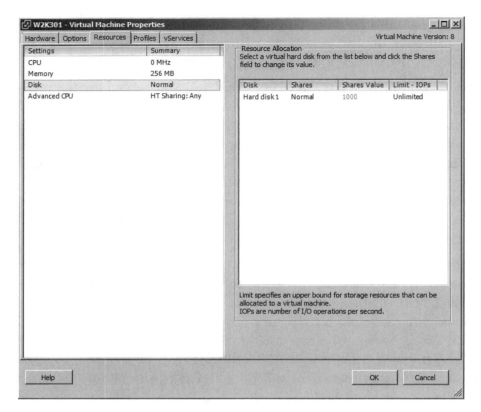

Figure 10.6
VM disk resources.

As you can also see, there is no place to configure the underlying storage device in this window. That's because we configured all those settings in the storage configuration area of the ESXi host as we showed in Chapter 8.

Network

Finally, you might be asking yourself how we control network resources. Throughout the book we've always coupled the CPU, RAM, disk, and networking resources together, so why is networking notably absent from this list? The reason is that VMware doesn't have an option to control networking resources on the VM settings screen. The only thing you can change at the VM level is the number of network cards assigned to the VM. Everything else is configured at the virtual switch level.

If you remember back to our discussions on Network I/O Control in Chapter 7, you'll recall that we can adjust the shares and limits of a VM's network. In vSphere 5 we also have the ability to establish Quality of Service (QoS) rules that behave like

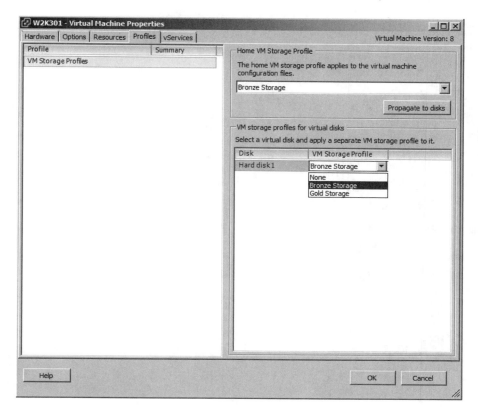

Figure 10.7
VM Storage Profiles.

shares. Instead of reserving a particular amount of bandwidth for a VM, we just give certain VMs priority if the network falls under contention. For more information, read about QoS and Network I/O Control in Chapter 7.

Managing Resource Pools

Resource pools can be created on hosts, but if you want to create a resource pool that spans multiple hosts (a cluster) you must license the Dynamic Resource Scheduler (DRS) feature. Since we haven't discussed clusters yet (they are covered in Chapter 11), we'll focus on how to do this at a host level. The process of creating and deleting resource pools remains the same whether the root is a host or a cluster. The difference lies in the resource planning as we discussed earlier in the chapter.

Creating Resource Pools

To create a resource pool, right-click on the host and then select New Resource Pool. A window will appear like the one shown in Figure 10.8. You'll need to enter a useful

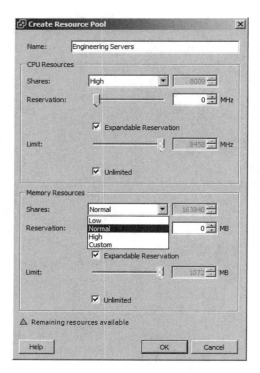

Figure 10.8
Creating a new resource pool.

name and then configure the size of the reservations for both CPU and RAM. Keep in mind that any reservation you set on this resource pool will automatically and immediately deduct that amount of CPU or RAM from the host's available capacity.

Note

If the option to create a resource pool is grayed out, the host is part of a cluster that does not have DRS enabled. If you want to use resource pools you can either enable DRS, or drag the host out of the cluster if you aren't using the cluster for High Availability (HA) purposes.

You can also create resource pools within other resource pools. Each time you do this, the available resources are carved up into smaller pieces, so don't use resources as organizational units or folders. That's what the folders in vCenter are for as we'll discuss in just a moment.

VM Power-On Restrictions
Be careful when configuring the reservations on your VMs and resource pools. If you configure reservations on VMs that are within resource pools, you must have a

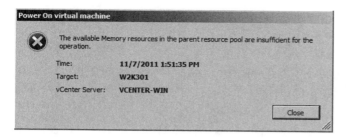

Figure 10.9
Insufficient resources error.

reservation on that resource pool large enough to satisfy the VM's individual reservation. To understand this, think of VMs and resource pools as buckets that hold a specific amount of RAM (or CPU cycles). The size of the reservation is the size of the bucket. You can't place a bigger bucket into a smaller bucket, and you can't place a VM with a 3GB reservation into a resource pool that only has a 2GB reservation.

For example, you configure a resource pool with a non-expandable reservation of 2GB of RAM (meaning you deselect the expandable reservation option). You then configure a VM inside that resource pool with a 3GB memory reservation. When you attempt to power on the VM, it will fail because the resource pool will be unable to satisfy the reservation and its reservation cannot grow. Fortunately the error message is descriptive to help you figure out what you did wrong. It will tell you that there are insufficient resources available, as shown in Figure 10.9.

Also, keep in mind that reservations are exclusive; two VMs can't share the same reservation. Going back to our previous example, your resource pool still has a 2GB memory reservation, but now you have allocated a 1GB reservation to VM1 and a 2GB reservation to VM2. You can power on either of these VMs separately, but not both simultaneously because together they require 3GB of RAM to be reserved in the resource pool.

Expandable Reservations

Now, there is a solution to the VM power-on problem, but is has a downside. The solution is called an expandable reservation. If enabled, it allows the resource pool to power on the VM that is requesting the additional RAM or CPU resources, but it pulls those extra resources from the resource pool's parent. That parent may be another resource pool if you had created a string of nested resource pools, or it may be the root resource pool. If you remember back to the Planning section of this chapter, the root resource pool is either the ESXi host or the cluster of ESXi hosts.

Either way, enabling expandable reservation can be a problem because it can allow an inexperienced vSphere administrator to sap all of a host's available resources by configuring his/her VM with a reservation that is just too big. Expandable reservations are enabled by default because VMware believes that under normal circumstances you shouldn't have this problem. Either you will have more than enough RAM in your ESXi hosts to accommodate all your VM reservations or everyone that you grant permissions to vCenter will be properly trained in how resource pools function. If that's not how your environment will work, you might want to disable the expandable reservations until you are certain you need them.

Permissions

Resource pools can be configured with permissions, but please keep in mind that they are not intended to be organizational units or folders. If you want to configure permissions on a resource pool, focus on permissions that have some impact on performance or resource control instead of access control. One example is the ability to alter the resource settings of the resource pool itself.

VMware includes a role called "resource pool administrator" that includes the necessary permissions to change the reservations, shares, and limits of a resource pool. You may want to assign a particular group of users the ability to modify their own resource pool settings. Do this by assigning those users/groups to the resource pool and using a role like the sample resource pool administrator role.

Caution

Don't grant this ability to inexperienced users. If you grant a user the ability to increase the reservation allocated to their resource pool, he/she could accidently create a resource shortage for other VMs or resource pools on your ESXi host (or cluster).

Configuring Reservations, Shares, and Limits

You can dynamically adjust the reservations and limits assigned to resource pools much in the same way you can adjust a VM's resource allocations. Right-click on the resource pool and then select Edit Settings to open a window similar to the one shown in Figure 10.10. You'll probably notice the settings screen looks identical to the one you used when you created the resource pool. Just adjust the sliders or enter the values you would like and then click OK. Notice that you can also enable or disable the expandable reservation as we discussed a bit earlier.

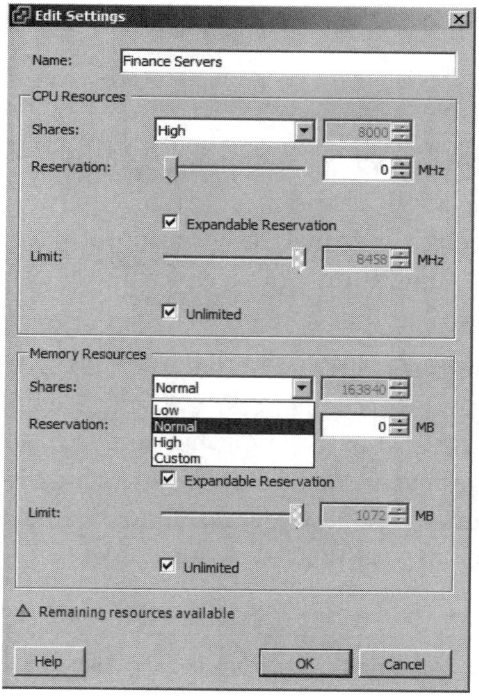

Figure 10.10
Editing a resource pool.

Make sure that you have the resources available before you make changes. The effects are immediate regardless of whether the effects will be good or bad. If you configured your resource pool with a reservation that was a bit too large, you might inadvertently starve a VM that didn't have a large enough reservation.

Tip

If you know that you need to make changes to resource pools often, you can schedule a task in vCenter to adjust resource pools. This is particularly useful for granting batch-processing servers extra resources during non-peak hours.

VM Optimizations

Monitoring resource utilization is important, but if you couple monitoring with some optimization techniques you may find that your systems run better and longer between reboots. There are many aspects to optimizing your VMs, starting with following the best practices of your application vendors. But application vendors can't possibly know every detail about *your* environment; so we've also included some advice that is a bit more general in nature. Use this advice to customize and create a best practice document of your own that applies to your specific organization.

Third-Party Application Best Practices

Nearly all the major application vendors provide best practices for their applications. Some are now giving special care to running their applications in a virtual environment. Some of these recommendations may involve the specific configuration of your virtual machines, or they may be more generic configuration practices for the guest operating system irrespective of virtualization.

The only thing constant about "best practices" among vendors is that they change often. There will always be documents that suggest best practices, and there will always be follow-up documents to replace them. The goal is to stay as current as possible, but also understand that making rapid changes every time a new best practice is released might cause you a lot of grief and downtime. Our best practice is to evaluate your vendors' best practices on a quarterly basis or as you upgrade your software.

Tip

Periodically check your vendor's best practices for updates. Sometimes new techniques are found that can have a significant impact in your virtual infrastructure.

Reduce CPU Waste

Here are some things you can do to reduce the amount of CPU overhead or waste in your VMs:

- Use single-processor VMs whenever possible. Only use multiple vCPUs in a VM if you have a multithreaded application in that VM.

- Remove unused virtual devices such as serial and parallel ports. These are typically found on VMs that were converted from physical machines.

- Use a hypervisor-based virus scanner (via the VM Safe APIs) instead of running the virus scanners in each VM.

Improve Memory Usage

RAM is critical to your VM's performance. Not having enough RAM can also cause performance issues on the disk and CPU due to excessive memory swapping. Here are some ideas related to RAM that may help improve your VM's performance:

- Allocate enough RAM to your VM to prevent the guest operating system from paging to disk excessively.

- Verify that the applications within the VM are configured to use the VM's RAM effectively.

- Deploy VMs that fit into a single NUMA node. Calculate your host's NUMA node size and size your VMs appropriately. This helps avoid having a VM span multiple NUMA nodes (which is slow).

- Grant at least a 25% reservation of memory to your VM. Increase the reservation if contention on the host causes this machine to give up its RAM at critical times.

Improve Storage Usage

The performance impact of storage can be easily overlooked, so to keep it from being a problem we need to consider several of the best practices we've talked about so far:

- Use the paravirtual SCSI adapter for your virtual disks in each of your VMs. The paravirtual adapter was discussed in Chapter 9, and it requires the VMware Tools to function properly. Even system/boot volumes are supported when using this adapter in vSphere 5.

- If your VM is I/O intensive, increase the spindle count of your storage array (or use SSD drives) to increase the maximum IOPS it can deliver to your VM.

- Defragment your virtual disks. This is something that goes well back into the day of physical servers. The only caveat: don't do this if you have a snapshot on your virtual disk—it could make your snapshot the same size as your virtual disk!

- For older guest operating systems, you may need to align your partitions appropriately. Windows 2003 and earlier, as well as some Linux distributions, can benefit from this process.

Improve Network Communications

While network performance typically isn't the bottleneck on most systems, there are still some adjustments that can improve your VM's network performance:

- Use the vmxnet3 network adapter for the NICs in each of your VMs. The vmxnet3 adapter was discussed in Chapter 9, and it requires the VMware Tools to function properly. You'll need to remove your VM's existing NIC, and then add a new NIC selecting vmxnet3 as the adapter type.

- Set up Network I/O Control in vCenter and use Quality of Service (QoS) for the VMs to guarantee a specific priority level for their network traffic.

- If your VM utilizes the network at rates of 90% or more, you may want to dedicate a physical network card to the VM. As you read in Chapter 9, you can do this via VM DirectPath I/O. The VM's network I/O stream will now bypass the hypervisor, which may give you a slight performance boost at the expense of not being able to use vMotion.

Note

The VM DirectPath I/O limitation on vMotion was lifted in vSphere 5 for the Cisco UCS hardware platform if you present one of Cisco's virtual Ethernet adapters to your VM instead of a dedicated Ethernet PCI card in the ESXi host.

Host Optimizations

Here are some optimizations that you can implement on your ESXi hosts to increase the performance of your Guest VMs. Not all of these suggestions will be applicable to your environment, so please research these topics in more detail before implementing them (even in a test environment, research comes first).

Enable Hardware Virtualization and EPT/RVI

Most CPU instructions called by a VM are directly executed on the ESXi host's physical processor; however, there are a few that are unable to execute properly unless the hypervisor helps out using a virtualization technique called binary translation. This mode involves overhead in the VMkernel because it must repackage the VM's CPU instruction(s). If you have hardware that supports hardware virtualization assistance you should enable it to reduce the need for binary translation.

On Intel CPUs, hardware virtualization assistance is referred to as "Intel VT-x," whereas AMD calls it "AMD-V." In either case it permits the ESXi hypervisor to operate at a higher than normal privilege in certain cases when the Guest VM needs to execute a privileged processor instruction. This enables the Guest VM to execute its instruction, while letting the hypervisor regain control of the physical CPU as soon as the VM is finished. In many cases this can result in a performance boost for your VMs because there is less overhead on the hypervisor.

Another hardware virtualization technique involves the management of the Guest VM's memory pages. Because the hypervisor doesn't grant the VM direct access to the physical ESXi host's memory controller, the hypervisor must account for and manage the VM's memory using a software solution known as shadow page tables.

This results in overhead for each VM, which can lead to performance degradation in highly active VMs.

The burden of guest memory management can be significantly lessened if you have an Intel processor that supports Extended Page Tables (EPT) or an AMD processor that supports Rapid Virtualization Indexing (RVI). The EPT and RVI additions to the processor provide hardware-level assistance by tracking the memory activity for the hypervisor. Memory-intensive VMs can see dramatic performance improvements because the hypervisor doesn't have to track the VMs' memory activity using software-based shadow page tables, therefore reducing the overhead.

Use NICs with TSO and Checksum Offloading for iSCSI

If you recall back to our discussions in Chapter 7 when we talked about networking, you will recall that if you intend to use the software iSCSI initiator, you can gain substantial performance improvements using hardware that assists in the TCP Segmentation of the packets. This technique is referred to as TCP Segmentation Offloading (TSO). If you use the software iSCSI initiator in ESXi, the hypervisor is responsible for the segmentation and processing of the storage packets. This results in excess overhead on the processor. You can avoid this by using NICs with TSO and checksum offloading capabilities.

Note

If you are using a hardware iSCSI HBA, the card should already support TSO, and possibly even the checksum offloading features.

Network Multipathing

Network multipathing can affect your performance if a VM is consistently reaching the barrier of a single 1Gbps NIC. You have a choice: You can either add another network card and implement the IP-hash load-balancing algorithm on your virtual switch or you can upgrade to a 10Gbps NIC. Why enable the IP-hash algorithm? Check out Chapter 7 for more details, but IP-hash is the only distribution algorithm that permits a VM to use more than one outbound NIC. It has caveats though, so you may be better off upgrading to a 10Gbps NIC where your VM can run well past the 1Gbps boundary.

Storage Multipathing

When possible, you should use storage arrays that support active-active multipathing. This ensures a better distribution of your storage I/O, and it can increase the throughput of your VMs because multiple controllers can service the request. If you have an active-active storage array, be sure to enable the Round Robin path selection policy on each datastore on your ESXi host(s) to take advantage of the additional storage paths.

Shut Down Idle VMs

True idle VMs are mythical because the only true idle VM is one that is powered off. Even a VM that isn't actively processing huge workloads will consume some CPU processing power and memory to handle basic operating system tasks such as time keeping. This extra CPU workload detracts from the available CPU resources of your ESXi host.

While one or two of these "idle VMs" may not be a big deal, as they add up, so will the unnecessary CPU usage. If you have VMs that are "idle," power them down if possible.

Caution

> Keep in mind that the hypervisor must consider all powered-on VMs in its resource scheduling even if the VM isn't doing anything "important." This can be problematic if the host falls under resource contention unexpectedly and you have several "idle VMs" with high memory or CPU share values.

Mitigating Contention

Even if you follow all the best practices to prevent resource contention, there will still be that time when everything goes wrong. VMware provides tools to solve contention problems quickly, and potentially without further downtime, so that your users can get back to work.

- **vMotion.** Move the VMs manually to another ESXi host without downtime.
- **Storage vMotion.** If the problem is disk-related, move the VMs to another datastore without downtime.
- **Dynamic Resource Scheduler (DRS).** Automate the load balancing of your VMs via vMotion.
- **Storage DRS.** Automate the load balancing of your storage I/O via Storage vMotion.
- **Power off or suspend any idle VMs.** While not ideal, sometimes it is your only option.

Understanding Performance Data in vCenter

We're changing topics now from the administration of the resources to the monitoring of those resources. We need to discuss how to work with the performance charts so that you understand where to look for trouble. We'll cover the details of what to look for in the next section.

Performance Charts

VMware vCenter has a performance chart section for each VM, host, cluster, resource pool, and even datacenter. The charts are divided into Overview or Advanced, as shown in Figure 10.11. The overview charts show multiple resources on the same page, but each resource is represented in a separate graph. Sometimes these are referred to as "At a Glance" reports because you can see all the major resources in one view.

Tip

If you ever have difficulties opening/viewing the Overview charts, check if the WebServices service is running on the vCenter server. These charts are dependent on the Tomcat engine installed on the vCenter server.

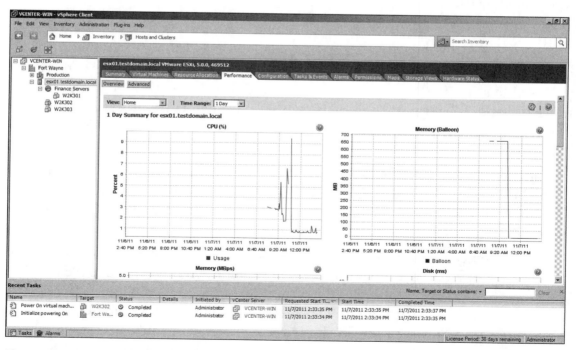

Figure 10.11
Performance charts—Overview versus Advanced.

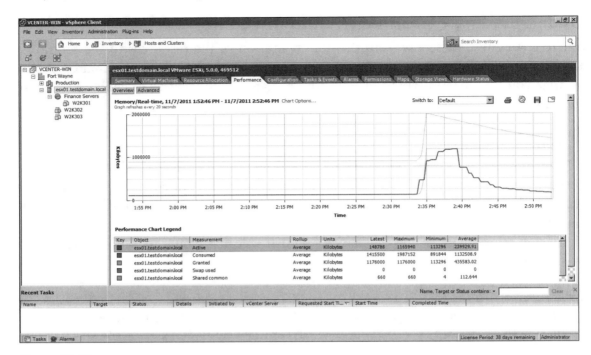

Figure 10.12
Advanced resource charts.

If you would like a bit more detail or the ability to customize the charts and graphs, you need to select the Advanced toggle button. This will bring you to a page similar to what you see in Figure 10.12. This chart is refreshed every 20 seconds, because that is the default interval that vCenter polls the ESXi hosts for its performance counters.

The advanced charts can display a great deal of information about the performance of the hosts as well as the VMs. To customize the advanced charts, click on Chart Options. The window shown in Figure 10.13 displays the advanced chart options for an ESXi host.

From here you can customize the chart to show only the counters and objects (VMs or hosts) that are relevant to your needs. For example, you might create a chart that shows the CPU Ready information for your VMs on a given ESXi host. If you find that you come back to view that report often, you can save the chart settings using the Save Chart Settings button in the lower-right corner. You'll have to specify a name for the chart settings, and then you can then use the Manage Chart Settings button to recall those settings later.

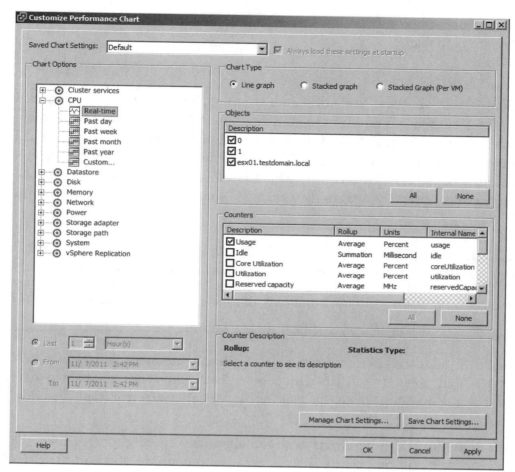

Figure 10.13
Advanced resource chart options.

Printing/Exporting Chart Data

Viewing the chart data in the vSphere Client is helpful, but there are many cases in which you may want to print or export the chart to give it to a colleague or keep it for trending and benchmarking purposes. Fortunately, there is a way to do both. You can print the chart by clicking the little Printer icon on the chart, but the more useful feature is exporting the data.

To export a chart, click on the Disk icon. You have the option to produce an image of the chart in JPG, BMP, GIF, or PNG. The image is great for presentations and charts. If you wanted to capture the data points, you also have the option to export the chart in XLS format. This last option doesn't include an image; instead, it gives you the ability to recreate the chart in Excel. Sometimes this is preferable to pasting an image file into a presentation because you can fine-tune the chart details to make the chart a bit more readable.

Performance Statistics

We've talked about all these statistics and counters, but we haven't explained where vCenter gets them. In addition to statistics about itself, an ESXi host gathers performance statistics about each VM it runs. The statistics are stored on the ESXi host until the vCenter agent collects the data and sends it to the vCenter database. The collection occurs every 20 seconds, which is why the advanced performance charts only refresh every 20 seconds (even if you click the Refresh button sooner).

Note

Clicking the Refresh button on the advanced performance charts doesn't actually gather new statistics from the ESXi host. The Refresh button only repaints the screen and refreshes the chart with data from the vCenter database. The hosts are only queried every 20 seconds, regardless of how many times you refresh.

As you saw in the advanced performance chart options, there are a variety of different chart types and counters available to choose. Each chart has predefined date ranges that include real-time stats as well as historical charts for daily, weekly, monthly, and yearly ranges.

You'll notice that the real-time charts will contain many more counters than the daily, weekly, or even monthly charts. This is because to conserve space in the database vCenter only retains certain counters for the historical charts. The idea is that most of the really advanced or detailed counters are only used during troubleshooting. The trending or historical charts typically focus on higher-level or overview counters such as CPU utilization, memory usage, and disk space.

Even though vCenter doesn't retain many of the more detail-oriented statistics by default, you can override the settings. vCenter uses different Collection Levels for each performance counter. The more detailed a counter is the higher the collection level. The highest collection level, Level 4, is reserved for the virtual device-specific counters, whereas CPU utilization is a Level 1 counter. Again, the lower-level counters typically contain the basic information that you would use when trending or creating historical baselines for your system.

If you configure vCenter to retain all the counters (Level 4 and below), the amount of performance data retained in the database also increases, resulting in a very large vCenter database.

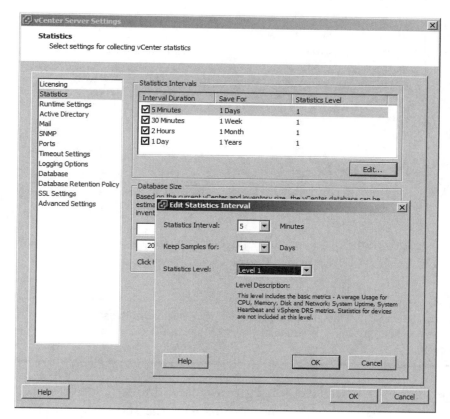

Figure 10.14
vCenter statistics settings.

To help you reduce the bloat in the database, vCenter automatically rolls up or summarizes the performance data throughout the day. The data is summarized multiple times, and at each time interval you can choose which performance counters are retained. The performance data is first rolled up, or summarized, every five minutes. The data is then summarized again after 30 minutes, then two hours, and finally after one day. These intervals are used as the basis for the historical charts (daily, weekly, monthly, and yearly, respectively). Again, each step of the way you can tell vCenter to retain a different level of statistics, as shown in Figure 10.14.

For instance, you may want to retain the Level 4 details at the 5-minute interval, which would allow you to select even the most detailed statistic when looking at the daily historical charts. At the 30-minute interval, you decide to select Level 3 because you don't require quite as much detail in your weekly charts. Finally, you select Level 2 for both the 2-hour and 1-day intervals so that you get a decent level of detail for both the monthly and yearly charts. Note that you can't set the 1-day interval to

Table 10.3   Example of the Statistics Levels and Estimated vCenter Database Size

Statistics Collection Level	Database Size
Level 1	1.04GB
Level 2	3.58GB
Level 3	6.89GB
Level 4	9.66GB

Level 4 if you have selected anything lower than Level 4 for the preceding intervals because you stripped out the Level 4 counters at one of the previous levels.

Tip

Setting the Statistics Level to 2 seems to be a happy medium in most environments because it captures much of the useful data without retaining device-level statistics that are typically only used during advanced troubleshooting.

Be aware that increasing the statistics level setting can have a dramatic effect on the size of your vCenter server database. Each time you increase the statistics collection level, your database size requirement increases, but you do get a lot of data for that cost. Hopefully you use it wisely because even a small increase in your database size has a lasting effect. Think about the impact to your database backup size and the required length of your database maintenance windows.

These are just estimates, but based on the database sizing calculator in vCenter, an environment of five hosts and 100 VMs can expect to see the database sizes in Table 10.3 after one year of operation at the respective statistics levels (if all four collection increments are set to the collection levels shown in the table.

Alarms

All of this monitoring is great, but who has time to watch a graph all day? If you said "me," you need a hobby. There is a better way, and likely a more accurate approach than watching a screen of charts. We can configure alarms in vCenter to let us know when things start behaving unexpectedly.

You can configure alarms on hosts, virtual machines, clusters, datastores, networks, and more. To work with the alarms, you must click on the Alarms tab of one of these objects in the vSphere Client. From here, you can see the triggered alarms and the alarm definitions. Alarm definitions are inherited through the vCenter hierarchy, meaning that you can create an alarm definition at one level and it will propagate to the child objects.

In the triggered alarms view, you can see any alarm that has been triggered for the selected object. In the alarms definition view, you can see any alarm defined on this object or inherited from a parent object. You can only edit alarms that are defined on the object you have selected in the hierarchy. If you want to edit an alarm that is being inherited, you must navigate to that object where the alarm was defined.

Alarms 101

vSphere has a large number of predefined alarms, but by default these alarms only display a notification in vCenter. It's up to you to configure the alarms to notify you or take other actions. If you want to notify different people or take different actions, you must edit the alarm definition, or create a new alarm. vCenter supports both SMTP for e-mail and SNMP traps for network monitoring applications. You can also configure vCenter to take additional actions, such as restarting a VM, but first we need to explain the anatomy of an alarm.

An alarm is composed of two key components:

- The trigger
- The action

Alarm Triggers

The trigger of the alarm can be a condition or an event. Conditions are typically (but not always) things that happen to VMs/hosts, whereas event triggers are typically related to actions that someone took. For instance, you can have a condition trigger if a VM's power state suddenly changes to "Off," and you can have an event trigger that monitors if a user changes the power state of the VM. You might be asking what the difference is, so consider this: In the case of the sudden power change, the host running the VM may have crashed, resulting in the VM's sudden power change. The event-based trigger wouldn't catch this because a user didn't initiate the power off, but the condition-based trigger would catch it. On the other hand, if a user powered off the VM, both the condition- and event-based triggers would catch the problem and report it.

Depending on the object type, you may be able to use a condition-based trigger, an event-based trigger, or both types of triggers. Refer to Table 10.4 for the details.

Table 10.4   Triggers by Object Type

Object	Valid for Condition Alarms?	Valid for Events?
Virtual Machines	Yes	Yes
Hosts	Yes	Yes
Clusters	No	Yes
Datacenters	No	Yes
Datastores	Yes	Yes
Datastore Clusters	Yes	Yes
vSphere Distributed Switches	No	Yes
Distributed Port Groups (on Distributed Switches)	No	Yes
vCenter Server	No	Yes

You can see the configuration settings in Figure 10.15. Note the column for condition length. This helps prevent false alarms because vCenter will only consider this condition "triggered" if the condition persists for a specified length of time. You can also configure both a warning and alert condition threshold. This can be helpful if

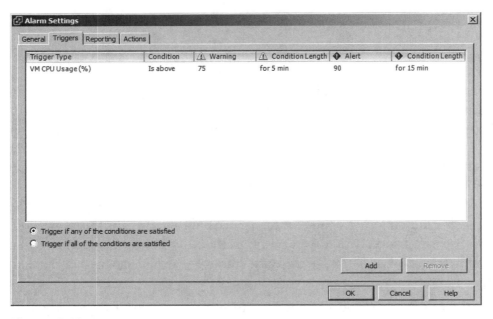

Figure 10.15
Condition-based triggers.

you want different actions to be taken depending on the level of problem severity. For instance, you may want to receive an e-mail if a VM's CPU crosses 75% utilization for a 5-minute duration, but if it remains above 90% for 15 minutes, you notify the on-call technician to investigate. Here are some examples of condition-based triggers:

Condition-based triggers for VMs:

- VM CPU Ready Time (ms)
- VM CPU Usage (%)
- VM Disk Aborts
- VM Heartbeat
- VM Memory Usage (%)
- Host Network Usage (kbps)
- VM Snapshot Size (GB)
- VM State

Condition-based triggers for hosts:

- Host Connection State
- Host CPU Usage (%)
- Host Disk Usage (KBps)
- Host Memory Usage (%)
- Host Network Usage (kbps)

Event-based triggers can be fine-tuned to only fire if a specific object experiences the event. For instance, as shown in Figure 10.16, you can configure an event-based trigger to watch for the creation of VMs that have a name beginning with "SQL." You might use this if your organization has a specific naming convention that can be predicted. Knowing when these VMs are created will help keep track of your VM growth and potentially your guest operating system or application licenses.

Event-based triggers for VMs:

- Event trigger
- Cannot migrate VM
- Creating a VM

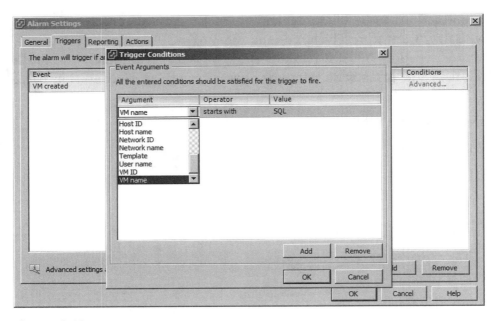

Figure 10.16
Alarms—Event-based triggers.

- Deploying a VM

- Guest OS shutdown

- Not enough resources for vSphere HA to start VM

- VM created

- VM is violating a DRS VM-host affinity rule

- VM powered off

Event-based triggers for hosts:

- Checked host for compliance

- Degraded storage path redundancy

- Duplicate IP detected

- Hardware health changed

- Host shut down

- Lost storage connectivity

- vSphere HA agent on a host has an error

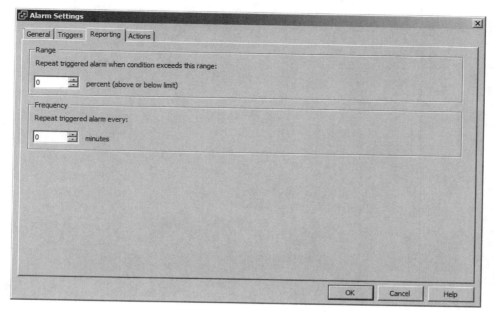

Figure 10.17
Alarms—Reporting options.

Reporting Options

The last thing you want is to become desensitized to alerts, meaning you see an alert, but discard it because it was probably just the system "crying wolf" again or alerting you to a problem that you already knew about. Fortunately, the alerts in vCenter can be tuned to reduce the frequency of alerts. We affectionately refer to the reporting options as the "anti-annoyance settings" because we can configure a tolerance rating for conditions, and we can configure a hold-down timer for alarms. Together these settings prevent alarms from alerting again within a specified time or until the condition passes a +/− percentage threshold. You can see the options in Figure 10.17. By default, both fields are set to zero, meaning the conditions have no tolerances and the alarm may be triggered whenever the alarm conditions are met without regard for how recent it may have already been triggered.

Actions and Frequency

Having an alarm is only helpful if it actually tells you something. The Actions tab, shown in Figure 10.18, is where you will configure the various alert actions for your alarm. You can configure vCenter to send an e-mail or SNMP trap, run a script, or even take specific actions like suspending or shutting down a VM.

The actions are executed based on the trigger level: all-clear, warning, or alert. The all-clear level is indicated by the green checkmark. The warning level is a yellow

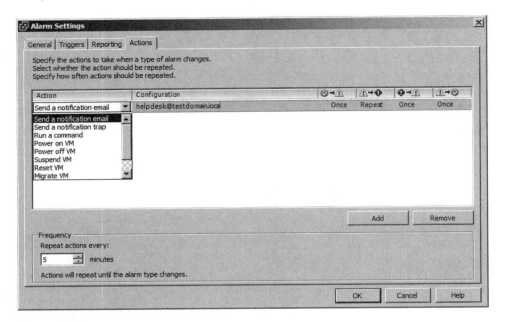

Figure 10.18
Alarms—Actions tab.

triangle, and the alert level is a red diamond. The actions are executed at the following events:

1. **All-clear to Warning.** Condition triggered warning, but not alert.

2. **Warning to Alert.** Condition triggered alert.

3. **Alert to Warning.** Condition improved, but still beyond warning threshold.

4. **Warning to All-clear.** Condition corrected.

You can configure many different actions, and each can be configured to fire at a different time. We recommend that you configure your notification actions (such as e-mail/SNMP) to trigger at least once at each event mark, and potentially "repeat" at the Warning to Alert level. If you configure the action to repeat, you should also configure the frequency of the repetition. This is specified in minutes using the option at the bottom of the Actions tab. Note that you can only set one repeat frequency value for all the actions specified in each alarm definition.

Clearing/Acknowledging Alarms

Go back to the triggered alarms view in the vSphere Client. As we said earlier, you can view any alarm that has been triggered on the currently selected object. If you believe that you have already corrected the problem, you can right-click on the alarm and choose "Reset to Green." This will allow vCenter to retest the alarm conditions and, if appropriate, trigger the alarm again if the problem still exists. Keep in mind that this resets the hold-down timer if you had specified one on the Reporting tab of the alarm definition.

Alternatively, you can "acknowledge" a triggered alarm. This is similar to pressing the silence button because the alarm is still active, but it no longer sends alert e-mails or notifications. Acknowledging an alarm is useful if you know about the problem, but you are unable to do anything to correct it at the moment. One common example is a datastore that is low on free disk space. Unless you can create free space, the acknowledge alarm feature is your best bet to avoid getting desensitized to the alarms.

Where to Configure SMTP/SNMP

Before vCenter can send you any alerts, you must configure it to talk to either your e-mail server (for SMTP) or your network monitoring software (for SNMP). You can do either at the main screen of the vSphere Client. Select the vCenter Server Settings icon, and then select the Mail or SNMP entry, as shown in Figure 10.19.

Caution

If you have virtualized your DNS server and you intend to monitor it using vCenter's alarms, you may wish to use the IP address of your e-mail server or network monitoring server instead of the host name. If the DNS server is offline, vCenter won't be able to resolve the name, and therefore you won't get notified.

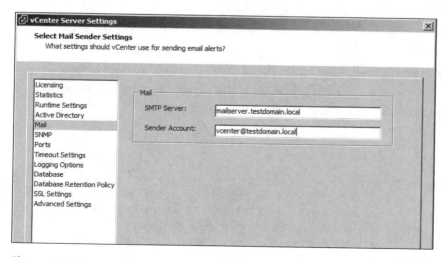

Figure 10.19
Alarms—e-mail server settings.

Tip

vCenter relies on anonymous access to send SMTP e-mail. Many e-mail systems today require authentication to prevent an open SMTP relay. If you're not sure about your system, check with your messaging administrator. You may be able to add an exception in your e-mail system for the IP address of your vCenter server so that it can send e-mail anonymously.

SNMP (Simple Network Management Protocol) is a standard that allows traps (messages) to be sent from monitored systems to a trap receiver (server) that is configured to accept them, often with its own alerting mechanisms. The general concept is to provide a central place where the organization can send these messages for centralized monitoring of all computers (or at least server, storage, and networking assets). An in-depth discussion of SNMP is beyond the scope of this book, but if you have such a system in place in your network, you can leverage it via vCenter to monitor your vSphere servers. To configure SNMP:

1. Go to the home screen in the vSphere Client, and then select vCenter Server Settings.

2. Select the SNMP link.

3. Enter the FQDN or IP address of your SNMP server in the Receiver URL text box.

4. Enter the port used by SNMP (162 is the default) in the box to the right of the URL.

5. Fill in the community string used in your environment. A community string is like a password for SNMP. Use the same community string that you configured in your SNMP trap receiver software.

6. If you wish, you may enter multiple trap receivers. vCenter will send a notification trap to each receiver. You might use this for redundancy or to send traps to different monitoring systems in your organization. To do this, select the Enable Receiver x checkbox, where x is a number from 2 to 4, and then fill in the details of that receiver as described in steps 3–5.

7. Click OK.

Caution

If you configure multiple SNMP receivers, they must be enabled in numerical order—first the primary, and then receivers 2–4. If you skip one or more along the way (such as entering a primary and only receivers 3 and 4), vCenter will skip all the receivers following the gap—though there is no visual cue that this is happening. In the previous example, only the primary trap receiver would be used as Receiver 2 was not configured, regardless that Receiver 3 and 4 were also configured.

TROUBLESHOOTING

A resource management chapter wouldn't be complete without a troubleshooting section. We could write complete books containing all the specific troubleshooting examples we've seen over the years, but specific examples aren't as helpful as they sound. Troubleshooting isn't about applying a specific technique or solution to a problem. To really troubleshoot and resolve a problem you have know what questions to ask. This section is going to equip you with those questions so that you can find the answers.

The Basics

A sound troubleshooting methodology is just as important as a solid planning methodology when your project begins. You can read books cover to cover without understanding where to begin when things break. Knowing how something works certainly helps, but knowing what to look for and asking the right questions will help even more.

It's exceedingly rare that anyone reports the actual root cause in their list of symptoms. It's typically up to us to determine what might have happened to get us to this point. Here are some questions that you need to ask:

- What symptoms were reported to you?
- When did the symptoms start?
- Is the problem reproducible, or does it happen at random?
- What will define "problem resolved" from the user's perspective?
- If the problem seems really obscure and it's hard for you to reproduce, how did the person figure out that there even was a problem?

All of these questions are very important because you are now playing the role of detective and even the subtlest pieces of evidence can change the story. Depending on how involved the problem is, you may have many more questions to ask.

Next we'll talk about how to monitor both VMs and hosts, looking for clues as to what happened.

Tip

Here is a great resource to help you identify problems in your virtual infrastructure. William Lam maintains a health check script that can be run from the vCLI or vMA. The script provides a wealth of information and is indispensible in any environment. Check it out here:

http://communities.vmware.com/docs/DOC-9842

Monitoring VMs

Now that you know how to find the performance data, it's time to talk about what we are supposed to be monitoring. This section is dedicated to monitoring the individual VMs. Next, we'll discuss monitoring the hosts.

A VM Has a Different View of the World

Have you ever seen a performance monitor within a VM report that the VM is using 100% of the CPU, but when you look in vCenter you see that the VM is really only using a small fraction of that power? It happens all the time. All it means is that the VM is using 100% of what the hypervisor allows it to use—not that the VM is lying. The opposite can also be true. A VM reports that it isn't using the processor, yet vCenter shows it using nearly 100% of a physical processor. In this case the virtual hardware is at fault, and it typically means that you have configured your guest operating system to use more than one processor, but you forgot to increase the number of vCPUs assigned to the VM.

So how can we know which system to believe, vCenter or the VM? You actually need to consider both sides. For basic reports and trending information you can generally rely on the performance data in vCenter, but if you suspect trouble in a VM, you need to take additional steps. By comparing vCenter's performance data to the performance data you collect in the VM, you can tell if the VM is being deprived of resources or if there is a misconfiguration. It may take a bit more time, but the results are far more useful than guesswork (and likely less risky).

VM-Based Monitoring Tools

So what tools can we use to monitor the guest operating systems? Try the built-in tools first. In Windows, these would be tools such as Task Manager, Performance Monitor, and Resource Monitor in 2008. In Linux we have tools such as top, ps, iostats, and vmstats. These tools are often overlooked as being too basic or non-relevant in a VMware environment, but we can assure you that they are very relevant, and serve as the backbone of many of our monitoring and troubleshooting practices. The built-in tools are generally very reliable sources of information on processor utilization, memory utilization, and even disk performance.

Remember, virtualizing your server doesn't mean that the operating system's tools are invalid. On the contrary, once you virtualize your servers, you will probably find more reasons to use these tools because now your server has to share its hardware resources with other servers, making it critical that each server uses its resources properly.

Aside from the built-in tools, we also have some excellent third-party tools, many of which are even free. Two very important examples include IOMeter and Wireshark. You may have just scratched your head about the inclusion of Wireshark. Trust us; it can be helpful when troubleshooting resource usage. How else will you know what is actually using your network card if you can't sniff the wire? IOMeter is another tool that allows us to measure the disk or network I/O on a server. It isn't just a monitoring tool though. IOMeter is often used to stress test storage and networks to determine whether the server can get the bandwidth that it was promised. Both of these are free tools and easily downloaded for both Windows and Linux VMs.

On the Windows side there is also xperf and the Performance Analysis of Logs (PAL) tool. These tools make it easier to aggregate your performance logs to compare your performance data to known benchmarks for several key Microsoft applications such as Active Directory, IIS, Sharepoint, Exchange, and SQL Server.

Windows Guests: PerfMon DLL from Tools

Finally, we have a note that only applies to Windows VMs. VMware included a special perfmon.dll file in the VMware Tools that gives the Windows Performance Monitor the ability to call back to the ESXi host controlling the VM to get more details on the VM's actual performance. You might recall that we said that a monitoring tool within a VM only reports what it can see. The noted exception is PerfMon with this DLL loaded. The DLL is automatically loaded if you install VMware Tools, and it gives you the ability to chart a couple new counters in PerfMon.

The counters are called VM Memory and VM Processor. They allow you to chart the CPU utilization that Windows sees against the CPU utilization that the ESXi host sees the VM using. Remember, these can be very different numbers. The idea is that you can use this simplified chart to compare the hypervisor to the guest, making troubleshooting a bit easier.

Tip

While there isn't an equivalent to the perfmon.dll on the Linux side, it is possible to script the retrieval of performance data from the ESXi host (or vCenter) via the vCLI in Linux.

Keep Your Baselines Up to Date

Think back to the last time a group of users told you their application was running slowly. Assume that you have never seen the application in question and have no inherent idea what fast or slow would look like. Now, how are you going to fix the problem? If you had a baseline showing the performance when the application was running correctly, you could easily compare today's performance statistics to that baseline to see what may have changed. Perhaps the CPU of the VM is running particularly high, or maybe it's abnormally low (meaning something isn't working at all).

A baseline is nothing more than a regularly created snapshot of the performance of a system. You create baselines when the performance is good because you want to use these baselines as the basis of your comparison when things aren't running well. Taking a baseline is easy once you get into the habit. In fact, you could even script the process if you're handy with the vCLI and your guest's performance monitoring tools. Yes, you have to collect both statistics from vCenter and statistics from the VMs. Otherwise, you may miss some important details.

The good news is that you really only need to do this after major upgrades or once a quarter, which ever comes first. Some people prefer to update their baselines monthly or even weekly. Do what is appropriate for your organization. If you are automating the process, weekly baselines may be easy. Another advantage of updating these baselines is that you can review them for trending data over time. Analyzing the various baselines, especially if they are taken at regular intervals, can provide great visibility into how your virtual infrastructure is growing and performing over time.

What Are We Looking for in vCenter?

There are a number of counters in vCenter that you can monitor to determine the health of your VMs. We've divided this list into counters for the CPU, RAM, disk, and network in an attempt to make it easier for you to reference. All of these counters can be found in the performance charts of vCenter, and most of these counters can be found using esxtop, the command line performance monitoring tool on the ESXi hosts. We'll talk more about esxtop in the Host Monitoring section of this chapter. In Figure 10.20, you'll see a sample of the VM chart options in vCenter.

While most of these counters aren't really black and white in terms of good values versus warning conditions, they are still useful for troubleshooting and monitoring. For example, seeing a VM's memory utilization at 80% may be perfectly normal if your applications are functioning well, but it can be reason to increase the VM's RAM if the applications are being paged to disk frequently. In some cases, counters have well-established thresholds that indicate problems. For example, a VM's average disk latency should be below 20ms when the system is performing properly. Numbers higher than 20ms typically mean the storage array is under too much I/O load.

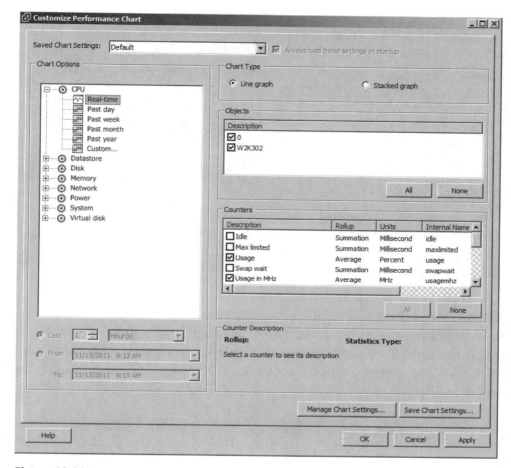

Figure 10.20
Advanced resource chart options for VMs.

Table 10.5 is a list of VM counters that we use when troubleshooting performance issues with VMs. It isn't meant to be an exhaustive list because there are many more counters to include, depending on what your VMs do and what applications they run. Where appropriate we have noted if we knew of a useful warning threshold for the counters.

CPU ready is the most definitive indicator that your VM isn't getting enough CPU time on the processor. It can be caused by too many vCPUs on a single ESXi host without sufficient physical CPUs to support the simultaneous demand. *Costop* is a measure of the time that a VM can't run because the hypervisor was unable to schedule all of the VMs vCPUs. If this value gets too large, you can either decrease the number of vCPUs on the VM or move it to another ESXi host that has more logical processors available. *Maxlimited* should never be greater than zero unless you have placed a CPU limit on the VM. If you have placed a limit on a VM, or its resource

Table 10.5   CPU Counters for Performance Troubleshooting

CPU Counters	Counter Description	Units	Warning Threshold
usage	Average percentage of total CPU usage	Percentage	> 95%
ready	Time the VM's vCPU is ready to execute, but unable to execute on a physical CPU	Milliseconds	> 2000ms
costop	Time the VM can't execute due to co-scheduling constraints (multiple vCPUs)	Milliseconds	> 500ms
maxlimited	The amount of time the VM attempted to execute, but its CPU Limit prevented it from running	Milliseconds	> 0ms
latency	Percentage of time the VM is unable to execute due to contention	Percentage	> 5%

pool, you can use this counter to see how often that limit is effecting your VM's performance. *Latency* is a general statistic that you can monitor to see if the VM is getting the physical resources it requests. This value may show a percentage point from time to time, but if it consistently reports above 5% you should consider rebalancing your ESXi server loads.

Table 10.6   RAM Counters for Performance Troubleshooting

RAM Counters	Counter Description	Units	Warning Threshold
usage	Percentage of RAM allocated by the guest operating system	Percent	(varies)
active	Amount of RAM recently accessed by the guest operating system (estimated)	Kilobytes	(varies)
granted	Amount of physical RAM allocated to the VM	Kilobytes	(varies)
latency	Percentage of the time the VM is waiting to access virtual (swapped) or compressed memory pages	Percentage	> 0%
vmmemctl	Amount of RAM inaccessible to the VM due to ballooning	Kilobytes	> 0
swapped	Amount of RAM swapped to disk (virtual memory)	Kilobytes	> 0

Usage is the amount of memory that the VM's guest operating system has addressed and allocated to its applications. Sometimes operating systems will allocate far more memory than they actually use, so VMware also has the active counter. The *active* counter is an estimate by the VMkernel as to how many memory pages are actively being used by the Guest OS. This value is most helpful when you compare it to the granted counter. *Granted* indicates how much of the guest's memory has been allocated to physical RAM. If the amount of granted is ever lower than the amount of active memory, your VM is experiencing delays. That's where the latency counter comes in. *Latency* is a good indicator of contention because it should only be greater than zero if the VM is experiencing delays due to having its memory swapped to disk or if the VMkernel has compressed its memory pages. While swapping can also occur if the VM has a limit on its memory, compression only occurs when the ESXi host is under contention. The *vmmemctl* counter shows the amount of physical RAM that has been taken back from the VM and given back to the VMkernel to use for other VMs. Any value above zero indicates the VM isn't getting all the memory you allocated to it. Ballooning is bad, but the worst problem is when the VM is swapped to disk and forced to use virtual memory instead of physical RAM. If *swapped* is ever above zero, your VM is accessing the disk for its memory instead of using physical RAM. This typically results in massive application delays on that VM.

Table 10.7   Disk Counters for Performance Troubleshooting

Disk Counters	Counter Description	Units	Warning Threshold
commandsAveraged	Average IOPS (read & write)	Number	(varies)
read	Average kilobytes of data read	KBps	(varies)
write	Average kilobytes of data written	KBps	(varies)
maxTotalLatency	Highest disk latency	Milliseconds	(varies)
commandsAborted	Number of SCSI operations aborted	Number	> 0
DAVG	Device Average Latency (SAN)	Milliseconds	25
KAVG	Kernel Average Latency (VMkernel)	Milliseconds	2
GAVG	Guest Average Latency (VM)	Milliseconds	25

The number of *commandsAveraged* is your measure of how many IOPS the VM is generating. You can use this number in connection with read and write to determine whether your VM is overloading your storage device. *Read* and *write* show the average storage bandwidth in kilobytes per second. If these values are particularly high as compared to your other VMs, you may want to investigate what application within the VM is utilizing the storage so heavily. If the storage becomes too slow, the *maxTotalLatency* number will increase, indicating that your storage device is overwhelmed. We didn't specify a threshold here because this counter can vary because it shows the maximum value, not an average value. You can have very high levels of I/O as long as the latency doesn't increase too dramatically. The one thing you cannot have is a lot of aborted SCSI commands. This is monitored in the *commandsAborted* counter. Aborted SCSI commands can come from contention or from errors in the storage network. If this value rises above zero, you may need to investigate your storage configuration. Device Average Latency (*DAVG*) represents the I/O latency from the ESXi host to your storage array. Values higher than 25ms indicate a possible performance bottleneck on your SAN (the array or the storage network). Kernel Average Latency (*KAVG*) represents the delay caused by the VMkernel before the I/O request is set to the disk system. If the KAVG value is higher than 2ms you may have a path problem, such as a failing HBA or other event that is causing the VMkernel to queue the I/O request instead of sending it immediately. Guest Average Latency (*GAVG*) represents the sum of KAVG + DAVG, and should match what the guest operating system's performance monitoring software reports as its own disk latency because the guest's I/O must pass through both the VMkernel and the storage array. Values higher than 25ms can lead to delayed write errors in the guest operating system.

Table 10.8   Network Counters for Performance Troubleshooting

Network Counters	Counter Description	Units	Warning Threshold
usage	Combined network bandwidth (read & writes)	KBps	(varies)
received	Average rate network traffic was received	KBps	(varies)
transmitted	Average rate network traffic was sent	KBps	(varies)
packetsRx	Number of incoming packets	Number	(varies)
packetsTx	Number of outgoing packets	Number	(varies)
droppedRx	Number of incoming packets dropped	Number	> 0
droppedTx	Number of outgoing packets dropped	Number	> 0

The *usage* counter provides a good overview of how much bandwidth the VM is currently using. You can further refine this by examining the *received* and *transmitted* counters to see a breakdown of sent versus received traffic. In some cases the bandwidth isn't the major concern; it is the number of packets the VM must handle. By analyzing the *packetsRx* and *packetsTx* counters you can see the ratio of sent to receive packets. The more packets you have, the more work the VM must do; even small packets take time to process. All of these counters are highly variable and don't really have any set thresholds for problem detection unless you approach the limits of the physical networking. On the other hand, dropped packets are always bad. If you see the *droppedRx* or *droppedTx* counters begin increasing, you have a problem. It may be contention related or problems in the VM.

Monitoring the Hosts

Let's switch gears now and talk about the ESXi hosts. While the VMs are important, and are typically the first place we look when we have trouble, a misconfigured ESXi host can be devastating for both performance and availability.

Like the VMs, there are multiple ways that we can monitor our ESXi hosts. Probably the easiest method is via the vCenter charts that we discussed earlier, but there are also tools we can use at command line. Once we discuss the various monitoring tools, we'll give you some important counters to monitor like we did with the VMs.

Using vCenter Charts

You may have noticed or guessed this before, but the vCenter charts can be used to monitor your ESXi host's statistics as well as the VMs. The same mechanisms that bring us the guest statistics also bring us the CPU, RAM, disk, and network counters for the host. Aside from clicking in a different location (on a host instead of a VM), you will find the ESXi host performance charts in the same place we discussed earlier. Click on the Performance tab and then choose between the overview and the advanced views.

If you open the Chart Options box on the Advanced charts, you'll see the window shown in Figure 10.21. This window is for a host. The last time you saw this window we had selected a VM. Notice that there are a few differences between the options available on a host versus a VM. You may want to flip back to Figure 10.20 as a comparison.

The categories on the left side of the chart are slightly different, adding things like Cluster services, Storage adapter, Storage path, and vSphere Replication. The only thing missing is Virtual Disk, which only applies to a VM. At the top of the Chart

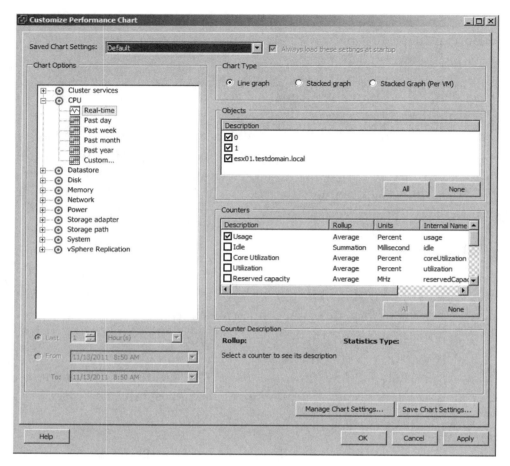

Figure 10.21
Advanced resource chart options for hosts.

Options window, you can also see a new option: Stacked Graph (Per VM). This allows you to display one (and only one) host-based statistic, such as CPU utilization, and then break down the usage of the CPU by the VMs running on that host. It's a brilliant way to see which VMs are consuming the host's resources in an easy-to-understand manner.

Counters

The counters that we need to monitor on our hosts are similar to the ones we talked about for the VMs. In fact, several of the counters we discussed earlier can also be monitored at the host level. In particular, the CPU usage and CPU ready counters are very valuable when viewed in the Stacked Graph (Per VM) view. Please refer back to the list of counters in the previous section for more details.

Command-Line Monitoring Tools: esxtop and resxtop

Let's face it, easier and faster tend to rule over complex and time consuming every day. If you have a choice between getting your information now versus waiting for it, which do you tend to choose? Probably the easier, faster route. What if we told you that doing things in the vSphere Client actually wasn't the easiest and fastest way to get your performance statistics? It's true, but the easier, faster route may not seem like it because you must use the command line.

Think back to the sample rates on our vCenter-based performance charts. These charts are updated every 20 seconds. Why? The vCenter server only downloads the statistics from each ESXi host that often. In reality, the statistics are available on a much more real-time basis, but we have to use a program called esxtop. For those of you familiar with Linux, this tool will be familiar to you because as you may have guessed, esxtop is based on the Linux `top` command. Also, note that when using the esxtop remotely, the command has a different name: `resxtop`. The "r" stands for "remote."

Note

> We have included a complete reference guide for `resxtop`, the remote version of the `esxtop` command, at the end of this chapter.

The `esxtop` command is very versatile. By default, we use it to view statistics interactively on a real-time basis, but you can also run the command in batch mode to collect statistics for later analysis. The output from this batch job can then be analyzed in a number of ways, which we'll cover in the very next section.

If you're not a command line aficionado, don't worry; we still have you covered. If you remember, back in Chapter 4 we talked about how you can use any of the following methods to gain access to the command line tools. Some methods are more limited than others, so refer back to Chapter 4 if you're not sure which method will be best suited for your needs. The methods available to us include:

- The vCLI tool set. It is installable on Windows or Linux workstations.

- The PowerCLI tool set, which includes the Windows PowerShell cmdlets. It is only installable on a Windows workstation with PowerShell installed. PowerCLI does not have a native `esxtop` or `resxtop` command; however, some information may be obtained using the `Get-EsxTop` cmdlet.

- The vSphere Management Assistant (vMA). This is a prebuilt Linux VM with the vCLI tools installed. VMA is deployed as a Virtual Appliance, and is available for free from VMware's website.

- You can use direct console access to the ESXi server via Local Tech Support Mode.

- You can use remote SSH access to the ESXi server via Remote Tech Support Mode.

Note

If you are connected to the ESXi server via the console or an SSH session, you can directly run the `esxtop` command; however, if you intend to collect your performance statistics via the vCLI or vMA, you will need to use the command `resxtop`. It serves the same purpose; it just has a slightly different command syntax because you must specify the remote server's name.

Analysis Tools

Once you have collected the performance statistics using `esxtop` or `resxtop`, you need a tool to view the data. Because the batch mode of these commands captures the data in a comma-separated value (CSV) file, you can use a variety of charting tools to analyze the data. One of the more straightforward tools is probably the basic Windows performance monitor. You can load the CSV file as a source, and then select the counters you want to monitor. You can do this both graphically using the charts, or as a report with summarized data.

VMware also provides a cross-platform tool called ESXPlot. It is located on the VMware Labs flings page here: http://labs.vmware.com/flings. The tool leverages python, so it will run on Windows, Linux, or even Mac OSX. It will help you graph your performance data and output the chart to a standard image file (great for presentations!).

Note

We talk about how to capture the data in batch mode at the end of this chapter in The resxtop Command Reference section.

Resource-Specific Troubleshooting

Sometimes it helps just to have a checklist of things to look for when trouble strikes. These lists aren't intended to solve your problem. Instead, we hope they help jog your memory of topics we talked about in earlier sections of the book, or even topics that you may have read elsewhere. To make the list a bit more reader-friendly, we've organized the list into the following sections: CPU, memory, storage, and networking.

CPUs

Here are some things that you need to check if you're experiencing CPU performance issues with your VMs or hosts:

- Does your ESXi host have hardware virtualization assist disabled?

- Have you assigned too many vCPUs to the problematic VM? Check the CPU utilization of each vCPU. They should be balanced.

- If the VM's vCPU load is uneven, are the applications in your VM multithreaded?

- Is HyperThreading enabled on the host? Try toggling it to see if the performance changes.

- Is your ESXi host's power management enabled? CPU speed throttling (for power management) can cause performance issues.

- Check the host and VM performance counter "CPU ready" to see if the VMs are limited or constrained by contention. The value should be under 10%.

- Check for excessive CPU usage on the host or VM. The value should average less than 80%.

- Are your guests' VM Tools up to date? This affects all the virtual hardware drivers, which can indirectly affect the ESXi host's CPU performance.

Memory

Many of the suggestions here involve checking or modifying the ESXi hosts. As always, research any unfamiliar terms before applying these changes as your system configuration will dictate whether these changes will help or hurt your VM performance.

- Is the VM ballooning or using VMkernel swap? If so, check for limits on the VM or memory contention on the ESXi host.

- Is the VM paging or swapping to disk excessively? If so, consider allocating more vRAM to the VM.

- Does the ESXi host support hardware virtualization that includes Intel's Enhanced Page Tables (EPT) or AMD's Rapid Virtualization Indexing (RVI)? If so, enable it to reduce the overhead of your very active VMs.

- Is the VM spanning multiple NUMA nodes? If so, migrate the VM to a larger host, power off the VM to reset its vNUMA configuration, or decrease the vCPU and vRAM allocation of the VM.

- How active is the VM's vRAM? If the percentage of active vRAM in the VM is consistently very high, you may want to increase the amount of vRAM allocated to the VM.

- It may be obvious, but check your applications for memory leaks and inefficient use of the VM's vRAM.

- If you know that VMkernel swapping on your ESXi host is inevitable (again, due to limits or expected memory contention), you can elect to use SSD drives for the swap files.

Storage

Tools such as IOMeter, vscsiStats, and your SAN management tools will give you visibility into the latency and quantity of your I/Os, but don't forget what we discussed earlier in this chapter. Review vCenter's performance charts and compare the data to what the VM's guest operating system reports to get the most accurate information.

- Check for high average latency values on your datastores and redistribute the virtual disks of your VMs accordingly.

- If your storage I/O or latency is unbalanced at the datastore level, consider implementing policy-based storage in vCenter to help automatically redistribute your VMs based on load.

- If you have high and unbalanced queue depths on your ESXi storage paths, consider redistributing your I/O across your ESXi host's storage paths or use the Round Robin path selection policy.

- If you are unable to get enough IOPS from your storage array, consider increasing its spindle count or using SSD drives instead.

- Check to see how your LUNs are mapped to the backend arrays in your SAN. Ideally you want to have one LUN per array, and one datastore per LUN. This ensures that your datastores aren't competing against each other for I/O performance on the backend.

- Consider switching your VMs to use the Paravirtual SCSI adapter. It has been improved in vSphere 5 and can be provide a nice performance boost over using the standard LSILogic controllers.

- Do you have network contention on your iSCSI network segment(s)?

- Have you enabled jumbo frames (increased MTU size) on your iSCSI network segment(s) and VMkernel port(s)?

- Check your storage network switches for errors. This applies to Ethernet switches and Fibre Channel switches, depending on your storage architecture.

Networking

Much like storage, we have several tools we can use to monitor our networking performance and troubleshoot when the performance becomes questionable.

- First, verify that you have installed the paravirtual VMXNet3 driver installed in your VM. Remember, this adapter requires at least virtual hardware version 7 (8 is preferred) and the VMware Tools must be installed in your guest operating system.

- Check the vCenter performance charts for excessive dropped packets on the network card of your ESXi host and each of your virtual network adapters in your VMs.

- Check the vCenter performance charts for high network utilization (high number of packets per second, and/or high Mbps throughput) on the network card of your ESXi host and of each of your virtual network adapters in your VMs. (Remember to check the statistics within your VM as well.)

- Are your physical network cards on your ESXi host "flapping"? That is, is their link state going up and down rapidly? If so, disable NIC failback on your virtual switches.

- If you are using the vNetwork Distributed Switches, you can reference the virtual port statistics of your switch(es) in vCenter's Networking inventory view. This will show you which of your VMs are sending/receiving the most traffic.

- If you need to know who your VMs are talking with, you can now use NetFlow in vSphere 5 to map the traffic of a VM all the way to its virtual network card. This requires vNetwork Distributed Switches as we discussed in Chapter 7.

- As you might recall from Chapter 7, Port Mirroring takes this to the next level, because in addition to mapping who the VMs are talking to, we can also capture their traffic to see what they are talking about. Use this in conjunction with a program such as Wireshark to see if the traffic is legit, or if the performance problem is just an application sending superfluous data.

The resxtop Command Reference

As we discussed earlier, the `resxtop` command is the "remote" version of the `esxtop` command, and it is used in the vMA or the vSphere CLI utility. The `resxtop` command is a very useful utility that provides a keen perspective on real-time utilization statistics returned by an ESXi host. These real-time counters can be related to the host itself, a VM that is running on the host, or memory usage by a process that is currently running on the host.

We will focus on the `resxtop` syntax, however, `esxtop` and `resxtop` are very similar. Both commands can operate in three different modes, the default being "interactive."

- **Batch Mode.** A non-interactive process that exports collected statistics to a CSV formatted file.

- **Replay Mode.** You can replay statistics previously captured using the `vm-support` command. This mode does *not* require you to use batch mode.

- **Interactive Mode.** Real-time statistics are displayed on the screen in columns and rows.

If no options are specified, `esxtop` and `resxtop` will operate in interactive mode. The `resxtop` command syntax follows. Refer to Table 10.9 for details on each option in the command syntax.

`resxtop [-a] [-b] [-c filename] [-d seconds] [-h] [-n iterations] [-R filename] [-server hostname] [-vihost hostname] [-portnumber TCP_port_number] [-username username]`

Table 10.9   The resxtop Command Syntax

Option	Description
a	Using this option will force `resxtop` to display all available statistics. Do not use with the `-c` option.
b	Instructs `resxtop` to execute in batch mode.
c	Loads a previously saved configuration file that defines the fields `resxtop` will display.
d	Defines the desired time interval between statistics samples. The default is 5 seconds, and the minimum is 2 seconds.
h	Displays the help screen.
n	The number of samples that should be taken. The batch file will exit when this number of samples has been reached.
R	Instructs `esxtop` to execute in replay mode. Requires the path and filename of the `vm-support` command's output file.
server	The specific server that the statistics should be gathered from (vCenter or an ESXi host).
vihost	This option is used when connecting through vCenter instead of directly to an ESXi host.
portnumber	The default TCP port for this connection is 443; this can be changed with the portnumber value.
username	The user account that should be used when connecting to the physical host.

Running resxtop in Batch Mode

You can run the `esxtop` command in batch mode, which allows you to collect the statistics on a scheduled basis. You can specify the sampling frequency to gather statistics at a specified interval, such as every five seconds. The output is comma delimited and works best if you redirect the command's output to a CSV file.

If you are planning to run `resxtop` or `esxtop` for many hours or even days, you may wish to limit the counters that ESXi records so the output file remains manageable. Before you run `esxtop` in batch mode, run it in interactive mode and create a configuration file that limits `esxtop` to display specific performance counters. You will then use this configuration file in your `esxtop` batch command to reduce the output file size (because you are removing fields from the collection). Refer to the sidebar for more information on configuring `resxtop` in batch mode.

Using resxtop in Batch Mode

Because it isn't the most straightforward process, here's a little guide for customizing `resxtop` for batch mode collection in the vMA (vSphere Management Assistant) appliance (for more details refer to the `esxtop` main page).

1. First, open an SSH session to the vMA appliance and log on using `vi-admin` or other appropriate credentials for your organization.

2. Run `resxtop` against the ESXi host using a command similar to this:

   `resxtop -server esx01.yourdomain.com`

3. In `resxtop`, use the "`f`" key to change which fields are displayed (and therefore output during the batch mode collection). You will need to adjust each of the following screens by pressing the associated menu letter, then pressing "`f`" to adjust the fields: cpu (c), memory (m), interrupts (i), network (n), storage adapter (d), storage device (u), virtual disk (v), and power states (p). You can then toggle the field selection in each of these views by pressing the letter to the left of each counter. Excluding counters will make your capture file smaller and more manageable.

4. When you have included/excluded your desired fields, you need to save the configuration as a file. Press the "`w`" (uppercase W) key and then specify a filename for the file. Be careful that you don't overwrite the default configuration file.

5. Exit the `resxtop` program by pressing the "`q`" key.

6. Now you need to run the `resxtop` command in batch mode, specifying your configuration file. Do so by running a command similar to this:

   `resxtop -server esx01.yourdomain.com -b -c myconfigfile -d 15 -n 40 > perf.csv`

7. When the command has finished running the specified number of iterations, it will exit to the command prompt. You will then need to transfer your newly created CSV file to another machine for analysis (see the next section for details).

The -server parameter tells resxtop which ESXi server to monitor (appropriate credentials are required). The -b parameter tells resxtop to run in batch mode instead of interactively. The -c parameter tells resxtop to load a custom configuration file that specifies which counters to gather. The -d parameter specifies the delay in seconds between collections. The -n parameter specifies the number of collections to gather. The > filename.csv parameter is how we output the command results to a text file. In the case of our example, we are going to gather performance statistics from the ESXi server every 15 seconds, over the course of 10 minutes (40 iterations, 4 iterations per minute).

Running resxtop in Replay Mode

As we've said, the resxtop command also has a mode that will allow you to replay the performance statistics. Using replay mode, an administrator can gather metrics during a specific time interval, and save the information for later evaluation. Instead of using the resxtop command in batch mode to gather the statistics, you use the vm-support command. Refer to the sidebar on the vm-support utility for more information.

Once you have gathered the performance snapshot information using the vm-support utility, resxtop can be used to replay the statistics. Use the command:

```
resxtop -R vm-support_export_filename
```

The available command-line options for the resxtop command can be found in Table 10.9.

Using the vm-support Utility with resxtop

The vm-support utility is a robust debugging utility that must be run from either the local or remote technical support interface on your ESXi host. It cannot be run from the vCLI or in the vMA. It gathers performance and process debugging metrics, and then saves the output in a compressed tar file named "esx-Date.PID.tgz," where the Date field is the date of the retrieval, and PID is the process ID of the process. We can also use the vm-support utility to gather performance statistics about a specific VM.

For resxtop replay mode purposes, we are only interested in the performance "snapshot" information that it creates. To use the vm-support utility for this purpose, follow the syntax guide below:

```
vm-support [-p] [-S] [-d duration] [-i interval]
```

Here is a brief explanation of the options used in the above command:

- The -p option specifies that the vm-support utility should gather performance snapshot information in addition to the process debugging information. Do not use this option with the -S option.

- The -S (uppercase S) option specifies that the vm-support utility should exclude process debugging information, and only collect performance snapshot information. This is the mode typically used to create resxtop replay files because the export files are smaller.

- The -d option sets the duration length in seconds of each sampling interval. The default is 300 seconds.

- The -i option specifies the amount of time in seconds the vm-support utility will wait between each snapshot. The default is "autodetect," which means the utility sets the interval to twice the length specified in the duration option. For example, if the duration is set to 300 seconds, the interval will be set to 600 seconds by default. In most troubleshooting cases you should manually set the interval value to 10 seconds.

Caution

VMware changed the vm-support command in vSphere 5. In previous versions of vSphere we used a -s instead of a -p to gather performance information.

Note

You must unzip and untar the export file generated by the vm-support utility before it can be used with the resxtop command. Use the command tar -xzf esx-Date.PID.tgz to expand the file into a directory named "esx-Date.PID."

Resxtop in Interactive Mode

If you run resxtop without a mode option, it will run interactively and show you real-time statistics about a variety of resources. There are eight different views of the resources accessed by the ESXi host and its VMs, and the view can be changed dynamically using one of the following hotkeys:

- Pressing "c" will change to the CPU statistics (the default view)

- Pressing "m" will change to the Memory statistics

- Pressing "p" will change to the Power statistics

- Pressing "d" will change to the disk adapter statistics

- Pressing "u" will change to the disk drive statistics

- Pressing "v" (lowercase v) will change to the VM disk statistics

- Pressing "n" will change to the network statistics

- Pressing "i" will change to the interrupts statistics

Also, the following hotkeys can help customize the displayed metrics and information:

- The use of "h" or "?" will display a help screen

- The use of the space bar will force the screen to refresh

- The use of the CTRL-L key sequence will cause the screen to delete the current contents and redraw the display

- The use of "F" or "f" will allow the user to add or remove columns from the displayed metrics

- The use of "O" or "o" will allow the sequence of the displayed columns to be modified

- Typing a "#" will allow for customizing the number of displayed rows

- Typing an "s" will allow the update time to be modified from the default of 5 seconds

- Using a "W" will write the current configuration to a file for reuse at a future date. This parameter is used when creating the batch mode configuration file.

When you run resxtop, you will be shown the CPU view by default. We show a sample of this in Figure 10.22. In the upper-left corner of the screen, resxtop displays the

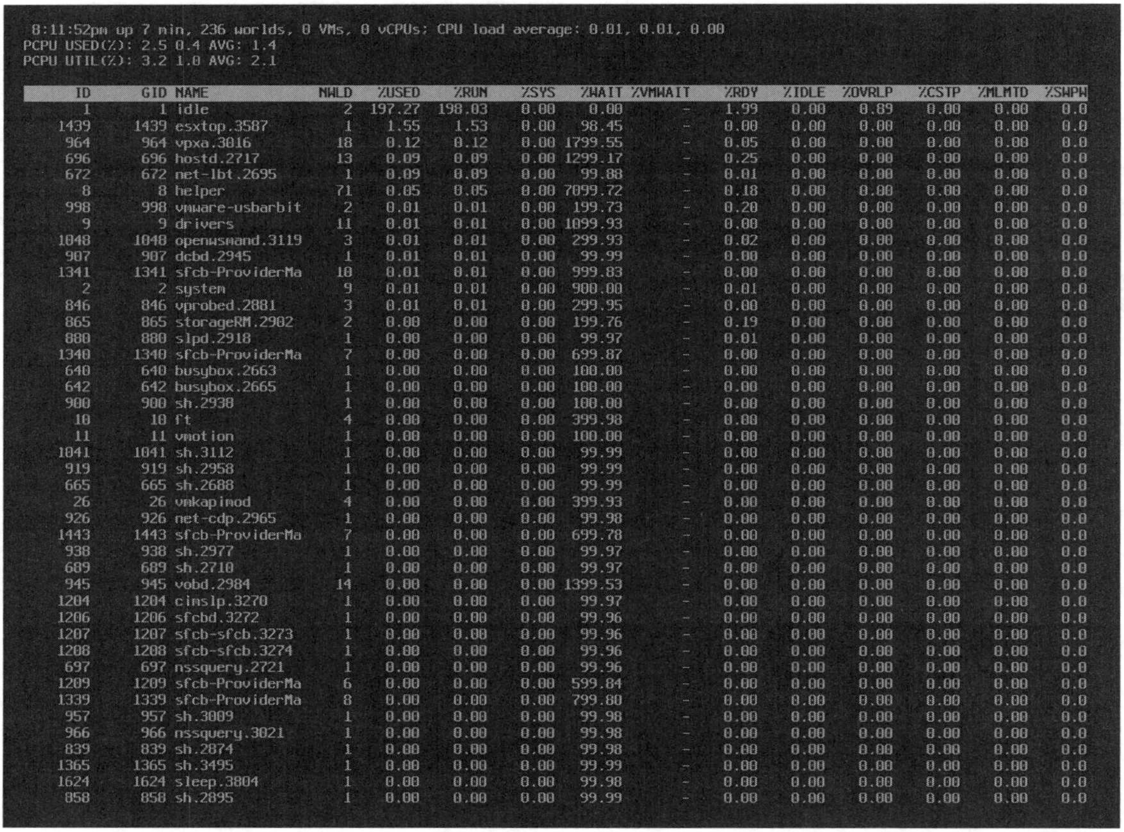

```
8:11:52pm up 7 min, 236 worlds, 0 VMs, 0 vCPUs; CPU load average: 0.01, 0.01, 0.00
PCPU USED(%): 2.5 0.4 AVG: 1.4
PCPU UTIL(%): 3.2 1.0 AVG: 2.1
```

ID	GID	NAME	NWLD	%USED	%RUN	%SYS	%WAIT	%VMWAIT	%RDY	%IDLE	%OVRLP	%CSTP	%MLMTD	%SWPWT
1	1	idle	2	197.27	198.03	0.00	0.00	–	1.99	0.00	0.89	0.00	0.00	0.0
1439	1439	esxtop.3587	1	1.55	1.53	0.00	98.45	–	0.00	0.00	0.00	0.00	0.00	0.0
964	964	vpxa.3016	18	0.12	0.12	0.00	1799.55	–	0.05	0.00	0.00	0.00	0.00	0.0
696	696	hostd.2717	13	0.09	0.09	0.00	1299.17	–	0.25	0.00	0.00	0.00	0.00	0.0
672	672	net-lbt.2695	1	0.09	0.09	0.00	99.88	–	0.01	0.00	0.00	0.00	0.00	0.0
8	8	helper	71	0.05	0.05	0.00	7099.72	–	0.18	0.00	0.00	0.00	0.00	0.0
998	998	vmware-usbarbit	2	0.01	0.01	0.00	199.73	–	0.20	0.00	0.00	0.00	0.00	0.0
9	9	drivers	11	0.01	0.01	0.00	1099.93	–	0.00	0.00	0.00	0.00	0.00	0.0
1048	1048	openwsmand.3119	3	0.01	0.01	0.00	299.93	–	0.02	0.00	0.00	0.00	0.00	0.0
907	907	dcbd.2945	1	0.01	0.01	0.00	99.99	–	0.00	0.00	0.00	0.00	0.00	0.0
1341	1341	sfcb-ProviderMa	10	0.01	0.01	0.00	999.83	–	0.00	0.00	0.00	0.00	0.00	0.0
2	2	system	9	0.01	0.01	0.00	900.00	–	0.01	0.00	0.00	0.00	0.00	0.0
846	846	vprobed.2881	3	0.01	0.01	0.00	299.95	–	0.00	0.00	0.00	0.00	0.00	0.0
865	865	storageRM.2902	2	0.00	0.00	0.00	199.76	–	0.19	0.00	0.00	0.00	0.00	0.0
880	880	slpd.2918	1	0.00	0.00	0.00	99.97	–	0.01	0.00	0.00	0.00	0.00	0.0
1340	1340	sfcb-ProviderMa	7	0.00	0.00	0.00	699.87	–	0.00	0.00	0.00	0.00	0.00	0.0
640	640	busybox.2663	1	0.00	0.00	0.00	100.00	–	0.00	0.00	0.00	0.00	0.00	0.0
642	642	busybox.2665	1	0.00	0.00	0.00	100.00	–	0.00	0.00	0.00	0.00	0.00	0.0
900	900	sh.2938	1	0.00	0.00	0.00	99.97	–	0.00	0.00	0.00	0.00	0.00	0.0
10	10	ft	4	0.00	0.00	0.00	399.98	–	0.00	0.00	0.00	0.00	0.00	0.0
11	11	vmotion	1	0.00	0.00	0.00	100.00	–	0.00	0.00	0.00	0.00	0.00	0.0
1041	1041	sh.3112	1	0.00	0.00	0.00	99.99	–	0.00	0.00	0.00	0.00	0.00	0.0
919	919	sh.2958	1	0.00	0.00	0.00	99.99	–	0.00	0.00	0.00	0.00	0.00	0.0
665	665	sh.2688	1	0.00	0.00	0.00	99.99	–	0.00	0.00	0.00	0.00	0.00	0.0
26	26	vmkapimod	4	0.00	0.00	0.00	399.93	–	0.00	0.00	0.00	0.00	0.00	0.0
926	926	net-cdp.2965	1	0.00	0.00	0.00	99.98	–	0.00	0.00	0.00	0.00	0.00	0.0
1443	1443	sfcb-ProviderMa	7	0.00	0.00	0.00	699.78	–	0.00	0.00	0.00	0.00	0.00	0.0
938	938	sh.2977	1	0.00	0.00	0.00	99.97	–	0.00	0.00	0.00	0.00	0.00	0.0
689	689	sh.2710	1	0.00	0.00	0.00	99.97	–	0.00	0.00	0.00	0.00	0.00	0.0
945	945	vobd.2984	14	0.00	0.00	0.00	1399.53	–	0.00	0.00	0.00	0.00	0.00	0.0
1204	1204	cimslp.3270	1	0.00	0.00	0.00	99.97	–	0.00	0.00	0.00	0.00	0.00	0.0
1206	1206	sfcbd.3272	1	0.00	0.00	0.00	99.96	–	0.00	0.00	0.00	0.00	0.00	0.0
1207	1207	sfcb-sfcb.3273	1	0.00	0.00	0.00	99.96	–	0.00	0.00	0.00	0.00	0.00	0.0
1208	1208	sfcb-sfcb.3274	1	0.00	0.00	0.00	99.96	–	0.00	0.00	0.00	0.00	0.00	0.0
697	697	nssquery.2721	1	0.00	0.00	0.00	99.96	–	0.00	0.00	0.00	0.00	0.00	0.0
1209	1209	sfcb-ProviderMa	6	0.00	0.00	0.00	599.84	–	0.00	0.00	0.00	0.00	0.00	0.0
1339	1339	sfcb-ProviderMa	8	0.00	0.00	0.00	799.80	–	0.00	0.00	0.00	0.00	0.00	0.0
957	957	sh.3009	1	0.00	0.00	0.00	99.98	–	0.00	0.00	0.00	0.00	0.00	0.0
966	966	nssquery.3021	1	0.00	0.00	0.00	99.98	–	0.00	0.00	0.00	0.00	0.00	0.0
839	839	sh.2874	1	0.00	0.00	0.00	99.98	–	0.00	0.00	0.00	0.00	0.00	0.0
1365	1365	sh.3495	1	0.00	0.00	0.00	99.99	–	0.00	0.00	0.00	0.00	0.00	0.0
1624	1624	sleep.3804	1	0.00	0.00	0.00	99.98	–	0.00	0.00	0.00	0.00	0.00	0.0
858	858	sh.2895	1	0.00	0.00	0.00	99.99	–	0.00	0.00	0.00	0.00	0.00	0.0

Figure 10.22
The CPU Metrics pane.

current date and time as well as the ESXi host's uptime. Also shown are the number of executing threads (or worlds), the percentage of PCPU (Physical CPU) used, and the current PCPU utilization. Each of the running processes and their associated process ID is displayed in the lower half of the screen, along with the relevant counters for each process.

The counters and their respective definitions are found in Table 10.10.

There are "hot keys" that can change the displayed statistics in the CPU view:

■ The use of the "e" key will alternate between expanded and unexpanded CPU metrics

■ The use of "U" (uppercase U) will sort the metrics based on the %USED values

■ The use of "R" will sort the metrics based on the %RDY values

■ The use of "N" will sort the entries based on the GID values

■ The use of "V" (uppercase V) will display the metrics relating to VMs only

■ The use of "L" will modify the length of the displayed values in the NAME column

The memory view, depicted in Figure 10.23, can be selected by entering an "m" at the resxtop screen.

The memory pane is designed to provide real-time utilization parameters related to memory processes. The counters and their definitions are found in Table 10.11.

There are several commands that can customize the displayed statistics:

■ The use of an "M" will sort the objects by the values in the MEMSZ column.

■ The use of a "B" will sort the objects based on the values in the Group MEMCTL column.

■ The use of an "N" will sort the objects based on the values in the GID column.

■ The use of a "V" (uppercase V) will display only the statistics for VMs.

■ The use of an "L" will modify the length of the values in the NAME column.

The Power statistics can be displayed by using the "p" key at the resxtop pane. In Figure 10.24, you can see this view displays the current CPU utilization and power consumption metrics for the physical CPUs. The default counters and their definitions are listed in Table 10.12.

Table 10.10 CPU Metrics in resxtop

Counter	Description
ID	The identifier of the resource pool, VM, or the world that is currently in execution.
GID	The unique identifier of the resource pool that is in execution.
Name	The name of the resource pool, VM, or world that is currently in execution.
NWLD	The number of objects in the resource pool, VM, or world that is in execution.
%USED	The amount of overall CPU resources being consumed by this resource pool, VM, or world.
%RUN	The amount of possible scheduled time consumed by this resource pool, VM, or world.
%SYS	The amount of time the VMKernel spends servicing requests and interrupts for this resource pool, VM, or world.
%WAIT	The amount of time that this resource pool, VM, or world was in the busy wait state.
%VMWAIT	The amount of time that this VM was in the busy wait state.
%RDY	The amount of time that this object was ready to execute, but there was insufficient resources available.
%IDLE	The amount of time that this object was in the idle state.
%OVRLP	The amount of time that this object was scheduled, and another object was scheduled as well.
%CSTP	The amount of time that this object was de-scheduled to maintain consistency with vSMP VMs.
%MLMTD	The amount of time that this object was de-scheduled to maintain consistency with the Limit configuration.
%SWPWT	The amount of time that this resource pool, VM, or world was waiting for the VMKernel to swap memory in order to free memory pages.
%AMIN	The configured Reservation for this object.
%AMAX	The configured Limit for this object.
%ASHRS	The configured Shares for this object.
Affinity Bit Masking	Indicates the scheduling affinity that is currently in execution.
HTSHARING	The current hyperthreading parameters.

(Continued)

Table 10.10   CPU Metrics in resxtop (*Continued*)

Counter	Description
CPU	The physical CPU that the object was executing on when the metrics were obtained.
HTQ	Indicates the quarantining state.
Timer/s	Displays that current timer rate for this object.
Power	Displays the current power utilization in Watts.
%LAT_C	The amount of time that this object was not scheduled due to CPU contention.
%LAT_M	The amount of time that this object was not scheduled due to RAM contention.
DMD	The amount of CPU load over the last 60 seconds.

```
8:13:01pm up 9 min, 236 worlds, 0 VMs, 0 vCPUs; MEM overcommit avg: 0.00, 0.00, 0.00
PMEM   /MB:   2047  total:     751    vmk,    89 other,   1205 free
VMKMEM/MB:   2037 managed:    122 minfree,  1494 rsvd,    542 ursvd,  high state
PSHARE/MB:     18  shared,     18 common:     0 saving
SWAP  /MB:      0   curr,      0 rclmtgt:            0.00 r/s,   0.00 w/s
ZIP   /MB:      0  zipped,      0  saved
MEMCTL/MB:      0   curr,      0  target,     0 max

   GID NAME             MEMSZ    GRANT   SZTGT    TCHD   TCHD_W   SWCUR   SWTGT   SWR/s   SWW/s  LLSWR/s  LLSWW/s  OV
   696 hostd.2717       43.76    34.15    0.00   34.15   34.15    0.00    0.00    0.00    0.00    0.00    0.00
   964 vpxa.3016        22.61    14.88    0.00   14.88   14.88    0.00    0.00    0.00    0.00    0.00    0.00
  1339 sfcb-ProviderMa  14.83    12.22    0.00   12.22   12.22    0.00    0.00    0.00    0.00    0.00    0.00
   945 vobd.2984         8.44     1.21    0.00    1.21    1.21    0.00    0.00    0.00    0.00    0.00    0.00
  1341 sfcb-ProviderMa   7.43     4.22    0.00    4.22    4.22    0.00    0.00    0.00    0.00    0.00    0.00
   685 vmsyslogd.2610    6.35     4.25    0.00    4.25    4.25    0.00    0.00    0.00    0.00    0.00    0.00
   604 vmsyslogd.2609    4.62     3.71    0.00    3.71    3.71    0.00    0.00    0.00    0.00    0.00    0.00
  1439 esxtop.3587       3.96     1.59    0.00    1.59    1.59    0.00    0.00    0.00    0.00    0.00    0.00
  1252 dcui.3323         3.75     1.30    0.00    1.30    1.30    0.00    0.00    0.00    0.00    0.00    0.00
  1443 sfcb-ProviderMa   3.73     1.49    0.00    1.49    1.49    0.00    0.00    0.00    0.00    0.00    0.00
  1209 sfcb-ProviderMa   3.11     1.58    0.00    1.58    1.58    0.00    0.00    0.00    0.00    0.00    0.00
   612 vmkeventd.2630    3.00     1.18    0.00    1.18    1.18    0.00    0.00    0.00    0.00    0.00    0.00
  1340 sfcb-ProviderMa   2.77     0.64    0.00    0.64    0.64    0.00    0.00    0.00    0.00    0.00    0.00
   865 storageRM.2902    2.73     1.36    0.00    1.36    1.36    0.00    0.00    0.00    0.00    0.00    0.00
   846 vprobed.2881      2.56     0.74    0.00    0.74    0.74    0.00    0.00    0.00    0.00    0.00    0.00
  1374 sh.3504           2.54     0.14    0.00    0.14    0.14    0.00    0.00    0.00    0.00    0.00    0.00
  1365 sh.3495           2.53     0.13    0.00    0.13    0.13    0.00    0.00    0.00    0.00    0.00    0.00
   998 vmware-usbarbit   2.50     0.35    0.00    0.35    0.35    0.00    0.00    0.00    0.00    0.00    0.00
   116 init.2146         2.40     0.12    0.00    0.12    0.12    0.00    0.00    0.00    0.00    0.00    0.00
  1275 sfcb-ProviderMa   2.38     0.71    0.00    0.71    0.71    0.00    0.00    0.00    0.00    0.00    0.00
   632 vmkdevmgr.2639    2.00     1.20    0.00    1.20    1.20    0.00    0.00    0.00    0.00    0.00    0.00
   672 net-lbt.2695      1.88     1.02    0.00    1.02    1.02    0.00    0.00    0.00    0.00    0.00    0.00
   907 dcbd.2945         1.52     0.72    0.00    0.72    0.72    0.00    0.00    0.00    0.00    0.00    0.00
   888 slpd.2918         1.24     0.47    0.00    0.47    0.47    0.00    0.00    0.00    0.00    0.00    0.00
   926 net-cdp.2965      1.06     0.43    0.00    0.43    0.43    0.00    0.00    0.00    0.00    0.00    0.00
  1206 sfcbd.3272        1.05     0.70    0.00    0.70    0.70    0.00    0.00    0.00    0.00    0.00    0.00
   908 sh.2938           1.03     0.14    0.00    0.14    0.14    0.00    0.00    0.00    0.00    0.00    0.00
   919 sh.2958           1.03     0.14    0.00    0.14    0.14    0.00    0.00    0.00    0.00    0.00    0.00
   665 sh.2688           1.03     0.14    0.00    0.14    0.14    0.00    0.00    0.00    0.00    0.00    0.00
   938 sh.2977           1.03     0.14    0.00    0.14    0.14    0.00    0.00    0.00    0.00    0.00    0.00
   689 sh.2710           1.03     0.14    0.00    0.14    0.14    0.00    0.00    0.00    0.00    0.00    0.00
   957 sh.3009           1.03     0.14    0.00    0.14    0.14    0.00    0.00    0.00    0.00    0.00    0.00
   839 sh.2874           1.03     0.14    0.00    0.14    0.14    0.00    0.00    0.00    0.00    0.00    0.00
   858 sh.2895           1.03     0.14    0.00    0.14    0.14    0.00    0.00    0.00    0.00    0.00    0.00
   991 sh.3061           1.03     0.14    0.00    0.14    0.14    0.00    0.00    0.00    0.00    0.00    0.00
  1007 sh.3078           1.03     0.14    0.00    0.14    0.14    0.00    0.00    0.00    0.00    0.00    0.00
  1204 cimslp.3270       1.01     0.64    0.00    0.64    0.64    0.00    0.00    0.00    0.00    0.00    0.00
   697 nssquery.2721     1.00     0.18    0.00    0.18    0.18    0.00    0.00    0.00    0.00    0.00    0.00
   966 nssquery.3021     1.00     0.18    0.00    0.18    0.18    0.00    0.00    0.00    0.00    0.00    0.00
```

Figure 10.23
Memory utilization of the physical ESXi host.

Table 10.11 Memory Metrics in resxtop

Counter	Description
GID	Global Identifier of the resource pool VM or world that is currently running.
Name	The unique name, or the resource pool, VM, or world that is currently running.
MEMSZ	The amount of physical RAM that is associated with a resource pool or VM.
GRANT	The amount of physical RAM presented to the guest.
SZTGT	The amount of RAM that a resource pool or VM has requested, and the VMKernel wants to allocate to that object.
TCHD	The estimated amount of used RAM for that object.
TCHD_W	The estimated amount of RAM used for writes by this object.
SWCUR	The amount of swap space in use by this object.
SWTGT	Estimated swap space usage by this object.
PMEM	Displays the memory usage statistics for the server based on the following: ■ **total.** The total amount of physical RAM in the server. ■ **vmk.** The RAM being consumed by the VMKernel. ■ **other.** The RAM in use by processes other than the VMKernel. ■ **free.** The amount of free RAM in the server.
VMKMEM	Displays the memory usage statistics for the ESXi VMKernel based on the following: ■ **managed.** The amount of RAM that the VMKernel is currently managing. ■ **min free.** The amount of free RAM that the VMKernel tries to maintain. ■ **rsvd.** The amount of RAM that resource pools are currently reserving. ■ **ursvd.** The amount of unreserved RAM in the server. ■ **state.** The available memory state of the server.

(Continued)

Table 10.11   Memory Metrics in resxtop (*Continued*)

Counter	Description
NUMA	Displays the memory usage statistics for ESXi NUMA architecture servers. The statistics are: ■ The current amount of RAM that the VMKernel manages within a particular NUMA node. ■ The current free memory within a particular NUMA node.
PSHARE	Displays the memory page sharing statistics for an ESXi host. These metrics are: ■ **curr.** The current amount of swap RAM In use ■ **rclmtgt.** The expected amount of RAM reclaimed by swapping or compression. ■ **r/s.** The swap in rate for this ESXi host. ■ **w/s.** The swap out rate for this ESXi host.
ZIP	Displays the memory compression statistics for an ESXi host. These metrics are: ■ **zipped.** The amount of current compressed RAM. ■ **saved.** The amount of RAM saved through compression.
MEMCTL	Displays the ballooning statistics for an ESXi host. These metrics are: ■ **curr.** The amount of RAN that is reclaimed through the vmmemctl driver ■ **target.** The amount of physical RAM that the ESXi VMkernel attempts to reclaim through the vmmemctl driver. ■ **Max.** The total amount of physical RAM that the ESXi host can reclaim through the vmmemctl driver.
AMIN	The configured memory Reservation for this object.
AMAX	The current configured memory Limit for this object.
ASHRS	The current configured memory Shares for this object.
NHN	The home NUMA node for this object.
NRMEM	The amount of RAM that is local to another NUMA node and is associated with this object.
N%L	The amount of local NUMA memory associated with this object.

(*Continued*)

Table 10.11 Memory Metrics in resxtop (*Continued*)

Counter	Description
%ACTV	The instantaneous value of memory utilized with this object.
%ACTS	The slow-moving average of memory utilized by this object.
%ACTF	The fast-moving average of memory utilized by this object.
%ACTN	An estimated value of memory utilized by this object.
MCTL?	Current state of the memory balloon driver.
MCTLTGT	The goal for reclaimed RAM through the use of ballooning.
MCTLMAX	Defines the maximum amount of RAM that the vmmemctl driver can reclaim.
MCTLSZ	The amount of ballooned RAM for the resource pool.
SWCUR	On a per-VM basis, the amount of swap utilization.
SWTGT	Anticipated swap usage for an ESXi host.
SWR/s	The current swap in rate for this object.
SWW/s	The current swap out rate for this object.
ZERO	The zeroed pages used by an object.
SHRD	The number of shared memory pages for this object.
SHRDSVD	The amount of physical RAM that is saved through page sharing.
OVHD	The amount of RAM that is used as management overhead for an object.
OVHDMAX	The maximum amount of physical RAM that could be allocated as overhead for an object.
OVHDUW	The amount of RAM that is consumed as overhead resources for a world.
GST_NDx	The amount of NUMA node x RAM provided to an object.
OVD_NDx	The amount of overhead RAM from NUMA node associated with an object.
CACHESZ	The amount of cache memory that is currently compressed.
CACHEUSD	The amount of cache memory that is currently compressed and is in use by an object.
ZIP/s	The amount of memory that is compressed per second.
UNZIP/s	The amount of memory that is decompressed per second.

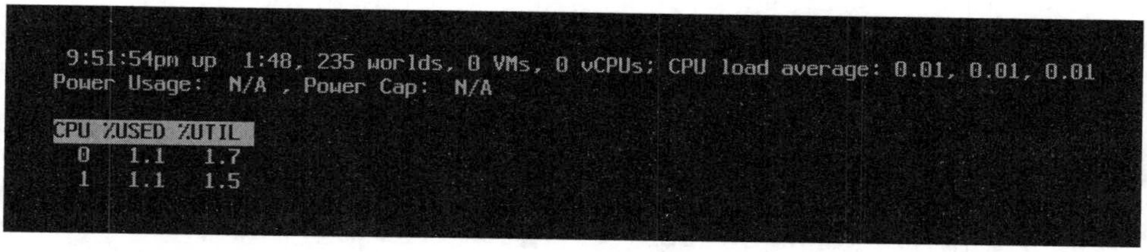

```
 9:51:54pm up  1:48, 235 worlds, 0 VMs, 0 vCPUs; CPU load average: 0.01, 0.01, 0.01
Power Usage:  N/A , Power Cap:  N/A

CPU %USED %UTIL
  0   1.1   1.7
  1   1.1   1.5
```

Figure 10.24
Current power statistics for the selected ESXi host.

Table 10.12 Power Metrics in resxtop

Counter	Description
Power Usage	The power consumption in watts
Power Cap	The cap for power consumption in watts
%USED	The physical CPU utilization since the last update interval
%UTIL	The amount of time that the physical CPU was not in an IDLE state
%Cx	Refers to the amount of time that the CPU was in power state "Cx"
%Px	Refers to the amount of time that the CPU was in power state "Px"
%Tx	Refers to the amount of time that the CPU was in power state "Tx"

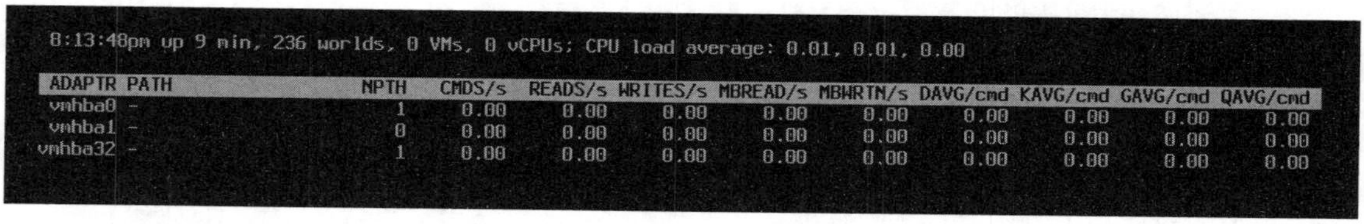

```
8:13:48pm up 9 min, 236 worlds, 0 VMs, 0 vCPUs; CPU load average: 0.01, 0.01, 0.00

ADAPTR PATH            NPTH  CMDS/s  READS/s WRITES/s MBREAD/s MBWRTN/s DAVG/cmd KAVG/cmd GAVG/cmd QAVG/cmd
vmhba0  -                1    0.00     0.00    0.00     0.00     0.00     0.00     0.00     0.00     0.00
vmhba1  -                0    0.00     0.00    0.00     0.00     0.00     0.00     0.00     0.00     0.00
vmhba32 -                1    0.00     0.00    0.00     0.00     0.00     0.00     0.00     0.00     0.00
```

Figure 10.25
Current storage metrics on a per-HBA basis.

The statistics for the storage adapter can be viewed by selecting "d" at the interactive `resxtop` pane. Note, these statistics are for the ESXi host's storage adapters, not each VMDK disk file. In Figure 10.25, the disk adapter statistics are displayed for all vmhba objects. Included are the metrics relating to multipathing and the I/O per second.

The available disk adapter statistics are found in Table 10.13.

Table 10.13 Disk Adapter Metrics in resxtop

Counter	Description
ADAPTR PATH	Indicates the specific vmhba.
NPTH	The current number of paths for this device.
CMDs/s	The number of SCSI commands per second for this adapter on a per-adapter basis.
READS/s	The number of read commands per second for this adapter on a per-adapter basis.
WRITES/s	The number of write commands per second for this adapter on a per-adapter basis.
MBREAD/s	The amount of data read in megabytes per second on a per-adapter basis.
MBWRTN/s	The amount of data written in megabytes per second on a per-adapter basis.
DAVG/cmd	On a per-command basis, the latency average displayed in milliseconds.
KAVG/cmd	On a per-command basis, the latency average for the VMKernel displayed in milliseconds.
GAVG/cmd	On a per-command basis, the latency average for the OS displayed in milliseconds.
QAVG/cmd	On a per-command basis, the latency average for the disk queue displayed in milliseconds.
AQLEN	The number of queued commands for this vmhba.
RESV/s	On a per-second basis, the SCSI reservations issued by this vmhba.
CONS/s	On a per-second basis, the SCSI reservation conflicts experienced by this vmhba.
DAVG/rd	During a read operation, the average latency expressed in milliseconds.
KAVG/rd	During a read operation, the average latency for the VMKernel expressed in milliseconds.
GAVG/rd	During a read operation, the average latency for the OS expressed in milliseconds.
QAVG/rd	During a read operation, the average latency for the disk queue expressed in milliseconds.
DAVG/wr	During a write operation, the average latency expressed in milliseconds.
KAVG/wr	During a read operation, the average latency for the VMKernel expressed in milliseconds.
GAVG/wr	During a write operation, the average latency for the OS expressed in milliseconds.

(Continued)

Table 10.13   Disk Adapter Metrics in resxtop (*Continued*)

Counter	Description
QAVG/wr	During a write operation, the average latency for the disk queue expressed in milliseconds.
ABRTS/s	The number of SCSI commands per second that are aborted.
RESETS/s	The number of SCSI commands per second that are reset.
PAECMD/s	On a per-second basis, the number of PAE commands issued.
PAECP/s	On a per-second basis, the number of PAE copy processes issued.
SPLTCMD/s	The number of SCSI commands per second that are split.
SPLTCP/s	The number of SCSI copy commands per second that are split.

There are hotkeys that can change the method in which the statistics are displayed. The hotkey combinations are:

- The "e" key will enable the administrator to view the statistics on a per-adapter basis. Choosing this option will prompt for the adapter to be viewed.

- The "r" key will sort the statistics based on the READS/s column.

- The "w" key (lowercase w) will sort the statistics based on the WRITES/s column.

- The "R" key will sort the statistics based on the MBREADS/s column.

- The "T" key will sort the statistics based on the MBWRTN/s column.

- The "N" will sort the statistics based first on the ADAPTR column, and secondly by the PATH column.

Pressing the "u" key from the main resxtop screen will display the device utilization statistics. As depicted in Figure 10.26, the Device Utilization view provides storage statistics based on the individual storage device. In the figure, the storage device is referenced as a "t10" device, which is a software iSCSI device.

The available counters for the device utilization are listed in Table 10.14.

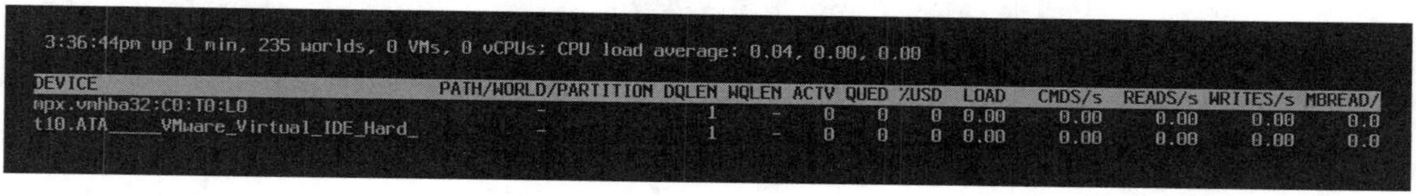

Figure 10.26
Device Utilization view.

Table 10.14   Device Utilization Metrics in resxtop

Counter	Description
DEVICE	The storage device name.
PATH	This is the logical path of the device.
WORLD	The world identifier for this storage device.
PARTITION	The partition identifier of this device.
DQLEN	Represents the active queue length for this device.
WQLEN	The active queue length for this world.
ACTV	The active commands in the VMKernel.
QUED	The active commands in the VMKernel that are queued for service.
%USD	The amount of total requests in the queue for the VMKernel.
LOAD	The queue length divided by the sum of the VMKernel active and queued commands.
CMDS/s	The number of SCSI commands per second for this adapter on a per-adapter basis.
READS/s	The number of read commands per second for this adapter on a per-adapter basis.
WRITES/s	The number of write commands per second for this adapter on a per-adapter basis.
MBREAD/s	The amount of data read in megabytes per second on a per-adapter basis.
MBWRITE/s	The amount of data written in megabytes per second on a per-adapter basis.
NPH	The number of available paths for this storage device.
NWD	The active worlds currently in execution.
NPN	The partition count for this device.
SHARES	The Share configuration for this device. Available when viewing worlds only.
DAVG/rd	During a read operation, the average latency expressed in milliseconds.

(Continued)

Table 10.14 Device Utilization Metrics in resxtop (Continued)

Counter	Description
KAVG/rd	During a read operation, the average latency for the VMKernel expressed in milliseconds.
GAVG/rd	During a read operation, the average latency for the OS expressed in milliseconds.
QAVG/rd	During a read operation, the average latency for the disk queue expressed in milliseconds.
DAVG/wr	During a write operation, the average latency expressed in milliseconds.
KAVG/wr	During a read operation, the average latency for the VMKernel expressed in milliseconds.
GAVG/wr	During a write operation, the average latency for the OS expressed in milliseconds.
QAVG/wr	During a write operation, the average latency for the disk queue expressed in milliseconds.
DAVG/cmd	On a per-command basis, the latency average displayed in milliseconds.
KAVG/cmd	On a per-command basis, the latency average for the VMKernel displayed in milliseconds.
GAVG/cmd	On a per-command basis, the latency average for the OS displayed in milliseconds.
QAVG/cmd	On a per-command basis, the latency average for the disk queue displayed in milliseconds.
ABRTS/s	The number of SCSI commands per second that are aborted.
RESETS/s	The number of SCSI commands per second that are reset.
PAECMD/s	On a per-second basis, the number of PAE commands issued.
PAECP/s	On a per-second basis, the number of PAE copy processes issued.
SPLTCMD/s	The number of SCSI commands per second that are split.
SPLTCP/s	The number of SCSI copy commands per second that are split.

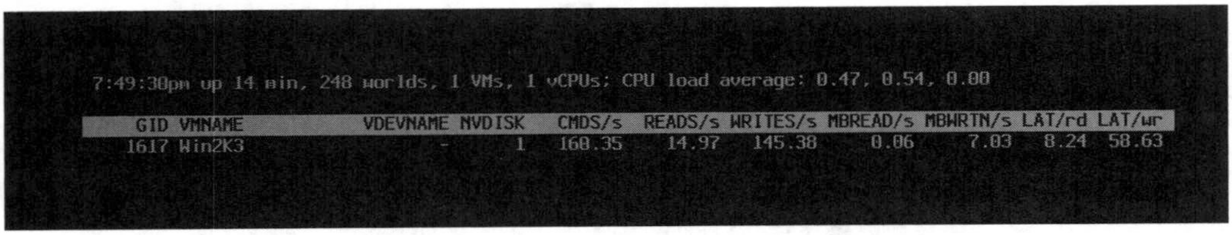

Figure 10.27
Storage statistics for a particular VM or for all VMs on a specific ESXi server.

There are also hotkeys that can optionally sort the displayed statistics. They are:

■ The "e" key will display storage statistics based on a particular storage device.

■ The "P" key will display storage statistics based on a particular path.

■ The "t" key will display storage statistics based on a particular partition.

■ The "r" key will sort the displayed data based on the READS/s column.

■ The "w" (lowercase w) key will sort the displayed data based on the WRITES/s column.

■ The "R" key will sort the displayed data based on the MBREAD/s column.

■ The "T" key will sort the displayed statistics based on the MBWRTN/s column.

■ The "N" key will sort the displayed statistics initially based on the DEVICE column, and then the PATH column, the WORLD column, and finally the PARTITION column.

■ The "L" key will allow the administrator to modify the length of the DEVICE column.

The storage information relative to VMs can be displayed using the "v" key.

Figure 10.27 shows the available information from resxtop relating to the VMs on this particular ESXi host. The available counters for VM storage are listed in Table 10.15.

There are also hotkeys that can optionally sort the displayed statistics. They are:

■ The "e" key will display storage statistics based on a particular virtual SCSI storage device.

■ The "r" key will sort the displayed data based on the READS/s column.

■ The "w" key (lowercase w) will sort the displayed data based on the WRITES/s column.

■ The "R" key will sort the displayed data based on the MBREAD/s column.

Table 10.15   VM Metrics in resxtop

Counter	Description
ID	The identifier of the virtual SCSI device or resource pool.
GID	The identifier of the resource pool.
VMNAME	The resource pool assigned name.
VSCSINAME	The VSCSI device assigned name.
NDK	The quantity of virtual SCSI devices.
CMDS/s	The number of SCSI commands per second for this adapter on a per-adapter basis.
READS/s	The number of read commands per second for this adapter on a per-adapter basis.
WRITES/s	The number of write commands per second for this adapter on a per-adapter basis.
MBREAD/s	The amount of data read in megabytes per second on a per-adapter basis.
MBWRITE/s	The amount of data written in megabytes per second on a per-adapter basis.
LAT/rd	The average read latency displayed in milliseconds
LAT/wr	The average write latency displayed in milliseconds.

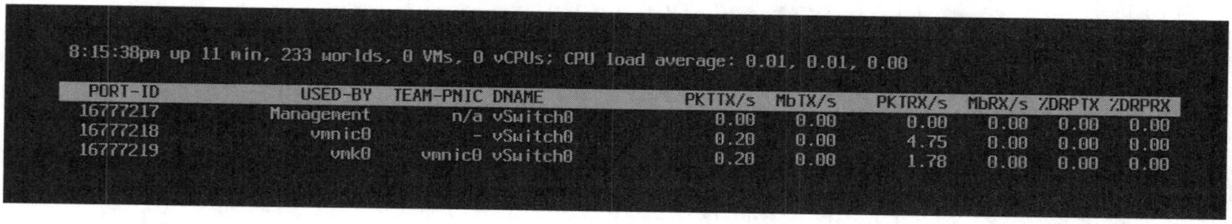

Figure 10.28
Networking statistics in `resxtop`.

- The "T" key will sort the displayed statistics based on the MBWRTN/s column.
- The "N" key will sort the displayed statistics initially based on the VMNAME column, and then the VSCSINAME column.

The networking statistics can be displayed by pressing the "n" key at the main `resxtop` screen as shown in Figure 10.28.

The available networking statistics are listed in Table 10.16.

Table 10.16 Networking Statistics in resxtop

Counter	Description
PORT_ID	The identifier of the virtual network port in use.
USED-BY	The current user of this virtual network port.
TEAM-PNIC	The physical network adapter used by this virtual team.
DNAME	The name of the virtual network device as assigned by the VMkernel
PKTTX/s	On a per-second basis, the quantity of transmitted packets.
MbTX/s	On a per-second basis, the quantity of Megabits transmitted.
PKTRX/s	On a per-second basis, the quantity of received packets.
MbRX/s	On a per-second basis, the quantity of Megabits received.
%DRPTX	The ratio of dropped transmitted packets to the total packets sent.
%DRPRX	The ratio of dropped received packets to the total packets received.
UPLINK	A "Y" here indicates that this is a physical network adapter; an "N" indicates that this is not a physical NIC.
UP	A "Y" in this field indicates that the link is in an "Up" state; an "N" indicates that no link pulse is detected.
SPEED	This is the connected speed in Mb/s.
FDUPLX	A "Y" in this field indicates that this is a Full Duplex connection; an "N" indicates that this link is not operating in Full Duplex mode.
DTYP	An "H" indicates that this is a Hub; an "S" indicates that this port is a switch.
DNAME	The name of the virtual device.
PKTTXMUL/s	On a per-second basis, the quantity of transmitted multicast packets.
PKTRXMUL/s	On a per-second basis, the quantity of received multicast packets.
PKTTXBRD/s	On a per-second basis, the quantity of transmitted broadcast packets.
PKTRXBRD/s	On a per-second basis, the quantity of received broadcast packets.

There are also hotkey combinations that can change the method in which the statistics are displayed:

- Pressing the "T" key will sort the displayed metrics by the Mb Tx column.
- Pressing the "R" key will sort the displayed metrics by the Mb Rx column.
- Pressing the "t" key will sort the displayed metrics by the Packets Tx column.
- Pressing the "r" key will sort the displayed metrics by the Packets Rx column.
- Pressing the "N" key will sort the displayed metrics by the values in the NAME column.
- Pressing the "L" key will allow the length of the DNAME column to be modified.

The interrupt statistics can be displayed by pressing the "i" key at the main resxtop screen. Here, the information related to the interrupts generated by hardware devices and services is displayed, as shown in Figure 10.29.

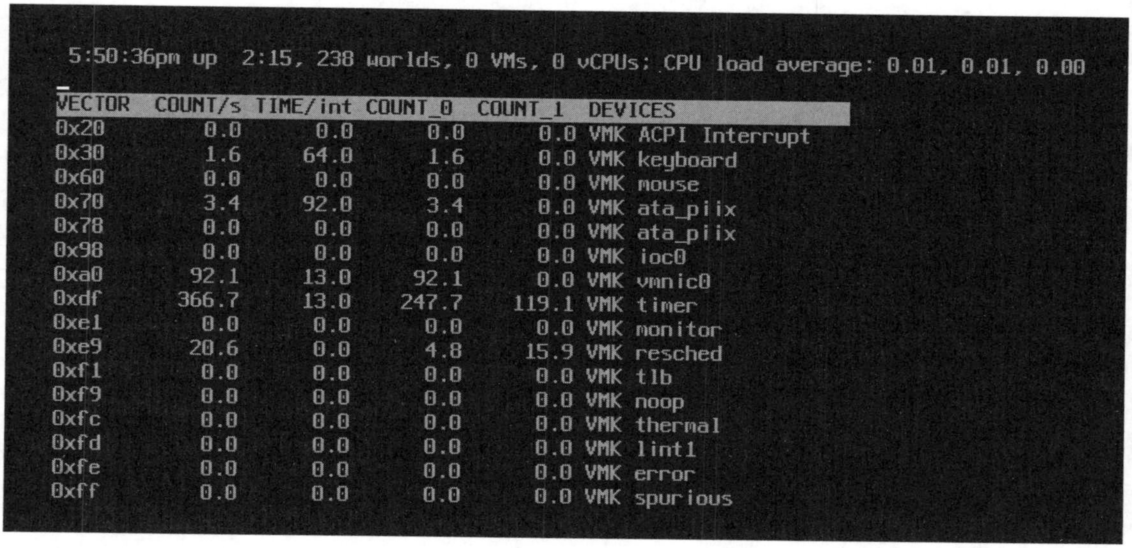

Figure 10.29
ESXi interrupts metrics.

Table 10.17 Interrupt Statistics in resxtop

Counter	Description
VECTOR	The identifier of the interrupt vector.
COUNT/s	The total quantity of interrupts generated per second over all CPUs.
TIME/int	The average time taken to process each interrupt.
COUNT_0	The total interrupts generated on CPU 0.
COUNT_1	The total interrupts generated on CPU 1.
DEVICES	The device that generated the interrupt.

The available counters that are related to the system interrupts are listed in Table 10.17.

Summary

Resource management is a hot topic for both seasoned and inexperienced vSphere administrators. The key to keeping things running properly is change control and up-to-date documentation. If you find yourself in troubleshooting mode, make sure you are documenting every little change you make. As you've seen, there are many different ways to adjust your resources, and not all of them will be helpful. In fact, some of the things you can change may cause you more grief than you expect. Recording what you change will help you later when you have to go back to undo your "fix."

This chapter contained a lot of information. Some of the information would be good to remember, while the rest makes this book a great reference tool. Just remember that VMware doesn't have an award for memorizing their whitepapers or manual pages. The most valuable administrators simply know where to find everything when they need it—as quickly as possible. Know where to find your resources like the back of your hand, and let Google handle the memorization.

In our next chapter, you'll learn how important resource management becomes when you have multiple hosts. You'll soon explore the details of the Distributed Resource Scheduler (DRS) and Storage DRS, both of which play a very important role in managing a cluster's resource configuration.

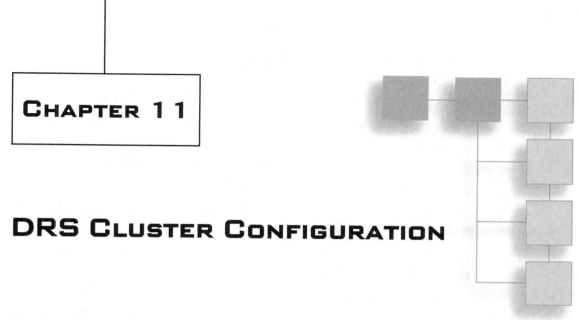

CHAPTER 11

DRS CLUSTER CONFIGURATION

The decision to deploy a DRS cluster involves some choices that will impact how the DRS cluster performs its duties. Careful evaluation and understanding of the current environment, including the applications and operating systems being virtualized, will prove invaluable in these decisions.

PLANNING

DRS stands for Distributed Resource Scheduler. Based on how you configure the cluster, the DRS cluster has three main functions:

- Automatically places all new VMs on the most appropriate physical host, based on resource utilization.

- Performs load balancing of the workloads across each of the physical ESXi hosts.

- Controls the power state of the physical ESXi hosts in an effort to conserve energy and cost.

To ensure that the new cluster can perform all of its processes as designed, consider the current environment and evaluate the servers that will be used as cluster nodes.

vMotion

When creating the DRS cluster, take nothing for granted; we must consider each physical server's configuration. In order for the DRS cluster to perform its duties optimally, each cluster member must be vMotion compatible. vMotion is the

VMware process that migrates the running state of a virtual machine from the memory of a source host to the memory of a destination server. If we design the cluster well, this process is completely transparent to any clients that are connected to that VM. From a physical server perspective, the vMotion requirements are:

- Each server must see the same datastores in exactly the same way (each server must see each datastore with the same unique identifier). This is a standard clustering requirement present in other vendor's clustering solutions.

- Each physical server must have access to the same physical networks. For example, if a VM is currently being accessed on the 10.1.1.x network, when it is moved to another host, it must still be visible on that same subnet.

- Each physical server must be CPU compatible with the peer cluster nodes (we will cover this in the next section in more detail).

- Each physical server must have at least one vMotion-enabled VMKernel port. This should be on an isolated network that does not carry other traffic such as print jobs, DNS or DHCP traffic, etc., and should not be the same network used for management traffic.

- If the vMotion VMKernel ports will be configured on Standard vSwitches, the name of the port group used by vMotion must be consistent across all cluster nodes or the vMotion process will fail. Remember that the Port Group name is an ASCII string, so capitalization and spelling are important.

From a virtual machine perspective, there are requirements that must be followed in order to achieve a successful migration:

- The VM must not be actively connected to a "virtual intranet." A virtual intranet is a vSwitch without an uplink or physical adapter. Note that the key phrase is "actively connected." The VM can be configured with the connection, but not currently connected (remember the "Connected" checkbox in the Network properties of the virtual machine).

- The VM must not have an active connection to a floppy drive, CD, DVD, or an .ISO image.

- The VM cannot have CPU Affinity configured.

- Virtual machines can be migrated if they are using a USB device, provided that USB device is configured for vMotion compatibility.

- The VM cannot be configured with an RDM that is part of a clustering solution.

- Just by reviewing these requirements, it should be obvious that a bit of planning when deploying hosts and virtual machines can go a long way toward a more efficient cluster.

So, how does vMotion work? The whole process can take only a couple of minutes, but there are several important steps to complete:

1. vCenter will evaluate the destination host to verify that sufficient CPU, RAM, and network resources are available. If so, vCenter then turns its attention to the virtual machine. Remember the requirements we covered for the VM above? The points that we mentioned are evaluated to determine if the migration may cause issues with the running applications within the VM. If there are no issues found, the migration moves forward.

2. A virtual machine is created on the destination ESXi server with the exact same resource usage as the original VM.

3. Once the destination VM has been defined, the memory contents of the source ESXi server that contain the host memory of the VM are copied to the destination server.

4. A second copy process will copy any memory pages that were changed during the initial copy.

5. This incremental copy process will continue until the memory contents are identical between the two servers.

6. At this point, the source VM is "stunned" or paused on the source ESXi host, and resumed on the destination.

Even though it may seem like magic and pixie dust, these steps are carried out very efficiently; remember, this is designed to be transparent to the end users. If you look at the steps very carefully, you will notice that if a virtual machine has a high amount of changes in the running memory content (a high transaction rate), the migration process may take longer than anticipated, and may be more efficiently performed in an off-peak time slot.

A key factor to mention here is if vCenter decides that the amount of incoming data is too great to copy; in other words, if more data is coming in than we can move across the network, vCenter will estimate the time required to move all remaining memory changes. If the calculated time is less than 100 seconds, vMotion will proceed. If the estimated time is greater than 100 seconds, the vMotion process will fail, rather than risk affecting the VM.

How do I migrate a VM? If you have satisfied all of the design requirements listed above, you can simply right-click on the VM, select Migrate, and select Change Host. You will be asked for:

1. The destination ESXi host

2. The destination resource pool (if you have resource pools on the destination)

3. The priority

If we have met all of the prerequisites, the virtual machine will move from the source host to the destination with no problem. If you want to verify the effect that a client will experience during this process, open a command prompt on the virtual machine and start an extended Ping test. You will see that the effect is negligible if we have done our homework.

We must ensure each server conforms to the vMotion requirements. First, verify that the physical servers all use CPUs from the same vendor, and if they have the same vendor, they must be feature compatible. Keep in mind that just because all of the physical servers have a CPU from the same vendor doesn't mean that the CPU's stepping and instruction sets are compatible. We must examine the available physical servers and determine which CPUs are compatible. This can be accomplished by accessing the following URL and downloading the CPUID (CPU Identification Utility) ISO:

http://downloads.vmware.com/d/details/cpu_identification_utility/ZHcqYmR0dGhidGRl

The ISO can be burned to a CD. Then we will boot each of the ESXi hosts using the ISO. The CPUID process will evaluate the physical CPUs and report its characteristics. They can then be compared to the other hosts to verify compatibility.

If the CPUs feature sets are similar, the DRS cluster will be able to vMotion the VMs without the end users being aware of the process. The whole goal of vMotion is that it is a transparent, background process that allows management processes to occur without causing client disruption.

One of the main indicators of whether a vMotion migration can succeed is the CPU in each host. If both hosts contain CPUs from the same vendor, and the CPUs are code set and feature compatible, the vMotion should proceed from a CPU perspective. Both of these factors can be verified using the CPUID utility.

Another way to verify the CPU vendor is the NX or XD bit flag. This status flag is vendor specific (Intel uses the XD or eXecution Disable bit, while AMD uses the NX or No eXecute bit). In both cases, when this flag is set, the CPU will prevent code from being executed within memory pages that have been configured as data-only. This helps reduce the occurrence of buffer overflow attacks.

This configuration can also indicate whether the source and destination CPUs are from the same vendor. This allows VMware to verify that the destination CPU is compatible with the CPU on the source ESXi server, and if the CPU vendors are not identical, a warning will be displayed in the Migration wizard, and the migration will fail.

You have the option to hide this status flag from the virtual machine through the properties of the VM, and this will allow the virtual machine to migrate between potential ESXi hosts, (as long as all other pre-requisites have been met), but the VM may "lock up" or "blue screen" as a result of being presented with a different instruction set on the new host. Remember, this vMotion process is supposed to be transparent to the end users.

vCenter can support a maximum of 32 hosts per cluster, and this includes DRS clusters. In the previous chapter, you learned that the root resource pool is predefined on the server when you installed ESXi, and this is comprised of the population of the server system board: all installed CPUs and all installed RAM. All VMs deployed on this server will share the same resources. When creating a cluster, the root resource pool becomes the aggregate resources of all cluster nodes. This can dramatically increase the amount of available resources. Keep in mind here that, in most cases, you will not want to "max out" the resources in the cluster. If the resources are completely allocated, the cluster will not have free resources to use when performing a vMotion to load balance the cluster. Consider planning the cluster so that the individual hosts are below 75% utilization. This will give DRS the most flexibility when making load-balancing decisions.

One of the most important deployment considerations is to ensure that any and all datastores that contain VMs are shared among all the ESXi hosts, and are viewed identically by each host. This means that each host will see the LUNs with the same LUN number. Shared storage is the foundation of vMotion, and DRS is dependent on vMotion for load-balancing operations. If there are any VMs that will live in the cluster, but are currently located on local storage, you can use Storage vMotion to move those local VMs out to a shared datastore, if there is sufficient free space.

Additionally, each of the ESXi hosts will require access to the same physical networks. If a virtual machine is being accessed via the 10.1.1.0 network on the source ESXi server, the destination ESXi server will also require access to the 10.1.1.0 network. This allows any clients that are currently accessing the VM to continue to have network access. Remember, if we vMotion a VM from one host to another, but the VM is unreachable by clients, we have achieved nothing.

At this point, it would be beneficial to review the prerequisites for vMotion that were discussed earlier in the chapter, as each of these prerequisites will still apply here.

When a VM is marked for movement, the vCenter instance will check the destination host for three initial resources:

- Sufficient free CPU resources to meet the VM's reservation
- Sufficient free RAM resources to meet the VM's reservation
- A free network port

If these host requirements are met, vCenter will evaluate the .vmx file of the VM to determine if there are any hardware requirements that will prevent a migration. These include an active connection to physical removable media, such as a floppy, CD, DVD, or an .ISO file, an active connection to an internal virtual switch, or if the VM is configured for CPU affinity. Non-compliance with any of these hardware configurations will render the VM unable to migrate, and will seriously impact the physical host's ability to enter Maintenance Mode.

Reservations

To understand the functionality of DRS, we must cover some fundamental concepts that play an integral part in DRS.

Contention

The term "contention" is applied to a cluster or to a single physical ESXi host that is experiencing high amounts of CPU or RAM utilization. You may also hear the term "overcommitment" used here. Short-term contention may be the result of an unanticipated workload generated within a virtual machine that impacts the host or cluster for a short period of time, or may exist as a long-term symptom. If this is a long-term situation, this typically results from "scope creep," in which hardware is procured with an anticipated number of virtual machines that are deployed. Later the decision is made to deploy more virtual machines, and now the budget will not support the purchase of additional hardware. The end result is that the performance and availability of the virtual machines cannot be sustained by the available hardware.

From a virtual environment perspective, contention means that virtual machines are contending for the available CPU and memory resources.

Entitlements

An entitlement is the amount of physical resources that a virtual machine or resource pool can use. These entitlements are computed by the local ESXi server and, if a DRS cluster is defined, by vCenter on an ongoing basis.

Static entitlement is the number of resources with which the virtual machine or resource pool is configured. These resources are represented by reservations, limits, and shares. The local ESXi host scheduler is responsible for providing resources to the virtual machine based on these configurations. If a virtual machine is configured with a reservation of 256MB, but is currently only actively using 128MB, the remaining 128MB can be allocated to other virtual machines on the same host. If a VM has a reservation, this does not mean that it automatically receives it; the virtual machine is allocated resources on demand. In the above example, if a virtual machine is using 128MB of RAM, it is assigned 128MB of physical memory pages. If it asks for more, and the request does not exceed a configured limit, the pages can be allocated to the VM.

Dynamic entitlement is the current resource demands of the virtual machine. These demands can change up and down, based on the workload that is running within the VM. If the cluster or ESXi host has an abundance of free resources, the virtual machine can use resources up to its limit or configured maximum. If limits are configured, the host scheduler must consider the limits as the VM requests resources, and can restrict the performance of the VM.

The resource usage of a virtual machine is computed using several metrics: for the CPU resources, %Run and %Ready are used. The %Run metric represents the total scheduled time for the virtual machine; the %Ready metric defines the amount of time that the virtual machine was ready to run, but insufficient CPU resources were available.

For dynamic memory usage, memory active (%ACTV) is the metric used. This represents the number of physical memory pages that are currently in use by the virtual machine. Remember that in a physical server, the operating system can allocate pages of memory to applications as they are opened, and those pages are returned when the application is closed. The exact same thing happens within the virtual machine. If a VM requests memory from the physical server, and if it does not exceed a limit, the memory is granted. Then, when the virtual machine no longer requires the memory, it is retained by the virtual machine as free pages. At this point it is helpful to understand that the hypervisor does not know what the VM is using the allocated memory for; it just knows that it is allocated to the VM. That is where the %ACTV metric comes in. This allows the scheduler to determine how much RAM is actually in use by the VM, and how much is idle. The virtual machine's overhead is also included in the active memory value.

Keep in mind that the dynamic entitlement is calculated by the host scheduler on an ongoing basis. vCenter, on the other hand, calculates the entitlement by default every five minutes. These two schedulers do not share or compare information; these values are determined separately.

Differences between Resource Pool Reservations and Virtual Machine Reservations

As discussed earlier, reservations can be configured at both the virtual machine and the resource pool level. The reservations that are applied at the resource pool are shared by all virtual machines that are currently powered on within the pool. If virtual machines are powered on, powered off, resumed, or added to the pool, these resources are re-evaluated, based on the allocations of each virtual machine, and the resources that are allocated to each virtual machine may change.

Reservations that are configured at the virtual machine level determine a "guaranteed level of performance" during a period of contention. If a virtual machine has requested memory above its reservation, the hypervisor can reclaim the extra memory through ballooning, but memory included in the reservation cannot be reclaimed. The only way that a reservation can be reclaimed is if the virtual machine is migrated to another host or is powered off. This means that if the host is running out of memory, a virtual machine with a reservation has an amount of memory that is guaranteed, providing a stable environment for that VM.

DPM

DPM is an additional component that initially made its appearance in VI 3.5, but was considered "experimental." With the release of vSphere, DPM was fully supported. DPM is an option that allows vCenter to manage the power state of each physical ESXi server. One of the main concepts of virtualization is that we can replace existing physical devices, and these can be desktops, notebooks, and servers with virtual replacements. This provides tremendous savings on power and cooling as well as a dramatic reduction in the physical space required.

Adding to this reduction in operating costs and space is the ability to determine when virtual machines are in a latent state, and migrate the VMs to a minimal number of physical servers. The remaining physical hosts can then be powered down. This occurs through the vCenter instance, and, like DRS, becomes unavailable if vCenter becomes inaccessible.

As a prerequisite to enabling DPM, we need to evaluate our environment to identify any potential issues. These include:

■ The cluster must have at a minimum two hosts that are running ESX 3.5 or later.

■ Each must have at least one functional vMotion interface that also supports Wake on LAN (WoL). As discussed earlier, this can be determined by highlighting the physical ESXi server, and selecting the Configuration tab. Select Network Adapters and the WoL-enabled column is on the right. It is important to note here that each physical server is tested for WoL compatibility as it is configured for DPM. If the server does not pass the analysis, it is not configured for DPM, and in fact, DPM is disabled for that server.

The HP's iLO interface can be described as a management interface that is embedded into the server system board of the server, whereas IPMI is a standardized interface for hardware-level access to a device. In both access methods, the system's baseboard management controller (BMC) is the management target. The BMC is one of the devices that still receives power, even if the main server is in a powered-off state. This allows an administrator to access the server using either a serial connection or a network interface.

As a prerequisite, the IPMI interface or the iLO interface must be configured with an IP address, subnet mask, and default gateway. If you are considering authentication, DPM does not support MD2 authentication, but will fully support plaintext. It will support MD5 authentication if it is used through the BMC. Note that for security reasons, if the physical server cannot support MD5 or plaintext authentication, the BMC cannot be used as a wakeup medium, and DPM will use Wake on LAN instead.

Resource Pool Hierarchy

Each physical server has a root resource pool that is made up of the CPU and RAM resources on the physical system board. And the virtual machines that are hosted on that server must work and play within those resource boundaries. A resource pool is simply a subset of those server resources.

A resource pool is a logical container to which we can add resources in the form of CPU and RAM. We can then deploy or move virtual machines into this logical container, and they can be restricted to using these resources exclusively. This allows us to deploy VMs in a manner that will:

■ Mimic the company's organizational chart

- Isolate one workgroup's resources from another
- Form the basis for chargeback, or pay-for-resources

In essence, resource pools can provide a building block for web hosting, isolation, organization, or to simply delegate authority.

If desired, we can further subdivide the resource pool by creating a child resource pool. Depending on the amount of resources provided to the parent resource pool, there could be multiple child resource pools, each with different permissions assigned, and with different CPU and RAM resources.

Like virtual machines, resource pools can have limits, reservations, and shares. These are used to provide physical resources to the virtual machines that are located within them.

As shown in Figure 11.1, when we create a resource pool, we can assign specific amounts of CPU and RAM resources to the pool, but we can also assign shares, reservations, and limits identical to those assigned to virtual machines.

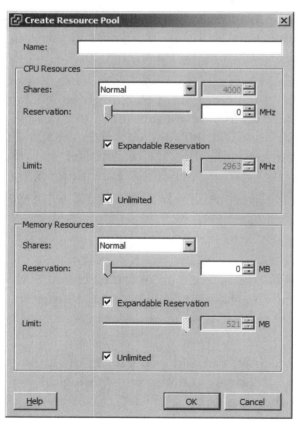

Figure 11.1
Resource pool creation.

Remember that shares are used to signify the priority for a specific virtual machine as compared to its peers, and that shares only apply if the resource is under contention. When the ESXi server begins to run out of a physical resource, in this case CPU and RAM, it compares the shares configuration for each VM when requests arrive for that resource. The shares are then compared to create a ratio.

For example, if there are three VMs, as depicted in Figure 11.2, each with 1,000 shares, for a total of 3,000 shares, during a time of contention, each VM will receive one-third of the remaining resources. However, if the shares value is modified for a given VM, the ratio will change.

In the scenario shown in Figure 11.3, one of the VMs now has 4,000 shares. The total number of shares is now 6,000 and the VM with 4,000 shares now receives two-thirds of the resources, while the other two VMs, each with 1,000 shares, will split the remaining one-third; each will receive one-sixth of the remaining resources. It is important to remember that this ratio will change as VMs are powered on, powered off, resumed, or migrated; the shares values themselves will not change, but the amount of resources that they are entitled to will change.

For CPU resources, we can select Low, which represents 2,000 shares; Normal, which represents 4,000 shares; High, which represents 8,000 shares; or Custom, in which you can enter a specific amount. These shares will be used to compete with peer resource pools in times of resource contention. When we configure shares for CPU

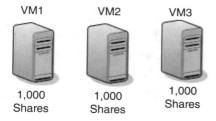

Figure 11.2
Equal reservations.

Figure 11.3
Different shares.

access, the local CPU scheduler will use the shares value to determine a MHz/Share ratio (MHz/Share = MHz Used/Shares). This allows the CPU scheduler to determine if the VM is ahead or behind on its entitlement. If it is behind compared to other VMs, it will be moved up in the queue, possibly pre-empting other VMs. If it is ahead of its entitlement compared to other VMs, it will be moved back in the queue.

Keep in mind that whatever the MHz/Share value, reservations will always outweigh shares. This is to verify that the VM will always receive the reservation specified by the administrator.

For RAM resources, we can select Low, which represents 81,920 shares; Normal, which represents 163,840 shares; High, which represents 327,680 shares; or we can also define a specific value by selecting Custom.

If desired, we can also configure a Limit for both CPU and RAM resources. This allows us to place a cap on the amount of those resources that can be consumed in the resource pool.

Note the term "Expandable Reservation." If this is selected, this resource pool can "borrow" resources from a parent pool. This grants the ability for a business group to deploy more VMs than originally planned to meet business objectives. The resources that are borrowed from the parent are returned when the borrowing VM is powered off.

However, this also means that an administrator for this resource pool can consume resources far beyond that which is intended. Conceivably, the administrator can consume enough resources from the root to cause a contention issue, possibly resulting in ballooning and swapping activity. If you are planning to use an expandable reservation, consider using a limit as well, to ensure that resources are conserved.

When we expand those resources through the deployment of a DRS cluster, the cluster root resource pool becomes the aggregate resource across all cluster nodes, and resource pools will then span physical servers.

As you add a physical host to a DRS cluster, vCenter determines whether the host has a resource pool hierarchy or if the VMs are in the root resource pool. If the VMs are located in the root of the new host, you will be asked whether you want to maintain the resource pools in their current configuration or destroy the resource pools and place the VMs in the root resource pool of the cluster.

If you want to maintain the existing resource pool structure, it will be moved into the root of the cluster resource pool, and the existing resource tree hierarchy will have

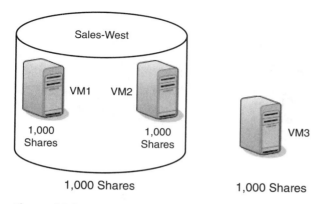

Figure 11.4
Shares between a resource pool and a virtual machine.

the term "Grafted from <FQDN or IP address>," describing the fact that it was copied intact when the ESXi server was added to the cluster.

What happens if a virtual machine competes with a resource pool? In Figure 11.4, we see that a virtual machine (VM3) is in the same root resource pool as a resource pool named Sales-West. The Sales-West resource pool contains two virtual machines (VM1 and VM2), each with 1,000 shares. In this situation, both the virtual machine and the resource pool have an equal number of shares, during a period of contention they are both entitled to 50% of the root resources. Within the Sales-West resource pool, the two VMs will compete for the 50% allocated to the resource pool.

Figure 11.5 shows a different perspective on the competition for resources using shares. In this example, the Sales-West resource pool has a child resource pool named Outside Sales. In the Outside Sales resource pool, there are two virtual machines, VM3 and VM4. VM3 has 5,000 shares and VM4 has 1,000 shares. Note that here, VM5 does not compete with VM3 and VM4 within the resource pool hierarchy; VM5 still directly competes with the resource pool, and the virtual machines in the resource pool will compete with each other for the 50% of the root allocated to the resource pool.

IMPLEMENTATION AND MANAGEMENT

As mentioned earlier, when considering the creation of a new DRS cluster, you need to evaluate the current utilization of the existing hosts, and determine whether additional servers will be required to efficiently host the VMs.

The deployment of shared storage is a critically important factor that must be considered. VMs that are stored on local storage cannot vMotion, and as a result, will

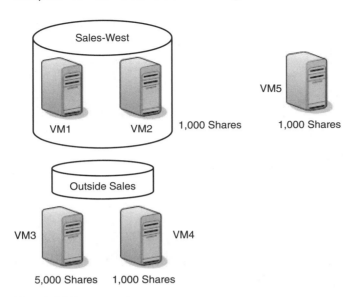

Figure 11.5
Competition between VMs.

impede DRS from maximizing the functionality of the cluster. This is important not only from a load-balancing aspect, but it is also a major factor in a host entering Maintenance Mode successfully.

Also, it is important to verify that each of the VMs is "vMotion compliant," meaning that it meets all the requirements to successfully vMotion. If a VM is designed with these constraints in mind, clustering is a much easier process. If a VM cannot vMotion for any reason, it impedes DRS from fully functioning. In the case of performing an update on an ESXi server, this means that the server will need to be powered down to complete the update, causing an outage to any VMs that it is hosting.

DRS Cluster Basics

DRS utilizes an algorithm that runs within the vCenter instance. Therefore, if vCenter is unavailable for any reason, the algorithm will not run, and DRS loses its functionality. This does not mean that the VMs become inaccessible; it simply means that the algorithm does not run, so there is no evaluation of the host utilization, and VMs remain on their current host.

When the DRS cluster is created, all of the local resources on each physical server are aggregated to provide the root resource pool for the cluster. A component called the DRS scheduler views the aggregate resources as though they were on a single server and uses the local ESXi server to fulfill the local resource requirements of each local virtual machine and resource pool. But can VMs in the same resource pool be on different physical servers?

Yes, because the resource pool spans the DRS cluster, VMs can be on separate physical servers. By default, DRS will copy the resource pool configuration that applies to each virtual machine to the physical ESXi server that is hosting it. This allows each ESXi server to provide the required resources to each VM, regardless of where it is migrated within the cluster. At this point, the local scheduling mechanisms will honor the cluster resource configurations, just as if the VMs had been deployed locally.

Calculations

The processes associated with DRS utilize a series of calculations to determine the status of the cluster hosts. By default, vCenter will evaluate the resource utilization of each host every five minutes, but they can be evaluated at any time by using the Run DRS link from the DRS tab.

Creating

There are two methods to create a DRS cluster. One is by using the vSphere Client to log in to vCenter, and a different method is to use the vSphere CLI. In both cases, the administrator will require the correct permission set to create the cluster.

If you are using vCenter to create and define the new cluster, right-click on the data-center object or folder in your vCenter inventory and select "New Cluster."

As shown in Figure 11.6, the first step in the Cluster Creation wizard is to define the functionality of the new cluster. Note that at this point you can choose DRS, HA, or both. Here, we are going to select DRS.

In Figure 11.7, we can define the level of interaction that we want to have with the cluster. The levels are as follows:

- **Manual.** In this level, the administrator is responsible for manually deploying any new virtual machines to the most appropriate host. The

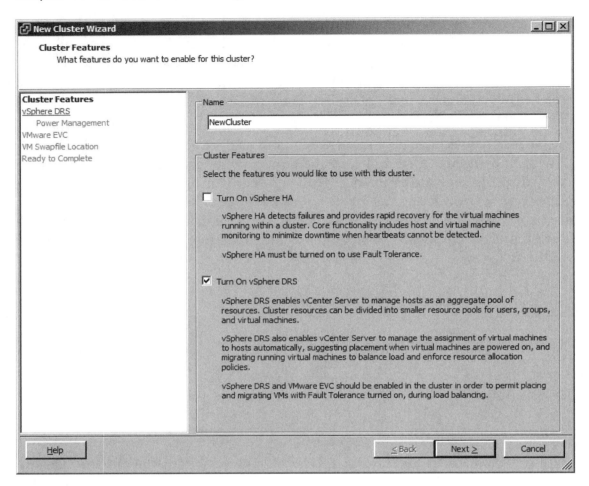

Figure 11.6
Cluster type.

administrator is also responsible for performing the vMotion processes for load balancing.

- **Partially Automated.** In this level, any new VMs that are deployed on this cluster will be automatically placed on the most appropriate host, based on resource utilization. However, vMotion processes are still performed manually.

- **Fully Automated.** In this level of automation, the cluster will automatically place all new VMs on the most appropriate host, and will automatically vMotion VMs based on the result of the DRS algorithm. If you select Fully Automated, you can also set the Migration Threshold for the cluster. The default value is 3.

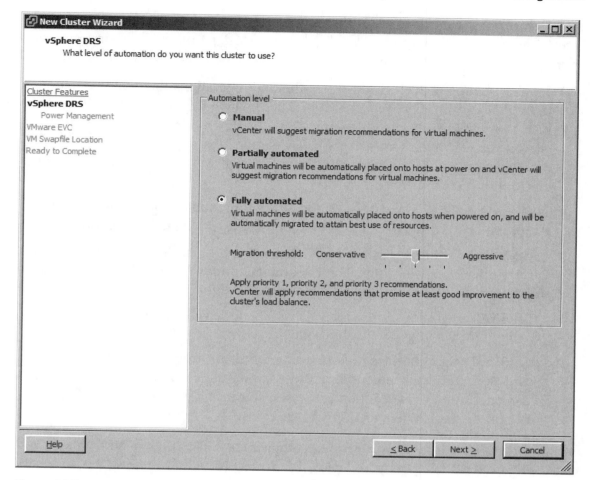

Figure 11.7
Defining the level of automation.

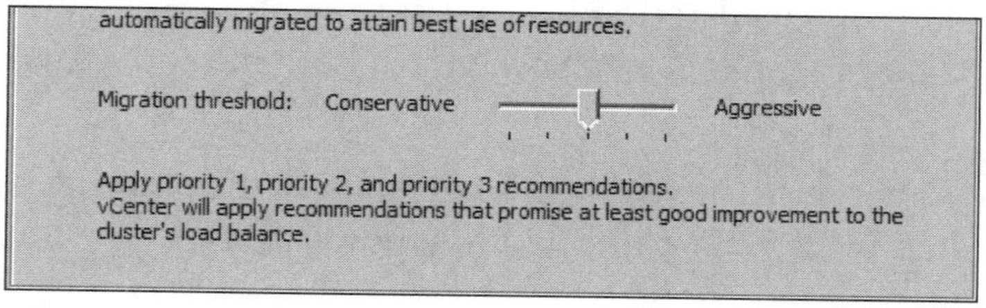

Figure 11.8
Migration levels.

The New Cluster wizard provides the options depicted in Figure 11.8 to define the level of automation that you would like the new cluster to use. There are five levels of migration that can be chosen:

■ **Level 1 (Conservative).** In this level, the only migrations that will occur are those that are considered mandatory. Those include migrations that will enable a host to enter Maintenance Mode or DPM standby mode, migrations that will alleviate an affinity or anti-affinity rule violation, and migrations that result from oversubscription of a physical host. This selection will result in a small amount of vMotion network traffic.

■ **Level 2.** Only Level 1 and Level 2 migrations (only those migrations that indicate the possibility of a significant improvement in cluster balance are performed).

■ **Level 3.** Those migrations listed for Level 1, Level 2, and Level 3 are performed. Level 3 migrations will provide a less dramatic improvement than Level 2 migrations. Level 3 is the default DRS configuration.

■ **Level 4.** All migrations for Level 1, Level 2, and Level 3, and those for level 4 which will result in good equalization.

■ **Level 5.** All migrations are performed for Levels 1 through 4 and those that will provide a slight improvement in cluster load balancing. This selection will result in a greater number of vMotion processes, and thus a higher amount of vMotion traffic on the designated VMKernel network.

As shown in Figure 11.9, if you decide to implement DPM in your DRS cluster, you can configure the settings as you deploy the cluster. Note that these settings are very similar to those used to configure the DRS automation level.

Those options are as follows:

■ **Off.** In this configuration, DPM does not evaluate the hosts for power savings, and will not make any recommendations.

■ **Manual.** In this mode, vCenter will evaluate the host's resource utilization and make recommendations as to hosts that could be suspended, but takes no action on its own.

■ **Automatic.** In this mode, vCenter evaluates each host's resource utilization and can evacuate the VMs and then place a host into the low power state.

As we discussed with DRS, when the cluster is configured for Automatic mode, the level of aggressiveness can also be configured.

As depicted in Figure 11.10, each virtual machine can also be configured with automation settings. Each individual virtual machine can be configured for Fully

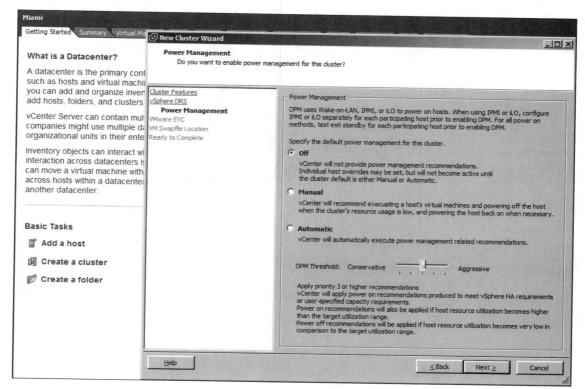

Figure 11.9
DPM settings.

Automated, Partially Automated, Manual, the cluster default, or Disabled. These settings will override the cluster settings for this VM. Choosing the Fully Automated option will cause this particular VM to automatically migrate to the most opportune environment as compared to its peers. In the Partially Automated setting, this VM will generate recommendations when powering on, resuming the VM, and for migration purposes. The VM can also be configured for a disabled state, in which the VM will not be included for migration as part of DRS load balancing considerations, and will always be restarted on the host where it is listed in the local inventory. Any VMs configured for a Disabled state will still be considered by the DRS algorithm when evaluating host resource utilization.

Using the PowerCLI to Manage the DRS Cluster

As we have found in previous chapters, you can use the PowerCLI to manage many of the objects in the vCenter inventory, and to automate frequently used tasks. The DRS cluster has several options for use with PowerCLI.

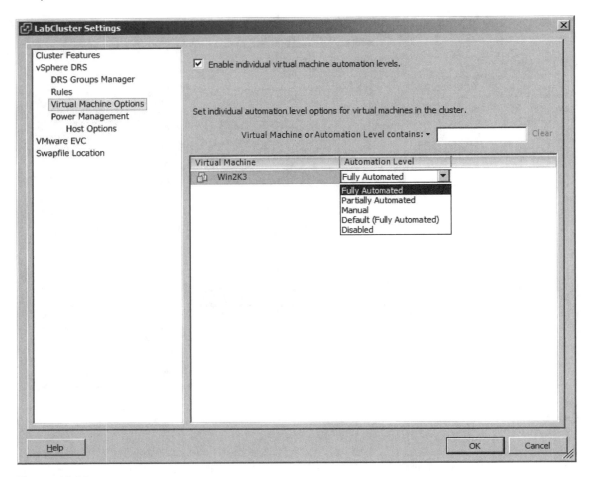

Figure 11.10
Virtual machine automation options.

Figure 11.11
Creating the DRS cluster with PowerCLI.

As shown in Figure 11.11, after you use the VI-Connect Server command to associate with a vCenter instance, you can use the New-Cluster cmdlet to define a new
cluster, enable DRS, and define the automation level.

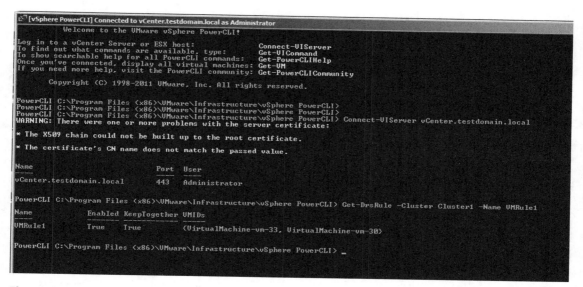

Figure 11.12
Run the DRS algorithm.

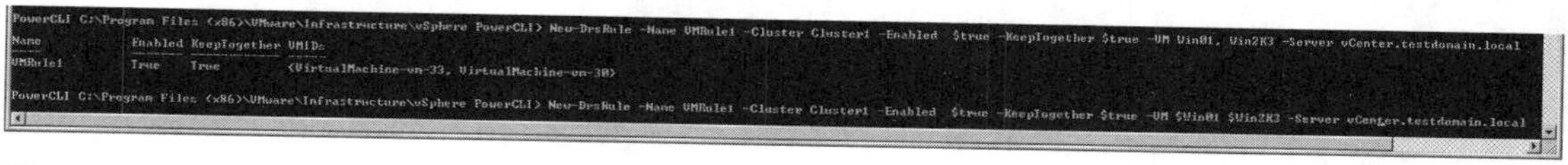

Figure 11.13
Create a New DRS rule with PowerCLI.

Figure 11.14
Obtaining DRS rule parameters.

As shown in Figure 11.12, even though the DRS algorithm runs by default every five minutes, it is possible to manually cause the algorithm to run through PowerCLI by using the Get-DrsRecommendation cmdlet.

As shown in Figure 11.13, you can also define a new affinity rule through the Power-CLI by using the New-DrsRule cmdlet.

As shown in Figure 11.14, you can also use the Get-DrsRule to display the details of a specific DRS rule. Here, we are queried for the properties of VMRule1.

EVC

EVC (Enhanced vMotion Compatibility) clusters allow the administrator to create a cluster in which vMotion processes may succeed even though there may be small differences in CPU features.

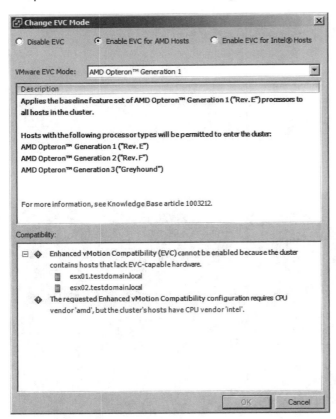

Figure 11.15
The EVC configuration for AMD-family processors.

In Figure 11.15, the AMD Opteron compatibility is listed. Note that the permissible processor levels for this cluster are as follows:

■ AMD Opteron Generation 1 Rev. E

■ AMD Opteron Generation 2 Rev. F

■ AMD Opteron Generation 3 Greyhound

In Figure 11.16, the Intel compatibility is shown. Note that the permissible processor levels for this cluster are as follows:

■ Intel Xeon Core 2 Merom

■ Intel Xeon 45 nm Core 2 Penryn

■ Intel Xeon Core i7 Nehalem

■ Xeon 32 nm Core i7 Westmere

■ Intel Sandy Bridge Generation

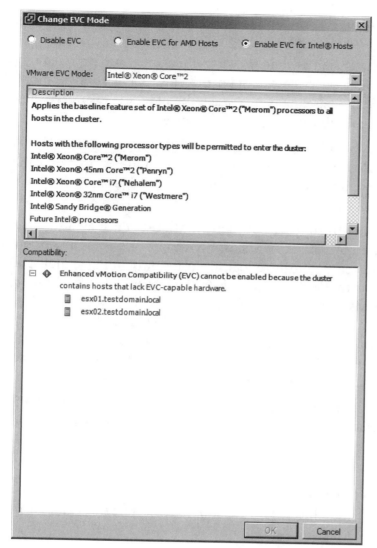

Figure 11.16
The EVC configuration for Intel-family processors.

The VMware optional configuration of EVC relies on functionality provided by AMD (in the form of AMD-V), also known as Live Migration, and Intel (in the form of Intel-VT), also known as Flex Migration. Both of these technologies use hardware extensions to allow the VMM (Virtual Machine Monitor) to hide CPU characteristics from the VM. The VMM also disables CPU features that are not supported by all cluster nodes. This assures that if a VM migrates from one host in the cluster to another, the instruction sets appear to be identical. This also has the effect that some of the features that are available in some of the servers (but not all) may be hidden from the VMs in the cluster; this is the trade-off to ensure vMotion compatibility.

If at some point the EVC mode is changed while the virtual machines are powered on, they will require a power-off/power-on cycle to obtain the latest CPU configuration. This does not apply if the EVC CPU baseline is increased; the old CPU characteristics will still be in use until the VM goes through a power-off/power-on cycle.

After EVC has been configured for a cluster, it may be disabled at any point. However, if any of the VMs on the cluster nodes are in an active or online state, the VMs will continue to function at the same instruction set and CPU configuration as when EVC was enabled.

If you have configured your cluster to support both DRS and HA, you may also have virtual machines that are protected by FT. As we will see in Chapter 12, FT is an option that is available within an HA cluster. FT creates a logical cluster by defining a duplicate VM that is located on another host in the cluster. The delta changes in the memory state are mirrored between the two VMs, and the .vmdk file is also shared between the VMs. The primary VM has read/write access to the .vmdk, while the secondary has read-only access. If an FT VM is hosted within an EVC cluster, DRS can not only produce initial placement recommendations for FT VMs, but can also migrate FT VMs to load balance the cluster. This capability was introduced with the release of vSphere 4.1.

This change is important for two reasons: the ability to migrate FT VMs helps DRS reach a load-balanced state earlier, and physical hosts can enter Maintenance Mode with fewer problems.

Swap File Location

As part of the Cluster Creation wizard, you have the option to define where the swap files for all of the VMs in the cluster will be stored. This screen is shown in Figure 11.17.

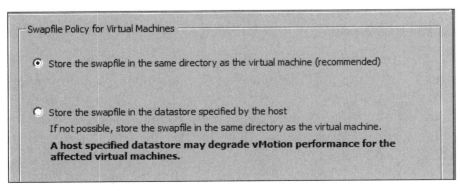

Figure 11.17
Defining the swap file location.

The swap file is created on a per-VM basis when the VM is powered on. Remember, you have no control over this process; this swap file will be created. As a best practice, locate the swap file on a shared datastore to ensure vMotion compatibility.

As discussed in Chapter 10, the size of this file is either:

- The size of the installed RAM if there is no reservation provided
- The result of subtracting the reservation from the limit

Note that if there is no reservation, a VM that has 32GB of installed RAM will have a 32GB swap file. You cannot disable this swap file, but you can determine where this file is located. You can configure the file to be stored:

- In the same folder as the VM
- In the location defined on the ESXi host
- In the location defined in the cluster properties

The final step in the cluster creation process is to review your choices on the Summary page, and then click Finish.

Removing a Node from a Cluster

If you decide to remove a host from the cluster, you will need to put the host in Maintenance Mode first. This means that all VMs that can vMotion are relocated to another host in the cluster. Any VMs that cannot vMotion for any reason will remain on the host, and you need to manually power the VM off and move it to another host.

Note that if there were any resource pools on the host when it was added to the cluster, they will remain with the cluster. Also note that the overall number of resources available to the cluster will be reduced by the amount of physical hardware on the host. This may result in the health of the cluster changing, as there may not be sufficient resources for the VMs that are in the cluster.

Resource Pools

As discussed in Chapter 10, resource pools can be used to divide CPU and RAM resources into smaller containers and then used to restrict the resource access of VMs that are placed in them. Resource pools can be created for myriad reasons:

- **Delegate authority.** This allows a department manager or workgroup leader to name someone in their department or workgroup to be responsible for managing the virtual machines and resources in their resource pool. This allows someone who is more familiar with the environment and the applications to manage those resources directly.

- **Chargeback.** This is the concept that departments and business divisions are charged a monthly fee to host their virtual machines. In essence, as long as the check doesn't bounce, their virtual environment will be accessible. This allows the IT department to recoup the money that was initially spent to deploy the environment.

- **To mirror a company's organizational chart.** For example, all of the Accounting group's virtual servers and desktops can be in the same logical container within the vCenter inventory.

This capacity is available in both stand-alone and clustered hosts.

Child Pools and Expandable Reservations

Remember that resource pools can be further sub-divided in to child resource pools to enhance delegated authority, mimic corporate structural design within the VM environment, guarantee resources to mission critical VMs, and so on. Keep in mind that if you choose to use a resource pool, you must fundamentally understand the real resource requirements of the virtual machines in order to provide sufficient resources to ensure acceptable client experiences.

You can also use a concept called an expandable reservation within a resource pool. This means that if you start enough VMs within a resource to consume all the local resources, attempts to start more VMs will require more resources than is contained in the resource pool. Normally, this will result in an "Insufficient Resources" message. The expandable reservation will allow the child resource pool to ask the parent pool if it can "temporarily borrow" additional resources. If so, additional VMs can then be started. If not, the child pool can ask the next level parent for those resources. This will continue until the pool obtains the requested resources or it exhausts the possibilities and the power-on process fails.

DRS

As stated earlier, when a DRS cluster is created, each of the cluster nodes' local resources then become a part of the cluster resource pool. Similarly, if a new host is added to a DRS cluster, the resources of that host are added to the cluster root resource pool. This means that resource pools can span physical hosts, but virtual machines will always run on one physical host at any given time.

Remember that DRS performs several processes, and we need to discuss these concepts in more detail. The first is the initial placement of new virtual machines within the cluster, and this also includes powering up or resuming a VM as well. This process is called Admission Control. DRS evaluates the reservations for the VM, and also the cluster resources available. This simply means that each VM has reservations; those that are configured by the administrator, and the overhead necessary to manage that VM and its virtual hardware. Even if no reservations are configured for the VM, there is still reservation in the form of the VMKernel overhead. This overhead represents the resources required by the VMkernel to manage the VM and its virtual hardware, and it is specifically used by the VMKernel to store the frame buffer for the VM and the VMKernel data structures. DRS looks at a worst-case scenario and assumes that the VM is 100% utilized. By taking this approach, DRS can bypass the requirement to understand the past workload for this VM. DRS then makes recommendations as to which physical server will be able to host that particular VM, based on current resource utilization.

If the cluster is configured for Manual automation level, when a VM is powered on or resumed, DRS evaluates the requirements for that VM and makes recommendations as to the most appropriate host for that VM. The administrator can accept those recommendations, and DRS will start the VM on that host, or he can manually start the VM on any cluster host that he chooses.

If the cluster is configured for Partially Automated or Automatic, DRS will start the VM on the most appropriate host on its own, without administrator invention.

Memory Overcommitment

VMware has utilized the concept of overcommitting physical memory to provide significant savings over the same application and operating system installation in a physical server. In a physical server, there are many instances in which memory is underutilized, resulting in wasted resources. VMware leverages this concept in several ways to maximize the use of physical RAM.

The first method of memory overcommitment is through Transparent Page Sharing. In many operating systems, the basic services and processes are loaded in every physical server and will typically occupy the same amount of RAM in each installation. If we virtualize these physical servers, why would we make multiple copies of identical RAM content? That seems like a tremendous waste of resources. VMware remedies this by making one copy of common RAM content and giving each VM a read-only pointer to that memory location. This maintains the perception on the part of the VM that it has complete control over its resources and that it has a contiguous memory space—both concepts are true in a physical installation.

How does the hypervisor know that the memory content is truly identical? When the hypervisor writes a memory page, it also calculates a CRC value that is written to the bottom of the page. The hypervisor compares memory pages, and if they look similar, it will compare the CRC values to be sure.

If one of the virtual machines that is sharing this common memory page sends a write request to that page, the hypervisor will make a copy of the memory page and give that VM a read/write pointer to that page, maintaining the illusion.

Note that this is an ongoing process, not only occurring when VMs are deployed, but constantly occurring in the background, looking for physical RAM pages that can be consolidated.

Transparent page sharing can be customized by navigating to the Configuration tab for your ESXi server and selecting Advanced Options. Under the Mem category, the following options are available:

- **Mem.ShareScanTime.** This setting configures the time between memory scans
- **Mem.ShareScanRate.** This setting configures the rate at which the memory is scanned for duplicate content
- **Sched.Mem.pshare.enable.** Enables and disables transparent page sharing

The second method of memory overcommitment is the concept of ballooning. Remember, we configure shares on a per-VM basis to indicate a priority for memory access if free resources begin to decrease. When we configure a value for RAM shares, the local memory scheduler will run every 15 seconds to determine the true resources in use by the VM. This polling information is made accessible to DRS and will be used to schedule the memory resources throughout the cluster. Remember, shares do not come into play unless the ESXi server begins to run out of free memory resources.

If the local server detects contention based on the amount of free RAM on that server, the memory scheduler can activate a component called the vmmemctl driver, also known as the balloon driver. The balloon driver is installed as a part of the VMware Tools installation, so it is a good idea to always install VMware Tools in every virtual machine on which it is supported by the operating system.

Each ESXi host regularly gauges the status of the memory subsystem by calculating the amount of free memory. If the amount of free memory is above 6%, the ESXi server does nothing as this is considered the "High" state—the amount of memory in use by virtual machines is less than the ESX installed RAM. If the amount of free memory drops to 36% of the High state, the ESXi server will attempt to reclaim free space by using the balloon driver.

In each VM that has VMware Tools installed, the balloon driver will request RAM from the installed operating system. For example, if the balloon requests five pages from the OS, the OS will respond by allocating five pages of RAM from its free memory pool. The balloon driver will then "pin" these pages, meaning that it indicates to the OS that these pages cannot be paged out to disk at any time. The balloon driver then relays the page numbers to the hypervisor, allowing it to reuse the physical pages that correspond to the pinned pages. This allows the OS to choose which pages are given to the balloon driver. This way the ESXi server can reclaim unused memory from each VM without negatively impacting performance of the VM. If, however, the VM requests to use the reclaimed pages, the hypervisor will allocate new physical pages and provide them to the VM. If the desired memory was reclaimed, and the contention issue has dissipated, the hypervisor can "deflate" the balloon driver, releasing the pages back to the VM.

In order to determine which VM to reclaim memory from, the hypervisor evaluates each VM and divides the shares for the VM by the page allocation for the VM and derives a metric called Shares per Page. Ultimately, the RAM will be gathered from the VM with the lowest share per page value.

If a VM is using its full limit of RAM, the balloon driver can remove 65% of the limit or down to the reservation, if one exists. If and when the ESXi free memory reaches the "Soft" threshold, or 64% of the High value, the hypervisor will opt to use either memory compression or swapping to relieve the memory contention.

Memory compression was introduced with vSphere 4.1 as an alternative to the performance impact of swapping. At this point, ballooning was not sufficient to free enough RAM to reduce the memory pressure. Now the hypervisor will be more aggressive in its efforts to reclaim memory. The hypervisor will begin to swap RAM from the VM that is active within the VM. Because this will present a negative performance impact on the VM, the hypervisor will examine the data that is being swapped to see if it can be compressed instead. If the hypervisor determines that there will be at least a 50% reduction in space, the data will be compressed within memory and stored in a memory compression cache.

For example, if possible, the hypervisor will take two 4KB pages of data, compress them to 2KB each, and store them in a single 4KB page. The logic here is that it is much more efficient to compress the data within memory than to write the data to a swap file, and then possibly have to swap it back in again.

By default, memory compression is enabled, but if desired, it can be changed by highlighting the ESXi server in vCenter, or by directly connecting to the ESXi server with the vSphere Client.

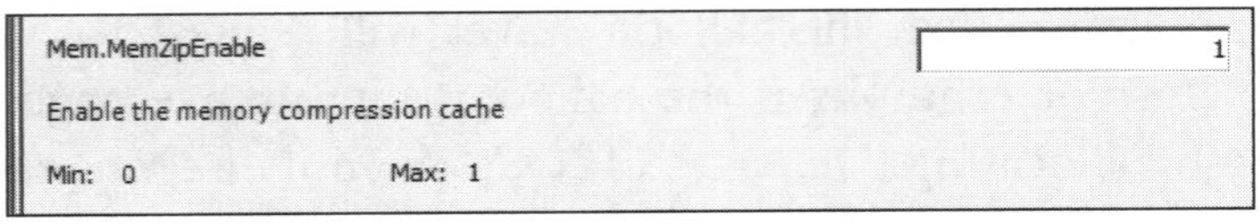

Figure 11.18
Enable the memory compression cache.

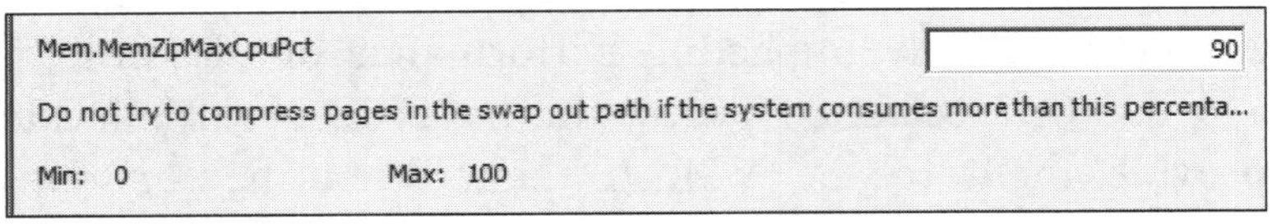

Figure 11.19
Configure the maximum compression cache.

As shown in Figure 11.18, navigate to the Configuration tab, and select Advanced Settings. In the Mem category, select the Mem.MemZipEnable entry. A "1" in this field will enable the memory compression cache, while a "0" will disable the feature. We can also change the default size of the memory compression cache.

As Figure 11.19 shows, this value is a percentage of the VM's memory size—10% by default. In the Advanced Settings of the ESXi server, the entry is the Mem.MemZipMaxPct option. It will define the maximum compression cache as a percentage of the virtual machine's configured memory size.

If compressing the data will not result in sufficient savings, the data will be swapped out to disk. This will present a significant impact to the performance of the virtual machine. In this scenario, the hypervisor will randomly choose the memory pages from the virtual machine that will swapped out to disk. This is where the VM's swap file comes in. Note that this memory content could come from an application, system file, data file, and so on and may need to be swapped back in to respond to a user request. This swap-out and swap-back-in present a significant impact to the performance of the VM.

With the release of vSphere 5, VMware has provided a way to minimize the impact of swapping to the VM. Of course, the best way to minimize this impact is to verify that you have enough physical RAM to satisfy the memory requirements of your environment. However, in the real world, due to factors such as scope creep, this is not always possible. If we must swap to disk, we can now configure and use Solid State Drives (SSD) drives as the swapping destination. This will drastically improve the cost to the VM in case hypervisor swapping is mandated.

Solid-state drives offer several dramatic advantages over rotational media:

- Solid-state devices read and write data to memory components, rather than rotating platters. This provides a huge performance advantage because solid-state drives offer access times in the range of 100 nanoseconds, while standard rotating drives offer access times in the range of 3 to 5 milliseconds.

- Solid-state devices require less power and therefore operate quieter while consuming less power.

- Solid-state devices do not have rotating components, and are more resilient to impact because there are no read/write heads that can bounce against media.

If the swapped-out data is required in the virtual machine, the data is retrieved from the solid-state device, and the swap space is then deleted from the cache to save space.

The SSD cache can be easily configured. Keep in mind that there must be at least one SSD datastore within the ESXi environment. To configure this option, highlight the ESXi host, and navigate to the Configuration tab.

1. In the Software section, click on the Host Cache Configuration link, select the SSD datastore that you wish to use, and click on Properties.

2. Select the size of the cache that you want to provide for host swapping purposes. Note, to disable this function, uncheck the Allocate Space for Host Cache option.

Modes of Operation

As discussed earlier, there are three different modes available: Manual, Partially Automated, and Fully Automated. In both Manual and Partially Automated modes, DRS will only make recommendations as to where the virtual machines should be moved; it is up to the Administrator to decide whether to accept those options or decline and manually make changes.

Affinity Rules (Host and VM)

When configuring the DRS cluster, you have the option of creating rules that will describe the placement and relationship of virtual machines and physical servers within the cluster. Virtual machines can be associated with an affinity rule that mandates that the virtual machines will always be on the same physical server. This allows us to take advantage of using internal server RAM to transfer data between the virtual machines as opposed to using physical networking devices to transfer the data.

The relationship between virtual machines and ESXi hosts can be defined and controlled through the use of an affinity rule that can be applied between virtual machines or between virtual machines and physical hosts.

An affinity rule that applies only to virtual machines mandates that within the cluster, a set of virtual machines will always be on the same physical server. This is usually configured to take advantage of the increased bandwidth available if VMs communicate within the same standard switch. Just to give you an idea of this advantage, tests have indicated that inter-vm network bandwidth can exceed 20GB/s because the traffic passes between memory cells, not through a physical network infrastructure, which can create collisions and retransmits.

This type of rule also has the benefit of grouping similar virtual machines on the same physical host to maximize savings on memory by leveraging transparent page sharing.

An anti-affinity rule mandates that any virtual machines that are related through an anti-affinity rule can never be on the same ESXi server. The only situation in which multiple virtual machines included in an anti-affinity rule will be on the same physical server is when all VMs are in a powered-off state. The moment that one of the VMs is powered on, it will be migrated, if possible, to another cluster node.

An anti-affinity rule is typically used to separate virtual nodes such as Microsoft DCs, front-end web servers, cluster nodes, and so on. With each of these options we are more interested in application or server availability than possible performance gains.

If a company employs multiple virtual administrators, it is possible that affinity rules that conflict with each other may be defined. If this is the situation, only one rule can be enabled. In this case, the first rule defined will be enabled, and the second will be disabled; DRS will ignore any disabled rules when evaluating the cluster environment. At this point, you should simply remove the conflicting rule.

As shown in Figure 11.20, to create a new Affinity rule, follow these steps:

1. Right-click on the Cluster and select Edit Settings.

2. Select the Rules link and then use the Add button to create a new rule.

3. Enter a name that defines the new rule in the Rule dialog box.

4. Using the Type drop-down box, select the type of rule that you are creating. This can be Keep Virtual Machines Together (VM-to-VM affinity), separate Virtual Machines (VM anti-affinity), or Virtual Machines to Hosts.

5. Click on the Add button to specify which virtual machines and/or ESXi hosts will be associated with this new rule.

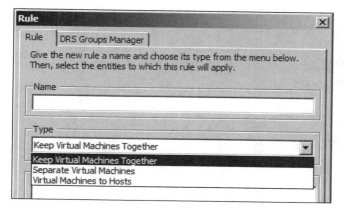

Figure 11.20
Creating VM-to-VM affinity rules.

You also have the option to define a VM-to-Host affinity rule. A Host-to-virtual machine rule defines the relationships between ESXi servers and virtual machines within the cluster. This type of rule can take several forms:

- A preferential rule is one in which one or more virtual machines should run on one or more ESXi servers, but will be allowed to run on other servers if the listed hosts are unavailable.

- A mandatory rule is one in which one or more virtual machines are required to run one or more ESXi servers exclusively. This option can result in VM unavailability if the physical servers included in the rule are experiencing hardware or connectivity issues.

In Figure 11.21, from the Edit Settings menu, select the Rules option. Click on the DRS Groups Manager tab. You have the option to list the virtual machines that will be associated with this rule, and the ESXi hosts that will host the virtual machines.

There are two types of groups that are defined in a VM-to-Host affinity configuration. The membership of a virtual machine DRS group will be those virtual machines whose ESXi host relationships are defined in the rule. A host DRS group defines the ESXi servers that are included in the rule. It is helpful to remember here that if a VM or a host is removed from the cluster, it is also removed from the appropriate group. If the VM or host is then re-added to the cluster, it is not automatically re-added to the respective groups.

There are also four types of rules that can be defined:

1. A Should Run on rule details that the VMs listed in the rule should run on the specified host, but may run on others if necessary.

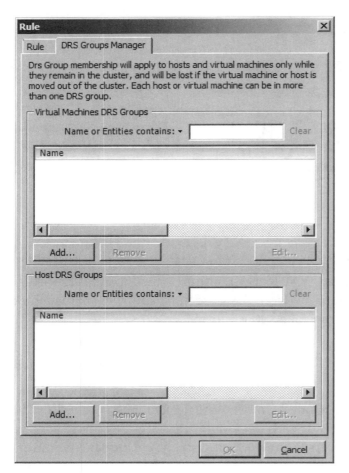

Figure 11.21
Creating a VM-to-Host affinity rule.

2. A Must Run on rule mandates that the VMs listed in the rule can only be hosted on the indicated hosts, regardless of the situation.

3. A Should Not Run on rule specifies that the listed VMs should not be hosted on the listed ESXi servers, but may if necessary.

4. A Must Not Run on rule mandates that the listed VMs cannot be hosted on the listed ESXi server, regardless of the situation.

If preferential rules are created, HA may violate the defined rules when restarting VMs due to a physical host failure. DRS will the make recommendations or migrate the VMs after the next execution of the DRS algorithm, to comply with the administrator defined rules.

However, if mandatory rules are defined, HA will honor these requirements when restarting VMs. In this situation, HA will leverage DRS to migrate virtual machines within the cluster so it can comply with the administrator-defined rules.

If a mandatory rule is defined by an administrator, that rule will remain in effect, even if DRS is disabled for the cluster. Any attempts to migrate a VM that would violate a mandatory rule will result in an error displayed in vCenter. The mandatory rule must be manually removed prior to disabling the DRS component of the cluster.

Keep in mind when considering a mandatory rule that it can directly impact the DRS cluster and its efforts to load balance the cluster.

As shown in Figure 11.22, clicking on the Add button for the Virtual Machines DRS Groups section allows you to specify which VMs will be associated with this rule. Highlight the desired virtual machines in the left pane, and click on the right arrow icon to add the VMs. Similarly, clicking on the Add button for the host DRS groups section allows you to specify which hosts are to be included in the rule.

After the virtual machines and the ESXi servers have been defined, you must select the rule that will associate with these objects.

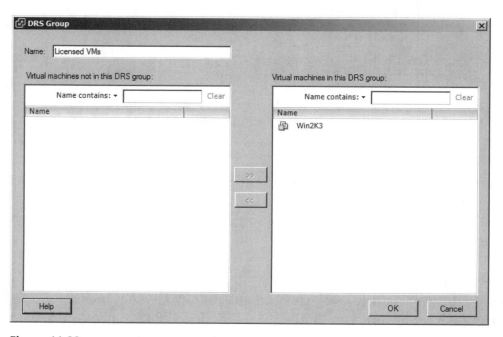

Figure 11.22
The adding VMs to DRS groups page.

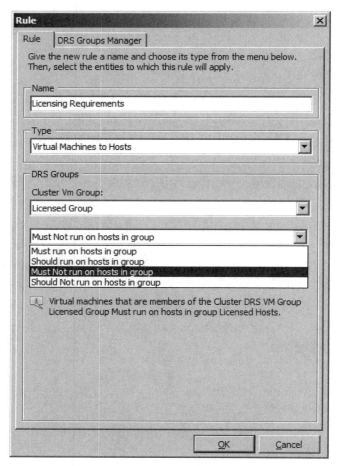

Figure 11.23
Specifying the rule.

As shown in Figure 11.23, insert a name for the rule that describes why the rule was created. In the Type section, this should be Virtual Machines to Hosts. When you click in the DRS Groups section, select the correct VM group from the drop-down menu, and then select the type of rule that is being defined.

DRS Interaction with FT Virtual Machines
Since the release of vSphere 4.1, DRS has been able to include fault-tolerant virtual machines when calculating cluster utilization; this includes all DRS functionality, load balancing, and initial placement. This calculation includes the requirement that the two VMs will always be on two separate physical servers.

DRS Info on the Summary Tab of the Cluster

In a virtualized environment, much like a physical server deployment, it is important to be proactive in your management of the hosts and devices. To this end, you can highlight the DRS cluster in the vCenter inventory, and by selecting the Summary tab, you are presented with an overview of the status of the DRS cluster.

As shown in Figure 11.24, the General pane displays the configuration of the cluster. For example, in Figure 11.24, DRS is enabled for the cluster, while HA is not enabled. Note that either DRS or HA can be enabled individually for the cluster, or can be configured at the same to maximize the functionality of the cluster. This particular cluster does not have EVC enabled as all of the physical hosts have CPUs from the same vendor.

Remember that when a cluster is created, the root resource pools for each of the physical servers are combined into a large, aggregate cluster resource pool. In this cluster, there are 7GHz of CPU resources, 4GB of RAM resources, with 2 physical ESXi servers, with a total of 4 CPUs.

There are also 2 datastores, and 2 virtual machines located in this cluster.

For further insight into the DRS cluster, the vSphere DRS provides additional information. In Figure 11.25, we can see that the migration level of the cluster is Fully Automated, and that DPM is currently disabled. There are currently no DRS recommendations and no DRS faults have been encountered. It is vitally important that you investigate any faults that are identified. These can be related to VMs that are not vMotion capable or hardware issues.

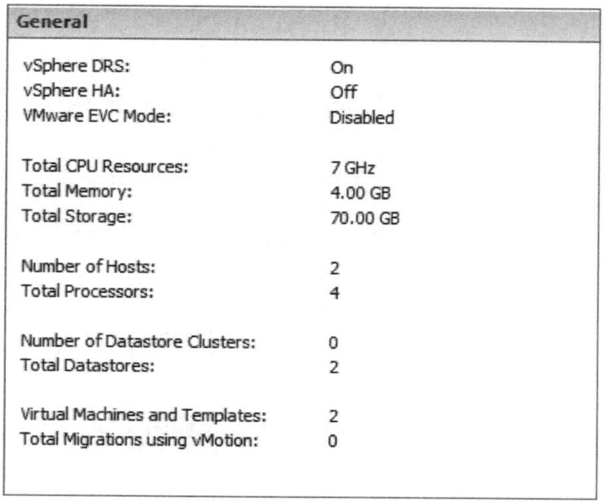

General	
vSphere DRS:	On
vSphere HA:	Off
VMware EVC Mode:	Disabled
Total CPU Resources:	7 GHz
Total Memory:	4.00 GB
Total Storage:	70.00 GB
Number of Hosts:	2
Total Processors:	4
Number of Datastore Clusters:	0
Total Datastores:	2
Virtual Machines and Templates:	2
Total Migrations using vMotion:	0

Figure 11.24
The DRS General information pane.

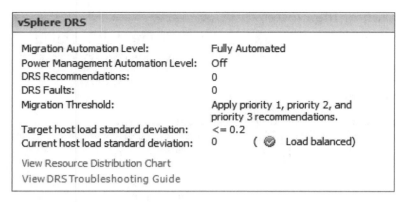

Figure 11.25
The vSphere DRS pane.

The current migration threshold is listed, and the target host load standard deviation is less than .2%. The host load standard deviation metric is calculated by adding the resource requirements of all virtual machines on a single host and dividing this by the resource capacity of that ESXi host.

This computation is performed on all cluster nodes and this becomes the average deviation for the cluster. The standard deviation is the variation in the calculated values across all cluster nodes.

Maintenance Mode

Placing a physical host into Maintenance Mode sets a flag on the host that tells vCenter that no VMs can be started on that host, nor can any VMs migrate to the host. In fact, the VMs that are currently in the host's inventory will be migrated to other hosts in the cluster. If this is not possible, Maintenance Mode will be suspended until an administrator powers off any VMs that cannot be migrated. As mentioned earlier, it is critically important that all VMs within a DRS cluster be compliant with each of the vMotion prerequisites.

There are several possible reasons you would place an ESXi host into Maintenance Mode:

- The possibility exists that a hardware component has failed and requires immediate replacement.

- The host could require a hardware upgrade, for example, to install an additional HBA to accommodate an increase in VM workload.

- That particular server may be scheduled for retirement, and will be replaced by a new server.

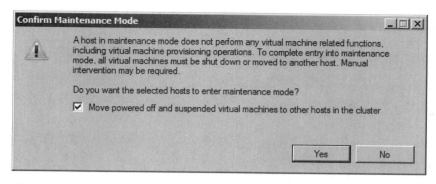

Figure 11.26
Entering Maintenance Mode.

- Remove a host from a DRS cluster.

- Update Manager leverages Maintenance Mode to update and patch ESXi servers. To be able to do this transparently to the end users, and remove the necessity for planned outages, Maintenance Mode is required.

While this is a necessary activity, remember that placing a host into Maintenance Mode reduces the CPU and RAM resources available to the cluster and may result in resource contention.

To place a host into Maintenance Mode, right-click on the ESXi server in Hosts and Clusters view and select Enter Maintenance Mode.

As shown in Figure 11.26, if the specified ESXi host is placed into Maintenance Mode, all VMs will be evacuated to other hosts in the cluster, if they can be migrated. If they cannot, an administrator must intervene to allow Maintenance Mode to continue.

For the host to exit Maintenance Mode, right-click on the ESXi server and select Exit Maintenance Mode. When the host exits Maintenance Mode, its resources are once again added to the cluster resource pool, and DRS will load-balance the cluster.

The Resource graph can provide a wealth of cluster-related information.

As Figure 11.27 shows, you can click on the View Resource Distribution Chart link to display the current resource utilization across each of the cluster nodes. For example, you can select to view the CPU or RAM utilization on the basis of resource percentage of use, or you can view the results in MHz (for CPU) or in MB (for RAM). Note that the display shows the metrics in a color-graded scale that starts with green if the cluster is currently providing all resources requested by the VMs, to red if the cluster is having trouble meeting VM requirements.

On the Resource Allocation tab, as depicted in Figure 11.28, the top pane will display the current CPU and RAM characteristics of the cluster, while the bottom of the

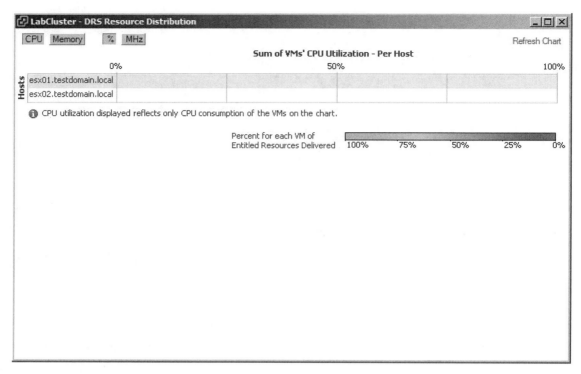

Figure 11.27
The resource distribution chart.

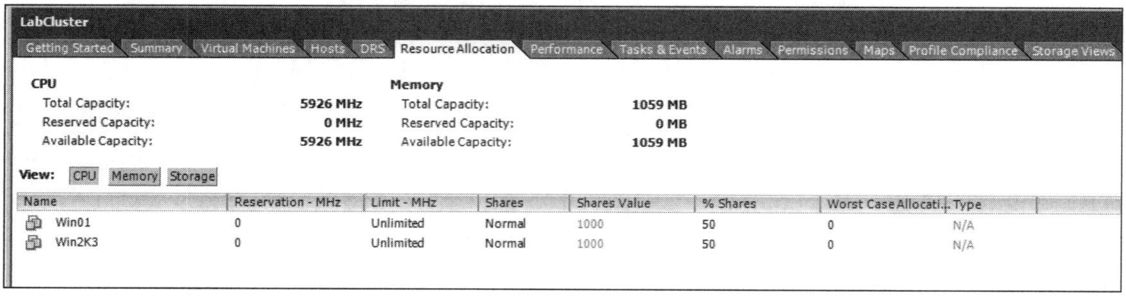

Figure 11.28
The Resource Allocation tab.

pane allows you to view the resource utilization of each of the virtual machines in the cluster, based on CPU, RAM, or storage resources.

With the release of vSphere 5, VMware improves on the concept of Maintenance Mode with the introduction of Cluster Maintenance Mode. Cluster Maintenance Mode is a feature that allows DRS to consider placing multiple cluster hosts in Maintenance Mode simultaneously. This means that Update Manager can perform remedial operations in a much more timely fashion, updating multiple ESXi servers within the same cluster simultaneously. This means that mandatory remediations will

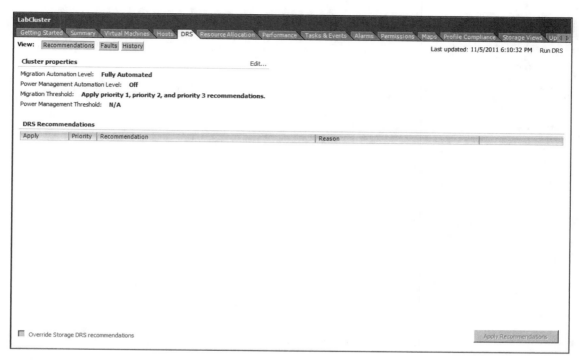

Figure 11.29
The DRS tab.

consume less time, and possibly affect the production environment to a lesser degree. Keep in mind that affinity and anti-affinity rules are still followed during this process. If enabled for the cluster, FT, DPM, and HA configurations will also be honored.

DRS Tab

The DRS tab is shown in Figure 11.29. In the upper-right corner, we can click on the Run DRS link to cause vCenter to run the load balance algorithm at any time. This can be as a result of deploying new VMs in the cluster, powering on one or more VMs, or as a result of changing the active workload in one or more virtual machines.

As stated earlier, this timeframe can be modified by adding the following entry to the vpxd.cfg (vCenter configuration) file:

```
<pollperiodsec>
300
</pollperiodsec>
```

Note that 300 is the default time interval of 300 seconds (5 minutes). The DRS algorithm will also be executed if a new host is added to the cluster or if a cluster node has been placed in Maintenance Mode. If this value is decreased (making the algorithm execute more frequently) there will be an increased overhead for the vCenter

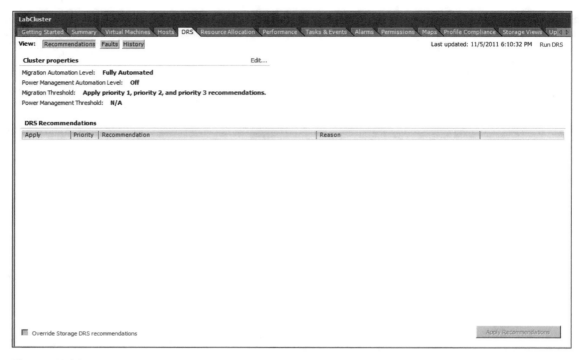

Figure 11.30
The Recommendations pane.

server, while increasing this value will cause the algorithm to execute at longer time intervals, decreasing the vCenter overhead.

Recommendations   As shown in Figure 11.30, at the top of the DRS tab there are three buttons that will display different perspectives on the DRS cluster. Selecting the Recommendations button allows the current cluster configuration to be viewed below the Cluster Properties heading, and the configuration can be edited by using the Edit link. Any current migration recommendations will be listed under the DRS Recommendations heading. If you select the Apply Recommendations button, all of the migrations listed will be performed.

Faults   If you click on the Faults button, as depicted in Figure 11.31, vCenter will display any faults that have occurred during the application of migration recommendations. These errors will be listed detailing the timestamp of the event, the error encountered, and the target of the migration.

By highlighting the fault events identified by vCenter that are listed in the upper pane, the problem and the recommendation that was affected are detailed.

History   As shown in Figure 11.32, if you click on the History button, the migration history of the cluster will be listed, including the event and the timestamp.

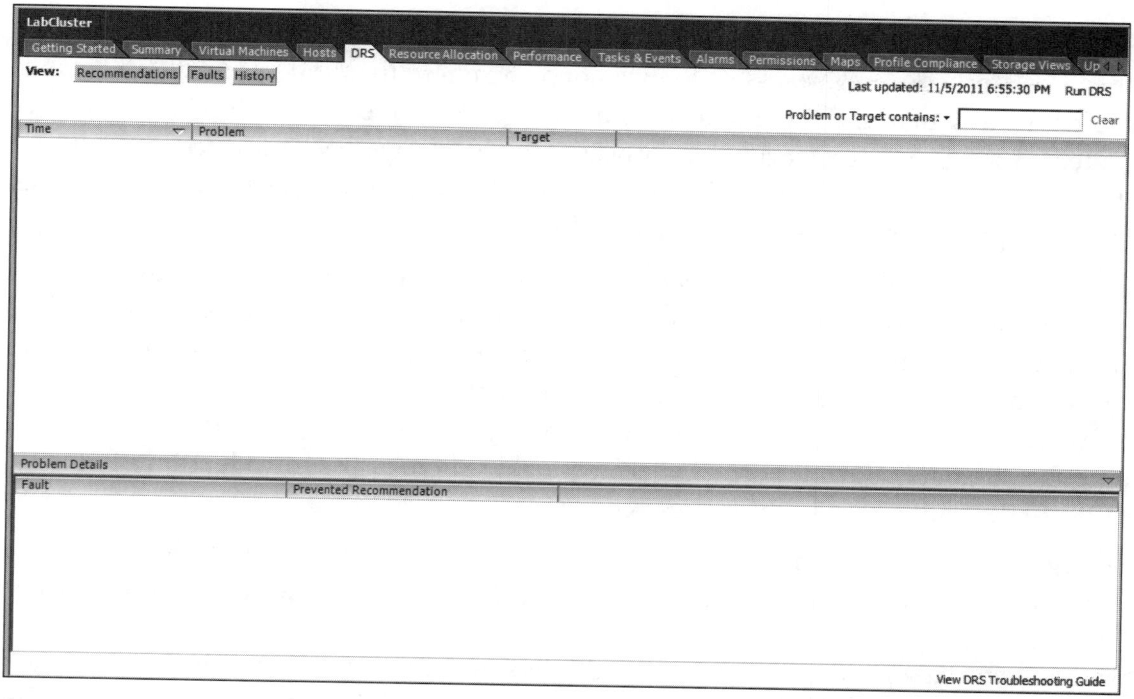

Figure 11.31
The Faults pane.

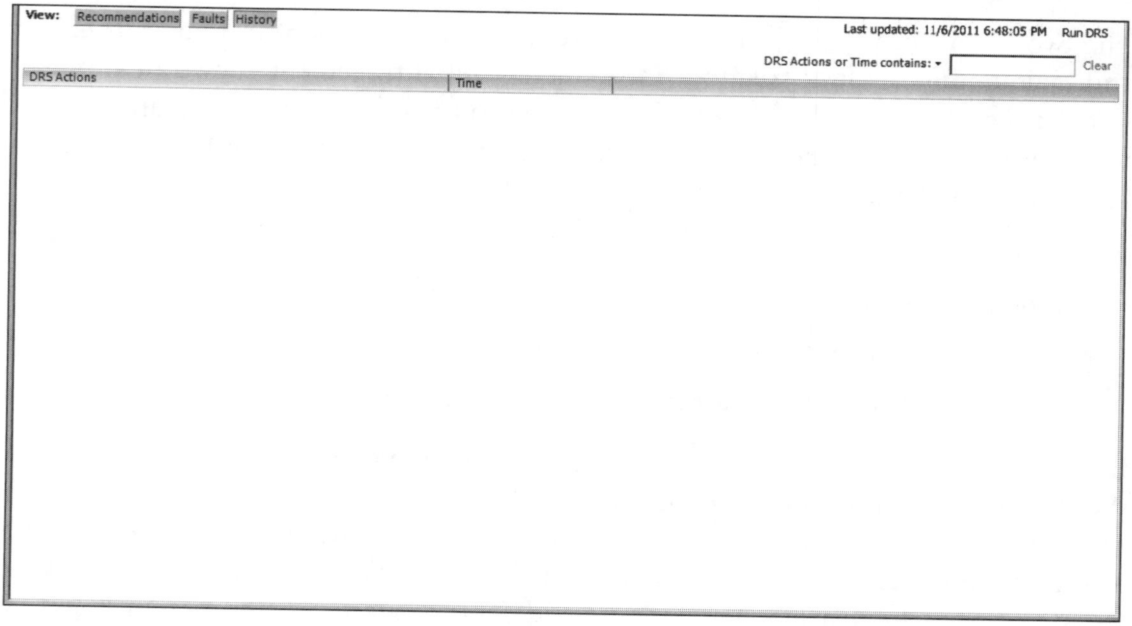

Figure 11.32
The History pane.

Storage DRS

It is a best practice, regardless of the version of vSphere that you are using, to balance the datastores that are presented to individual ESXi servers and those that are presented to a vCenter instance. This process should always be performed while using the storage vendor's performance analysis utility; you must view the performance from the perspective of both the SAN and vCenter.

To this end, virtual administrators and SAN administrators are tasked with the prospect of maintaining storage performance and maximizing storage capacity flexibility. In many cases, this can become an overwhelming task. If the storage is planned well, the performance may be satisfactory, but the datastores run out of available space unexpectedly. Or, there may be plenty of free space, but the VMs experience a high amount of latency during normal processes. In vSphere 5, the introduction of Storage DRS (SDRS) addresses both of these concerns.

Storage DRS allows administrators to group datastores with similar characteristics, such as RAID level, type of disk, number of disks, and so on into a datastore cluster. These datastores can be physically on the same SAN or located on different SANs, if we desire to balance the load across multiple storage systems. Note that these datastore clusters can be expanded on the fly by simply adding more datastores to the cluster, or we can also remove a datastore from the cluster, without causing an outage or a maintenance window.

The two main functions of Storage DRS are the initial placement of virtual machines and maintaining the load balance of the cluster. Initial placement allows an administrator to pre-provide datastores with the appropriate performance characteristics prior to initiating the virtual machine process. An administrator can specify a datastore cluster as the destination for any of the following events:

- When a new virtual machine is created
- When a new disk is added to an existing virtual machine
- When a virtual machine is resumed from a suspended state
- When a VM will be the target of a Storage vMotion

In each situation, vCenter then evaluates each of the member datastores to determine the best target. This evaluation includes both space considerations and free I/O capacity. This can be a tremendous advantage for administrators who may not have a working knowledge of how each datastore is configured. There are enterprises that allow an SAN administrator to configure and deploy datastores, and present them to each ESXi host. The datastore is then labeled with a description of the anticipated workload, and then is added to a cluster so the administrator simply chooses the datastore cluster with the desired I/O characteristics.

Similar to DRS, initial placement is utilized to make the decisions surrounding the location of a new virtual machine a much less daunting task. The initial placement evaluation will execute when a new virtual machine is created, a new VMDK is added to an existing virtual machine, a Storage vMotion process migrates a virtual machine into the cluster, or when a VM is cloned and the datastore cluster is selected as the storage destination.

The administrator simply selects a datastore cluster as the storage destination, allowing vCenter to evaluate the individual datastores, and places the new VMDKs on the most appropriate datastore. During this decision-making process, vCenter looks at both I/O utilization and free space as determining factors. This allows vCenter to choose the datastore that not only has sufficient free space, but also can efficiently handle the additional I/O workload. This allows the administrator to be sure that the virtual machine changes will not adversely affect the running environment. If this initial placement occurs within a DRS cluster, the initial placement will examine the datastores that are connected to all ESXi hosts in a DRS cluster first; the SDRS will evaluate the datastores that are connected to a subset of the cluster nodes.

Load balancing takes over where initial placement leaves off. Load balancing monitors the latency and space utilization within the datastore cluster. In many situations, administrators make a "best guess" or simply do not consider the effect of a new virtual machine on the virtual machines that are already located on that datastore. It is interesting that evaluating the workload of the new virtual machine, and the current performance and free space of the destination datastore are "too much trouble," yet if the performance is not as expected, it is "the storage guy's fault." SDRS addresses these situations by providing an analysis of the existing datastores in the cluster and either placing the new VM on the most appropriate datastore or by displaying a series of recommendations as to the best placement. Additionally, the load balancing aspect of the datastore cluster verifies that the datastore I/O latency and space capacity are within user-defined thresholds. If the cluster exceeds these thresholds, SDRS looks at the cluster configuration, and if the cluster is set for Fully Automated, SDRS migrates virtual machines to alleviate the situation. If the cluster is configured for Manual mode, SDRS makes recommendations to remedy the imbalance.

The administrator can decide that he or she will make space and load balancing decisions for a specific virtual machine. This can be accomplished by selecting the "Disable Storage DRS for this virtual machine" option. This also means that the administrator will be responsible for manually migrating this virtual machine.

If the SDRS algorithm detects that a datastore has exceeded its user-defined threshold, SDRS must verify that a Storage vMotion that relieves pressure on one datastore does not apply pressure on another datastore that is also nearing capacity. In this case, SDRS utilizes a setting called the "space utilization ratio difference" threshold that specifies the minimum difference in free space between the source and the intended destination. This value is 5% by default, and can be modified in the Advanced Options for the datastore cluster.

Affinity Rules

Storage SDRS also provides affinity and anti-affinity rules that dictate which virtual machine disks should never be on the same datastore, and anti-affinity rules specify which VMDKs are never allowed to be on the same datastore. These rules should be configured with an understanding of the workloads and perhaps the workload schedules of the virtual machines involved, or they may reflect an organization's standard best practices for the applications. In its default setting, each virtual machine's disks are kept on the same datastore.

Within the datastore cluster, Storage DRS will create a mandatory migration recommendation if an affinity or anti-affinity rule has been exceeded, if a member datastore runs out of free space, or if a datastore has been marked for Maintenance Mode. At other times, the Storage DRS algorithm executes at the default time interval of 8 hours to evaluate the load balance within the cluster and the capacity utilization of the member datastores. Storage DRS will also make recommendations based on the administrator-configured options for the cluster.

Decisions, Decisions, Decisions

When deciding whether to migrate a virtual machine, SDRS carefully examines the virtual machine before evaluating possible migration destinations. SDRS looks at each of the virtual machine's VMDKs, identifying the I/O profile of the applications and processes at work within each disk, the provisioned size of each disk, and the amount of I/O that each disk receives. During the migration process, each of the writes that are received by the VM will need to be written to the destination datastore as well to maintain data consistency. This will help determine the length of the migration process and the overhead that will be placed on the system. This provides SDRS with the ability to determine if migrating the virtual machine is likely to cause the destination datastore to run out of space within the next 30 hours. This 30-hour window is the default value and can be modified using the Advanced Options feature of the datastore cluster.

There are several considerations that SDRS "keeps in mind" as it evaluates each VM. The first consideration is that it is less overhead on the system if SDRS chooses to migrate a virtual machine that is currently in a powered-off state, than if it opts for a powered-on VM. If the VM is not actively receiving I/O during the migration, there will be no I/O duplication to the target datastore. Secondly, SDRS will attempt to move a virtual machine that approximates the size of the imbalance; it is less overhead to move a single virtual machine than to migrate multiple VMs.

Evaluation

In order to gather accurate information regarding the latency experienced by a datastore, SDRS uses a technology known as the injector. The injector is a part of the Storage I/O Control mechanism, and it is used to generate random read I/O to a selected datastore. In an effort to minimize any impact to clients, this I/O is presented during a period of inactivity. The injector can recognize when client I/O is accessing the datastore and it will pause until a later time. This "I/O injection" is comprised of different workloads at each sampling period, and the latency is measured for each pattern. This allows SDRS to understand the performance profile of the datastore, and generate better recommendations for load balancing.

SDRS uses the I/O latency to each datastore and the benchmark to determine whether a migration is required to balance cluster resources. SDRS will query vCenter to retrieve metrics such as the size of each I/O presented to the datastore, the level of random I/O (how far each I/O is from the physical location of the previous I/O), the queue depth (the number of I/Os queued from the device), and the read/write ratio for this datastore. SDRS will evaluate this data over time; it takes 18 hours after being enabled to have sufficient data to make recommendations. This enables SDRS to bypass temporary fluctuations in I/O, providing a more accurate perspective of the I/O profile.

Datastore Maintenance Mode

If an administrator selects a datastore within the cluster for Maintenance Mode, SDRS contacts vCenter to discover the virtual machines that "live" on that datastore. SDRS will evaluate the current status of the datastores, and will either make recommendations for the new home of the VMs or will migrate the VMs itself.

If the migration process encounters any issues during this datastore evacuation, the administrator is notified, and he or she must address the reported issues by cancelling the Maintenance Mode attempt, or by manually migrating the virtual machines. It is important to remember that this migration will consider datastores within the cluster; "free agent datastores" will not be considered as possible destinations.

Keep in mind that this will decrease the amount of space available and will decrease the I/O capacity of the datastore cluster. This will likely result in higher utilization at the datastore level, and this may be reflected back to the VM in the form of disk read and write latencies.

If a datastore is placed into Maintenance Mode, SDRS will evaluate the cluster based on free space characteristics alone; I/O latency is not considered at this point.

Storage I/O Control

Introduced with vSphere 4.1, Storage I/O Control provides a mechanism to actively gather latency metrics from datastores. While vCenter could simply retrieve storage statistics form the database, it is far more accurate to periodically measure latency at intervals through the day, changing the workload to simulate different applications. When Storage I/O Control (SIOC) is enabled on a datastore, the datastore handles the prioritization through the use of disk shares configured at the VM level. When SIOC is not enabled, the individual ESXi hosts are responsible for resource prioritization, again through VM shares.

Reviewing the Virtual Machine Disk I/O Flow   When the virtual machine issues storage I/O, it first is processed through the client I/O stack and will be queued according to the virtual SCSI device that is presented to the VM in the form of virtual hardware. The I/O is parsed based on the virtual SCSI driver in the O/S, and the queue depth is set to 32 for the LSI HBA or 64 for PVSCSI devices through the O/S device driver. At the virtual HBA level, the queue depth is limited by the hypervisor to 128 I/Os, and the PVSCSI is limited to 255. From this point, it is up to the SAN device. Each front-end port on the SAN will have a queue depth that is determined by the SAN vendor.

The I/O moves through the VMM to the hypervisor where the client I/O is placed in the HBA buffer area. Each physical HBA will have a queue depth limit that is configured through a vendor-supplied utility. In general, these limits vary based on the access protocol and the HBA in use: Fibre Channel is typically 32, iSCSI is 128, NFS and any local devices have a maximum queue depth of 256. At this point, the data is sent to the SAN device where the front-end port also has a queue depth that is defined by the SAN vendor.

The local disk scheduler becomes involved when I/O is sent from a VM to the HBA. When two or more virtual machines are issuing I/Os to the same datastore, an advanced parameter, `Disk.SchedNumReqOutstanding`, will limit the number of I/Os that each VM can send to the datastore. It is important to remember that the I/Os from the virtual machines enter the queue on a first-come, first-served basis; the VMKernel does not re-sequence the client I/Os. The `Disk.SchedNumReqOutstanding` value becomes a factor when a counter known as `Disk.SchedQControlVMSwitches` has been met. This value is configured at a default value of 6 and indicates that throttling should occur when the VMKernel discovers at 6 time intervals that the VM which sent the current I/O is not the same VM that sent the prior I/O. This value then indicates that there is a level of contention for the datastore access.

In general, the value of `Disk.SchedNumReqOutstanding` should match the queue depth configured at the physical HBA in the ESXi server. This will provide the ability of each virtual machine to have its I/O processed in the most efficient manner. However, if you have an environment in which smaller virtual machines share a datastore with a VM that has a very high workload, and the other VMs are experiencing a high degree of storage latency, then you may want to drop the `Disk.SchedNumReqOutstanding` value. This will provide more queue access and drop the latency for the smaller VMs. But keep in mind that the high I/O VM may now experience latency. Since there is a finite amount of queue depth available, we have to take it away from one VM in order to give it to another.

At this point, we are managing virtual machine datastore access at the individual ESXi server level.

At the datastore level, it is equally important to verify each virtual machine is granted access to the datastore, but that the VM is not given the opportunity to monopolize the datastore. SIOC determines whether to enforce share-based access by using the true latency and IOPs as reported by each physical ESX host. Periodically, each ESXi server will report the average latency and IOPs that it is experiencing to a shared file on the datastore. The ESXi hosts can then add up the average latencies and configure its queue depth appropriately.

When the latency exceeds the threshold of 30ms, the datastore scheduler determines the priority of each VM based on their shares value. This threshold is configurable in the Advanced button on the Properties page of the datastore.

As shown in Figure 11.33, you have the option to configure a latency threshold that more accurately reflects the type of drives that are in use for the datastores. Note that it is a good idea if you are going to deviate from the default value, to monitor the performance over time to verify that this change does not adversely change the performance of the datastore.

VMware has recommended the following values as a starting point, but the true virtual machine workload, the SAN cache configuration, and the type and number of disks that make up the datastore, will all play a part in the performance of this

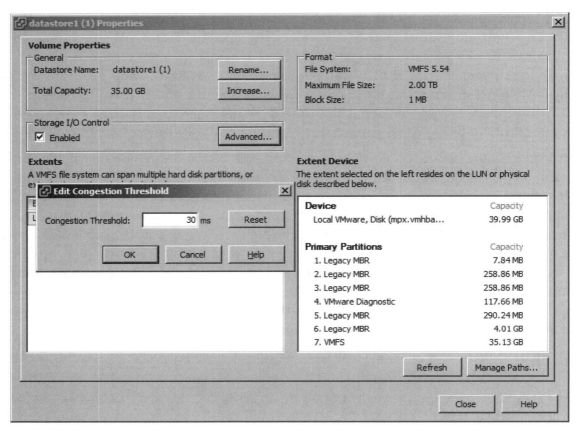

Figure 11.33
The SIOC Advanced Options dialog box.

datastore. For a Fibre Channel SAN device, start with a value of 20ms to 30ms. The starting point for SAS devices is also in the range of 20ms to 30ms. If you are lucky enough to have solid-state devices (SSD or EFD), start with value in the range of 10ms to 15ms. Since SATA devices tend to present a lower level of performance, start with a value in the range of 30 to 50ms. Many vendors also have the ability to automatically evaluate the I/O workload and place it on the most appropriate level of disks within the SAN device. For these "auto-tiering" storage devices, use the value recommended by your storage vendor. If the vendor does not have a recommendation, use the value that represents the slowest disk type that is installed in your array.

In an ideal situation, configure the threshold and monitor the latency and IOPs over a period of time. If there are still unacceptable latencies, make a small change and again, monitor the performance.

As a result, when the latency exceeds this value, virtual machines that have a lower shares value will receive a smaller amount of access to the HBA buffers than their counterparts with higher shares values.

There are two important points at this point: the amount of I/O that is generated by the virtual machines cannot exceed the buffer space of the HBA. If this happens, the I/O requests are stored in the Kernel RAM until it can be placed in the HBA buffer space. This latency can be viewed through the vCenter performance charts and through the `esxtop` command line utility. Secondly, SIOC cannot "automagically" increase the amount of available bandwidth, but it will take capacity from the lesser-prioritized virtual machines and allocate it to higher-prioritized virtual machines; we have to take the resources away from one set of VMs to be able to give it to another.

Modes of Operation

To configure Storage DRS, we create a series of datastore clusters. These datastore clusters are configured from a series of datastores with identical storage characteristics. A datastore cluster is a collection of datastores with shared resources and a shared management interface. The datastore cluster is the management object for Storage DRS.

Similar to the clustering of physical ESXi servers, when a datastore is added to a datastore cluster, or when a new datastore cluster is created, the individual datastore's capacity and I/O workload capacity are part of the datastore cluster's resources. As we discussed when creating a DRS cluster, when we create the cluster, we can also define cluster policies that will define how the cluster will function.

As is the case with the operation of a DRS cluster, you can configure policies that dictate how the initial placement of new, migrated, and cloned virtual machines is handled. If the cluster is configured for Manual operation, the administrator is responsible for accepting the Storage DRS cluster recommendations.

Before creating the Storage DRS Cluster, you should deploy the LUNs from your storage system(s) and present them to the vCenter instance. At this point, remember that these datastores will be shared datastores, and should be seen by all cluster hosts identically.

As shown in Figure 11.34, select the Datastores view in vCenter. This can be accomplished by using the Inventory > Datastores and Datastore Clusters path, or simply by using the CTRL-Shift-D key sequence. From the Datastores and Datastore Clusters view, right-click on the Datacenter and select New Datastore Cluster.

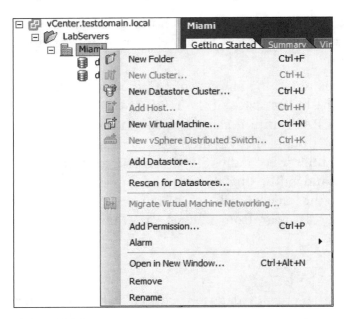

Figure 11.34
Creating the Storage DRS cluster.

As shown in Figure 11.35, the cluster must be named, and the name should follow a naming standard that has been put into place by the organization. The naming of datastores as days of the week, favorite Star Wars characters, or Greek and Roman deities does nothing to indicate to the ESXi hosts what will be presented with this datastore, nor does it indicate its function. As with any object defined within vCenter, the name should indicate the function of the object to assist in troubleshooting at a later date.

As shown, placing a check mark in the Enable Storage DRS box grants vCenter the ability to monitor and manage this datastore cluster.

Figure 11.36 shows the two options for Storage DRS cluster automation. If the Manual option is selected, Storage DRS will make recommendations to improve the space utilization or the I/O load balance within the member datastores, but will take no action on its own—it is up to the administrator to decide to accept those recommendations. Note here that when compared to the cluster settings available for DRS, there is no partially automated mode.

If the Fully Automated option is selected, Storage DRS will automatically perform a migration of the VM or VMs that will achieve the desired load-balancing equalization.

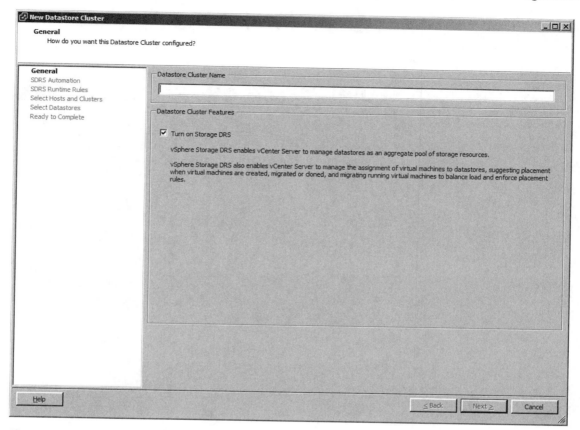

Figure 11.35
Enabling Storage DRS.

In Figure 11.37, the next step in the creation for the SDRS cluster is to determine how the Storage DRS algorithm will proceed. This first option is to include the I/O metric as part of the cluster evaluation. Note that if any ESX/ESXi vSphere 4.x or earlier hosts are presented with the datastore cluster, this setting is disabled. If this option is not selected, datastore capacity will be the only metric considered when making evaluations.

Next are the Storage DRS thresholds. The first is the Utilization threshold and it can be configured in the range of 50%–100%. This is determined by adding up the datastore space utilization of each cluster member and dividing it by the total amount of datastore space available on that datastore. The default value here is 80%. This means that the total used capacity of this datastore cannot be allowed to exceed 80%.

The next option is the I/O latency. This option is in the range of 5ms to 100ms and defines the point at which load balancing is considered to minimize the I/O latency

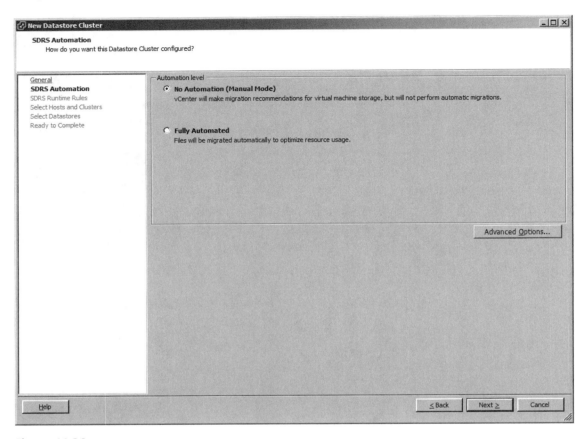

Figure 11.36
Storage DRS automation level.

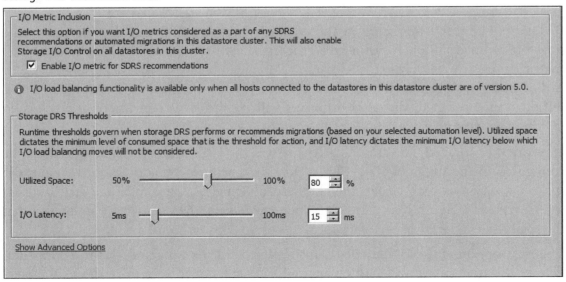

Figure 11.37
Storage DRS runtime rules.

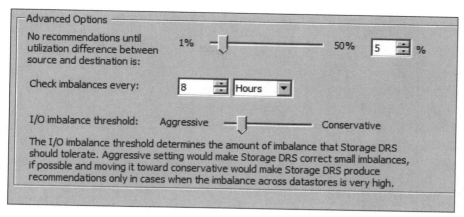

Figure 11.38
Advanced options.

of the cluster member datastores. The default latency setting is 15ms. This setting should be carefully considered and monitored over time to ensure that all applications and virtual machines are performing within expectations.

As shown in Figure 11.38, if you click on the Advanced options link on the Storage DRS Runtime Rules page, you have the ability to further define the SDRS cluster operation. The first option is the level of space utilization imbalance that will be tolerated between datastores. This value can range from 1% to 50%. The default value is 5%.

The second option here is the frequency with which the load-balancing algorithm will execute. If left at the default setting, SDRS evaluates the datastore cluster at eight-hour intervals. This means that SDRS will re-evaluate the cluster I/O latency and space utilization and either make recommendations or begin to Storage vMotion virtual machines, based on the findings. If an administrator has configured the cluster for manual mode, any recommendations that the administrator ignores is deleted. However, SDRS may make the same conclusion if the load or space imbalance still exists at the new evaluation interval.

The range of values is between 1 hour and 30 days. A smaller value here will result in more calculations and possibly more Storage vMotion processes, but may result in faster I/O and space issue resolution. A larger number will result in fewer calculations and less frequent Storage vMotion processes but may resolve problems in a slower manner. If the value is configured at 0, the load balancing mechanism is disabled.

In addition to the designated interval, SDRS will re-evaluate the cluster balance when an administrator modifies the cluster configuration, datastores enter or exit Maintenance Mode, datastores are added to or removed from the cluster, when space and I/O values are over the configured threshold values, or if an administrator manually

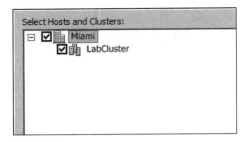

Figure 11.39
Selecting the hosts.

initiates the algorithm. Compared to DRS in which a host enters or exits Maintenance Mode, SDRS will not evaluate the datastore cluster based on I/O latency if a datastore is placed into Maintenance Mode; it will only consider space utilization.

As depicted in Figure 11.39, we must select the cluster of ESXi servers that will be presented with the datastore cluster. Note that only the clusters from a single vCenter instance are displayed; a datastore cluster cannot span multiple vCenter instances.

As shown in Figure 11.40, now that we have the cluster parameters configured, we need to add the datastores that will be cluster members. It is important to remember

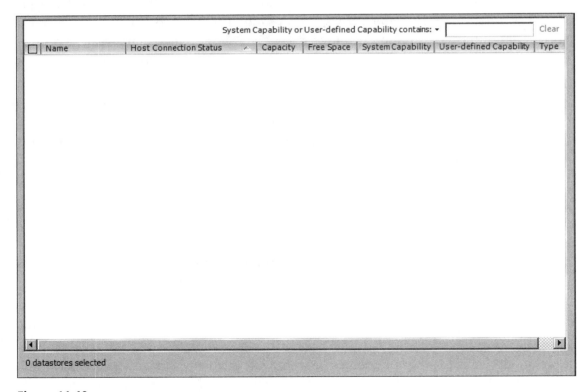

Figure 11.40
Selecting the datastores.

here that the datastores that are selected should have the same I/O and space capacity, same RAID levels, and they should also use the same type of disks. You should never mix performance or capacity characteristics within the same datastore cluster.

By default, the only datastores that are visible are those that are shared by all cluster hosts. Select the datastores that will be cluster members and click next. The Summary page will indicate the properties that have been defined in the wizard, and the datastore cluster will be created when you click Finish.

The final option on this page is the I/O Imbalance Threshold. If this is configured in the Conservative setting, this causes storage migrations to occur only if they will equalize a large I/O imbalance. The Aggressive setting will cause migrations to occur to resolve a much smaller imbalance.

Storage Awareness

In vSphere 5, VMware has made a new set of APIs available called the vSphere Storage APIs—Storage Awareness (VASA) that directly apply to storage. This set of APIs allows a storage vendor to make array-based information available through an object called a storage vendor.

A storage vendor is a software component that is written by an SAN vendor to integrate with that specific vendor's arrays. This software vendor is installed on a Windows or Linux physical device or is also available as a virtual appliance that can be downloaded from the vendor's website. It is important to remember that the provider cannot be installed on the vCenter server, and, once registered, exposes array capabilities such as the different tiers of storage that are available from an SAN device. Depending on the vendor and the storage device, the administrator can view the categories of LUNs that have been deployed and made available from that specific SAN. For example, if a RAID 0 set is deployed, this would be described as "Unprotected." A category of storage called "Capacity" might be comprised of less expensive, but larger SATA drives configured in a RAID 5. A category such as "Performance" might be a RAID 10 set with SAS or FC drives. Another category such as "Extreme Performance" or "High Performance" might be a RAID 5 or a RAID 10 made from SSD devices. Note that these descriptions are very useful to the VM administrator as he or she can deploy virtual machines to the datastore with the most appropriate characteristics. This SAN-based information forms the basis for a new VMware concept: Profile-Driven Storage.

Prerequisites for VASA

To utilize the VASA interface, each physical host must be managed through an instance of vSphere 5, all hosts must be running a minimum of ESX or ESXi 4.0, and the storage array must support the VASA plug-in. Note at this point, FCoE is not supported, but VASA is fully supported for both block- and file-type storage using either FC or iSCSI.

It is possible for a single vCenter instance to utilize multiple vendor providers, and, if the environment is utilizing a single, large storage system, multiple vCenter instances can use the same vendor provider.

In addition to providing the characteristics of a storage array to vCenter, the vendor provider is also able to export events and alarms from the array to vCenter. These events might include changes to the status of a datastore, such as the failure of a physical disk in a redundant RAID set. The events surrounding the creation, deletion, or expansion of a LUN might also be made available, depending on the storage vendor. If this is a single physical ESXi server, the Events tab will display these events as reported by the vendor provider; if the host is managed through a vCenter instance, these events will be available from the tasks and Events tab for that host.

Before deciding to install, update, or remove a vendor provider, it is a best practice to consult the vSphere Compatibility Guide from the VMware website to verify revisions and compatibility.

Register a Storage Provider

The process of integrating the vendor provider for the storage involves navigating to the Administration toolbar in vCenter and selecting the Storage Provider icon.

At the Storage Providers screen, select Add from the upper-right corner.

As shown in Figure 11.41, enter the connection information for the vendor provider, including the name and URL that can be used to communicate with the vendor provider, and the credentials for authenticating with the vendor provider. Also, you can import a certificate from the vendor if desired.

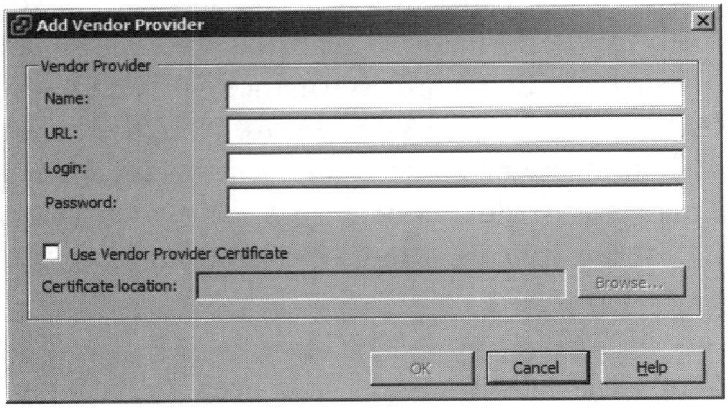

Figure 11.41
Registering the storage provider.

What about Security?

If desired and/or mandated by corporate datacenter standards, the communication between the vCenter and the vendor provider can utilize SSL if certificates are installed from an internal CA or from a third-party provider.

When the vendor provider is registered with vCenter, the administrator has the opportunity at that point to import a certificate, or it can be added at a later date by using the Use Vendor Provider Certificate from the Add Vendor Provider configuration window. At this point, the certificate is added to the vCenter truststore and SSL communication is possible.

Performing an Update for a Storage Vendor

If a storage vendor updates their provider to expose more information or new features, those new provider characteristics must be updated within vCenter as well. Select the Storage Provider icon from the Administration toolbar, highlight the vendor provider in the listing, and select SYNC.

Removing a Storage Provider

If, for example, a company were to change their storage vendor, an administrator can always remove legacy providers by using the Storage Providers icon in the vCenter Administration.

Profile-Driven Storage

The process of defining profile-driven storage begins with understanding the actual storage characteristics of the datastores that are presented to the ESXi host. In previous versions of vSphere, it was the responsibility of the VM administrator to communicate with the storage team to determine how each LUN would perform under a given workload. This could be time consuming and inefficient. vSphere 5 provides the capability to dynamically determine these characteristics, and to place VMs intelligently based on true storage characteristics. This begins with the vendor provider that we discussed earlier. The vendor provider provides performance and redundancy properties of each LUN to vCenter.

Restrictions Each datastore can utilize only one storage capability that is defined through the use of VASA and one user-defined capability at any time. Therefore, if a datastore has been configured to span multiple extents, the resultant datastore will exhibit the storage capability of one of the extents, not the sum.

As shown in Figure 11.42, navigate to the Management toolbar in vCenter and select "VM Storage Profiles." Click on the Manage Storage Profiles button on the top management bar. The current Storage Profiles are listed below.

Figure 11.42
View the current storage profile.

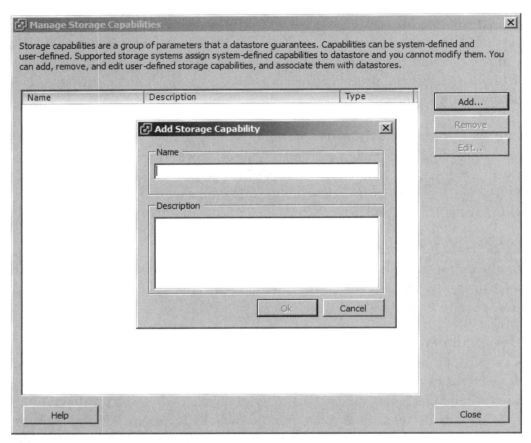

Figure 11.43
Adding a storage profile.

Adding a Storage Profile As shown in Figure 11.43, from the VM Storage Profiles icon, you can add a new storage profile by selecting Manage Storage Profiles and then clicking the Add button. Provide a name for the new profile and also consider entering a description for the profile that details the specific SAN, RAID characteristics, and properties for the datastore. Keep in mind that you should verify that the datastore really exhibits the storage characteristics that you describe here; misconfiguration can result in unpredictable storage performance.

After the user-defined storage profiles have been created, we can now create a link between the user-defined capabilities and a datastore. Since a user-defined capability cannot be assigned to a datastore cluster, it is important to verify that all datastores

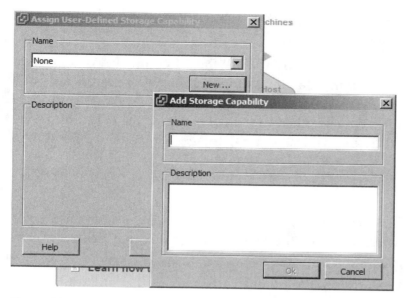

Figure 11.44
Assigning a user-defined capability to a datastore.

in a cluster have the same capabilities, as the cluster will derive its capabilities from its component datastores.

To add a user-defined capability to a datastore, navigate to the datastores and datastores inventory or use the CTRL-Shift-D key sequence. Right-click on the desired datastores and select Add User Defined Capability.

As shown in Figure 11.44, select the appropriate user-defined storage capability from the drop-down box and click Next. Note that is it possible to define the capability by selecting the New button and applying the name and description of the new capability. The new capability can then be selected from the drop-down box.

DPM

One of the main reasons that companies consider deploying a virtualized environment is the hardware savings that can be gained through consolidation. Simply put, this means that we can run multiple application servers within a single physical server; the savings in power, cooling, and administrative costs are considerable.

But what if we could improve on this power and cooling savings? VMware DPM allows us to save even more by allowing virtual machines to be consolidated on a minimal number of physical servers during times of low utilization. We can make a very compelling argument in that there are few environments in which servers and applications are accessed in a true 24/7 fashion. So, if the servers are unused for a large portion of the day, why do they run at full power and consume resources even though no users are accessing them?

Similar to DRS, DPM leverages vCenter to evaluate the CPU and RAM utilization across the cluster and make recommendations as to which physical servers are good candidates for consolidation. In order to do this, the VMs that are hosted on those physical servers must be moved to another host in the cluster prior to any server power changes. Of course, this means that shared storage is mandatory for this to work correctly.

Resource Utilization

In order to ascertain whether a cluster host can be placed in a low power state, DPM evaluates each physical host to discover the level of utilization that exists on each ESXi host within the cluster.

On a per-host basis, DPM determines the number of resources that are available for virtual machines by subtracting the resources consumed by the Hypervisor from the installed hardware set. Then DPM adds up the resource utilization of each VM on that host and divides it by the total resources in use by the total available resources. This shows the level of utilization for that host. When making a decision to power down a physical host, DPM looks at the resource utilization over the past 20 minutes to verify that the value is representative of the true utilization and not an aberration.

DPM calculates the resource utilization of an ESXi host based on the virtual machine demand and the available ESXi host capacity. The available capacity of a host is the number of resources remaining after subtracting the resources required for running the virtualization layer. DPM calculates the resource demand as the sum of each active virtual machine over a historical period of interest plus two standard deviations. DPM uses different historical periods for recommending power-on recommendations and for recommending power-off recommendations.

These calculations rely on two basic values. The first, the `DemandCapacityRatio Target` is the "ideal" resource utilization for all physical hosts in the cluster. By default, this value is 63%. The second value, `DemandCapacityRatioTolerance Host`, defines the acceptable range from the `DemandCapacityRatioTarget`, either higher or lower. The default value is 18%.

In the default values, this means that DPM will try to maintain each ESXi host at 63%, with a tolerance of 18%, or between 45% and 81%.

In the DRS cluster, if the utilization of an ESXi server drops below 45%, DPM will consider whether to recommend powering down this server. If the utilization of an

ESXi server rises above 81%, DPM considers powering up an ESXi server within the cluster that has been placed in a low power state.

When a period of low utilization is detected, vCenter will begin a 20-minute counter, waiting to see if any more I/O is presented to the VMs before consolidation processes are considered. If no I/O is detected, vCenter will examine the cluster configuration to determine how to proceed: if the cluster is set to Manual or Partially Automated, vCenter will make recommendations as to which physical servers can be placed in a low power state. If the cluster is configured for Fully Automated operation, vCenter will consolidate the VMs on a minimal number of hosts, and place the remaining physical servers in a low power state.

This low power state is known as ACPI (S5), or Advanced Configuration and Power Interface, state 5. In state 5, the CPU, the system clock, and the NIC still remain powered on. This is a minimal hardware set, and is enough logic to allow the server to be brought out of the low power state remotely. This is based on the fact that, in most cases, physical servers use 60% of their peak power utilization when they are in an idle state.

Once the algorithm has been completed, and the minimum number of hosts has been determined, DRS will load balance the virtual machines across the remaining physical servers. Keep in mind that all affinity and anti-affinity rules are followed during this process.

At this point, each physical server evaluates its local power needs and can place any unused CPU cores in a low power state as well, saving additional power. To add to the possible savings, each ESXi server can use a concept called Dynamic Frequency and Voltage Scaling (DVFS) in which the clock frequency and supply voltage can be dynamically adjusted based on the demand. Less voltage and clock speed may result in less heat generated by the CPU, meaning the internal fans of the server will run less frequently.

The operation of the DVFS component can be modified from its default configuration, disabled by using the `Power.Cpu.Policy` advanced option. Note that the physical server has to support the use of DVFS; you may wish to consult with your server vendor before enabling this option.

If desired, an administrator can modify these values on a per-cluster basis.

As shown in Figure 11.45, the administrator can edit the properties of the cluster to change these values. Right-click on the cluster and select Edit Settings. Click on the Advanced Options button, click in the appropriate textbox, and enter the new cluster values.

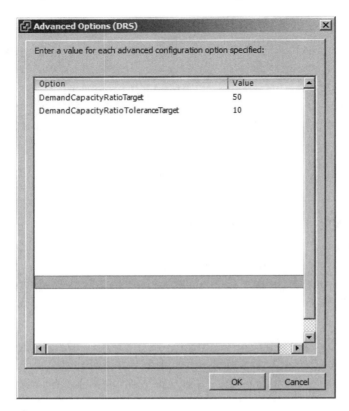

Figure 11.45
DPM Advanced Options.

In Figure 11.45, we have configured the cluster to maintain 50% utilization and a tolerance factor of 10%. This means that the host's utilization can fluctuate between 40% and 60% before DPM steps in.

Wake-Up Options
When this threshold has been reached, DPM will use vCenter to send a "wake-up" signal via (in order of preference): IPMI (for Dell and IBM servers), iLO (for HP servers), or Wake-on-LAN for those servers that do not support either the iLO or the IPMI interface. When the hosts have resumed, DRS will perform load balancing according to the cluster configuration.

Host Configuration
In order to resume a host, at least one physical host in the cluster must remain online, and it will be used to "wake up" the hosts. The administrator will need to configure each host with the MAC address and IP address of the host by the vSphere Client to log in directly to an ESXi host or vCenter.

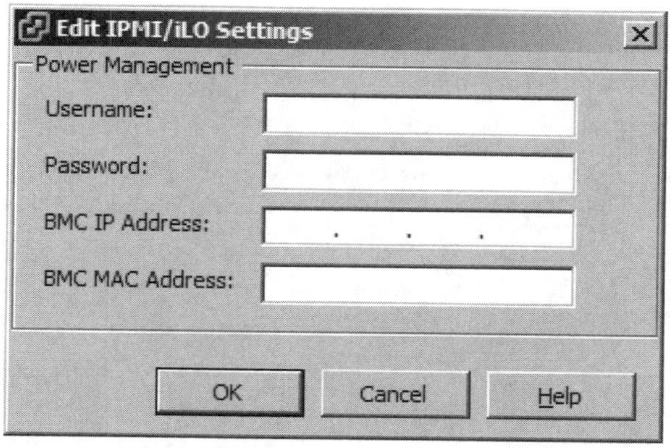

Figure 11.46
Configuring the ESXi power settings.

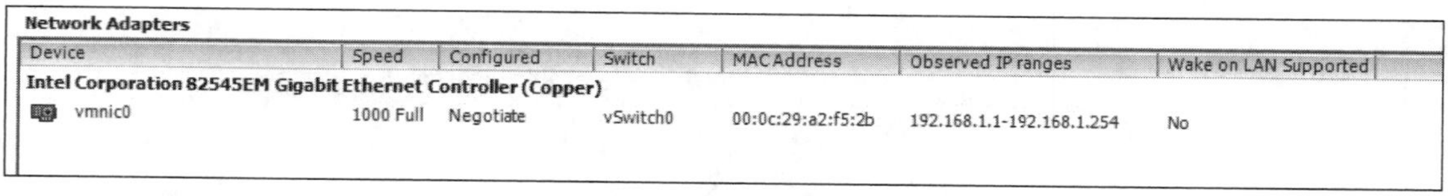

Figure 11.47
Network Adapters pane.

As shown in Figure 11.46, the administrator must highlight the ESXi server in the vCenter inventory or in the vSphere Client, select the Configuration tab, and click on the Power Management link.

Here, the administrator will enter his or her credentials, the IP address, and the Mac address of the desired interface. This interface will be the DRAC for Dell servers, or the iLO for HP servers. DPM can also use simple Wake on LAN (WoL) if the server does not support the iLO or DRAC.

As shown in Figure 11.47, if desired, the administrator can verify whether each physical NIC supports Wake on LAN by navigating to the Configuration tab for the ESXi host, selecting Network Adapters, and the WoL status will be listed in the right column. In any case, this interface will be used as the wake-up interface when the utilization exceeds the threshold.

Cluster Configuration

As shown in Figure 11.48, to configure the DPM options, right-click on the Cluster and select Edit Properties. Highlight the Power Management link and the DPM Settings pane appears.

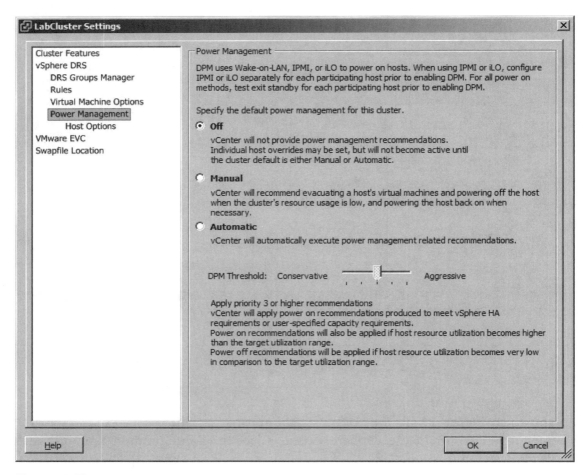

Figure 11.48
DPM cluster options.

Notice that, just like the configuration of a DRS cluster, you have the option to configure the level of automation that your cluster will use. The Off selection disables DPM and its algorithm. This is the default selection.

The Manual selection means that the vCenter instance will execute the algorithm, and will make recommendations, but will take no action on its own; you still have to apply the recommendations.

The Automatic selection gives DPM the ability to evaluate the power usage within the cluster and to automatically place ESXi servers into a low power state, and to resume those servers when the utilization increases.

Thresholds: Conservative–Aggressive

When we discussed DRS we found that there are aggressiveness settings that we can configure that will dictate how aggressive DRS will be in its efforts to load-balance the cluster.

Figure 11.49 shows the available levels of aggressiveness that can be applied through DPM. If you configure DPM at the Conservative setting, DPM will generate recommendations that will accommodate existing HA policies, or to satisfy capacity requirements that have been put into place by an administrator. In this setting, DPM will not display power-off recommendations, but will power on ESXi servers if the cluster utilization will interfere with the HA or cluster configuration.

Like DRS, using the Aggressive setting will generate recommendations to power down the ESXi servers if there will be a strong return in power savings.

Once the DPM settings have been entered, you can highlight the Host Options link from the Cluster properties drop-down, and you can configure individual settings for each ESXi host

As shown in Figure 11.50, each ESXi server can be configured with a DPM setting that will override the cluster-wide setting. Also, notice the "Never Exited Standby" column. If you are serious enough about power management, doesn't it make sense that you test each ESXi server to verify that vCenter will be able to resume it from a

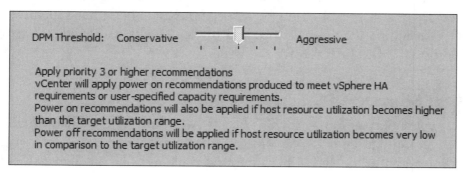

Figure 11.49
DPM aggressiveness settings.

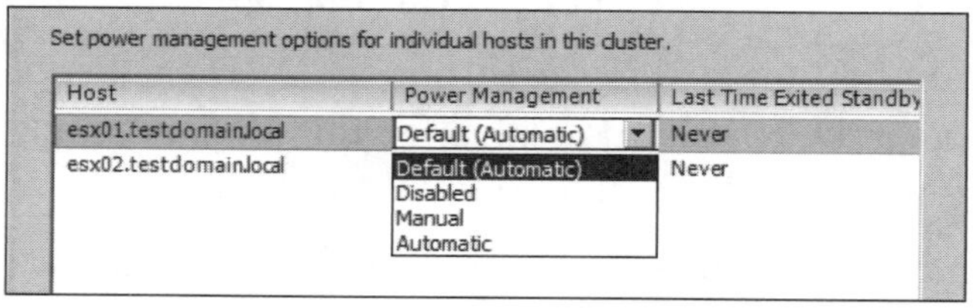

Figure 11.50
Individual ESXi server settings.

low power state? This is a must if you are going to place DPM into a production environment. Once each host has been resumed from the low power state, this column will display a "Yes."

TROUBLESHOOTING

Troubleshooting DRS should start with the virtual machines in the cluster. Are they vMotion capable? This simple factor can cause DRS to lose the capability to load balance the cluster and to allow hosts to enter Maintenance Mode; note the initial placement functionality will still work, however. An examination of the virtual machine properties can readily indicate whether it can vMotion or not. Simple things such as placing the VMDKs on a shared datastore, rather than local storage, or disconnecting the VM from an ISO file or physical media that is located on a CD or DVD device can also stop vMotion. Check the network configuration of the ESXi hosts: is there a VMKernel port with the correct networking settings for each host, and is vMotion enabled for the port? A fundamental cluster design issue is whether all of the clusters are CPU-compatible. Even though the CPUs in each server are from the same vendor, this doesn't necessarily mean that vMotion is possible between the hosts. As discussed earlier, use the CPU utility from VMware to accurately determine CPU compatibility between all cluster and prospective cluster nodes. Highlight the ESXi server in vCenter and select the DRS tab. Use the Faults button to determine whether the repetitive issues occur at a specific time, or a specific cluster node has repetitive vMotion errors. If so, examine the vCenter logs and the logs for that individual host to gather further information to help resolve the issue.

Troubleshooting Storage DRS

The process of troubleshooting Storage DSR begins with examining the virtual machines. A look at the configuration of the VM can help eliminate potential conflicts with Storage DRS. For example, the virtual machine's swap file must be on shared storage or Storage DRS will be disabled for this particular VM. Similarly, if the virtual machine is currently a participant in a vMotion or a manual Storage vMotion process, Storage DRS must wait until those processes complete before it can migrate that VM.

If the VM boots from a floppy drive, an .ISO file that is stored on CD/DVD media, or if the VM has a separate data disk, Storage DRS will be disabled for this VM. Planning will make a big difference in the outcome when deploying a virtual machine.

Storage DRS works well with DRS and HA, but it will also respect the configuration of those clusters. For example, if the VM is restricted by an anti-affinity rule, or is involved in a FT configuration, Storage DRS will be disabled for that VM.

As discussed earlier, the administrator has the option to place a datastore in Maintenance Mode if, for example, the datastore is being upgraded or enlarged on the SAN. However, if Storage DRS is disabled for this datastore, or if there are affinity or anti-affinity rules that are prohibiting the virtual machine from moving to a new datastore, the DRS functionality may be severely limited. In case of emergency maintenance, an administrator can configure the following settings to tell Storage DRS to ignore anti-affinity rules when placing a datastore in Maintenance Mode:

Open the Advanced Options pane and add `IgnoreAffinityRulesForMaintenance` and set the value to a 1.

If the datastore is shared with ESX/ESXi hosts that are running a legacy version of VMware, or if the datastore has been made available to host that is not currently using Storage I/O Control, Storage DRS will not be able to gather latency and performance metrics that are complete and accurate for this datastore. Rather than try to manage the latency without the full accurate workload, Storage DRS will not be able to manage this datastore.

Note that if you are considering migrating virtual machines between datastores, there must be enough free space on the destination datastore, or the migration will fail. The same is true if Storage DRS attempts to perform a migration. If the destination datastore runs out of free space before the migration completes, an error will be generated that indicates an "Insufficient Data Space" situation.

Troubleshooting DPM

Distributed Power Management utilizes the management IP and MAC address for each ESXi server in order to be able to manage the power state. Care must be taken here to verify that the networking information is correct and that there are no typos when entering the information for each host. If incorrect information is entered, DPM may be unable to bring the ESXi server out of the low power state, and this may result in resource contention on the remaining hosts.

This issue may be compounded when HA is added to the cluster as there may be insufficient space to restart VMs in the event of a physical host failure. Ultimately, this means applications that are hosted within those virtual machines will be unavailable until the physical host(s) are resumed.

Keep in mind that if HA is enabled for the cluster, DPM will not place an ESXi host into a low power state if doing so will violate the HA configuration for the cluster. In this scenario, the administrator can configure DPM with a more aggressive threshold, or by editing the Advanced Options of the DRS cluster and adding the following entries:

■ Adding the `MinPoweredOnCpuCapacity` entry with a value of 1 will allow the administrator to define the minimum amount of CPU resources to be maintained by the cluster.

■ Adding the `MinPoweredOnMemCapacity` entry with a value of 1 will allow the administrator to define the minimum amount of RAM resources to be maintained by the cluster.

SUMMARY

As you can see, deploying a DRS cluster can involve a lot of planning. However, the capability to perform automatic load balancing of the cluster can provide a more efficient environment for your virtual machines. Maintenance Mode provides the option to perform maintenance tasks during production hours without impacting client access. In the physical world, these same maintenance tasks, such as adding PCI adapters or adding DIMM modules or CPU modules, would have required an outage to accomplish.

We must also consider the option to power down physical servers when the resources are not required. Distributed Power Management can save money, power, and physical resources.

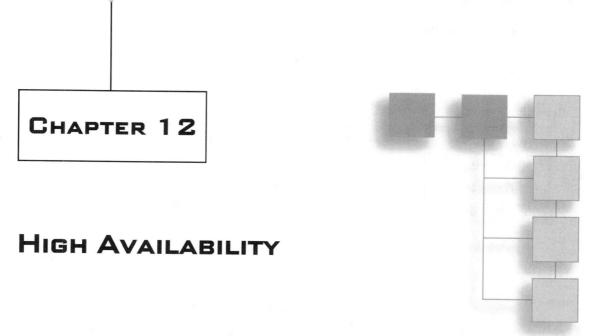

CHAPTER 12

HIGH AVAILABILITY

High availability can be defined in very simple terms—a VM, service, application, server, etc., is available when you want it to be. Usually, this is expressed as part of a SLA (Service Level Agreement), a simple way to define how much of the time the component in question will be available and any penalties to the owner of that component if they are not. Most commonly, people want 100% uptime (don't we all?) until the cost for that uptime is calculated (which can be in the millions of dollars or more). We thus need to balance the desire for uptime (or in other words the cost of downtime) with the cost of providing that level of uptime. This is typically expressed as the number of 9s of reliability, as shown in Table 12.1.

"Five 9s of reliability" is considered the holy grail of availability and is usually very expensive. This chapter will cover the various options for providing availability, from very low cost to more expensive add-on software (which is bundled with higher versions of vSphere). Most of the chapter will review the conceptual underpinnings that are required to implement the various features—the actual implementation of the various features is fairly simple.

Before we look at these options in detail, let's start with a brief overview of how vSphere provides availability solutions at all levels—by handling failures from the component level to entire sites. This is shown in Figure 12.1. You'll note that we have talked about several of these already—multipathing storage (Chapter 8) and NIC teaming (Chapter 7) at the component level, vMotion (Chapter 10) and DRS (Chapter 11) at the platform level, Storage vMotion (Chapter 8) at the storage level, and Alarms (Chapter 10) at the component, server, and storage levels. This chapter will focus on HA and FT. Site Recovery Manager (SRM) is not included in any

Table 12.1   Annual Downtime Allowed for Number of 9s of Reliability Desired

Reliability	Downtime (Per Year)
99% (two 9s)	87 Hours (3.5 Days)
99.9% (three 9s)	8.76 Hours
99.99% (four 9s)	52 Minutes
99.999% (five 9s)	5 Minutes

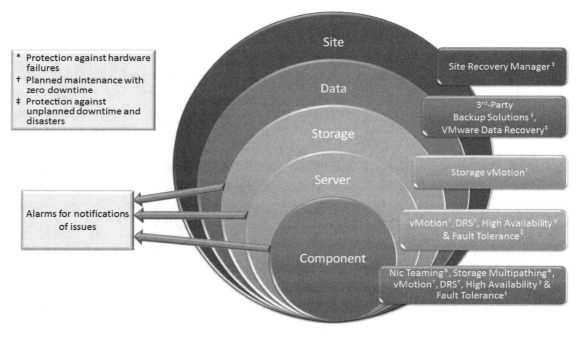

Figure 12.1
High availability options.

vSphere bundle and will thus be covered in Chapter 15 with other VMware products that can be used with vSphere.

One other thing you'll notice in Figure 12.1—we've chosen to illustrate the relationship between the components in a Russian doll–type diagram. The idea is that providing basic component reliability automatically provides for better server availability, and so on through the levels all the way up to having site resilience by having multiple sites in case a site should fail. You'll also notice that some of the products we mentioned can provide better availability at multiple levels.

PLANNING

We're going to begin by introducing vSphere 5's availability options (all of which were also available in vSphere 4, but which have been upgraded to a greater or lesser degree). Some options are fairly reactive and/or manual in nature, while others are more proactive and automatic. After we provide a brief overview of the options, we'll cover the HA and FT options individually. Each option involves trade-offs and costs, and they can be used in any combination to provide more robust solutions and notifications.

Alarms versus HA versus FT versus DR

vSphere includes four different options for providing varying levels of high availability, as listed in Table 12.2.

HA

HA requires some careful thought and planning to work well. It works out of the box, but with a little time spent optimizing it, it can be even better. This section will cover why HA exists, the basic architecture of HA, and how HA handles various failures that could occur. Our goal for HA in this book is to discuss the design and implementation of HA for typical scenarios for most administrators. For an in-depth review of the subject by two experts in HA (and employees of VMware), refer to *VMware vSphere 5 Clustering Technical Deepdive* by Frank Denneman and Duncan Epping.

Purpose

In the physical server world, if a server crashes, you lose one server, but you probably have many other servers to keep things running through the outage. In the virtual world, you typically have many VMs on a single server, so if that server fails, it will take many other VMs with it. This will cause more widespread disruption to the environment unless careful DRS rule planning is undertaken, and even then, a large percentage of the reserve capacity for various services may be affected. To minimize the disruption, HA has been designed to do the following:

- If a physical ESXi server fails, restart the protected VMs (generally the VMs it was running) on other hosts in the HA cluster.

Table 12.2 Overview of Availability Features

Feature	Included With	Automation Level	Capabilities
Alarms	vCenter	Automatic notification, manual response by an administrator	Monitor disk, network, CPU, memory, VMs, network configuration, etc., and take automatic actions (for example, send an e-mail or run a script).
High Availability (HA)	All vSphere license levels except Essentials (New in 5)	Automatic failure detection and VM restart	Monitor ESXi hosts, VMs, and possibly individual services and restart the VM if a failure is detected (for host failures, restart the VMs it hosted on other hosts).
Fault Tolerance (FT)	vSphere Enterprise or higher	Automatic failure detection and transfer active VM to secondary VM	Monitor hosts, running a VM on two hosts in parallel such that if one host fails, the VM will run with no loss of data or downtime on the second host. Automatically create a second copy of the VM on another host whenever only one is running.
VMware Data Recovery (VDR)	All vSphere license levels except Essentials	Schedulable backups; manual restore as needed	Backup and recovery tool that can back up VMs and restore VMs, individual .vmdk files, or even individual files.

- If a VM fails, restart the VM on the same host.

- If properly configured, it can also detect failures of individual services and restart the VM if they fail.

- Work with DRS (Distributed Resource Scheduler—covered in Chapter 11) to optimize the VMs on each server to provide the capacity to failover VMs after a host failure.

VMware recommends, as do we, that you protect all of your VMs with HA to minimize the impact of any failures in the environment (with the possible exception of some low-priority VMs, such as those used in development).

Architecture

While the HA functionality is similar to vSphere 4's, the underlying architecture has been completely redesigned in vSphere 5. Let's begin with a quick look at the components of HA in vSphere 5, as shown in Figures 12.2 and 12.3. We'll look in detail at each of the components later, but for now, a quick overview of the roles and responsibilities will help us understand HA at a high level.

- **Master node.** Master of the cluster, it sends commands to each slave to perform tasks such as restart VMs. It communicates with the vCenter server to update the configuration of the cluster and the list of protected VMs. There's normally only one master node per cluster.

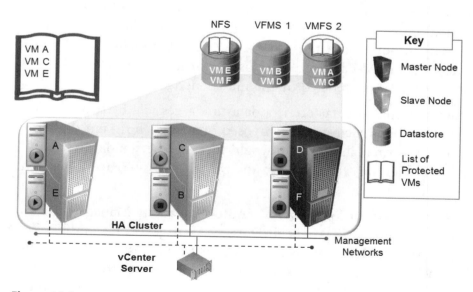

Figure 12.2
HA Architecture-1.

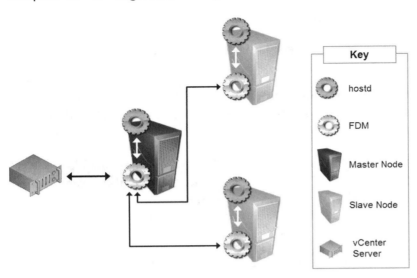

Figure 12.3
HA Architecture-2.

- **Slave nodes.** All other nodes in the cluster are slave nodes to the master and follow the directions issued by the master node. Each slave node also listens for heartbeats from the master, and if none are received, the slaves can get together and have an election for a new master.

- **Protected VMs list.** The list of VMs protected by HA, or in other words the VMs that will be restarted by HA after a failure. A VM will be protected when it is powered on and unprotected when it is powered off unless an administrator has configured HA to not protect the VM at all. This list is maintained by the master node on each shared datastore that has one or more protected VMs running on it, and the list is updated by the master node.

- **Shared datastores.** A shared datastore is a datastore accessible by two or more hosts (or one host if the HA cluster is composed of a single host, but there wouldn't be much HA capability in that, would there?). The standard recommendation is to have all datastores used in the cluster accessible by all hosts in the cluster.

- **FDM agent.** The replacement for the AAM (Auto Availability Manager) used in previous versions of vSphere, FDM (Fault Domain Manager) is responsible for all HA activities on the node. It interfaces directly with the hostd process on the same server and with the other FDM agents on the other nodes (depending if it is acting as the master or a slave node). Note that unlike previous versions, it does not interface directly with the vCenter agent (vpxa).

- **Hostd.** The master management process on each node, hostd carries out whatever commands are requested by vCenter (through the vpxa) or other processes (such as the FDM agent).

- **vCenter.** vCenter maintains the state of the cluster, tells the master node which VMs are protected or unprotected as they are powered on and off, updates the nodes as cluster parameters change, and deploys the FDM agent when an HA cluster is created. It does not, however, get involved with any HA activities such as VM restarts, eliminating vCenter as a single point of failure for VM restarts in the event of a server failure, especially if the vCenter instance was on a VM on the host that failed.

As you can see in Figure 12.3, the interaction between the components is as follows:

- vCenter only talks to the FDM on the master node for any changes; it does not directly communicate with any of the slave node's FDMs. It will deploy the FDM, however, when the HA cluster is created or a new node added.

- The master node FDM communicates with each slave node FDM and the slave node FDMs communicate with the master node. Specifically, the following happens:

  - Each slave node sends a heartbeat over each VMkernel port that has been enabled for management to the master node. This is a unicast packet.

  - The master node sends a heartbeat packet to each slave node (so they can verify the master node is functioning).

- The master node communicates with hostd on each node to determine the state of each VM and initiate the various actions required (such as powering on or off VMs).

ESXi Server Responsibilities   Most of the work done by HA takes place on the individual ESXi servers, as shown in Figure 12.3. This ensures that there are no dependencies on vCenter for proper operation, which is especially important if vCenter is a VM as it may be running on the server that goes down. The master and slave nodes have specific responsibilities and obviously these roles are hosted by physical servers.

Each ESXi node has specific responsibilities in HA, but most fundamental is making sure heartbeats happen. There are two heartbeats that HA uses in vSphere 5 (up from just network heartbeats in vSphere 4), as described in the sections below.

Figure 12.4
HA warning—no network redundancy.

Network Heartbeats   As previously described, network heartbeats are unicast packets that are sent from each slave to the master node and from the master node to each slave node. This is a much simpler design than in previous versions where secondary nodes sent heartbeats to each primary node (a primary node was roughly equivalent to the master node now and a secondary node was roughly equivalent to a slave node now; vSphere 4 supported up to five primary nodes, with all other nodes being secondary nodes). Primary nodes were in a full mesh architecture where each primary sent heartbeats and cluster configuration information to every other primary node.

For maximum fault tolerance on the network, it is recommended that you have at least two heartbeat networks or use NIC teaming and at least two NICs on the virtual switch that contains the VMkernel ports used by HA (which are all those enabled for management). This reduces the false positives of failure caused by network interruptions. In fact, if you enable HA on a server that is not configured in one of these ways, the server will appear as shown in Figure 12.4 to remind you that you still need to address the issue. One quick note on this—the server appears with an exclamation point, just like an alarm creates, but if you look on the Alarms tab, it is not a true alarm. It is just a configuration warning.

Storage Heartbeats   Network heartbeats are the primary way that HA keeps track of the other nodes to ensure that all are alive. If network heartbeats are not seen, the system can fall back on a new mechanism introduced in vSphere 5, the datastore heartbeat. The basic premise is that each server in the cluster will update the datastores that it is connected to so the master node can check a different way to see if a possibly failed server (one with no network heartbeats) is still alive. The mechanism is slightly different depending on whether the datastores use NFS or VMFS.

When VMFS is used, a special area of the datastore, known as the heartbeat region, is used by all servers connected to the datastore to allow other servers (primarily the master node) to know that the server is alive. This is done so that the virtual machines it hosts are not taken over if it is isolated on the management network(s), making it invisible across the network by the other nodes in the cluster but is still running, or conversely if it has truly failed to let other hosts take over the VMs it was running. VMFS was built with this concept in mind; NFS, a general-purpose file-sharing protocol, does not have the same capability.

To accomplish the same end result with NFS, a tiny file is accessed every few seconds that updates the last accessed time. By doing this, the master node can, by checking the last accessed time, determine if the node is still functioning.

Datastore heartbeats are not required, but they do provide an additional measure of protection from false positives about a host being down when it is in fact just isolated. This feature is enabled by default and can be modified if needed (as discussed in the Implementation and Management section). That having been said, however, datastore heartbeats work best when separate physical networks are used for storage and management purposes. In scenarios where the same NICS and/or physical switches are used for both, failure of the NIC (or switch) will take down both mechanisms at once, so the level of HA provided by this feature is minimal at best.

vCenter Responsibilities   vCenter, while not required for failover of VMs, is nevertheless important to several facets of HA deployment and operation. Among the roles and responsibilities of vCenter relative to HA are the following:

- vCenter is the only component that can create cluster objects with ESXi servers located in them.

- vCenter automatically deploys the FDM agent to each node when it joins an HA cluster and then proceeds to distribute the cluster configuration to the node.

Note

New in vSphere 5, deployment of the agent is done in a parallel fashion if multiple hosts are to be protected at once instead of the sequential method used previously, making the process of enabling HA much quicker.

- vCenter requests that the master node protect a VM when it is powered on and unprotect it when it is powered off. It is the master node's responsibility to actually update the file that contains the list of protected VMs and report that back to vCenter—in fact, as far as HA is concerned, a VM is not fully protected or unprotected until vCenter has requested it, the master has committed the change to disk, and an acknowledgement has been sent back to vCenter.

- vCenter displays the protection state of a VM (located on the Summary tab of the VM), based on the request for and acknowledgment of protection by the master node.

- If a host is disconnected from the vCenter server, vCenter will request that the master node unprotect any VMs that were hosted by the ESXi server that is no longer in vCenter.

- vCenter enforces Admission Control for HA, the necessary feature that reserves some spare capacity in the cluster for restarting VMs after a server failure (this is discussed more fully in the Implementation and Management section).

- vCenter is the final and only source of the state of the cluster. In fact, if vCenter isn't available, no changes to the cluster can be made. Among the things that vCenter maintains as part of the cluster state are the following items:

  - The hosts in the cluster.

  - The list of VMs that are protected (anything not on the list is therefore unprotected).

  - Cluster configuration parameters (some of these will be discussed in the Implementation and Management section).

  - VM to host compatibility information (based on DRS rules, VM size requirements, etc.).

- vCenter is required to be available (along with Auto Deploy—discussed in Chapter 5) for stateless (i.e., PXE booted) ESXi servers when those servers also are connected to a Distributed Virtual Switch.

vCenter always communicates with the master node in performing its duties and responsibilities (with the exception of pushing out the FDM agent, which obviously involves every node in the cluster).

As you can see, while vCenter is not involved with restarting VMs after a host failure, it is critical to the functioning of HA.

How ESXi Server Failures Are Handled

In this section, we'll cover the possible failures that could take place within an HA cluster and how HA responds in each case. We'll start with the simplest (and most common) situation, the failure of an ESXi host; then we'll move on to host isolation (where the server is still running, but has lost connectivity with the cluster). Next, we'll discuss network partitioning (where the network inadvertently gets split into two or more parts that can't communicate with each other). We'll conclude the section with a brief wrap up on the time frames involved in the failure scenarios to better understand when each task takes place and how long the overall process will take.

In all cases, the vSphere 5 response is better than previous versions due to the architecture update.

Server Failure   As simple as it sounds, there are actually two different kinds of server failures to discuss in this section, namely the loss of a slave node and the loss of the master node. In either case, vSphere will respond well, but the response will be a little different.

Let's briefly set the stage for these two scenarios. Figure 12.5 shows the cluster configuration. Note the following about this scenario:

- All VMs are running as shown, with VMs A and E on the first server, VMs C and B on the middle server, and VMs D and F on the last server (which is also the master node in the cluster).

- VMs A, E, and C are on the NFS volume, while VMs B, D, and F are on the VMFS volume named VMFS 2. There are no VMs running on VMFS 1 at the moment.

- The list of protected VMs (shown in the large book) contains all of the protected VMs and is stored on all datastores that have at least one running VM, hence at this point the NFS and VMFS 2 datastores.

- HA prefers VMFS volumes instead of NFS volumes for datastore heartbeats; the two datastores used for this are VMFS 1 and VMFS 2.

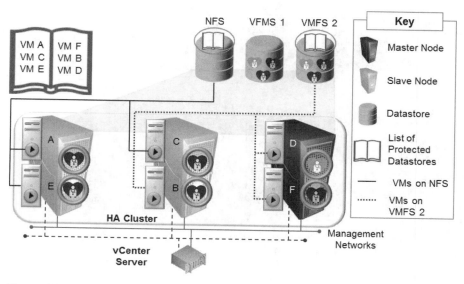

Figure 12.5
HA cluster—initial.

- Network heartbeats are sent and received by the nodes (as previously described) as noted by the hearts in green circles (we know the figure is in grayscale—it appears lighter than the red circles that will appear in later figures).

All is well at this point and this is the normal state of the cluster. The various scenarios below all start from this point and describe different failures that can occur and how HA responds to each. The exception to this starting point is the partition example which is a different scenario altogether.

Slave Server Failure Let's start with the simpler and more common (because there are more nodes in a cluster that are slaves [up to 31 of them] than the single master) scenario—a slave fails. Figure 12.6 shows what happens initially when the slave fails:

1. The slave fails and thus stops sending heartbeats to the master. This is illustrated in the figure as red (darker) circles on the server on the left as well as on the VMs it was hosting. The VMs have crashed at this point and are off. In addition, the red circle on the master indicates that it is not receiving heartbeats from the one failed slave node.

2. The master node notices it has not received any heartbeats from the slave and checks for datastore heartbeats from the node to ensure it is not simply isolated (which is another scenario we will cover a little later in this chapter).

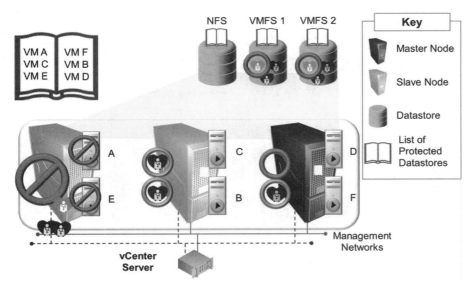

Figure 12.6
Slave Failure-1.

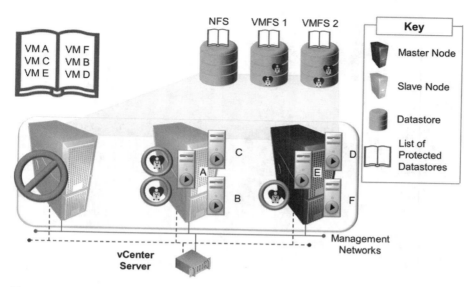

Figure 12.7
Slave Failure-2.

3. As shown in Figure 12.7, the master node now assigns either itself or another slave node (in this case the only other node) to restart the various VMs that were running on the failed node. In this example, the slave gets VM A and the master gets VM E.

4. The master node stops sending heartbeats to the failed node and looking for datastore heartbeats on the datastores. At this point, the new normal with a two-node cluster begins. When the failed node gets repaired, it will automatically rejoin the cluster and DRS (covered in Chapter 11) could then rebalance the load if needed.

Master Server Failure   On the other hand, the master can also fail. This is a more complicated scenario. We have to first elect a new master from among the slaves and then determine which ESXi servers are working. Once that is determined, the VMs on the failed host or hosts can be restarted as required. As with the previous scenario, it begins with the cluster working properly, as shown in Figure 12.5; when the master fails, Figure 12.8 illustrates what happens next:

1. Since the master server has failed, it is unable to send heartbeats to any of the slaves (as represented by the red circles on each slave), and obviously doesn't receive heartbeats from the slaves either (represented by the red circles on the master). In addition, there are no datastore heartbeats from the master on the

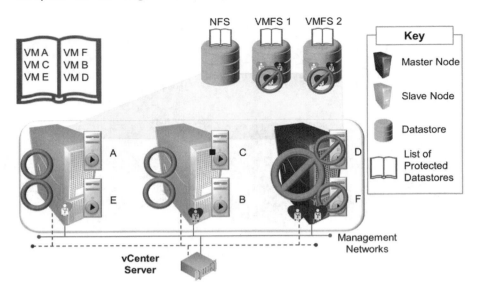

Figure 12.8
Master Failure-1.

datastore heartbeat datastores. Note, however, that the slaves are still sending heartbeats normally.

2. When the master node crashed, the VMs it was hosting (D and F) crashed as well.

3. As illustrated in Figure 12.9, after the slave nodes realize that they are not receiving any network heartbeats, they determine that the master has crashed (they do not check the datastore for heartbeats first, unlike the failed slave scenario). At this point, they hold an election and one of the slave nodes will become the new master.

4. Finally, as shown in Figure 12.10, the new master is the node on the left, and it will read the list of protected VMs, determine which VMs are running, and then restart the failed VMs from the old master—in this case, starting VM D on itself and VM F on the remaining slave node.

These two scenarios are the most common, but others are possible. The next most common scenario is server isolation, which we'll discuss below.

Server Isolation   The next scenario is one in which the network heartbeats are not seen on the network, but datastore heartbeats are detected. Datastore heartbeats are not checked unless network heartbeats are not seen, as it increases the load on the storage (though by a very tiny amount at best) but does not change the HA level.

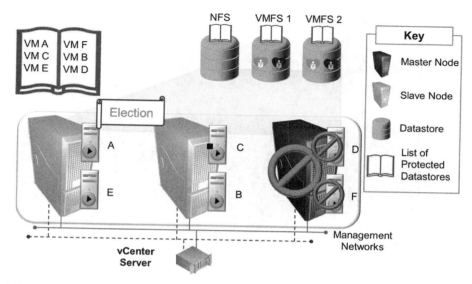

Figure 12.9
Master Failure-2.

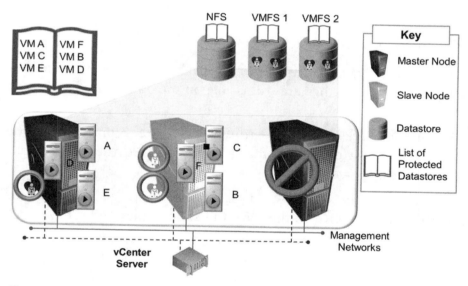

Figure 12.10
Master Failure-3.

As can be seen in Figure 12.5, each slave will send heartbeats on the heartbeat networks to the master, while the master will send heartbeats to every slave. In addition, each node will update the heartbeat information on the two heartbeat datastores as a backup measure.

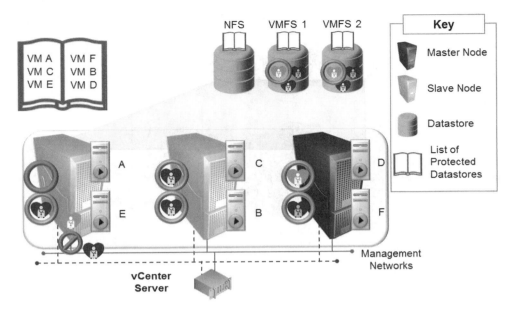

Figure 12.11
Server Isolation-1.

In Figure 12.11, the process begins, as follows:

1. One NIC fails in the host, causing the host to not see heartbeats from the master on one of the networks, but as they are still visible on the other, no effect is seen from the slave side.

2. When the NIC fails, vSphere will send heartbeats out to the second NIC, so the master continues to see heartbeats from the slave and doesn't realize there are any issues with the host.

3. In Figure 12.12, the second NIC fails. At that point, vSphere can't send (or receive) heartbeats over any NIC, so the slave thinks the other nodes have failed and the master thinks the slave has failed.

4. The master node then checks the datastore heartbeats, finds the host is still updating the heartbeats on the heartbeat datastores, and realizes the host is still running, thus leaving it to the slave to determine what to do with its VMs (see Step 6 below for options).

5. The slave will proceed to force an election, and since it has experienced a network failure, will not hear from any other node. It will then declare itself as the master. At that point, the slave will ping the default isolation address (by default, the default gateway for the network), and if it gets a response, it will assume that

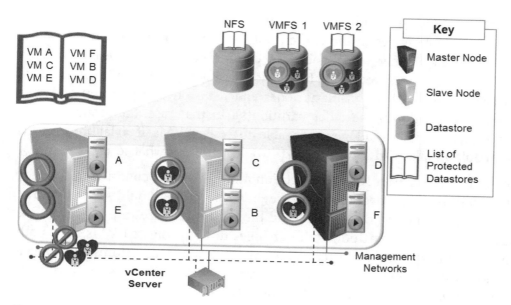

Figure 12.12
Server Isolation-2.

all other nodes have failed and will try to restart them. In this case, however, the NIC has failed (or the cables to it). It will not get a response and will declare itself isolated (and not the master node either).

6. Once the slave declares itself isolated, it can choose to leave its VMs powered on (as illustrated in Figure 12.12), power them off (not a graceful shutdown—it basically just kills power in each VM), or shut them down (using VMware Tools to request the guest OS to shut down gracefully). The advantage to powering off the VMs is that HA can restart the VM faster, but the downside is that it is just like a power failure in the real world and may leave the data in a state that requires recovery actions (such as rolling back or forward logs in a database or scanning the file system for errors) before the VM is fully functional when powered on again. Shutting down VMs takes a little longer to shut down, and thus to be restarted, but the restart will be clean and may be substantially faster overall. If it leaves them powered on, they function like normal, just like no failure had occurred. If the VMs are powered off or shut down, the master node will note that the VMs are off, but they were not ordered to do so by vCenter and thus are still protected. At this point, the master will act as if there had been an actual slave failure and restart the VMs, as explained in Figure 12.7.

Network Partition   Our final situation is a little different from the others. In this scenario, there are multiple nodes in the cluster, but for some reason, the nodes can't all communicate with each other (each node can communicate with at least one other node, but no node can see everyone). In previous versions, HA would not respond very well, especially if all of the primary nodes ended up on one partition and there were only secondary nodes in the other partition(s). In that case, the group of nodes that had only secondaries would never be able to restart VMs if a failure occurred because they couldn't talk with a primary that would tell them what to do.

In vSphere 5, there is a master for each partition and HA would continue to function, although it would be a little degraded because only one master could see the vCenter server. That brings up a question—how would the master that sees the vCenter server tell the master in the other partition about changes to the protected VMs list or otherwise communicate with that master? The answer: via the datastores. As long as communication with storage still exists, the master that sees vCenter can make changes and the other master can then find out about those changes.

Let's explore this scenario through a sequence of figures.

The initial scenario, in which everything is working, is shown in Figure 12.13. Note the following about this figure:

1. A master node (Node 4) and three slave nodes (Nodes 1–3) are all working properly. Heartbeats are being sent from the slaves to the master and from the master to each slave.

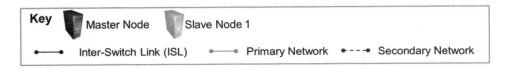

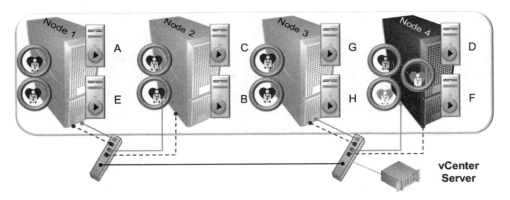

Figure 12.13
Network Partition-1.

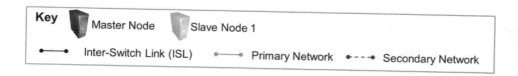

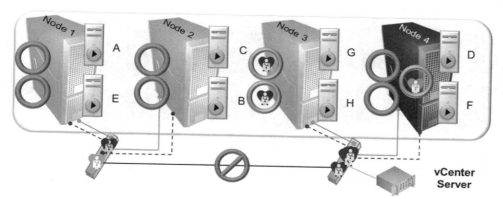

Figure 12.14
Network Partition-2.

2. There are two network switches with an ISL (Inter-Switch Link) between them.

3. Nodes 1 and 2 are connected to the switch on the left and Nodes 3 and 4 are connected to the switch on the right.

4. In Figure 12.14, the ISL between the two switches fails, causing two separate network segments. Nodes 3 and 4 still work, though the master thinks that Nodes 1 and 2 have failed or have become isolated.

5. At the same time, Nodes 1 and 2 think that either the master has failed or that they each have become isolated.

6. The original master node will check the datastore heartbeats and find that they are still there for Nodes 1 and 2, and then continue.

7. In Figure 12.15, Nodes 1 and 2 realize that they can communicate with each other and hence are not isolated. They discover this during the master election process and a new master is elected for their partition.

8. Figure 12.16 shows that Node 1 has been elected the master of its partition (consisting of Nodes 1 and 2) while Nodes 3 and 4 continue as they were, communicating with each other.

9. Any hosts or VMs that fail at this point will restart properly, as a master is available to instruct the two nodes (itself and the slave) in the partition to restart the

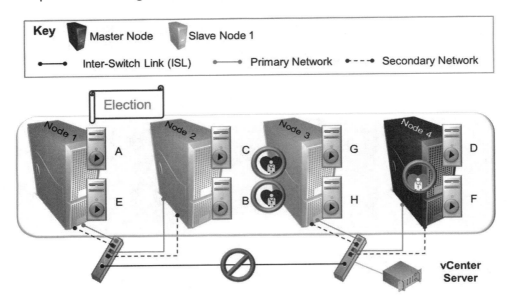

Figure 12.15
Network Partition-3.

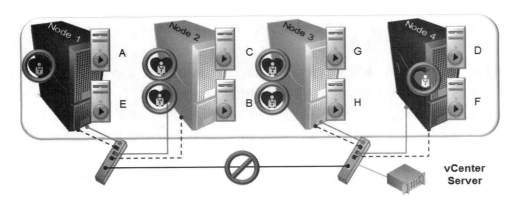

Figure 12.16
Network Partition-4.

failed VMs. Note that it is possible that a master could own a VM in another partition; in that case, the two masters will communicate using the datastores, and the owning master will inform the master in the partition of the need to restart the VM, which will then be done.

10. As Figure 12.17 shows, once the ISL is fixed, the temporary master (Node 1) will be demoted back to being a slave. Nodes 1 and 2 will communicate with Node 4. Node 4 will resume sending heartbeats to the entire cluster again.

Failures Summary   That was a lot of information, and it is easy to get lost in the details. Let us summarize the various faults that could occur and show the results of each in Table 12.3.

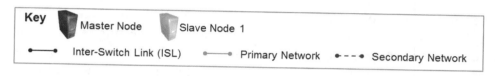

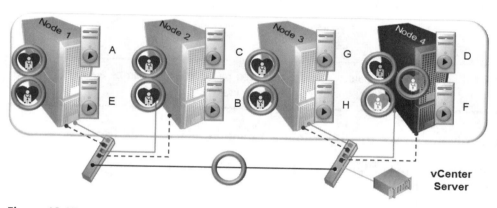

Figure 12.17
Network Partition-5.

Table 12.3   Possible Failures and Node State Summary

Network Heartbeat State	Storage Heartbeat State	Ping Response	Node State
Yes	N/A	N/A	Running (Normal)
No	Yes	No	Isolated or Partitioned
No	No	No	Failed
N/A	N/A	No	FDM Agent Down

The difference between isolated and partitioned is the number of hosts involved. If a single host can't see anyone else, it is isolated; on the other hand, if multiple nodes can see each other, but not the master, and at the same time the master can see some but not all of the nodes in the cluster, it is partitioned.

Note the special case where the FDM agent crashes in the bottom row of the table. Normally, there is a watchdog process that will restart the FDM agent if it fails. However, if it stays down for whatever reason, the node will not create or respond to heartbeats (network or storage), but if pinged it will respond. In this case, we know the node is alive and functioning, but HA is not.

Server Failure Timelines   Okay, so now that we know the basic process of what occurs when we have a master or slave failure, the question naturally becomes, how long does the process take to work? How long before my VMs are available again? That depends on whether the master or a slave has failed, as electing a new master takes additional time. Of course the timelines described in this section are the times before the restart is initiated, not before the VM is available. That will take additional time to complete, depending on the OS, application(s) installed, etc. Let's look at both scenarios.

Note

The times listed below assume default values for advanced parameters that can be adjusted if needed. Only change these parameters if you understand the repercussions of doing so.

In Figure 12.18, you can see the following actions take place at the indicated times:

- At T0, the master server fails, starting the chain of events described in the timeline.

- At T+10, the slaves have not heard from the master in ten seconds (missing ten heartbeats) and initiate the election process.

Figure 12.18
Master Failure timeline.

- At T+25, one of the slaves has assumed the role of master and begins acting in that role. It will begin by reading the list of protected VMs from the datastore (left by the previous master) to see what should be running and check with all the nodes in the cluster to determine what is actually running. It also informs vCenter that it is the new master to reestablish that link.

- At T+35 the new master begins assigning VMs that were running on the failed master node to itself and/or various slave nodes and then each node will power on any failed VMs that were assigned to it and were previously protected (this will include at least those that were running on the failed master and possibly other VMs if multiple hosts failed at the same time).

In Figure 12.19, the timeline is shorter as we don't have to worry about a master election, nor confirm what is or isn't running after the new master takes over. The time frame is as follows:

- At T0, the slave server fails, starting the chain of events described in the timeline. Note that there are two possible sub-scenarios illustrated here, one where datastore heartbeats are used (shown above the timeline in the darker boxes), and one where there are no datastore heartbeats in use (shown below the timeline in lighter colored boxes).

- At T+3 seconds, if datastore heartbeats are being used, the master node gets concerned that is has not heard from the slave over the network and begins monitoring datastore heartbeats to determine if it has failed or if it is isolated.

- At T+10 seconds, a continuous ping is sent (in either scenario) to the slave. This continues for five seconds looking for a response (and checking for the special case where the FDM agent has failed).

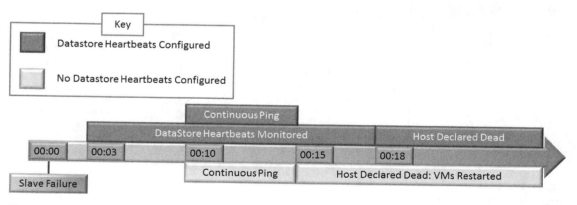

Figure 12.19
Slave Failure timeline.

■ If datastore heartbeats aren't in use, at T+15 seconds the node is considered failed and VMs are assigned to other nodes in the cluster and started by the master as needed (as previously described).

■ If datastore heartbeats are used, at T+18 seconds the node is considered failed and VMs are reassigned to other nodes and powered on as needed. This is ten seconds after heartbeat monitoring began, allowing time for the node to update the heartbeat at least once (usually this is done every five to seven seconds).

Server Isolation Timelines Now that we know the basic process of what goes on during a master or slave failure, we have to determine what changes if the node is functioning but the network is isolated instead. As with our previous description of master and slave failures, the timeline described here is the time before the power-on request is initiated, not before the VM is available.

In Figure 12.20, you can see the following actions take place at the indicated times. We'll start by looking at how the isolation of the master node (the top line in the darker boxes) works:

■ At T0, the node becomes network isolated (bad NIC, failed cable or switch, etc.), starting the chain of events described in the timeline. At that point, the master node begins to ping the default isolation address.

■ At T+5 seconds, the master node declares itself isolated and begins the isolation response. Slave nodes would then hold an election, just as with a master failure.

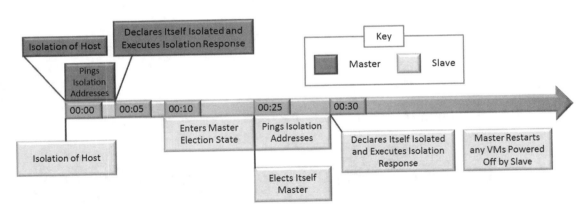

Figure 12.20
Server Isolation timeline.

On the other hand, the isolation of a slave (the bottom line in lighter boxes) has more tasks that need to be accomplished and thus responds differently, as described here:

- At T0, the node becomes network isolated (bad NIC, failed cable or switch, etc.), starting the chain of events described in the timeline.

- At T+10 seconds, not hearing from the master node, the slave node assumes the master has failed and starts the election process, just like the master actually had failed.

- At T+25 seconds, not having heard from any other slaves (and thus assuming they have all failed along with the master), the isolated slave node elects itself master. It then begins a sanity check to make sure the rest of the nodes have failed by pinging its isolation address. If it gets a response, it assumes it has network connectivity and thus is the only remaining node still functioning.

- At T+30 seconds if it hasn't received a response from the isolation address, it declares itself isolated (and not the master) and undertakes the configured isolation response.

- If the isolation response is to either power off or shut down the VMs, once the process is complete and the locks are released, the master node will see that the VMs are powered off and yet are still on the protected list (thus not shut down by the user) and will power on the VMs as previously described.

VM and Application Failures

HA can protect against not only physical host failure, but also VM failures, and even application failures (if you're using the SDK [Software Development Kit] from VMware for HA or if you have purchased software, such as Symantec's Application HA). Application monitoring will not be discussed in this book because it requires extra software or special application design. However, VM failures will be discussed in the Implementation and Management section as there is not much planning required. The remaining portion of the Planning section for HA will describe options for host-level failures.

Failover Options

In this section, we'll look at the three options that can be used with HA to plan for and handle host failures. The first, "Host failures the cluster tolerates" has been around as long as VMware has had HA, while the other two, "Percentage of cluster resources reserved as failover spare capacity" and "Specify failover hosts" were introduced in vSphere 4 and upgraded in version 5.

These settings are all designed to reserve some resources in the cluster to handle the loss of one or more ESXi hosts. The information in the Admission Control section below is also important as it determines if these reserved resources are not allowed to be used in normal operation (the recommended setting) or if they can be used (meaning that if an actual failure were to occur, there may not be enough resources left to restart all the VMs that were previously running).

It is important to think and plan properly to ensure that VMs on a failed server (or multiple servers if you are more paranoid) can be restarted on the remaining nodes in the cluster. Not only must this be planned for when HA is initially deployed, but as the cluster grows and changes (more or fewer hosts or VMs, changes in CPU or RAM per host, etc.), this needs to be revisited to ensure that the desired level of spare capacity is held in reserve.

Host Failures the Cluster Tolerates Let's begin with the oldest option, "Host failures the cluster tolerates." This option is designed for simplicity—it has the lowest overhead on the vCenter server and is very simple to configure. There are two important points regarding this option:

- **vCenter Overhead.** The overhead on the vCenter server is minimal with this option. It uses a one-size-fits-all philosophy for calculating the resources each VM requires. This algorithm will be described below.

- **Algorithm is Pessimistic.** HA assumes that the largest server is the one that fails, so if you have a quad socket, quad core server, and a single [dual socket] core server, HA will assume the quad core will fail and thus reserve a large percentage of the resources of the cluster to handle this possibility.

Tip

Best practice: Use uniformly sized servers (same amount of CPU and RAM on each).

Please refer to the sidebar on slots and slot sizes to understand these terms before proceeding with this section.

Slots and Slot Sizes

Slots are used extensively in the "Host failures the cluster tolerates" mechanism and the default settings are also used by the "Percentage of cluster resources reserved as failover spare capacity" option when no VMs are running (otherwise HA uses actual CPU and memory reservation values for the VMs running in the cluster). Slot size is calculated as follows:

- The VM with the highest memory reservation determines the memory slot size (slot size is that reservation + the overhead memory for that VM). If no VMs have reservations, memory slot size is set to the VM with the largest amount of overhead memory.

- The VM with the highest CPU reservation determines the CPU slot size (this can be from a different VM than the previous step). If no VMs have a CPU reservation, 32 MHz is used (prior to vSphere 5, 256 MHz was the default).

Once the slot sizes have been calculated, the system needs to calculate how many slots are available in the cluster. It does so as follows:

1. Round down the CPU capacity of each node in the cluster/CPU slot size. Add them up for the number of CPU slots in the cluster.

2. Round down the memory capacity of each node in the cluster/memory slot size. Add them up for the number of memory slots in the cluster.

3. The number of slots in the cluster is the smaller of Steps 1 and 2.

4. If admission control is enabled, reserve the percentage of memory and CPU specified, or the number of slots in the largest *n* hosts if the "Host failures the cluster tolerates" policy was specified, where *n* is the number of host failures selected.

This can get confusing, so let's look at two examples, using the same configuration in each, but with different HA policies. In the cluster there are four hosts (all with HyperThreading disabled to simplify the scenario—typically HyperThreading is enabled):

- Host 1 has 64GB of RAM and dual quad core 2.5GHz processors (for a total of 20GHz).
- Host 2 has 96GB of RAM and quad hex core 3.0GHz processors (for a total of 72GHz).
- Hosts 3 and 4 each have 48GB of RAM and dual quad core 3.0GHz processors (for a total of 24GHz).

The cluster thus has a total of 256GB of RAM and 140GHz (or for simple math 140,000MHz).

Table 12.4 describes the VMs in the cluster.

Note that the domain controllers will use 32MHz for CPU calculations and their overhead memory (we'll use 150MB for this example) for memory calculations.

Let's start with the traditional "Host failures the cluster tolerates" scenario. In this example, the CPU slot size will be 15,000MHz and the memory slot size is 40,000MB. Following the steps above, these are the slots in the cluster:

- Host 1: 1 CPU and 1 memory slot.
- Host 2: 4 CPU and 2 memory slots.

Table 12.4   VM Configurations for the Example Scenario

Number	Purpose	CPU Reservation	Memory Reservation
2	Domain Controllers	0	0
5	Web servers	200MHz	512MB
1	Oracle server	15,000MHz	40,000MB
1	vCenter server	6,000MHz	4,000MB

- Hosts 3 and 4: 1 CPU and 1 memory slot each.
- Total: 7 CPU and 5 memory slots.
- Using the smaller value, there are thus five slots in the cluster.

If the value of 1 was selected for "Host failures the cluster tolerates," the system will remove host 2 (which contributes 4 CPU slots and 2 memory slots to the cluster), leaving three slots in which to run VMs, meaning a total of three VMs could be run from the list of nine. This behavior wastes a lot of resources by default (though advanced parameters we'll discuss in the Implementation and Management section can make this more reasonable).

On the other hand, with the "Percentage of cluster resources reserved as failover spare capacity" option, if 25% CPU and 20% memory were selected, the system would see total CPU used of: (32MHz * 2) + (200MHz * 5) + 15,000MHz + 6,000MHz for a total of 22,064MHz or 16% utilization and thus could continue to power on VMs until 105,000MHz was reserved. On the memory front, the following is the consumption: (150MB * 2) + (512MB * 5) + 40,000MB + 4,000MB for a total of 46,860MB (excluding the overhead memory for all but the first two VMs, which would have to be added to this total, or 18% utilization and thus could power on VMs up to 192GB).

The upside to this approach is that it is very simple to calculate the slots available and determine if a VM can be powered up, but the downside is that unless the VMs are sized similarly (in terms of CPU and memory reservations), a lot of resources can be wasted.

Tip

This mechanism works best when all the VMs are similarly sized so that each VM uses the slot size efficiently.

You may be wondering how many host failures you can specify. In previous versions, you could specify four, because there were only five primaries and you had to guarantee that at least one primary would be left available to restart VMs. In vSphere 5, the maximum number that can be selected is 31, as at least one node still needs to be on in the cluster to run VMs. But boy would this be a pessimistic administrator! The waste of resources would be enormous: 3% used and 97% in case of failure!

Percentage of Cluster Resources Reserved as Failover Spare Capacity This option works by using the actual CPU and memory reservations set on the VMs, not a one-size-fits-all approach. New in vSphere 5, the percentage of resources reserved for CPU and memory can be different (for example, 25% CPU and 20% memory). In vSphere 4, one value was used for both settings. If a node fails, then the CPU and RAM it contributed to the cluster are removed from the calculation and new values are calculated and used until the failure is rectified.

Tip

VMware recommends that this method be chosen in most scenarios, especially where CPU and/or memory reservations vary widely between VMs.

Specify Failover Hosts   This approach, also introduced in vSphere 4, allows a failover host (or new in vSphere 5 multiple failover hosts) to be specified. The specified nodes are always on and consuming resources, but will never host any VMs unless another node fails. The failover node(s) also will not have VMs moved to it/them by DRS; will not be powered off by DPM; or do anything but consume resources unless and until a failure occurs, at which point it/they will run the VM(s) from the failed node(s). When the node failures are fixed, the VMs will return to the other nodes in the cluster, and the failover node(s) will become standby node(s) again. We like to think of this like a mortician, who does nothing unless/until someone dies, at which time he swings into action, takes care of the body, then returns to waiting for the next death. In a large city, there is always work to be done (and the same is true in vSphere—statistically there will be more work to do [more failures] in a large cluster), while in a small village, there may not be much work at all (small clusters statistically have fewer failures due to fewer nodes).

The question logically follows: What if the failover node fails? The answer: There is no impact on the cluster as it didn't host VMs previously. But what if a failure happens elsewhere in the cluster while it is also failed? HA will simply look to any other standby hosts, and if there are none, or they are all at capacity, HA will try to use the other hosts (i.e., not those dedicated as standby hosts) in the cluster.

Tip

VMware recommends that this setting be used only when required by organizational policy. It will increase the CPU and memory load on the cluster instead of spreading the load across all of the servers in the cluster with additional headroom on each server (that can be used by VMs as needed unless a failure has occurred and the surviving nodes are running extra VMs to cover for the failed node(s)).

Admission Control in HA

In an HA cluster, admission control is the ability to strictly reserve the capacity specified in one of the three foregoing policies to ensure (as long as the values were set correctly and more failures than expected haven't occurred) that all of the VMs on the failed node(s) can be restarted elsewhere in the cluster.

Note

Admission control is managed exclusively by vCenter (not the individual nodes—in fact, the FDM agent is unaware of this setting). In other words, when a VM is powered on in vCenter, vCenter will first check to see if there are sufficient resources left reserved after the VM turns on to meet the minimum specified. If there are, it will turn the VM on; if not, no host will know that a request to power on a VM was made.

This feature can be enabled or disabled. If enabled, the reserved capacity will always be available in the cluster (except during failure events). This capacity requirement is observed and respected by not only vCenter when powering on VMs, but also by DRS and DPM as they power off hosts to save power or move around VMs. On the other hand, if it is disabled, you can start as many VMs as you want, subject only to the physical limit of the cluster's resources to start them. In this state, however, there is no guarantee that there will be enough spare resources to restart any or all of the VMs from the failed node(s).

Tip

We strongly recommend that this setting always be left enabled unless an extraordinary event exists (such as a node that is out for maintenance or a new VM needs to be made available and additional memory, CPU, or entire nodes are on order and you are awaiting delivery). If it is routinely disabled, why bother having HA configured at all? On the hope that it might be able to restart something?

FT

FT (fault tolerance) was a new feature introduced in vSphere 4. The basic premise is to provide a higher level of availability than HA alone. Any failure of a host in an HA cluster will automatically mean downtime for VMs that were on that host. HA will minimize it as much as possible, but there will still be downtime. FT (which can only be used in an HA cluster) goes a step further—the goal is zero downtime and zero data loss for protected VMs.

Use cases include VMs that must always be available (though understand that if a VM blue screens, FT will not protect it as it will do so on both hosts—HA can still restart the VM in this case) or when other clustering options are either too complex or are not available at all. FT can also be enabled and disabled on demand for situations where availability is critical only sometimes (during high sales periods, at the end of a quarter for financial systems, etc.).

In this section, we'll begin by looking at how it works, then we'll look at the requirements to implement it (and current limitations when using it), and then finally we'll look at the required vCenter configuration.

Operation

So how does FT work? Let's begin by looking at it at the macro level—how it creates the secondary VM and handles failures—and then we'll drill down to the micro level, namely how the VM is kept in lock step (synchronized) across two physical hosts.

Figure 12.21 shows six VMs running on a four-node cluster. One of these VMs (VM A) running on host Node 1 is considered critical and thus begins the following sequence of events:

1. FT is enabled for the VM, causing this VM to be known as the primary VM.

2. As soon as it is enabled, vCenter will use vMotion technology to create a second copy of the running VM, known as the secondary VM (pointing to the same storage) on a different host (Node 2), only instead of turning control of the VM over to that host when the process completes, it leaves it running on both hosts. If the VM had been powered off instead, it would have started the VM on both hosts when the user requested the primary to be booted.

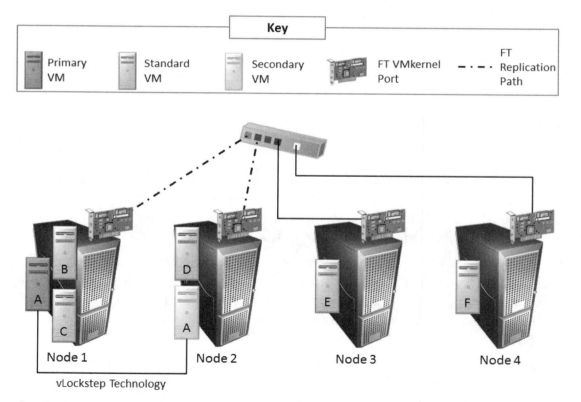

Figure 12.21
Functionality-1.

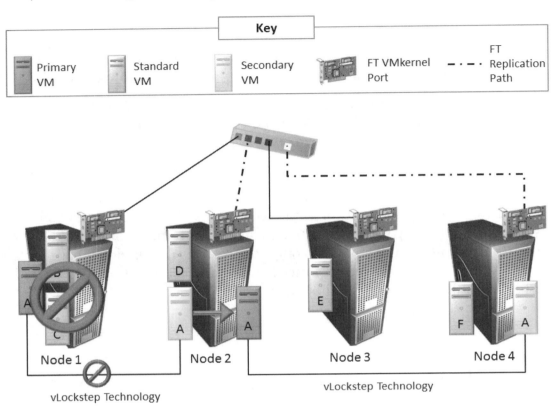

Figure 12.22
FT Functionality-2.

3. Once the two VMs are up and running on both hosts, vLockstep Technology is implemented over the FT VMkernel ports (as shown by the dotted lines for the NICs on Nodes 1 and 2) to keep them synchronized. This technology will be described in more detail later in this section.

4. Figure 12.22 illustrates what happens when the host that is running the primary copy fails (Node 1). Of course, the primary VM (along with VMs B and C) will fail because the host they have been running on has failed. The standard VMs B and C would be restarted by HA, but are not shown restarting elsewhere in the figure.

5. FT notices the loss of heartbeats between the nodes (heartbeats will be discussed later in this section as well) and promotes the secondary VM (on Node 2) to be the new primary as indicated by the arrow showing the promotion from secondary to primary.

Note

For a couple of seconds VM A will not be responding, but the clients will probably never notice as that is within the TCP retry interval, so they will assume that the network packet(s) just got lost in the network and retransmit it/them. Once the secondary has been promoted, it will receive any retransmitted packets and process them, and the client will have no idea anything happened. If the client was using a UDP-based protocol (such as is often used in audio and video streaming), they may see a momentary flicker or hesitation like when a DVD is scratched, but otherwise will not notice anything.

6. The new primary (on Node 2) creates a new secondary (on Node 4) and synchronizes them as described in Steps 2 and 3. At this point, the situation is back to normal.

Okay, so how does vLockstep Technology keep the two copies of the VM synchronized? Figure 12.23 shows the basic configuration involved. There are five phases shown in the diagram (the numbered circles), as described here:

1. Non-deterministic input (keystrokes, mouse movement and clicks, network I/O, and/or disk I/O) comes into the primary copy of VM D on the host on the left. In this example, mouse input was followed by network I/O, which was followed by keystrokes.

2. As the input came into the VM, the VMM (Virtual Machine Monitor—the component that makes a VM a VM) will see these inputs happen and will copy the

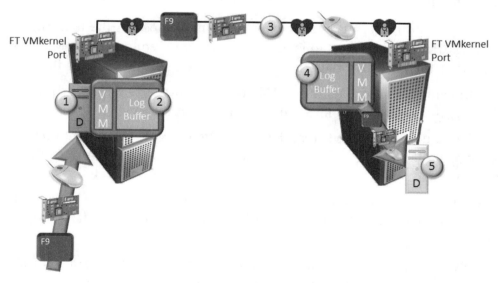

Figure 12.23
FT Functionality-3.

mouse clicks, network packets, and keyboard presses in order into the log buffer used by FT.

3. These inputs, along with heartbeats between the FT VMkernel ports, are then sent across the network to the host on the right. The exact timing and sequence used on the primary VM are copied to the secondary so nothing is lost between them. Heartbeats are sent between the nodes every 100 milliseconds by default, but they are never visible outside the FT framework. In the diagram, a heartbeat occurred. Then in the 100 milliseconds before the next heartbeat, mouse I/O occurred; then another heartbeat; then network I/O and a key press; then another heartbeat.

4. On the receiving side, the log buffer receives the I/O, processes the heartbeats, and sends the remainder of the I/O to the secondary copy of VM D.

5. VM D receives the inputs and processes them in the exact same way that they were handled on the primary with the exact same results. Thus the two VMs are identical to each other, though the secondary VM will always be a few milliseconds behind the primary.

You may have noticed that Figure 12.23 showed all of the acceptable input types except for disk I/O. By default, disk I/O is handled in the same way, but this can cause a strain on the FT network if a lot of disk I/O occurs. To handle that possibility, FT can be configured to do all disk input on the underlying LUN directly. This process is illustrated in Figure 12.24 and utilizes the same five-step process.

1. Disk I/O comes into the primary copy of VM D on the host on the left. In this example, a disk read request was followed by a disk write request. The VM reads and then writes the necessary data to the disk per the requests made of it.

2. As the input came into the VM, the VMM sees these disk I/O requests in order and will place the I/O requests into the log buffer used by FT.

3. The disk I/O requests—not the actual data from the requests—along with heartbeats between the FT VMkernel ports are then sent across the network to the host on the right.

4. On the receiving side, the log buffer receives the I/O, processes the heartbeats, and sends the remainder of the I/O (the disk requests) to the secondary copy of VM D.

5. VM D receives the I/O requests and the VM then processes the read requests handling the read like the primary did (causing actual disk I/O; hopefully read cache on the disk array will reduce the performance impact on the

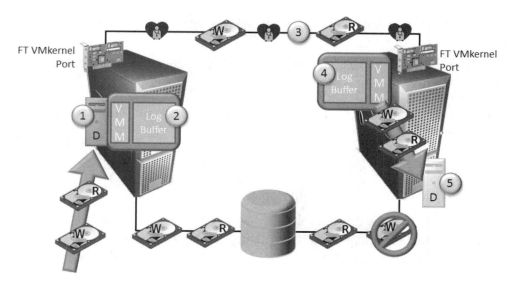

Figure 12.24
FT Functionality-4.

underlying disks). It also attempts to carry out the write request, but the VMM silently blocks the write (though when the acknowledgement of the write occurs on the primary, it will be forwarded to the secondary, and the secondary will have no idea that it didn't actually write the data). Thus the two VMs are identical to each other.

Requirements

With the understanding of how FT works behind the scenes, we are now ready to look at the requirements to implement it at the vCenter, host, and VM level.

Unfortunately, there is a fairly long list of requirements for FT to work, at the vCenter, host, and VM level. In this section we'll examine them to help ensure FT works properly when deployed. In the Implementation and Management section we'll discuss how to configure the major requirements.

vCenter   Let's start with vCenter requirements. They include:

- FT and vMotion VMkernel ports for spinning up the secondary and then keeping them synchronized (more on this in the vCenter Configuration section below).

- Host certificate checking (enabled by default on new installations of vCenter 4.0 and later, but not on upgrades from previous versions).

- Hosts in the same HA cluster with access to shared storage and common networks.

- The same version of FT on the nodes that will use it (for ESX(i) 4.1 and later) or the same ESX(i) build for vSphere 4.0.

Not so bad, right? For most people this list is fairly obvious (with the exception of host certificate checking).

Host Let's continue on and look at the host requirements. They include:

- Enterprise license level or higher for the hosts.

- Hardware virtualization features enabled in the BIOS (though if the memory virtualization features are enabled [Intel's Extended Page Tables—EPT—or AMD's Rapid Virtualization Indexing—RVI] they will automatically be disabled for any FT-enabled VM).

- FT-compatible processors (most processors in the last few years are); for a complete list, refer to http://kb.vmware.com/kb/1008027.

Tip

You can see if a host is FT capable by looking in the Fault Tolerance box on the host; if it is not, clicking on the "thought bubble" icon will list the reason(s) why FT is not supported.

VM Finally, there are some requirements that the VM must meet. Among the requirements:

- It must use either an RDM in virtual compatibility mode or a .vmdk file that is Eager Zero thick provisioned (both of which were described in Chapter 8).

- It must run a supported OS (which includes Netware, Linux, and Windows NT 4 or higher). For a complete list, refer to http://kb.vmware.com/kb/1008027.

Limitations

That doesn't sound too restrictive, right? Well there is also a substantial list of vSphere features and capabilities that are not compatible with FT. Some of the more commonly used features that are not compatible include:

- **Virtual SMP.** In other words, the critical VM must have only a single vCPU. This is a deal breaker for many for using FT, but SMP is at least an order of magnitude harder to accomplish. VMware has demonstrated SMP FT in the lab, but as of the writing of this book, it is not available. The demonstrations that have been done also included a requirement of at least 10 Gb Ethernet (GbE) for the FT link, versus the 1GbE that is required for a uniprocessor VM.

- **VMware snapshots.** You can't back up the VM using the vStorage APIs for data protection (including VMware's own VMware Data Recovery [VDR]). If the previous item was not a deal breaker, this one often is. You could still back up the VM using storage-based snapshots or by using a traditional agent inside the VM that backs up the VM over the network.

- **Storage vMotion.** This can't be used either, meaning the VM can't be relocated to different storage while protected. You can, however, disable FT temporarily, move the VM, and then re-enable FT.

- CD or floppy connections to anything other than a floppy image or .iso file located on shared storage.

- USB, sound, and the vlance network card are not supported, nor are serial or parallel ports.

- Hot plugging any device, including changing the port group to which a virtual NIC is connected.

- 3D-enabled video.

There are more limitations as well, but those listed are the most common. For the above reasons, FT is considered by many to be a niche solution. When some of the major limitations, like a single processor and no snapshots, are removed, we expect to see wider implementation of this feature, but we have no idea how long it will be before this becomes reality.

vCenter Configuration

The details of how to configure vCenter and your ESXi hosts will be covered in the Implementation and Management section; for planning purposes, it is just important to note that you will need not only a vMotion link, but also an FT link between the hosts in the cluster. These links are just VMkernel ports configured for either vMotion or FT—separate links are strongly recommended (required to be supported) when 1Gbps NICs are used, while with 10Gbps NICs, they can share the same physical link.

One other note about the links—the data sent is unencrypted and could contain passwords, network and disk traffic of a sensitive nature, etc. We thus strongly recommend that you keep it on a private network accessible only by the ESXi hosts themselves. This can be accomplished using separate physical switches (or better yet, a pair of switches for better availability) or at least by using a dedicated VLAN.

It makes sense, but it should be stated that the primary and secondary VM can't run on the same host (there is an implied—not explicit—anti-affinity DRS rule that keeps them separate). At the same time, if any host affinity rules are assigned to the primary VM, the secondary will have to abide by the same restrictions, so be sure to leave enough servers for FT to function properly.

While we're on the subject of DRS, FT does not require DRS to function, only HA, but will leverage DRS if it is configured. If the HA cluster has been configured with EVC (Enhanced vMotion Compatibility), and DRS is configured in either partial or full automatic mode, it will automatically place the primary and secondary VMs on appropriate hosts and will load balance them (in fully automatic mode) as needed. On the other hand, if EVC is disabled, FT will automatically disable DRS for the VMs and will start the primary VM on the host it is assigned to (last run on) and start the secondary on any other host.

IMPLEMENTATION AND MANAGEMENT

Whew! We finally got all of the planning issues out of the way, so let's get into the "how" section and cover the steps involved in implementing these features. We'll discuss the features in the same order we discussed their planning, namely HA and then FT. Ready? Let's get started.

VMware HA

VMware HA is designed to protect against host, VM, and application failures, though application failures require either custom programming or third-party applications to implement and thus won't be discussed in this book. What we will cover is how HA handles host and VM failures, some of the advanced options that can be used to tune HA, and how HA can leverage DRS to work better. It is important to note that much of the background surrounding HA was covered in the Planning section; this section of the book will focus much more on the how than the why.

Host Failures

The original purpose of HA, and still the primary purpose in our opinion, is to automatically restart VMs when a physical server fails. We'll look at how to create a cluster and the host and VM options as a single sequence of steps, but will look at the other sections individually.

To create an HA cluster, do the following:

1. Right-click the desired datacenter or folder object in Hosts and Clusters view, and select New Cluster.

2. Give the cluster a name, check the Turn On vSphere HA checkbox, and then click Next.

3. Verify (and check if necessary) the Enable Host Monitoring checkbox to enable HA to detect failures and restart VMs. This should always be selected unless you are doing maintenance tasks that could cause false failure detections (such as network maintenance that might disrupt the management network).

Admission Control Options   Admission control in HA is a mechanism for reserving resources to enable VMs to be restarted after a host failure. It should not be confused with the vSphere definition of admission control, which relates to not starting a VM if its reservation cannot be guaranteed. This HA feature should *always* be left on unless there is a specific, short-term reason to disable it, such as when a critical VM needs to be deployed and used that requires some of the reserved resources to function and more memory, a new host, etc., is on order to rectify the situation. Whenever this is unchecked, you run the risk of not being able to restart all of the VMs from a failed host. Checking this does not guarantee that they will all be able to be restarted (either due to incorrect sizing of the reserved resources or to multiple simultaneous failures), but it does dramatically increase the odds of them being restarted.

To enable admission control:

4. Click the "Enable: Disallow VM power on operations that violate availability constraints" radio button.

Failover Options   Next, you'll select the mechanism for reserving failover resources. We discussed them in the Planning section, and thus this section is just going to review the specific options for each choice. There is a separate sub-section for each option. Even though each option has its own step number, you can only select one of them.

Host Failures the Cluster Tolerates   This is the original and most conservative option. You specify the number of concurrent failures you want the cluster to be able to handle, and the system will reserve the number of slots that number of servers has (starting with the largest servers if the servers differ in CPU and/or memory capacity). In previous versions of vSphere, you were limited to four failures maximum; now you can specify up to 31 (though that is very pessimistic and not very realistic—31 spares for a single host). To select this option:

5. Click the "Host failures the cluster tolerates" radio button and then specify the desired number to the right of the option (1 is the default).

6. Click Next and skip to Step 13.

Percentage of Cluster Resources Reserved as Failover Spare Capacity This option was introduced with vSphere 4 and has been enhanced in version 5 with the addition of the ability to specify separate values for the amount of CPU and memory the cluster will reserve. It is also VMware's recommended option for most circumstances. To use this option:

7. Click the "Percentage of cluster resources reserved as failover spare capacity" radio button, then enter the desired percentages for CPU and memory in the associated boxes (25% for each is the default).

8. Click Next and skip to Step 13.

Specify Failover Hosts The final option dedicates one or more ESXi hosts to be strictly used in failover scenarios—they will never be powered off by DPM (Distributed Power Management) to save electricity and cooling, used by DRS to better load balance, etc. This option is recommended for organizations that have a policy that requires one or more standby nodes. New in vSphere 5, multiple standby hosts can be specified. To use this option:

9. Select the "Specify failover hosts" radio button, then click the Click to Edit link to specify the desired host(s).

10. From the Available Hosts list on the left, select one or more ESXi servers then click the >> button to add them to the Failover Hosts list.

11. Click OK. The system will report in the blue link text next to "Specify Failover Hosts" the number of hosts selected.

12. Click Next.

Virtual Machine Options: Restart Priority and Isolation Response The next step in the wizard is to set VM options, both at the cluster level to set defaults for every VM in the cluster, as well as, optionally, on individual VMs if they require a different setting than the cluster default. Let's briefly review the settings and the implications, then we'll look at how to set them.

The first setting is the "VM restart priority." The higher the priority of a VM (relative to the other VMs' priorities), the better chance it will restart if resources are scarce and there are not enough resources to restart all failed VMs. Remember, this is a relative setting, so setting all VMs to High will have no more effect then setting them all to Low, unless you manually override the settings of individual VMs to create different values for different VMs. Disabled can also be selected, so that no VMs will automatically restart. You may wonder why anyone would choose that. It would most likely be used in a development cluster where only a few infrastructure VMs for the developers (such as domain controllers or SQL servers) should automatically be restarted (by setting it on a VM-by-VM basis). We rarely see the Disabled option set in the field.

HA will restart all VMs that are set to High, followed by those set to Medium, followed by those set to Low. If there are insufficient resources to restart all of the VMs within a given priority level, they will be restarted alphabetically by VM name until resources are gone (so a VM named DC would be restarted before a VM named SQL), and obviously any VMs at lower priority levels would not be restarted at all.

Tip

We have seen cases where people place a number before a VM name (such as 1-SQL) to influence the restart priority if resources are expected to be scarce under normal conditions.

The other setting is "Host isolation response." This is the default response (which again can be overridden on an individual VM basis if necessary) that HA will take after a host has declared itself isolated (as described in the Planning section). There are three options: "Leave powered on" (the default), which makes sense if you think most interruptions will be brief and/or the networking for VMs is separate from the networking for management (and possibly storage); "Power off," which hits the virtual power button—this may be used if restart time is the most important factor to consider, realizing that it will not be a clean shutdown and the restart time for the VM may be longer if transactions need to be rolled forward and/or backward; and "Shut down," which makes sense if you think the failure is likely going to last for a while and/or VM networking uses the same network cards and infrastructure as management and storage, and when you want a clean shutdown followed by a clean restart. Remember, this option only works if the host declares itself isolated and not when an actual unplanned failure occurs.

Note

If the server loses access to storage, this setting does not matter because the lock will expire and HA on other nodes will restart the VMs anyway.

13. In the "VM restart priority" drop-down list, select Low, Medium, or High, or choose Disabled if you don't want most VMs restarted. Medium is the default.

14. Select the desired isolation response from the three previously described.

15. If desired, change the restart priority and/or isolation response for individual VMs from the drop-down options to the right of the VM names (all VMs default to "Use cluster setting").

16. Click Next.

VM Failures

vSphere can also handle VM (and even application) failures that may occur. We won't be discussing application recovery options as that group of features requires either a third-party product or use of the HA SDK to add that functionality to your own applications. Note that even if either of these application solutions is implemented, the result is the same as a failed VM—restart the VM.

As for VM monitoring, the next step in the wizard, it is fairly easy to configure. To do so:

17. In the VM monitoring drop-down list, select one of the following:

   ■ **Disabled.** (the default) HA does not monitor for VM failures [other than those caused by host failures]) and skip to Step 21.

   ■ **VM Monitoring Only.** To monitor for VM failures (but not applications and/ or services within the VM).

   ■ **VM and Application Monitoring.** To monitor for both, as described in this section.

Options   If VMs (and/or applications) are being monitored, you can set a monitoring interval on a cluster-wide default basis, and then override the cluster defaults on a per-VM basis as needed, similar to the host isolation response and restart priority options previously described. To set these options:

18. Set the monitoring sensitivity using the slider from Low to High (with an unnamed setting in the middle), or check the Custom checkbox to set your own settings, as described in Table 12.5.

Note
_____

The meaning of each of the settings will be described at the end of this sequence of steps (in this section).
_____

19. If desired, you can override the cluster defaults just specified on a per-VM basis. Go to the VM row and in the VM Monitoring column, set any of the options

Table 12.5   Monitoring Sensitivity Definitions

Setting	Failure Interval	Minimum Uptime	Maximum per-VM Resets	Maximum Resets Time Window
Low	2 Minutes	8 Minutes	3	7 Days
Medium	1 Minute	4 Minutes	3	24 Hours
High	30 Seconds	2 Minutes	3	1 Hour
Custom	1–100,000 Seconds (almost 28 hours)	0–100,000 Seconds	1–1,000	Either "No Window" (in which case the Maximum per-VM resets is an absolute number after which no automated resets will be performed) or 1–1,000 Hours (more than 41 days)

previously described to "Cluster default" or to "Disabled" (to not monitor the specified VM for failures).

20. Click Next to continue to the next step in the wizard.

Screenshots   One of the nice features of vSphere 4 and 5 in relation to VM restarts is that before the action is taken, a screenshot of the console (not any remote sessions, just the native console) is taken and stored in the same directory as the VM so you can determine what was on the screen when the reboot took place—did you see a blue screen or other error message? Did it look okay (maybe a VMware Tools failure or a VM that had frozen)? vSphere will keep the latest ten screenshots for review by an administrator.

Datastore Heartbeats

As described in the Planning section, heartbeat datastores provide a backup mechanism to the network heartbeats to determine if a host is isolated. In addition, some minimal information can be communicated to other nodes if they are isolated or between master servers in a partitioned network using this technique. We previously discussed that VMFS volumes are preferred over NFS volumes. It is possible to configure your own preferences regarding which volumes should be selected as heartbeat volumes if you want as well. To do so:

21. On the Datastore Heartbeating step of the wizard, select one of the three choices from this list (no matter how many are selected, the system will only choose two [by default] to actually become the heartbeat datastores for the cluster):

    ■ **Select only from my preferred datastores.** This option restricts HA to only selecting from the datastores you specify. All others will be excluded, even if there are not enough datastores to meet other HA settings or the datastores are not accessible to all hosts (though all datastores should be shared datastores in an HA cluster for it to work properly).

    ■ **Select any of the cluster datastores.** The system will select from all current and future datastores presented to the cluster using the preferences described in the Planning section.

    ■ **Select any of the cluster datastores taking into account my preferences.** The best of both worlds (and the default), it will select from your preferred datastores if possible, but if not can select any other datastore the system needs.

22. If you selected either "Select only from my preferred datastores" or "Select any of the cluster datastores taking into account my preferences" in the previous step, select the preferred datastores that you'd like HA to use; if you select the first option and don't select any datastores, you've effectively disabled datastore heartbeats.

23. Click Next.

EVC and Swapfile Options

The EVC settings are irrelevant for a pure HA cluster as it only applies to vMotion, which HA does not use (though it could if FT is also configured). Likewise, swapfile location is not critical for HA, though it could have an impact, preventing a VM from starting if a datastore for a host was selected for the swapfile and that location did not have enough free space to create the swapfile on power on. We discussed these options in Chapter 11.

Advanced Options

There are quite a few (35 in vSphere 5) advanced options that can be used with an HA cluster to modify default behaviors. Most have limited application, and thus are beyond the scope of this book. However, a couple of settings are more commonly used and will be discussed here. Before we get to the individual settings though, this is the general process to configure them:

1. Right-click the cluster you want to change the parameters on and select Edit Settings.

2. Select the vSphere HA step from the available steps.

3. Click the Advanced Options button.

4. Click in the first available row in the Option column, then click again to allow the option's name to be specified.

5. Type the name of the option; all options begin with "das."

Note

das stands for distributed availability service, the internal name of HA before it was released and officially named HA.

6. Press the Tab key to move to the associated Value column.

7. Type the desired value for the parameter.

8. Repeat Steps 4–7 as necessary.

9. Click OK to exit the Advanced Options (vSphere HA) dialog box, then OK to exit the Cluster Settings dialog box.

Slot Size   As described in the Planning section, slot size is used by HA to determine how many VMs it should allow to run in the cluster and how many resources to reserve as spare capacity. The point of this section is not how the values are calculated, but rather how to view the current values and change the slot size defaults.

Let's begin with how to view the current slot size values (this is only valid for the admission control policy of "Host failures the cluster tolerates"):

1. Select the HA cluster and then select the Summary tab.

2. On the right side of the information displayed, you'll see the vSphere HA box, as shown in Figure 12.25. Select the Advanced Runtime Info link.

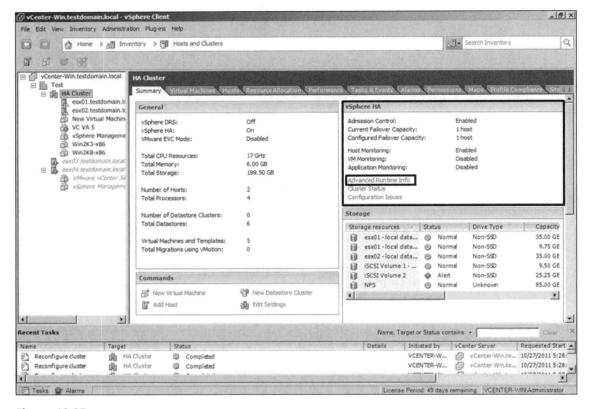

Figure 12.25
vSphere HA box.

3. The vSphere HA Advanced Runtime Info dialog box will be displayed, as illustrated in Figure 12.26. Note the following things:

■ The CPU slot size is 32MHz (the default in vSphere 5) because there are no VMs with CPU reservations.

■ The memory slot size is 534MB because the largest memory reservation set was 512MB and the overhead memory on that VM was 21.71MB, so rounded up the total was 534MB.

■ Based on the size of the ESXi hosts and these slot sizes, there are a total of two slots in the cluster, of which one was currently used (only one VM was powered on).

■ There are no available slots because we are using one and the other is reserved for failover use only. No more VMs can be powered on.

4. Review the information, then click OK when finished.

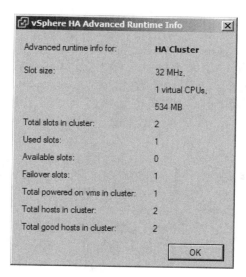

Figure 12.26
Advanced Runtime Info.

Now that the slot size can be viewed (for the Host Failures option), let's discuss what you can do to change the defaults—both the default slot size values and the maximum slot sizes. There are four parameters that control these behaviors, as described in Table 12.6.

Table 12.6   Slot Size Parameters

Parameter	Applies to Host Failures Option	Applies to Percentage of Cluster Resources Option	Description
das.vmMemoryMinMB	Y	Y	The default slot size for memory.
das.slotMemInMB	Y	N	The maximum slot size for memory (important when you have VMs with large memory reservations).
das.vmCpuMinMHz	Y	Y	The default slot size for CPU.
das.slotCpuInMHz	Y	N	The maximum slot size for CPU (important when you have VMs with large CPU reservations).

You can use the procedure outlined in the Advanced Options section above to set these parameters as needed.

You might be wondering what happens if a VM has a reservation of 8GB of RAM, but you set das.slotMemInMB to 1GB and are using the Host Failures option. The answer is that the VM will use 8 slots (or more if the CPU reservation versus slot size requires it). This doesn't matter for the Percentage of Cluster Resources option as it uses actual values.

Isolation Addresses The other common parameters for HA revolve around what happens when the host is network isolated. By default, the system will ping the default gateway for the VMkernel to determine if it isolated or if all other hosts have failed. But what if you don't have a default gateway? What if you do, but only for one of the management networks and you have multiple management networks on different subnets for redundancy? What do we check on those networks? There are two parameters that come in handy in these situations, namely:

■ das.usedefaultisolationaddress tells HA whether to use the default VMkernel gateway. If it's set to "true," it will be used as the first isolation address; if it's set to "false," it will not.

■ das.isolationaddress [x] specifies the address or addresses a host should ping before declaring itself isolated or not. Valid values for x are 1–10 (duplicate values for x are not allowed). We recommend one isolation address on each network that will be used by HA so that each network has an IP that should always be available. For example, if you used the IP storage network, set the IP to the management IP of the SAN or NFS box you are using.

More on the advanced parameters can be found in this VMware KB article: kb.vmware.com/kb/1006421 or in the VMware Uptime Blog at: blogs.vmware.com/uptime/2011/09/index.html (note that all of the topic blogs have been combined into the VMware vSphere Blog with sub-communities for each specialty as of November 2011; you can reach it here: blogs.vmware.com/vsphere/).

Integration with DRS

A cluster can be used with HA, DRS, both, or neither. "Neither" would often be used to enable EVC for easier vMotion only. While HA does not require DRS to be used, HA will leverage DRS if it is configured. This leveraging is done by vCenter (not the FDM agent used in most other HA operations as only vCenter can perform DRS tasks). For example, if the slot size is reduced as described previously and a VM requires multiple slots, and there are enough slots available in the cluster, but not enough on a single host, HA will inform DRS that a power-on request was unsuccessful and request it to defragment the cluster so that there are enough slots on a single host (if possible). DRS will then move the VMs as needed and HA will try again. This will lengthen the time before the VM starts, but at least the VM will start. Another example: If DPM (Distributed Power Management) is used and it has powered off one or more hosts to conserve power and reduce the cooling load, and a host failure occurs, HA can request DPM to power on a host to provide sufficient computing power to run the VMs in use on the cluster.

Note

As of vSphere 5, DPM will now keep a minimum of two hosts running in HA clusters with admission control disabled. In previous versions, only one host had to be left powered on (depending on the load).

VMware FT

That brings us to the other section in the Implementation and Management section. In this section, we'll review the configuration tasks necessary for Fault Tolerance and also discuss how to vMotion primary or secondary VMs, as well as how to confirm that FT is indeed working properly. Please refer to the Planning section for details on requirements and how it works.

Configuration

When it comes to configuring FT, there are many requirements that must be met, but they were described in the Planning section, and the prerequisite procedures described elsewhere in this book. The purpose of this section is to cover procedures not described elsewhere in this book. As such, we'll look at how to configure FT logging, how to configure a virtual disk for use with FT, and how to actually enable FT on a VM.

FT Logging Before you can do anything with FT, you must create a VMkernel port on each node in the cluster for use with FT. If you have busy VMs and or multiple VMs on a single host, you may want to use 10GbE instead of the standard 1GbE.

To configure FT logging:

1. Create a virtual switch (Standard or Distributed) as described in Chapter 7 (or at least a VMkernel port on an existing switch) for vMotion.

Note

VMware recommends a separate network (physically or at a minimum a separate VLAN) for vMotion as memory contents are sent unencrypted between the nodes. The same applies for the VMkernel ports used for FT logging.

2. Repeat Step 1 and create a separate switch or at least VMkernel port and check the Enable FT Logging checkbox as shown in Figure 12.27.

Note

VMware also recommends using separate networks for FT Logging and vMotion, as both can be bandwidth intensive; in fact, if you select the same VMkernel port for both vMotion and FT Logging (as we did in Figure 12.27 to point out the two checkboxes needed), you will get the warning message shown in Figure 12.28.

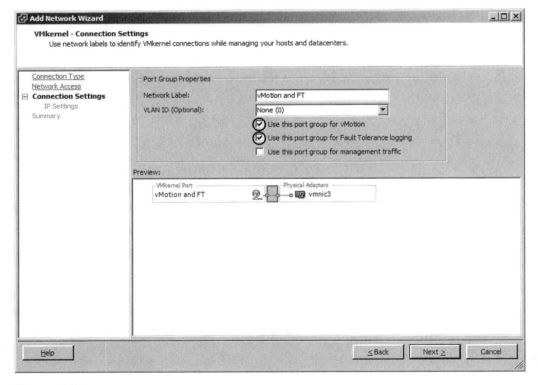

Figure 12.27
FT Logging.

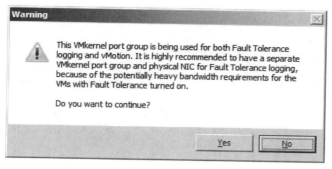

Figure 12.28
Separate VMkernel ports recommeded for FT logging and vMotion warning message.

FT Version Requirements between Nodes   When FT Logging is enabled, a new
Fault Tolerance box will be displayed (if it is not already) on the Summary tab for
the ESXi host, as shown in Figure 12.29. You should also see in the General box
that both vMotion Enabled and Host Configured for FT should say Yes.

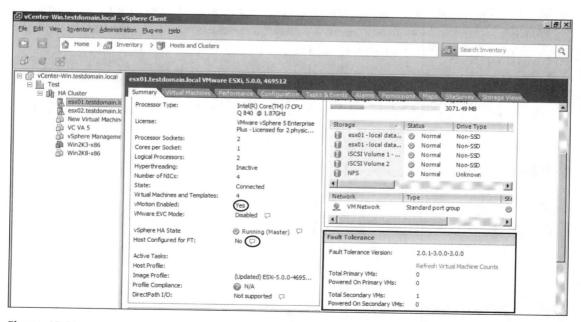

Figure 12.29
FT version.

Tip

If it does not show Yes to the right of Host Configured for FT, click on the "thought bubble" to the right of No to find the reason(s) why it is not (in the screenshot, Host Configured for FT is No because it is running in a VM).

Note that the Fault Tolerance version is displayed, along with the total number of primary and secondary VMs (both powered on and off as well as powered on only) hosted on this node.

Eager Zero Thick Disk and Memory Reservation Requirements   One of the VM requirements is that any virtual disks must be in the Eager Zero thick format. If you have thin provisioned disks or disks that are Lazy Zero thick provisioned (see Chapter 8 for a discussion of disk types), you will get the message shown in Figure 12.30.

Note that you will be told that Eager Zero thick disks must be used (what the dialog box calls "disks with all blocks zeroed out") before FT can be enabled, which will require more space if the disk is thin provisioned. The simplest way to make the change is to click Yes in the dialog box. This will take some time and disk I/O to complete.

Second, FT requires setting the memory reservation on the VM (and thus both the primary and secondary copies of the VM) to the amount assigned to the VM (in other words, if the VM was given 1GB of RAM, the reservation will be for 1GB each on two physical hosts—the primary and secondary copies). This is required as long as FT is enabled on the VM. In addition, the amount of RAM assigned to the VM can't be changed (up or down) as long as FT is enabled.

Enabling FT on a VM   Enabling FT requires just a couple of clicks:

1. Right-click on the VM that you want to enable for FT and select Fault Tolerance > Turn On Fault Tolerance.

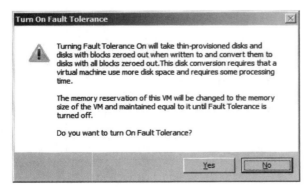

Figure 12.30
Enable FT changes.

2. You will see the dialog box shown in Figure 12.30 (or an abbreviated version that does not mention thick provisioning if it is already Eager Zero thick provisioned); click Yes to enable FT.

3. If any requirements for FT are not met (as described in the Planning section of this chapter) you'll get an error message—review it and make the necessary changes and try again until it completes successfully.

You'll note a slightly modified icon for the VM and a new Fault Tolerance box on the Summary tab. Note the following about Figure 12.31:

- The host the primary runs on is shown in the General box next to Host (in this case esx02.testdomain.local), while the secondary location is listed in the Fault Tolerance box next to Secondary Location (in the figure it is esx01.testdomain. local).

- The Fault Tolerance Status is currently Not Protected because the VM is not running.

- The other FT settings are either zero or N/A because the VM is off and thus consuming no resources.

- The icon for Win2K3-x86 is darker than the other VMs (though this may be difficult to see in grayscale).

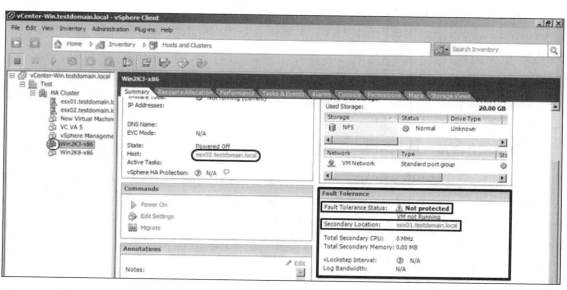

Figure 12.31
FT Box on VM—VM powered off.

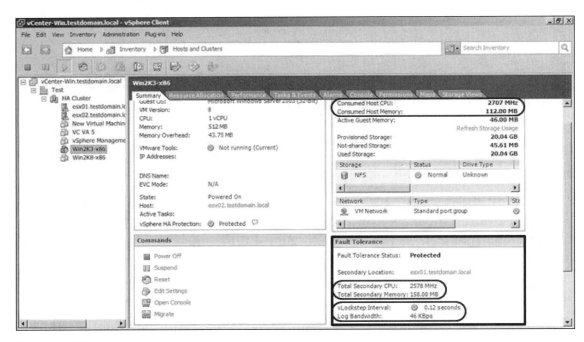

Figure 12.32
FT Box on VM—VM powered on.

Once the VM is turned on, the status will change to Need Secondary VM, followed by Protected once the VM is up and running. Once the VM is fully functional on both hosts, you'll see the Fault Tolerance box become populated with information, as shown in Figure 12.32, including:

- Fault Tolerance Status is now Protected, indicating that primary and secondary are working properly. If that changes for some reason, an alarm will be triggered alerting you to the change in FT status.

- The Total Secondary CPU and Total Secondary Memory values are populated and indicate the load the VM is causing on the secondary host (at the top of the screen in the Resources box you can see the load the VM is causing on the primary node). The memory should be the same on both nodes as the VM had a memory reservation set when FT was enabled; in this example, the primary is using 112MB for the VM plus 46MB in overhead memory, for a total of 158MB, the exact same value you see in the Fault Tolerance box. CPU may differ due to different times at which performance data is gathered, what the secondary is doing at the moment relative to the primary, etc. In this example, the primary CPU is higher than the secondary, but it may be the other way as well.

- The vLockstep Interval indicates how far behind the primary the secondary is. At this point they are within the tolerance for the normal level (green checkmark) at .12 seconds (120 milliseconds). If the secondary continued to lag, it would go to warning, then alert levels and the primary would be slowed down by FT to allow the secondary to catch up and keep them in sync.

- Log Bandwidth displays how much bandwidth this VM is consuming on the FT Logging VMkernel port. This VM was booting, so not much was required on that NIC, but the load at other points could be more substantial, depending on what was occurring in the VM.

vMotioning Primary or Secondary VMs

Once the VM is running (on both servers), you vMotion the primary exactly like you would any other VM, by right-clicking on it and choosing Migrate. vMotion was discussed in Chapter 10.

On the other hand, there is no VM to right-click on and migrate when referring to the secondary VM, so an alternate method needs to be used. To migrate the secondary VM, do the following:

1. Right-click on the Primary VM, select Fault Tolerance, and then Migrate Secondary as shown in Figure 12.33.

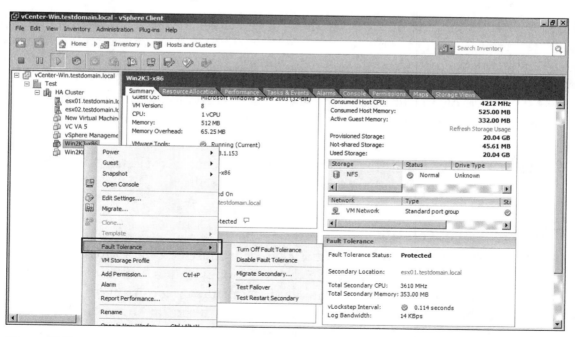

Figure 12.33
FT menu.

2. Select Change Host (the only option) and then proceed through the wizard the same as a standard vMotion with one exception: the Select Resource Pool step of the wizard is omitted. The secondary VM and the primary VM are in reality just one VM and thus can't be in different resource pools.

Note

You can't select the node that is hosting the primary VM as the two copies can't be on the same node; if you try, you'll get a validation error.

3. At the end of the process, the secondary VM will be on the new node, just like a standard vMotion.

Confirming That FT Is Working Properly

Finally, how do you know that FT is working properly and will work as expected in the event of a failure? You can see the VM has a status of Protected, but that just tells you it is protected; how can you be sure that it really will failover as expected?

There are two possible failure scenarios that can be envisioned for an FT-enabled VM. The first is the failure of the server hosting the primary, and the second is the failure of the ESXi host that the secondary runs on. To test these options, do the following:

1. Right-click on the Primary VM, select Fault Tolerance, and then Test Failover to test the failure of the primary, making the secondary the primary node and then the new primary will create a new secondary.
   OR
   Right-click on the Primary VM, select Fault Tolerance, and then Test Restart Secondary to test the failure of the secondary, making the primary create a new secondary.

2. There are no questions to be asked when either choice is selected; it simply does the indicated action and allows you to see the results.

TROUBLESHOOTING

Now that we're reaching the end of the chapter it must be time to look at troubleshooting issues and techniques. While there are many things that could go wrong, VMware has tried to plan for and handle many of them, and many of the rest are well beyond the scope of this book, often involving technical support. There are a couple of common areas that we can address here. We'll begin with a brief look at the various logs and configuration files used by HA and then we'll touch on some issues that may arise with FT and how to manage them.

HA Configuration Files and Logs

One of the best sources for troubleshooting any problem is the log file or files the application creates. This is very true for HA, where there are many logs created. Table 12.7 lists the various log files that are created, where they are located, and what they contain.

Table 12.7 HA Configuration Files and Logs: Location and Purpose

Location	Name	Contents/Purpose
/etc/opt/vmware/fdm on each HA-enabled ESXi host	fdm.cfg	One of two primary FDM configuration files; we recommend you not change this manually unless working with technical support as you could break HA. It is an XML file. The working directory for FDM, logging configuration, and other advanced parameters are located here.
	hostlist	This file contains the list of all hosts that are part of the cluster, including the host's name, MAC and IP addresses, **MOID** (**M**anaged **O**bject **ID**; referenced later in this section), and configured heartbeat datastores. It is also an XML formatted file.
	compatlist	This is a binary file that contains all of the hosts that each protected VM can run on to ensure that the VM will restart in a location where it can run.
	clusterconfig	This is a binary file that contains the cluster configuration options made in the GUI (such as VM restart priority, isolation response settings, etc.). It also acts as a cached copy of the cluster configuration in case vCenter is unavailable.
/var/log/ on each HA-enabled ESXi host	fdm.log	The typical log file created by most VMware components, it details the operation of the FDM agent.

(continued)

Table 12.7   HA Configuration Files and Logs: Location and Purpose (*Continued*)

Location	Name	Contents/Purpose
On all datastores with at least one protected VM on it[†]	protectedlist	This file contains all of the protected VMs on the datastore on which it resides. HA will restart these VMs (if possible) in the event of a failure. The file is created, owned, distributed to the appropriate datastores, and locked by the master node of the cluster.
On each heartbeat datastore[†]	host-*X*-hb[‡]	This file is created by each host and kept open (for VMFS datastores, keeping the heartbeat region of a VMFS datastore updated that the host is alive) or timestamp updated (for NFS datastores). The master node can thus look at the appropriate region or file and determine if the host is available by seeing if the timestamp is within the last few seconds.
	host-*X*-poweron[‡]	This file, created and maintained by each host in the cluster, contains the list of powered-on VMs on that node. It can also be used in the event of isolation for a slave to communicate with the master that it is isolated and which VMs (if any) it has powered off so that they can be restarted on other nodes. This file is in plain text and can be viewed—but don't modify it! If the top line in the file contains a 0, it is functioning normally, but if it is a 1, it is isolated.

[†]The HA logs on the datastores are located under /.vSphere-HA/<Directory per cluster this datastore is associated with>. Usually there will only be one cluster and thus one directory to look at.
[‡]The *X* in the filename refers to the MOID assigned by vSphere to the host. The simplest way to obtain the name of the host and its matching MOID is to look in the hostlist file referenced in the table.

Troubleshooting FT

Many of the issues that arise with FT are caused by not carefully reviewing the requirements and limitations of the product as it currently exists. Before you spend a lot of time reviewing this section, go back and review these areas in the Planning section of this chapter. Really. Review them carefully now—maybe even open the documentation (and read—crazy!) and double-check the requirements and limitations.

Okay, now let's move on and look at the other issues. VMware provides several recommendations to make FT work better.

First, it is recommended that you disable all power management features of your CPU (AMD's PowerNow! Or Intel's Speed Step) so that it runs full speed all the time. This is not a requirement, but will reduce problems. If the primary is on a server that is running fast and the secondary is on a server that is running slower (maybe to save power), the secondary could fall further and further behind the primary. If it gets too far out of sync with the primary, vSphere will slow down the primary (and thus the speed of the running applications) to give the secondary time to catch up. How far behind the secondary is from the primary can be seen by looking on the Summary tab of the VM in the Fault Tolerance box and checking the vLockstep Interval (in seconds—multiply by 1,000 to determine how many milliseconds the secondary is behind the primary). As the value increases, the green checkmark before the time will be replaced with a yellow warning, and then finally a red alert symbol, letting you know that the primary is running slower to allow the secondary to catch up.

Second, VMware recommends that there be no more than four primary or secondary VMs (total) per physical server. That is a total of four, not four primary and four secondary VMs. The reason for this is partly resource consumption (the cost is twice a standard VM as it is running on two hosts at the same time), but mainly the load on the Fault Tolerance VMkernel port(s). This is helped somewhat if 10GbE is used. It is also helped if jumbo frames are implemented.

Finally, VMware actually has a tool called VMware Site Survey that is designed to let you know if FT will work in the environment based on the host configuration; but it will also list all the VMs and any issues with them that would prevent any of them from using FT (many of which would also prevent vMotion, HA, and/or DRS from working properly).

To get it, simply go to www.vmware.com/download/shared_utilities.html and download the utility and installation instructions (which are one page long). After you install the utility, open your vSphere Client, select a host or cluster, go to the new SiteSurvey tab and click Run SiteSurvey. A few minutes later, you'll see a report describing issues that prevent hosts from running FT. Below that you'll see a list of all your VMs and either a green checkmark or a red X in a bunch of categories allowing you to quickly see what needs to be done to implement FT (and for many of the columns the information can help you with troubleshooting the other tools previously mentioned). Just remember to rerun the utility after configuration changes are made.

Summary

Now that we've looked at how to provide high availability to your environment, let's turn our attention to how to keep everything patched and up to date.

CHAPTER 13

CONFIGURATION AND PATCH MANAGEMENT

In most IT environments, there is a designed patch management solution that allows for the automated patching of physical servers. Many system administrators consider patching to be a mandatory management process for operating systems and for hardware revisions. If patching has a level of importance in the physical world, does the importance of maintaining a patch level diminish once the servers have been virtualized? Absolutely not. In most situations, both physical and virtual servers require a regular, planned update procedure. The same level of care and testing will be invested when patching and updating both virtual and physical servers.

There are several approaches that can be used to update physical servers and their operating systems. Most vendors, including Microsoft and Red Hat, offer solutions that can be leveraged to perform patching and updating as new releases are made available. For example, Microsoft's WSUS (Windows Software Update Service) is utilized in many environments to deploy tested and verified updates to desktops and servers throughout the enterprise. Several third-party solutions are also available and have gained wide acceptance. From an enterprise perspective, patching and updating server-related components cannot be ignored in the grand scheme of things. We will always encounter incompatibilities and new hardware that require kernel modifications to fully access and use.

In previous versions, VMware Update Manager provided the means to perform updates on the operating systems of virtual machines, and even update applications that are installed within the virtual machines. That capability has been diminished in vSphere 5, although we can still update VMware Tools and the virtual machine hardware for each VM in the vCenter inventory.

PLANNING

It is a best practice to establish a documented, verifiable method of updating ESXi servers, and additional VMware components, such as the virtual machine hardware, VMware Tools, and virtual appliances. Not only will this allow the administrator to patch and address possible security issues, but it also allows the most updated virtual hardware to be made available to production and test virtual machines. Update Manager from VMware provides an enterprise-level tool to perform these updates from a centralized interface.

Capabilities

The addition of Update Manager to the vCenter environment provides you with the capability to design an automated solution for patching ESXi hosts, upgrading and updating VMware Tools and virtual machine hardware for VMs, and updating any virtual appliances that may be deployed.

Update Manager allows you to:

■ Create baselines that represent the patching level that you want to maintain.

■ Scan hosts and VMs for compliance with those baselines.

■ Perform remediation of those hosts, VMs, and appliances either manually or based on a schedule.

■ Install drivers and software extensions available from third-party vendors.

No Internet Access

To implement Update Manager, there must be an opportunity to access the Internet as Update Manager must be able to download updates and metadata relative to the updates and patches. However, deciding to grant Internet access to Update Manager may be strictly a security concern rather than an Internet issue. Many organizations have blanket security procedures that restrict Internet access only to those devices that require it due to a business need, and all others are denied access by default.

If you are in one of these high-security environments, and still desire to use Update Manager to perform update processes, you can deploy UMDS (Update Manager Download Service).

The VMware vSphere UMDS can be installed on a physical or virtual server and then employed to download the metadata, patches, and related notifications. This information can be exported to a USB or other removable device. We can then import these objects to the Update Manager server after they have been approved or scanned by the local security team. We will see how to configure the Update Manager Download Service later in this chapter.

Also of concern is the level of patching that we will need to maintain on our environment. You can always deploy the latest update or patch, regardless of the objects that are modified, or you can choose to remain at a certain revision, due to application support. Are there applications, perhaps developed in-house, that require a specific revision level to function appropriately?

Sizing

To install Update Manager, you must provide a database to store the downloaded metadata and associated patches and upgrades. Similar to vCenter, Update Manager can use either SQL or Oracle as its database. In many cases, you will choose the same vendor for the Update Manager database as you did for the vCenter database. The Update Manager database instance cannot be the same database instance as is used for vCenter; it can be on the same database server, but not the same actual database. Keep in mind that the best results will be gained if you install the database on the same server as Update Manager, but at a minimum, the database must be always accessible.

If you are going to deploy a small environment, you can use the included SQL Server 2008 R2 Express database to store the content for a maximum of 5 hosts or 50 VMs. If your environment will scale beyond those values, you will need to use either a full instance of SQL or Oracle as your database.

To make the sizing of the database much easier, VMware has provided the "VMware vSphere Update Manager Sizing Estimator." This estimator is an Excel spreadsheet that allows you to input such variables, as:

- The number of legacy hosts (ESX 3.x, 4.x, ESXi 3.x, 4.x, etc.)
- The number of VMs in the inventory
- The number of concurrent ESXi upgrades that you plan
- The anticipated frequency of scanning and patching
- The location of the Update Manager database

The Update Manager Sizing Estimator can be downloaded from the following URL: http://blogs.vmware.com/performance/2010/08/vmware-vcenter-update-manager-41-sizing-estimator.html.

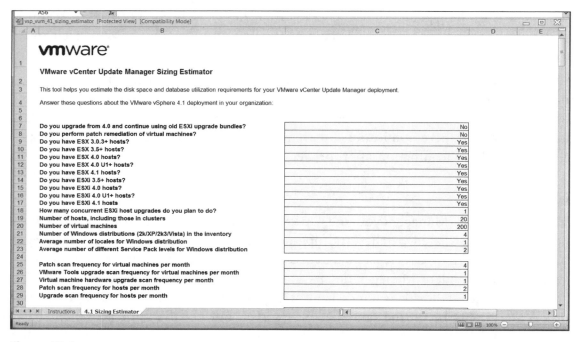

Figure 13.1
The Update Manager Sizing Estimator.

As shown in Figure 13.1, VMware provides the Update Manager Sizing Estimator to help provision the database for Update Manager. This will enable you to properly size the data to contain the metadata and all available patches and updates.

To accurately input these variables, you must analyze your current inventory, and the anticipated inventory. You may want to consider the long-term perspective of your deployment: how many hosts and VMs do you anticipate over the next 18 to 24 months? If we can plan for an estimated value, we can deploy a database of sufficient size to accommodate the data associated with the environment.

Remember at this point that Update Manager no longer supports the patching of VM operating systems; Update Manager can still update the virtual machine hardware and VMware Tools within each VM. Operating system patching was supported in previous versions of Update Manager, but is no longer supported.

In order to allow Update Manager to perform its functionality, Update Manager requires network connectivity with a vCenter instance. The Update Manager service can be installed on the same server as vCenter or on a separate device, but it must remain in contact with vCenter at all times. After Update Manager has been installed, you must also install the Update Manager plugin in your vSphere Client.

Currently, Update Manager can upgrade both ESX and ESXi hosts, including upgrades to vSphere 5, as well as any virtual appliances that have been created using a minimum version 2.0 of VMware Virtual Studio.

Planning to use Update Manager as a patching mechanism is a three-fold process:

1. What type of database will be used?
2. How will Update Manager access the Internet?
3. What is the level of patching and update that we want to achieve?

Host Profiles

Another concept that debuted with the release of vSphere 4 was Host Profiles. This addition to the set of available tools provides the capability to quickly and accurately bring a freshly installed ESXi host into corporate compliance with just a few steps and minimal additional management and time. This convenience does come with a price: you must have purchased the Enterprise Plus license to utilize this tool.

Host Profiles allow an administrator to install a new ESXi server, configure it according to corporate guidelines and standards, and then use this configuration as a blueprint for future server configurations. This can greatly benefit web hosting providers as they can create a separate configuration for each hosting client, and then deploy new servers for that client with a minimum of time and effort. Consider this option: there are environments in which port management is key. It is mandated by corporate standards that certain ports are allowed to be open, and the rest are closed. You can use a Host Profile to verify compliance in a very short period of time with no downtime and no impact to client virtual machines. Configuring and scanning with Host Profiles will be discussed later in this chapter.

IMPLEMENTATION AND MANAGEMENT

As we mentioned, the first step in the configuration of Update Manager is to deploy a database to contain the metadata, patches, and updates. Once that is completed, we can install the Update Manager package. Remember that this installation can be on the same server as the vCenter server, or it can be on a separate device. At this point it should be noted that this does not have to be a physical server; it will provide the same functionality if it is installed within a VM.

After the Update Manager package has been installed, you will need to install the vSphere Client plugin to complete the installation.

To install the Update Manager plugin for the vSphere Client:

1. Log in to the vCenter instance.

2. Use the top toolbar and select Plugins > Manage Plugins.

3. Click on the blue highlighted link to install the plugin.

VMware Update Manager (VUM)

We have discussed the capability of Update Manager to automatically download patches and extensions from the Internet, and we can schedule these Internet accesses based on business needs. For example, we may be replicating data across the link to a DR site between the hours of 6PM and 6AM, so we have to tell Update Manager to use the link at other hours, but there are other options. We can download the new packages manually and store them in what is termed a "shared repository," which can simply be a network share. The only requirements are that there is enough free space to store the content, and that Update Manager can reach the share across the network.

Update Manager downloads different types of content that are categorized under the heading patches, updates, and extensions. These types of data are:

- **Metadata.** Data that describes the package and any dependencies that may be required.

- **VIB.** Defined as containing a single update.

- **Bulletin.** More than one VIB in a single package.

- **Depot.** An online resource that contains multiple VIBs and associated metadata.

- **Extension.** A package that is designed to add functionality to an ESXi host, may be comprised of multiple VIBs and metadata, and is typically available from a vendor.

- **Host Upgrade.** Typically defined as an ESXi image package that can be downloaded and used by Update Manager to upgrade a physical host from one version to another.

- **Offline Bundle Zip.** A single package that contains multiple VIBs, associated metadata, and is usually applied when the host is in an offline state.

- **Patch.** An update that addresses a specific issue or provides increased functionality.

- **Rollup.** A single package that contains multiple VIBs.

- **VA Upgrade.** A single package that provides an upgrade for a virtual appliance.

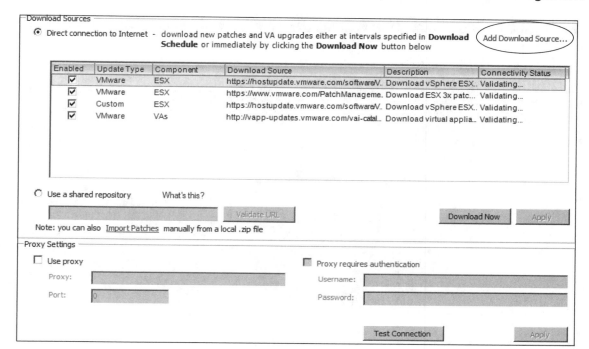

Figure 13.2
The default download sources.

In Figure 13.2, when Update Manager is installed, it is configured with default locations that it uses to access update and patch content. It uses https://hostupdate. vmware.com/VUM/PRODUCTION/main/vmw-depot-index.xml and https://hostupdate.vmware.com/software/VUM/PRODUCTION/csco-main-index.xml as a source for VMware ESX and ESXi updates, https://www.vmware.com/PatchManagementSystem/patchmanagement for patches, and http://vapp-updates.vmware.com/vai-catalog/ index.xml as a source for virtual appliance upgrades.

Note that you can also add sources for third-party applications by using the Add Download Source line to specify new download destinations.

As shown in Figure 13.3, you have the option to modify the default download schedule from a daily interval at 11:35 PM to a more compatible time frame that matches the normal utilization of the Internet connection. This is very useful in environments where a single link is shared among several business units, and conflicting processes must be taken into consideration.

To configure the download schedule:

1. Log in to the vCenter instance.

2. Select the vCenter instance and select the Update Manager tab.

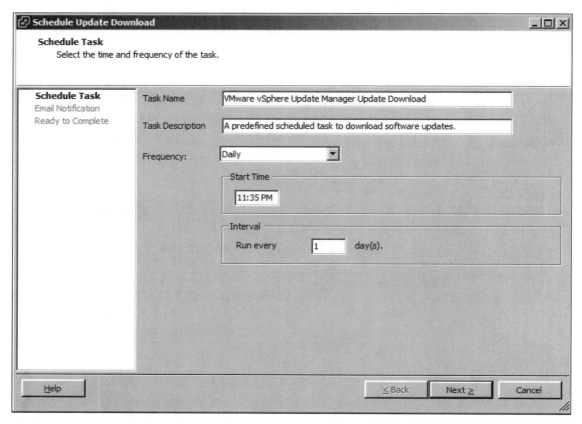

Figure 13.3
Defining the download schedule.

3. Click on the Admin view link in the upper-right corner.

4. Click on the Configuration tab.

5. Click on the Download Schedule link.

If you have a third-party vendor that is supplying drivers or extensions, you can add their download site to the regular schedule through the Add Download Source link.

Also, you can use the Download Now link to manually check for updates at any time.

As shown in Figure 13.4, you have the option to download the update packages and store them on a network share. You will need to tell Update Manager the location of the update packages, and then use the Validate button to verify that Update Manager can access the share.

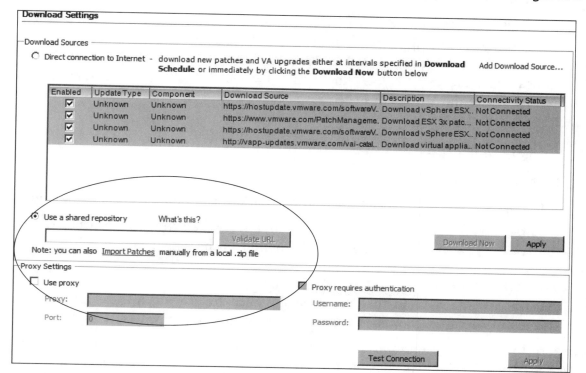

Figure 13.4
Defining the shared repository.

To configure the download schedule:

1. Log in to the vCenter instance.

2. Select the vCenter instance and select the Update Manager tab.

3. Click on the Admin view link in the upper-right corner.

4. Click on the Configuration tab.

5. Click on the Download Settings link.

6. Select Use a Shared Repository.

7. Enter the URL for the network share and select Validate to verify accessibility.

Update Location Configuration

When you install the UMDS component, you will define a location that will be used to store the metadata and updates that are downloaded from the Internet. If, at a future time, you decide that another location would be better suited, you can change the location.

The default location is found in C:\Documents and Settings\All Users\Application Data\VMware\VMware Update Manager\Data. If you modify the default location, you will need to manually move any updates, patches, or virtual appliances to the new location. Note that as you choose the new location, the location must be on the server where the UMDS has been installed.

To move the patch repository:

1. Log in to the vCenter instance.

2. Open a command prompt.

3. Change to the current patch repository location using the DOS `cd` command.

4. Enter `vmware-umds -S --patch-store new_patch_repository_location` ("S" means to set the provided option as the new default)

Proxy Configuration

Depending on the method that has been designed to provide Internet access, you may need to configure a proxy server in order to download updates.

Figure 13.5 shows the location that is used to define the proxy configuration required to access the Internet. This does not mean that you must use a proxy server to access the Internet, but if your environment specifies proxy server use, for example, to record websites that are visited, or to restrict Internet usage to a selected group of individuals, that server must be specified here.

Configuring the Notification Schedule

Periodically, VMware releases notifications regarding updates and patches. These can include recall notifications that tell Update Manager to discontinue deployment of selected packages.

As shown in Figure 13.6, the schedule to check with VMware for possible recall information can be changed from the Notification Check Schedule link. As shown, the default time frame is 47 minutes after each hour.

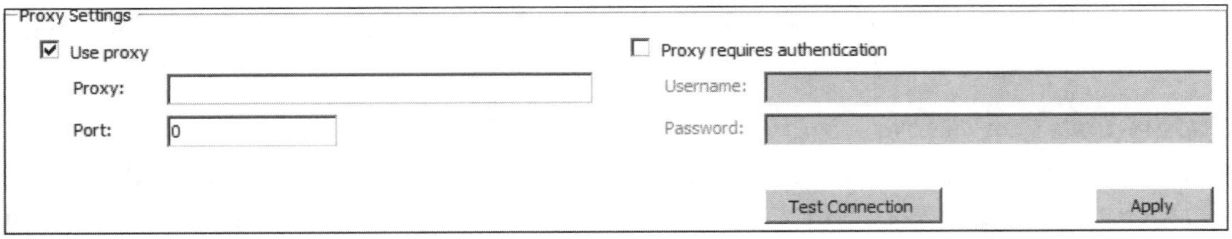

Figure 13.5
Configuring the Proxy server.

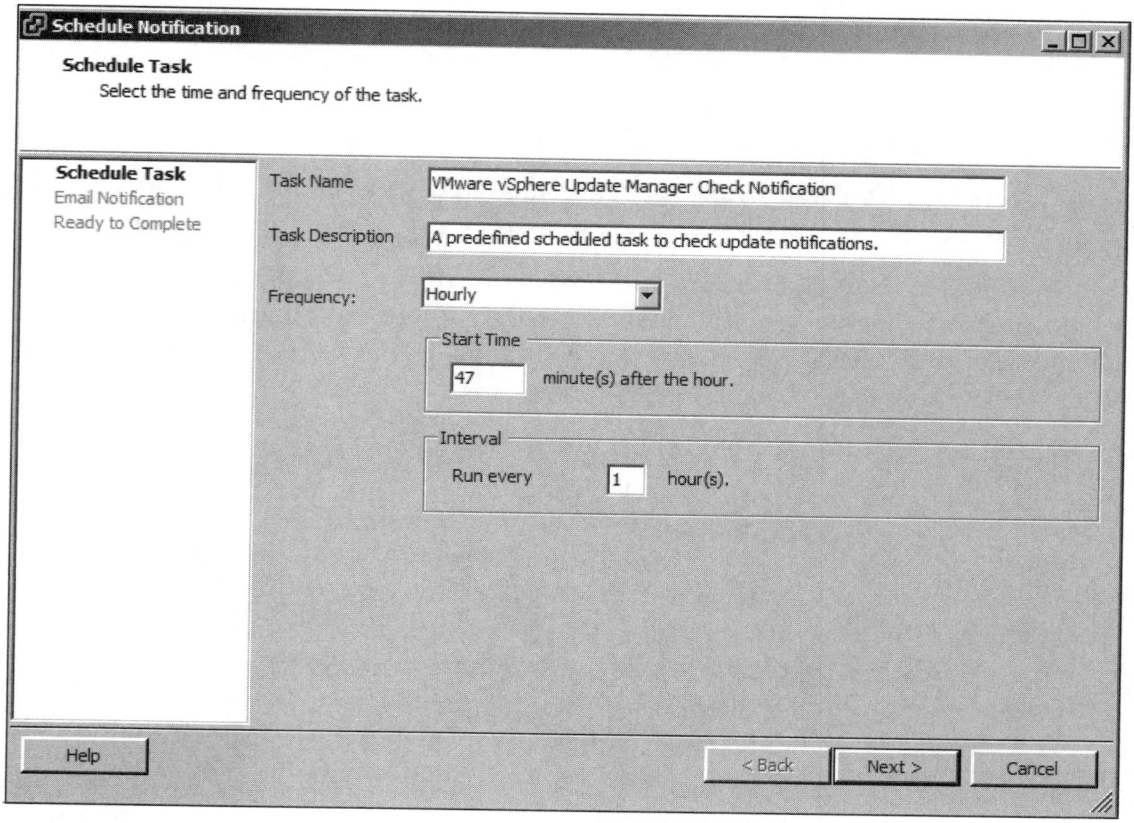

Figure 13.6
Notification schedule.

Installing and Configuring the UMDS

If you are considering the prospect of installing the UMDS, keep in mind that there is no upgrade path from a vSphere 4.x version to the new vSphere 5 revision. You can, however, reuse the old database with the new installation by specifying the old database during the new installation. For best results, uninstall the old version before installing the new vSphere 5 version.

To install the UMDS, you will need the vCenter 5 distribution media. The actual installation files are found in the UMDS folder. When you have completed the installation, you can begin to populate the UMDS content.

If this installation is on a 32-bit host, open a Command Prompt and locate the C:\Program Files\VMware Infrastructure\Update Manager folder. If the UMDS host is a 64-bit operating system, the correct folder is C:\Program Files (x86)\VMware Infrastructure\Update Manager.

In either case, you can use the `vmware-umds -S --enable-host --enable-va` command to configure the Download Service to access all content relative to all ESXi host and virtual appliance metadata, patches, and upgrade packages. If you want to focus on ESXi content exclusively, use `vmware-umds --S --enable-host --disable-va`.

If you want to download virtual appliance upgrades without the ESXi updates, use `vmware-umds -S --disable-host --enable va` from the command line.

Note that the preceding command will download patches and upgrades for ESX/ESXi 3.5x as well as vSphere 4.x and vSphere 5.x hosts. If your environment does not contain any legacy ESX/ESXi 3.5x hosts, use the following command to bypass those particular updates: `vmware-umds -S --enable-host`

`vmware-umds -S -d esx-3.5.0 embeddedEsx-3.5.`

Once you configure the types of updates and content that you want to download, start the process using `vmware-umds -D`.

You will notice that the initial download is extensive: approximately 5GB of content. The next process is to copy the new data to a removable disk and import it to the Update Manager server. To export the downloaded content use the `vmware-umds -S --default-export-store F:\Export` command to configure the default export location, and the `vmware-umds --E` command to actually export the updates.

As shown in Figure 13.7, if you are in an environment in which Internet connectivity is not extended to the datacenter itself, you can manually download the updates in .zip format and place them on a network share or a USB key.

Also available is an option to use the Update Manager PowerCLI to initiate a download. After installing the Update Manager PowerCLI, there are a limited number of cmdlets that are provided exclusively to manage Update Manager processes.

Figure 13.8 shows that you can use the Update Manager PowerCLI package to automate the process of downloading update and patch content. Here, use the syntax `Download-Patch --Server vCenter.testdomain.local` to download patch content. In this example, replace `vCenter.testdomain.local` with the FQDN of your vCenter server.

As depicted in Figure 13.9, you also have the option to manually upload ESXi images into Update Manager from a local or network source.

You also have the option of leveraging Microsoft's IIS components to provide access to the downloaded update content. If you are currently utilizing IIS to deploy and

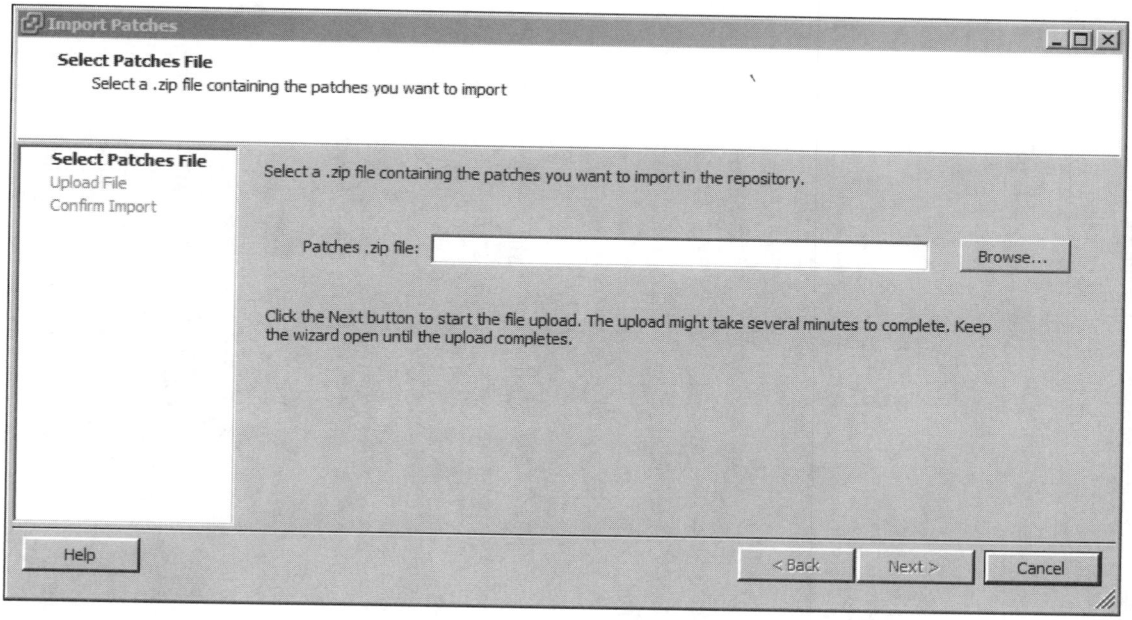

Figure 13.7
Importing update content from a local or network location.

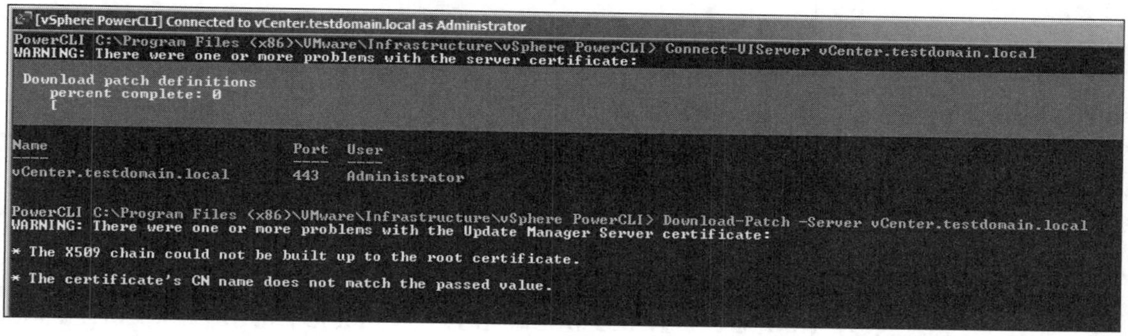

Figure 13.8
Using PowerCLI to download patches.

provide content access in your environment, this can provide a verified method of accessing the updates from a centralized location.

In this scenario, you will install IIS on the same server that is hosting the Update Manager Download Service. As previously discussed, you will need to install the UMDS components on a server that is accessible to the Update Manager server.

Once both the UMDS and IIS packages have been installed, you need to create a local folder that will be used to host the updates and metadata. Now, instead of exporting

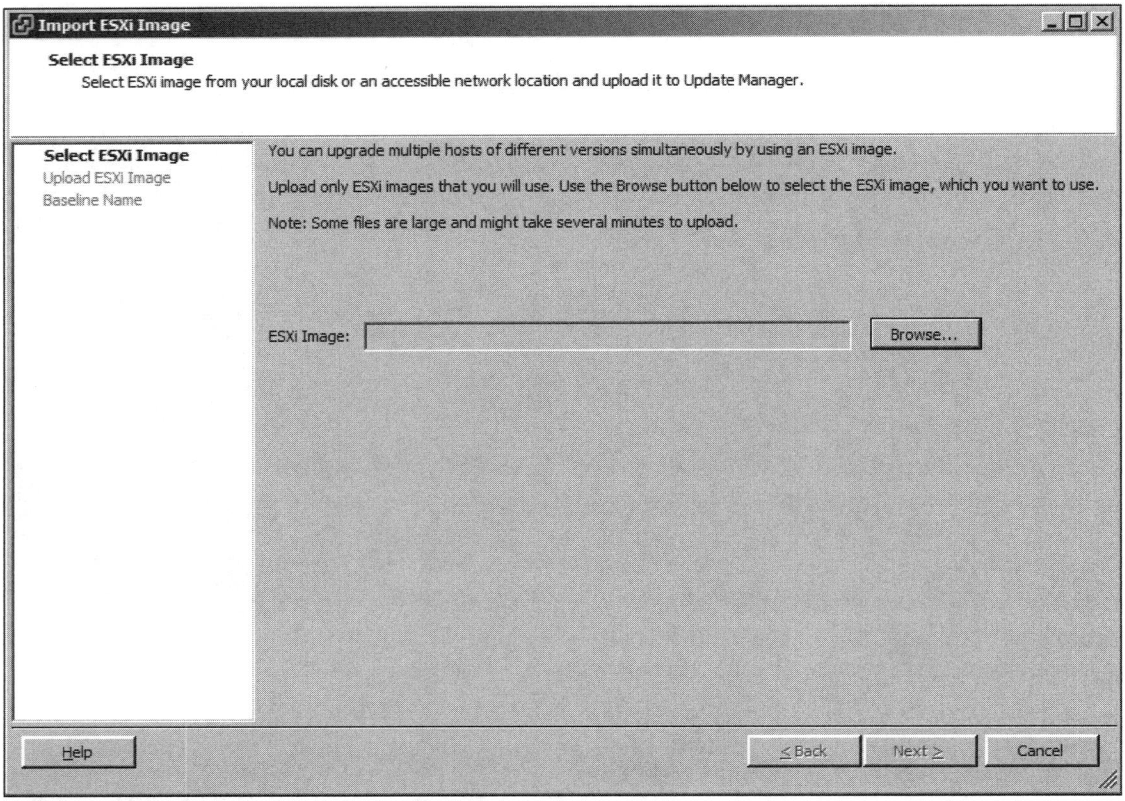

Figure 13.9
Importing an ESXi image.

the content to an external storage device, the data is exported from UMDS to the designated share folder.

As shown in Figure 13.10, the command line options available for the `vmware-umds` CLI (Command Line Interface) utility are displayed. From the previous example, the command is `vmware-umds -E --export-store C:\inetpub\wwwroot\Export`, assuming the shared folder is named "Export."

As shown in Figure 13.11, as the export progresses, you can follow the status, but the entire process requires approximately 5GB of free space.

As shown in Figure 13.12, when you have completed the export of the downloaded content from the UMDS server to a removable device, you can then use that storage as a shared repository. Click on Use a Shared Repository, provide the URL of the new content, and select Validate. After Update Manager has been able to locate and associate with the new device, you will see a green checkmark with the Connected message.

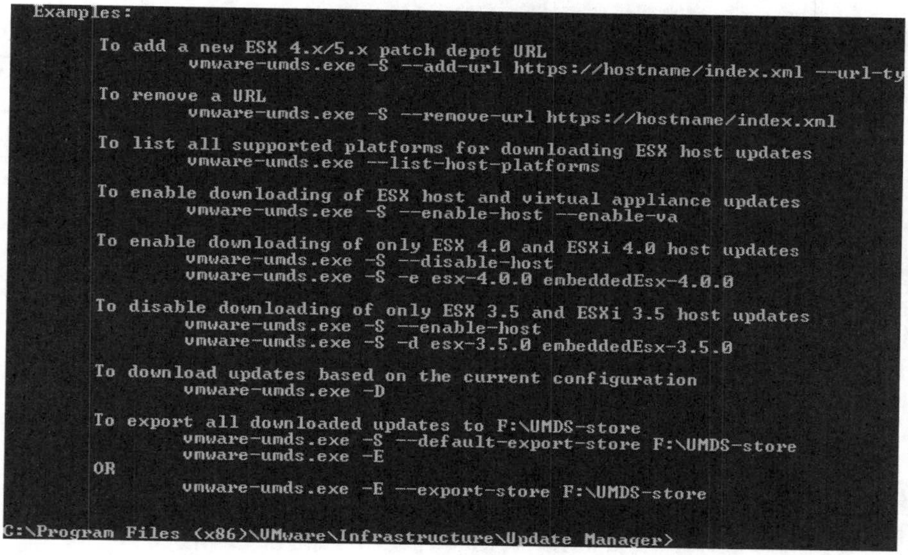

Figure 13.10
The syntax for the `vmware-umds` command.

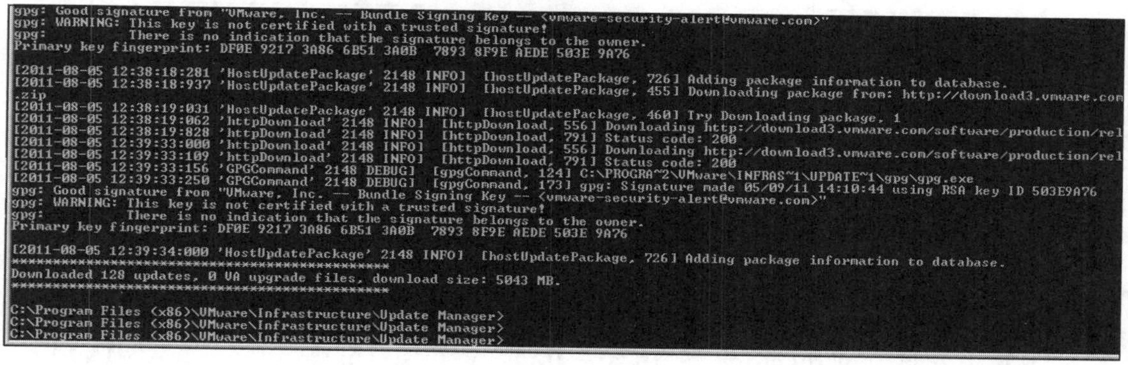

Figure 13.11
The completion of the export process.

Scanning

At this point, we have Update Manager installed, the location where we want to store the downloaded metadata and patches has been defined, and we have scheduled our notifications. But how do we put Update Manager to work?

If you have what is termed a "hybrid environment," or an environment in which there are vSphere hosts of different revision levels, Update Manager supports the following scenarios:

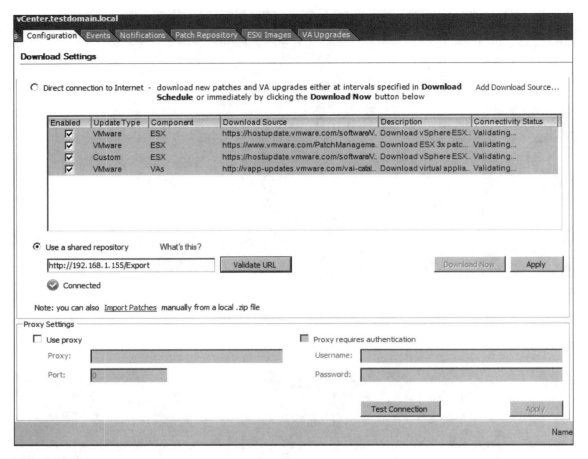

Figure 13.12
Connecting to the imported content.

- If you have ESX and ESXi 4.x hosts, Update Manager can upgrade VMware Tools and virtual machine hardware, upgrade hosts, and migrate hosts from a previous version to a newer version.

- If you have ESX or ESXi 3.5 or later hosts, Update Manager can perform host patching processes.

Note that this compatibility extends to both the scanning and remediation of hosts and related components.

First, we have to create a baseline. A baseline is a collection of updates and patches that we want to install on a single host, or across a cluster of hosts. In other words, it becomes a standard revision in our environment for selected ESXi physical servers, virtual machines, and appliances.

When Update Manager is installed, there are pre-defined baselines that are included as part of the installation and these are typically the most frequently used. However, you do have the capability to create a custom baseline that more directly meets your environments' requirements. Two of the baselines affect the virtual machines, and two affect the physical ESX/ESXi host. The last is directed at any virtual appliances that may be deployed.

The predefined baselines for virtual machines are:

- **VMware Tools Upgrade to Match Host.** In this baseline, the version of VMware Tools that is presented to the VM can be upgraded if the hosting ESX/ESXi host is at a minimum level of vSphere 4.x.

- **Hardware Upgrade to Match Host.** In this baseline, the version of virtual machine hardware that is presented to the VM can be upgraded to revision 8 if the physical host is at a minimum level of vSphere 5.

Of the remaining pre-defined baseline, two are directed at the physical ESX/ESXi hosts:

- **Critical Host Patches.** In this baseline, the physical host is compared to a list of critical packages provided by VMware.

- **Non-Critical Host Patches.** In this baseline, the physical host is compared to a list of non-critical packages.

The final pre-defined baseline is solely for virtual appliances:

- **VA Upgrade to Latest.** In this baseline, the VMware virtual appliances are compared to the latest revisions available from VMware.

To create a baseline:

1. Log in to the vCenter server.

2. Highlight the vCenter instance in the inventory and click on the Update Manager tab.

3. Select the Baselines and Groups tab.

4. Note at this point that there are two buttons at the top of the pane. One is labeled Hosts, and the second is labeled VMs/VA. The Hosts button will allow you to create a baseline that will be assigned to clustered or stand-alone ESXi hosts, and the VMs/VA option will create a baseline for virtual devices. There are also default baselines that are installed as part of the Update Manager deployment. For ESXi hosts, the default baselines are Critical and Non-Critical

Host Patches; and for VMs and virtual appliances there are VMware Tools Upgrade to Match Host, VM Hardware Upgrade to Match Host, and VA Upgrade to Latest. In the Baselines area, click the Create link.

5. On the Baseline Name and Type pane, specify the name for the new baseline, and select the type of baseline. Baselines can be defined for ESXi host patches, upgrades, or extensions, or upgrades for virtual appliances.

6. On the Patch options pane, you have two available types of baselines: Fixed and Dynamic. A fixed baseline reflects the same updates and packages, regardless if any new updates have been downloaded. Dynamic baselines will be updated to include any packages that match the baseline.

As shown in Figure 13.13, when you select the Fixed baseline option, you select the individual patches that will be contained in this baseline. To add a patch to the

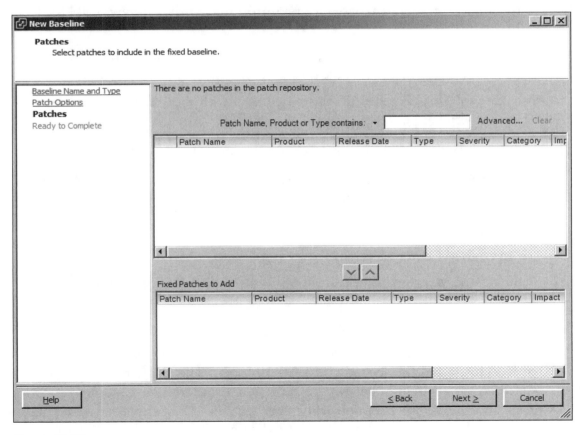

Figure 13.13
Fixed baseline options.

baseline, highlight it in the upper pane and click the arrow pointing down. To remove a patch from the baseline, highlight it and click the up-facing arrow.

1. The Patch screen allows you to specify the patches that will be included in this baseline.

2. At the Ready to Complete screen, review your choices and click Finish.

As depicted in Figure 13.14, if you choose to utilize a dynamic baseline you must also specify the vendor and the product referenced in the patch, the severity level or the category of the update, and a time frame that references the release date of the updates.

Baseline groups are collections of baselines that we want to deploy as a group. You can deploy baselines individually, or as a baseline group.

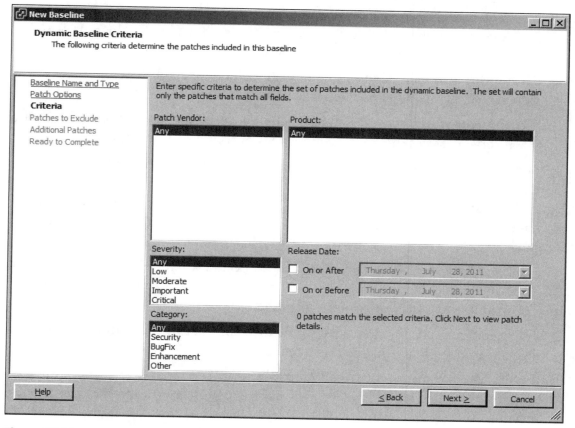

Figure 13.14
Dynamic baseline options.

To create a baseline group:

1. Log in to the vCenter server.

2. Highlight the vCenter instance in the inventory and click on the Update Manager tab.

3. Select Admin View.

4. Click on the Baselines and Groups tab.

5. Select Create.

6. Specify whether this will be a baseline that is applied to ESXi hosts, or to virtual machines, and enter a name that describes why this baseline was created. (Is this for ESXi hosts? VMs? What is the update that is being applied? Which cluster does this reference, etc.?)

7. On the Upgrades screen, if this baseline will reference a previously created Upgrade baseline, you can specify it on the Upgrades screen. If there are no baseline groups defined, you can use the "Create a new Host Upgrade Baseline" link. Select the appropriate baseline and click Next.

8. On the Patch screen, if this baseline will include a default baseline that is to be applied, select the baseline and click Next.

9. On the Extensions screen, if this baseline is to include extensions for physical ESXi servers, select the appropriate extensions(s) and click Next.

10. Review your configuration on the Summary screen and click Finish.

Figure 13.15 shows the summary screen to verify the options that we have chosen for our baseline. After reviewing, click on the Finish button. The baseline is now ready to be applied.

Now that we have created our baseline, we can decide where this baseline is applied. This is termed attaching the baseline. To attach the baseline, we click on the Compliance view link, and view the available baselines.

As shown in Figure 13.16, after we have defined the baseline, we can attach it to the vCenter inventory object that is the intended target. This object can be a vCenter folder, cluster, ESXi host, VM, or virtual appliance.

After we have defined a baseline, we can make a logical association between a vCenter inventory object or group of objects and a baseline. We can right-click on the vCenter instance, a folder, cluster, and select Scan for Updates.

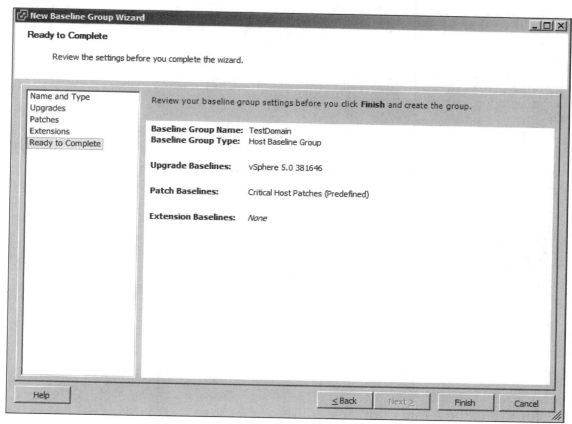

Figure 13.15
Creating a baseline.

As shown in Figure 13.17, we must tell vCenter whether we are scanning for patches and extensions, or whether we are scanning for upgrades.

As shown in Figure 13.18, depending on the type of updates that are planned, you can choose to scan the object(s) for compliance with the designated baseline. For example, you can either shut down the VM or place it in a suspended state prior to placing the host in Maintenance Mode.

If the remediation is to occur within a cluster, we can temporarily disable DPM, HA admission control, or FT. Also in vSphere 5, you have the option to perform parallel remediations within a cluster. If parallel remediations is selected, vCenter will evaluate the cluster and determine the optimum number of simultaneous remediations that can occur within the cluster. Or you have the option to manually specify the number of parallel processes that occur.

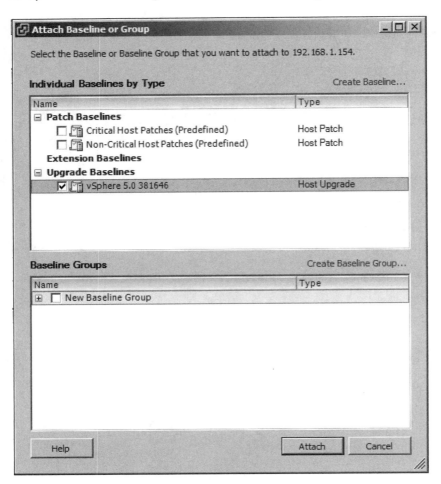

Figure 13.16
Attaching the baseline.

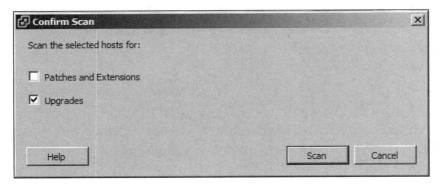

Figure 13.17
Patches vs. Upgrades.

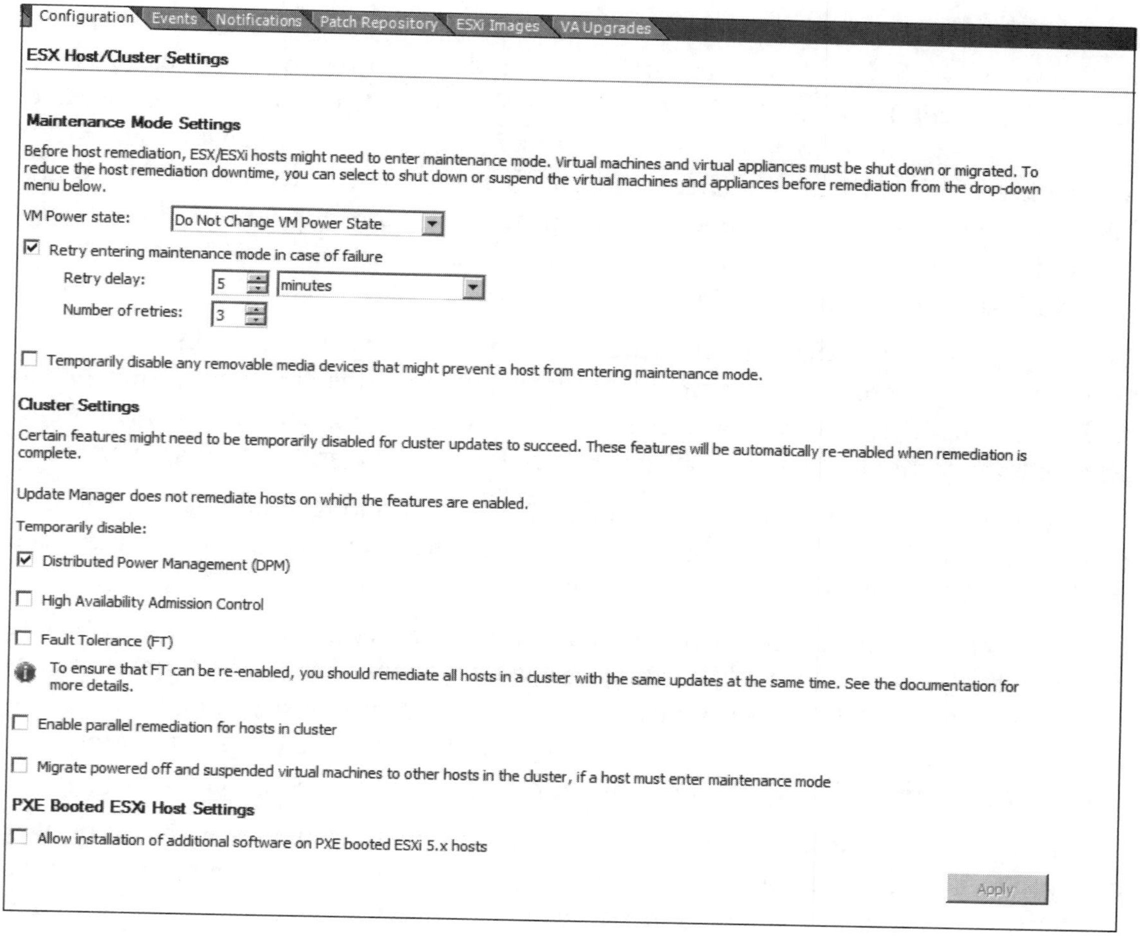

Figure 13.18
Host and Cluster Settings.

If you are using PXE boot to deploy the ESXi hosts, you can leverage Update Manager to patch and update to these hosts as well.

Staging

In a normal production environment, maintaining client access to server-based resources is a priority. At the same time, keeping the patching at a current level is an equally important process. The concept of "Staging" is one method to reduce the time necessary to apply updates to physical servers. Staging will copy updates, patches, and extensions locally to the ESXi hosts, eliminating the copy time from the repository to each host. Once the packages have been copied locally, the updates can be performed at a time when the activity level is lower, reducing the impact to production.

Remediation

At this point, we have defined the patches and updates that we want to deploy across our environment through the creation of a baseline. Simply deciding the level of patching and updating that we want to maintain can be a time-consuming process as we have to consider dependencies that may already exist in the environment, and how these new updates may affect existing processes. Hopefully you have the luxury of a test lab in which you can test your baseline without actually deploying it on production hosts and virtual machines.

We have scanned our devices for compliance with our baseline, and discovered that there are some objects that require an update. But how does the application of our updates occur? This is known as remediation. Remediation means that Update Manager will apply the designated packages to our hosts, VMs, and virtual appliances.

It is helpful to note at this point that Update Manager no longer supports the process of updating VM-based operating systems and applications. That process has been moved to VMware Configuration Manager.

Update Manager can update virtual machines by upgrading the version of VMware Tools or the version of virtual machine hardware presented to a VM. These updates can occur if the VM is currently powered on, powered off, or suspended. For example, if a VM is in a suspended state, the VM will be resumed from that state, the update will be applied, and the VM will be returned to the suspended state.

You can remediate hosts, virtual machines, and appliances in much the same way that you can scan them. As with scanning, you can remediate single hosts, virtual machines, or virtual appliances, and you can also initiate remediation on the folder, cluster, or datacenter level.

If you are considering the use of Update Manager as a part of a migration strategy, in other words, moving from a previous version of ESX/ESXi to vSphere 5, Update Manager supports migrating any ESX or ESXi 4.x hosts to the new revision. Please consult the upgrade module for details on migrations from an earlier revision.

These migrations are also performed through the use of baselines. The first step in this migration is the uploading of the new ESXi image(s) into Update Manager. We found in Figure 13.8 that we can use the Import ESXi Image link from the ESXi Images tab to add the new images into Update Manager. We can now create a baseline or a baseline group, depending on the number of hosts that are to be upgraded, to apply the upgrade package.

In a normal situation, ESX and ESXi hosts are placed into Maintenance Mode in order to apply the upgrade or patch. If this update is intended for a stand-alone host, this means that you will manually migrate any running VMs in the host's inventory to other ESXi hosts in order maintain client availability.

Implementing Host Profiles

The first step in utilizing Host Profiles is to decide what set of configuration parameters will become the model for the Host Profile. Host Profiles can be created from a new, function-specific installation, an existing production server, or imported from a file. The main concern is that you configure all of the parameters that you want to implement; for example, you can specify that vmnic0 is always created on a specific physical network adapter. One thing to keep in mind: if you define multiple IP addresses, such as multiple management networks or VMkernel networks (for vMotion and/or IP-based storage), you will want to consider creating a spreadsheet that will contain all the IP addresses that you will be using. As the Host Profile is applied, the process will stop and wait for you to input networking information before continuing; if the networking information is not provided the process will fail.

If you have a hybrid environment (one where there are hosts that are running VI 3, VI 3.5, and 4.x), there are caveats to using Host Profiles. The most definitive is that Host Profiles will not work with ESX 3.x hosts. As a general principle, you may want to upgrade these legacy hosts before continuing. If legacy hosts are required in the environment, perhaps to support a particular process or business unit, keep the following in mind:

- ESX/ESXi VI 3.x hosts cannot be used as the basis for a Host Profile.
- ESX/ESXi VI 3.x cannot be a target of a Host Profile.
- If your environment contains a mixed cluster, the Host Profile will report a failure when the cluster compliance is validated.

Creating

As stated earlier, decide which ESXi server will serve as the reference for your new Host Profile. You have the option of creating the profile from an existing ESXi host, or you can also import the profile from a removable storage device.

Creating a Host Profile can be performed in several methods: by using the View > Management > Host Profiles link, by right-clicking on the host in the vCenter inventory and selecting Host Profiles, or by using the Ctrl+Shift+P key sequence and selecting the Create button in the upper-right corner.

Figure 13.19
The Host Profile interface.

As shown in Figure 13.19, the Host Profile interface allows you to create a new profile, clone a profile, edit an existing profile, delete a profile, or attach a profile to a host or a cluster.

To create a new Host Profile:

1. Click the Create button.

2. Indicate whether this profile will be created from an existing host or imported from a file.

3. Browse to the source host.

4. Specify the name and document the profile.

5. Click Finish.

As shown in Figure 13.20, the completed Host Profile will appear beneath the Host Profiles folder.

Modifying an Existing Profile

Once the Host Profile has been defined, you can always edit the profile to accommodate changes in host requirements, or new configuration changes in the production environment.

As an alternative, as shown in Figure 13.21, you can also right-click on the ESXi host, and select Host Profile, and then you have the option to manage an existing profile, create a new profile from this ESXi host, check this host for compliance against a host profile, and apply a profile to this ESXI host.

Figure 13.20
Completed Host Profile.

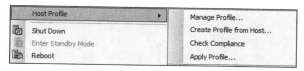

Figure 13.21
Host Profile options.

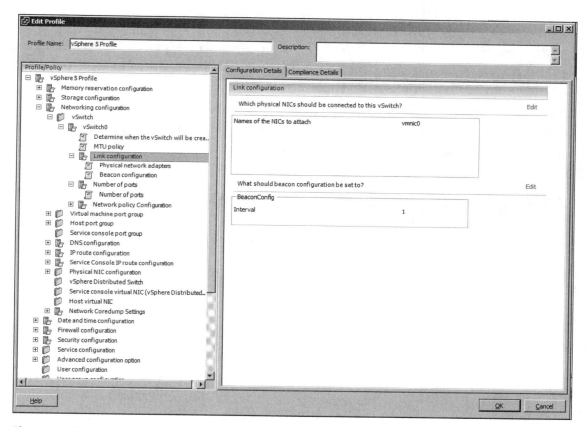

Figure 13.22
Editing a Host Profile.

From the Host Profile management interface, if you select the Edit Profile button, you can modify the individual settings as shown in Figure 13.22. Here, you can be very granular in the configuration, even going down to defining whether the virtual network adapter should be created, and if so, what its parameters should be.

Assigning the Profile to Hosts and Clusters

To make this Host Profile available to hosts and clusters, you must attach the profile to the appropriate host or cluster.

To attach a Host Profile to a host:

1. Click the Attach Hosts/Cluster button.

2. Browse to the correct host or cluster and click the right-facing arrow.

3. Click OK.

Scanning and Applying the Host Profile

For the profile to be applied successfully, the host must be placed in Maintenance Mode. This will evacuate the host and vMotion all VMs to other hosts, if possible. Right-click on the host and select Apply Profile.

When the profile has been attached, the host will be evaluated against the configuration specified in the profile, and any discrepancies will be noted. As shown in Figure 13.23, our profile has found that the DNS configuration is not the same as that found in the profile. When we click Finish, the host will be remediated.

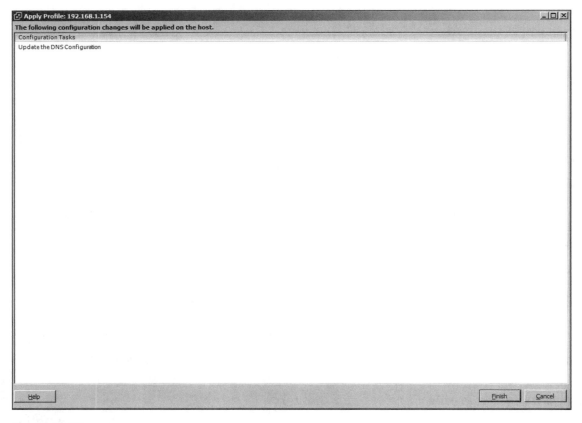

Figure 13.23
Attaching a profile to a host.

TROUBLESHOOTING

The use of Update Manager to update the ESXi servers, upgrade VMware Tools, and revise virtual machine hardware is an often-overlooked tool that can help maintain a stable environment. But, as we have seen in previous chapters, the need to troubleshoot the updating of a cluster or downloading the latest updates may still arise. In this section, we will look at some basic troubleshooting concepts related to Update Manager.

Troubleshooting Update Manager

As we discussed, the first thing that you should consider when troubleshooting Update Manager is whether the Update Manager services are currently running. Check Services.msc on the hosting Windows Server to verify that the two Update Manager services, Update Manager and Update Manager UFA, are started. If they are currently in a "Not Started" state, restart them and retry Update Manager to check whether functionality has been restored.

If the services are indeed running, check connectivity with the vCenter server. If the Update Manager server has network access with the vCenter server, is the vCenter service running? If the vCenter service has stopped, all functionality within vCenter comes to a screeching halt.

If addressing either of the previous scenarios does not reveal anything, it is time to retrieve the log bundles from the Update Manager server and the vCenter server. This can be accomplished by using the All Programs > VMware > Generate VMware Log Bundle. These log files are gathered together and placed on the user's desktop in .zip format where they can be easily reviewed to determine the cause of the problem. Remember, the log files should be the first source of troubleshooting information. If necessary, the log files can also be uploaded to VMware for further analysis.

If there is no additional baseline metadata available, check the accessibility of the Internet from the Update Manager server or the UMDS server. Has the proxy configuration been modified, if one is required to access the Internet?

Issues with Host Updates

Verify the functionality of DNS and that the correct information is contained in the DNS resource records for the Update Manager server and all hosts that are scheduled for scanning and remediation. All vCenter components rely strongly on the ability to resolve host names to function correctly.

Verify that all required ports are open between the Update Manager server and the clients. If the ports are blocked, Update Manager will be unable to scan and remediate the hosts.

Another common issue occurs when a virtual machine is remediated to update the version of VMware Tools that is installed in the VM. This remediation process will fail if VMware Tools is not currently installed in the VM. In this case, the upgrade requires an existing installation before VMware Tools can be upgraded.

If you have scheduled the update of an ESXi host, and the remediation process fails, verify that the ESXi host has at least 10MB of free space in its /tmp folder. In some cases, this host will indicate that the upgrade was successful, but in reality the package was not applied correctly. This free space is required for local processing of the update package. Delete sufficient files or make the datastore bigger and retry the update.

Lastly, verify that the ESXi host has enough free space to contain the updates. If the local disks are full, the update will fail.

Summary

In this chapter, we discussed how Update Manager can be utilized to download and update VMware components, such as virtual appliances, VMware Tools, and virtual machine hardware, along with the updating of both stand-alone and clustered ESXi hosts. We found that Update Manager can be used to directly access the Internet to download update packages, but Update Manager can also be used in a very secure environment through the installation of the Update Manager Download Service on a separate server. We discussed how the use of Host Profiles can streamline the deployment of new servers by applying a standard configuration, and can be used to verify if a server is within corporate standards by scanning servers non-disruptively.

In the next chapter, we will take a look at the process of migrating from physical servers or from another virtualization platform to a VMware virtual machine.

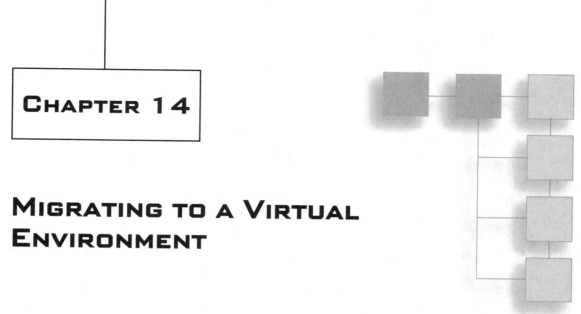

CHAPTER 14

MIGRATING TO A VIRTUAL ENVIRONMENT

Wouldn't it be great if all your existing servers and data could just magically appear in your new virtual environment? Everything would just work, all your users would be happy, and you just sit back and relax while the magic happens. Well, it isn't quite that perfect, but physical to virtual migrations have come a long way in the last few years. We're going to help you figure out the best approach for you to get those old (or maybe even new) physical servers into your virtual environment.

PLANNING

Before you start cloning and copying data all over the place, let's take a step back and talk about what you intend to migrate. There are many different methods to migrate physical and virtual servers into vSphere 5. We need to talk about your objectives, your options, and then discuss some of the caveats that affect migrations both before and after the operation.

What Is Your Objective?

To migrate a machine into a virtual environment you can use a variety of means. Note we didn't specify virtual or physical machine. That's because we can migrate VMs from other VMware products or even other vendors' products. We can also migrate third-party disk images to VMs as well as some backup software images. We'll explore each of these categories so that you understand your wide variety of options.

Physical Server to VM Migration (P2V)

A Physical to Virtual (P2V) migration is the most common type of migration, and is likely the one you think of most often when anyone mentions migrating VMs. The physical servers are typically part of an existing infrastructure, and tend to be aged hardware and software either ready for a refresh or even long overdue.

The most important question in the P2V area is whether you intend to migrate only a few physical servers or if this will be a major project including dozens or hundreds of servers. Though small projects still involve gathering the same type of performance and resource information required in the larger projects, the methods we use to collect that information can vary greatly. For example, if you are planning to migrate only one or two servers, you might consider logging into each of the physical servers to gather the necessary statistics manually. On the other hand, if you're working on a fairly large project, you may want to engage a VMware partner to help you size your environment properly using a piece of software called VMware Capacity Planner. This tool automates the process of collecting performance data from your physical (and virtual) servers and helps you determine the appropriate size of your virtual environment. Virtualizing a physical server may seem easy after listening to all the marketing hype out there, but we can tell you that there is much more to the process than running a wizard. Most of the real work is done up front in the form of planning and information gathering. The converting and migrating part is typically straightforward (again, if you've done the right planning and preparation). The more time you spend gathering information before your migration, the better your final result will be after the dust has settled.

VM to VM Migration (V2V)

Another popular migration strategy involves moving from one Virtual Machine to another Virtual Machine (V2V). The source could be a VMware-based VM, such as from VMware Workstation, Fusion, Server, or even ESXi, or it could be a VM from a Microsoft Hyper-V server or a Citrix XenServer. At this time, the VMware Converter product (that we'll describe later) doesn't support a direct migration from XenServer. However, there are third-party software packages that can convert these VMs.

We talked about a popular use case for this type of migration earlier in the book when we discussed VMDK disk sizes. While you can't shrink a VMDK, you certainly can use Converter to migrate the VM to a new VM, reducing the resulting virtual disks in the process.

Restore a Backup to VM

Let's say that you have a very old server backup tape that you need to recover. The server has been gone for years and you have no hardware like it anywhere. You manage to find a tape drive that can restore the data, but now you're stuck trying to find hardware to use for the server restore. In many cases, you can use a VM as the replacement hardware if you are able to redirect the restore process to another disk. vSphere 5 supports some very old operating systems, so there is a good chance you can build a new VM, and then restore your data into it.

This even applies to some backup methods. The now-retired VMware Consolidated Backup (VCB) framework enabled administrators to create VMDK-based backups of their VMs, but it had no native restore functionality. The resulting backup was a sparse-format VM, complete with VMX files. You can restore these backups using VMware Converter, essentially performing a V2V on the backup image. VMware replaced the VCB framework with the VMware Data Recovery (VDR) appliance, which now has a built-in method to restore VMs.

Restoring backups to VMs is also a great way to check the quality of your backups. You can create a sandbox environment that has a fenced-in network area so that your restores do not affect your production environment. Then you restore things like Domain Controllers, database servers, and file servers to confirm that your back-ups function as expected. It's a great way to see if your backups missed critical files before it's too late to fix the problem.

What Are Your Options?

As we've discussed, there are many reasons you may wish to perform P2V or V2V operations. We have different methods to achieve each of those goals, some involve using conversion software, but software isn't always the answer. There are even third-party solutions to help you with P2P (Physical to Physical) and V2P (Virtual to Physical), but that falls outside the scope of this chapter (migrating to a virtual environment).

Manual Rebuild

Believe it or not, there are cases where converting a machine to a VM isn't the most appropriate option. There is no shame in manually rebuilding a server natively as a VM. Some applications just don't respond well to migration due to license keys or hardware issues. Others may convert to a VM only to perform poorly or cause other issues within the infrastructure. Still, sometimes a manual rebuild is the only possibility because the guest operating system isn't supported as a conversion source.

VMware Converter

Fortunately, a free software program known as VMware Converter can very effectively handle the vast majority of the conversions we perform. VMware Converter is an application that enables administrators to clone running physical (or virtual) machines to virtual disks and then converts the result to running VMs. The tool can also import disk images from several third-party backup vendors.

VMware changed the Converter product with the release of vSphere 5, removing the version of the product that integrated into vCenter. VMware Converter version 5 is only available as a stand-alone product, but it remains a free download from VMware's website. There had always been a gap between the functionality of the stand-alone product and the vCenter-integrated product. With the latest release, VMware merged some of the functionality to improve the cloning operations and security aspects of the stand-alone product.

We'll talk more about these options in just a moment, but VMware Converter version 5 can only migrate machines that are currently running. This is referred to as a hot clone operation, very similar to what we described back in Chapter 9 when we talked about the different VM cloning methods. The other method, cold cloning, enabled us to clone machines using a special boot CD method. It was particularly useful when the guest operating system was either unstable or too out of date to support hot cloning. The cold clone boot CD is still available for download for customers who had purchased the VMware Converter Enterprise product. It was also available for customers of vCenter server 4.0, so it may be found on the Internet if you have an appropriate license.

Architecturally speaking, VMware Converter is a one-off product. You don't integrate it with anything, and it can be installed on a workstation. The software serves as a middle manager that controls the cloning process from the source machine to the destination ESXi server, and then processes the conversion routines to allow the cloned machine to boot as a VM. There are no permanent hooks into the ESXi server or vCenter, but VMware Converter must be able to communicate with both of them, and the operator (you) must have the appropriate permissions on both the source machine and in vCenter/ESXi to create the destination VM.

The product can convert a number of operating system types including the more recent releases of Window and Linux; however, because the live migration process in Windows requires the presence of VSS, versions of Windows prior to XP are not supported. Also, Linux machines cannot be reconfigured automatically. VMware Converter does a great job despite the fact it is free. For extra functionality, you should consider purchasing a third-party conversion tool.

Third-Party Products

When we go outside of the traditional Windows migrations, we have to look to third-party software vendors for support. A couple of major players provide support for those complex migration projects. Some can even automate the conversion operations so that you can tackle mass migrations.

Alternatively, you can use imaging software such as Symantec Ghost, the open source G4L project, Acronis True Image, Symantec BackupExec LiveState Recovery, ShadowProtect, or even Microsoft's VHD format. All of these formats can be used with VMware Converter to create a VM from the backup image. For a complete list of supported third-party image formats (with version numbers), refer to the Implementation and Management section of this chapter.

Pre-Migration Considerations

Now before you begin migrating anything, there are things you need to consider. Well, actually there are many things to consider. P2V and V2V operations are simple to learn, but hard to master, because each server is different and each migration brings with it new challenges. Here are some topics you should consider:

- Licensing
- Mass migrations
- Pre-migration performance benchmarks
- VM architecture
- Application consistency
- Hot clones and cold clones
- Cloning bandwidth
- Reducing copy times via RDMs
- Changes to the machine's hardware

Licensing

While we are not lawyers, we'd like to remind you of your legal obligations. Each software vendor has its own rules, typically called the End User License Agreement (EULA). You may be permitted to migrate the software to new hardware, or you may need to relicense the software.

Microsoft, for example, does not permit you to migrate an OEM copy of Windows. You must purchase either a retail or a volume license version of the product. In the case of Windows Server, the Enterprise and Datacenter editions provide licensing for multiple VM instances on a single ESXi host. If you are virtualizing many Windows servers, you may want to investigate these licenses further.

In addition to Microsoft, many vendors bind their software licenses to hardware. Some do this using CPU serial numbers or Ethernet MAC addresses, while others just state the limitation in their license agreement. Even if the software can be moved technically, if the license agreement dictates otherwise, contact the vendor to see what options you have. Some vendors will reissue license keys without a charge, while others may require you to purchase the software package again for the new hardware.

Mass Migrations

As we mentioned at the beginning of this chapter, if you are migrating a large number of VMs, you may want to retain the services of a VMware partner organization. These partners have the ability to use a piece of software known as VMware Capacity Planner to analyze your physical equipment and make recommendations on how the virtual environment should be constructed. Also, these partners may be able to provide you with assistance in the automation and planning of the migrations.

Pre-Migration Performance Benchmarks

Benchmarking is a very helpful step to take before you begin converting machines, because after you have converted you have no means to assess how the machine performed. This can be particularly useful when shortly after the migration performance issues surface that may or may not be directly related to the migration. Having a solid benchmark of the server's prior performance goes a long way when defending your migration methodology and virtualization design.

Also in the process of benchmarking the source machine, you may learn that the resource consumption of the VM is much greater than expected. For instance, a file server may experience very little activity during the day; however, during its nightly backup process the server saturates the disk I/O channels.

For that reason, we recommend creating several charts of performance data. Don't worry; you only collect the data once. The additional reports are all in the presentation of that data. You start with a daily collection of CPU, RAM, network, and disk performance statistics at 5-minute intervals for a 24-hour period. This data collection process should really run for several days to ensure that you get a good sample because many servers (like users) have good and bad days. You want to know the worst that this server can dish out so that you don't size the VMs too small.

When you're done, you should be able to show an average workday with 5-minute granularity and a workweek at a 15-minute granularity level. Don't forget to monitor the backup windows and any other system maintenance windows, because these processes aren't likely to go away just because you virtualize the server.

VM Architecture

Once you know what your VMs should look like, you can proceed with the architecture of your virtual environment. What? You've already bought the hardware and you didn't realize that we needed to benchmark first. Well, you may be going back to the money tree. You don't want to shortchange your long-term success (read: your career) by squeezing your organization's infrastructure into a solution that was improperly designed (or not designed). The truth is that many organizations face this dilemma because it is very easy to just buy hardware and then start packing VMs into it. The trouble: all VMs aren't equal; in fact, there are some VMs that will never play well with others because they need far too many resources.

There really isn't a one-size-fits-all model in virtualization. Every server workload should be considered based on its resource utilization and relative importance to the organization. Placing a critical e-mail server next to a critical database server, both of which require tremendous amounts of disk I/O and CPU usage, will prove very stressful for both you and your users.

The key is to document the exact requirements of each virtual workload as it exists today, or if the VM will be brand new, consult the vendor's performance recommendations and sizing information. From there you can design appropriate computer resources (CPU/RAM) and storage silos that match the demands of the VMs before you have performance issues.

Tip

> Remember, just because you have 2TB of free space, doesn't mean you have to fill up the volume. Sometimes we have to let disks sit partially unoccupied from a space perspective so that one or two applications can get as much I/O speed as possible from those disks (without fighting other VMs).

Application Consistency

Application consistency or integrity is something we seem to take for granted when backing up our data or when making copies of data. We assume that whatever we back up we can restore in perfect condition. But, what if the data was in use when you backed it up? Can you get a perfect copy of that data? The answer isn't clear, nor is it obvious, because different applications handle open files in very different ways.

When we migrate machines to VMs, we have to be aware of the state of the source machine and all of its associated data files. This means that we need to know if the server contains data that could be in use, and if it is in use how we can back it up or copy it effectively. For instance, database servers will have their databases open at all times that the database engine is running. If we want to back up that data, we can either shut down the database engine or we can tell the database engine to export the data to a backup file that won't change.

In Windows systems, we can use a snapshot behavior that releases locks on files so that we can back them up. This feature is called Microsoft Volume ShadowCopy Services (VSS), and it exists on Windows XP and later, and on Windows Server 2003 and later. If VSS is operational you may be able to back up a live database; however, we still caution you to consider the impact if the copy were to be incomplete or inaccurate.

In most cases, we recommend that you shut down the applications prior to the cloning operations just to be safe. This does present downtime, but a little downtime during the migration process beats a lot of downtime later if the copy process doesn't go so well.

Hot Clones and Cold Clones

We talked about the concept of hot cloning and cold cloning earlier in this chapter, and we said that it is a lot like the hot and cold cloning we did with VMs back in Chapter 9. The hot clone is when the source operating system is fully booted and running; whereas the cold clone leverages a boot CD so that we can get a 100% consistent clone.

The cold clone process is certainly the more reliable and consistent version of the two, but what are its limitations? For one, the cold clone is a boot CD. That means you must have physical access to the source server or you must have a hardware/ firmware remote control solution that permits remote ISO booting. Either way, the operating system is shut down and the machine is rebooted, causing downtime until the clone is complete. The clone operation pushes the virtual disk data to the ESXi server directly where it is recomposed as a VMDK for the VM. When the clone operation has completed, the converter software can reconfigure the VM to boot from the virtual hardware presented by ESXi.

Cold cloning has a couple advantages though too. One is that you do not have to install anything on the source machine. Hot cloning requires agents to move the data; cold cloning uses a boot CD that can see the entire file system. Another advantage is related to the visibility of the file systems; the cold clone process can migrate operating systems that do not support VSS or snapshotting because the files are all closed. This means we can use cold clone migrations for legacy operating systems where the hot clone would fail.

Hot cloning, of course, has its advantages too. One being that it does not require the operating system to be stopped, but it is still advisable to stop the application services on the source machine due to file locking. This procedure is agent-based, meaning the administrator must have credentials on the source machine to install the agent.

Hot cloning is certainly the more convenient option, but it can be disastrous if not done perfectly. For example, in VMware Converter 5, multiple copy passes are conducted during a hot clone operation to minimize the number of changed files that are missed during the migration. This was one of the features that VMware merged in from the vCenter version of Converter.

Cloning Bandwidth

Regardless of whether you choose hot cloning or cold cloning, the copy process is network intensive. The time and bandwidth required are directly related to the size of the data volumes that you are migrating. The larger the volume, the longer the time, and the more bandwidth that will be required to decrease that time.

Why is the bandwidth of the clone process important? It defines how long the copy will take, which if you are using cold clones, defines how much downtime you will have during the migration. If you are using a hot clone copy process, the bandwidth is still important because it affects how much data may have changed on the source since the copy was initiated. Again, the more bandwidth you have, the less downtime you have, or the fewer changes that must be recopied after the initial clone has been completed.

Reducing Copy Times via RDMs

If you calculate, based on your maximum downtime window, that your source machine will require more bandwidth than you have available, you need to find a way to reduce the amount of data being copied. One method for this involves the use of Raw Device Mappings (RDMs), discussed in Chapters 8 and 9. RDMs, as you may recall, require that the storage on your source machine is stored on a SAN. If this is true, you may be able to clone only part of the source machine, leaving the bulk of the data on the SAN, and then linking the VM to the rest of the data on the SAN using an RDM.

If you choose to do this, place the RDM in virtual compatibility mode, because in this mode you can later use Storage vMotion to migrate that data from the SAN to a VMDK file on a VMFS datastore. Remember, Storage vMotion is noninvasive and does not incur downtime for the VM, whereas the cloning process of the P2V or V2V process likely will incur downtime.

Changes to the Machine's Hardware

Following the migration from a physical machine or even a differently formatted virtual machine, your VM may have very different virtual hardware. This can alter the behavior of applications and even disrupt the licensing of your software. Before converting a machine to a VM, check carefully that the software installed in the machine is not tied to any hardware addresses or special hardware devices. Here are some samples to consider:

- CPU model/Serial numbers
- Ethernet adapters and MAC addresses
- Video cards/Sound cards
- Disks and partitions
- SCSI/IDE controllers

Post-Migration Challenges

The migration process really isn't complete when the wizard finishes. No, you'll still have some clean up to perform within the guest operating system of the VM. The cleanup varies by operating system, but typically involves removing old software and drivers, perhaps even "ghosted" hardware devices that existed in the previous system, but are now inactive. In addition, you need to consider how you will back up the new VM, and whether your traditional methods will change because of virtualization.

Remove Software and Drivers

Both Windows and Linux are affected by the problem of extra software, but Windows usually takes the spotlight because it also retains all past hardware devices in an inactive state. The drivers for old physical hardware can be removed from the VM, but exercise caution because it is possible for software to depend on other software; removing the bottom layer could make the top layer unstable.

If you have a VM that has a lot of software to clean up, you might consider cloning it or placing a temporary snapshot on it in case things don't go so well. The removal of software should include anything that required special hardware devices, such as:

- Network card teaming/management software
- SNMP management agents (unless they also manage software inventories)
- Specialty hardware monitors
- Video card management tools
- Sound card management tools

This list is by no means complete, but it will give you an idea of what to look for. We find it is often easiest to start by removing the software and then go back to remove any leftover drivers. In many cases, the software management applications also remove the drivers.

Once you have removed the various software packages, we still have to contend with ghosted hardware (at least in Windows). Windows systems track hardware devices in the registry. If you remove a device, the registry still contains references to that device and any customized settings you had applied to it. Normally this isn't an issue, but there is one particular type of device that causes us a bit of grief: network adapters. Refer to the Troubleshooting section at the end of this chapter for details on how to remove these non-present devices.

Backup Software Changes

Don't forget about your backup software. We discussed a variety of backup solutions in Chapter 9, including leaving your existing backup software agents in place. Before you start your migration to virtualization, you should consider how to back up your data. Here are a few questions that you should consider:

- Will you continue to use an agent-based system?
- If so, will the IP addresses change for the backup network (if you have one)?
- Will we need to reinstall the backup agent software after the P2V/V2V?
- Will there be sufficient bandwidth on the VM network to use an agent-based backup or do you need more uplink ports on the ESXi servers?
- If you use an image-based backup, how do you create database backups?

Security Considerations

Yes, even P2V and V2V operations have security considerations. After all, you are copying your data over the network and you are essentially moving the server from one datacenter to another. The fact that the new datacenter is a virtual one doesn't remove the necessity for security—depending on your environment, it might actually increase the need.

Security During the Clone

The security of the data transfer should always be placed ahead of the speed of the copy process, because compromised servers tend to lead to résumé-generating events. You can provide end-to-end security in a number of ways, the most common being physical separation. Unfortunately, modifying the physical network architecture is usually not an option when we work with P2V operations. The next best option would be to encrypt the data transfer. In VMware Converter 5, the data stream between source and destination is now encrypted to provide that extra level of protection.

Securing the VM after the Clone

Unfortunately, the transfer of the cloned data is only part of our security concerns. We still need to apply appropriate access control permissions within vCenter to avoid the casual observer from accessing or exporting our new VM.

Once the vCenter security has been established and tested, double-check the guest operating system security level, including patches and remote connectivity. If you altered the IP address of the VM, you may also need to change the firewall settings within the OS or even in physical firewall appliances in your network.

What about the Old Hardware?

Finally, we come to the old hardware. Don't wipe it out yet because you may need it, but certainly put a time limit on that server's existence; it shouldn't stay on a shelf forever because that too creates a risk when other people forget that there is data on the hard drives. That brings us to our next point. Unless you want to find your organization's private data on the Internet, keep these servers under lock and key. The data on that server must be maintained in the same manner that it was maintained when it was in production.

Once you are certain that the server is no longer needed, use a secure erase application to remove your data from the hard disks and follow your organization's policy on the proper disposal of the equipment (sell, donate, or discard). Just remember, your data is on those hard drives and there are companies that specialize in reconstructing data from hard drives that have even survived building fires. Surely they could reconstruct the data from drives that you didn't properly erase (even if you smashed the disks with a hammer). Trust us.

IMPLEMENTATION AND MANAGEMENT

Now that we have discussed the planning aspects of your P2V/V2V process, let's talk about how to actually put the plan into motion. First, we're going to cover an overview of the process, and then we'll investigate the major areas, focusing on areas that we've found easy to overlook.

Overview of the Process

The migration process can be broken down into several major steps, starting with the selection of the source machine and ending with its decommissioning after the migration has been completed and tested.

1. Pick the virtualization candidates.
2. Design the target VM environment.
3. Prepare the source machine.
4. Create third-party image (optional).
5. VM migration operation (VMware Converter).
6. Post-migration VM management.
7. Sanitize the source machine.

Choose the Virtualization Candidates

Choosing candidates isn't really an implementation discussion, but it does bear repeating because of its importance. Choosing appropriate virtualization candidates shouldn't be a random selection process because not every physical server in your environment is going to be a great virtualization candidate. Some servers will be very easy to virtualize, because they consume very few resources and have a more tolerant downtime window. Other systems may operate with dedicated storage and networking systems due to their importance or performance requirements. You may eventually achieve virtualizing 100% of your servers, but there is no harm in starting small and choosing the easy ones first. Not everything works well in a shared I/O environment.

Design the Target VM Environment

We discussed in the Planning section of this chapter how to properly assess your existing workloads and collect that information. Once you have your statistics assembled, you can determine how much CPU, RAM, disk I/O and space, and network bandwidth to allocate to your VM.

Check Available CPU Resources

CPU and memory requirements are typically the easiest things to fix if you get it wrong during the design, because we can easily add more RAM to a VM, or even add more CPUs if needed. That doesn't mean you should toss the design to the wind and over allocate CPUs and RAM to everything. We recommend starting small and working up because it is typically easier to add CPUs and memory than remove it later.

We also don't want to see you starve your VMs for resources. We discussed the impact of starving a VM of RAM in Chapter 10. If you recall, it has the effect of increasing the VM's CPU resources while it tries to page/swap memory to disk, which then increases our disk I/O load. We impact two resources because we restricted one. The key is to right-size everything. Know how much RAM your application needs and allocate that amount. Check to see how often the VM is paging to disk and increase the RAM if the paging activity becomes too frequent.

Check Available Storage Capacity and Speed

Disk capacity is usually easy to see, but it can be hard to fix if you have no free space. Disk I/O on the other hand is often very difficult to see and fix. Improperly sized disk systems can cause problems that appear to originate in other areas. For example, a slow disk array will increase your storage latency, slowing down all your processing times. It will appear that the CPU isn't fast enough to handle the workload, but if you check the CPU you will see that it is waiting on the disk subsystems.

Before you size your storage, check the Disk Reads and Disk Writes on each of your source machine's volumes. That will tell you the number of IOPS required for that workload. Use this information to see if the workload can fit into the remaining I/O in your SAN. If not, dedicate a new set of disks to this workload.

Prepare the Source Machine

Just before the cloning process begins, you need to prepare the source machine for the migration. This includes shutting down any non-essential services, and any services linked to data systems that may keep files open during the cloning process. We want to make sure that all the data files are properly closed and that the system is ready for migration.

If you are unable to stop these data services or close the appropriate applications, you should investigate the possibility of creating database or file dumps of the data. This way, you will get a consistent copy of the data before the migration begins. The trouble will be capturing any changes that occur after the backup has been completed. Our recommendation is to keep those services offline so that no users can access the data during or just before the clone operations. Again, a little downtime during the clone is better than a lot of downtime later if the data is corrupted or invalid.

If there is just no way to shut down the data services, and no backup can be made that can easily be restored, you may want to consider using a cold clone process. If you choose to use the cold clone, you must ensure that the cold clone boot CD has the appropriate drivers to allow the cloning software to see the volumes on your server. A common problem with cold clone CDs is that they do not contain the RAID or SCSI drivers for every card known to man. That means you'd need to specify a driver for your boot CD to work, and that can be a challenge.

Create a Third-Party Image (Optional)

Third-party images can be very helpful if you are attempting to clone a machine that is very old or that is completely inaccessible to the cold clone boot CDs. If you intend to use VMware Converter to import the third-party image for conversion, you should check the VMware documentation of the latest version of Converter. Here are the supported versions as of version 5.0:

- Acronis True Image Echo 9.1, 9.5, and Acronis True Image Home 10 and 11 (.tib).

- Microsoft Virtual PC 2004 and Microsoft Virtual PC 2007 (.vmc).

- Microsoft Virtual Server 2005 and 2005 R2 (.vmc).

- Norton Ghost version 10.0, 12.0, and 14.0 (.sv2i format only).

- Parallels Desktop 2.5, 3.0, and 4.0 (.pvs and .hdd). Compressed disks are not supported.

- Parallels Workstation 2.x (.pvs). Compressed disks are not supported. Parallels Virtuozzo Containers are not supported.

- StorageCraft ShadowProtect Desktop, ShadowProtect Server, ShadowProtect Small Business Server (SBS), ShadowProtect IT Edition, versions 2.0, 2.5, 3.0, 3.1, and 3.2 (.spf).

- Symantec Backup Exec System Recovery (formerly LiveState Recovery) 6.5, 7.0, 8.0, and 8.5, LiveState Recovery 3.0 and 6.0 (only .sv2i).

Typically, you can create the image by booting to a special boot disk provided by the manufacturer of the imaging software. Like the cold clone boot CD, the boot disk must have driver support for your SCSI or RAID controller before you will be able to create an image of the disks. The advantage here is that many of the vendors supporting image-based backups also have tremendous support for different SCSI/RAID cards.

You should create a separate image file for each hard drive in the source machine. This will make the migration to a VM easier because you can convert the images into individual virtual hard disks. Some imaging software may have difficulties reading dynamic disks in Windows or custom partition types in other operating systems.

Check with the application vendor to determine the limits of their support before purchasing a product.

Once you have the image file(s), you will need to move them to a location where you can run the VMware Converter product against them. This could be on a network share, but it might be faster if you copied them to a workstation running the VMware converter software locally. The converter software will then move the expanded data up to an ESXi server during the import process.

VM Migration Operation (VMware Converter)

We've completed the preparations for the source machine, so now it's time to start the actual conversion work. That means it's time to install VMware Converter.

Installing VMware Converter

You can only install VMware Converter on a Windows system, but it can be a workstation or server. The Converter product has both a client and a server component. Both may be installed on the same machine or you can separate the installations if you would prefer to centralize the server and install the client application on your workstation. If you choose to separate the client from the server, ensure that TCP port 443 (HTTPS) is open between them.

The Converter server (and/or client) may be installed on these operating systems:

- Windows XP Professional (32-bit and 64-bit) SP3
- Windows 2003 (32-bit and 64-bit) SP2, R2
- Windows Vista (32-bit and 64-bit) SP2
- Windows Server 2008 (32-bit and 64-bit) SP2
- Windows Server 2008 R2 (64-bit)
- Windows 7 (32-bit and 64-bit)

Note

The Converter server must have 525MB of free space for the agent files, server files, and client files.

Caution

If you install the VMware Converter client/server application on your vCenter server, you must change the Converter service's port numbers because port TCP/443 and TCP/80 are both in use by vCenter. Remember, this change may affect your firewall rules and any remote Converter clients. It's better to install VMware Converter on a separate machine.

The Converter server component requires connectivity to the ESXi server, the vCenter server (if used), and the source machine. The agent that copies the data from the source machine to the target VM does not pass through the VMware Converter server, but there is still control information and customization processes that need to occur. Refer to the Troubleshooting section of this chapter for details on the TCP/UDP ports required as well as the permissions necessary in vCenter to import the VMs.

Initiating the Conversion Process

The first step in the conversion process is to launch the VMware Converter product. Next, you'll want to click on "Convert Machine" from the toolbar. This launches the wizard, shown in Figure 14.1, which allows us to initiate both P2V and V2V migrations.

We will now discuss the five different migration types:

- Powered-on machine (P2V)
- VMware infrastructure VM (a VM located in ESX/vCenter)
- VMware workstation or other VMware VM (file-based)

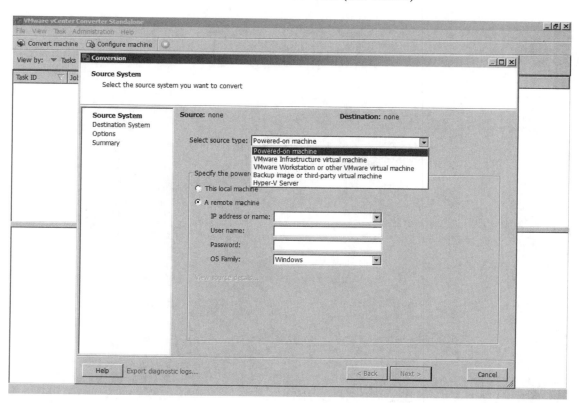

Figure 14.1
Initiating the P2V Migration wizard.

■ Backup image or third-party VM

■ Hyper-V server

Powered-on Machine (P2V)

Here are the steps in the Migration wizard for powered-on machines:

1. Choose the source machine. Is it this machine or a remote machine? Enter credentials and continue. Click "View Source Details…" to confirm this is the correct source machine.

2. Choose the destination type. Will this go to vCenter/ESXi or to a workstation format? If you choose workstation format, you will be given the option to specify the path and the VM Hardware type. If you specify Infrastructure, you must specify the server name and credentials.

3. Choose the destination VM name and folder

4. Choose the destination VM host, datastore, and hardware version, as shown in Figure 14.2

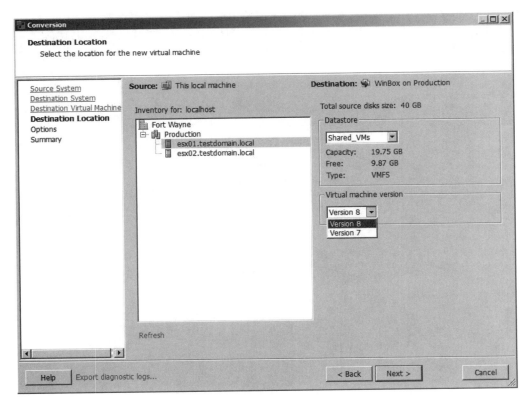

Figure 14.2
Selecting the P2V destinations.

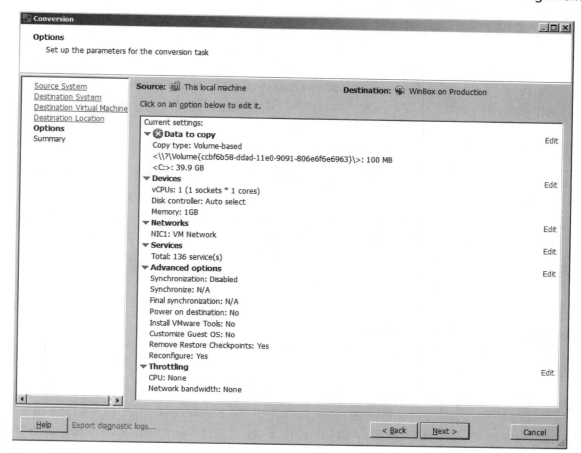

Figure 14.3
Adjusting the P2V migration options.

5. Configure the options for the migration process, including adjusting the VM hardware, the size of the VM disks, and whether to start/stop services prior to the migration. These options are shown in Figure 14.3.

6. Confirm the process and submit the job for migration.

VMware Infrastructure VM

Here are the steps in the Migration wizard for VMs currently contained on ESXi or vCenter servers:

1. Choose the source machine. Enter credentials for vCenter or the ESXi server and continue.

2. Select the VM to import. The VM must be powered off. Click "View Source Details..." to confirm this is the correct source machine.

3. Choose the destination type. Will this go to vCenter/ESXi or to a workstation format? If you choose workstation format, you will be given the option to specify the path and the VM Hardware type. If you specify Infrastructure, you must specify the server name and credentials.

4. Choose the destination VM name and folder

5. Choose the destination VM host, datastore, and hardware version, as shown in Figure 14.2

6. Configure the options for the migration process, including adjusting the VM hardware, the size of the VM disks, and whether to start/stop services prior to the migration. These options are shown in Figure 14.3.

7. Confirm the process and submit the job for migration.

VMware Workstation or Other VMware VM

Here are the steps in the Migration wizard for VMs that have been exported to a file system:

1. Choose the source machine. Choose the VMX file using the file system browser. Selecting a VM on your local storage will likely be quicker than importing from a remote file server. Click "View Source Details..." to confirm this is the correct source machine.

2. Choose the destination type. Will this go to vCenter/ESXi or to a workstation format? If you choose Workstation Format, you will be given the option to specify the path and the VM Hardware type. If you specify Infrastructure, you must specify the server name and credentials.

3. Choose the destination VM name and folder.

4. Choose the destination VM host, datastore, and hardware version, as shown in Figure 14.2.

5. Configure the options for the migration process, including adjusting the VM hardware, the size of the VM disks, and whether to start/stop services prior to the migration. These options are shown in Figure 14.3.

6. Confirm the process and submit the job for migration.

Backup Image or Third-Party VM

Here are the steps in the Migration wizard for VMs that have been exported to a file system:

1. Choose the source machine. Choose the image file using the file system browser. Selecting an image on your local storage will likely be quicker than importing from a remote file server. Click "View Source Details..." to confirm this is the correct source machine.

2. Choose the destination type. Will this go to vCenter/ESXi or to a workstation format? If you choose workstation format, you will be given the option to specify the path and the VM Hardware type. If you specify Infrastructure, you must specify the server name and credentials.

3. Choose the destination VM name and folder.

4. Choose the destination VM host, datastore, and hardware version, as shown in Figure 14.2.

5. Configure the options for the migration process, including adjusting the VM hardware, the size of the VM disks, and whether to start/stop services prior to the migration. These options are shown in Figure 14.3.

6. Confirm the process and submit the job for migration.

Hyper-V Server

Here are the steps in the Migration wizard for VMs currently contained on a Hyper-V server:

1. Choose the source machine. Enter credentials for the Hyper-V server and then continue.

2. Select the VM to import. The VM must be powered off. Click "View Source Details..." to confirm this is the correct source machine.

3. Choose the destination type. Will this go to vCenter/ESXi or to a workstation format? If you choose Workstation Format, you will be given the option to specify the path and the VM Hardware type. If you specify Infrastructure, you must specify the server name and credentials.

4. Choose the destination VM name and folder.

5. Choose the destination VM host, datastore, and hardware version as shown in Figure 14.2.

6. Configure the options for the migration process, including adjusting the VM hardware, the size of the VM disks, and whether to start/stop services prior to the migration. These options are shown in Figure 14.3.

7. Confirm the process and submit the job for migration.

Guest Customization

With each of these formats, you can optionally choose to customize the guest operating system. While it's unlikely that you want to rename the machine you are working with, you may want to change the IP address of the VM. For example, if your source machine was in a different IP subnet that your ESXi hosts cannot use, you may not be able to use the VM's original IP address.

Post-Migration VM Management

The migration task progress may complete successfully, but was the migration a success? Sure, you can just power up the new VM, shut down the old server, and let users begin to work. But, what if the new VM didn't work perfectly? Say there were multiple applications on the server, but only one was properly tested. You allow users to connect to the server, change data, and resume normal activities. Then you learn of the failed applications. You can't easily roll back to the original source server because there is changed data on the new server now.

This underscores the importance of a checklist for all services and applications that must be tested thoroughly before releasing the server to the production network. You will likely have a checklist for every major server, but you could have a collective checklist for servers that share a similar role, such as web servers. Once everything checks out, release the server. It may not be perfect, but having some sort of checklist will likely catch most of the surprises.

Following the migration, you will need to clean up the hardware and software on the VM. If you remember, we talked about this in the Planning section. You need to remove any hardware drivers that do not exist in the virtual world—things like network card teaming software and video adapter drivers. There may also be services that need to be uninstalled. Once you have removed all the software, be sure to reinstall the VMware Tools to ensure that the VM's new drivers have not been negatively affected by the clean-up phase.

Sanitize the Source Machine

This step is largely a matter of your organizational policy. We recommend taking the most secure position, which is to erase the hard disks of the source machine using a multiple-pass erasure program. These programs typically write 1s and 0s multiple times across the disk to reduce the likelihood that someone could recover data from the disks. Once you have wiped out the disks, sell, donate, or discard the old equipment—again, depending on your organization's security policy.

TROUBLESHOOTING

P2V and V2V operations can be tricky, especially if the source machine isn't in the most stable condition from a software or hardware perspective. You could write a book just on troubleshooting the plethora of situations where P2Vs fail, so we opted to keep this brief. We've decided to use this section to ask you questions rather than give you answers. The idea being, the question may jog your memory and help you look in a particular direction. At the end of this section, we have included several networking-related tips that we find ourselves using quite often during these migrations.

VMware Converter Permissions in vCenter

If you're having difficulty migrating machines into a vCenter environment using VMware Converter Standalone edition, you might check your permissions. These are the minimum permissions required at the Datacenter level in order for you to import a VM (hot or cold) into vCenter:

- Datastore.Allocate Space
- Virtual machine.Inventory.Create new
- Virtual machine.Configuration.Add new disk
- Virtual Machine.Interaction.Power On
- Virtual Machine.Provisioning.Allow Disk Access
- Resource.Assign Virtual Machine To Resource Pool
- Network.Assign network

VMware Converter TCP/UDP Port Requirements

These are the ports that are required for VMware Converter Standalone to convert a source machine to a VM in a vCenter environment.

Windows Source Machine (P2V)

Double-check the Windows Firewall settings to ensure that the ports found in Table 14.1 are open.

Table 14.1 Firewall Ports for Windows P2V Migrations

Communication Pathway	Protocol/Port	Function
Converter Server* to Source*	TCP/9089, TCP/445	Agent installation and communications (if NetBIOS is not enabled)
Converter Server* to Source*	TCP/9089, TCP/139, UDP/137, UDP/138	Agent installation and communications (if NetBIOS is enabled)
Converter Server* to vCenter	TCP/443	vCenter Communications (required only if vCenter is the destination)
Converter Client* to vCenter	TCP/443	vCenter Communications
Source* to ESXi	TCP/443, TCP/902	Converter Clone Process (only TCP/902 is required if vCenter is the destination)

* For readability in the table, the following terms were abbreviated:
"Converter Server" is the VMware Converter Standalone Server component
"Converter Client" is the VMware Converter Standalone Client component
"Source" is the Physical Windows Source Machine (powered on)

Linux Source Machine (P2V)

Double-check the Windows and Linux Firewall settings to ensure the ports shown in Table 14.2 are open.

Virtual Source Machine (V2V)

Double-check the Windows Firewall settings to ensure the ports shown in Table 14.3 are open.

Hot Cloning Failing?

Hot cloning operations are tricky because they require security, stability, and you are typically using them because you are short on time. If you are having hot clone issues, ask yourself these questions:

- Is the converter agent installed properly?
- If not, does my user ID have administrative rights to the source machine?
- Check the event logs on the source machine. Is there any mention of the converter agent?

Table 14.2 Firewall Ports for Linux P2V Migrations

Communication Pathway	Protocol/Port	Function
Converter Server* to Source*	TCP/22	Agent installation and communications
Converter Client* to Converter Server*	TCP/443	Client/Server communications
Converter Server* to vCenter	TCP/443	vCenter Communications (required only if vCenter is the destination)
Converter Server* to ESXi	TCP/443, TCP/902, TCP/903	ESXi Communications (only ports TCP/902 and TCP/903 are required if vCenter is the destination)
Converter Server* to Helper VM*	TCP/443	Conversion Control
Helper VM* to Source*	TCP/22	Converter Clone Process (SSH)

* For readability in the table, the following terms were abbreviated:
"Converter Server" is the VMware Converter Standalone Server component
"Converter Client" is the VMware Converter Standalone Client component
"Helper VM" is a transient VM used by Converter during the migration
"Source" is the Physical Windows Source Machine (powered on)

- If the source is a Windows machine, is the converter agent successfully initiating a Windows VSS snapshot?
- Have you checked the source machine's firewall configuration?
- Are the appropriate TCP/UDP ports open?
- Does your User ID have the appropriate vCenter/ESXi permissions to import a VM?

If you are unable to make the hot clone function, you should try to use a boot CD and perform a cold clone. This will eliminate several of the variables, but it will require physical contact with the source machine.

Cold Cloning Failing?

Many of the problems that plague the hot clone process do not apply to the cold clone process, but we still have to maintain a connection to ESXi and vCenter, and

Table 14.3   Firewall Ports for V2V Migrations

Communication Pathway	Protocol/Port	Function
Converter Server* to File Server*	TCP/445	CIFS communications (if NetBIOS is not enabled)
Converter Server* to File Server*	TCP/139, UDP/137, UDP/138	SMB communications (if NetBIOS is enabled)
Converter Client* to Converter Server*	TCP/443	Client/Server communications
Converter Server* to vCenter	TCP/443	vCenter Communications (required only if vCenter is the destination)
Converter Server* to ESXi	TCP/443, TCP/902	Converter Clone Process (only TCP/902 is required if vCenter is the destination)

* For readability in the table, the following terms were abbreviated:
"Converter Server" is the VMware Converter Standalone Server component
"Converter Client" is the VMware Converter Standalone Client component
"File Server" is the Server hosting the file share that contains the source VM files

we must still have the requisite permissions. Plus, we now have to concern ourselves with appropriate drivers for the physical server's storage adapters.

- Does the cold clone boot CD detect the volumes on the physical server?

- If not, do you have the correct storage adapter (RAID/SCSI) drivers installed in the boot CD?

- If you are unable to migrate the VM to vCenter, try migrating directly to an ESXi server without specifying vCenter.

- If you are attempting to migrate to a vNetwork Distributed Switch environment, try migrating to a vStandard Switch instead (then move the VM later).

- Does the physical server have enough RAM to handle the cold clone? It should have at least 264MB of RAM (yes, that is an unusual number). Really old servers may not have this much memory.

- Are the appropriate TCP/UDP ports open?

- Does your User ID have the appropriate vCenter/ESXi permissions to import a VM?

If you are still unable to make the cold clone process work, you may need to use a third-party tool like Norton Ghost or Acronis True Image to create an image of the hard disks. You should then be able to use VMware Converter to import the disk image(s).

Trouble after the Migration

Below are a couple suggestions that can apply to either P2V or V2V migrations. For more information on performance issues, refer back to Chapter 10.

Performance Is Horrible

There are a couple things that can easily contribute to poor performance immediately following a P2V or even a V2V migration, and both relate to the drivers and virtual hardware. The first is to check the VMware Tools in the VM. Remember, the VMware Tools package isn't just an application; it's the drivers for the VM's new hardware. Without the tools properly installed, Windows or Linux will have significant performance issues.

Another common problem comes from migrating a physical machine that had more than one CPU/core, but you configured the VM to have only one vCPU. The source machine had the multiprocessor kernel or Hardware Abstraction Layer (HAL) loaded, which expects to see multiple physical processors. If it doesn't find the right number of processors, it constantly polls the virtual system board, dragging down performance and making the VM appear in vCenter as though it were using 100% of a CPU.

Finally, you might consider upgrading the VM's virtual hardware devices. We discussed the VM Hardware version in Chapter 9, and we talked about the various para-virtual adapters that you can use in your VM instead of the emulated ones that are provided by default. Just remember, if you swap out the network adapter, you will need to reconfigure the IP address on your VM, and you may want to remove the old ghosted hardware if you are running Windows (refer to the last section in this chapter for details).

VMware Tools Not Available?

It turns out that not every operating system that VMware supports actually has (or needs) VMware Tools. VMware updates the supported list with each release of vSphere. As of the release build of vSphere 5 these operating systems, while supported as guest operating systems, do not have a matching VMware Tools installation package:

- Windows Preinstallation Environment
- Windows Recovery Environment

- MS-DOS 6.22 and Windows 3.1x
- eComStation 2.0
- eComStation 1.0
- IBM OS/2 Warp 4.5.2
- IBM OS/2 Warp 4.0
- SCO OpenServer 5.0
- SCO UnixWare 7
- Solaris 9 Operating System x86 Platform Edition
- Solaris 8 Operating System x86 Platform Edition
- VMware ESXi 5.x
- VMware ESX 4.x

Networking Changes

Here are some useful commands that you may need after migrating your physical machine to a VM. The first entry, removing hidden network adapters in Windows, is something that you may also need to use when switching from the e1000 NIC to the vmxnet3 adapter. The final sections on changing your Ethernet MAC address are handy if you have software licensed to a particular MAC address. Note that most of the MAC address changes (from inside the guest operating system) are not persistent across reboots. If you want a permanent solution, you can modify the MAC address of the VM in the vSphere Client.

Tip

In vSphere 5 we can now change the MAC address of VMs right from the vSphere Client. This was partially possible in vSphere 4, but the GUI only permitted us to modify the last three octets of the MAC address; all six octets are editable now in vSphere 5!

Hidden Network Cards in Windows

You may have seen this before. You're editing the TCP/IP settings for a network adapter in a VM, and as you click OK to save your settings, Windows displays a pop-up message stating that another adapter in the system has the same IP address. Knowing that you have only one network adapter, you click past the pop-up, but every time you edit that adapter, the message comes back. How do we fix it?

This problem is caused by old, non-existent devices still listed in the Windows registry. The old device has that same IP address assigned to it, and we need to remove it. You can remove devices in the Windows Device manager, but non-present devices don't appear automatically because Windows masks them from the device list. The solution is to run a couple of commands at the command prompt to force Windows to display those devices:

```
set devmgr_show_nonpresent_devices=1
devmgmt.msc
```

Tip

For more information, refer to Microsoft's Knowledge Base article on this topic at: http://support. microsoft.com/kb/315539.

This will first set an environment variable, and then it launches the Windows Device Manager, but there's still one more step. You must click View > Show Hidden Devices. Now the devices should be visible, albeit grayed out. Remove the grayed-out devices and your mystery network card messages will be gone. Just make sure to only remove the grayed out or "ghosted" devices.

Changing the Ethernet MAC Address in Windows

You can use `ipconfig` from the command line to verify which Ethernet adapter to use. This process does not require a reboot, and the new configuration will remain persistent across reboots.

1. Open Windows Device Manager and expand the Network Adapters section.

2. Right-click on the network adapter and select Properties.

3. Click on the Advanced tab, and then select the property named Network Address or Locally Administered Address.

4. Enter your desired Ethernet MAC address without any dashes or colons.

Changing the Ethernet MAC Address in Linux

You can use `ifconfig` to verify which Ethernet (eth0) port to use (i.e., `eth0`, `eth1`). In most cases, the port you want to modify is `eth0`. First, bring the port down, then change the MAC address, and then finally bring it back online. This setting is non-persistent and will revert after a reboot.

```
ifconfig eth0 down
ifconfig eth0 link 01:23:45:67:89:0A
ifconfig eth0 up
```

Changing the Ethernet MAC Address in Mac OS X

You can use `ifconfig` to verify which Ethernet (en) port to use (i.e., en0, en1). In most cases, the port you want to modify is en0. It is not necessary to bring down the interface prior to changing the MAC address. This setting is non-persistent and will revert after a reboot.

```
sudo ifconfig en0 ether 01:23:45:67:89:0A
```

Changing the Ethernet MAC Address in BSD

You can use `ifconfig` to verify which Ethernet (xl) port to use (i.e., xl0, xl1). In most cases, the port you want to modify is xl0. First, bring the port down, then change the MAC address, and then finally bring it back online. This setting is non-persistent and will revert after a reboot.

```
ifconfig xl0 down
ifconfig xl0 link 01:23:45:67:89:0A
ifconfig xl0 up
```

Summary

As you've seen, migrating to a virtual environment can be an involved process, but with the right plan you can avoid many of the pitfalls we mentioned. The key to any successful project is carefully analyzing the situation and planning your steps *before* you take action. You've learned what options are available, how to start your migration project, and how to clean things up if it didn't go as you'd planned.

In the next chapter, we'll explore how you can leverage your virtual environment in even more areas by adding products such as vCloud Director or View. We won't go into great depth because that goes outside the scope of this book, but it will give you some ideas for your next project.

PART IV

WHERE DO WE GO FROM HERE?

This final part of the book is a little different from all of the preceding parts of the book. In this section, we'll look at other VMware products and how they fit in with vSphere. They are designed to work together to solve many of the problems that businesses experience.

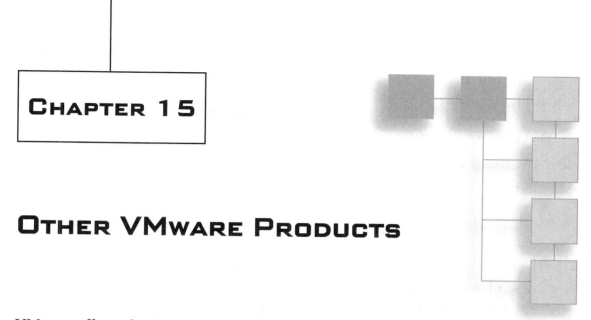

Chapter 15

Other VMware Products

VMware offers a large suite of products, as summarized in this chapter. The headings have been organized in the same way that VMware organizes the list on their website as of the writing of this book.

Datacenter & Cloud Infrastructure

This group of products is primarily focused on cloud offerings, which are expected to grow over time. VMware is investing a lot of time and money in taking their best-of-breed virtualization tools and leveraging them as the basis for cloud deployments. At this point, many of the cloud offerings are in their early iterations and thus don't have all of the functionality one might desire, but they are a great starting point to begin experimenting with cloud computing. "Go" is the other tool in this category, and it is designed to simplify many of the processes that IT must go through to provision a virtual environment, manage patches, and track licensing, etc.

Go

This group of web-based tools is used to deploy vSphere; create VMs; use Converter; manage patches; track software licenses; track hardware assets; and create, manage, and report on help desk tickets. It is designed to simplify IT for the small to medium business.

vCloud Director

This product is designed to create public, private, and/or hybrid (public/private) clouds based on vSphere and vCenter that can support multiple tenants (departments, divisions, or even customers). The idea is to deliver Infrastructure As A Service (IAAS), allowing customers to outsource some or all of the IT infrastructure.

Each tenant can create, manage, and delete its own VMs via a URL created by vCloud Director when the tenant was set up, and the provider builds and maintains the appropriate vSphere infrastructure to support it. Each tenant is completely isolated from every other tenant, so there is no data, network, or other leakage between them. Thus, competing companies could be hosted in the same cloud and no one would ever know except for the provider.

vCloud Director integrates with vCenter Chargeback (described below) to track the costs for providing the service (the provider decides what to charge for, such as storage space used, CPU consumed, network bandwidth used, etc., and how much to charge for each).

SECURITY

This group of products, all part of the vShield suite of products, are designed to provide various forms of security to VMs. Some protect the network while others protect against viruses, malware, etc. They are all managed with the vShield Manager application. All support various forms of logging, and may also support auditing.

vShield App

This add-on product to vSphere provides a firewall based in the VMkernel of vSphere servers that inspects all of the packets in and out of virtual NICs in the VMs. Firewall rules can be based on network, port, protocol, etc. It also supports vMotion, thus as VMs are migrated between hosts, the protection migrates with the VM. Traffic can be monitored between VMs on the same host as well as VMs or physical machines elsewhere in the network.

vShield Edge

This product is implemented as a VA instead of as a driver in the VMkernel (as vShield App is), acting as a firewall for the datacenter. Firewall rules can be based on IP address, protocol, and/or port. vShield Edge also supports both NAT and DHCP and can be used to provide site-to-site VPN services based on IPSEC. It can provide load balancing services for network traffic as well as control traffic between port groups.

vShield Endpoint

This tool allows you to remove anti-virus/anti-malware applications from inside each VM and replace it with a dedicated security appliance (provided by a third-party partner), reducing the load in each VM while still providing the necessary protection.

A module in the vSphere kernel manages the traffic between the VMs and the security VM. Remediation can be enforced by policies using vShield Manager.

DESKTOP AND END-USER COMPUTING

This book has focused primarily on server virtualization, but the same infrastructure that supports server virtualization can also be used to support desktop virtualization (VMware's solution is via View). Application virtualization can be deployed easily, separating the application from the OS in much the same way that server virtualization separates the OS from the underlying hardware. Horizon App Manager provides a simple mechanism to access both Windows- and web-based applications from any device anytime. For those who don't want or need dedicated ESXi hosts, Workstation can be used to create and work with VMs on top of Windows or Linux (for Macintosh users, Fusion is the equivalent of Workstation). With VMware's Mobile Virtualization Platform, even mobile phones are not beyond virtualization with all of its benefits. Finally, if you are looking for a collaboration and e-mail platform, Zimbra is the VMware product for you.

View

This product is VMware's tool for VDI (Virtual Desktop Infrastructure) and is designed to manage virtualized Windows (XP, Vista, or 7) desktops running on vSphere. It integrates with Active Directory, so a user can log in once to the client and be automatically logged into any VMs assigned to him/her. A gold-image VM can be created and then, using linked clone technology, copied tens or hundreds of times very quickly. With linked clones, only the differences between the source VM and the user's disk actually consume disk space, much like how VM snapshots work. Changes can be made to the source VM (patches, new software, etc.), and those changes can be propagated to all the VMs with just a few clicks. Provisioning the VMs is a simple and quick process, and can also leverage ThinApp (described below) to deploy apps to the VMs all through the View interface.

Security functionality built into the product allows remote access over SSL. View also includes the ability to check out a virtual desktop to a laptop and take it on the road and run it in a customized version of Player. When the user gets back to the office (or hotel or whatever), the user can sync any changes with the virtual copy in the datacenter and either keep it checked out or check it back in to be run online again.

The virtual desktops (or physical PCs, or even Terminal Services desktops) can be accessed from PCs, Macs, a web browser, or even an iPad, as well as thin (or zero) clients.

ThinApp

Application virtualization can be used with either physical or virtual environments and can make it easier to use applications in multiple versions of Windows or even to run multiple versions of an application side-by-side on the same system (for example, IE 6, 7, 8, and 9). It makes them easier to deploy and upgrade, especially when used in conjunction with View. In addition, the space required to deploy an application can be minimized, which is especially useful in a virtual environment. ThinApp requires no software or agent to be installed on the client computer. Not only that, nothing will be installed when the application runs and the application will execute in user mode, so no special privileges are required to run any ThinApped application. It also supports running apps in a "sandbox" in a terminal services deployment so multiple users can run the same app on the same server without any conflicts. It can be integrated with AD, restricting application execution to those members that belong to specified AD groups, as well as with View, making it very simple to deploy apps to specified groups of desktops.

Horizon App Manager

Horizon App Manager is a new tool designed to provide secure access to applications from any device—from PC to iPad—and report on the usage to meet compliance and auditing requirements. It can also manage all of your ThinApped applications, including tracking user licenses, a thing that ThinApp can't natively do.

Workstation

This tool is different from ESX(i) in that it is a hosted hypervisor; in other words, a hypervisor that runs on top of Windows or Linux, instead of on the hardware directly. In many ways, it is cutting edge—many features are pioneered and tested first on Workstation and then later incorporated in vSphere (such as multi-core support). It can even run ESXi as a VM, making it simple and easy to create a simple lab environment with very little hardware; in fact, our lab environment consists of a laptop with a quad-core, hyper-threaded Core i7 processor and 16GB of RAM that runs Workstation on top of Windows with VMs for ESXi, vCenter, etc. It is simple, easy to set up and maintain, and portable. It is often used by developers, but it is also used by sales people to demonstrate features to customers and teachers and other technical trainers.

Player

Player is a simple version of Workstation, just like PowerPoint Viewer is a simple version of PowerPoint. In PowerPoint, presentations can be created and modified, whereas in

Viewer, they can only be viewed. Similarly, VMs can be created and modified in Workstation, while Player provides minimal options to create, modify, or run them. Player provides a better, more powerful option than XP mode in Windows 7. It also works with any Guest OS on multiple versions of Windows or Linux, not just XP in Windows 7.

Zimbra

Zimbra is an enterprise-level application environment for e-mail, calendaring, and collaboration based on open-source standards. It can be accessed either online or offline via a browser, the Zimbra Desktop client, or other third-party clients such as Microsoft Outlook. It has some features similar to SharePoint for collaboration, including document check in and out with versioning support. It can be deployed in the cloud, on a physical server, or as a VA in vSphere.

Mobile Virtualization Platform (MVP)

This product is in the early phases of existence, but the concept is to do for mobile phones what Workstation or Player does for user access on PCs; namely it is designed to allow users to have a single mobile phone with two platforms on it. One platform, the native phone environment, is for personal data (contacts, applications, etc.) and a second platform is a virtual machine that can be secured with appropriate policies for the company's contacts, work, etc. This design allows users to choose a single device of their choice instead of carrying around separate devices, one for personal use and one for company use. A single management interface for all devices further simplifies management for IT.

Fusion

Fusion is similar to Workstation, but it is built for the Macintosh platform, with many similar features and functionality (although it is not as full featured). In addition, it includes migration utilities that convert your existing Windows-based computer to run inside of Fusion, making the migration from PC to Mac simpler. Fusion integrates copy-and-paste and other functionality native to the Macintosh platform making it seamless to move from one (native) platform (Mac) to the other (Windows) and share data between them. No more is it PC or Mac; it can be both.

INFRASTRUCTURE AND OPERATIONS MANAGEMENT

This group of products helps the datacenter work better. Configuration Manager is a tool that automates configuration management across both physical and virtual servers and desktops, including the ability to report on changes from established policies. Server and software provisioning can also be automated with this tool.

CapacityIQ is a tool used to monitor resource utilization and analyze the data to predict resource needs in the future. vCenter Operations is the big brother to CapacityIQ and can also see across applications and infrastructure components to more rapidly resolve problems. It can also provide a quick view into regulatory compliance issues across both physical and virtual servers. It also includes some features of Configuration Manager.

Lab Manager is a tool used by developers and trainers to set up and deploy needed environments more efficiently. vCenter Heartbeat provides high availability for vCenter server (and if desired, the SQL database that the configuration data is stored in). Site Recovery Manager is used for Disaster Recovery (DR) between sites.

Configuration Manager

Configuration Manager will analyze an entire IT environment, including vSphere, UNIX, Linux, and Windows workstations and servers, storing the data (including security and configuration settings—over 80,000 of them!) it collects in a database. This allows early and easy detection of changes or variance from established policies. These policies can come from VMware, Apple and/or Microsoft security and/or hardening best practices, industry or governmental groups and governance boards (such as Sarbanes-Oxley, HIPAA, DISA, ISO 27002, 802-53 Basel II, PCI DSS, and NIST), or even your own internal best practices. The output of this data can be displayed in dashboard or report formats, and items that are out of compliance will be highlighted. A simple mouse click is all that is required to bring the items in line with the specified policy. The fix can be applied to that server only, a group of servers, or all servers in the organization.

This tool can also be used to provision vSphere on to bare-metal servers and then deploy operating systems (including Windows, Red Hat, and SUSE) in VMs on the newly deployed vSphere servers as well as deploy various operating systems (again including Windows and Linux) to physical servers directly via PXE. Software can then be layered on top of the physical or virtual systems, and if critical software (such as antivirus) is missing, it can automatically be reinstalled. Patches to the operating systems or applications can also be managed centrally and deployed to desired systems. The repository of software can be distributed and used throughout any part of the organization, even in different geographic areas.

Configuration Manager can also monitor Active Directory (AD) for changes, access control, and group membership modifications, and so on, and report the changes to a central console.

CapacityIQ

This tool employs dashboards, charts, and graphs to provide quick and easy views of past, present, and predicted capacity needs. One-off events can be added to the mix to determine what impact they would have on the environment. CapacityIQ also provides reports with detailed recommendations for capacity changes, such as VMs that are oversized (given too many resources for the work they are doing) or powered off.

vCenter Operations

vCenter Operations provides information about real-time performance as well as capacity and configuration management features to spot problems quickly, with a goal of spotting trends and other issues before they impact production. This allows time and resources to be budgeted in advance of a drop off in performance or a crisis. Root cause analysis is also provided for many of the problems, helping managers fix the problem, not just a symptom of the problem. The product will analyze the environment and, from watching over time, determine what "normal" is for your specific environment, making it easier to know when things are abnormal—without a baseline of what's normal, how will you know when things are abnormal? Many templates are included to quickly configure the environment with security and hardening best practices as well as for implementing various industry compliance standards.

Many of the features of CapacityIQ are also included in vCenter Operations, making it easy to perform various what-if scenarios quickly and easily. vCenter Operations can also spot underutilized, oversized, and other VMs that are consuming needless resources. Both physical and virtual servers can be monitored to ensure policy compliance. According to VMware, most vCenter Operations users realize 15%–80% utilization improvements and run 300%–500% more VMs on the same hardware.

Lab Manager

Lab Manager is a tool used for quickly and easily deploying VMs, such as a group of VMs for use in training, or a set of VMs used by development, sales, or help desk teams. This group of VMs can be quickly provisioned with just a few clicks by the users who need them via a self-service, web-based portal. The state of the VM can be saved and replicated so, for example, a development team can see an error discovered by the QA team and address it. Lab Manager uses Linked Clone technology (similar in concept but different in implementation) to View or reduce the space required to store the VMs, both the template versions (the VMs that are copied for each use) as well as those currently in production (used by the team that created them from the templates). Storage leases can also be implemented so that after a project is over, the space consumed by those VMs will be automatically reclaimed.

Many of Lab Manager's features have been incorporated into vCloud Director (though VMware states that vCloud Director doesn't replace Lab Manager). Lab Manager will be going End-of-Life in May of 2013, but is still available as of the writing of this book.

vCenter Server Heartbeat

As described throughout this book, vCenter is the primary tool for managing and reporting on your vSphere environment. While VMs will continue to run after a vCenter failure, all of the features that depend on vCenter, such as vMotion, DRS, and alarms, will be inoperative until the failure is resolved and vCenter is brought back online. For many environments, making vCenter a VM and protecting it with HA is good enough; for those that need better availability, VMware created vCenter Heartbeat. This tool, a collaborative effort between NeverFail and VMware, provides high availability to vCenter, whether physical or virtual, by utilizing a second instance to failover to. It is also possible to have one of each (i.e., a physical primary and a virtual secondary or vice versa). vCenter server Heartbeat can also protect the SQL database that vCenter depends on for greater tolerance to disruptions within the environment. It requires two installations of vCenter (primary and secondary) and they can be deployed on separate storage (even local storage) so a storage outage won't take down vCenter. The vCenter instances can both be local or you can separate them across a WAN if desired.

vCenter Heartbeat recognizes all of the standard VMware components (including View Composer for linked clones and VUM). It replicates the data between the two instances automatically and will failover when a failure is detected, or the failover can be manually initiated by an administrator for a planned outage. The tool is managed by a web interface that can manage multiple vCenter Heartbeat installations for different vCenter installations from a single console.

Note

As of the writing of this book, vCenter server Heartbeat can only protect the Windows-based version of vCenter, not the vCenter VA.

Site Recovery Manager

Site Recovery Manager (SRM) is a tool designed for disaster recovery, but can also be used to facilitate datacenter moves between locations. It requires two separate, independent environments, including installations of vSphere (ESXi and vCenter) as well as SRM, two databases on each side (one for vCenter and one for SRM), and storage-based replication pre-configured between the two sites (for example, Clariion or EqualLogic on both sites). SRM 5 introduces the ability to replicate data at the vSphere level, so storage-based replication is no longer required (but still supported if you want to use it); this allows different vendors or even types of storage to be used in the different sites, as well as allowing individual VMs to be replicated. SRM leverages the replicated volumes or VMs to failover VMs between the two sites in the event of a disaster. Note that as of SRM 4, it is possible to have multiple sites failover to a central site as well, making it simpler and cheaper to handle failover for many distributed sites to a central site (previously, it would have required many SRM, vCenter, and ESX/ESXi installations to handle multiple failures to a single site).

Planning is the key to any successful implementation, and nowhere is this more evident that with SRM—it requires a lot of upfront planning, but that planning pays huge dividends. VM placement (which VMs on which LUNs if using storage-based replication) and network design are two of the most important things to consider. Once the planning is complete, and any necessary network issues are addressed and storage replication is properly configured (if it is being used), the actual installation of SRM is fairly straightforward. You define the VMs you want to protect, and SRM will create "place holder" VMs on the remote site.

One of the great advantages of SRM is that you can non-disruptively test failover at any time to determine how it performs and to allow you to prove that failover will work in the event of an actual disaster. Scripts can be run and messages displayed on the console for the administrator on the recovery site as part of the process, providing even greater automation, data validation checks, and so on. This can be done as often as desired and the results of each test are saved so you can prove to your boss, regulators, and so on that failover does indeed work as planned. If any errors are discovered, they can quickly and easily be addressed before there is an actual emergency.

When VMs are failed over, the following steps take place:

1. Protected VMs are shut down on the production side (for actual failovers only, assuming the site is still functional to allow for a clean shutdown).

VMs are shut down starting with the lowest priority and ending with the highest priority to minimize downtime for the high-priority VMs.

2. For storage-based replication implementations only, storage is made visible on the remote side. If you are performing a test, the remote site will use a snapshot or clone of the secondary copy for the test (depending on the storage manufacturer and how they implement things). However, if you are performing an actual failover, the secondary copy on the remote site will become the primary copy, the datastore will be resignatured, and all of the .vmx files will be updated with the new UUID from the resignaturing process.

3. If desired, low-priority VMs on the recovery site can be suspended to make more capacity available for the failover (or test).

4. VMs are restarted in priority order (high; medium; low; and no-power on, meaning that they are failed over, but left powered off, such as for a VM that is only used occasionally). Within each priority, VMs are ordered from highest to lowest priority.

5. For a test failover, a message is displayed prompting the admin to verify that everything works and to then click a button in the message when testing is complete to reset the environment.

6. For a test failover, VMs on the recovery site are powered down and reverted to their "place holder" status, any suspended VMs are resumed, and (if storage-based replication is used) storage is reset for the next test (the clone or snapshot is removed).

SRM is a great DR tool, typically used for major disasters rather than local failures (a VM, blade, server, etc.). In addition, this tool is great at testing and failover, but failback after the disaster has been cleaned up and the original datacenter put back in working order is a manual process in SRM 4 and below that typically involves configuring SRM in the opposite direction, failing everything back over, and then reconfiguring SRM back to its original configuration. This has been automated to a great degree with SRM 5.

APPLICATION MANAGEMENT

The tools in this category are designed to discover the applications in your network and the relationships between them (Application Discovery Manager), optimize and alert you when there are application performance issues (AppSpeed), and help you create vApps and OVF files from existing VMs (Studio).

Application Discovery Manager

This tool uses an agentless design to monitor network traffic to discover the applications on the network and the other applications that they connect to (if any). Due to the monitoring of network traffic, both physical and virtual machines can be analyzed. In addition, because Application Discovery Manager (ADM) is always monitoring network traffic, the data is always up-to-date. If even more detailed information is needed, active application discovery can be used with credentials to dig deeper into any necessary systems; however, the design is still agentless.

Through the use of *Application Fingerprints*, many common applications are automatically recognized, including many n-tier applications (which are automatically grouped together to make it easier to see the relationships). By using deep-packet inspection techniques, it can also determine URLs, database table names, and so on to help further define the relationship between the applications.

This information can be useful in DR planning, for example, to make sure that all of the component pieces of an important application failover as a group, or to make sure there are no lingering references to test/dev equipment when the VM is moved into production. ADM can also be a useful tool to see not only what is deployed for license and legal reasons, but also to understand the relationships between applications so you don't decommission a server or database unintentionally, thereby breaking another application in the environment.

AppSpeed

AppSpeed is designed to make performance monitoring and management a much simpler process by leveraging the native vSphere capabilities; gathering performance metrics (such as latency and utilization) and comparing them to baselines that are automatically generated by the program (thus automatically determining what "normal" is in your environment) and alerting you when those values are exceeded; and displaying the results in easy-to-use dashboards.

While AppSpeed will analyze your system to determine the baselines and thus thresholds for normal, these values can be manually overridden by an administrator to set the required SLAs in your environment. The values generated range from broad (the application level) to specific (individual transaction latency levels, for example). The reported values can be further zoomed in on to determine the components of the latency issue (for example, to determine if the issue is with the server, clients, network, or the application). Systems can be moved automatically into color-coded status conditions based on these thresholds.

This tool, unlike many others on the market, utilizes native vSphere metrics and packet monitoring to do its job, not agents, code modifications within your applications, or the use of made-up transactions to gather and monitor the performance. It can monitor http/https traffic, as well as database traffic to/from Oracle, SQL, and MySQL. The performance information can be viewed either with the normal vSphere Client (on a new tab) or using a web browser, giving you the freedom to choose the best tool for any situation.

Studio

Studio is a free tool for administrators and developers who want to create and/or convert VMs into vApps (multiple VMs that are packaged and deployed as a unit, usually in multi-tier applications) and VAs in the OVF format. It can include an agent in the guest operating system (either Windows or Linux) to perform initial setup and customization that can be managed with a branded web interface. It is controlled through one of three interfaces: a web interface (mostly used by administrators); a command line interface (CLI, most often used for automation by either administrators or developers); or an Eclipse plugin for developers that uses the Eclipse IDE (Integrated Development Environment), a common platform for Java development. The vApps and VAs can be run in Workstation, Fusion, vSphere, and vCloud Director, among others. It is primarily designed to be used by developers to make package creation and distribution easier.

IT BUSINESS MANAGEMENT

The applications in this category are focused on the business side of IT—managing costs and determining what those costs are, including invoicing customers, business units, etc., for IT services provided if necessary.

vCenter Chargeback

Chargeback can be used with either vSphere/vCenter or vCloud deployments to monetize the cost of providing IT services to customers using several different (and customizable) cost models. Most users today think of VMs as "free," so if creating a new one is free, why not create as many as desired and load them up with resources? Once the true cost of providing those services is provided to customers, they can make more intelligent decisions.

Chargeback can be used to show various divisions/departments the service costs (showback) and/or to integrate with third-party invoicing solutions to bill customers, departments, etc., for the cost of providing those services. This simple change can make IT a profit center instead of a cost center.

You can charge customers for variable costs such as CPU, memory, network, and disk consumption (including base rates and "peak" rates if they go beyond certain thresholds); fixed costs (such as licensing); other one-time costs (such as the cost to provision a VM); as well as power and cooling and other costs that are often not included when billing for IT services. It also allows for charging in different currencies, allowing the cost to be put in local currencies for global operations. The metrics can be saved and applied to new deployments, and different models can be used with different groups of VMs, departments, etc.

Reports can be customized and branded, automatically scheduled to be created and delivered to designated business managers, and can include data derived from multiple vCenters (for very large deployments, as well as many DR scenarios). Among the reports that can be generated are the "most expensive <n> VMs" to see if they really bring the value they should for their cost.

Chargeback can be accessed and configured from either the vSphere Client or a web interface.

Service Manager

Service Manager is a tool for helping you implement ITIL (IT Information Lifecycle) best practices and providing tools for the help desk. Among the help desk–oriented features are the ability to provide better help through a self-service portal to end users as well as a knowledge management database that can be accessed by the help desk. It can also integrate problem management functions with change and release management processes to address problems as they are discovered. Reporting and dashboards can also be utilized. This tool can be combined with VMware service professionals to implement the best practices required by specific industries as well.

vFabric Cloud Application Platform

The products in this category are primarily designed for developers. They help implement Platform as a Service (PaaS), as opposed to the IaaS that vCloud Director makes possible. They are built around the Spring platform (VMware acquired SpringSource, the company behind the Spring platform, in August 2009), an open-source platform for Java and web application development. VMware then acquired RabbitMQ in April of 2010, followed by GemStone Systems in May. As this book is aimed at IT administrators instead of developers, each product will be treated in less detail than those previously described.

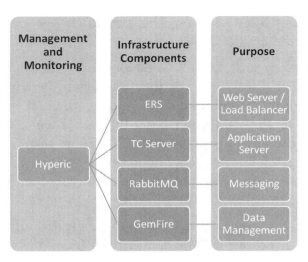

Figure 15.1
vFabric Application relationships and purposes.

These products are related, as shown in Figure 15.1.

vFabric tc Server

This product is an enterprise version of the Tomcat server often used in Linux application development. It has been optimized to reduce resource consumption and the Spring components have been preinstalled.

vFabric GemFire and vFabric SQLFire

GemFire is a data storage platform that is database-like, but designed to scale more easily in a cloud deployment. SQLFire is similar, except it uses standard SQL interfaces and commands that are more familiar to many developers. Functionality is similar in both cases.

Data can be spread across nodes and the storage can be pooled and accessed as needed. A disk or single-node failure will not affect data access. It supports data partitioning (keeping parts on different nodes); automatic rebalancing across nodes; and automatic, dynamic load balancing.

vFabric Hyperic

Hyperic is a web application monitoring tool that can locate, analyze, resolve, and prevent performance issues. It can gather over 50,000 metrics across physical and virtual environments, different operating system and application servers, and so on, including the following:

- Operating systems: AIX, HP/UX, Linux, OS X, Solaris, and Windows.
- Databases: DB2, Informix, MySQL, PostgreSQL, MS SQL Server, and Sybase.
- Application frameworks: J2EE, LAMP, .NET, and Spring.
- Directory services: Active Directory and OpenLDAP.
- Hypervisors: Xen Server and vSphere.
- Application servers: Tomcat, ColdFusion, WebSphere, JBoss, .NET, and Oracle Application Server.
- Mail Servers: Exchange, qmail, Sendmail, and Zimbra.

For technologies not listed above (or other technologies listed on their website), a plugin provides the ability to integrate new platforms as they are deployed in the environment. Also, Hyperic can find new VMs automatically as they are brought into the environment, making sure the entire environment is always monitored. The agents can be very quickly configured, keeping the IT (or developer) overhead low.

vFabric Enterprise Ready Server

Enterprise Ready Server (ERS) is a web server and load balancer based on Apache. Via various plugins, SSL decryption (including via add-in hardware cards); applications based on PERL, C, and PHP; FTP; and authentication options can all be implemented. VMware employs Apache developers as well, so security vulnerabilities are noticed early and often fixed before the vulnerability is made public. VMware provides indemnification against IP infringement at the platform level. VMware has optimized the platform as much as possible—up to 100% over the standard non-optimized builds.

RabbitMQ

RabbitMQ is a message handling system applications use to communicate with each other over standard protocols (not APIs, which would link the application to a specific platform and/or development environment). It is based on AMQP (Advanced Message Queuing Protocol), an open standard for messaging. It includes interfaces for Java, .NET, Ruby, and many more, and was designed for use in the cloud where applications may be hosted in completely different sites.

Cloud Foundry

Cloud Foundry is the first (according to VMware) open PAAS offering. It is designed for creating applications in the cloud, and is based on VMware infrastructure in a vCloud environment, but the applications are all standards based, so they can be moved between public and private clouds, even clouds from different vendors using different underlying technologies (such as Amazon Web Services or Google's AppEngine). The commercial version is at www.cloudfoundry.com, while the open source version is at www.cloudfoundry.org. There is also a "Micro Cloud" version for designing and testing apps locally (to later be ported to the cloud), as well as a product offering for enterprises and service providers to allow them to create their own PAAS clouds.

SUMMARY

Well that is quite a list of other products in the VMware ecosystem—and it is not even a comprehensive list! Whether you are interested in management (from a performance or business perspective), VDI, DR, cloud computing, or development, VMware has tools designed to work together and build on the basic vSphere infrastructure and tools described in this book. With the world moving more to the cloud and access from any kind of device, VMware has made a big push in tools and technologies to help make the transition and then to manage the infrastructure, applications, and devices.

As big as this book is, it does not cover all that vSphere can do, but does provide a great foundation for wherever your needs and requirements may take you. Enjoy!

INDEX

License Agreement/Notice of Limited Warranty

By opening the sealed disc container in this book, you agree to the following terms and conditions. If, upon reading the following license agreement and notice of limited warranty, you cannot agree to the terms and conditions set forth, return the unused book with unopened disc to the place where you purchased it for a refund.

License

The enclosed software is copyrighted by the copyright holder(s) indicated on the software disc. You are licensed to copy the software onto a single computer for use by a single user and to a backup disc. You may not reproduce, make copies, or distribute copies or rent or lease the software in whole or in part, except with written permission of the copyright holder(s). You may transfer the enclosed disc only together with this license, and only if you destroy all other copies of the software and the transferee agrees to the terms of the license. You may not decompile, reverse assemble, or reverse engineer the software.

Notice of Limited Warranty

The enclosed disc is warranted by Course Technology to be free of physical defects in materials and workmanship for a period of sixty (60) days from end user's purchase of the book/disc combination. During the sixty-day term of the limited warranty, Course Technology will provide a replacement disc upon the return of a defective disc.

Limited Liability

THE SOLE REMEDY FOR BREACH OF THIS LIMITED WARRANTY SHALL CONSIST ENTIRELY OF REPLACEMENT OF THE DEFECTIVE DISC. IN NO EVENT SHALL COURSE TECHNOLOGY OR THE AUTHOR BE LIABLE FOR ANY OTHER DAMAGES, INCLUDING LOSS OR CORRUPTION OF DATA, CHANGES IN THE FUNCTIONAL CHARACTERISTICS OF THE HARDWARE OR OPERATING SYSTEM, DELETERIOUS INTERACTION WITH OTHER SOFTWARE, OR ANY OTHER SPECIAL, INCIDENTAL, OR CONSEQUENTIAL DAMAGES THAT MAY ARISE, EVEN IF COURSE TECHNOLOGY AND/OR THE AUTHOR HAS PREVIOUSLY BEEN NOTIFIED THAT THE POSSIBILITY OF SUCH DAMAGES EXISTS.

Disclaimer of Warranties

COURSE TECHNOLOGY AND THE AUTHOR SPECIFICALLY DISCLAIM ANY AND ALL OTHER WARRANTIES, EITHER EXPRESS OR IMPLIED, INCLUDING WARRANTIES OF MERCHANTABILITY, SUITABILITY TO A PARTICULAR TASK OR PURPOSE, OR FREEDOM FROM ERRORS. SOME STATES DO NOT ALLOW FOR EXCLUSION OF IMPLIED WARRANTIES OR LIMITATION OF INCIDENTAL OR CONSEQUENTIAL DAMAGES, SO THESE LIMITATIONS MIGHT NOT APPLY TO YOU.

Other

This Agreement is governed by the laws of the State of Massachusetts without regard to choice of law principles. The United Convention of Contracts for the International Sale of Goods is specifically disclaimed. This Agreement constitutes the entire agreement between you and Course Technology regarding use of the software.